The **Intext** Series in

SECONDARY EDUCATION

consulting editor   **JOHN E. SEARLES**
Pennsylvania State University

THE SECONDARY
SCHOOL CURRICULUM

CONTENT AND STRUCTURE

THE SECONDARY SCHOOL CURRICULUM

CONTENT AND STRUCTURE

WELDON BECKNER

JOE D. CORNETT

Texas Tech University

INTEXT EDUCATIONAL PUBLISHERS

College Division of Intext

Scranton   San Francisco   Toronto   London

U-R-RI

LIBRARY OF CONGRESS
CATALOG CARD NUMBER 73–185823

ISBN 0–7002–2415–7

To our wives and children

BETTY

BRENDA, MARILYN, GAYLA AND **JAN**

ELAYNE

JEFFERY AND **CARA**

PREFACE

Educators today, especially those directly concerned with curriculum development and teaching methodology, almost universally stress the importance of "structure," "process," and "inquiry." "Concepts" and "generalizations" are seen to be basic to educational efforts which utilize these ideas. The "new" programs, first in mathematics and science, and now developing in social studies, language arts, and other areas of study, emphasize these ideas in selecting and organizing curriculum materials. The "disciplines" are considered to be the sources of knowledge from which we should draw in defining and organizing curriculum content.

This is all well and good—but what does it mean in terms of the everyday work of classroom teachers, curriculum workers, and school administrators? Educators seem to have a congenital weakness for jargon, and the jargon of today is in many cases no better understood by those involved than was the "pedagese" of the Progressive Education era. We all learn to speak the language, but classroom operations all too often seem to show little evidence of the concepts which are tossed around at professional meetings and in professional education courses.

The authors are convinced that ideas about disciplinary structure and inquiry or discovery learning have enormous promise for helping educators develop much more effective programs and methods for the classroom. However, for this promise to be fulfilled the typical teacher and school administrator must have a clear and usable understanding of the concepts and implications involved. To the achievement of this understanding we have directed our efforts in the construction of this book.

The major purpose of this text is to take ideas about disciplinary structure and apply them as specifically and concretely as possible to the selection and organization of content for the secondary school curriculum. The theoretical background for this has been rather thoroughly developed by Jerome Bruner, Hilda Taba, Arno Bellack, Philip Phenix, and others, but there is still considerable confusion and misunderstanding about the implementation of the theories. Using them in the classroom is not necessarily easy, but we are finding that the more we learn about how to apply these theories the more successful are our teaching efforts.

The book begins with an introductory chapter designed to examine some of the ideas about disciplinary structure and how they may be applied to the school curriculum. From this brief theoretical exploration is developed the basic approach of this book, utilizing a somewhat traditional grouping of knowledge into four major categories—mathematics, the natural sciences, the social studies, and the humanities. The greater portion of the book is then devoted to identifying the major disciplines within each of these categories, their content and structural elements (concepts, generalizations, and methods of inquiry), and examples of their application to classroom practice.

To help students gain a better overall understanding of the secondary school curriculum, a large part of the book is devoted to a study of the foundations of curriculum (especially as related to curriculum goals), components of the curriculum which do not fall into the disciplinary fields of knowledge, organization and administration of the curriculum, and curriculum evaluation and improvement.

It is not possible to recognize all of the sources of information and understanding which have contributed to the authors' efforts in an undertaking of this nature, but considerable care has been exercised to note those sources which were most specifically drawn upon or extensively quoted. To each of the sources documented in the text, as well as the many not mentioned, we acknowledge our debt and appreciation. Special notice is due colleagues at Texas Tech University for their contributions and encouragement, especially Professors Charles Rebstock, Holmes Webb, Gerald Skoog, and B. J. Fallon. And only our wives, Betty and Elayne, know the depth of appreciation due them for patient encouragement and assistance of many kinds.

WELDON BECKNER
JOE D. CORNETT

Lubbock, Texas
January, 1972

CONTENTS

xi

part IV / Other Components of the Secondary School Curriculum

CHAPTER 11 VOCATIONAL AND TECHNICAL SKILLS . . 369

CHAPTER 12 STUDENT ACTIVITIES 396

part I

Introduction

CHAPTER 1

AN APPROACH TO CURRICULUM DETERMINATION AND ORGANIZATION

What is education? How does a person become educated? What should be taught in schools? How should what is taught be organized? These and other similar questions are the concern of those who study the programs offered by schools to provide educational activities and experiences for young people. All of those activities and experiences of pupils which occur under the guidance and direction of the school as a result of the planned school program are a part of what we call the school curriculum. Some may not agree with this definition of curriculum, but it fits the authors' ideas on the subject and will doubtless be evident in the rather broad and comprehensive content of this book. Rather than attempting a more detailed discussion or more specific definition at this point, we will encourage the student to develop his own definition as he studies the bases and components of secondary education in the United States.

The questions indicated above are basic to all curriculum study, and through-out this text the focus of attention will revolve around them. There are many subsidiary and component questions, but they all derive their origin from: (1) What shall the schools teach? and (2) How may we best organize that which should be taught in order to achieve optimum results? The resolution of these two questions we will call curriculum determination and curriculum organization.

As we approach the questions of secondary school curriculum determination and organization, there are several fundamental problems that must be considered. Consideration of these problems necessarily involves investigation of the approaches which have been utilized in attempts to resolve them. These various types of efforts must be described, analyzed, and evaluated in our attempts to determine the best answers to questions of curriculum determination and organization.

The concept of disciplinary structure and ideas related to it hold much promise in developing curriculum content and organization for our society today. Since these concepts form the nucleus of this text, we will devote considerable attention to defining and developing them, showing how they may be applied to the classroom, and relating them to the type of secondary school curriculum judged necessary to the preservation and development of American society and civilization.

Major Problems in Curriculum Determination and Organization

People involved in public education often complain that it seems they are continuously going in circles in working to resolve the many questions related to the school curriculum. Such efforts often seem to result only in more confusion and uncertainty. One problem leads to another, and the myriad of considerations involved in each seem to defy logical organization or attack. Perhaps the principal barrier to these efforts is an inability to "see the woods for the trees." An atomistic approach to curriculum evaluation and revision may lead to short-range and limited improvements in specific areas, but long-range, sweeping betterment is unlikely when the people involved are afflicted with this fragmented type of vision.

A broader, or "holistic," view of curriculum determination and organization would seem to include only a few "big" questions or problems. Three of these seem pertinent to our discussion at this point.

Conflict Between Social Needs, Individual Needs, and Demands of the Disciplines

We have long recognized the conflict that often results when we try to give adequate consideration in public schools to both individual student interests and the needs of the society. A third element enters into this situation if the demands of the discipline or disciplines involved—their elemental structure, basic concepts, required skills, and pertinent facts—are given the consideration they deserve. If one of these elements is emphasized at the expense of the others, situations which are less than desirable may develop, such as:

1. The approach usually required to satisfy individual student desires may overemphasize practical use and severely limit what can be accomplished in transmitting basic factual and conceptual knowledge about a subject, and it may be that national or social needs of the time may discourage the inclusion of the subject in the curriculum at all.

2. Concentrating on teaching too many facts and too much theory in attempts to adequately transmit basic elements of the discipline may fail to appeal to student interests and result in very limited learning.

3. Excessive attention to local or national social demands is likely to cause severe limitation of instuction in certain disciplines or the lack of atten-

tion to the type of organization most likely to encourage basic understanding of subject matter and application of the subject matter to individual concerns.

Traditional or "academic" approaches to curriculum development have tended to stress subject content, while advocates of "progressive" education have emphasized the individual and his functioning within the social and physical environment. Perhaps somewhere within the framework of these three ideas about curriculum design there exists a concept that will enable us more adequately to combine and incorporate all three types of needs—social, individual, and disciplinary.

Student-Centered and Subject-Centered Approaches to Organization

Although many variations have been developed, traditionally there have been only two basic approaches utilized in curriculum organization. The subject-centered approach has long been the most accepted procedure. With this approach, subject matter is compartmentalized and taught in rather discrete divisions, with little or no attempt made to teach relationships and correlations among the subject areas. Because many educators were not satisfied with this divisive way of organizing what was to be taught, various schemes were utilized to broaden the focus of classroom activity through organizational innovations variously labeled with terms such as "correlation," "fusion," "broad field courses," and "core curriculum." These innovations fall into the category of "problem-centered" approaches, as opposed to the "subject-centered" traditional organization. The problems most often recognized as the appropriate foundation for curriculum development by "progressive" educators (as they were called) were usually those related rather directly to student needs and interests.

The battle lines of curriculum organization have thus formed behind the ideas of subject-centered and student-centered approaches to teaching and learning. The attempts to integrate and broaden the subject-centered curriculum by "core" or other similar organizational devices were usually clumsy and ineffective, due to the background and habits of teachers and the lack of basic understanding concerning the nature of the separate subject fields being integrated. The worthy goal of having students "draw upon" various subject matter as needed was seldom fulfilled, because the content of the disciplines was not organized to facilitate such an approach to teaching and learning. Consequently the recent trends have been in the direction of increased reliance upon subject-matter division in organizing the school curriculum, especially at the junior high and high school levels.

The Relationships Between "Content" and "Process"

Educators tend to think of teaching as being composed of two primary elements—subject (content) and method (process). Consequently teacher-preparation programs, in-service improvement efforts, and most writing about the subject have followed a dichotomy which is difficult to defend and impossible to follow. Those who teach college courses designated as "curriculum" or "methods" have long labored under the frustration of attempting to separate the two. Because the two cannot really be separated, there has inevitably been much confusion and duplication. Handicapped with this background in their preparation, public school teachers have entered on their careers thinking in terms of a separation between content and method—or at least unable without help to gain adequate awareness of the relationships that exist between the two. Good teachers eventually learn to put the two together, but only through trial-and-error or intuition rather than through a basic understanding of the interrelatedness of subject and method.

Realization that content and process cannot be really separated in thinking about curriculum—that they combine to form the curriculum—has brought about several attempts by various authorities and curriculum workers to reconcile this artificial dichotomy. Such a reconciliation seems to come about best by adopting a concept which accepts "process" as an inherent and inevitable part of "content." This idea is well stated by Parker and Rubin:

> The substance of our proposition is that process—the cluster of diverse procedures which surround the acquisition and utilization of knowledge—is, in fact, the highest form of content and the most appropriate base for curriculum change. It is in the teaching of process that we can best portray learning as a perpetual endeavor, and not something which terminates with the end of school. Through process, we can employ knowledge not merely as a composite of information but as a *system* for learning.[1]

The currently popular concept of "discovery" in teaching provides an excellent example of how content and teaching processes must be combined to provide adequate learning opportunities. Learning by discovery involves the teaching of an association, a concept, or rule (subject content) by leading students to individually arrive at personal concepts of the association or concept or rule through an ordering and patterning of evidence and experiences. Thus the "structure" of the discipline being studied comprises the "content" of the lesson, but "structure-finding" through utilization of the "discovery" method of teaching (process) is an inherent and basic ingredient which is inseparable from the subject matter or content. The process is part of the content.

Ways to Select and Organize the Curriculum

Proposals concerning how best to select and organize for instruction have assumed many varying positions. In the interests of simplicity, let us place two basic ideas at each end of a continuum and recognize the fact that many variations in opinion exist between these extremes. At one extreme we may place the

[1] J. Cecil Parker and Louis J. Rubin, *Process and Content: Curriculum Design and the Application of Knowledge* (Chicago: Rand McNally, 1966), p. 1.

concept that the school's responsibility is the intellectual training of children, and the curriculum should, therefore, be limited to academic subjects—the typical subject curriculum. At the other extreme we set the idea that the school should accept full responsibility for the entire range of intellectual, social, physical, and vocational needs of youth, and that it should provide a broadly expanded program to meet these needs. The subject-centered versus student-centered question mentioned earlier forms the basis for this dichotomy. Probably no one advocates either extreme position, although several theorists have taken positions near these extremes. Between the extremes may be placed the many combinations and variations of the two basic concepts.

Arno Bellack describes two contrasting approaches to curriculum selection and organization which illustrate similar extremes of opinion, although the second position he describes does not divide the curriculum into discrete subjects to the extent demanded by the extreme subject-centered approach.

> First, there is the point of view that curriculum content should be selected and organized on the basis of categories of life functions or youth needs. This position, which has gained wide acceptance among educators during recent years, in effect calls for a curriculum that deals with life situations as they are faced by adolescents and makes a direct assault on the problems of living as they are encountered by youth. Accordingly, instruction is organized around problems or topics dealing with health, family relations, civic affairs, community life, recreation, and the like. Resources of the culture—generalizations, skills, concepts, techniques and methods—are selected on the basis of their relevance to the topics under study and their contribution to the solution of personal and social problems faced by students.
>
> Another group . . . contends that all youth live in multiple environments—the changing ones of the world of nature, those of social organizations and interest communities, and the personal environments of introspection that each one lives in with himself. The intellectual tools to interpret and deal with these aspects of the environment are to be found in the great organized fields of human inquiry and creativity. Therefore, the argument runs, a functional program is one that introduces youth to the areas of inquiry and creativity that correspond roughly to the three interrelated aspects of the environment—the social sciences, the natural sciences, and the humanities.[2]

The extreme positions described above may also be viewed in terms of the theoretical versus the practical, with the intellectual or subject emphasis being considered more theoretical in nature and the emphasis on student needs the more practical. John Dewey recognized the conflict which usually develops in attempting to recognize both concepts when working to develop the school curriculum. He contended that the practical and theoretical elements are both necessary, forming mutually reinforcing ingredients in a functional program for young people.[3]

[2]Arno A. Bellack, "Selection and Organization of Curriculum Content: An Analysis," *What Shall the High Schools Teach?* (Washington, D.C.: Association for Supervision and Curriculum Development, 1956), pp. 104–105.

[3]John Dewey, *How We Think* (Lexington, Mass.: Heath, 1933), pp. 228–229.

In developing another plan of curriculum study and improvement, Hilda Taba first described four levels of knowledge to be recognized:

1. Specific facts, descriptive ideas at a low level of abstraction, and specific processes and skills.
2. Basic ideas and principles, . . . ideas which describe facts of generality, fact that, once understood, will explain many specific phenomena.
3. Concepts, such as the concept of democracy, of interdependence, of social change, or of the "set" in mathematics.
4. Thought systems . . . composed of propositions and concepts which direct the flow of inquiry and thought.[4]

It is proposed that each discipline and each subject within a discipline offers something distinctive to the education of students at each level of knowledge. Each level of knowledge implies somewhat differing methods of teaching and fundamentals to be acquired. The concept of scope appropriate to thinking in terms of levels of knowledge goes beyond the traditional ideas of "coverage" and views the content fields as a way of understanding a limited number of basic ideas rather than treasures of knowledge to be transmitted. Learning of facts need not necessarily precede learning to think (they may proceed simultaneously), and the integration of knowledge occurs more readily when knowledge is viewed by levels.[5]

A seminar sponsored by the National Education Association in 1962 drew scholars from the several disciplines together to consider the problems and possibilities of curriculum selection and organization, and from this conference there emerged another recommended approach to reconciling the demands of disciplines and the needs of our culture and society where they are competitive. The proposed plan would recognize that at each level of school the curriculum consists of two parts—the *nuclear* curriculum and the *cortical* curriculum. The nuclear curriculum would be designed to fulfill those objectives of education which are determined primarily by the needs of youth and the demands of our society. The cortical component would consist of materials chosen specifically because of their direct relationships to the major disciplines, and emphasis would center around the more important conceptual frames of each discipline, its techniques of discovery and verification, and the variety of problems to which it addresses itself. The ratio of nuclear to cortical components in the curriculum would vary from about 90 percent nuclear–10 percent cortical in the earlier grades to the reverse ratio in the upper levels of high school, with an overall ratio probably being about 60 percent nuclear–40 percent cortical.[6]

James B. Conant, who has gained considerable respect among both educators and interested laymen in recent years, has proposed that the high school cur-

[4]Hilda Taba, *Curriculum Development* (New York: Harcourt, 1962), pp. 174–181.
[5]Taba, *op. cit.*, pp. 181–192.
[6]*The Scholars Look at the Schools* (Washington, D.C.: National Education Association Project on Instruction, February 1962), pp. 51–52.

riculum, in its effort to provide a good general education for all students, should include three major areas of study:

1. The Humanities—art and literature.
2. The Study of Man—ethics, political science, economics, psychology, sociology and anthropology. History and philosophy are fields of study that form the connecting link between these subjects and the humanities.
3. The Natural Sciences.[7]

He emphasizes that in carrying out this program of studies constant attention should be given to helping students see the relevance of their academic studies to the world around them and to their personal lives.

Harry Broudy has taken a similar stand pointing out that students need to gain an understanding of the physical environment, the social environment, and the "life of the self." To help young people achieve an understanding of their relationships to these aspects of the environment, he proposes that the curriculum should be organized around the three major areas of (1) the natural sciences, (2) the social studies, and (3) living with the self, or self-science.[8]

Joseph J. Schwab has identified the existence of at least three "great genera of disciplines." These "genera" are another approach to grouping knowledge into broad fields possessing basic similarities. Schwab calls them

1. The investigative (natural sciences).
2. The appreciative (arts).
3. The decisive (social sciences).[9]

Disciplinary Structure and the Curriculum

As one studies the different proposals being made for revising and reorganizing the secondary school curriculum it becomes rather obvious that three major purposes lie at the heart of these attempts: (1) to understand the basic relatedness of knowledge (the structure) inherent within the disciplines, (2) to establish relationships among the disciplines, and (3) to establish relationships between the disciplines and life situations. Serious attempts are being made to reconcile the old arguments about the relative value and place of subject matter demands versus student and social needs in the curriculum, and significant progress is evident as better understanding is gained of the concepts of disciplinary structure and how these concepts may be applied to everyday teaching and learning.

Defining Disciplinary Structure

Many of the writers concerned with the concept of disciplinary structure make it appear unnecessarily abstract and difficult to understand. The structure

[7] James B. Conant, *Education in a Divided World* (Cambridge, Mass.: Harvard U. P., 1948).
[8] Harry Broudy, *Building a Philosophy of Education* (Englewood Cliffs, N.J.: Prentice-Hall, 1954), Chapter 7.
[9] *The Scholars Look at the Schools, op. cit.,* p. 3.

of anything refers to its parts and the ways in which they are interrelated. Similarly, the concept of disciplinary structure refers to the connections and derivations within the field of knowledge that make one idea follow from another. In the words of Bruner:

> Grasping the structure of a subject is understanding it in a way that permits many other things to be related to it meaningfully. To learn structure, in short, is to learn how things are related.[10]

Each discipline has a fundamental structure, which, if understood, will allow the student to draw implications and relationships from his study instead of just memorizing a body of factual subject knowledge which he may neither understand nor be able to use intelligently.

We have traditionally divided knowledge into many separate subjects, such as American history, world history, government, physics, chemistry, literature, grammar, and so on. Disciplines obviously have a natural order and structure which separate them, but we have tended to make too many artificial divisions. The resulting separation of disciplines into numerous subjects is unnatural and defeats many of our expressed purposes in education.

> . . . [students] graduate from junior high school, and . . . from senior high school as well, imbued primarily with one gigantic falsehood: *Subjects consist of little discrete pieces of knowledge that have almost no discernible relationship either to each other or to the whole of one's living environment.*[11]

The concept of disciplinary structure suggests that we may integrate knowledge most efficiently by maintaining the broadest possible disciplinary organization within which the method of inquiry and structure are such as to produce the perception of "wholeness" in the minds of students.

Broad knowledge division such as "social studies," "mathematics," and "science," may be utilized rather than the more narrow and limited divisions denoted by the terms "world history," "physics," and "algebra." A statement by Dorothy M. Fraser illustrates the justification for this approach to curriculum organization:

> A discipline is more than a collection of information; it is a body of knowledge organized around basic concepts. These basic concepts form the structure of the discipline. That is, they provide a structure or perhaps several complementary structures within which the relationships of specific facts can be established and the meaning of the facts understood.[12]

[10]Jerome S. Bruner, *The Process of Education* (Cambridge, Mass.: Harvard U. P., 1960), p. 7.

[11]Theodore Brameld, "A Philosopher Looks at the Current Values and Changing Needs of Youth," *The Current Values and Changing Needs of Youth* (Hartford: Connecticut State Department of Education, 1966), p. 39.

[12]Dorothy M. Fraser, *Deciding What to Teach* (Washington, D.C.: National Education Association, 1963), pp. 21–22.

An adequate definition of disciplinary structure has proved an illusive goal of scholars and groups studying curriculum, and writers usually skirt the problem by describing and illustrating some of the elements of the concept, as we have briefly attempted above. Perhaps reference to one more approach will be sufficient at this point.

Philip H. Phenix has stated that a discipline must consist of knowledge which is organized in such a way that it may be taught. Three fundamental features are thus required of a discipline: (1) analytic simplification, (2) synthetic coordination and (3) dynamism.[13]

Analytic simplification means that diverse and apparently disparate elements of experience are integrated into a common framework of ideas. Analysis is discernment of similarities and differences among the objects or concepts being studied. This leads to simplified understanding of the body of knowledge through the establishment of certain techniques, models, and theories which are characteristic of the discipline. Rather than requiring an increasing burden of accumulated knowledge, advanced study of a discipline should achieve an increasing simplicity and understanding.

> If . . . it can be made clear that, like Christian in Bunyan's allegory, the academic pilgrimage aims at release from the burdens of merely accumulated experience and leads to intellectual salvation through the insightful and revelatory concepts and theories contained in the traditions of the disciplines, how eager students become to learn and how ready to exchange their hampering ignorance for liberating understanding.[14]

Synthetic Coordination makes it possible for concepts to be seen in their interconnections and relationships rather than in isolation. This function of a discipline, then, is to reveal significant patterns and relationships. A hierarchy of ideas is established through the discrimination of similarities through analysis. The organization of curriculum by disciplines thus facilitates the teaching of the subject matter contained therein.

> Whatever is taught within a discipline framework draws strength and interest from its membership within a family of ideas. Each new idea is illuminated by ideas previously acquired. A discipline is a community of concepts. Just as human beings cannot thrive in isolation, but require the support of other persons in mutual association, so do isolated ideas wither and die, while ideas comprehended within the unity of a discipline tend to remain vivid and powerful within the understanding.[15]

The third quality of a discipline, *dynamism*, refers to the power to encourage further understanding, the ability to invite further analysis and synthesis. The concepts of a discipline will suggest new structures of understanding which

---

[13]Philip H. Phenix, "The Use of the Disciplines as Curriculum Content," *Educational Forum*, 26 (March, 1962), pp. 273–280.

[14]*Ibid.*, pp. 276–277.

[15]*Ibid.*, p. 277.

enable the student to make new generalizations and further simplify and coordinate the body of knowledge.[16]

Components of a Discipline

The above attempts to arrive at a description of a discipline have included references to the composition of a discipline—the elements which combine to form it. It appears that three primary ingredients are included in the make-up of disciplines: content, structure, and methods of inquiry.

The *content* of a discipline is usually understood to mean the data and factual information which are combined in a logical and natural way to form the *structure*, which we have described as a combination of basic concepts and generalizations. The *method of inquiry* refers to a discipline's particular approaches, tools, and methods for discovering and ordering information. None of these can be fully understood in isolation from the other, but their individual existence and relationships to each other need to be recognized to facilitate a fuller understanding of the disciplinary concept.

When we recognize and understand the various disciplines we may logically develop a curriculum for instructional purposes. This curriculum should carefully adhere to the fundamental content, structure, and method of inquiry of the discipline. Although it will contain several subject areas to aid in the translation of the discipline into patterns of learning, this translation should be constantly evaluated and revised. Arthur Foshay has stated this admonition very well:

> . . . [H]ow good is the translation? Is the subject of mathematics as we conceive of it in school true to the discipline of mathematics as a mathematician sees it? . . . In a good many cases our attempts to translate the discipline into viable subject matter that can be learned in school are a mistranslation, in the sense that learning method that we have developed has taken the place of the discipline. We have become subject-centered in fact; the subject is no longer relevant to the discipline. Our objection to the artificial and largely arbitrary nature of much school subject matter is derived from the fact that it is arbitrary, superficial material. It fails properly to represent the discipline out of which it came.
>
> Listen to a series of charges. We have taught prosody in the name of poetry, thus killing an interest in poetry for ourselves and our descendants. We have taught grammar in the name of composition, destroying the possibility of a widespread ability to write good essays or even good expository prose. We have taught computation in the name of mathematics, and now we commonly say to one another, "The trouble is, the youngsters can do it, but they don't understand it." When we have taught phonics in the name of reading, we have produced in the early grades word-callers, not readers. We have taught place geography in the name of geography, almost killing this subject in the schools. No geographer says that this is what geography is. We have taught dates and battles in the name of history; I would say instead of history. An historian does not describe

[16] *Ibid.*, pp. 277–279.

his discipline thus. Only in school do you get preoccupied with these matters—never again. We have taught facts and principles in the name of science; but science is a mode of inquiry, and the scientists now say what we are doing is not only out of date, but it is not science.[17]

Identification of Disciplines

Before we can progress further in our discussion of disciplines and their structure, the disciplines must be identified, and it is at this point that writers on the subject part company.

Knowledge has commonly been grouped for pedagogical purposes into several categories. Each group has been called in many cases a discipline; at other times a subject or course of study. History, anthropology, and sociology, although exhibiting many similarities of structure and purpose, are treated as separate "disciplines." Teachers may seek to establish relationships among these groupings, but the separation usually remains rather definite in the minds of both teachers and students. The umbrella concept of "literature" may be utilized to hold poetry, prose, and drama together to some extent, but how do grammar, composition, and spelling fit into the picture? Physics, biology, chemistry, and geology each occupy a world of their own in the minds of too many teachers and students, despite the efforts of recent study committees and textbook writers. Music and art are well-established curriculum elements, but where do they fit into the total picture—even when grouped into "fine arts"? Add to this confused galaxy the fields of business education, physical education, and other similar occupants of school schedules and the picture becomes almost hopelessly blurred. In the absence of broad unifying concepts, it is no wonder that teachers become subject-bound and students graduate from high school and college wearing a highly efficient set of subject-tinted blinders.

PROPOSALS CONCERNING THE DESIGNATION OF DISCIPLINES. A preceeding section of this chapter discussed some of the proposals concerning the selection and organization of curriculum materials and described several of the ideas about how subject matter should be divided and organized. A brief examination of three additional proposals about how knowledge should be divided for teaching and learning may serve to widen our perspectives and help lead to a plan of disciplinary organization which may be best applied in the secondary school curriculum and which may serve as a basis for organizing the discussion in this text.

As part of the justification for proposing organization of the curriculum

---

[17]Arthur Foshay, "Education and the Nature of a Discipline," in Walter B. Waetjen (ed.), *New Dimensions of Learning* (Washington, D.C.: Association for Supervision and Curriculum Development, National Education Association, 1962), pp. 5–6.

around "families" of closely related disciplines, Alice Miel suggested in the 1963 Yearbook of the Association for Supervision and Curriculum Development that a block of time devoted to the disciplines should provide at least four different kinds of experiences:

> (a) for learning the domain and the key concepts of the disciplines; (b) for rediscovering (or possibly discovering) knowledge in the disciplines; (c) for taking on the structures of the disciplines (some of the most significant, interrelated facts making up that body of knowledge); and (d) for seeing likenesses and differences among disciplines in the same category and becoming aware of their relation to the totality of knowledge.[18]

These types of experiences would be provided by arranging the study of the disciplinary "families" into three "cycles" which would be spread from grade four through grade twelve, as follows:

Cycle One

Grade 4	The arts (graphic and plastic, fine and industrial, music, dance, poetry).
Grade 5	The natural and physical sciences (human biology, physiology, chemistry, physics, physical geography, geology, climatology, astronomy) and mathematics (arithmetic, geometry, algebra).
Grade 6	Social sciences (history, anthropology, sociology, economics, political science) and ethics.

Cycle Two

Grade 7	Communication (linquistics, semantics, mathematics, statistics, art forms).
Grade 8	Social sciences (history, human geography, political science, economics).
Grade 9	Natural and physical sciences (biology, chemistry, physics).

Cycle Three

Grade 10	Communication and aesthetics (literature and the arts).
Grade 11	Social sciences (sociology, psychology, social psychology, anthropology).
Grade 12	Religion, philosophy, and ecology.[19]

Harry S. Broudy identifies six areas and functions of knowledge and groups the disciplines serving them ". . . to indicate six distinctive strands of the curriculum, each organizing knowledge in a different way in order to achieve somewhat different school and life outcomes."

1. The symbolic tools of learning, thinking, and communication: language of ordinary discourse; language of quantity (mathematics); language of art (drawing, painting, musical performance, etc.)—all as influenced by modern developments in linguistics, logic, and information theory.
2. Systematization of basic areas of knowledge: physics, chemistry, astronomy, geology; biology, physiology, botany; psychology, sociology.

[18]Alice Miel, "Knowledge and the Curriculum," *New Insights and the Curriculum* (Washington, D.C.: Association for Supervision and Curriculum Development, 1963), p. 95.
[19]*Ibid.*, p. 96.

3. Organization of the past: evolutionary account of cosmos; evolutionary account of human groupings (family, communities, and types of state); evolutionary account of institution sciences, technologies, art and value systems.
4. Modes of analyzing and coping with the problems of the future—the role of agriculture, medicine, engineering, and other arts based on knowledge—also the regulative sciences of law, political science, economics, administration and management, and the sciences of information distribution such as education, library science, journalism, and mass communications.
5. Value systems that synthesize and integrate man's knowledge and strengthen his aspirations—philosophy and fine arts.
6. Personal problems.[20]

Philip H. Phenix has identified six "realms of meaning" and proposes that the curriculum be organized to correspond with these basic disciplines which "exhibit distinctive structures or patterns of meaning." In studying each discipline, Phenix suggests that the main questions to be asked are:

1. What does it mean to know in this discipline?
2. How is knowledge gained in this subject, and how is it validated?
3. How does knowledge in this discipline differ from and agree with knowledge in other disciplines?

To answer these questions, analysis of the discipline must proceed along four main lines: the *general logical character* of the field, the distinctive *subject matter* of the discipline, the *representative ideas* of the discipline, and the *methods of inquiry* used in the discipline.[21]

On the basis of the above concepts, Phenix identifies the six fundamental patterns of meaning as follows:

1. The first realm, *symbolics,* comprises ordinary language, mathematics, and various types of nondiscursive symbolic forms, such as gestures, rituals, rhythmic patterns, and the like.
2. The second realm, *empirics,* includes the sciences of the physical world, of living things, and of man.
3. The third realm, *esthetics,* contains the various arts, such as music, the visual arts, the arts of movement, and literature.
4. The fourth realm, *synnoetics,* embraces what Michael Polanyi calls "personal knowledge" and Martin Buber the "I-Thou" relation. The novel term "synnoetic" . . . derives from the Greek *synnoesis,* meaning "meditative thought," and this in turn is compounded of *syn,* meaning "with" or "together," and noesis, meaning "cognition." Thus synnoetics signifies "relational insight" or "direct awareness."
5. The fifth realm, *ethics,* includes moral meanings that express obligation rather than fact, perceptual form, or awareness of relation.
6. The sixth realm, *synoptics,* refers to meanings that are comprehensively integrative. It includes history, religion, and philosophy. These disciplines combine empirical, esthetic, and synnoetic meanings into coherent wholes.[22]

---

[20]Harry S. Broudy, *Building a Philosophy of Education,* 2d ed. (Englewood Cliffs, N.J.: Prentice-Hall, 1961), pp. 314–315.
[21]Philip H. Phenix, *Realms of Meaning* (New York: McGraw-Hill, 1964), pp. 53–54.
[22]*Ibid.,* pp. 6–7.

A Retreat to Tradition. Early in the development of Western thinking about knowledge, four major categories were established for grouping the various fields of learning—the *humanities*, the *social studies*, *mathematics*, and the *natural sciences*. Each of these groupings exhibits distincitive although not necessarily entirely unique types of content, structure, and methods of inquiry. In short, each contains the three components of a discipline we identified earlier in this discourse, and these three components seem to rather adequately include other ideas suggested by scholars in the field. Within the *humanities* may be grouped the study of literature, language, music, art, and drama. *Social studies* may include history, sociology, government, anthropology, and similar disciplines. Algebra, geometry, trigonometry, calculus, and other related divisions may be combined within the concept of *mathematics*. The *natural sciences* category groups the study of chemistry, physics, geology, biology, and other similar categories of knowledge into a more meaningful whole.

One or more of the recent attempts to identify basic areas of knowledge may be more accurate and inclusive in the light of modern understanding. Yet, because most students of education are more familiar with the traditional groupings and would find it difficult to think in some of the more drastically different terms suggested, and because each of these categories seems to rather adequately fulfill the concepts of disciplinary wholeness which we have developed, discussion in the chapters that follow will be organized primarily around these four groupings, which we will call classes of disciplines: the humanities, the social studies, mathematics, and the natural sciences. The traditional subject divisions may be grouped into these disciplinary classes rather easily (although several must be included to some extent in more than one class), and the disciplinary elements of content, structure, and inquiry method embodied in each category make it possible to organize learning activities and courses around instructional purposes in such a way that both teachers and students may view the world, its inhabitants, and its physical elements as a more meaningful whole, rather than as unrelated parts. Within each class of disciplines, the subdivisions of *disciplines*, *subjects*, and *courses* will serve to provide the subgroupings necessary for logical and efficient teaching and learning. For our purposes, a "subject" will be viewed as a subdivision of a "discipline," and the term "course" will refer to a series of encounters typically planned for an age, grade, ability, or interest group of students.

In order to include consideration of parts of today's secondary school curriculum which do not lend themselves to grouping within the above four classes of disciplines, those learning activities commonly termed vocational or technical will be grouped under the heading of vocational and technical skills, although it must be emphasized that each of these "vocational" and "technical" instructional categories includes elements of the "disciplines." Student activities, guidance and counseling services, organization of the curriculum in terms of time and space allocations, and curriculum evaluation and improvement are alloted additional chapters to facilitate the consideration of their special place and function in the total school teaching and learning program.

Selected References

Bellack, Arno A., "Selection and Ogranization of Curriculum Content: An Analysis," in *What Shall the High Schools Teach?* ASCD 1956 Yearbook. Washington, D.C.: Association for Supervision and Curriculum Development, 1956, pp. 97–126.

Bruner, Jerome S., *On Knowing: Essays for the Left Hand.* Cambridge, Mass.: Harvard University Press, 1962. Part II "The Quest for Clarity."

———, *The Process of Education.* New York: Vintage Books, 1960, Chapter 2, "The Importance of Structure," pp. 17–32.

Conant, James B., *Education in a Divided World.* Cambridge, Mass.: Harvard University Press, 1948.

Dewey, John, *How We Think.* Lexington, Mass.: D. C. Heath & Company, 1933.

Doll, Ronald C., *Curriculum Improvement: Decision-Making and Process.* Boston: Allyn and Bacon, Inc., 1964. "Reconsidering Subject-matter as Learning Content," pp. 79–84.

Foshay, Arthur W., "Education and the Nature of a Discipline," in Walter B. Waetjen (ed.), *New Dimensions of Learning.* Washington, D.C.: Association for Supervision and Curriculum Development, 1962.

Fraser, Dorothy M., *Deciding What to Teach.* Washington, D.C.: National Education Association Project on Instruction, 1963, Chapter 2, "Learning, the Disciplines, and the School Program," pp. 15–49.

King, Arthur R., Jr., and John A. Brownell, *The Curriculum and the Disciplines of Knowledge.* New York: John Wiley & Sons, Inc., 1966.

Miel, Alice, "Knowledge and the Curriculum," in Alexander Frazier (ed.), *New Insights and the Curriculum,* ASCD 1963 Yearbook. Washington, D.C.: Association for Supervision and Curriculum Development, 1963.

Parker, J. Cecil, and Louis J. Rubin, *Process and Content: Curriculum Design and the Application of Knowledge.* Chicago: Rand McNally & Company, 1966.

Phenix, Philip H., *Realms of Meaning.* New York: McGraw-Hill Book Company, 1964.

———, "The Architectonics of Knowledge," in Stanley Elam (ed.), *Education and the Structure of Knowledge.* Chicago: Rand McNally & Company, 1964, pp. 44–74.

Schwab, Joseph J., "Problems, Topics, and Issues," in Stanley Elam (ed.), *Education and the Structure of Knowledge.* Chicago: Rand McNally & Company, 1964, pp. 4–42.

Shulman, Lee S., and Evan R. Keislar (eds.), *Learning by Discovery: A Critical Appraisal.* Chicago: Rand McNally & Company, 1966.

Taba, Hilda, *Curriculum Development.* New York: Harcourt Brace Jovanovich, Inc., 1962. Chapter 12, "The Nature of Knowledge," pp. 172–192.

The Scholars Look at the Schools. Washington, D.C.: National Education Association Project on Instruction, February 1962.

part II

The
Foundations
of Curriculum

The Relation of the Curriculum to the Objectives of Education

Chapter 1 began by asking some questions related to education and schools. Two questions were identified as basic to all study and work concerning schools. One of these was, "What shall the schools teach?" Before this question can be answered we must decide just what schools and teachers are trying to accomplish through teaching. In other words, what are the goals, purposes, objectives, or aims of teaching? Questions of curriculum determination cannot very well be settled until the more basic questions about purposes have been identified, studied, and solved to some degree of satisfaction.

The teacher, through teaching, tries to help students master the curriculum, and his teaching is evaluated accordingly. Teaching may be successful, however, without the students becoming satisfactorily educated. How can this be? It will occur if the curriculum does not fit the established educational purposes. The curriculum must be evaluated, then, according to the effectiveness with which it promotes the achievement of the school's objectives. It is thus readily apparent that before we concern ourselves with teaching methods or before we attempt to establish a school curriculum we must first give careful attention to the purposes and objectives of education.

Education is a value process in that those involved exercise value judgments about what should be included and what should be attempted. Purpose is always involved, whether consciously or unconsciously. As pointed out by Romine,

> The decision to be made . . . is not whether objectives will be established, but whether they shall come about through careful planning cognizant of both the end-product sought and the process of attaining it, or by default because of failure to give adequate consideration to these factors.[1]

Objectives then are the starting point for all educational criteria. They give the sense of direction and the standards for evaluation which are required to guide the efforts of all educators.

Levels of Educational Goals

An understanding of the different levels and types of educational goals will help the student of education to better relate goals to the curriculum and other facets of the educational process. Educational objectives may be classified as ultimate, intermediate, or immediate, thus providing a better perspective of the relationships that exist among these types or levels of

[1]Stephen A. Romine, *Building the High School Curriculum* (New York: Ronald, 1954), p. 158.

21

objectives. Sometimes the terms *general* and *specific* are used to denote this difference in levels of objectives.

The more general, or ultimate, goals might be illustrated by objectives of self-realization, improved human relationships, a sense of civic responsibility, and economic efficiency. "The ability to think" or other identifications of ultimate goals which have been stated by various groups and individuals may provide the ultimate or overall goals for the educational process.

The intermediate goals of education are embodied in the school curriculum—the subjects that are taught and the experiences that are provided. These subjects are useful instruments in the teaching-learning process, but they are not the end products. "They are not *what* the teacher teaches but are what the teacher teaches *with*."[2]

The more specific or immediate goals of education may be illustrated by daily lesson objectives such as "Learn how to spell *cat*," "Know the procedure for obtaining the volume of a cylinder," or "Understand the causes of the American Civil War."

Within this hierarchy of objectives there must be established a relationship that results in the objectives of the lower ranks leading to the achievement of the objectives which are more ultimate or general in nature. The ultimate goals of secondary education, the goals of the social studies program, the goals of the year or semester, the goals of a particular unit of instruction and the goals for one day must be given their proper place in the total curriculum so that the goals at a lower level combine to equal the objectives at a higher or more general level.

Sources of Educational Goals

How are educational goals established? Who decides just what our schools should be trying to do? How did we come to accept those goals as pursued by teachers and their students? Some understanding of the sources of educational goals is necessary if we are to intelligently evaluate the objectives of secondary education or satisfactorily translate them into teaching and learning activities.

Tradition and historical practice may well be the most powerful influences on curriculum goals. This is not necessarily bad, because the "tried and true" certainly deserve a place in our schools. On the other hand, tradition in itself may prove a detriment to improvement of curriculum practices. Recognition and understanding of historical sources of curriculum purposes is required of those who wish intelligently to study what is taught in schools.

Philosophy as a source of educational goals is closely tied to historical

[2]Harl R. Douglass (ed.), *The High School Curriculum*, 3d ed. (New York: Ronald, 1964), p. 25.

precedent, from the standpoints of both cause and effect. Concepts of the nature of truth, ultimate values, and first causes are inevitably tied to education. Although teachers may not consider themselves philosophers, they depend on philosophy for direction—either their own philosophy or that of others.

The nature of the learner provides a third major source of educational purposes. The interests, needs, and problems of the individual student, how he learns, his growth and development, and his behavior determinants all form a base for curriculum development which educators cannot afford to slight in their study of educational determinants. Attitudes, ideals, habits, and sensitivities are woven into the fabric of individual behavior, and it is individual behavior that should most concern those responsible for formal education.

The nature of the social order, which has established the educational process to achieve its preservation and improvement, forms the fourth major source of educational purposes. As is true with the individual, the society also has interests, needs, and problems that go into the makeup of the educational process. These sources of educational objectives originate in the social dynamics of our civilization, and they, too, must be understood if we are to competently develop aims and purposes for secondary curriculum development.

The disciplines of knowledge make up a fifth source of purposes in education. These include the traditional academic subjects, but knowledge also includes areas of learning outside the academics, such as vocational and technical knowledge. In using these sources for educational efforts, their structure provides the basic foundation for learning. Achieving student understanding of concepts, generalizations, and methods of inquiry in the disciplines of knowledge should provide prime objectives for the secondary school curriculum. This topic will be the focus of attention in Part III of this text.

CHAPTER 2

HISTORICAL
FOUNDATIONS OF SECONDARY
SCHOOL CURRICULUM

To preserve the species, man has been required from his earliest existence to pass on to the younger generation the knowledge and skills he has acquired which enable him to adequately meet his needs for food, clothing, shelter, and safety. For prehistoric, primitive man, this "education," as we would call it, was largely a matter of the father passing on to his son (or mother to daughter) the customs and skills which had been transferred from generation to generation to insure adequate provision of the necessities of life and preservation of folkways or religious customs.

One of the earliest purposes of this education was doubtless to see that the younger members of the group would respect and care for the needs of their elders when age and its infirmities prevented their adequately caring for themselves. This meant that youthful aggressiveness and natural tendencies of rebellion had to be kept under firm control. Radical departure from accepted practice threatened this control and so was discouraged, if not forbidden.

The folkways that governed the conduct of primitive peoples changed very slowly, because it was felt that safety and prosperity were dependent upon adherence to established practices, whether related to rules of warfare, skills of the hunt, treatment of other family and tribal members, sexual practices, interpretation of natural phenomena, or other aspects of daily living. Acceptance and preservation of the status quo, therefore, became a prime purpose of primitive education, and any change was suspect until thoroughly proven and accepted by those in authority.

The earliest forms of what we would call formal education came about because of the need to involve all members of the tribe or community in religious dances, chants, or other observances. Teaching these to the group became the responsibility of a priest, medicine man, or witch doctor—the first professional

25

teachers. Religion and education thus came to be thought of as interdependent and reciprocal elements of life.

When the individual reached the group standards of prowess in hunting and warfare, courage, knowledge of the various customs, and the like, his education was considered complete. To mark this stage in the individual's life, a ceremonial (often involving the choosing of a mate) initiated the young "graduate" into the adult world with "all the rights and privileges appertaining thereto."

As we move on to consideration of more recent and "civilized" developments in educational practices, we must assume, then, that most if not all of these practices are rooted in the dim past of pre-history. Tracing these roots may not be practical or necessary, but the knowledge that they exist is at least humbling.

Oriental and Hebraic Contributions

There is no way of knowing just how influential oriental practices were in the development of Western civilizations, but it is not hard to see many similarities in educational purposes and practice. These early civilizations placed extreme importance upon the preservation and acceptance—even reverence—of custom and tradition. External authority, as verified from the past, was not to be questioned. Education existed to see that each man fit into his proper place in the established social order, and individual development was sacrificed to existing standards.

The teachings of Confucius, the most influential teacher of the Far East, provide a prime example of the early educational practices developed in that part of the world. Moral training was emphasized, focusing upon the concept of a noble life. A doctrine of personal submission—subject to ruler, son to father, wife tc husband, friend to friend—was the basis for teaching human relationships, duty, order, and morality. The home was the center for most of this training and is still today the prime source of responsibility for such practical education.

Confucius was a pragmatist, maintaining close contact with his pupils to assure maximum influence and stimulation. After his death, however, his followers began to move away from this example of utility and personal relationships between teacher and pupil. Education became formalized and took on an abstract and meaningless character because of practices that developed which required memorization of the traditional texts, without application.

The Hebrews formed a link between oriental civilization and those that grew up in the Western world. In the field of education, they mark a transition from Far Eastern practices to those coming later in Europe and America, and the precedents they set were especially important in later Christian educational practices.

Hebraic law and custom established the most extensive educational system of ancient times and the only one that aimed to make all members of the culture literate. The Jews saw education as necessary to the maintenance of a national identity. Universal, compulsory education was prescribed by God, and religious training was accepted as its first purpose.

Hebrew education accepted the oriental subjection to external authority, but this authority, instead of being tradition or ancestoral prescription, was the authroity of Jehovah. On the other hand, it was democratic in the sense that all members of the group were educated.

The system adopted by the Hebrews to carry out the divine mandates concerning education placed much importance on family responsibilities for education of children. The patriarchal authority given to the father in the home carried with it the responsibility for teaching the children. The mother played an important part, especially in the training of the daughters, and shared the responsibility for family education.

A formal educational system existed alongside the family responsibility, and was also closely related to the religious practices and institutions. The Jewish boy in ancient times usually began his formal education in a school attached to the synagogue when he was about six years old. He was first taught to read and write and then was trained to develop a mastery of the laws and customs of his people. The school day was long, usually consuming the daylight hours, and the only respite during the year was for religious holidays. Priests formed the teaching staff.

Ancient Hebraic education had some very practical aspects, its two primary purposes being vocational training and education designed to preserve the culture and religion. With the passage of time, however, the synagogue schools became places for rote memorization of the Mosaic law and accepted interpretations of that law. Training in ritualistic observances largely took the place of more useful education.

Ancient Greece

From the civilization of the ancient Greeks we can more readily trace the threads of educational philosophy and practice. It is not at all difficult to recognize in the educational systems of the city-states of Sparta and Athens the basic controversies and questions that plague us today; the importance of history in understanding contemporary educational problems becomes even more evident.

Greek civilization and education may be logically divided into two periods, commonly called the old and new periods. During the early period education was almost wholly designed to serve the purposes of the state, whereas the later period, at least in Athens, allowed more consideration of the individual. The question of individual versus state needs, a question still very much with us, thus occupied the ancient Greeks, and doubtless those before them.

The Earlier Period

Education to serve the purposes of the state took two different forms during the earlier period of Greek civilization. The system developed by the Spartans contrasted rather dramatically with the Athenian system because the two forms of government were quite different. Sparta was surrounded by hostile neighbors and found it necessary to wage an almost constant war of survival. The system of government developed in Sparta very logically stressed promotion of the Spartan state, and laws written to form organized education aimed to submerge the individual in his duties to the state. Spartan education purposed to produce good soldiers—men who were courageous, physically strong, skilled in the arts of war, and completely loyal to the state.

The Spartan state's complete control over the life and education of its people began at birth, when an inspection committee determined if the babies appeared to be physically and mentally strong enough to be good warriors or mothers of warriors. If not, they were not allowed to live. Babies that passed this examination were left with their mother until age 7, at which time they became wards of the state. From age 7 through age 18 or 19 they lived in a barracks under the supervision of state officials and received the prescribed training.

The Spartan educational curriculum consisted primarily of exercises, games, gymnastics, hand-to-hand combat, running, jumping, throwing, and other prerequisites of fighting prowess. Instruction in civic virtues and responsibilities to the state was given at the mess tables, with intellectual training being largely limited to memorization of the accepted laws and excerpts from Homer, particularly those glorifying war.

Upon completion of his barracks training, the young Spartan was granted recognition as an apprentice soldier and entered the service of his country. At age 30 he gained the status of warrior and attained the rights and duties of citizenship, which included an obligation to marry and produce more good soldiers.

The education of girls in Sparta was given more attention than at any future time until the nineteenth century. So that they might produce strong and capable soldiers, girls underwent rather rigorous physical training as well as preparation for running the household. The mother was required to assume most of the responsibility for education in these household skills.

Athenian education had little in common with that of Sparta, except its devotion to serving the purposes of the state and the development of good citizens. Instead of placing total reliance on the development of physical and military skills, the Athenians purposed to produce a citizenry educated in every aspect of culture and personality. There was a unity of educational experiences which involved the emotional, intellectual, and physical in a symmetrical pattern.

Although reserved for male *citizens*, a rather small proportion of the population, Athenian education set the stage for later Western educational practice.

Instead of destroying the family, as in Sparta, Athens preserved it and gave it much of the responsibility for education. The concept of the liberal arts (education for a free man, and the idea of a well-rounded education) came to us largely as formed in Athens.

The training of Athenian citizens to age 7 was left in the hands of the family, at which time private schools took up the responsibility. Only the last two years of education, when the boys were age 16–18, were provided by the state.

Education in the private schools took two main forms and was provided by two types of schools. The *palaestra*, or gymnastic school, emphasized physical development, but stressed grace and harmony of body rather than physical strength and skill as a warrior. The *didascaleum*, or music school, included reading, writing, the literary element of education (poetry, drama, history, oratory), science, training in citizenship, and music.

What might be called secondary education in the early Athenian period was under the direct control of state officials, and was designed as military training. It consisted largely of physical training at the gymnasium, an exercising ground on the outskirts of Athens, and was followed by two years of military service. After they completed their two years of military service, the boys became citizens of the state.

The Later Athenian Period

Following the Persian Wars (380 B.C.), democratic ideas gradually developed in Athens, opportunity for advancement in politics accelerated, and the expansion of trade and other financial endeavors afforded the accumulation of individual wealth on an unprecedented level. Men were able to win fame and fortune for themselves, with little regard for the welfare of the state or society, and individualism became more important than the state.

A new type of education became popular which catered to the particular needs and desires of individuals and the demands of the times. Wandering teachers known as *Sophists* taught (for a fee) any who would listen. The type of learning most desired was usually related to success in life, since this was often best acquired through careers in politics. Skill in debate and public speaking, therefore, became the most popular educational objective.

The formal Athenian schools were influenced by the mood of the times and altered their programs so that the former emphasis on athletics and physical training yielded to the study of grammar and rhetoric, reading classic writings and speeches, and development of skill in speaking and debate. Athenian education began to lose its well-rounded and "liberal arts" character in favor of whatever seemed at the moment most likely to lead to personal success.

Controversy between conservative elements, who viewed the new trends in education as a national disaster, and the followers of the Sophists led to somewhat compromising proposals by philosophers such as Socrates, Plato, and Aristotle.

The admonition "know thyself" formed the foundation for Socrates' teachings. Progress toward this goal was achieved through a system of guided questions and answers designed to inductively lead the student to understanding and wisdom (a procedure known today as the "Socratic method" of teaching). He maintained that education should have for its immediate goal the development of the power to think, not simply the imparting of knowledge. Knowledge was not considered unnecessary, however, because Socrates also propounded the idea that "knowledge is virtue" and possesses universal validity.

Plato sought to develop concepts about an ideal social system in which each individual would be placed according to his abilities so that the best service to the state would be achieved. He pointed out that people vary in their abilities and interests, that these variations fit them for different places of responsibility in life, and that education should have as its goal the best preparation possible for each individual so that he might optimally fill his place in the system. Three types or classes of citizens were proposed, each with an appropriate educational background. Those who were to comprise the laboring class of people would be afforded a basic education of four to six years, similar to earlier ideals of Athenian education. Those with more ability would be selected to be civil servants, guardians, and minor state rulers. They would be educated for an additional two or more years according to the places they were to fill in the state. A "higher education" was reserved for the privileged ruling class. Schooled in the best traditions in philosophical, scientific, and political learning, this intellectual elite was to be prepared to rule by wisdom, rather than the word of the law, and according to the best interests of all concerned. An aristocracy of ability was to be developed through at least ten additional years of study including arithmetic, geometry, music, astronomy, logic, and philosophy. Although Plato's ideas did not gain wide adoption during his time, his influence can be plainly seen in later developments. Special note might be made of his lack of concern for the practical value of the study required for his "philosopher-kings" and his contention that they were designed to discipline a person to think, a concept of mental exercise still prominent in the twentieth century.

Aristotle, one of Plato's pupils, also attempted to describe the ideal state and the education needed to prepare good citizens of that state. His main concern, however, was with the development of moral and intellectual virtues, which he believed would also make the most effective citizens. He proposed that physical development of a child should be followed by nurture of the irrational soul (by means of music, gymnastics, and literature), and then culminated in training of the rational soul (through mathematics, science, and dialectic). An objective and scientific method was proposed, rather than Plato's philosophical emphasis. He did not advocate education for all citizens, and saw no need for educating the working classes and little purpose in educating women. The negative effect of some of these ideas as well as Aristotle's development of the sciences and of the laws of thought or reason profoundly influenced later education, especially in the late Middle Ages.

As Athens gained a reputation for learning and teaching, men from all parts of the civilized world gathered there to study. This led eventually to the development of an intellectual community which gradually organized as the University of Athens. Aided in its spread throughout the world by the conquests of Alexander the Great and the later Roman empire, the latter days of Athenian greatness witnessed a system of education roughly similar to the elementary, secondary, and higher education we know today.

Rome

Following the conquests of Alexander the Great, the seat of Western civilization moved westward, as the armies of Rome extended that empire toward the limits of the known world. As the Greek city-states were overrun, many of the educated Greeks were taken back to Rome as slaves. Through the influence of these imported Greeks and the general results of contact with the Greek civilization, many changes were introduced into the Roman system of life and education.

Roman education provides a good example of the liberal versus vocational conflict in education. From their earliest days, the Romans were a practical people. Before the arrival of the Greeks, the primary aim of all education was the rearing of sons who would be good citizens and soldiers to serve the state. The home was the center of this training and parents were responsible for its being carried out satisfactorily. The duties of Roman citizenship were stressed through study of the laws of the Twelve Tables, which clearly described the rights and duties of Roman citizenship. Stories and songs about Roman heroes of the past strengthened this instruction. What we would consider to be the "basic skills" of reading and writing were considered unnecessary "frills."

Greek influence gradually brought about the development of more formal systems of education in Rome. An elementary type of school called the *ludus* first evolved to teach six through ten-year-old children the rudiments of reading, writing, simple calculation, and the Twelve Tables. This was later extended, probably because of the many translations of Greek classics into Latin during the second and first centuries B.C., to form a grammar school which took up the education of children from age 10 through 15. This grammar school reminds us of the "middle school" concept becoming popular today, as it included both elementary and secondary school elements. The curriculum consisted primarily of training in grammar (both Latin and Greek) and in literature. Some of Plato's suggestions for the training of philosophers—arithmetic, geometry, astronomy, and music—seem to have been included in some of the later grammar schools.

Roman emphasis on the ideal of service to society and the state brought about another extension of formal education known as the school of rhetoric. These schools of rhetoric were founded on the belief that an ideal education would produce a man who knew his duties as a citizen and who could speak convincingly about them. They offered training in the substance, arrangement, style, memorization, and delivery of speeches to boys from about ages 16–18. This included a broad expansion of the study of grammar and literature to develop the "excellence of mind" and "perfect orator" desired. Many educational historians trace the "Seven Liberal Arts" of the Middle Ages and subsequent times to the Roman schools of rhetoric, as they showed definite signs of the ideals of the "liberal education" so lauded in the centuries that followed.

It should not be concluded that the Romans had a well-developed-and well-organized system of education, even though there were schools of several types. There was no systematic plan of education supported by the government, although one or two attempts were made in that direction by at least one emperor. Only a very small minority of the young people had any opportunity for education—those whose parents were in a political and economic position to see that their children were educated. Emperor Antoninus (86 A.D. 161) decreed that all towns should pay the salaries of teachers with local tax funds, but most of the establishment, support, and control of schools seems to have been a private matter within the wealthier community of citizens.

Despite its weaknesses, the Roman system of education set many precedents and provided the basis for much that came later. The greater part of the Greek system of thought and education was preserved and passed on—though in diluted and corrupted form—to the Middle Ages and later Western civilization, and we must credit them with giving added emphasis to training for vocational and other practical purposes.

The Middle Ages

The rebuilding of any form of formal education was very slow after the fall of the Roman Empire and the barbarian invasion. The church survived as practically the only educational agency and changed the educational emphasis entirely. During Greek and Roman times the major controversy concerning education was related to whether emphasis should be given to education for the welfare of the individual or for the welfare of the state. The Church rejected both of these focuses of purpose as worldly, and established the idea that the ultimate purpose of education must be otherworldly—the salvation of souls.

The greatly deteriorated remains of Roman education were rejected and replaced first by the catechetical and cathedral schools which offered simple instruction in Christian doctrine and morality, some Greek philosophy, and a few other essentials for the training of clergy. As the monasteries came into being, they too established elementray forms of education, teaching to read and write and to do simple calculation.

Some of the monks became dissatisfied with such rudimentary education and returned to the Roman and Greek classics still available to them, arguing that it was only the spirit of pagan education that was wrong, the form and substance of it being just as valuable to servants of God as to Greek philosophers or Roman orators. From this movement developed the curriculum known as the "Seven Liberal Ats," which formed the foundation for education throughout the Middle Ages and greatly influenced the curriculum of schools until today. This curriculum consisted of the *quadrivium* (arithmetic, astronomy, geometry, and music) and the *trivium* (grammar, rhetoric, and dialectic). The influence of Plato's curriculum for philosophers may be detected in the *quadrivium*, while the *trivium* exhibits obvious similarities to the Sophist and Roman school of rhetoric programs to train orators for political success. Most of the subject matter was diluted and corrupted, however, because the monastic and cathedral schools were not all interested in developing philosophers, orators, or statesmen. The fear that pagan learning might corrupt the faithful squeezed the *trivium* quite empty. Grammar was concerned with the Latin language and the forms of literature, and its mediocrity may be illustrated by the fact that the elementary grammar text used for over 800 years consisted of only fourteen pages. Rhetoric degenerated to a study of rules for letter writing and record keeping. Dialectic was formal logic used mainly for heresy hunting. Within the *quadrivium*, arithmetic usually involved little more than the calendar calculations necessary to determine holy days (at least partially due to the difficulty of calculating with Roman numerals). Geometry included the writing of Euclid, geography and natural history, and some study of medicines to be derived from plants. Music encompassed the theory and practice of church music. Astronomy dealt with the courses of the stars and involved more superstition (astrology) than science.

Few of the schools attempted to instruct in all the above areas. They usually focused their attention on either the *quadrivium* or the *trivium*. Some attempted to add study in ethics and theology above the "Seven Liberal Arts," but it was all a far cry from the thought and learning of the ancient Greeks.

With the development of the customs and rules of chivalry which grew out of the feudalistic system of the Middle Ages, there came a need for a different kind of education. The rules of war, courtship, etiquette, the tournament and other aspects of life as prescribed by chivalry pertained primarily to members of the nobility, but each noble generation had to be educated for life as knights or ladies. A system was developed for training the boys which included about seven years' training in the home, another seven with a family of higher rank in the nobility, and then seven years as squire attending the lord in battle and caring for his various needs. Following the teaching which accompanied this service, the squire was ready for knighthood. Girls were taught household arts and the manners of chivalry at home or as maids-in-waiting to the ladies at court.

Chivalric education is another in a long list of examples which illustrate the development of schools or systems of education more related to practical needs. The cathedral and monastery schools were not meeting the needs of feudalism, so chivalric education attempted to fill the gap. It too had religious aims at its core, because the knight was considered a defender and servant of the church, but it was a nonintellectual education, because the more formal system failed to adjust to practical demands of the times.

Another type of education came into being in the later Middle Ages because of the failure of traditional educational forms to meet developing needs. With the renewed interest in trade, commerce, and industry, the growth of towns, and the development of various skilled craftsmen, groups of tradesmen, merchants, and craftsmen organized guilds, which were similar in many ways to our modern associations and labor unions. The apprenticeship system, whereby a boy learned a skill or trade from a master, served to pass on the knowledge and skills from one generation to the next. In addition, local priests were later utilized as teachers for apprentices and other children. Reading, writing, and arithmetic for business calculations made up the curriculum, and a significant change came with the substitution of the vernacular for Latin as the language of instruction in many of these guild schools. Even though the guild schools maintained religious and moral training along with their more materialistic purposes, they were strongly opposed by the church. This opposition brought about more and more use of lay teachers and started the trend toward later secularization and civic control of education.

Among the intellectuals of the later Middle Ages, there developed a movement known as scholasticism, which came about primarily as a result of the rediscovery through Moslem scholars of the writings of Aristotle. His use of scientific reasoning as the approach to the discovery of truth conflicted with the accepted assumption that the church possessed all ultimate truth through Biblical revelation. The controversy that resulted finally culminated in the writings of St. Thomas Aquinas, who formed a synthesis of faith and reason by showing that there is no inconsistency between them if one simply uses faith as a final check on reason. The revival of learning which was an outgrowth of scholastic education served as a beginning for man's journey out of the Dark Ages and into the cultural and intellectual revolution which was to come.

At the close of the Middle Ages, then, there were several types of schools, and they were relatively numerous, even though the percentage of people afforded any kind of education was still minute. The control of education was passing from the monasteries and church authorities. Scholasticism had brought a revival of interest in the study of logic and rhetoric, ancient writing and knowledge from other parts of the world. Only a new spirit was needed to bring the blossoming of modern education.

Renaissance and Reformation

Although it began earlier, the revival or "rebirth" of classical learning and the renewed interest in individuality know as the Renaissance became prominent about the fourteenth century. This revival of learning came about as a result of the desire to free man from the bonds of theological and political tyranny under which he lived and to overcome his ignorance and fear of himself and the world about him. Great interest developed in the world of the ancient Greeks and Romans, the subjective world of the emotions, and the natural world. These interests were almost unknown in the Middle Ages, and they led to an intensive study of Greek and Latin literature. Introspective study of the emotional life encouraged new creativity in art and literature and a new interest in contemporary life.

In Italy the curriculum of schools was more a study of authors than of subjects, because knowledge had not been organized into subjects as yet. The ability to memorize was considered very important, although an understanding to accompany rote learning was deemed necessary, and it was thought that good physical condition and personal bearing should accompany intellectual development.

In Germany things took a somewhat different turn, culminating in the *Gymnasium*, a school based upon formal humanism. The idea developed that one narrow aim—Latin eloquence—should be the supreme purpose of secondary education. Other subjects received little or no attention.

England and France continued the trend toward a curriculum of the classics, with emphasis on Latin. As has happened so often, confusion developed concerning means and ends. The curriculum of humanism came to be an end in itself. Language and literature, especially, became the goals of education, rather than the way to effective and happy living.

Ciceronianism is the term used in referring to the formalized drill on Latin style which followed the earlier functional study of languages and literature. Many philosophers and educators objected to the fossilized education of Ciceronianism, and although they did not achieve immediate reforms, their influence was important later on. Three types of these objectors are commonly identified: humanistic realists, social realists, and sense realists.

The humanistic realists, such as François Rabelais and John Milton favored a return to the vitality of the humanistic school. They recommended practical subjects such as agriculture, natural history, and geography—taught by reading the works of the ancient authors in these fields.

Social realists, of which Michel de Montaigne is an example, gave priority to those subjects that would help in getting along in the world—etiquette, dancing, horsemanship, modern languages, and travel, for example. The influence of Medieval court school practices seems evident in these ideas, and several private schools were developed to carry them out.

Sense realists, as represented by John Comenius and Francis Bacon, were forerunners of our modern scientific movement in education, as they placed new emphasis on science and vernacular languages. From their proposals came the development of the *Realschule* in Germany, which included in its curriculum the study of geography, history, writing, arithmetic, economics, drawing, and manu-

factures. This trend toward the scientific and utilitarian in education pointed the
way to the American academy and similar trends of later years.

Probably the most important contributions of the Renaissance to modern
education may be summarized in two concepts—liberal education and humanism. These concepts included those studies worthy of a free man, those that tend
to develop virtue and wisdom, more emphasis on practical affairs, and a new
regard for the aesthetic. They advocated a return of individuality, freedom of
thought, creativity, and human values as opposed to otherworldly values, and they
idealized the concept of the "whole" man—the versatile and well-rounded person
created through the harmonious development of mind, body, and morals.

The sixteenth-century revolt against the established church and the general
moral decadence of Europe is known as the Reformation, and the leaders of this
movement gave some final twists to the educational ideas that were to be soon
exported to the New World. Martin Luther and John Calvin, the most prominent of the reformers, both strongly believed that the individual should be able
to read and interpret the Bible for himself, so that he might understand and
follow the Biblical requirements for salvation. This suggested that education must
be universal and compulsory. In addition, it should be removed from the control
of the Church and redefined to promote secular as well as religious purposes.
Instruction in the vernacular should be added to a broad humanistic plan of
education which would include the traditional subjects plus history, science, and
music. These ideas gained considerable acceptance and were put into practice to
some extent, although many secondary educators of the Reformation period
simply superimposed the ultimate aim of Christian salvation upon the traditional
memorization of rules of Latin and Greek grammar, excerpts from the writings
of Cicero and other similar formalized practices.

Education in Colonial America

The American colonists coming from England and Europe brought with
them the educational practices with which they were familiar, and it was many
years before something different evolved. The secondary school curriculum which
was transplanted consisted chiefly of Latin and Greek, some English, writing, and
arithmetic. This was usually provided in the Latin Grammar School, which
typified the deteriorated humanist Ciceronianism to which the reformers had
reassigned religious and moral motives. Nothing new was added to provide for
the different political, economic, and cultural environment of the new world.

In colonial America there was no universal, publicly supported system of
education. At the secondary level, the Latin Grammar School, supported by
tuition, was primarily for prospective ministers and politicians. A few of the
transitional English Grammar and private venture schools were operated by
businessmen to care for the general needs of young apprentices in commerce and
industry. Forerunners of the academy and modern educational practices, their

curriculum usually included offerings such as reading, writing, ciphering, higher mathematics as needed, merchant's bookkeeping, surveying, navigation, and sometimes local geography and history. Formal school needs were less than today, because educational needs were less complex, and the home, the farm, the shop, and the community functioned as educational agencies. Even so, the Latin Grammar School, as the only secondary school usually available, failed to meet the needs of the day.

Because the narrow curriculum of the Latin Grammar School was inadequate, and because it refused to change, a type of secondary school known as the academy began to develop during the early eighteenth century, spread throughout the colonies, and became the dominant form of secondary education by 1800. Benjamin Franklin had been one of the first to propose this type school and suggested a curriculum including such things as writing, drawing, arithmetic, accounting, geometry, astronomy, the English language, history, natural science, mechanics, commerce, and health (classical languages were considered unnecessary). Each student would take the courses most useful to him.

Few general statements can be made about the academies, because each one developed to serve the needs of the particular group supporting it. Religious groups often developed academies to serve sectarian interests; some academies had as their main purpose the provision of tutorial education for college preparation, and others served the special interests of the expanding industrial and business establishment. Whatever their major purpose, ties to the past were strong and deviation from traditional curricula came slowly. Change that did occur usually took the form of addition to the old rather than substitution of newer curricula for the traditional. Although well over a hundred different courses were offered in addition to the traditional subjects at various academies during their prominence, the core of the academy education remained the old classical curriculum of Latin, Greek, and mathematics; primarily because the major portion of the student body of most academies was composed of students preparing for college. Reversion to older practices was a constant threat to innovation and change.

The Nineteenth Century

Largely because the academies failed to fulfill their early promise to offer the type of secondary education required to meet the more practical needs of a new and expanding nation, the public high school concept began to materialize with the establish of the Boston English High School in 1821. Encouraged by the democratic ideals favoring equal opportunity for all citizens, and promoted by men like Horace Mann, mass secondary education gradually became an accepted part of American life. After the Kalamazoo decision of 1874 had established the legality of using public tax money for secondary schools, the public high school rapidly displaced the academy as the most popular form of secondary education.

By 1900 more than 20,000 such high schools were in operation, but although this was a worthy improvement of secondary education opportunity, the large majority of American youth received little if any education at the secondary level until after the turn of the century.

As with the academy, one of the primary reasons for the development of the public high school was to provide a more practical education—one not so tied to the classics. But again as with the academy, little deviation actually materialized. Some courses were added, and most schools offered two or more parallel curricula (similar to what we now call "tracks"), but theories of mental discipline and the college preparatory emphasis retarded any serious curriculum revision.

Near the turn of the century, various kinds of vocational subjects began to multiply. Commercial subjects, manual arts, agriculture, and home economics began to appear in quite a large number of public high schools, although it could not be said that they were common.

During the latter 1800's, concern and controversy about the purposes and program of public high schools led to the establishment of various committees to study and make recommendations about the course the high school curriculum should follow. Prominent among these was the Committee of Ten, which recommended in 1893 that the secondary school program should consist of five groups of studies headed by the languages. Four parallel curricula were recommended as acceptable: (1) classical, (2) Latin-scientific, (3) modern language, and (4) English. The modern-language program included no Latin or Greek and the English program included only one foreign language, and it was pointed out in the report that these programs were considered distinctly inferior to the other two. The report recognized the terminal role of high school, but still said: "Every subject which is taught at all in the secondary school should be taught in the same way and to the same extent to every pupil so long as he pursues it, no matter what the probable destination of the pupil may be, or at what point his education may cease."

Other study committees which met and reported near the turn of the century strengthened the contention of those who continued to maintain that the classical and traditional subjects should be emphasized. This college preparatory type of emphasis was also reinforced by the standardization of college entrance requirements, adoption of the Carnegie Unit, accrediting associations, and general domination of high schools by the colleges. Consequently, educational practices continued to be very slow to change.

The Twentieth Century

The curriculum study committees prior to 1900 were all characterized by an emphasis on two aspects of education—preparation for college and preparation for life. They tended to be very slow to recommend any substantial change from the traditional and classical curriculum, which consisted of primary emphasis on languages and mathematics. Some change was initiated, however, due to several developments and investigations. It was noted that a huge number of students dropped out after the sixth grade because of a lack of interest in the traditional curriculum. The changing needs of society and compulsory school attendance laws brought more recognition of individual student needs. Charles W. Eliot and others pointed out that verbal methods are not the best way to learn things that must be done in actuality in the world.

One of the more important trends was the tendency to pay more attention to the broader philosophy of John Dewey, which included the concept of "education as life" rather than just "preparation for life." The subject approach to curriculum study began to be influenced by ideas about the aims of education, as related to social and individual realities.

Numerous committees were established in attempts to establish some purpose and direction for public schools. Probably the best known of the reports coming from these various committees was the one released in 1918 by the Commission on the Reorganization of Secondary Education, which recommended that seven objectives serve to guide the selection and organization of school subjects. These objectives illustrate the growing concern for things other than subject matter of the traditional type, and may be summarized as: (1) health, (2) command of fundamental processes, (3) worthy home membership, (4) vocation, (5) citizenship, (6) worthy use of leisure, and (7) ethical character.[1]

Others pointed out the need to reorganize the curriculum to include science, industry, physics, and aesthetics. Inclusion of more materials to stimulate oral expression and to fit student interests was urged as protests rose against formal rhetoric and the piecemeal analysis of literary masterpieces. Dewey was not the only one to emphase the fact that the traditional curriculum had little or nothing to do with life, and although change came slowly, curriculum revision did become somewhat more common.

Junior High Schools

The various reports and studies made around the turn of the century pointed out several things which indicated a need for changing the 8-4 organizational plan to something which would allow better provision for the early adolescent and better articulation between elementary and secondary school. Some of the first pressure to extend the secondary school program downward to include a junior high school came from the Committee of Ten reccomendation that more than four years was needed to adequately impart the broad liberal arts education needed for success in college. Other education pointed to the massive dropout rate during the first year of high school, suggesting that a better transition was needed from the self-contained classroom of the elementary school to the depart-

---

[1] *Cardinal Principles of Secondary Education,* Department of Interior, Bureau of Education Bulletin, 1918, No. 35 (Washington, D.C.: Government Printing Office, 1937).

mentalized and highly academic high school. Psychologists proposed that early adolescents have unique needs and interests which could be better met in a special school for this age group.

Beginning about 1910, the junior high school movement allowed experimentation with ideas about individual needs, socializing experiences, and overall adolescent development which influenced the high schools as well as the developing junior high school movement. Because they were less bound by college requirements and accreditation standards, more innovation with class schedules, course content, and curriculum organization has been possible in junior high schools, although the sad fact is that they have usually not lived up to early expectations of those who hoped they would provide a much broader and pragmatic type of educational opportunity for the early adolescent.

The Period 1920–40

The more rapidly changing world of the twentieth century, especially after World War I, brought more and more demands for a change in school curriculum practice. Urbanization, population mobility, transportation, industrialization, universal compulsory elementary education and the growth of secondary and higher education, technological changes, the loosening of home and family ties, and other symptoms of a changing social and economic milieu made it necessary for education to change. Nothing revolutionary occurred, but change was evident in developments such as the guidance movement, student activities programs, vocational education, and attempts to ease subject lines of separation through "fusion," "correlation," "broad fields courses," and "core curricula."

Attempts to ease the boundaries which existed between the subject areas took many forms during the first three or four decades of the twentieth century. Many of the combinations formed courses which are still common in our schools, such as general mathematics, biology, general business, social studies, civics, and general science.

Areas of learning previously considered "extracurricular" worked their way into the regular program and were better correlated with the academic subjects. Art, music, health, and physical education programs eventually gained a permanent, although still some-what frowned-upon, place in the secondary curriculum.

Vocational education received added impetus with the passage of the Smith-Hughes Act in 1917. This was followed in later years by other acts designed to encourage and strengthen education in the fields of agriculture, home economics, and similar areas of study.

The Eight-Year Study

Dissatisfaction with the traditional strongly college-preparatory program found in most high schools encouraged considerable experimentation and deviation in curriculum organization prior to World War II. One of the best known and perhaps most significant pieces of research in curriculum revision conducted in the mid-1930's is commonly known as the Eight Year Study. This study attempted to compare the success in college of high school students who received the traditional college-preparatory secondary school education with the college performance of an experimental group graduating from schools unhampered by college entrance requirements and differing in several respects from the typical high school.

An agreement was reached between thirty high schools and more than 300 colleges which freed the high schools from the necessity of meeting the usual unit or examination requirements for college admission. The thirty schools differed widely in the extent to which they experimented, but some developed rather radical and nonacademic programs. A total of 1,475 graduates of the experimental schools were matched in terms of scholastic aptitude, interests and socioeconomic background with an equal number of graduates from traditional high schools and the college success of the two groups was compared. Success in college was defined to include grades earned, certain "intellectual characteristics" not necessarily measured by grades, citizenship in the college community, and the attainment of personal goals.

Comparison of the 1,475 matched pairs of students revealed that those who graduated from the experimental high schools were somewhat *more* successful in college than those coming from the traditional college preparatory secondary school programs. Perhaps even more significant was the finding that the graduates of the most experimental schools were strikingly more successful in college than their counterparts from traditional high schools.

> Clearly, among the Thirty Schools, the more experimental the school, the greater the degree of success in college. Furthermore, although students of high aptitude seem to have profited most from experimental education, students of low aptitude profited as much from experimental programs as their matchees did from conventional schooling.[2]

Life Adjustment Education

Following World War II, renewed interest in the ideas of John Dewey and his followers culminated in a movement known as Education for Life Adjustment. It included a considerable broadening of the high school curriculum to achieve ". . . that (education) which better equips all American youth to live democratically with satisfaction to themselves and profit to society as home members, workers, and citizens."[3]

Although the term "Life Adjustment Education" has been severely criticized

---

[2]Dean Chamberlin, Enid Chamberlin, N. E. Drought, and W. E. Scott, *Did They Succeed in College?* (New York: Harper, 1942), p. 209.

[3]*Life Adjustment Education For Every Youth*, U. S. Office of Education, Federal Security Agency, Bulletin 1951, No. 22 (Washington, D.C.: Government Printing Office, 1951), p. 4.

in recent years, the emphasis on guidance, vocational education, student activities, and other special programs has carried over into almost every modern high school program. Dewey advocated a curriculum based on problems, and he defined a problem as anything that gives rise to doubt and uncertainty. Such problems to be studied should be significant and important both to the culture and to the individual student. Most of his followers misinterpreted Dewey's ideas, and this led to a much more narrow interpretation of "problems."

Recent reforms in the science and mathematics curricula involve problems that must be solved by students utilizing the scientific method and stress "discovery" of relationships and "inquiry" into the "structure" of the world of things and ideas—all part of Dewey's concepts.

Recent Criticisms and Developments

The Progressive Education movement, including life adjustment and similar ideas, has been criticized since it first gained recognition. Because Progressive educators view subject matter as a means to an end, rather than an end in itself, some have maintained that the curricular developments they have proposed are "soft" and neglect the "essentials" of education. Some critics have accused curriculum reformers of wanting to do away with the academics in the interests of Progressive Education, although it has been stated and demonstrated time and again that this is not the case. Conservative elements have objected to the addition of courses designed to meet immediate and practical needs of students. They have been especially critical of most student activity programs and nonclassroom experiences. Most criticisms of this type are closely related to concepts of "mental discipline" and the value of accumulating knowledge for possible future use.

With the advent of the first Russian Sputnik in 1957, the criticisms and voices of alarm turned with renewed vigor to blaming the schools for most if not all of our national problems. The schools were accused of incompetence and malpractice through national publications, television and radio, and other mass media. Most critics blamed the "failure" of American education on the "new" practices and advocated a return to emphasizing the traditional "hard" or "basic" subjects. In their search for a scapegoat on which to place the blame for an apparent failure of the United States to maintain its leadership in all scientific and international affairs, many people found the schools a convenient victim. The renewed interest in education which resulted from recognition that Russia was making rapid advances in the scientific and military world has resulted in increased support for education, but it has also made it more difficult for those interested in educational reform to experience very much success in making our schools more relative to current times and student needs.

While many of the critics of public education have been primarily noneducators and have operated outside the established educational framework, others have been more constructive in their approach and have worked with educators to bring about what they considered to be needed reforms. Instead of charge and countercharge between reformer and educator, an attitude has developed which is directed at cooperation and collaboration in the study and improvement of secondary education. Prominent among these is James B. Conant, whose comprehensive survey of American high schools culminated in a report recommending that our secondary schools should accomplish three complementary goals: (1) provide a good general education for all students, (2) make available elective programs to develop useful skills, and (3) adequately educate the more academically talented students through advanced academic subjects.[4]

Conant's report was well received by most of those interested in public education, possibly because it is a moderate compromise of the views advocated by the more conservative and more liberal reformers. He has proposed no radical changes in the basic pattern of secondary education, but rather a strengthening and broadening of the typical program of a good comprehensive high school.

Since the first massive entry of the federal government into public education with the National Defense Education Act of 1958, there have been increasing efforts to include education in national efforts to improve the nation's social, economic, and military condition. "Upward Bound," "Job Corps," "Headstart," and similar programs are examples of attempts on a nationwide scale to improve the educational opportunities afforded our young people, especially those who fall into the category known as "disadvantaged." Scientific education has also reaped large benefits from national programs to keep up or surpass other world powers in certain areas. Funds to support a large variety of projects to upgrade public education have been allocated by Congress. More money is now being spent each year by the federal government for the support and improvement of public education than was spent in all the years prior to 1965, and it appears that this trend is not likely to be reversed.

Brief mention of other current "innovations" and trends may serve to indicate the direction in which the American secondary school curriculum is going. It is difficult to define or describe these activities, because they exhibit so many variations. Our limited space here allows only a listing of some of the more common types of experimentation and renovation currently in progress. These include:

1. Modular and flexible scheduling.
2. Subject matter reorganization for instructional purposes, such as the "new" math, PSSC physics, BSCS biology, structural linguistics, Chem-bond chemistry, and aural-oral foreign language techniques.
3. Nongrading or continuous progress, organizational practices.
4. Team teaching.
5. The "Middle School."

[4]James B. Conant, *The American High School Today* (New York: McGraw-Hill, 1959).

6. The addition of courses such as psychology and sociology to the secondary school curriculum.

7. Increased availability of vocational and technical training.

8. Independent study provisions in curricular organization.

9. Other approaches aimed at individualizing instruction.

Only the very brave or the foolhardy would attempt to predict the future course of our secondary school curriculum at this time. There are some indications of additional reversion to theories of mental discipline and the accumulation of knowledge, while other trends seem to indicate that efforts to develop a more vital and functional curriculum will continue and perhaps prevail over the forces of conservatism and the status quo. The future of our nation and its culture is at stake, so let us not take our task as professional educators lightly as we assume our roles in determining curriculum adequacy.

Historical Tendencies in Secondary School Curriculum

From a study of the history of education and the school curriculum, it is readily apparent that certain questions, problems, and tendencies recur in every nation and every era of Western civilization. The identification of some of these recurring phenomena will perhaps serve to summarize this brief look at the history of the secondary school curriculum.

1. *Veneration of the Written Word.* Since man first learned to put his thoughts into writing the written word has possessed an authority and influence which it may not have deserved intrinsically. This tendency may also be noted in the tendency to emphasize textbooks and textbook teaching in the schools.

2. *The Individual versus Social Needs Question.* Statesmen, philosophers, and educators since the time of Sparta and Athens have debated the relative merits of emphasizing in the educational program the needs either of individual students or of the state or society. From time to time and from nation to nation the emphasis has changed, and we must still face this crucial question in determining the purposes and objectives of the secondary school curriculum today.

3. *Deterioration and Formalization of Previously Useful Practices and Materials.* When they were introduced into the curriculum, every subject or method possessed functional and vital characteristics. With the passing of time, there has tended to develop a confusion of means and ends, so that the usefulness and vitality of these subjects and methods is replaced with a dry formalism exhibiting few if any of the original practical attributes.

4. *Devotion to the Old and Resistance to the New.* Throughout history our secondary schools have been oriented toward traditional practices and have proved difficult to displace, even when needs and times were obviously different and demanded innovations in subject matter or teaching method. Probably most of the secondary school curriculum today exists because of tradition rather than current need.

5. *Thoughtless Adoption of Innovations.* A tendency which seems to be in contrast to the traditional orientation toward the past is commonly called "getting on the bandwagon." However, it would appear that mass adoption of current innovations or "new" practices and thoughtless clinging to the past are both examples of action without logical purpose or careful evaluation of the outcomes.

6. *The Use of Education to Maintain an Elite or Ruling Class, Ignoring Needs of the Common People.* Education has historically been reserved to a privileged class—the wealthy, the clergy or the aristocracy. Consequently college preparatory purposes have dominated secondary education, a goodly portion of the curriculum has been maintained for intellectually decorative purposes, and practical needs of the noncollege-bound students have been neglected.

7. *Constant Battle Between Contrasting Ideas.* All history, and education is no exception, seems to exhibit a "pendulum" action, in that one group is continuously rebelling against another. This too often results in the defense of extreme positions with little or no effect to maintain a satisfactory middle ground. Narrow versus broad programs of education and useful versus formalized curricula are examples of this tendency.

8. *Education for Mental Discipline and Character Development.* Most of the "hard" subjects are defended on the basis of their value in "strengthening the mind" or "developing character," either because their original purpose is no longer valid or because more valid purposes are not being achieved with current teaching practices. The tendencies to venerate the written word and cling to the past are related to this phenomenon.

9. *Authoritarian versus Democratic Control.* The question of the degree of control which should be exercised, either by local authorities over the activities of teachers or by teachers over pupils is another of the recurring educational problems. This controversy has exhibited the "pendulum" qualities described above, in that educators seem to be continuously involved in a reaction against a tendency to lean in one direction or the other.

10. *College Domination of Secondary Education.* The practices and purposes of secondary schools have seldom escaped the control of higher educational institutions, partially because of other tendencies described above. This has severely limited the range of innovation and change available to those attempting to improve the secondary school.

11. *Ties Between Education and Religion.* Education has usually developed strong ties to the religion of a nation, both in terms of educational purposes and support. The question of the proper relationship between education and religion (church and state) has assumed new significance in recent allocation of public taxes for aid to private school students.

12. *Curricular Changes by Accretion.* Changes in the curriculum have usually occurred in the form of addition to the old rather than substitution of newer curricula for the traditional. Because of this tendency, at least one-half of today's

secondary school curriculum could probably be eliminated without harm to the student or society.

Other historical tendencies in secondary education and the curriculum in particular can be identified, but these will serve to illustrate the power of tradition and precedent in shaping modern educational practices. To the student and future teacher is left the responsibility for applying this knowledge of historical pressures as he attempts to improve today's secondary school curriculum.

Selected References

Atkinson, Carrol, and Eugene T. Maleska, *The Story of Education*. 2d ed. Philadelphia: Chilton Book Company, 1965.

Beckner, Weldon, and Wayne Dumas (eds.), *Readings in Secondary Education: A Foundations Approach*. Scranton, Pa.: Intext Educational Publishers, 1968, pp. 1–76.

Brubacher, John S., *A History of the Problems of Education*. New York: McGraw-Hill Book Company, 1947.

Clark, Leonard H., Raymond L. Klein, and John B. Burks, *The American Secondary School Curriculum*. New York: The Macmillan Company, 1965, Chapter 1.

Cubberley, Elwood P., *History of Education*. Boston: Houghton Mifflin Company, 1920.

Doll, Ronald C., *Curriculum Improvement: Decision-Making and Process*. Boston: Allyn and Bacon, Inc., 1964, Chapter 1.

Dumas, Wayne, and Weldon Beckner, *Introduction to Secondary Education: A Foundations Approach*. Scranton, Pa.: Intext Educational Publishers, 1968, Chapter 1.

Eby, Frederick, *The Development of Modern Education*. 2d ed. Englewood Cliffs, N.J.: Prentice-Hall, Inc., 1952.

Kandel, I. L., *History of Secondary Education*. Boston: Houghton Mifflin Company, 1930.

Orlich, Donald C., and S. Samuel Shermis (eds.), *The Pursuit of Excellence: Introductory Readings in Education*. New York: American Book Company, 1965, pp. 224–240.

Romine, Stephen A., *Building the High School Curriculum*. New York: The Ronald Press Company, 1954, Chapter 3.

Ulich, Robert, *Education in Western Culture*. New York: Harcourt Brace Jovanovich, Inc., 1965.

Wood, Hugh B., *Foundations of Curriculum Planning and Development*. Seattle: Cascade-Pacific Books, 1960, Chapter 2.

PHILOSOPHICAL FOUNDATIONS OF THE SECONDARY SCHOOL CURRICULUM

The astute student will have noted in the previous chapter that throughout the history of education certain ideas and value concepts have been instrumental in the development of educational practices. One cannot intelligently discuss the history of education without including the philosophy of the men who were influential in shaping educational purpose, content, and methodology. It may be that many teachers and school administrators cannot be classified as philosophers, but they have been guided by the ideas and proposals of philosophers.

The word *philosophy* frightens many teachers into avoiding consideration of something which they conceive to be so scholarly and difficult to understand. In actuality, all teachers act upon some philosophy, either their own or that which they have adopted from someone else. A philosophy of education refers to the guiding principles that determine a person's concepts of value and appropriateness in choosing goals and means for educational efforts. It includes a systematic and orderly approach to thinking about education, as opposed to an aimless, haphazard approach. The establishment of priorities in choosing what to teach will be either uniform in terms of educational philosophy or it will be disconnected and inconsistent because of the absence of guiding principles. All educational questions are rooted in philosophy and all philosophy has implications for education. We dare not fail to include some consideration of this cornerstone in a discussion of the secondary school curriculum.

Most educational problems are closely related to *general* philosophical questions—questions concerning the "good" life, the nature of man, the nature of society, and the nature of reality. The philosophy of education guides educational theory and practice in dealing with these problems. Kneller has identified three primary ways this guidance occurs: ". . . (1) it orders the findings of the disciplines relevant to education, including the findings of education itself, within a compre-

47

hensive view of man and the education itself, within a comprehensive view of man and the education that befits him; (2) it examines and recommends the ends and general means of the educational process; and (3) it clarifies and coordinates basic educational concepts."[1]

Since the focus of this textbook is the secondary school curriculum, the brief discussion of educational philosophy which follows will stress curricular relationships, but we must recognize that the curriculum cannot be logically examined without also touching upon methodology and other elements of education. Objectivity in describing various philosophies will be attempted, but the authors feel an obligation to point out advantages and disadvantages inherent in these philosophies, and this identification must inevitably include some personal preference.

The student is encouraged to evaluate carefully the various aspects of different philosophies and construct his personal philosophical system according to his own best judgment. Such a construction will doubtless include an element of eclecticism—and rightly so. A word of caution is in order, however, because certain elements and unique core concepts of the different philosophies directly contradict each other, and the student who attempts to combine conflicting elements in his own philosophy of education will succeed in achieving only confusion and indirection.

The Elements of Philosophy Related to Education

As we attempt to utilize philosophy in our study of education in general and the secondary school curriculum in particular, it would seem that we should identify the elements of general philosophy which have particular significance for education. As we gain some understanding of these elements perhaps we can apply them to those questions which face us in education.

Philosophy takes the disciplines in both their theoretical and practical stages and attempts to explain and establish relations among them, seeking coherent meaning within the whole domain of human thought and existence. Three major components of philosophical endeavor may be identified:

1. *Speculation.* Because of his need to organize ideas and find meaning within the whole of reality, man attempts to think in the most general way about everything in the universe. Philosophy, then, is a way of thinking, using intellectual procedures and practices designed for the purpose.

2. *Prescription.* The speculative element of philosophy normally leads to recommendations or criticisms. Values and ideals are examined with the purpose of establishing *what should be* as well as *what is*. The determination of good and bad, right and wrong, beautiful and ugly all fall within this prescriptive aspect of philosophy.

3. *Analysis and Criticism.* This third side of philosophy is especially con-

[1]George F. Kneller (ed.), *Foundations of Education*, 2d ed. (New York: Wiley, 1967), p. 72.

cerned with assessing various concepts and ideas with the purpose of clarification and identification of inconsistencies.[2]

All kinds of philosophy are important, although one type normally is given more attention than the others at certain times or in certain parts of the world. To yield the optimum results, a balance must be maintained, for as Kneller points out, "Speculation unaccompanied by analysis soars too easily into a heaven of its own, irrelevant to the world as we know it; analysis without speculation descends to minutiae and becomes academic and sterile."[3]

Epistemology and Education

Epistemology is the area of philosophy which deals with how we know and the sources of knowledge. Philosophers have commonly accepted one or more of the following as acceptable springs of truth.

1. *Revealed Knowledge.* Knowledge disclosed to man through divine revelation, although it can usually be neither proved nor disproved, emperically, is, to many people, an unquestioned source. Such knowledge must be accepted by faith and buttressed whenever possible by reason and critical experience.

2. *Authoritative Knowledge.* This is accepted as true because it comes from those considered to be experts.

3. *Intuitive Knowledge.* This occurs on the subliminal level, beneath the "threshold of consciousness." It is intimately connected with feeling and emotion and contrasts with the logical processes associated with conscious thought. Many view intuition as the only true source of knowledge—others consider it closely akin to superstition. Jerome S. Bruner, a widely accepted authority on education, calls intuition "the intellectual technique of arriving at plausible but tentative formulations without going through the analytic steps by which such formulations would be found to be valid or invalid conclusions.[4] He adds, however, that one must be familiar with the scope and structure of the knowledge involved before there can be substantial intuitions about it. Schools tend to emphasize analytical thinking, but as Bruner asserts, intuition is an "essential feature of productive thinking, not only in formal academic disciplines but also in everyday life," and the intuitive power of a student should be cultivated as a genuine source of creativity. On the other hand, intuition is probably not a reliable source of knowledge unless it is checked by reason and analysis.[5]

4. *Rational Knowledge.* Those of the "rationalist" philosophy view reason as the best source of knowledge. From this source may be derived universally valid judgments that are consistent with one another. The senses contribute facts, but the intellect must interpret and organize these pieces into reliable knowledge.

[2]Adapted from Kneller, *Foundations of Education,* pp. 46–48.
[3]*Ibid.,* p. 48.
[4]Jerome S. Bruner, *The Process of Education* (Cambridge, Mass.: Harvard U.P., 1960), p. 13.
[5]*Ibid.*

Such a source of knowledge is limited by abstractness, prejudices, interests, and inclinations.

5. *Empirical Knowledge.* Characterized by the view that knowledge comes from the senses, empiricists say "look and see," as opposed to the rationalists admonition to "think things through." Prejudices, conditioning, and the limitations of our senses weaken this source of knowledge, although it is perhaps the most widely accepted in this day of scientific emphasis. The "scientific method" involved in utilizing the empirical sources of knowledge involves testing theories through experiments in order to arrive at tentative conclusions.

METAPHYSICS. Metaphysical questions frequently underlie class discussion in many subject areas. In teaching biology, for example, any discussion of the theories of creation and evolution involves the metaphysical question of whether human life has any purpose, and if so, what that purpose is. The question of whether a teacher teaches a *subject* or the *child* brings up the problem of determining the ultimate purpose of teaching the subject. Educational psychology must consider the nature of mind and whether it is different from the body. Scientific studies of the brain give us some information, but many questions remain unanswered if we rely only on empirical evidence. Perhaps the greatest value of metaphysics to education is that it allows intelligent discussion of questions and problems for which we, at least at present, do not have scientifically proved answers.

APPLICATION TO EDUCATION. Since education is largely concerned with the discovery and transmission of knowledge, it is important for the teacher to be able to assess the grounds on which claims to knowledge are made. Several types of teacher activity are related to this. For example, the teacher can help students distinguish between opinion and fact or between belief and true knowledge. He can also help students gain an understanding of the methods by which knowledge may be acquired—through revelation, authority, intuition, reason, the senses, and experimentation. He should be able to show students how the various ways of acquiring knowledge may be used together and how they complement each other in our search for truth. This again illustrates the importance of a teacher's philosophy of education, because different philosophies stress different types of knowledge and different teaching methods.[6]

Axiology and Education

The general study of values, including ethics and esthetics, is referred to in philosophy as *axiology.* Moral, aesthetic, and economic values are of vital concern to teachers in secondary schools as they strive to help students establish personal

---

[6]George F. Kneller (ed.), *Foundations of Education,* 2d ed. (New York: Wiley, 1967), pp. 53–68.

standards and acquire the elements of character required of good citizens and happy individuals.

In studying values, attention is usually given to three main questions:

1. *Are values objective or subjective?* Are they impersonal or personal? Objective or impersonal values possess intrinsic value and exist regardless of man's personal feelings and desires—truth, goodness, and beauty, for example. Conversely, subjective or personal values are relative to personal desire; truth and goodness depend on the particular circumstances and situations that apply to them.

2. *Are values changing or constant?* Absolute values are constant and unchanging, while changing values respond to man's immediate needs—they are relative, and always subject to revision.

3. *Are there hierarchies of value?* A person's general philosophy determines whether or not he believes in a hierarchy of values. The idealist exalts the things of the spirit, while the realist values the physical and mathematical sciences highest—he ranks higher those things which help man in a practical way. The pragmatist does not establish a fixed hierarchy, saying that their value changes.

ETHICS. The philosophic study of moral values and conduct is known as *ethics.* Concepts about the good life for all men or how men should conduct themselves are included. They determine rightness and wrongness of actions, thereby justifying or condemning behavior.

Most ethical systems are closely related to a religion, tending to be absolutist and unchanging. Today, however, although deriving from religious beginnings, ethical systems often justify themselves on grounds other than religious—practical, naturalistic, or relativistic.

Ethical values are believed to be understood either through an intuitive apprehension without benefit of factual considerations (intuitionism), or through interests, needs, and desires of the individual (naturalism). Naturalistic values are evaluated by an empirical study of the consequences of human actions, while values derived by means of intuition come from an inborn sense and require no justification.

ESTHETICS. The study of values related to beauty and art is known as esthetics. Such values are the hardest to evaluate, because they are likely to be personal and subjective and because they relate to imagination and creativity. Who is to judge the rightness or wrongness of one's artistic appreciation? Who can say whether art should be imitative and representative of natural phenomena or the product of one's private perception and imagination?

APPLICATION TO EDUCATION. The importance of ethics and values to education is easily illustrated. Many educators view character development and the instilling of proper values to be more important in teaching than the teaching of cognitive subject matter. They are concerned more with moral and spiritual values needed to make the world a better place in which to live than they are with the designation of specific subject matter to be taught.

Every teacher is faced with questions related to the general axiology of his philosophical system. Which should be emphasized, the subject matter to be taught or the pupil (do we teach students)? What type of moral behavior should be urged upon the students? Should a teacher yield to the beliefs and values of the community in which he teaches, or should he teach according to his own beliefs about right and wrong? How may certain character traits deemed desirable be taught? Such questions cannot be ignored if a person wishes to become a good teacher.

Logic and Education

Logic, the science of correct reasoning and orderly thinking, is another essential element of philosophy which is important to educators. Perhaps the aspect of logic most applicable to education concerns the two major types of logical reasoning—deduction and induction.

1. *Deductive logic* leads to the drawing of conclusions from one or more preliminary statements or premises. Particular conclusions are derived from general premises. The importance of this type of reasoning lies in the ability to determine that a conclusion is unavoidable from the premises.

2. *Inductive logic* results in a generalization or prediction being inferred from particular facts. The conclusion is never completely certain, only probable. The teacher must help students to avoid generalizing from insufficient evidence.

APPLICATION TO EDUCATION. The most recent statements from professional education organizations have placed teaching the ability to think at the top of the list of educational goals. Few would argue the importance of this goal, but reaching it is a difficult matter. Many people do not think logically. They allow emotions and personal biases to interfere with the correct analysis of a situation.

Students must be made aware of the fact that the words used in communicating may carry emotional connotations which hinder effective communication or careful consideration of ideas. Feelings and subjective opinion get in the way of objective and logical reasoning about a topic of discussion.

Students must also be made aware of the difference between studying about evaluations and actually making them, as in the studying of communism, colonialism, or evolution. The study of religions or sex education involve many of the same tendencies to allow emotion or personal feeling to distort logical consideration and evaluation.

Logic is essential to teachers as they organize and carry out teaching activities. In order to achieve a desired learning goal, the teacher must follow a logical and orderly sequence in the presentatign of subject material. Students must be helped to see the various steps by which results are attained, along with the reasons and relationships behind them. Principles and prime ideas must be focused upon and the subject matter logically related to them.

Other logical operations in which the teacher is involved include the definition, interpretation, and explanation of terms. Ambiguous uses of words and misinterpretation by students negate all too many teaching efforts.

The Major Philosophies and Education

Because most educational problems are closely related to philosophical problems, it is important that the student of education gain at least a minimum understanding of the different philosophies and how they relate to education. Educational research and the human sciences often produce conflicting data which must be ordered and interpreted in developing purposes of education and the means to seek achievement of those purposes. Analysis and evaluation of educational efforts also depend on philosophy for guidelines and standards. Educational ideals must be consistent with our other ideals, and the achievement of educational goals must fit into the total pattern of personal and social goals.

Philosophy is a complex study, because no two people follow exactly the same philosophy. Yet in order to study the realm of ideas, philosophies are typically grouped according to the major concepts which go to make up the total philosophy of an individual. The risks of oversimplification are inherent in this practice, but it greatly facilitates the study of men and their ideas.

In attempting to relate philosophy to education, we will categorize the philosophies according to common practice, including the traditional philosophies of idealism, realism, and pragmatism and the more recent existentialism. In each case particular attention will be given to indicating how these general ways of thinking relate to education and educators.

Idealism

This oldest of all Western philosophic systems may be traced to Plato and more recently to such men as Johann Herbart and Herman Horne. According to their concepts, knowledge exists independently of the human mind, and man is obligated to continuously seek a better understanding of the "ultimate reality" which underlies all existing things and is therefore common to them. The idealist maintains that those things with which science and our senses acquaint us may be real enough to us, but they are not *ultimately* real. They are only our conception of the universal, spiritual mind which we constantly strive to better understand. Plato's allegory of the cave, contained in *The Republic*, is the classic example of this type of thinking.

The idealist views the pupil as a spiritual being whose prime purpose in life is to express his own unique nature, and education should help him in this attempt. Students are not viewed as storehouses of information, but as individuals seeking to attain unique spiritual and personal maturity according to their inborn potentialities.

Idealists generally maintain that truth is best discovered through reason. The mind imposes meaning and order on the confused mass of information presented by our senses. The purpose of teaching, therefore, is not simply to familiarize the mind with a mass of information, but to facilitate the discovery of meaning according to the individual's own concepts and ideas as they have been shaped by his previous experiences.

To the idealist, values are absolute and unchanging—it is only man's understanding of values that changes. School practices must be based on the enduring principles of the good, the right, and the beautiful. The child should learn to live by permanent values, so that he may fit into the ultimate moral and spiritual universe into which he was born.

The role of the teacher is particularly important to the idealist, because he serves as an example of the values being taught. The teacher is seen as the one responsible for developing the potential existing within each student rather than to "pour in" knowledge and understanding. Idealist teachers should be seekers after a perfection which they know to exist in a higher mentality and to be available to the mind of man through intuitive contemplation.[7]

The teacher tries to inspire his students and open their minds through his personality and his handling of classroom activities. Student interest is the very essence of good education and the foundation of educational method. To capitalize on natural interests and allow the fullest individual development, the ideal teacher places greatest importance on how the student develops from within, maintaining that it is not what we do for and to him, but what he does for and to himself that provides the stimulation needed to achieve, to understand, and to manage himself. Nakosteen's description of the idealist teacher seems to summarize this concept.

> He encourages the creation of beautiful objects and the carrying on of debate and discussion, tolerates individual taste and bent of mind, and gives way to freedom, initiative, individuality, purpose, aim, and inner satisfactions and realizations. Not that effort and drill find no place in the idealistic teacher's method of approach, but to him they are outward expressions of that inner reality he calls "interest." Where there is interest there is always effort requiring drill and discipline, but effort, drill, and discipline are interconnected with the very life of the individual rather than merely parts of a mechanical relationship going on between the environment and the nervous system.[8]

[7]Wayne Dumas and Weldon Beckner, *Introduction to Secondary Education: A Foundations Approach* (Scranton, Pa.: Intext, 1968), p. 58.
[8]Mehdi Nakosteen: *The History and Philosophy of Education*, copyright © 1965 (New York: Ronald), p. 573.

The purposes of education as seen by the idealist are directly tied to the ultimate goal of life, which is to develop the natural man as a free and moral agent into the ideal man, as determined within the purpose of the Universal Mind. More specifically, the objectives of education include "health, character, social justice, skill, art, love, knowledge philosophy, and religion.[9] The achievement of these goals requires a unique combination of human and educational elements:

> . . . the ideal pupil is one possessed with the "will to perfection"; the ideal teacher, one who can help cultivate and perfect human personality; the ideal curriculum, one that gives direction and substance to this development and contributes to accomplishment of the purposes . . . ; the ideal school, one motivated and directed not by the passing whims and interests of the child but by the fundamental universal purposes that govern and shape our lives; and the ideal method, that which stimulates the cultivation of these basic human goods.[10]

Realism

The realist philosopher differs from the idealist in that he sees the universe and its various parts not as a foggy impression of the ultimate, but as reality. Trees, hills, and animals exist in concrete form; they are not an illusion of the ideal. There are several schools of thought within the realist concept, but they all agree that the material world is real and exists outside the minds of those who observe it.

The major differences within this philosophy involve the determinination of true reality. One group believes that knowledge of reality can best be gained through revelation from God, verified and understood by means of reason and experience (religious realism and classical realism). The other group (natural or scientific realism) follows ideas which developed with the rise of science in Europe during the fifteenth and sixteenth centuries. They stress the value of science in determining the real and disregard the necessity for tempering scientific findings with Divine revelation.

Because he believes that the universe and its components exist independently of human conception and operate according to unchanging laws, the realist maintains that it is essential for us to know certain things about this universe and the people who inhabit it. Education must, therefore, include a basic core of subject matter which will acquaint the pupil with the unchanging world in which he lives. The religious realist adds the necessity for understanding the relationship of God to the universe. The purpose of education for the realist is to equip the pupil so that he may become a well-adjusted person who can live in harmony with the world around him.

The teacher who follows the realist philosophy will not lose sight of his

---

[9]Herman H. Horne, "An Idealistic Philosophy of Education," in Nelson B. Henry (ed.), *Philosophies of Education*, Forty-first Yearbook of the National Society for the Study of Education, Part I (Chicago: U. of Chicago Press, 1942), p. 182.

[10]Nakosteen, *op. cit.*, p. 570.

primary goal, which is to impart substantive knowledge of the actual world. Students must learn from the experts, and, lest they drift away from the most important things to be learned, they must not be allowed too much freedom to choose what they should know. It is the teacher's responsibility to decide what the student should learn, and if at the same time his interests and curiosity can be satisfied, so much the better. Pupil desires are not the primary guide for study, however, the intellectual discipline is a necessary ingredient of education.

The school curriculum favored by the realist usually emphasizes the sciences, mathematics, and foreign languages as the central elements of education. As described by Wild, this position may be recognized as the core of most contemporary school programs.

> There is certainly a basic core of knowledge that every human person ought to know in order to live a genuinely human life as a member of the world community, of his own nation, and of the family. This should be studied by every student and should be presented at levels of increasing complexity and discipline throughout the entire curriculum. First of all (a) the student should learn to use the basic instruments of knowledge, especially his own language. In order to understand it more clearly and objectively, he should gain some knowledge of at least one foreign language as well. In addition, he should be taught the essentials of human logic and elementary mathematics. Then (b), he should become acquainted with the methods of physics, chemistry, and biology and the basic facts so far revealed by these sciences. In the third place (c), he should gain some familiarity with the great classics of his own and of world literature and art. Finally (e), in the later stages of this basic training, he should be introduced to philosophy and to those basic problems which arise from the attempt to integrate knowledge and practice.[11]

Realists agree that values do not change and that education should adhere to certain "truths." Teaching related to moral and esthetic concepts should not be influenced by contemporary deviations but should adhere to the enduring concepts which have proved themselves throughout history. Right and wrong, good and bad, beauty and ugliness have been established through the experience of mankind or guidance from God and should be clearly understood and followed by students.

Development of the intellectual powers of reason is another component of the philosophy followed by most realists and especially those known as classical realists or classical humanists. Because of their emphasis on developing man's rational powers, those who stress this aspect of realism are often referred to as "rationalists." The ultimate purpose of education is seen to be development of the intellectual powers of reason, and concessions to "practicality" or "vocationalism" serve to take school time which could be better used to strengthen the intellect. The rationalist insists that wisdom and intellectual power are best

---

[11]John Daniel Wild, "Education and Human Society: A Realistic View," in *Modern Philosophies of Education*, Fifty-fourth Yearbook of the National Society for the Study of Education (Chicago: U. of Chicago Press, 1955), pp. 34–35.

cultivated by studying certain traditional subjects (the "liberal arts"), and by reading what wise men of the past have written.

Because of their view that all men are basically the same in their need for intellectual development, and because they also maintain that this unchanging need can best be met by an essentially unchanging educational program, the term "perennialist" is often applied to those of this philosophical bent. The following quote summarizes the rationalist or perennialist position favoring the liberal arts curriculum.

> What was once the best education for the few is now the best education for the many. In essential aim and in essential content, liberal education is unchanged. It consists in the cultivation of the intellect, the refinement of taste, and indirectly, the development of character and personality through the mastery of the liberal arts and the study of the basic problems of man and society, past as well as present.[12]

The ultimate purpose of education in the eyes of a realist, then, is to lead students to understand the universe in which he lives so that he might better fit himself into that unchanging combination of human and physical elements. This requires a basically traditional, academic, liberal-arts curriculum for all students, regardless of their intellectual ability, individual interests, or goal in life.

Pragmatism

The philosophical ideas identified by the term pragmatism came into modern prominence around the turn of the century. Although they were preceded in their ideas by Charles Peirce, it is William James and John Dewey who are given the most credit for developing and promoting these ideas, with Dewey usually getting the most praise (or blame) for their application to education.

Pragmatic philosophy is a revolt against the thinking which constantly seeks for first causes and universal principles. Instead, the pragmatist is primarily concerned with "last things"—fruits, consequences, and facts. The name pragmatism itself comes from the principle that the final test of any concept or process is whether or not it succeeds in application. If an idea works well in achieving desired ends, then it is a good and correct idea.

Other terms are often used in referring to this general philosophy and its application to education, including instrumentalism, functionalism, and experimentalism. Regardless of the term used, there are commonly five principal themes of this philosophy: ". . . (1) the reality of change over permanence; (2) the relativity of values; (3) the social and biological nature of man; (4) the importance of democracy as a way of life; and (5) the value of critical intelligence in all human conduct."[13]

---

[12]Mortimer J. Adler and Milton Mayer, *The Revolution in Education* (Chicago: U. of Chicago Press, 1958), p. 96.

[13]George F. Kneller, (ed.), *Foundations of Education*, 2d ed., (New York: Wiley, 1967), p. 85.

CHANGE VERSUS PERMANENCE. Pragmatists agree with the realists that the world exists in concrete form understandable to man, not as a shadowy mental conception, but they reject the proposition that the world is changless and independent from man. They believe that reality is created by the interaction of man with his environment, and that we cannot be sure that anything will remain unchanged forever. Science and the scientific method are accepted as the route to truth, but the pragmatist uses the scientific problem-solving approach to find temporary solutions to immediate problems, rather than as a means to search for universal principles and natural laws which are not expected to change.

THE RELATIVITY OF VALUES. Values and "truth" are considered to be relative to the times and to new knowledge. Changes bring new truths, because true knowledge works and gets things done in a constantly evolving world society. The ever-changing relationship between man and his environment prohibits the establishment of permanent values.

SOCIAL AND BIOLOGICAL CONSIDERATIONS. Dewey's life view was founded on the Darwinian biological and social concepts of struggle for survival in a constantly renewing world. To Dewey and the pragmatists who follow his thinking, intelligence is the method derived from experience to deal with the problems of life, and knowledge provides the auxiliary tools needed in the operations of intelligence.

THE IMPORTANCE OF DEMOCRACY. Education is viewed as a social process, and the student must be given every opportunity to learn to live cooperatively and productively with other human beings. Knowledge about the nature of group behavior and group processes becomes a necessary tool of teaching and learning. Democratic ideals fit naturally into this philosophy and are essential to its fulfillment.

CRITICAL INTELLIGENCE. Only one absolute may be identified in the philosophy of John Dewey and other pragmatists: suspicion (and usually denial) of absolutes, finalities, and fixed patterns. The world and man's relationship to both the physical and social environment in which he lives are in a constant state of flux and change, and adjustments required for successful living in such a world require an attitude of critical analysis and intelligent reaction to environmental uncertainties.

Existentialism

This, the most recent of the major philosophies, developed largely as a revolt against established philosophies and systems. It is a reaction to conventionalism, traditional ideas, and prescribed values or concepts of all kinds.

Existentialists maintain that the universe has no innate order or logic, and consequently man possesses complete freedom to make of himself and the universe what he considers best. This also means, however, that he is therefore responsible for himself and his universe. He cannot place the blame for his mistakes on his environment, parental influence, or any other external environmental factor. Man is simply the sum of his own actions because he could always have chosen otherwise. "Man is nothing other than what he makes himself."[14]

Existentialists believe that philosophy should be more than just an intellectual exercise; it should be a passionate encounter with the recurring problems of life. Man's feelings as well as his intellect should be utilized in his search for knowledge and meaning in the world. He should be particularly careful to avoid doing what the "crowd" proposes or what is "acceptable," unless he feels individually inclined to accept such external determinants of behavior.

Modern Educational Theories

Theories about education as they relate to various philosophies have been included to some extent in the previous discussion of the major philosophies. In the following summary, at the unavoidable risk of oversimplification, modern positions related to educational concepts will be grouped according to their tendency to stress either the traditional and time-honored approaches to education or those which have developed during the twentieth century and which tend to place less emphasis on traditional educational ideas and practices. Wherever possible, some curricular implications will be given special attention, and the astute student will doubtless be able to identify others. For want of better terms, the two groups of theories will be categorized as either traditional or nontraditional.

Traditional Theories

The traditional, or conservative, theories of education contain elements of the older philosophies, especially idealism and realism, and may be found throughout the history of Western educational thought. Considerable attention is given to the subject matter to be taught, and consequently less emphasis is placed on the student, his needs and interests. The terms rationalism, perennialism, and essentialism are commonly used in referring to the dominant groups classified here as traditional.

Rationalism contains a strong element of Plato's idealism and his advocacy of preparation for life through development of the intellect. According to the rationalist, the best type of social leadership can be provided by those whose powers of reason have been developed to the maximum, and this development can best be achieved through rigorous intellectual study and discipline. The ability to solve all types of human problems is found in those individuals who have

---

[14]Jean-Paul Sartre, *Existentialism* (New York: Philosophical Library, 1947), p. 18.

attained a high degree of ability to reason and intellectually arrive at conclusions and courses of action. It is impossible to equip students to cope with problems and situations of the future which are still unknown and even unimagined today, so we must prepare their minds to function in such a way that they can assess each situation as it develops and intelligently devise proper courses of action. Typical vocational training is only an exercise in futility, because of the highly diverse and rapidly changing needs of business and industry. The proper training for a vocation—any vocation—is development of the rational powers of the intellect.

Rationalists tend to prefer the study of language and mathematics as the best means to intellectual development. Mental discipline is accepted as a valid component of learning, and strengthening of the mind is the goal of all educational effort. Other subject areas need not be neglected, but in no case should they take precedence over those studies which will "develop the power to think." Student activities and other nonessentials are considered unnecessary and time-consuming "frills."

Perennialism is founded philosophically in realism, especially in those concepts which maintain that the basic principles of education are changeless. Opposing the contentions of the pragmatists that change is inevitable, perennialists insist that education should be based on certain universal truths. Human nature, the good life, and moral principles do not change, because human nature remains essentially the same throughout the history of mankind. Robert M. Hutchins, one of the better-known and more articulate of this group, has stated the position well in the following quotation:

> Education implies teaching. Teaching implies knowledge. Knowledge is truth. The truth is everywhere the same. Hence, education should be everywhere the same.[15]

Kneller has identified six basic principles which seem to summarize the perennialist position:

1. Since human nature is constant, the nature of education remains constant, too.
2. Since man's most distinctive characteristic is his ability to reason, education should concentrate on developing the rational faculty.
3. The only type of adjustment to which education should lead is adjustment to the truth, which is universal and unchanging.
4. Education is not a replica of life but a preparation for it.
5. Children should be taught certain basic subjects that will acquaint them with the world's permanencies, both spiritual and physical.
6. These permanencies are best studied in what perennialists call the "Great Books."[16]

[15]Robert Maynard Hutchins, *The Higher Learning in America* (New Haven: Yale U. P., 1936), p. 66.
[16]George F. Kneller (ed.), *op. cit.*, p. 93.

It may be noted that perennialism and rationalism have several things in common, and they are many times combined in discussions of educational theory and practice.

Essentialism is difficult to associate with any of the traditional philosophies, because it developed more as a revolt against the extremes of progressivism than as an outgroth of a particular philosophy. It can be and is supported by adherents of several variations of conservative philosophical thought. The most generally accepted educational practices today are related to the theories of essentialism and their emphasis on the accumulation of a fund of knowledge as the most important function of education.

Essentialists maintain that there is a basic fund of knowledge, facts, and skill which must be passed on and understood by each generation, because it is impossible for each generation to discover for itself what man has spent centuries learning. Each generation can build on the accomplishments of the past and thus achieve a progressively better civilization only if the most important elements of what has been learned in the past are preserved and transferred to each succeeding group of young people. The term "conservationist" is also applied to this position, since the primary purpose of education is conceived to be the conservation and transmission of the accumulated knowledge of mankind.

Those who take this position are principally concerned with determining the essentials of curriculum and establishing the teacher as the controlling factor in the classroom. They feel that the accumulated knowledge of mankind is contained in the basic subject matter of the traditional curriculum—English, mathematics, history, science, foreign language, and the like. Subject matter is viewed as the core of education, although the ideas of the perennialists relating to the unchanging validity of certain subject matter and the stress on the writing of certain "authorities" as being always appropriate is rejected.

Nontraditional Theories

The nontraditional theories of education tend to favor pragmatic philosophical ideas, rather than idealism or realism, and usually give special attention to the learner in the educational scheme of things, with consequent lesser emphasis on subject matter. This is not to say that subject matter is considered unimportant. It is accepted as a vital part of education, but the attempt is made to keep it in the proper perspective as a means to achieving educational goals rather than tending to become an end in itself.

As with traditional educational theories, there are many variations in the way different educators perceive the tasks and methods of teaching. Several broad categories may be identified, however, and most theories can be fit into these categories more or less satisfactorily. We will consider four types of educational theory which tend to offer a contrast to the traditional concepts and include most of the significant nontraditional educational ideas. These four categories will be identified with the labels *progressivism, reconstructionism, structuralism,* and *existentialism.*

Progressivism is probably one of the most poorly defined, poorly understood, and most misused terms in the English language, particularly that part of the English language used in referring to educational activities. The twentieth-century movement which became identified with the term progressivism aroused so much interest and so much controversy that the term is now almost hopelessly embedded in semantic difficulty and confusion. Enthusiasm for the movement on the one hand and almost violent opposition on the other have involved so much emotion and personal feeling that objective evaluation or neutral consideration of the concepts involved is almost impossible. Those who oppose some practice in schools almost invariably label them "progressive," whether they really fall into that philosophical category or not, and many advocates of change in education consider anything outside the realm of what they term "progressive" education to be automatically outdated and of little value. Those who carried progressive ideas to extremes have brought down the wrath of critics upon the heads of educational innovators who were many times on very firm ground, both philosophically and educationally.

The roots of progressive education may be found far back in the history of education. Aristotle stressed learning by direct experience and following the growth patterns of the child—both progressive principles. Quintilian, Froebel, Pestalozzi, Rousseau, and Herbert all contributed important concepts to the system later put together by John Dewey and his disciples. In the late 1800's Francis Parker, as superintendent of schools at Quincy, Massachusetts, instituted many reforms which provided examples and inspiration for later progressive educational thinkers. Good teachers for centuries had followed similar principles, although they would usually not dare openly to criticize the established traditional curriculum or methods of teaching. John Dewey simply served as the catalyst and publisher of these ideas—ideas that fit naturally into the developing twentieth-century American social scene.

Progressivism is essentially the application of pragmatism to education; indeed, the philosophy of pragmatism was largely created out of experience in education. Change, not permanence, is seen as the dominant factor in human existence, and so education is always in the process of change and development. Rather than being adjustment to society, the external world, or unchanging truth, education is viewed as that which allows us better to understand the change and variety of daily living in such a way that past experience will better enable us to correctly determine future behavior. As Dewey put it,

> We thus reach a technical definition of education: it is that reconstruction or reorganization of experience which adds to the meaning of experience, and which increases the ability to direct the course of subsequent experience.[17]

[17]John Dewey, *Democracy and Education* (New York: Macmillan, 1916), p. 89.

From this rather abstract definition, progressive education has developed in several directions, but for our purposes, it may be stated that the following principles form the cornerstone for all true progressive educational endeavors:

1. Individual differences among children must be recognized.
2. We learn best by doing and by having a vital interest in what we are doing.
3. Education is a continuous reconstruction of living experience that goes beyond the four walls of the classroom.
4. The classroom should be a laboratory for democracy.
5. Social goals, as well as intellectual goals, are important.
6. A child must be taught to think critically rather than to accept blindly.[18]

To state it in negative terms,

> Pragmatic education is opposed to the traditional idealist and realist education in the pragmatic's outright rejection of external impositions and disciplines; authoritative use of texts and teachers; acquisition of mental drills divorced from life's situations; static aims and ready-made educational materials; subordination of the immediate experience of the child to an unknown, unrealized, and perhaps unattainable future in this or another world; and finally, imposition of the ideas, skills, and ideals of the old on the young, without due respect for freedom of choice and meaningfulness of this transmission in the experience of the receiver.[19]

Dewey and other progressivists do not say, however, that tradition or past educational practices should be disregarded, or that each individual or generation must begin to work out its own society and destiny without reference to past learning and accomplishment. Rather, he shares the belief that ". . . the present holds the past in retrospect and the future in prospect." Lessons and values from the past should be considered in working out the problems of the present, but they should not be allowed to dictate absolutes and block the development of newer and improved ideas and practices.

Reconstructionism had its origin in the confusion and dissatisfaction of the 1930's in the United States, and combines ideas from pragmatic and scientific philosophies. It carries the ideas of Dewey and other progressives much further than they seem to have intended in declaring that to meet the cultural needs of our times education should have as its chief aim the reordering of our society. The basic values of Western civilization must be interpreted in the light of modern scientific findings to identify the true goals of education. Progressive ideas about methods and procedures of education are accepted, but it is proposed that pragmatic philosophy provides no definite goals toward which progressive means should be aimed.

[18]Carroll Atkinson and Eugene T. Maleska, *The Story of Education*, 2d ed. (Philadelphia: Chilton, 1965), p. 78.

[19]Mehdi Nakosteen: *The History and Philosophy of Education*, copyright, © 1965 (New York: Ronald), pp. 611–612.

Two of the big questions that have historically concerned educators form the core of reconstructionist theory:

1. Should educational efforts emphasize the interests and concerns of the culture (social-centered) or of the individual (child-centered)?
2. Should public schools serve to reflect the values of society, whether static or changing, or should they actively take part in changing values, social concepts, and social practices?

Reconstructionists take the position on the first question that our society and its schools have placed too much emphasis on individualism, resulting in abuses of private enterprise ideas and the "rugged individualist" concept. The "child-centered" emphasis in schools is a prominent manifestation of this overemphasis on individualism, and it should be replaced by a concern for broader social needs. The major purpose of education should be to change society along lines that would allow the development of a "socialistic democracy." Such a democracy should provide for more equal opportunity for all citizens, the public control of the major institutions and resources, and comparative equality of material conditions.

Concerning the second question, reconstructionist theory proposes that teachers, through the schools, should assume an active and positive role in changing society so that the goals of a "socialistic democracy" are achieved. Reconstructionists thereby accept the means of education suggested by progressivists and add what they consider to be the necessary ends. The new social order must be achieved without delay, and so teachers should impress upon their students the necessity and urgency of the prescribed social reform so that a Utopian world culture may be soon a reality. In other words, the reconstructionist would ". . . turn the school into the central forum for social criticism and establish it as the headquarters of social reform and cultural reconstruction."[20]

Structuralism has already been discussed at some length in Chapter 1 of this text and forms the base for later exploration into the heart of the curriculum. Further delving into the concept at this point would seem unnecessarily repititious, although perhaps it should be pointed out again that the ideas contained in the structuralist approach are closely related to pragmatic philosophy, even though they perhaps place more emphasis on subject matter than one would expect from such a derivation.

Existentialism breaks rather abruptly with other theories of education, although it contains some things in common with them, principally pragmatism. Existentialists maintain that the purpose of education is to further the opportunities for individual freedom and uniqueness. Individual activity and development are favored above group activity, although it is recognized that group activity of

---

[20]Van Cleve Morris, *Becoming an Educator* (Boston: Houghton, 1963), "The Philosophy of Education," p. 80.

certain types may contribute to individual development and freedom. The major objection to group education is that it impedes the progress of able and imaginative students while moving too fast for slower students and thus hampering their development also.

According to the existentialist, each student should be allowed and helped to develop his own set of values freely and without adult dictation. The teacher may present the principles on which he bases his own beliefs and the reasons for his position, but he must leave the student free to either accept or reject those beliefs. To avoid moral anarchy, the student must be convinced of the fact that he cannot escape the consequences of his beliefs and acts.

The teacher's role is not to serve as a personality to be emulated (idealism), to impart knowledge (realism), or to serve as a consultant in problem situations (pragmatism). He is to serve each student individually as needed to help him acquire an individualism and complete self-realization.

The existentialist does not reject all traditional subject matter, but rather insists that it be mastered and used as necessary to understand the world and how to best achieve individuality within it. It is viewed as a means for the cultivation of the self, not as an end in itself (essentialism and the like) or as an instrument to prepare the student for life (progressivism). They absolutely oppose practices which require students to subject themselves to dictation concerning what they should learn and how they should learn it.

The existentialist is especially concerned that good education in the humanities be afforded each student so that he may better understand the nature of man and his relation to the universe, including other men. Overspecialization is shunned, because this tendency, especially as related to particular vocations, hinders the person's achieving understanding of the total universe and freedom within that universe.

Summary of Philosophical Questions Related to Education

Throughout this chapter questions of philosophy have been examined for their application to education. To summarize the implications of philosophy for education, the more important and obvious of these questions will be listed. This list is by no means exhaustive; neither is the order of listing of any particular significance.

General Philosophical Questions

1. What is the nature of man?
2. What is the "good life?"

3. What is the nature of society?
4. What is the nature of reality?
5. What are the sources of knowledge?
6. What are the determinants of value?
   (a) Are values objective or subjective?
   (b) Are values changing or constant?
   (c) Are there hierarchies of value?
   (d) What moral values are superior?
   (e) How is beauty determined?

Questions of Educational Philosophy

1. What goals should education seek to achieve?
2. Is education a preparation for life or an integral part of current living?
3. For what purpose should subject matter be utilized: the development of the intellect, the acquisition of knowledge, or for practical use?
4. To what extent should education be autocratic or democratic?
5. What should be done to best "improve the mind," or "develop the intellect?"
6. To what extent should the needs of the individual be honored in preference to the needs of the group or of the society?
7. What type of education best serves a democratic nation?
8. How can "better citizenship" be cultivated through education?
9. To what extent should education be subject-centered or student-centered?
10. What subject matter is of prime importance (what knowledge is of most worth)?
11. How much should the vocational purposes of education be considered, and what is the place of subject matter in vocational preparation?
12. How should subject matter be organized for teaching and learning?
13. To what extent should the curriculum be oriented to past educational practices, unchanging in their universal and perennial value?
14. What studies should be common for all boys and girls?
15. What studies should be differentiated according to student individual differences, and how should such differentiation be determined?
16. Should discipline be taught through imposition and authoritarian mandate, or should it be democratically developed to achieve self-direction?
17. Should education seek to develop an intellectual elite?
18. Should teachers stress information or process?

19. Should education accept the world as it is and help students adjust to it, or should education seek to actively improve the world in which we live?
20. To what extent should students be allowed or assisted to freely develop their own systems of value and purpose?

Selected References

Atkinson, Carroll, and Eugene T. Maleska, *The Story of Education.* 2d ed. Philadelphia: Chilton Book Company, 1965.

Beckner, Weldon, and Wayne Dumas. *American Education: Foundations and Superstructure.* Scranton, Pa.: Intext Educational Publishers, 1970.

Bode, Boyd H., *Modern Educational Theories.* New York: The Macmillan Company, 1927.

Brameld, Theodore, *Philosophies of Education in Cultural Perspective.* New York: Holt, Rinehart and Winston, Inc., 1955.

Broudy, Harry S., *Building a Philosophy of Education.* 2d ed. Englewood Cliffs, N.J.: Prentice-Hall, Inc., 1961.

Bruner, Jerome S., *The Process of Education.* Cambridge, Mass.: Harvard University Press, 1960.

Dewey, John, *Democracy and Education.* New York: The Macmillan Company, 1916.

Dumas, Wayne, and Weldon Beckner, *Introduction to Secondary Education: A Foundations Approach.* Scranton, Pa.: Intext Educational Publishers, 1968.

Henry, Nelson B. (ed.), *Modern Philosophies of Education.* Fifty-fourth Yearbook of the National Society of Education. Chicago: University of Chicago Press, 1955.

———— (ed.), *Philosophies of Education,* National Society for the Study of Education Forty-first Yearbook, Part I. Chicago: University of Chicago Press, 1942.

Hutchins, Robert M., *The Conflict in Education.* New York: Harper & Row, Publishers, 1953.

Kilpatrick, William H., *Philosophy of Education.* New York: The Macmillan Company, 1951.

Kneller, George F. (ed.), *Foundations of Education.* 2d ed. New York: John Wiley & Sons, Inc., 1967, p. 72.

Lee, Gordon C., *Education and Democratic Ideals.* New York: Harcourt Brace Jovanovich, Inc., 1965.

Nakosteen, Mehdi, *The History and Philosophy of Education.* New York: The Ronald Press Company, 1965.

Phenix, Philip H., *Philosophy of Education*. New York: Holt, Rinehart and Winston, Inc., 1958.

Sartre, Jean-Paul, *Existentialism*. New York: Philosophical Library, 1947.

Thut, I.N., *The Story of Education*. New York: McGraw-Hill Book Company, Inc., 1957.

Ulich, Robert, *History of Educational Thought*. New York: American Book Company, 1950.

CHAPTER 4

FOUNDATIONS
IN SOCIOLOGY

One of the sources—and possibly the most important source—of educational aims and objectives is the particular culture and society which the educational program serves. An analysis of its problems, needs, and requirements serves to identify what the society demands of the individuals living in it. The competencies and qualities necessary to equip individuals for life in the society must be developed to a considerable extent in the schools, since the schools are the major organized institutions operated by the society to meet social educational needs. George S. Counts, one of the earlier advocates of social emphasis in educational goal determination, stressed the importance of social considerations more than thirty years ago:

> The historical record shows that education is always a function of time, place, and circumstance. In its basic philosophy, its social objective, and its program of instruction it inevitably reflects in varying proportion the experiences, the conditions, and the hopes, fears, and aspirations of a particular people or cultural group at a particular point in history. In actuality it is never organized and conducted with sole reference to absolute and universal terms.[1]

Those engaged in curriculum planning and teachers involved in carrying out those plans must possess a broad knowledge of the society and culture which they serve if they hope to meet their social responsibility. Such a knowledge will include at least basic understanding in areas such as

1. The fundamental beliefs, values, and moral principles of the American people.
2. The mores, traditions, expectations, and value patterns of the citizens of a school community.
3. The philosophy, points of view, and recommendations on education of pertinent professional, civic, and patriotic organizations, and of leading authorities and officials in the field of education.

[1]George S. Counts, *The Social Foundations of Education* (New York: Scribner's, 1934), p. 1.

69

4. Social, economic, and political conditions.
5. The home and family situation of pupils.
6. Legal mandates, requirements of superior agencies, and admission requirements of colleges, universities, and other postsecondary educational institutions.
7. The psychology and sociology of cultural change.[2]

If educators hope to acquire an adequate understanding of these and other pertinent social considerations they must devote considerable time to a continuing study of current problems and developments. Because of obvious limitations common to all textbooks we cannot fully explore here the social foundations of curriculum planning for secondary schools. An attempt will be made, however, to indicate the major areas of social understanding required of educators, including the more important principles and considerations. The discussion will be divided into four areas of inquiry: the nature of society and culture, social roles of the secondary curriculum, social forces affecting the curriculum, and current social trends and problems affecting the curriculum.

The Nature of Society and Culture

Because man is characterized by a desire to associate with other members of his kind, we say that he is a social creature. Such association may be accidental or temporary or it may be more permanent. The term society is used to indicate the more lasting associations which occur because the members share common bonds of sentiment or feeling—similar tastes, interests, experiences, and concerns. They share a mutual or reciprocal service and cooperate for mutual benefits.

A human society does not exist unless the culture is passed on from one generation to the next. Culture then refers to the "patterns and products of learned behavior: the etiquette, language, food habits, religious and moral beliefs, systems of knowledge, attitudes, and values; as well as the material things and artifacts producted—the technology—of a group of people."[3]

Those ways of life which are shared by nearly all Americans make up the overall American culture. In addition to this overall culture, there exists a set of subcultures. Each subculture includes ways of life that differ from other subcultures. There are subgroups based upon country of origin, geographic location, social or economic class, religion, and other characteristics. Members of these subgroups share a certain subculture when they have common practices, beliefs, or attitudes that are not held by other American groups.

[2]Galen J. Saylor and William M. Alexander, *Curriculum Planning for Modern Schools* (New York: Holt, 1966,) pp. 102–103.
[3]Robert J. Havighurst and Bernice L. Neugarten, *Society and Education*, 3d ed. (Boston: Allyn and Bacon, 1967), p. 8.

Social Role and Role Expectations

Each of the members of a society must learn a set of social roles in order to fit himself into the society. By social role we are referring to a pattern of behavior common to all persons who fill a particular place in society. A mother, teacher, preacher, or businessman is expected to behave according to certain role expectations while filling the particular role. A person may be expected to conduct himself in various ways at different times, depending upon the role he is filling at a particular time. For instance, a teacher is expected to carry out a certain type of role while at school, even though he may be expected to behave differently at other times, as when he may be filling the role of father, husband, church member, or citizen.

The structure of various parts of the society may be described according to the social roles of the participants. For example, the school may be recognized by the social roles prescribed for the pupils, teachers, principal, superintendent, school board member, and parent. The business community includes roles for customer, proprietor, wholesaler, and employee. Likewise, churches, civic clubs, and other elements of the society include various roles and role expectations for the members of the society included in each group.

"Communal" and "Mass" Societies

A "communal" society is one in which a relatively small, closely knit group, such as the neighborhood, the extended family, or the religious denomination serves to maintain clusters of values and beliefs and takes care of virtually all the needs of its members. Tradition is the main source of values and beliefs and change comes very slowly if at all. Youth are expected to look to their elders for instruction and guidance, fulfilling the expectations of the older generation in every respect. In turn, the younger generation expects those who follow to similarly follow their directions and traditions. The American society near the turn of the century was largely of this "communal" type.

Contemporary American society, by contrast, may be described as a "mass" society. Huge, centralized bureaucracies more often than not carry out the social needs relative to education, health, religion, recreation, or production. An impersonality and loss of individual identification seem inevitable, as people become lost in a vast conglomerate of organizations and institutions. Change can occur much more rapidly, but fewer people have very much to say about what change will occur, because only the powerful institutional and organizational leaders have access to the sources of power necessary to institute significant change in the society. There develops the serious danger that people will feel a loss of security, meaningfulness, and purpose in this "mass" society unless the importance of the individual can be maintained.[4]

Personality and Culture

Most of the earlier efforts to study and understand human personality came under the heading of "psychology" and focused upon the individual's seemingly innate abilities and how physical and mental maturation affect personality. Much study has gone into efforts to determine how we learn, the causes of behavior, and individual personality development. These psychological attempts to understand personality have made significant contributions to education, but recently there seems to be increased concern with the social sources of personality. The culturally standardized aspects of personality, the effects of group pressures on individual development, and the modal personality which the individual shares with other members of his culture seem to provide several clues to educators.

The culture of a society tends to make a type of human being. The character, personality, and behavior of those who comprise the society correspond with the elements of the culture. Individuals tend to behave in a characteristic fashion, depending on the *social motives* engendered by their culture. Aggressiveness, friendliness, dependence, competitiveness, or other tendencies are largely culturally inspired and developed.

One's self-concept is also largely determined by his culture and his relations with associates. This self-concept in turn strongly influences a person's aspirations, attitude toward others, and overall personality. It even seems to affect measurable levels of ability and aptitude.

Typical descriptions of American culture indicate that it values independence, material success, achievement, work, and getting along with other members of the society. Motivation and a desire to get ahead are thus valued above self-minimization and achieved material position takes precedence over inherited wealth or social status. These and other basic goals of socialization in the American culture must be more adequately understood if we are to successfully understand individual personality and the school curriculum required to best develop that personality into a productive and happy member of the society.

American Society and Culture

The contemporary American social order may perhaps be best characterized as one of diversity, and it may be readily seen to encompass many subcultures. Even though predominantly one language is spoken, facilities for the communication of ideas are fantastic, and the population is very mobile, there is still great

---

[4]Harry S. Broudy, B. Othanel Smith, and Joe R. Burnett, *Democracy and Excellence in American Secondary Education* (Chicago: Rand McNally, 1964), pp. 24–28.

diversity within the overall culture and among the subcultures. It is impossible to identify all of the reasons for this heterogeneity, but a few may be rather quickly recognized.

The American colonists came to this country searching for freedom, and their example has been followed in many respects ever since. Religious freedom and differences in belief have led to unparalleled religious diversity and a multiplicity of denominations. Our democratic ideals of government have encouraged freedom of political belief and action. The development of a complex technological society resulted in the proliferation of occupations, each of which includes a set of values and ways of thinking. Differences in national origin, regional differences, and differences due to social status have added more cultural variety.

In addition to being diverse, the American social order may be characterized as one of contradictions. Inconsistencies within the core elements of American social structure and cultural value system create numerous problems to individuals as they seek to find reliable guides for behavior. Success goals and achievement motivation, for example, often conflict with traditional ideals of human values, democracy, and Christian ethic. Individual independence is advocated on one hand, while conformity required on the other. Ideals of individuality clash with norms of behavior, dress, and habits. The idea of equality is basic to our democratic system, but other cultures and subcultures within our own society often bear a stigma of inferiority. Excellence and the virtues of competition war with ideals of cooperation, teamwork, and helpfulness.

Adolescents in our American society are especially subjected to this tendency toward inconsistency. They exist in the no-man's land between childhood and adulthood, and nobody seems to know just what type of behavior is most appropriate for them. One moment they are reminded that they should act grown-up, while the next they are admonished to subject themselves to adult jurisdiction. They are admonished to make themselves useful in the society, but society has no place for their labors. A natural desire for developing independence is first encouraged and then put down when it reaches some adult-prescribed limitation. Maturity is expected at an increasingly early age, but compulsory school attendance is prolonged, the right to vote is denied, and every effort is made to keep the adolescent out of the labor market. Is it no wonder that this victim of cultural inconsistencies becomes confused, impatient, and rebellious?

A third characteristic of contempory American culture may be termed *other-orientation*. In contrast to either the tradition-directed or inner-directed person, one subject to this tendency relies on his contemporaries for his source of direction. Conformity is ensured by this tendency to follow the expectations of others. These expectations may be sensed by personal contact, through mass media of communication, or some other means, but in any case they become internalized and provide the source of guidance and direction.

Even though other-directedness may be most common, there continue to be tradition-directed and inner-directed people within the American society. This forms another source of conflict within the society and within individuals, as tradition, inner compulsion, and contemporary practice vie for dominance.[5]

Social Classes

The American social system incorporates several different types of social groups, with each group exhibiting certain ways of behaving and believing, which we term a subculture. There are subgroups—each with its own subculture—based upon point of origin, race, geographic location, religion, and social position. Each of these types of groupings has some significance for educators, but social-class subcultural groups are of particular importance. Social-class groupings cut across ethnic, racial, and other subcultures in that people from the same social class have much in common, even though they may come from different religious or racial subgroups. They usually live in much the same kinds of houses and neighborhoods, dress in similar fashion, have similar eating habits, prefer similar literature and forms of recreation, and have about the same amount of education.

Knowledge of social-class membership of his students is especially important to a teacher, because it rather accurately allows him to anticipate important characteristics of individuals within the group, such as

1. The general level of educational achievement.
2. The educational aspirations (for example, whether the majority will be interested in job training, or in college entrance).
3. The drive for achievement, and the willingness to postpone gratification (that is, to do things that are difficult or uncomfortable in the expectation that they will bring future gain).
4. Some of the experiences the child will have had in his family before he entered school as well as some of the experiences in the family and the neighborhood that he is likely to have during his school years.[6]

Armed with this knowledge about the probable characteristics of his students, a good teacher will be able to plan his work much more effectively.

Many studies have been carried out by sociologists in communities across the country during the past two decades. These studies have resulted in the generally held conclusion that there are basically five classes in the American social structure: the upper, upper-middle, lower-middle, upper-working, and lower-working classes. Although there may be considerable variation among specific communities, towns, and cities, the percentage of a community's population included in each class tends to be as follows: upper class: 1 to 3 percent; upper-middle class: 7 to 12 percent; lower-middle class: 20 to 35 percent; upper working class: 25 to 40 percent; and lower-working class: 15 to 25 percent.[7]

---

[5]David Riesman, *The Lonely Crowd: A Study of a Changing American Character* (New Haven: Yale U. P., 1950), pp. 19–35.
[6]Robert J. Havighurst and Bernice L. Neugarten, *Society and Education*, 3d ed. (Boston: Allyn and Bacon, 1967), p. 10.
[7]*Ibid.*, p. 19.

A complete description of the subculture common to each of the social classes is not possible here, but a brief exploration of this useful and interesting topic may serve to encourage further study. Any description of subcultural characteristics may be said to apply to the majority of the people composing a social class, even though it may not apply to every person in the class.

Upper-class people have usually inherited wealth and can trace a family tradition of wealth and leadership back several generations. They belong to the most exclusive social clubs and are listed in the local *Social Register.* They belong to the boards of directors of exclusive colleges, art museums, symphonies, charitable organizations, and chambers of commerce. Their church affiliation is likely to be Presbyterian, Episcopal, Congregational, or Unitarian. Young men go into business or one of the higher-status professions such as law, medicine, or architecture. Education of their young people is usually at private preparatory schools and prestige Ivy League or women's colleges. The term "graceful living" may best describe this subgroup of our society.

Upper-middle-class members of the American society may be said to be the "doers." At least half of them have climbed to their present status from lower levels, and they are concerned with continuing to "produce." They are active, ambitious people who place much importance on work and success. Most of the leadership positions in business, civic, and professional organizations are held by members of this group. They are strong believers in making use of the latest innovations and conveniences, especially as they serve to insure an even better future. Money is a prime concern of this class, and although some may be classified as wealthy, more usually the income is enough to pay for a comfortable home, a good automobile, adequate insurance and pension plans, college education for the children, and a modest investment in stocks and bonds or some other likely source of future gain. Church affiliation is almost a requirement, with the favored churches being Presbyterian, Methodist, Baptist, and Congregational-Christian. Numerous Roman Catholic, Lutheran, and Jewish families may also be identified with the upper-middle class. Education is extremely important, because these people see education as the prime stepping-stone to future financial and personal success. This education is usually received at public schools and a state university. The suburbs have become the living area for the upper-middle class, although some may live in the "better" neighborhoods of towns and cities.

Lower-middle-class groups are composed of white-collar clerical and sales workers for the most part, although factory foremen or other upper-level working families, such as farmers, small contractors, railroad engineers, and other "labor aristrocracy" may be included. The members of this group compose the "national average" in areas such as income, interests, recreational preferences, and size of home. "Respectability" is their theme song, and it includes a stressing of thrift, economic independence, and law. They travel a great deal by automobile, although travel abroad is not common, as it is with the upper-middle-class group. The bulk of the membership in the Protestant and Catholic churches, fraternal organizations, and the PTA come from this group, and they furnish much of the leadership for these organizations. Most members of the lower middle class have finished high school and almost half of their children go to college—often a junior college. Schooling is considered important, at least through high school, and the children tend to be obedient, hard-working students.

Upper-working-class people are the skilled and semiskilled "blue-collar" workers. They are viewed as "respectable working people" in contrast to the lower working class or "lower element of society." Parents of many of this group were immigrants, and pride of advancement in social and economic status is a dominant feature of their thinking. Church affiliation is common, although a large minority are not church members. Many are Catholics, there are considerable numbers who belong to fundamentalist Protestant groups such as the Assembly of God, Pentecostal, and Holiness churches, and Baptist and Methodist affiliation is also common. In the big eastern cities, these people commonly live on "the wrong side of the tracks," although they often own their small homes and take good care of them in their spare time. Modern gadgets and conveniences attract their money, sometimes at the expense of what some would consider more important things. Wives often work to supplement the family income, although this cannot be said to be an attribute of only this class, by any means. Working-class adults have typically less than a high school education, but they recognize the importance of education in obtaining good employment and urge their children to go further in school. About half of the children complete high school and a few go on to college. Because of his semiskilled status, the worker does not have much hope for improving his economic status significantly and reconciles himself to a life of routine labor, relieved by mass media and spectator recreation.

Lower-working-class members of our society are looked down upon and generally considered to be the most prominent source of crime, juvenile delinquency, and sexual promiscuity. They usually live in slums, low-income public housing, or various kinds of shacks and cabins. The unpleasant stereotype held of this group is often accurate, but there is a substantial percentage who hold steady jobs and maintain stable family lives, even though their income is below the "poverty" level. Lower-class people may come from families that have been at the bottom of the social structure for several generations, or they may be the newest immigrants, currently primarily Puerto Rican, Mexican-American, or Negro. They have few skills and usually less than a grade-school education, and their color causes great difficulty in finding jobs. Because they are "the last to be hired and the first to be fired," a business recession will quickly put many out of work and on the relief rolls. Work, when it can be found, does not bring personal satisfaction, and debt is often a constant burden. The belief that diligence and thrift have little to do with financial advancement is common. Instead, they tend to believe that only "luck" or "connections" bring financial betterment. Some lower-working-class people are church members—usually fundamentalist Protestant or Catholic, but many are not attached to any church and most are not very active in church life or any other type of community organization. A large percentage of the "problem" children in schools come from this group, including the slow learners, the truants, the delinquent, the aggressive, and the dropouts. They are now getting a good deal of attention from school authorities because of the national "antipoverty" program and related educational efforts.[8]

Some authorities do not agree on the five-class social structure described above, preferring some variation, but it seems to adequately describe the situation and provides a good basis for teachers' consideration in planning and carrying out classroom activities.

American Democratic Principles

To many people, democracy is a system of government, but although it does include ideas about government, the concept of democracy encompasses all of social living. Democracy is actually a set of values or principles which guide economic, social, educational, religious, governmental, and other practices of the members of a society. When accepted by the members of the society, the principles of democracy have important implications for all aspects of living together in that society.

Individual interpretations of the concept vary to some extent among the American people, but certain basic beliefs may be identified which tend to be accepted by most members of our society. Any attempt to identify and describe these principles may be expected to inspire disagreement, but the·following statements seem to accurately define contemporary American democratic principles.

RESPECT AND VALUE FOR THE INDIVIDUAL. This principle has long been advocated by educators in their admonition to "individualize" instruction. It is a sad fact, however, that more lip service than effort has been given to the idea. If educators live by this principle, they will value rather than decry diversity in talents, abilities, and interests of students. They will provide the opportunities for students to develop individual strengths instead of trying to mold each student to some imaginary ideal. Educational accomplishment will be recognized to exist in ways other than academic, and the traditional prestige of academic studies will be applied equally to what we call vocational and technical training. The student who is handicapped by physical, social, or economic circumstances will not only be given treatment equal to the more fortunate child, he will be given the extra attention required to overcome his inherited or acquired handicaps. Freedom of thought and expression will be guaranteed, so long as they do not infringe upon the individual freedoms of others. This concept does not deny the necessity of some conformity to social standards and moral principles required for satisfactory group living, but total conformity is foreign to democratic ideals and stifles the creativity and innovation which have advanced all aspects of our society. In summary, each person is seen as an important part of the society, he is respected as an individual, and he is recognized to be a source of contribution to society which must be developed to the fullest extent.

[8] *Ibid.*, pp. 14–31.

CONCERN FOR GROUP WELFARE. If democracy is to function as it should, concern for the individual must be balanced by an equally strong concern for the group and other members of the society. Such a concern will balance individual rights with responsibility and a concern for the welfare of others. The social consequences of one's acts will serve to temper satisfaction of personal desires. Educators encourage the development of these attitudes when they encourage various school groups in service activities, when plans are made to help the student who is new to the school, when students are encouraged to help each other with their studies, or when lessons from academic studies are used to illustrate the importance of concern for others. Although often ignored or neglected, this essential element of democracy must be purposefully and intelligently included in our school programs.

FAITH IN THE INTELLIGENCE AND JUDGMENT OF THE PEOPLE. Democratic philosophy includes the idea that man has the ability to develop intellectually to the point that he can govern himself wisely. This idea implies the need for the total population to have good opportunities for education. This education must include skills in problem solving and the information required to intelligently consider problems of democratic living. Because of this belief, education has from the beginning of our nation been considered the cornerstone of personal and national success, and schools have received public support seldom matched elsewhere. In fact, we have sometimes placed so much faith in education that we have neglected other essential elements of social progress.

Inconsistencies in the application of this principle may be identified, even though probably every American citizen would uphold its validity. Indoctrination, censorship, book burnings, and refusal to teach about communism or evaluate the capitalistic system are examples of the reluctance to fully follow this principle which we often encounter in American schools. Such examples of a lack of faith in the intelligence and judgment of an informed populace are fortunately becoming less common as we learn to more fully live by the principles of democracy.

A BALANCE BETWEEN COMPETITION AND COOPERATION. One of the problems often encountered in thinking about democracy is the tendency to think of competition and cooperation as being antithetical. It is not true that moving toward more cooperation necessarily requires a diminishing of competition, or vice versa. Cooperation and group decision making are important to our society, and they should be taught throughout our school programs. On the other hand, competition and the "free enterprise" system are also basic to American democracy and deserve much credit for the successes we enjoy. Democratic competition is not the "dog-eat-dog" type of situation tried early in our history, however, because it must include other American ideals of fairness and equitable opportunity. Our schools have been slower to move away from this unfair concept of competition than the business world, as evidenced in such practices as inflexible academic expectations and grading practices; inequitable competition in the gymnasium, in music and in dramatics or debate, and overemphasis on winning rather than improvement or effort. It is very likely that much of the failure experienced by teachers in attempts to encourage cooperation among students is a result of unfair competition in the classroom and on the playing field.

CONTROL FROM WITHIN THE GROUP. The principle related to faith in the intelligence and ability of the people which was mentioned previously is directly related to this precept. The generally accepted idea that those who are affected by decisions or those who are expected to carry them out should have a part in making them, rests on the supposition that they can intelligently and wisely make such decisions. Again, we are faced with the importance of an educated populace, and schools must accept as a major responsibility the task of helping young people develop the skills and understandings required of an active and thoughtful participant in the democratic processes—both in government and other aspects of daily living. This cannot be done by refusing to recognize that students are capable and willing to assume increasing responsibility for their actions as they move through the secondary school program. They cannot learn the skills of self-control and self-government without practicing them, and all too few of our schools and teachers are allowing students enough opportunity to learn these skills through guided practice in student council, athletic, club, or other school organizations. Human beings are not endowed with a natural ability to wisely govern themselves, and they do not learn to do this merely by being told about democratic principles in a civics class. This must be learned, however, if the democratic principle of control from within the group is to be exercised effectively.

Social Roles of the Secondary School Curriculum

Schools are expected to produce learning. This is not a very startling or enlightening statement, but if we consider just what type of learning they should be expected to produce we encounter some difficulties. The acquisition of certain skills, such as reading and writing, and the accumulation of certain bodies of knowledge, such as history, have traditionally occupied the prime attention of those responsible for the operation of our schools. Learning in this context assumes a rather narrow definition and the task of the school is very limited. Psychological theories of learning generally operate within this context, and consequently they are most concerned with learning as an individual process. Behavioristic theories predominate among educational psychologists, even though these theories are more appropriate to the laboratory and its controlled environment than to the classroom and wider culture which influence classroom activities.

The conventional theories of learning tend to largely disregard social and cultural influences, perhaps because they are so complex and difficult to fit into a consistent theory of learning. Current social problems and obvious evidence of inadequacies within our educational system may be an indication that the conventional theories are inadequate and require revision in terms of social concepts if our educational efforts are to achieve satisfactory results. Perhaps there is need to define education in terms more in line with the thinking of sociologists, who see the ultimate aim of education in terms of providing both younger and older members of the society with habits and patterns of behavior by which they may live most satisfactorily. This approach will lead to defining learning as essentially a "need-fulfilling, goal-seeking, and tension-reducing process."[9]

Social psychologists and others who study the ways in which social learning occur have not developed a theory of social learning as yet, but several ideas about the nature of behavior and learning have been formulated.

1. Human behavior is learned through the impact of social environment and the controls within the environment which act to modify behavior according to established models or standards.
2. Learning is primarily social, in that a person's innate or previously acquired tendencies are modified, suppressed, or encouraged according to social demands acting upon him from his surrounding culture.
3. Human learning potential is limited by cultural expectations and culturally determined motivation patterns rather than by natural ability. Self-concepts and ideas about appropriate occupations and ambitions are conditioned by what the surrounding culture values and encourages.
4. Most human activity, and most learning, is motivated as a result of cultural influence. These secondary drives are usually accompanied by strong feeling and are difficult to change.
5. A variety of cultural agents influence the socialization of individuals. The strongest of these is the family, but the school, the job, religion, and other social groups continue the process of socialization throughout life. Inconsistency among the various socializing agencies is the source of much anxiety and frustration as the individual attempts to develop a meaningful life pattern.[10]

Agents of Social Learning

The learning involved in socialization is promoted and influenced by many social institutions, groups, and individuals. The interpersonal relations resulting from contact with these agents of social learning provide the source of cultural approval or dissapproval, acceptance or rejection, which determine the development of an individual's life pattern. The degree of a particular agent's influence may vary from person to person, depending on its acceptance and relative strength, but to understand the social learning that goes into an individual's development we must have some knowledge of the various agents which act to create that learning.

[9]Hilda Taba, *Curriculm Development* (New York: Harcourt, 1962), p. 132.
[10]Adapted from Taba, *Curriculum Development*, pp. 130–131.

The basic socialization of a child occurs in early childhood under the influence of the family, and for this reason much emphasis has been given to the importance of the family in social learning. The basic personality, system of values, and modes of learning probably do owe their origins largely to influences from the home. Many cross-cultural studies have pointed out the fact that cultural differences develop because of differences in patterns of child rearing, and so it is probably true that a well-adjusted parent in a healthy milieu is the first requirement for the development of a healthy personality.

Without denying the importance of the family as an agent of social learning, there is increasing support for the idea that later changes from sources other than the family are common and increasing in importance. The peer group, the school, the community, the church, governmental agencies, the neighborhood, and friendship groups all exercise a certain amount of influence on various aspects of social learning. We cannot delve into the specific ways in which each of these agents encourages social learning, but the student of education and human development should give considerable attention to familiarization with this topic, especially as sociologists and educators learn more about the part each agent plays in social learning.

THE SCHOOL'S TRADITIONAL ROLE. When the task of education became too complex for the home to handle alone, schools were organized and more formal educational efforts began. The earlier schools in our Western pattern of civilization were extensions of the church and functioned primarily to fulfill religious objectives. Knowledge of the Bible was considered essential to personal salvation, and so the ability to personally read and understand the Bible was basic to educational purpose. Moral training was definitely considered to be a most important part of formal schooling, although the family still assumed the prime responsibility for such training.

As the complexity of our society increased, additional duties were delegated to the schools. Preparation for higher education and the professions was the guiding motive for determining the secondary school curriculum, although with the growth of industry some attention was given to more practical and immediately useful skills. Twentieth-century social problems provided the impetus for concern with education for citizenship and social living. John Dewey and others proposed an "education for life" which gained much general acceptance, but the changes required to actually achieve such an education were slow to come, if at all.

The school's traditional role as an agent of social learning has thus been primarily as a supplement to the home and the church in moral and religious training. Its influence has been largely conservative in nature, and educators have neither been asked nor permitted to lead in fostering social change or improvement. Where conflict between the school and other social agencies developed, the school was expected to make the adjustment needed to remove the conflict.

Any change in educational policy has been automatically subject to suspicion, and when educational activities or ideas conflicted with religious or home practices, the school was expected to make the adjustment. Learning was viewed as an individual process, and the effects of social learning were largely ignored.

THE SCHOOL'S CHANGING ROLE. As our society became more complex, so did the public school responsibilities. All of our society's institutions have been required to make changes in their assigned roles, and schools are no exception. Most of the changes required of schools have been in addition to earlier responsibilities; seldom have there been any reductions in function.

Many of the added school responsibilities have come as a result of a lessening in the influence of the family and church. Character development, moral training, mental hygiene, sex education, narcotic and alcohol education, training in etiquette and social graces, dating and premarital education, and health education are some of the more obvious examples of duties now considered part of the school's role as an agent of social learning. Many of these tasks have traditionally been a part of the school's role to some extent, but educators have been asked to assume a much greater share of the responsibility for this type of training in recent years.

As our nation's social problems have assumed added prominence, schools have been asked to keep students aware of the changes occurring in our society and how they must adjust to such changes. They have been asked to help students develop a more thorough understanding of our democratic principles and how they fit into today's social scene. Adjustment to social change is recognized as a skill required of today's citizen, and schools must help their students develop a sense of security while adjusting to cultural change. Cultural, religious, and class prejudice is recognized as undesirable, and schools are expected to reduce this prejudice, sometimes by means of artificial school boundary changes or other physical adjustments. Schools are no longer simply a mirror of social change, they are expected to be prominent agents and promoters of that change.

The Secondary School Curriculum as a Socializing Agent

A somewhat more detailed and specific examination of the functions of the school and its curriculum as a socializing agent may help the student better understand the relationships between our society and curriculum development. It would appear that the secondary school curriculum faces four major roles as a socializing agent.

The Conservative Role

This conception of education and the curriculum focuses on the school's responsibility to collect, preserve, and transmit the cultural heritage to each developing generation. A certain amount of refinement and interpretation is implied, but implementing social values receives preference over evaluation or criticism. The conservative role is essential in its contribution to cultural preservation, like-mindedness, consistency, and narrowing of the "generation gap." The danger is inherent, however, that too much attention to this function will result in extreme orientation to the past, satisfaction with the status quo, and social stagnation.

The Evaluative Role

A second major role of the curriculum involves constructive criticism and questioning of cultural elements and institutions. To some extent, this role is in conflict with the conservative role, in that students are taught less to accept and more to question and evaluate in the light of valid criteria. Participation in social change replaces willing acceptance of either the status quo or variation in cultural practices. In many cases evaluation of older values may result in a rededication of them and further preservation of the traditional, but often it may result in rejection of established ways and a seeking for better modes of living. Modern living requires choices, and making these choices requires a critical evaluation and decision making based on intelligent use of valid criteria.

The Transforming Role

John Dewey and many of his followers (especially George Counts) took the position that the school through its curriculum has as one of its major responsibilities the transforming or reconstructing of society. This view emphasizes the changing nature of our culture and proposes that the school should help young people adjust to changing conditions and find new ways of dealing with current problems. Traditional practices are not ignored; they are used as a base of operations from which evaluation and adjustment may be made. If this role for the school is accepted, the curriculum will become a positive force in reshaping the culture and generally improving our society.

The Countervailing Role

It is now widely recognized that a significant number of the young people growing up in our society are handicapped because of the subculture into which they are born or disadvantages due to economic, family, health, and other conditions. Because the influence of other socializing agents is absent, or weakened in today's world, the school must assume new or increased responsibilities for counteracting the forces which handicap many students. Development of the individual (or self-realization) is a widely accepted goal of education, but to achieve this goal some young people must be given much extra attention and special opportunities for overcoming handicaps and problems. The student and his background must be thoroughly studied and understood by the teacher and other school authorities if the curriculum is to be designed to help the child overcome gaps or weaknesses that occur in his development because of his background in the social structure, his physical endowments, or other individual characteristics.

Social Forces that Influence Curriculum Development

In discussing the nature of our society and the social roles of the secondary school curriculum, we have already mentioned some of the social forces that affect the secondary school curriculum. A better understanding of curriculum development may result if we quickly consider several more of these forces.

Tradition

Tradition has been accurately termed both a boon and a detriment to curriculum development. It is a boon in that it prevents attempts to discard the tried, tested, and true unnecessarily, but on the other hand it often restrains desirable change.

Three important types of traditional forces may be identified which rather directly affect the curriculum. Legal authority in the form of laws enacted by various legislative groups rather rigidly prescribes certain educational practices, especially in terms of required subjects, textbook selection, and class-time requirements. Laws which at one time may have served a useful purpose often hamper curriculum revision long after they have outlived their usefulness. Special-interest groups with legislative influence sometimes manage to legislate educational practices which may or may not be in the interest of the society as a whole. Legislators with an inadequate understanding of educational practice often act to prescribe school practice in ways that may handicap educators for years to come. Many states have constitutional limitations or requirements which hamper schools, and these are especially hard to change.

A second force which is often very powerful exists in the realm of generally agreed-upon principles of value—right and wrong, good and bad, beautiful and ugly. Ideas about property rights and individual rights, boy-girl relations, dress, and interpersonal conduct have come from our Judaeo-Christian heritage and are in many cases virtually immutable. Most of us would agree that these traditions are valuable controls on educational practice, but sometimes they do not allow education to change with changing needs of students. If change is allowed, it usually is slowed and thus fails to meet immediate student needs.

Psychological resistance to change forms a third force which supports traditional curricular practices. Human beings seem to naturally resist change, and teachers sometimes seem more prone to this tendency than the general population. Even though they may not be able to show that their curriculum and methods of teaching are actually functioning effectively in improving learning, many teachers will resist with all their might any effort to move them away from these traditional practices.

Home and Community Forces

The home and family still exercise the greatest socializing force on the lives of most young people, although their influence has weakened in recent years. Identification with the family and its ways comes early in the life of a child; the attitudes, ideas, and customs instilled in the home follow him throughout life. Neatness and cleanliness, obedience to authority, value of schooling, vocational expectations, social activities, race prejudice, sex attitudes, political concepts, and the value and use of money are examples of the mores and attitudes which get their major impetus from the home. The type of punishment which the child receives in the home and the strength or weakness of the affection which he has for his parents may have much to do with his attitudes toward teachers and school. A happy atmosphere in the home may determine his general attitude toward life and his happiness throughout adulthood. All of these factors and others are meaningful in relation to a student's school life, and teachers must know about them and understand their implications if he is to be of maximum help to the student.

Although its influence has weakened along with that of the family, the church is a strong force in the lives of most young people. Group pressure is brought to bear through the church in regard to personal attitudes, beliefs, wishes, and aspirations. Ideas about spiritual rewards and punishment, right and wrong, and relations with others come to a large extent from the church, and although adolescents may question them and even reject them, their imprint remains throughout life. Of special significance to educators is the conflict and confusion which often develops in the minds of young people as they question or reject religious principles and practices. This may have its effect on the whole life of the student, affecting his attitude toward the school and school authorities, and it is part of the school's task to help in the adjustments which are required.

Besides the church, there are various other community organizations which commonly act upon the school curriculum. Service clubs may wish to sponsor writing contests related to certain topics, or they may recognize those students who make particular contributions to the school and community. Patriotic organizations are often especially forceful in their desire to foster "correct" attitudes toward the nation and national ideals. Leisure-time agencies, either commercial or noncommercial, may encourage certain types of activities and discourage others. Various special-interest groups constantly seek to use the captive audience within the school as a means to further their particular concern because they recognize that young people are in their formative stages and particularly susceptible to influence as they develop lifelong attitudes and ideas. As with tradition, these forces may be either helpful or detrimental to the school program, and it is an important responsibility of the teacher to see that a proper balance is maintained and the overall objectives of the school are furthered.

Students

Students influence the curriculum indirectly in that school activities are adjusted to meet students' needs and desires, or at least they should be. There is no longer any question about whether there are differences in young people —differences that affect their learning and their needs relative to education. There is considerable disagreement about the types of adjustment that should be made by the school because of these student differences. To make wise decisions concerning these questions requires the utmost in teacher preparation and responsibility: the good teacher will never cease to study students and the implications for the school of what we know about students. A more direct influence on the curriculum is exercised by students as they express their preferences concerning the school program. Through the student council and other student groups, through their disapproval of certain teachers or courses, through influence with their parents, by talking with teachers, and in other ways, students wield a force in curriculum development that may be more potent than is generally recognized.

Professional Forces

Perhaps it is unnecessary to mention again the effect teachers have on curriculum development, but it should be recognized that they constitute a social as well as an educational force. Individually and through various teacher organizations, directly and indirectly, probably no other force is as powerful in the determination of curricular practices. This again points up the importance of their being well prepared and highly capable people. No amount of development of "new" academic programs and techniques, no number of new buildings, and no collection of materials and equipment will have a significant effect upon the school program in the absence of proper teacher competence in the classroom.

Accreditation agencies provide another professional force acting upon the curriculum. Various associations of schools and colleges throughout the country cooperate to ensure that high schools offer and carry out a satisfactory educational program, especially in the area of college preparation. Through self-evaluations and checking by committees of professionals from outside the school, acceptable standards of curriculum organization and implementation are enforced. The regional accrediting associations are composed of schools who voluntarily submit to accrediting procedures, but states also enforce at least minimum standards of accreditation as a prerequisite to obtaining state financial aid.

Colleges and universities influence public school practices through their membership in accrediting associations and through their teacher education programs, but they also exert considerable influence by means of entrance requirements, scholarships, and general prestige. The original secondary school in the United States was almost exclusively a college preparatory institution, and it was not until the second and third decades of the twentieth century that any significant change was made in this regard. With the advent of a larger percentage of the population to secondary schools due to compulsory attendance laws and tendencies to value more education, it became more and more apparent that the standard college preparatory program was not sufficient for a large proportion of the high school population. "Progressive" education influences and a recognition of the need for a broader curriculum brought some expansion of the curriculum during the 1930's and 1940's, but cold war fears, expansion of technological development, and increased demand for college graduates have recently resulted in a return to increased emphasis on the college preparatory portion of secondary school programs.

Textbook writers and publishers provide other forces acting upon the secondary school curriculum. Our traditional reverence for textbooks and tendency to slavishly follow them in teaching has increased the influence that those who write and publish textbooks have on what is taught. Lack of financial support results in most teachers being limited to the use of only one textbook, although improvement in library facilities and classroom supplementary materials has helped in recent years. Situations are still all too common, however, like that in which a teacher was observed to suggest to students that they "prove" the answer to a question in the textbook by stating the page in the textbook on which the answer was found.

Another potent force acting upon the curriculum is found among the curriculum "specialists" and special study groups set up to revise school practices and materials. Local "curriculum directors" as well as personnel from outside the district wield considerable influence through the development of curriculum materials, recommendations concerning organization of the school program, and in-service teacher training programs.

The above discussion of professional forces which serve to mold the secondary school curriculum is not exhaustive by any means, but perhaps it will illustrate the kinds of influence of which we must be aware—not that they are necessarily bad, but so that we may intelligently assess and utilize appropriate contributions while at the same time making adjustments necessary to counteract unnecessary or undesirable forces.

Governmental Forces

Both direct and indirect influence is exerted on the curriculum by various levels of governmental authority. Through legislation and administrative policy, direct influence is brought to bear, while financial support, furnishing information and consultant service, and various other activities serve to indirectly guide educational decisions.

The federal government exerts little direct control over education in the

United States, because the Constitution leaves the primary responsibility to the states, but more and more indirect influence is being exerted. This is done for the most part by making money available for certain types of programs and to support particular fields of study. The Morrill Act of 1862, which established land-grant colleges, the Smith-Hughes Act of 1917 and other enactments in support of vocational education, WPA projects of the Depression era, the GI bill following World War II, the National Defense Education Act of 1958, and the Elementary and Secondary Education Act of 1965 all trace a continuing and growing participation on the part of the federal government in the support and direction of public school programs. Curriculum materials and advisory services made available through the United States Office of Education also contribute to the influence of the federal government in education. All indications are that this influence will continue to grow, and curriculum leaders must be ever ready to counteract undesirable pressure from this source as well as to make use of the various assistance programs.

State control over education is constitutionally the most extensive and most influential of governmental educational activity. State legislatures have tradition- ally prescribed to a greater or lesser degree what should be in the curriculum. In some states this has reached the point that half or more of the required high school program is state-prescribed. This leaves little opportunity for local adap- tion in view of special needs or preferences. State Departments of Education exercise general control over the selection of textbooks, make curriculum studies, suggest legislative action, license teachers, administer federal funds, and generally supervise the curriculum and instruction in the schools of the state. State influ- ence seems to be increasing, especially where local school authorities have failed to adequately take care of educational needs, and this is almost everywhere.

At the county level, control of school activities is generally decreasing. The county board of education and county superintendent of schools usually have little to do with the operations of the larger independent school districts, and as smaller districts grow in size or consolidate to form larger units it is likely that the county function will disappear. In some states this is already happening. Exceptions to this are occurring where the intermediate unit of school operations is taking on a service role and providing consultant services, equipment and materials, cooperative purchasing services, and other services to the smaller dis- tricts in the county. The county unit of government as a direct force on the school curriculum seems to be disappearing as the needs it once filled are being taken over by either local school districts or the state.

Although the state has final authority over local school activities, it delegates much of the authority for detailed operation of school districts to the local school board. The local board of education operates within rather broad limitations in establishing administrative policies, hiring and placing teachers, approving the budget, authorizing curriculum materials, setting course requirements, and gener- ally determining the scope and quality of educational efforts in the community.

Professional school personnel may have more or less influence with the school board as they make their decisions, but in the final analysis it is the local board that has the authority to make crucial decisions. In so doing it serves as a funnel for the various forces within the community, and to some extent those outside the community, which have an interest in the educational program of the schools.

Economic Forces

The complex activities related to the nation's economy exert various kinds of influence within the society and on the schools. Labor, management, agriculture, and science and technology encompass the major economic groups, and each has its own special interests which they wish to further through public education.

Labor organizations and the people included in them have been primarily interested in furthering the educational opportunities for their young people, eliminating undesirable child-labor practices, and reserving jobs for adults. Labor early supported the movement toward free public education and compulsory education laws. No doubt their motivation was related to the wish for better educational opportunities for their children, but the desire to keep young people off the labor market was also a factor. Some of the results of compulsory education and limitations on the employment of youth have been less than desirable, in that there is now little constructive work available for youth who are younger than eighteen—or even twenty. Those who finish high school early or drop out when they reach the compulsory age limit (usually sixteen), find little demand for their services in the labor market. Apprenticeship or other job-training programs are scarce or nonexistent, even though there is little demand for unskilled labor in most communities. Even part-time work—for young people who need some income to allow them to stay in school or who would like to work during their spare time to earn money for personal wants—is difficult to find in most communities. The frustration thus encountered in looking for work may easily lead to juvenile delinquency, discouragement, and habits more related to idleness than constructive labor.

Labor also represents many small taxpayers who cannot pass on the tax burden to customers, and their concern with taxes is often expressed through the school board's actions. Labor is concerned that good vocational programs are offered in the schools, and special emphasis on the problems of labor is considered a necessary part of academic course content. Counteracting the views of management is a concern of labor groups, and they have sometimes been responsible for legislation designed to uphold the dignity of labor through the school and what is taught in the classroom.

Management largely controls the financial, material, and business resources of the community, and may thus powerfully influence school operations. Concern for conservation of tax dollars may overshadow requirements for good educational opportunities, and young people will be those who suffer the consequences of inadequate educational preparation. Management is also usually interested in the perpetuation of ideas supporting private interprise and opposing the growth of government or public enterprise.

Studies showing the correlation between money spent on education and the per capita income within the community have tended in recent years to weaken the traditional reluctance of management to approve of increased taxes for schools. They have also encouraged the establishment of funds and foundations supporting scholarships, experiments, research, and gifts to universities and colleges. This support is welcome, but care must be exercised to see that undue influence does not result in the overall weakening of the educational efforts of communities and the nation as a whole.

Agriculture is still a potent force in curriculum development, even though the dominance it once exercised over American life has weakened. Most state legislatures are still controlled by rural interests and local governmental units also usually feel their influence very strongly, except in urban areas. Agricultural interests were powerful in the early development of our school programs, and curricular provisions instituted at that time are often perpetuated today, even though the needs of the community and the students may be entirely changed. Some course offerings, and even the school calendar, are examples of this early-day agricultural influence on today's schools.

Science and technology seem to be assuming the dominant role in our society once held by agriculture. With all of its benefits to mankind, this movement also contains some threats and problems. Major changes in our way of life, and the problems of adjusting to these changes, may be one of these more serious threats. It may also be that our enthusiasm for things of science may overshadow other equally important aspects of life and the school curriculum. Government programs of support for education vividly illustrate the fact that some aspects of the school program may be grossly neglected if other parts of the curriculum receive all of the attention and support. Maintaining a balance between the things of science, the humanities, and other crucial elements of the educational program may prove to be the biggest challenge that educators have faced in modern times.

Mass-Communication Media

For the most part, modern means of communication simply facilitate the spreading of ideas from various sectors of the society which we have already mentioned as forces acting upon the curriculum. Those forces which manage to achieve the most effective use of these mass media are thus able to best encourage acceptance of their ideas. In this respect, mass media do not in themselves constitute a force upon the school curriculum, but they enable other forces to more effectively exert their influence.

However, those who work within the mass-media organizations must inevitably exercise their own judgment and preferences in choosing the topics and means of presentation. Even if they sincerely wish to remain objective, some personal preference and prejudice will be evident in what is presented and the light in which the presentation is made. Editorializing, both purposeful and accidental, will thus exert a tremendous influence on the general population and at least secondarily on the school. The general population is vitally interested in schools, so newspapers, television, and other mass-communication media have a valid purpose in including education as an integral part of their coverage. Those who control the mass media are thus in a position to exert a powerful influence upon school boards, administrators, teachers, parents, and students, who in turn strive to gain the adoption of their acquired ideas. It is necessary, therefore, for educators to become aware of the viewpoints of those behind the mass-media communications so that their influence may be recognized and either encouraged or counteracted as professional judgment dictates.

National and International Movements

Organized groups and agencies have become more effective in recent years in promoting various viewpoints and ideas. Many of these are very worthwhile and deserve the support of educators; others may be less desirable and require counteraction on the part of educators. For example, the civil rights movement must be recognized as a powerful force acting in our society today to correct obvious flaws, whether or not one agrees with the methods being used. Attempts to correct economic handicaps, health problems, and other situations are also being carried on by various groups, often in cooperation with each other. At the international level, communism may be cited as an example of a movement which must be recognized and dealt with appropriately. Agreeing on what should be done relative to these various national and international movements is often the biggest problem faced by educators and other leaders, but sitting on our hands while we wait for agreement to come from some unknown source does not constitute professional competence and responsibility.

Social and Cultural Change

Throughout this discussion of the forces that influence the secondary school curriculum, the changes that are occurring in every realm of human activity have been evident. Perhaps it is the change itself which is causing most of our problems in education and other aspects of daily living. Adjustment to modification of all aspects of our society is obviously at least a major, if not the primary, problem faced by our people and our institutions. In order for educators to meet the curricular demands of these changes, we must be aware of them and their implications for the school program. The final section of this chapter will deal in more detail with the social trends and problems currently affecting the secondary school curriculum.

Current Social Trends and Problems Affecting the Curriculum

One of the characteristics of American life and philosophy has historically been a faith in the future and a tolerance for change. It seems there is a strain of conservatism and a fondness for the status quo in all human beings, but in America this tendency has been overshadowed by an optimism and hope for tomorrow that not only accepts change but sees it as essential to progress and increased prosperity. Perhaps this enthusiasm for things new and different is overdone at times, but it remains an essential ingredient of American life and society. For this reason the successful educator must be constantly striving to keep up with changes that occur, and he then must analyze them in terms of their implications for the school and its curriculum. Failure to do so will soon result in an obsolete school program which fails to provide the education needed by young people going into a world of flux and constantly varying social realities.

No treatment of social changes and problems can be complete, and the following treatise is of necessity brief, but the major types prevalent today will be quickly explored in the hope that such an introduction will encourage the student to continuously study the society of which he is a part and for which he helps prepare young people in today's secondary schools.

International Relations

The United States of the twentieth century is confronted with international problems and responsibilities of an international power and world leader to which it is not accustomed. Our people, until the mid-twentieth century, were accustomed to maintaining an isolationist attitude toward the rest of the world. With today's means of transportation and communication, this is no longer possible, and our strength as a world power has cast us in a role of world leadership which we cannot shirk even if we wish to. This means that we must gain an understanding of other people and international relations that few school programs are currently able to provide.

The curricular implications of the world situation and our position of world leadership are not difficult to identify. We must teach the student today, who will occupy an even smaller world tomorrow, about international relations and the problems involved in living as next-door neighbors to the rest of the world. Recent history of Africa and Asia must be added to the traditional historical offerings. World geography and economics as related to the international setting can provide additional sources of international understanding. Tolerance and respect for people, regardless of race, religion, or creed, can and should be woven into several areas of the traditional school curriculum. This requires that the humanities be reemphasized, not at the expense of science and technology but to supplement them and provide guidelines for their use. It is not easy to gain acceptance for curricular revision of any type, but perhaps this phase of the school program needed today and tomorrow will be the most difficult to institute because of a strong undercurrent of isolationism and hypernationalism which still pervades our nation.

The Community

At times there has been a great deal said about how the curriculum should be molded to the needs of the community it serves. This worthy motive has been too narrowly construed at times and thus unwisely restricted the school program, but it is still true that local problems and concerns should be considered in developing the school program. Most communities in the United States are similar in many ways. They have problems of poverty as well as affluence, prejudice and intolerance, population mobility, growth or a lack of it, government and the local economy. But while there are similar problems among the nation's communities, each has its own peculiar concerns and areas of greatest need. Some suffer from too little money, others from too much. Some are old and well established, others are very young and suffering the ailments of all youth. Some are growing rapidly, others are losing population. Industry is most important to the welfare of the economy of one community, while agriculture assumes the dominant role in another. As we further explore social problems that exist throughout the United States, implications for local community concern and school involvement will be apparent.

Home and Family

Much as been written about changes in home and family life, and alarmists would have us believe that our civilization is crumbling because of these changes. No doubt there are serious implications to be drawn from some of these changes, although change does not necessarily mean catastrophe, and some of these implications are directly related to educational needs.

Since the main business of schools is education, probably the developments in home and family life more pertinent to schools relate to educational activities. Many educational responsibilities once carried out by fathers and mothers in the home have now been passed on to the schools. Sons don't usually learn a vocation from their fathers, neither do daughters learn homemaking skills from their mothers in many instances. Father works in an office somewhere and mother may also be out of the home a great deal of the time. Children, too, are gone from home much of the time, so opportunity for teaching in the home is often severely limited. This means that schools must take on more responsibility for vocational and homemaking education.

Because families are not together nearly as much as they once were, and because almost 50 percent of our children live in broken homes, the closeness which facilitated other types of teaching and learning is often absent. Moral and religious training, sex education, human relations skills, and preparation for marriage are prime examples of the kinds of teaching which must now be largely carried out in school rather than at home. Much of this type of education cannot be done in the traditional academically oriented classroom. Academics need not be abandoned, but these other necessary learning activities must be woven into the educational program, not necessarily as separate courses, but as an integral part of the academic program. Actually, this will benefit the academic studies, because students will take a greater interest as their practical and immediate needs are met in conjunction with more formal studies.

The Individual

Probably the most pressing problem faced by our society relative to the individuals who make up the society is what may be termed "alienation of the self" or "loss of individuality." We have become so society-minded, so conformist, so "other-oriented" that there is serious danger of dehumanization. Man loses his "humanness" when he is deprived of the opportunity for creativity, inventiveness, and autonomy, and even though an efficient society requires a degree of conformity and mutual adjustment, there must remain the opportunity for an individual to be an individual without losing his place in history.

The loss of individuality described above has been termed the "estrangement of the person from his selfhood through society." In addition, there is the danger of "estrangement of the self from society."[11] In this type of case the individual becomes estranged from society by his own choice. The delinquent, the criminal, the heretic, the "hippie," and the alcoholic are examples of this situation, and each requires a particular type of preventive which may at least be partially applied in our schools.

Discrimination because of racial or class prejudice is the most serious type of alienation found in our society today. Illustrated by the social situation confronting the blacks, the newly arrived immigrants, or minority religious and ethnic groups, such estrangement is usually beyond the control of the individual. Contemporary civil rights and equal opportunity movements have as their purpose the alleviation or elimination of such situations, but their methods sometimes only create increased and intensified prejudice. Many experts subscribe to the belief that only through education and a new generation can these situations be improved to any extent. The implications for schools and the curriculum are obvious and pressing, even though we might be inclined to avoid meeting the challenge because of its difficulty.

[11]J. Galen Saylor and William M. Alexander, *Curriculum Planning for Modern Schools* (New York: Holt, 1966), p. 118.

Population Changes

Among the more serious and pressing problems facing our society and its educational system are those related to the human components of that society —the people. Population growth, redistribution of age groups, urbanization, mobility, and the changing student population—all of these aspects of our changing population require solutions and imply changes in our schools.

The figures related to population growth in the United States and other parts of the world are alarming to say the least. It has been estimated that by 1985 there will be at least 54 million *more* people in the United States than there were in 1965. This would forecast an increase of 4.75 million more children in elementary school, almost 2 million more in high school, and a 3.5 million increase in the college-age group. By 1990 this country's population is expected to be at least 262 million, and the increase is forecast to continue to a minimum of 291 million in the year 2000 and 322 million by 2010.[12] Simple arithmetic shows what this implies for school needs.

Predictions of world population increases provide even more reason for concern. Estimates prepared by the United Nations indicate that the mid-1960 world population of about 3 billion will increase to between 4.88 and 6.9 billion by the year 2000.[13] A complicating factor is the tendency for the least industrialized and least advanced nations to increase at a much faster pace than the more advanced nations. At present rates of increase, the less developed areas of the world will double their populations in 20 to 40 years, while the industrialized countries will require 50 to 100 years to double in population.[14]

These predictions indicate, among other things, a need for including study of population problems in the school curriculum—rates of growth, population control, and the like. They point up the importance of continuing emphasis on problems of international cooperation and international relationships, the maintenance of peace despite national rivalries and nations' needs for more land and more natural resources. Providing educational opportunities for all of these people in itself presents a staggering problem.

In addition to problems created by the population explosion, there are those resulting from changes in the distribution of age groups. During the next ten to twenty years the population of the United States will be composed of an increasing percentage of younger and older people, with a corresponding decrease in the percentage of those in the middle-age ranges—those who must produce and provide for both the young and the old.

---

[12]Jacob S. Siegel, Meyer Zitter, and Donald S. Akers, *Projections of the Population of the United States, by Age and Sex, 1964 to 1985*, Current Population Reports, Series P-25, No. 286, July 1964 (Washington, D.C.: Government Printing Office, 1964), Tables 1 and 3.

[13]*The Future Growth of the World Population*, United Nations Publication No. St/SOA/Ser. A/28 (New York: United Nations, 1958).

[14]Philip M. Hauser, "Man and More Men: The Population Prospects," in Ronald Freedman (ed.), *Population: The Vital Revolution* (New York: Doubleday, 1964).

Along with the rapid increase in numbers, our population has become highly mobile. Part of the American tradition has been the idea that if success eludes you at the present there is another day and another place in which it may be achieved. "Moving on" is seen as a possible solution to most problems and results in a constant changing of residence for thousands of Americans. The more serious problems resulting from this population mobility have come from the less well educated and poorer groups who move from the rural areas and the South to the cities and especially to the Northeast and West Coast areas. Slums have mush-roomed, and caring for this largely nonproductive group of people presents an almost insurmountable problem for metropolitan areas. Movement of the better-educated and more prosperous families also brings its problems of adjustment to new homes and neighborhoods, new customs, and generally unfamiliar surround-ings. These and other implications for schools and government agencies provide additional challenges to the ingenuity and resourcefulness of educators and other public servants.

Most of our population mobility has been in the direction of the cities, resulting in increased urbanization. Whereas we were once predominantly rural dwellers, the majority of us now live in large cities. These cities tend to develop similar subdivisions with similar problems. There is the old central core area of the city which usually is a slum area. There are fringe slum districts between the central core and the outer, newer parts of the city, which may be salvaged and improved more easily than the core slum districts. And there are the suburban areas where the more affluent city dwellers have fled to escape the blight which is so typical of older parts of town. Each of these areas of our cities presents problems that can at least be partially solved through proper education. In the slum, juvenile delinquency and school dropouts present a challenge we have only begun to find out how to meet. The traditional curriculum is woefully inadequate for young people from the disadvantaged homes of the slum or ghetto, and we are just beginning to recognize the necessity of more personal, more relevant, more intensive, and much more expensive educational opportunities for these young people. The suburban youngster also has problems, notably the pressure resulting from parental desires, college entrance requirements, and social activi-ties. Distortion in the educational program is all too common as a result of the inordinate academic pressure resulting from too much parental ambition. The social pressures brought on by an ever earlier and more active social life for young people also provide teachers with the necessity of doing more than teaching the academics as they assist young people in the painful process of growing up.

The student population of our secondary schools has itself undergone signifi-cant change in recent years. Whereas once the high school students were typi-cally a small percentage of high school age youth, today a large percentage of these people are in school. The high school is now the "common school" rather than a school for the privileged few, and for the most part the typical secondary school curriculum has failed to adjust to this fact. We still concentrate on those studies which are appropriate for the college-bound, the academically capable, and the academically interested. Vocational training and similar programs occupy an inferior status if they exist at all, even though it is obvious that there is much more need for this type of instruction than for purely academic preparation. Our society has no constructive use for the adolescent in its economic organization, so we must provide better reasons for his staying in school than that of simply keeping him off the streets and out of the labor force.

Government

Several recent developments and trends in governmental operations are having rather direct and far-reaching effects on the educational system. As mentioned earlier, many of these evolve from the tendency of central governmental agencies to give more attention to the educational system. This has resulted in an increased amount of federal aid and control, and it appears that this trend will continue.

Largely as a result of increased governmental activity in education, the schools seem to be giving more attention to the needs of the society, sometimes at the expense of individual needs. The old question of social versus individual needs is not a thing of the past, and although fulfilling one type of need may help meet the other, watchfulness is required to assure that one emphasis does not overbalance the other.

Governmental concern for social problems and their alleviation is evidenced in the educational efforts going into helping those who are labeled as "disadvantaged" or "deprived." Medical and health care for this element of the population is being included in the educational program as welfare agencies cooperate with the schools to upgrade the living standards for the portion of our population which still lives below the accepted minimum. These types of activities are good examples of the way in which attempts to meet the needs of individuals and the society as a whole often complement each other or are even identical in their operation.

The judicial as well as the legislative and executive branches of government is exercising increasing influence in the operations of individual school districts and the total educational system. In the interests of civil rights, civil liberties, equitable treatment under the law, the separation of church and state, and similar causes, the courts are acting to influence school operations in individual districts and across the nation.

The Economy

An increased need for knowledge about our economy and how it works is causing one of the more noticeable developments in today's secondary school curriculum. The laws of supply and demand, national banking policies, taxation practices, and similar topics form areas of study which must be mastered to some extent if tomorrow's adults are to understand the world in which they live and be able intelligently to influence economic practices by means of political action. The price of gold, use of the gold standard, cooperation or competition with the European Common Market, devaluation of currencies, and the balance of trade are topics of common conversation among well-educated people today, and young people want to know more about the questions and possible answers which surround these economic questions.

Changing employment patterns require educational preparation of young people which differs markedly from that of a few years ago. Technology, automation, population shifts, changing consumer demands, and a need for more capable workers mean that the demand for unskilled and less educated laborers decreases while that for technical, clerical, managerial, and professional workers increases. Brain power now takes precedence in most occupational areas over muscle power, and employers are constantly increasing their demands for better-educated employees. Even in occupations where a high level of formal education is not a necessity, the trend toward more years of formal education causes employers to demand more highly educated job applicants, and as the percentage of young people finishing college increases, employers will continue this trend and expect many of their employees to have graduate degrees. This trend may not be entirely justified, but it is part of our American faith in education and will probably continue.

Rapidly changing employment patterns and the need for continually evolving skills also indicate that schools must prepare future employees in a way that will help them to learn new skills and change to new types of jobs throughout their lives. Preparation for a job immediately after high school or college graduation is not enough; the citizen of the future must be able and willing to continue to learn throughout his life, so that he may keep his job skills in line with changing needs of business and industry. It may be, therefore, that one of the most important tasks of schools is to teach students to learn, and this involves much more than teaching certain specified subject matter.

Consumer education is also gaining more support as it becomes obvious that consumer confusion costs the average American citizen hundreds of dollars each year. The abundance of material goods to buy, the techniques of modern advertising, the use of credit, and other complexities of buying and budgeting in an age of deficit spending illustrate the need for more education in the use of personal and family financial resources.

One other area of economic education that is demanding increasing attention in our schools will perhaps sufficiently illustrate the need for constant reevaluation of this part of our school curricula. More and more attention is being given to the wise use of natural resources—their conservation. Smog, water and air pollution, litter, and unnecessary waste on every hand are forcing us to recognize and do something about the tragic misuse and contamination to which we are subjecting the natural environment which sustains both our physical and psychological well-being. Schools cannot afford to continue their traditional neglect of this educational need.

Science and Technology

Probably the most importance forces acting to change the society in which we live emanate either directly or indirectly from the discoveries and changes resulting from scientific and technological advancement. Nuclear and atomic physics, space exploration, electronics, the development of synthetics, medical advancements, computers, industrialized farms, and innumerable other modern scientific advancements have a profound influence on the school curriculum, many times in ways which we do not readily recognize. The education of people to continue this advancement, to make use of modern scientific developments and—possibly most important—to live in a scientific world challenges the school system as never before.

Transportation and Communication

Part of the advancement in science and technology has been related to transportation and communication facilities. Air transportation, in particular, is enabling people to go places and do things undreamed of only a few years ago. As the world grows smaller because of improved means of rapid communication and transportation, the need for developing the ability among our people to live with other peoples of the world becomes ever more urgent. The social studies and studies in the humanities assume increased importance as we try to help young people develop an understanding and appreciation of other people which will allow them to live together in peace and mutal benefit.

Of perhaps greater significance to education are changes in mass media of communication and entertainment. Television, radio, newspapers, and magazines all clamor for the attention of every American. Their influence on developing minds is incalculable, and education must make adjustments to both counteract and capitalize on offerings of mass communication media.

Expansion of Knowledge

It is not just in the fields of science and technology that the growth of knowledge is staggering to the imagination. It has been said by some authorities that it took two thousand years for the fund of man's knowledge to double from the time of Christ to the beginning of the twentieth century. Since that time, our body of knowledge has increased at least threefold, and more liberal estimates place the increase at a doubling every decade of this century. Since schools are given the responsibility of passing on this knowledge to each succeeding generation, the task soon assumes astronomical proportions.

The schools may take either of two approaches to meeting the challenge of the "knowledge explosion." We may either attempt to cram more and more of this expanding body of knowledge into the heads of boys and girls, or we may place emphasis on the understanding and use of knowledge rather than its accumulation. To require that students accumulate this body of knowledge in their minds will require either an impossible pressuring to learn more or an increased specialization in the accumulated knowledge of a particular field of study. We have enough nervous breakdowns and suicides among our students now to discourage the approach of forcing more and more accumulation of a broad field of knowledge, and specialization obviously includes the danger of warped minds which lack judgment and the broad view required for man to live in peace and harmony with his fellow man. The alternative is to see education as ". . . primarily a process by which we become more able to organize those things that we do know in such a way as to cause them to have meaning and applicability."[15] Unless we take this approach, it would appear that future generations of young people will be faced with the necessity of using all of their time to learn an ever more exasperating expanse of disjointed, meaningless facts. This would undoubtedly result in a drouth of understanding, wisdom, and ability to successfully use what is "known."

Religion and Values

Most writers on the subject seem to agree that the United States is experiencing a decrease in church attendance and church activity among its population. Whether or not this indicates a decreased concern in the values and basic tenets of Christianity is not clear, but there certainly seems to be less response to religious urgings because of fear, less emphasis on denominational differences, and less concern with religious training and family worship in the home. There is also less fear of the results of easing the traditional maintenance of church and state separation, as evidenced by recent legislative and judicial decisions allowing more organized and more extensive support of parochial schools with public tax money.

Because religion and values have always been closely interwoven in our culture, we sometimes equate changes in religious practices with changes in our value system, although they do not necessarily go together. Whether or not they are connected with changes in religious concepts, there are certainly some changes in the value system of our society which may be noted. The pioneer emphasis on independence, self-reliance, and initiative is being softened, although probably not replaced, by more concern for cooperation and acquiescence to the demands of communal living. An extreme concern for power and for material things is being recognized as a weakness of the American system, and schools are being asked to replace this with something which is more compatible

[15]Wayne Dumas and Weldon Beckner, *Introduction to Secondary Education: A Foundations Approach* (Scranton, Pa.: Intext, 1968), pp. 90–91.

with democratic ideals and more likely to lead to the genuinely happy life. Secular morality is tending to replace religious morality to some extent, and as this occurs, relativism and the "new morality" gain favor with many individuals. The questioning of traditional values and rejection of past concepts in many cases leave a void which the schools must perhaps assume some responsibility for filling.

New Leisure

Our modern mechanized and automated society has produced leisure time in abundant quantities, a phenomenon seldom if ever faced by man before, and one opposed to some of our traditional values and religious concepts. The average work week of the American laborer has been reduced in less than a century from about 70 hours to 40 or less, and forecasters predict that this will dwindle further in the near future, perhaps to 20 hours per week before we begin the twenty-first century. But instead of being a utopian development, this phenomenon is proving to be a major social problem. As John I. Goodlad phrases it: "The rate of freeing man from his daily labors far surpasses the pace of freeing man to indulge fully in the rich and productive use of his leisure."[16]

This new leisure possesses vast possibilities for good, but it also points to a need for learning to use leisure intelligently. The problem is magnified because of the fact that leisure is most available to those who are least prepared to make use of it. The more highly educated professional elements of the population tend to experience a crowded schedule, while the less well-educated groups are in danger of being engulfed with poorly used leisure time. For half a century educators have accepted the "worthy use of leisure" as a major goal of education, but most school programs show little evidence of progress in the actual achievement of such a goal. Most critics of education scoff at the idea of education in the wise use of leisure time, and those who know letter seem disinclined to challenge these critics and the forces of inertia which support them.

Social Class Problems

Social class is in itself a powerful force upon the development of appropriate school programs for various groups, as discussed earlier in this chapter. The average person's desire to move upward socially adds a complicating factor, because successful social mobility requires that the person making the change understand and adopt most of the values and mores of the group into which he moves. Education is seen as the most promising aid to upward social mobility, but it must also help the individual to understand and accept the concepts and customs of the group into which he wishes to move.

A person's desire to move upward socially is not often easily achieved, and

[16]John I. Goodlad, *School, Curriculum, and the Individual* (Waltham, Mass.: Blaisdell, 1966), p. 151.

it appears that upward mobility is becoming more difficult. Educational and living standards have increased and raised the level of the various classes so that persons aspiring to new levels must reach higher standards than in the past. Increased requirements in the areas of technical and service vocations provide avenues for lower-class and lower-middle-class youth to rise socially, but predictions of a surplus in the supply of technical and professional workers within the next ten years indicate that competition for middle-class positions will become severe and upward social mobility extremely difficult.

There will probably always be a lower-class group of people in the society, and their inability to move out of this class will require that educators more adequately provide for the needs of those who do not move out of the lower classes. This has been a traditional weakness of our schools, and it has contributed to many of the problems of intergroup relations, civil rights, crime, and delinquency discussed below.

Intergroup Relations

We are a nation of many groups and it may be that this diversity has been one of the sources of our strength. On the other hand, there is considerable evidence that continued and even growing cleavages between ethnic, racial, social, religious, and other groups may lead to tragic consequences. Highly diverse groups have trouble coexisting amiably, and modern developments in transportation and communication have placed differing groups in ever closer contact with each other. Hatred, fear, cruelty, persecution, and violence are too often the result of intergroup relations in these United States, and it would appear that these relations are likely to get worse before they get better.

There have been times in history when intergroup tensions were relieved by the disintegration of one or more of the groups, by the development of a caste system, or by the integration of the groups. The first two solutions are obviously inappropriate in our country, and the third seems unlikely of accomplishment because of strong tendencies to maintain group characteristics. A pluralism seems unavoidable, and to make this situation a strength rather than a weakness provides an impressive challenge for the whole society and especially for our schools.

Civil Rights Conflicts

When the term "civil rights" is used today, we usually think of racial integration, fair housing practices, equal employment opportunities, and other problems faced by the American Negro. Current questions of civil rights tend to focus on this aspect of the concept, but the ideal of "inalienable" rights proposed by our founding fathers was much broader, and efforts to assure the achievement of these ideals have taken several directions during American history. Initiated with the passage of the Bill of Rights in 1791, the idea was forwarded by the gradual elimination of property and religious requirements for voting and office holding, the abolishment of slavery, the attainment of equal rights for women, free and fair access to public schools, equal treatment under the law, and the 1954 Supreme Court decision destroying the legality of mythical "separate but equal" practices in schools. Legislative actions and court decisions continue to rapidly expand efforts to guarantee that all citizens benefit from those humane and just principles which we have long given lip service but poorly practiced.

Most of the current problems related to civil rights pertain to unequal opportunities for minority groups. Black, Puerto Rican, Mexican and other "hyphenated" Americans are becoming increasingly impatient with the slow progress evident in their attempts to achieve equal educational, employment, housing, cultural, and social status. "Moderate" methods espoused by leaders such as the late Martin Luther King are being abandoned by many of the more "militant" members of these groups in favor of more direct and violent tactics. "Law and order" admonitions on the part of the majority are countered with cries for "justice" and accusations of "police brutality" from minorities. Campus riots and other forms of student revolt call our attention to biased and paltry treatment of minorities in history books, literature, music, and other aspects of college programs. "Black power" is put forward as the only really effective means for countering tradition, prejudice, and unfair treatment under the law. Never since the Civil War has our nation been so threatened with internal revolt and conflict among its citizens.

The cherished right of "dissent" is closely connected to most of the activities mentioned above, particularly in the form of protest and civil disobedience. "Sit-ins," marches, and other forms of protest have become so common that they sometimes fail to make the newspapers. Protests directed at military conscription, national foreign policy, and domestic governmental actions result in demonstrations involving draft-card burning, flag-burning, deliberate violations of law, and other means for dramatizing disagreement with current practices, policies, and judicial actions. Few in this nation would deny the right of dissent, but serious doubts exist among a large proportion of the population about the limits of freedom which must be maintained even in a democracy and the relationships that should be observed between freedom and responsibility.

Education may not be the answer to all of our national problems relating to civil rights, but its potential is yet to be fully explored in this regard, and it would appear to promise better results than the legal and forceful measures most prevalent to date. Simply providing "equal" educational opportunities for all will not suffice, however, because the neglected and downtrodden elements do not have an equal start. As has been stated before, "There is nothing so unequal as the equal treatment of unequals," and to make up for past negligence and past mistakes we must now allot unparalleled amounts of money and other forms of support to the educational opportunities afforded the disadvantaged groups in our society. In addition, these efforts must take drastically different forms and make use of revolutionary innovations in form, content, and method if satisfactory progress is to be achieved in the years ahead.

Crime and Delinquency

Little can be said about our problems of crime and juvenile delinquency that has not already been said many times. The situation is staggering when studied objectively, and the cost in lives and dollars almost surpasses comprehension. Conservative estimates of the monetary cost of crime in the United States approach $20 billion per year. Much of this is organized crime, but perhaps a more serious aspect of the problem concerns the fact that a substantial proportion of crime is perpetrated by ordinary citizens—shoplifting, petty embezzlement, employee theft, and the like. Statistics in the field of delinquency also vary considerably, but most authorities are agreed that there has been a sizable increase in the delinquency rate since World War II. Estimates may vary from two or three youths per hundred to six or seven per hundred who are actually picked up by police.[17] The Children's Bureau of the United States Department of Health, Education and Welfare reports that approximately 555,000 different young people were brought before juvenile courts in 1962 and about 1.1 million were dealt with directly by the police but not brought into court, excluding traffic cases. An increase of over 100 percent in the number appearing before the courts was recorded between 1950 and 1962.[18]

Most experts agree that just as normal personality is the product of culture, so is deviant personality. Both crime and delinquency are caused, at least partially, by inadequacies of the educational system. School authorities persistently rely on negative solutions, such as repressive discipline, and fail to utilize the more positive approaches long used by group workers to utilize gang leadership and develop worthwhile activities characterized by cooperation. Teachers' attitudes too often are not characterized by the warmth and understanding required to positively counter behavior problems, perhaps at least partially because most teachers do not understand the subcultures from which many of their students come. Inadequate emphasis is given in the curriculum to those matters that will help the coming generation to work out solutions to social problems so that fewer situations leading to deviant behavior and delinquency will exist. Too little attention is given to developing skills in helping people live amicably with each other, as pointed out earlier in the discussion of intergroup relations. Inadequate provision is made for the development of the ideals and practices leading to good family living which will produce good future citizens.

[17]Ralph L. Pounds and James R. Bryner, *The School in American Society*, 2d ed. (New York: Macmillan, 1967), p. 290.
[18]Richard Perlman, Chief, Juvenile Delinquency Statistics Section, Children's Bureau, "Statistical Aspects of Antisocial Behavior of the Minor in the United States" (Washington, D.C.: U. S. Department of Health, Education and Welfare, 1963), pp. 3,8,11.

Selected References

Backman, Carl W., and Paul F. Secord, *A Social Psychological* View of Education. New York: Harcourt Brace Jovanovich Inc., 1968.

Beckner, Weldon, and Wayne Dumas, *Readings in Secondary Education: A Foundations Approach.* Scranton, Pa.: Intext Educational Publishers, 1968, Selections 15–17, 21–25.

Broudy, Harry S., B. Othanel Smith, and Joe R. Burnett, *Democracy and Excellence in American Secondary Education.* Chicago: Rand McNally & Company, 1964, Chapters 1–5.

Clark, Leonard H., Raymond L. Klein, and John B. Burks, *The American Secondary School Curriculum.* New York: The Macmillan Company, 1965, Chapter 4.

Connell, W. F., R. L. Debus, and W. R. Niblett, *Readings in the Foundations of Education.* Chicago: Rand McNally & Company (no date), Part III.

Counts, George S., *The Social Foundations of Education.* New York: Charles Scribner's Sons, 1934.

Doll, Ronald C., *Curriculum Improvement: Decision-Making and Process.* Boston: Allyn and Bacon, Inc., 1964, Chapter 3.

Douglass, Harl R. (ed.), *The High School Curriculum.* 3d ed. New York: The Ronald Press Company, 1964, Chapters 4,5,7,9.

Dumas, Wayne, and Weldon Beckner, *Introduction to Secondary Education: A Foundations Approach.* Scranton, Pa.: Intext Educational Publishers, 1968, Chapter 3.

Gezi, Kalil I., and James E. Myers, *Teaching in American Culture.* New York: Holt, Rinehart and Winston, Inc., 1968, Chapters 2 and 3.

Goodlad, John I., *School, Curriculum, and the Individual.* Waltham, Mass.: Blaisdell Publishing Company, 1966, pp. 148–157.

Gross, Carl H., Stanley P. Wronski, and John W. Hanson, *School and Society.* Lexington, Mass.: D. C. Heath & Company, 1962.

Hass, Glen, and Kimball Wiles, *Readings in Curriculum.* Boston: Allyn and Bacon, Inc., 1965, Section 1.

Havighurst, Robert J., and Bernice L. Neugarten, *Society and Education.* 3d ed. Boston: Allyn and Bacon, Inc., 1967.

Kneller, George F., *Foundations of Education.* 2d ed., New York: John Wiley & Sons, Inc., 1967, Part II.

McLendon, Jonathan C. (ed.), *Social Foundations of Education: Current Readings from the Behavioral Sciences.* New York: The Macmillan Company, 1966.

Morris, Van Cleve, et al., *Becoming an Educator.* Boston: Houghton Mifflin Company, 1963, Chapter 3 (Robert J. Havighurst, "The Sociology of Education").

Pounds, Ralph L., and James R. Bryner, *The School in American Society.* 2d ed., New York: The Macmillan Company, 1967.

Romine, Stephen A., *Building the High School Curriculum*. New York: The Ronald Press Company, 1954, Chapter 4.

Saylor, Galen J., and William M. Alexander, *Curriculum Planning for Modern Schools*. New York: Holt, Rinehart and Winston, Inc., 1966, Chapter 3.

Smith, B. Othanel, William O. Stanley, and J. Harlan Shores, *Fundamentals of Curriculum Development*. Rev. ed. New York: Harcourt Brace Jovanovich, Inc., 1957, Chapters 1–4.

Stone, James C., and Federick W. Schneider, *Readings in the Foundations of Education*. New York: Thomas Y. Crowell Company, 1965, Section 1.

Taba, Hilda, *Curriculum Development*. New York: Harcourt Brace Jovanovich, Inc., 1962, Chapters 3–5, 10, 11.

Thayer, V. T., and Martin Levit, *The Role of the School in American Society*. New York: Dodd, Mead & Company, 1966.

Westby-Gibson, Dorothy (ed.), *Social Foundations of Education*. New York: The Free Press, 1967.

CHAPTER 5

FOUNDATIONS IN PSYCHOLOGY AND HUMAN DEVELOPMENT

Teaching obviously existed long before anything related to what we think of as psychology came into being. But just as scientific knowledge has helped us to understand and control natural phenomena which have existed through the ages, so psychology has helped us to better understand and improve upon teaching and learning activities. The "scientific" aspects of teaching are largely dependent upon psychology as a source of knowledge, and as this relatively young science matures it will doubtless provide more accurate and useful information for the educator.

Growth and Development of Psychology

Historically, we may date psychology from the conflicting views on human nature of Plato and Aristotle. The Greek work *psyche* means "soul," and so we might assume that psychology originally meant the study of the soul. However, the Greeks did not ascribe any religious implications to the "soul." The concept meant no more to them than does the word "mind" to us. They had, however, advanced in their thinking to the point of recognizing a mysterious something, an unseen element within the human being which determined his behavior. That mysterious unseen element they named *psyche.*

To fit into his general philosophy, which included a belief that the universe is divided into a spiritual and material world, Plato developed the idea that human nature likewise consists of spirit (soul) and matter (body). This dual approach led to his belief that ideas reside in the body during life, being innate at birth and developed throughout life as a result of sensations coming through the senses which arouse corresponding ideas that have been in existence but inactive since birth. To Plato, the mind contributes ideas to the learning process while the body contributes sensations. Any source of error in thinking is thus due to the senses. Through their limitations they handicap the mind.

From these basic concepts, Plato developed the notion that the purpose of teaching is to bring out that which has been within the learner since his birth, and misconceptions coming from this idea have plagued education since his time. To questions related to the relative importance of heredity and environment in the development of the human being Plato ascribed answers strongly leaning toward the importance of heredity, again directly influencing future educators.

Aristotle varied from Plato's ideas in his belief that mind and body coexist and are dependent upon each other. He held that human nature is a compound of vegetative, animal, and human characteristics. It was his opinion that man's vegetative nature grows, reproduces, decays, and dies in similar fashion to plant life; his animal nature has desires, sensory impressions, and active movement similar to those of all animals; but reason is possessed only by man and gives him his distinctive characteristic. This theory accounted for Aristotle's oft-repeated contention that "man is a rational animal."

The Renaissance Approach

Through the centuries much controversy revolved around the differences in these philosophies, but by the time of the Renaissance there developed wide support for describing the *psyche*, or soul, in terms of its functions, or faculties. Disagreement centered primarily around the correct number of faculties and their precise description. In the absence of modern scientific methods, arguments were largely limited to philosophical ideas and logic, resulting in support for from as few as one to as many as twenty-four faculties. Over a period of time, attention tended to focus on three faculties identified by Aristotle (knowing, feeling, and willing) and four which have become very familiar to teachers: judgment, memory, imagination, and attention.

For centuries the mind was conceived of as a collection of these faculties, each of which existed separately and functioned independently. Each faculty was discussed as if it existed and functioned entirely independent of other faculties. Psychology, then, was a study of these mental faculties, or "powers." "Development of the powers of the mind" was seen as the supreme aim of education, the classics and mathematics being considered to be most valuable for this purpose.

John Locke

With its emphasis on the role of the intellect in learning, faculty psychology neglected the use of the senses in learning, causing needless difficulty for students through the years. The abstract and mentally difficult were consistently favored at the expense of the experimental and concrete, a tendency that is still all too prominent in our schools.

Closely akin to ideas of faculty psychology, "formal discipline" was another strong influence on teaching methodology for hundreds of years. John Locke

(1632–1704) stated this idea in *Some Thoughts Concerning Education,* and he has ever since been closely identified with the notion, although many argue that this is an unjustified association. At any rate, his words clearly express the essence of this theory: "As the strength of the body lies chiefly in being able to endure hardships, so also does that of the mind." Many a teacher has seemingly interpreted this to mean that it doesn't matter so much what a person studies, so long as it is difficult—and preferably unpleasant.

Although we may not agree with some of Locke's statements, it is from his efforts that many date the study of educational psychology. Locke believed that ideas and knowledge come through the senses from experiences of the external world, impressing themselves upon the mind, which is originally blank—a *tabula rasa.* This type of belief required that more attention be given to development of all the senses through appropriate experiences.

As studies of how the mind works led to investigation of child development, vigorous opposition developed to the common practice of imposing adult standards upon children. This eventually resulted in better understanding of learning processes, new teaching methods, and improved teacher training.

Jean Jacques Rosseau

If Locke is recognized as the father of educational psychology, Jean Jacques Rousseau (1712–78) must be given credit for really breaking away from the tradition of his day and launching educational psychology into its modern period. Revolting against the Calvinists' belief that a child is wicked by nature and must be trained so as to transform him into a more Godlike being, Rousseau went to the other extreme in claiming that education is a matter of the free and unrestricted development of natural inclinations and powers of the individual. Going under the general term of "naturalism," these kinds of ideas were eventually proved to be impractical and too wasteful, as they were largely dependent on learning by trial and error and disregarded experiences of a child's elders.

Johann Heinrich Pestalozzi

Influenced by Rousseau, Johann Heinrich Pestalozzi (1746–1827) provided the patterns which led to modern teaching practices, although his influence was greater in elementary schools than in secondary schools. He believed that the natural instincts of a child should provide the motives for learning, with cooperation and sympathy, rather than compulsion or physical punishment being the proper means to achieve discipline. To allow the natural powers of the child to develop, he maintained that the teacher should adapt instruction to each individual as his particular changing, unfolding nature required at various stages of development. Sense perceptions were considered essential in this process, calling for observations of actual things and natural objects rather than upon books and reading. Advocating proceeding from the concrete to the abstract and from the particular to the general, Pestalozzi used everyday objects like animals, plants, and tools to develop an entire series of "object lessons" as aids to instructing in the fundamentals of language, number, and form.

Johann Friedrich Herbart

At the secondary school level, Johann Friedrich Herbart (1776–1841) made significant psychological contributions to education with his stress upon social and moral character building and his formulation of systematic teaching methods. He emphasized the development of clear ideas and concentration by the teacher on student interests. History and literature were considered to be the most effective subject matter for developing proper social attitudes, with other studies correlated around this "core."

Herbart is credited with the theory of learning which is considered by many to be the threshold of modern "scientific" psychology. Usually called "apperception," this theory rejects the idea of faculties and powers and proposes that the mind is composed of "apperceptive masses" which tend to attract (learn) that which is compatible with or closely related to earlier experience. The new learning is thereby integrated into the apperceptive mass. If an experience is not compatible with or closely related to the existing experience fibers in a "mass," then the new experience will tend to be rejected or not learned. According to Herbart's theory, learning becomes a process of progressive evolution of the "apperceptive mass" or "masses" from the lowest and most primitive levels of experience and thought to the highest. To facilitate this progression, education must constitute an orderly sequence of experiences, presented and then synthesized from birth throughout life. The principle of association was employed by Herbart throughout this process and led to its prominence in psychological thought of later years.

Modern Scientific Psychology

With impetus from the ideas of Charles Darwin and more general acceptance of scientific methods of inquiry, the late 1800's and early 1900's saw the rise of modern scientific psychology and its application to education. One of the early leaders in this movement was G. Stanley Hall (1846–1924), who tried to tie theories of biological evoluation to the human mind and soul. His theories of recapitulation and catharsis have been disproved, but Hall did make a significant contribution to education by emphasizing the need to focus educational efforts on the individual child at his stage of development, thus bringing on the "child-centered" movement of the early twentieth century.

Edward L. Thorndike (1874–1949) is given prime credit for bringing educational psychology from the realm of conjecture and simple inquiry into that of "scientific" inquiry. Thorndike's goal was to make teaching a science, so that students would form habits of exact study and learn how to apply their findings to all educational problems. In his efforts to apply methods of exact science to certain educational problems, Thorndike virtually created a new subject matter field—educational psychology. His work during the early 1900's challenged the educational world to develop objective approaches for discovering answers to problems about the original nature of children, their learning capacities, and individual differences.

John Dewey and Others

From the ideas of the pragmatists and progressives came the next significant development in educational psychology. Upon a foundation laid by Charles Sanders Peirce (1839–1914) and William James (1842–1910), John Dewey (1859–1952) led in the development of psychological philosophical, and methodological concepts which have had immeasurable impact on educational practice around the world. Pragmatism emphasizes and deals with real things, stressing results as standards in conduct. James developed this somewhat uniquely American philosophy to education, pointing out that interest, attention, selection, purpose, bias, desire, emotion, and satisfaction all affect our thinking processes. An individual's thought is both personal and purposive, leading inevitably to judgment which is prompted by motives and inspired by personal interest. Dewey blended these and other similar ideas with new scientific evidence about learning, showing the necessity of connecting the school with life outside the classroom, and of giving children an intelligent understanding of the world in which they live.

Dewey held that real education must be based upon the nature of the child and that knowledge is only a part of one's intellectual equipment and resources. Learning is a process, a growing and continuing affair, and it proceeds best through actual experience. To learn to do a specific thing, one must do it, not talk about it or watch someone else do it.

Dewey also stressed the idea that the psychological nature of a child must not be divorced from the society in which he lives. By bringing the meaning of past experiences to bear on the interpretation of new situations, a student best develops his ability to think, and at the same time he is directing his energies into socially useful channels.[1]

The Influence of Psychology

As we learn more about human beings, their minds, and how they work, educational psychology assumes a more and more prominent place in the thinking of all educators. The remainder of this chapter will be concerned with the application of psychology to various educational problems, but a few examples at

[1]Carroll Atkinson and Eugene T. Maleska, *The Story of Education*, 2d ed. (Philadelphia: Chilton, 1965), pp. 70–78, 275–291.

this point may serve to illustrate the application of modern psychology to teaching and learning.

The influence of psychology is readily apparent in attempts to adapt teaching to individual differences. Grouping practices of various kinds and the nongraded or continuous school are examples of this. Even in the absence of special grouping practices, knowledge about psychology and learning have led to remedial teaching, acceleration of various kinds, and enrichment programs. Team teaching, independent study opportunities, and other similar innovations are further illustrations of the attention now being given to individual differences—a need unrecognized before modern psychology came on the scene.

Attention to the educational development and educational needs of the disadvantaged has led to the recognition that readiness is not primarily an innate quality but rather something that is taught and learned. Educational adaptation to this knowledge is taking the form of compensatory programs of many varieties.

Educational technology is being used to make better use of other kinds of educational adaptations in the light of current knowledge. Programmed learning, with or without machines, computer-based instruction, active response programs and plans utilizing continual feedback and correction all owe much to insight provided by educational psychology.

The psychologist's role is further in evidence in the area of curriculum development. Reforms in mathematics, science, social studies, and language arts all are founded on increased knowledge of learners and the learning process.

Educational Psychology Defined

To conclude this introductory material on educational psychology, perhaps it would be well to settle on a definition for what we have been discussing and will be going into further. Just what is educational psychology? The brief description we have included on the development of this field of learning may in itself serve as a definition, but it would seem appropriate for us to attempt a common understanding before going on. A recent statement from a standard educational psychology textbook seems to adequately describe psychology, although each student should attempt a more acceptable definition from his own point of view.

> Psychology is two things: an academic discipline and a technology. As an academic discipline, psychology is the scientific study of the behavior of human beings and of animals. As a technology, psychology is the means of changing behavior by applying the findings of academic psychology, combined with intelligent guesses where knowledge is lacking.[2]

Both the academic study of psychology as related to education and the technological application of psychology to education come under the general

[2]B. Claude Mathis, John W. Cotton, and Lee Sechrest, *Psychological Foundations of Education* (New York: Academic, 1970), p. 1.

term educational psychology. Towo major divisions or areas of study are usually recognized—growth and development, and learning theory. We will group our further discussion accordingly, with special attention to the secondary school student—the adolescent.

Adolescent Growth and Development

The students enrolled in secondary schools are generally called adolescents. But what is an adolescent? Is he similar to those younger and older than he, or is he a species unto himself? Adolescence was practically unknown in primitive societies. Even in rather modern societies it has been of very short duration. After a short period of puberty, the child was expected to become a married man or woman with adult responsibilities. It has been only since the coming of our modern industrial development that economic necessity has required an adolescent period of eight to ten years, and recent indications are that this period in increasing in length. Older workers simply do not want competition from younger persons when there are a limited number of jobs. Technological developments and other requirements calling for increased education have also served to lengthen the adolescent period in the lives of young people.

It seems that we must settle on a rather general definition of the tern "adolescent." Webster defines adolescence as "the period of growing from childhood to maturity." It may be indentified in similar fashion as the period between childhood (when a person is relatively dependent) to adulthood (when a person becomes relatively independent). These kinds of definitions, although probably as accurate as any, are not much help. What we really need to know is what changes occur in an individual during this period and how these changes should affect the educational efforts made in his behalf. As we proceed to explore these questions, we will consider adolescent growth and development from four perspectives—physical, intellectual, emotional, and social.

Early Misconceptions

As mentioned earlier, G. Stanley Hall was primarily responsible for beginning the study of adolescence. He developed some theories which were an advance for his day, but some of their inaccuracies have had serious repercussions ever since. His "recapitulation" theory gained wide acceptance, perhaps because it was rather simple. According to this theory, each individual in the stages of his life "recapitulates" the progress of man from primitive society to modern civilization. Adolescence represents the stormy precivilized stage of man's history when he was captive to the baser emotions and traits, such as selfishness, greed, and possessiveness. The undesirable traits of this period were considered to be a normal condition which all must live through before reaching a more civilized state, and teachers must resign themselves to accepting the adolescent without trying to change him. Desirable change would come naturally with time.[3]

Hall's influence is also evident in a variation of the recapitulation theory which was developed at about the same time. This theory saw adolescence as a period of cataclysmic change, during which a child changed almost overnight to something quite different. This change brought higher and human traits, powers of reasoning and judgment, and moral and religious concerns. Efforts to define the peculiar traits of adolescence which came into being at this time resulted in many myths; they also helped bring on the junior high school movement, for it was felt that this different type of person required a different type of school than that appropriate for elementary age children or older high school students.[4]

Physical Growth and Development

Physical changes occurring in adolescence are probably the most obvious of the developmental processes which take place in young people at this time, and they may very well be the most influential in the total development of a young person. The psychological repercussions of these changes are in many respects more important than the changes themselves.

Following a period of slow growth, children experience a spurt of rapid growth about six months prior to puberty. Until they are about ten years old, boys tend to be taller than girls, but girls tend to forge ahead between the ages of eleven and fourteen. Girls mature on the average about eighteen months earlier than boys, although there is great variation among adolescents relative to the time of physical maturation. Those whose maturation is markedly ahead or behind the average are likely to experience various kinds of tensions, worries, and insecurities. Sexual maturity can occur anytime between the ages ot ten and seventeen, but twelve, thirteen, or fourteen is the most common period.

A group of changes often referred to as secondary sex characteristics accompany the physiological attainment of sexual maturity. These outward and readily noticeable changes are often most influential on general psychological development. Such changes include an increase in perspiration, change in voice, growth of body hair, and in girls, development of the breasts. Some physical disabilities often occur also, such as more rapid tooth decay, poor posture, and skin problems.

Intellectual Growth and Development

Intellectual growth and development during adolescence may be approached from two directions. We may consider growth in intellectual quantity, as measured by mental tests, or we may study the development of qualitative or cognitive abilities which determine the nature of adolescent thought and how it compares

[3]G. Stanley Hall, *Adolescence* (New York: Appleton, 1905).
[4]Harold W. Bernard, *Psychology of Learning and Teaching* (New York: McGraw-Hill, 1954), pp. 258–262.

with child thought. We will briefly consider both of these aspects.

It is generally agreed that the growth of intelligence is most rapid in infancy and early childhood, tending to increase thereafter at a progressively decreasing rate. However, there is considerable evidence of an increased intellectual growth rate during early adolescence, contrary to the generally decreasing rate of mental growth from infancy to adulthood. Little if any decrease in intellectual ability occurs before advanced old age, although the efficient *use* of intellectual ability may occur before that time.[5]

The mind is typically most imaginative and most creative during the late teens and early twenties. During adolescence there is also a definite increase in specialization (or differentiation) in ability due, not to education, but to maturation. Abilities in some areas become more pronounced, while in others there may be little improvement. For this reason, ability tests can be designed for adolescents which may predict the probability of success in a given field such as medicine, mathematics, the arts, science, and the like.

There are wide variations among individuals in intellectual growth, just as in physical growth. Among most young people, the growth rate is rather steady, but in some there seems to be an irregular pattern of intellectual development, with regressions actually occurring at times. As would be expected, the difference between the brighter and the duller boys and girls becomes greater with age.

In addition to types of intellectual development more related to quantity, educators must also consider qualitative developmental changes. Piaget's concepts are particularly appropriate in this respect, as he suggests that during late childhood and early adolescence students move from the *concrete* to the *formal operations* level of intellectual competence. This brings about abilities related to hypothetical thinking. The person is able to deal with logical relations and the operations necessary for their verification or refutation. He can consider what might occur, as well as what does occur. He is better able to process large bodies of organized and potentially meaningful bodies of information so that they may be better used in making choices and decisions. He develops an intuitive grasp of formal logic that may be used to obtain an understanding of new relationships among events, which allows the testing of alternative hypotheses. He develops the ability to grasp qualitative growth patterns include increases in the breadth and depth of subject-matter knowledge and the ability to organize this knowledge into more meaningful wholes.[6]

In discussing intelligence, questions inevitably arise concerning sex differences. Final conclusions are not possible yet, but the evidence at this time indicates that sex differences in general intelligence tend to be negligible. Differ-

[5]Luella Cole and Irma Nelson Hall, *Psychology of Adolescence,* 7th ed. (New York: Holt, 1970), pp. 158–162.
[6]Francis J. DiVesta and George G. Thompson, *Educational Psychology* (New York: Appleton, 1970), pp. 559–560.

ences between the sexes in specific cognitive abilities seem to be larger and more significant than in general ability, and tend to increase with increasing age. Girls tend to have superior ability in word fluency, rote memory, and reasoning, while boys tend to be superior in spatial and quantitative ability. However, most of these differences are not evident at the preschool level, so it may be that they are for the most part culturally determined. The differences that do appear between the sexes seem to be more evident during early adolescence, when girls are generally more mature physically. At this stage of development, girls are consistently superior on such verbal items as vocabulary, language usage, analogies, memory, and clerical ability. Boys are superior in working with spatial relations, in mechanical aptitude, and in arithmetic (in later adolescence).[7]

Another aspect of intellectual development deserves our brief attention—the question of heredity versus environment (nature versus nurture). A considerable number of varying methods have been used in an attempt to answer this question, but conclusive evidence is still lacking. For some time, however, it has been widely agreed that the bulk of evidence indicates that the influence of heredity is greater.[8]

Heredity imposes absolute limits on possible levels of cognitive attainment, but it must be quickly pointed out that the possible is profoundly influenced by environmental conditions. Limiting and stimulating influences from culture, social class, and family have many ways of influencing the level of cognitive development attained, regardless of the potential.

> By providing more or less opportunity for training and experience, by offering more or less encouragement and stimulation, and by selectively valuing and rewarding intellectual attainment, the operation of these factors leads to substantial differences in ultimate outcome among individuals with comparable genic potentiality. Personality variables of temperamental and environmental origin play a similar role. Especially important in this connection are: (a) such determinants of *task-oriented* motivation as intellectual curiosity, activity level, and venturesomeness; (b) intensity and area of ego-involvement; (c) such correlates of ego-enhancement motivation as need for achievement, competitiveness, responsiveness to prestige incentives, level of ego aspiration, goal tenacity, frustration tolerance, and anxiety level; and (d) need for volitional and executive independence.[9]

These kinds of environmental conditions rather than hereditary forces also account for differences in intellectual attainment sometimes found among racial or ethnic groups.

[7]David P. Ausubel, *Educational Psychology: A Cognitive View* (New York: Holt, 1968), pp. 241–243.

[8]David P. Ausubel and Floyd G. Robinson, *School Learning: An Introduction to Educational Psychology* (New York: Holt, 1969), p. 221.

[9]Ausubel, *op. cit.*, p. 244.

Emotional and Social Development

The emotions experienced by adolescents are of a similar nature to those experienced in earlier years, but an adolescent's emotional development is centered around a number of unique drives (primarily sexual in nature) which have not been apparent to him previously. These emotions are often more intense in the adolescent than in younger children, and they almost always have social ramifications.

The adolescent must identify his sex role as an adult and adjust to behavior expectancies in heterosexual activities. A large part of his time, and often an even larger portion of his fantasies, is concerned with the opposite sex. Fantasies often take the form of imagination and even worship of a "dream boy" or "dream girl," and these dreams can later lead to unrealistic perceptions and expectations of love and marriage partners. Adolescents typically "fall in" and "fall out" of love rather frequently. Dating and "going steady" give the benefits of experiences that might help them test their thoughts and feelings about the opposite sex. In many respects girls of courting age have a more difficult time than boys in that boys have more freedom and opportunity to exercise the initiative, while girls must seek to be attractive and at the same time avoid extremes and dangers leading to unwise premarital sexual relations. Most girls suffer unpleasant and sometimes shocking experiences with boys during these years, but popularity with the opposite sex is very important to them, probably more so than with boys in most cases.

The typical adolescent desires independence, but at the same time he needs to be relatively dependent at times on parents or other adults. He needs protection and security at the same time that he needs to operate under his own will. These contradictory drives often lead to early "steady" dating and teen-age marriages, as young people may attempt to gain independence from parents and satisfy needs for being accepted, which they seek to find in a member of the opposite sex. Teen-agers often demand adult privileges before they are willing to accept a corresponding degree of responsibility, and this leads to additional conflicts with parents and other adults.

Adolescents are strongly influenced by other members of their peer group, often more so than by their parents or other adults. The typical adolescent conforms to the group in large areas of his thinking and behavior, as evidenced by the cyclical fads and style changes in dress, hair style, slang, and the like. The adolescent population does not, however, operate as a single peer group with one group of forces acting to control behavior. There are subgroups or subcultures, each demanding its own particular type of conformity. There are also differences in the standards and expectations that prevail in lower as compared with higher socioeconomic levels.

An increased desire for excitement and novelty is also apparent in most adolescents. New experiences for their changing mental and physical characteristics are sought, experiences that create excitement and novel sensations. As more varied experiences are vailable to younger children, desire for ever increasing levels of excitement and novelty in adolescence may lead to dangerous experimentation with drugs or illegal activities.

At this time there is also an increased awareness of the world around them, as adolescents seek to better understand their environment, what makes it "tick," and ways to make it better. Idealism and curiosity work together, leading toward the development of value standards, personal and social ideals, and religious convictions. Standards upon which to base decisions about behavior and goals prove illusive but necessary objects of attention.

All human beings wish to be recognized, respected, envied, feared, and loved by other human beings, and adolescence is also the period during which these desires are coming into maximum evidence. It may be achieved through recognition by adults in the family that the adolescent is no longer a child and that he deserves a more mature status in the family. It usually takes the form of independence from adults, particularly parents. Acceptance by peers and those of the opposite sex are important to feelings of recognition. Increased physical strength, attractive personality and physical characteristics, and material possessions such as clothes or a car all are likely to make their contribution in this respect. It is easy to see, then, how damaging to this need are things like satire, ridicule, open or sharp criticism, frustration and failure in school tasks.

All in all, adolescence is a period of conflict, confusion, and ambivalence, especially in the emotional and social realms. It is an in-between stage, during which the adolescent is something of a marginal creature in a no-man's land between childhood and adulthood. If he acts too "grown-up," he is reminded of his immaturity; if he acts like a child, he is admonished to act more "grown-up." He is urged to make good use of his time, while being denied a useful place in the world of work; there is not even much he can do around the home today that is very useful or from which he can achieve a feeling of accomplishment and contribution to the welfare of the family. Confusions in the culture around him aggravate his personal confusion. He sees traditional moral values being rejected, with no new ones identified to take their place. Both plenty and poverty exhibit themselves on every hand. Cooperation and "brotherly love" are given lip service while ruthless competition is evident on every side. Intelligence is advocated as the best means for decision making and democratic government, but he sees everyday evidence of momentous decisions being made on the basis of political favor, prejudice, selfishness, and temporary inclinations. Tolerance is preached, while prejudice and violations of human dignity are practiced. He is taught that citizenship is all-important, but he also notices that voter apathy and disregard for the law are the rule rather than the exception in the adult world around him. Perhaps we should wonder that adolescents are as well adjusted to their world as they are. In any case, it is obvious that they need understanding and guiding hands to help them find their way through the maze erected by their predecessors.

Studying Adolescents

Studies on how best to understand and help adolescents through the school curriculum have typically attempted to identify important needs (often stated in the form of problems or interests) or "developmental tasks." A brief look at both of these approaches to the problem may point out the desirability of incorporating something from each of them into any attempt to understand adolescents and to develop a school curriculum in their best interests.

NEEDS OF ADOLESCENTS. Identifying the "needs" of youth as a way of understanding them achieved considerable popularity during the thirties and forties and is still considered a valid procedure. Educators and social workers have attempted to identify these needs by means of interviews and various kinds of questionnaires, although the weaknesses of both procedures are readily recognized.

The first attempts in this respect were made with the tenets of progressive philosophy in mind. This required that what was taught in the schools must relate directly and immediately to the learner. In fact, there were many who believed that effective learning was likely to occur only when there was a natural drive or tension within the learner for which a particular learning experience would provide. It was also felt that if the learner could meet his immediate needs and learn to solve his present problems he would be better able to adapt to future conditions. This resulted in primary attention being given to basic or "felt" needs having their origins in the psychological and biological nature of the human organism.

Many attempts were made to identify and categorize these basic human needs, and although there is doubtless a limit to which they should be utilized in curriculum determination, their contribution is worth our attention. One of the earlier categorizations of basic psychobiological needs was developed by P. M. Symonds in 1934. It included the following:

1. Need to be with others.
2. Need to gain attention.
3. Need for approval.
4. Need to be a cause.
5. Need for mastery.
6. Need to maintain self.
7. Need for security.
8. Need for affection.
9. Need represented by curiosity.[10]

About a decade later, A. H. Maslow suggested from his analyses of human drives a hierarchy of needs. According to his theory, there is a priority in basic needs, and first-order needs (physiological needs), if not fulfilled, will serve as an

---

[10]P. M. Symonds, "Human Drives," *Journal of Educational Psychology* 25 (1934), p. 694.

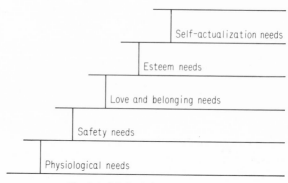

Fig. 5–1. Maslow's hierarchy of needs.

obstacle to the development and fulfillment of second order needs, and so on. Maslow's hierarchy (Fig. 5–1) proceeds from physiological needs (the most primitive) through needs for safety, love and belonging, esteem, and finally to those of self-actualization. Accordingly, requirements for food, clothing, and shelter must be achieved before adequate attention can be given to those related to safety and avoiding danger. Upon the achievement of these requirements, attention can be more adequately given to the need to be loved by others and to belong within some group. Then come esteem needs, both positive opinions by self and others, and ultimately the need for self-actualization, which encompasses such things as the need to master, to create, or to express oneself.[11]

Other studies followed, with varying degrees of agreement in the findings. A recent summation of the conclusions from various studies conducted before 1963 pointed out that adolescent needs focus around the following:

Learning what is permitted, what is expected, and what is not approved of in the role of a given sex.

Identifying with one's own sex, and changing one's relationship with the opposite sex.

Seeking ways to relate oneself to adult society in a constructive and satisfying manner.

Seeking to learn one's own potentialities and abilities.

Seeking adult status.

Wanting independence and protection.

Seeking acceptance by peers.[12]

Although it was acknowledged that earlier studies had made significant contributions to understanding adolescents, many educators believed that pro-

---

[11]A. H. Maslow, "A Theory of Human Motivation," *Psychological Review* 50 (1943), pp. 370–396.

[12]Kimball Wiles, *The Changing Curriculum of the American High School* (Englewood Cliffs, N.J.: Prentice-Hall, 1963), p. 50.

gram developers needed a more comprehensive view of needs as a guide. They pointed out that the school is a social institution and must therefore pay attention to the demands of the society as well as those coming from the felt needs of young people. It was proposed that the adolescent needs concept was too attentive to the whims and immature desires of youth, with a consequent lack of attention to needs of the society.

Attempts to occupy a middle ground between the more personal needs of the adolescent and those of the society took many forms. One of the more influential statements was developed by the Educational Policies Commission of the National Education Association and issued in 1944. It identified ten "Imperative Needs of Youth."

1. All youth need to develop salable skills and those understandings and attitudes that make the worker an intelligent and productive participant in economic life. To this end, most youth need supervised work experience as well as education in the skills and knowledges of the occupations.
2. All youth need to develop and maintain good health and physical fitness.
3. All youth need to understand the rights and duties of the citizen of a democratic society and be diligent and competent in the performance of their obligations as members of the community and citizens of their state and nation.
4. All youth need to understand the significance of the family for the individual and for society, and the conditions conducive to successful family life.
5. All youth need to know how to purchase and use goods and services intelligently, understanding both the values received by consumers and the economic consequences of their acts.
6. All youth need to understand the methods of science, the influence of science on human life, and the main scientific facts concerning the nature of the world and of man.
7. All youth need opportunities to develop their capacities to appreciate beauty —in literature, art, music, and nature.
8. All youth need to be able to use their leisure time well and to budget it wisely, balancing activities that yield satisfactions to the individual with those that are socially useful.
9. All youth need to develop respect for other persons, to grow in their insight into ethical values and principles, and be able to live and work cooperatively with others.
10. All youth need to grow in ability to think rationally, to express their thoughts clearly, and to listen with understanding.[13]

DEVELOPMENTAL TASKS OF ADOLESCENCE. Robert J. Havighurst of the University of Chicago and his Committee on Human Development have approached the problem in a somewhat unique manner, one which has gained much support

[13]National Education Association of the United States, Educational Policies Commission, *Education for All Youth* (Washington, D.C.: National Education Association of the United States, 1944), pp. 225–226.

in recent years. He has defined adolescent needs in terms of "developmental tasks" as follows:

> The tasks the individual must learn—the developmental tasks of life—are those things that constitute healthy and satisfactory growth in our society. They are the things a person must learn if he is to be judged and to judge himself to be a reasonably happy and successful person. A developmental task is a task which arises at or about a certain period in the life of the individual, successful achievement of which leads to his happiness and to success with later tasks, while failure leads to unhappiness in the individual, disapproval by the society, and difficulty with later tasks.[14]

The analysis of adolescent needs in these terms is probably the most comprehensive and useful available to educators. The needs were identified through the integrative analysis of biological, psychological, and cultural demands upon the adolescent, and stated in a sequence of developmental tasks proceeding from infancy to old age. Those pertaining to adolescence, with the nature of each task, are stated as follows.

The Adolescent Peer Group
  1. Achieving New and More Mature Relations with Agemates of Both Sexes.

  Nature of the Task. The goal: to learn to look upon girls as women and boys as men; to become an adult among adults; to learn to work with others for a common purpose, disregarding personal feelings; to learn to lead without dominating.

  2. Achieving a Masculine or Feminine Role.

  Nature of the Task. The goal: to accept and to learn a socially approved adult masculine or feminine social role.

The Development of Personal Independence
  3. Accepting One's Physique and Using the Body Effectively.

  Nature of the Task. The goal: to become proud, or at least tolerant, of one's body; to use and protect one's body effectively and with personal satisfaction.

  4. Achieving Emotional Independence of Parents and Other Adults.

  Nature of the Task. The goal: to become free from childish dependence on parents; to develop affection for parents without dependence upon them; to develop respect for other adults without dependence upon them.

  5. Achieving Assurance of Economic Independence.

  Nature of the Task. The goal: to feel able to make a living, if necessary. This is primarily a task for boys, in our society, but it is of increasing importance to girls.

  6. Selecting and Preparing for an Occupation.

---

[14]Robert J. Havighurst, *Developmental Tasks and Education* (New York: Longmans, 1948), p. 2.

Nature of the Task. The goal: to choose an occupation for which one has the necessary ability; to prepare for this occupation.

7. Preparing for Marriage and Family Life.

Nature of the Task. The goal: to develop a positive attitude toward family life and having children and (mainly for girls) to get the knowledge necessary for home management and child rearing.

8. Developing Intellectual Skills and Concepts Necessary for Competence.

Nature of the Task. The goal: to develop concepts of law, government, economics, politics, geography, human nature, and social institutions which fit the modern world; to develop language skills and reasoning ability necessary for dealing effectively with the problems of a modern democracy.

Developing a Philosophy of Life

9. Desiring and Achieving Socially Responsible Behavior.

Nature of the Task. The goal: to participate as a responsible adult in the life of the community, region, and nation; to take account of the values of society in one's personal behavior.

10. Acquiring a Set of Values and an Ethical System as a Guide to Behavior.

Nature of the Task. The goal: to form a set of values that are possible of realization; to develop a conscious purpose of realizing these values; to define man's place in the physical world and in relation to other human beings; to keep one's world picture and one's values in harmony with each other. Definition: a value is an object or state of affairs which is desired.[15]

Learning Theory

How do we learn? How can teachers best facilitate learning? What hinders learning? How do we retain what we learn long enough to make the best use of it, and what enables us to use learning from one point in time or one type of experience at a later time or with a different type of experience? These and other similar types of questions fall within the domain of learning theory.

Many attempts have been made to define learning, but no single effort seems to have met with complete success. A common and generally accepted type of definition is, "An enduring or permanent change in behavior as a result of experience."[16] A more detailed attempt describes learning as "a modification of behavior as a result of experience, which causes acquisition of information, formation of concepts and generalizations, development of physical and intellectual skills, and formation or modification of attitudes."[17]

It seems that instead of attempting to arrive at a single definition of learning

[15] *Ibid.*, Chapters IX, X, XI, and *passim*. From Harold B. Alberty and Elsie J. Alberty, *Reorganizing the High-School Curriculum*, 3d ed. (New York: Macmillan, 1962), pp. 133–134.

[16] Francis J. Di Vesta and George G. Thompson, *op. cit.*, p. 112.

[17] Willis D. Moreland (ed.), *Social Studies in the Senior High School* (Washington, D.C.: National Council for the Social Studies, 1965), p. 34.

we should perhaps consider the idea that no single definition can be adequate, because there are many types of learning. There is little similarity between the child learning to say his first word and advanced study by a student of linguistics. Learning to distinguish triangles from rectangles and learning to demonstrate that the sum of the internal angles of a triangle is the same as a straight angle also show striking dissimilarities. Learning to spell a word like "interdependence" is not the same as understanding the various concepts related to that word.

> Despite the prevailing emphasis on fundamental similarities of process in various learning situations, investigators of learning have always recognized certain "types" of learning. There is "trial-and-error learning," "discrimination learning," "paired associate learning," "concept learning," "conditioned response learning," and so on. . . . But these varieties of learning have tended to be identified with certain kinds of stimulus situations generated by particular equipment or materials, like the bar-pressing apparatus, or the memory drum with verbal syllables, or the maze with choice points. The tendency has *not* been for these types of learning to be distinguished in terms of the *kind of change in capability* they imply.
>
> The existence of differentiable performances as outcomes of learning naturally leads to the inference that different kinds of capabilities are established by learning; . . . [and] the identification of these different kinds of performance, together with the different kinds of capability they imply, suggests that there may be at least as many different kinds of learning. And if this is so, it may be supposed that there exist an equal number of *conditions of effective learning* to correspond with each variety. A theory of instruction, then, cannot be maximally useful if it concerns itself with only those conditions that are general to all classes of learning. Instead, such a theory must concern itself in an individual manner with each of the types of learning.[18]

Acceptance of the above ideas about learning makes teaching a complicated matter indeed, but it appears that anything less is inadequate. Before we despair, however, perhaps a brief look at some of the more common theories and ideas about learning will be helpful.

Basic Theories of Learning

Because learning is complex, there is today no coherent theory that encompasses consistently all aspects of learning. As indicated above, there are many different kinds of learning, such as mastering motor skills, memorizing information, learning feelings, concepts, and intellectual skills—generalizing, scientific inquiry, and problem solving, for example. Learning theories have been developed relating to these different kinds of learning, yet the findings of each specific type of learning theory are applied to all types of learning. Consequently, many theoretical disputes have been generated.

[18]R. M. Gagné, "Instruction and the Conditions of Learning," in L. Siegel (ed.), *Instruction: Some Contemporary Viewpoints* (San Francisco: Chandler, 1967), pp. 296–300.

Early Theories

At the beginning of this chapter we discussed the early belief that the mind is divided into faculties, compartments, or powers. This faculty theory, and its related ideas about mental discipline, held that the mind inherently contains all the necessary attributes and that the task of education is to bring them forth and strengthen them through certain types of intellectual exercise and manipulation. Acquisition of knowledge, with special value ascribed to the "hard" subjects like Latin and mathematics, was held to be the basis of learning. Once these mental faculties were developed (especially the powers of observation, reason, and memory), faculty psychology proposed that they could be applied in life as they were needed, with no special attention needed by teachers to the application of knowledge. According to faculty psychology, practice and drill are important for their disciplinary value. Motivation is not important, and individual differences are irrelevant. The training of the mind is general, so learning Latin or mathematics makes a better lawyer, as well as a better banker or scholar.

Herbart's theory of "apperceptive mass" was developed in opposition to faculty psychology and set the stage for modern learning theories. According to this theory, what an individual is able to learn is in large measure determined by the knowledge that has already taken shape through the learner's experience. New learning must be compatible with or closely related to earlier experiences so that it may become integrated into the apperceptive mass. Education must then be designed to facilitate the orderly acquisition of experiences and knowledge required to develop a mature mind.

Associationism

The first modern attempts to study and understand learning are identified with the terms "stimulus-response," "associationist," or "behaviorist." Strictly speaking, the theories associated with each of these terms are not the same, but their similarities warrant our grouping them together in this brief study of learning theory.

Associationist theory sees learning as a somewhat mechanical process by which a simple association is established between some environmental stimulus and a desired response, whether verbal, physical, or emotional. Major understandings or behavior complexes (the whole) result from the progressive addition of simple learned responses (the parts). The whole is thus the sum of its parts, according to this view.

Ivan Pavlov, the famed Russian physiologist, developed during the first decade of the twentieth century the basic ideas behind stimulus-response theories of learning. Working with dogs, he found that when the dogs were presented with meat powder (the stimulus) the measured increase in saliva was significant (the response). He then found that tapping a tuning fork just prior to the presentation of the meat powder created a connection between the sound of the tuning fork, even without the presentation of meat powder. This phenomena he called a "conditioned response." Pavlov had succeeded in substituting a new stimulus for the natural one in order to bring forth the desired response, and he proposed that human behavior is likewise subject to conditioning. He then theorized that human responses could be controlled by manipulating stimuli in relation to various responses.

Edward L. Thorndike gave the stimulus-response learning theory its impetus in America, but he called his theory *connectionism*. According to this line of thinking, learning is a process by which connections or bonds are formed between stimuli and desired responses, and his research centered on attempts to discover what factors facilitate the establishment of such connections and what factors are obstacles to the establishment of connections. Thorndike's conclusions are framed in three primary and several secondary laws or principles of connectionism.

Thorndike's first principle was that of *multiple response*, which held that learning basically occurs through a process of trial and error. Faced with a new situation (stimulus) for which we have no learned response, we try many responses until we find one which is satisfactory. By restricting the range of responses to stimuli, a teacher may cause learning to be more efficient.

A related principle developed by Thorndike was that a bond or connection between a stimulus and a response tends to be established or strengthened because of the *law of effect*. According to this principle, bonds are established or strengthened when the making of a response produces satisfaction. His earlier speculations led to the idea that annoyance would weaken a bond, but later work convinced him that this was not always true.

The *law of exercise*, as formulated by Thorndike, seems to have had considerable influence, judging from past and present school practices. This principle stated that connections between stimuli and responses are strengthened through use and weakened through disuse, all other factors being constant. To be effective, however, practice must be accompanied by continued rewards, success, and satisfaction to produce a stronger bond. Aimless practice, drill, or review, will not produce stronger bonds between stimuli and desired responses.

The *law of readiness* was developed by Thorndike to state that making a connection or bond between a stimulus and a response is dependent upon the readiness of the learner to make this particular connection. By readiness, Thorndike originally meant the establishment of *mental set*. This is a temporary predisposition to engage in the learning task, and may be determined by things such as the learner's physical condition (sleepy, hungry, cold), by competing events in the classroom, by situations at home or otherwise outside the school, or some other condition affecting him. Thorndike's interpreters have added maturation and experience to the law of readiness to provide considerations of neurological development, changes in interests, and other maturity factors.

One of the more important supplementary principles proposed by Thorndike was the principle of *analogy*. This idea suggested that when an individual is faced with a new stimulus or situation for which he has learned no response, he will react as he learned to react to some earlier similar stimulus. Ideas about transfer and generalization follow from this principle, as it recognizes the value of a person's learning to note similarities or relationships between the multitudes of stimuli in order to respond in a satisfying way to them, without reinstituting a process of trial and error in each new circumstance.

Behaviorism is a more modern adaptation of stimulus-response and connectionist ideas, and through the ideas of men such as Mowrer and Skinner it has assumed considerable importance among many educators. According to these theories, the higher mental functions have a very small place, as learning takes place largely by trial and error and by conditioning. The system of establishing responses is more important than thought and individual differences in it. Even motives, the behaviorists propose, can be controlled from without by conditioning, punishments, and rewards. Practice and drill are essential, and are most effective when accompanied by appropriate rewards and punishments. According to behaviorists, psychological data consist solely of observable behavior, and so knowledge and understanding must be studied indirectly, since they are not observable behaviors.

Skinner has extended the principles involved in the Law of Effect through what he calls *operant conditioning*. He replaces emphasis on the stimulus with emphasis on the reward as the more important reinforcing element in a learning situation. The response is thus strengthened through the reward, whereas according to Thorndike's Law of Effect a bond or connection between a stimulus and a response is strengthened. Skinner believes that human behavior can be *shaped* by giving attention to the reinforcement of those units of a behavioral chain leading to a desired total response.

Skinner's ideas have led some educators to overemphasize his techniques for classroom instruction, due to their relative simplicity. On the other hand, they have stimulated much serious and fruitful thought about units and sequences of learning activities which may lead to ultimate desired outcomes. They have brought considerable attention to the need for specific behavioral objectives designed to guide instructional activities and their evaluation, and they have been particularly important as applied to the use of programmed instruction and teaching machines.

Cognitive-Field Theory

Beginning early in the twentieth century, theories of learning variously named but generally classified as cognitive or field theories achieved considerable popularity among educators. Instead of viewing learning as a series of somewhat mechanical processes by which the whole (major understandings or behavior complexes) results from the progressive addition of simple learned responses, this view proposed that learning should be *approached* from the whole of what is ultimately desired. Their common feature is that they assume that cognitive processes—insight, intelligence, and organization—are the fundamental characteristics of human response. A house is more than a random collection of bricks, timbers, mortar, and pipes without concept or architectural design. In similar fashion, the cognitivist sees learning as more than an accumulation of conditioned responses, facts, or simple relationships. It must begin with the whole and proceed from it to the component parts and the organization of these as necessary to form a meaningful whole.

Cognitive-field theories of learning came into being through the work of three German psychologists, Max Wertheimer, Kurt Koffka, and Wolfgang Köhler. They used the German term *gestalt* to identify their theory, a word meaning "configuration" or "pattern." This word carried with it the idea of an undivided, articulated whole which cannot be made up by mere addition of independent elements. In the Gestalt, each part is not an independent element but a member of the whole whose very nature depends upon its membership in the whole. For example, a tone has a different character when it appears in two different musical settings; it influences and is influenced by the other tones.

Gestalt psychology provides the basis for most of the ideas current in field theories. The major ideas may be summarized as follows:

1. Stimuli do not occur in isolation, as implied by S-R bond psychologists, but occur in complex patterns which are never entirely reproduced.
2. Individuals respond not to simple stimuli within a pattern but to the whole pattern, their response depending upon the organization of stimuli within the pattern, and their perception of it.
3. An individual's perception of stimuli within a pattern is dependent upon his perceptual field, his perception of self and his previous and immediate perceptions of his environment.
4. Individuals respond to patterns of stimuli with their whole being and are forever changed by the experience—any further response to such a pattern would be influenced by the change produced in the individual by the previous experience.
5. Learning and behavior are influenced by individual goals. Human behavior cannot be entirely controlled by the environment, as stimulus-response would suggest. The way in which an individual responds to a pattern of stimuli is determined by his goals.
6. Human learning is not dependent upon such painfully inefficient procedures as trial and error and conditioning, but may occur through insight, which may be defined as immediate understanding or mastery of a concept, through the organization of its component parts into a meaningful whole.[19]

---

[19]Wayne Dumas and Weldon Beckner, *Introduction to Secondary Education: A Foundations Approach* (Scranton, Pa.: Intext, 1968), pp. 130–131.

Problems and Issues

Innumerable questions may be raised relative to how we learn, and most of these questions are appropriate for study by educators. Some of these issues are particularly pertinent to the study of curriculum foundations, and we will consider several of them at this point.

COGNITIVE VS. AFFECTIVE LEARNING. Statements of goals for public education in the United States have almost universally included several references to the need for developing accepted attitudes and values in students. The most important ones have usually been associated with citizenship, one's role in a democratic society, moral values, ethics, and the like. However, these "affective" aspects of learning have typically been neglected by most teachers in favor of learning in the "cognitive" domain—that which is more related to what we think of as knowledge or the acquisition of information. Recently much more attention has been given to learning in the affective domain, and teachers are attempting to find better ways to lead students into studying and establishing attitudes, values, and standards. It is not intended that learning in the cognitive domain should be neglected in this process, but rather that the two areas may be combined and teaching occur in such a way that learning in one domain supplements and complements learning in the other.

PERCEPTION. According to a substantial and growing number of educators, the way a person "perceives" a situation is a dominant factor in what he learns. This perception is influenced by attitudes and values (pointing out the importance of affective learning), physical condition, previous experiences, level of learning in related areas, and self-concepts. Arthur Combs, a prominent proponent for the importance of perception in learning, defends his position as follows:

> . . . All behavior is a product of the perceptual field of the behaver at the moment of action. That is to say, how any person behaves will be a direct outgrowth of the way things seem to him at the moment of his behaving. To change behavior in this frame of reference requires that we understand the nature of the individual's perceptual field. Knowing the meanings that exist for a particular person, we may then be able to create the conditions which will facilitate changes in his behavior and personality.[20]

Acceptance of this viewpoint requires that much more attention be given to individual student experiences, background, and needs. It points up the fact that the curriculum is actually that which pupils perceive and learn individually, not that which teachers and curriculum planners plan to teach or think they are teaching.

[20]Arthur Combs, "A Perceptual View of the Adequate Personality," *Perceiving, Behaving, Becoming*, Association for Supervision and Curriculum Development Yearbook, (Washington, D.C.: American Society for Curriculum Development, 1962), p. 50.

RETENTION AND FORGETTING. Students and teachers alike are plagued with the problem of being unable to retain learning which has occurred. Unless it can be recalled and used when needed, learning has little if any value. Consequently, it would seem that teachers should give just as much attention to helping students remember what they have learned as they do to seeing that the students achieve initial learning.

The major factors influencing retention and the rate of forgetting are summarized below. It may be recognized that many of these factors are closely related to the various aspects of learning discussed previously.

1. Those things which have personal meaning to the learner will be retained longer than those which do not. A simple illustration of this may be found in the classic experiment which compares the learning and retention of nonsense words and those which have meaning to the learner. Nonsense words are learned only with great difficulty, and within twenty-four hours few of them can be remembered, while a much larger percentage of the words with meaning to the learner will be retained.

2. If the learner sees that which is to be learned as being either immediately or ultimately of value to him, the motivation thus aroused will greatly facilitate remembering. Otherwise, it will be remembered only long enough to repeat it on a test or to fulfill whatever other temporary purpose may be required.

3. In accordance with Gestalt theories of learning, that which is learned in the context of a pattern or whole will be retained better than isolated elements, even those which have meaning and value to the student.

4. Innate intelligence directly influences the rate of learning and forgetting to a high degree. Higher intelligence allows more rapid learning and longer retention of what is learned, other things being equal.

5. Interference is widely recognized as probably the most helpful explanation of forgetting. One kind of interference (retroactive) occurs when any activity interpolated between the time of learning and the time of needed retention affects recall of the initial learning. This type of interference is especially troublesome when the learning tasks are similar. The importance of another type of interference (proactive) has been recently recognized. This occurs when previous experience has deleterious effects on ability to retain new learning.

6. Overlearning strengthens memory and facilitates retention. When practice, drill, and review are extended beyond the point of initial master, retention is more long-lasting and more complete.

7. Frequent use or exercise of that which is learned causes forgetting to occur more slowly. Such use may be in life outside the classroom or as a foundation for more advanced learning within the classroom.

TRANSFER OF LEARNING. Teachers hope that what is taught to students in school will somehow be used in later life, even though they know that activities in the classroom cannot be a replica of life outside the classroom. This use of classroom learning in life or in future classroom learning is commonly referred to as "transfer" and provided one of the earliest and most important concerns of psychologists and educators.

Transfer can be of two types—positive or negative. Being able to apply scientific reasoning learned in one lesson to new problems is an example of positive transfer (facilitation). Developing a dislike for science from the study of scientific reasoning is an example of negative transfer (interference). In either case, current learning is affected by previous learning. There is a "transfer" of previous learning to the immediate situation.

Earlier ideas about transfer of learning proposed that transfer would occur automatically from the study of certain subjects, such as mathematics, Latin, and philosophy, because these studies would "strengthen" the faculties of the mind. Through "mental discipline," it was felt that the basic powers of the mind (reasoning, memory, recall) would be developed and could then be used later as needed. This cornerstone of "faculty psychology" has been thoroughly refuted by psychologists, but its influence can still be seen in most classrooms.

Studies by William James, Edward L. Thorndike, and others discredited the theories about transfer which came from faculty psychology and led to the conclusion that there is no general transfer, either from general training of the mind or from the study of specific subjects. They showed that improvement in any single mental function rarely brings about equal improvement in any other function, no matter how similar. The conclusion was that transfer is possible only if there are identical elements in the content involved or in the process of training —in the method or attitude involved in the training procedure.

From these studies developed theories of transfer which shifted attention away from producing general understanding to teaching specific knowledge and skills. Training in specific processes was intensified. Spelling and arithmetic, for example, became drill subjects, and many practical subjects were introduced in an attempt to offer knowledge and skills which were as near to the actual context of use as possible. "Life adjustment" ideas became popular and functional, concrete education became the goal.

This movement served to free the American schools from some of the rigidity and aridity of the classical curriculum, but its stress on immediate utility overlooked the possibility that some ideas and mental processes might have wider transfer value.

More recent research has indicated that both of the earlier types of theories concerning transfer of learning were inadequate, and continuing study progressively increases our knowledge of this important aspect of education. The following statements summarize the basic ideas which are common today concerning transfer of learning.

Student Ability. Students vary in ability to transfer learning, depending primarily on their general intelligence. Some have more of an aptitude for forming generalizations and for seeing new relationships than others, no matter how the material is taught.

Previous Experience. The student's previous experiences and learning accomplishments are important to the achievement of transfer of new learning. A background of knowledge and understanding is required for each new type of learning.

Understanding Relationships. To the extent that a new situation has things in common with an earlier one for which responses have been learned, these responses will be employed again in the new situation. This points to the need for students to discover and recognize relationships within and between experiences inside and outside of the classroom.

Functional Similarity. Positive transfer results when two tasks are functionally identical, while the greatest amount of negative transfer occurs when two tasks appear to be similar but are functionally dissimilar. Learning from in-school situations does not transfer to real-life situations unless the two settings are functionally equivalent, unless the pupil sees where, when, and how the learning is to be applied.

Perception of the Whole. As stressed in field theory, it is important that new situations be perceived as integral parts of earlier learned patterns of stimuli and responses.

Importance of Structure. Some form of organization is essential to transfer. In most cases the best organization can occur through the use of generalizations and principles. From isolated experiences or facts which are of limited applicability in life, students must be helped to formulate generalizations or principles of broad applicability.

Discovery. Principles which the student himself discovers are understood more clearly, retained longer, and used more effectively. This also has implications for teaching procedures.

Ideals and Values. Ideals, values, and attitudes, although they may be considered a type of generalization or principle, provide a means for achieving transfer of learning. Personal ideals such as tolerance, industriousness, appreciation of beauty, cooperativeness, and democracy may be developed in the classroom and then applied in many areas of life.

Teaching for Transfer. Transfer of learning depends to a large extent on curriculum materials and educational processes being addressed to transfer. When more attention is paid to the principles underlying specific processes (such as principles for deriving a square root) or generalizations combining otherwise unrelated facts, transfer is more assured and learning itself becomes more stimulating and productive.

MOTIVATION. If there is no desire to learn on the part of a student, he will learn little, if any. This required desire to learn we call motivation, and although there has been an enormous amount of research conducted on the topic, we still really know very little about it. However, we have learned enough through research and the experience of teachers through the years to draw some general guidelines for improving motivation and learning in the classroom.

Intrinsic and Extrinsic Motivation. Those things which elicit a natural interest, without teacher encouragement, provide intrinsic motivation. Through extrinsic motivation, the teacher attempts to stimulate the learner toward a particular educational objective where previously there was little or no natural or intrinsic interest. Learning under intrinsic motivation is more effective than learning under extrinsic motivation. Extrinsic motivation based on grades, rewards from parents, future occupational success and the like can be temporarily effective, and in some situations they seem necessary. They should, however, be used as tools leading to intrinsic motivation.

General and Specific Motives. Motives are both general and specific. The desire to learn and the need for achievement, for example, are more general motivating factors, while the desire for a certain reward or to avoid a threatened punishment are specific motivators. Both types have their place in education.

Reward and Punishment. Learning under the control of reward is usually more effective than learning under the control of punishment. Rewards serve as incentives, they help set the goal desired, and by providing feedback information to the student they help him discriminate between appropriate and inappropriate responses. Rewards also tend to reinforce desired behavior and set a proper response in the learner's mind.

Some forms of punishment do seem to have their uses, however. In the form of nonreward or failure to obtain the reward, punishment may furnish direction and provide information about direction toward a goal–in terms of what should be avoided. Punishment of this type also tends on a long-term basis to weaken the motivations energizing the behavior that is punished. It may also weaken the probability of undesirable response recurrence.

True punishment, as contrasted to nonreward, may also be useful. It may take various forms—reproof, blame, reprimand, undesirable work assignments, physical pain, threat of failure in school, and the like. Although extreme care in its use is required, this type of punishment may contribute in similar fashion to nonreward.

It should be remembered that both reward and punishment are forms of extrinsic motivation and subject to its limitations.

Intense Motivation. Motivation that is too intense may create harmful emotional states, so that effective learning is inhibited. Anxiety, for example, is an effective motivational device in some instances, if used in moderation, but for most people very much anxiety decreases their ability to function effectively. Some students are especially susceptible to anxiety, as evidenced by their inability to perform well on classroom tests.

Learning as Motivation. Motivation is an effect as well as a cause of learning. "Cognitive drive" (the desire to know and understand, to master knowledge, to formulate and solve problems) provides its own reward and is potentially the most important kind of motivation. Cognitive drive and considerations relative to intrinsic motivation and needs for success provide support for attempts to help all students feel that they have learned something or made progress. Learning itself then becomes a type of intrinsic motivation. Human beings are naturally curious and desire to know more about their surroundings, and capitalizing on these inclinations may be one of the most effective motivational devices.

Classroom Climate. The social structure and the general climate in the classroom can either inhibit or encourage learning. They affect participation and communication among the students and between teacher and students, both of which are important to motivation. Aspirations and norms of behavior, ego expectations and roles, are all influenced by the general atmosphere—positive or negative, cooperative or distrustful, cheerful or gloomy.

Mental Set. The mental set most conducive to learning includes several of the things discussed elsewhere concerning motivation, such as interest, attitude, and classroom atmosphere. In its broader definition, mental set is the total readiness or preparation for a particular type of activity to the exclusion of others. To induce this mental set is the teacher's challenge.

Ego Enhancement. Another important ingredient of motivation may be termed ego enhancement, because it is concerned with achievement as a source of primary or earned status. The kind of status that an individual earns is ego enhancing according to how adequate he feels as a result of his achievement. His feelings of self-esteem and adequacy are thus a function of his perceived achievement. Motivation resulting from ego enhancement is thus directed both toward the attainment of current scholastic achievement, or prestige, and toward the future academic and career goals that depend on current academic success. Approval from teachers and parents supplies the most common source of ego-enhancement information, and we suffer an overemphasis on academic marks or grades because these comprise the usual language of communication to students about their achievement.

Affiliative Drive. Students are also motivated to achieve by their desire to please some person or persons with whom they identify in a dependent sense. Status in this case is not determined by the learner's perception of his achievement but by the acceptance of him and his achievement by the person(s) with whom he identifies. Conseuqnetly, the student is greatly influenced by the superordinate person's standards and expectations. During childhood, affiliative drive is usually most closely related to parent expectations or teacher desires. During late childhood and adolescence affiliative drive diminishes in intensity and is redirected from parents and teachers toward peers. Academic competition against the opposite sex group or toward agemates may be a powerful motivating force during adolescence. It may also depress academic achievement, however, if the valued persons do not perceive academic achievement as desirable. Social class variations relative to the value placed upon academic achievement are important in this respect.

Knowledge of Progress. A student's performance can be improved by giving him knowledge (preferably as soon as possible) about how he performed on a test or an assignment. Records or graphs which show a student's progress over a period of time can also be motivational, although care must be exercised to avoid emphasizing his progress in comparison to that of others. It is also more likely that a positive approach, which focuses on progress and success rather than failure, will be most effective.

DIFFERENCES IN INTELLECTUAL ABILITY. Common sense would seem to indicate that even under ideal motivational circumstances there are limits to possible learning among students. Simple observation seems to also indicate that these limits vary among individuals. Intelligence is the word we use in discussing these phenomena, and studies over a period of several years have now given us much useful information about this aptitude for learning.

We need to first draw some distinction between capacity and performance in the determination of ability to learn. Theoretically there may be great capacity for learning, due to biological make-up of an individual, with very little actual performing intelligence. Scientists are more concerned with this innate capacity than are practicing educators, because it is at the performance level that teachers must work. We cannot hope to measure capacity, but we can achieve some success in measuring performance, and from this we can only infer capacity.

In line with the idea that educators must focus their attention on performance in a learning situation, we may accept as a working definition the idea that intelligence is "a measurement construct designating general level of cognitive functioning." It is a functional manifestation of cognitive ability expressed in terms of individual performance or capacity differences.[21]

An early theory proposed by Thorndike suggested that intelligence is comprised of many independent abilities, including *social intelligence* (the ability to deal effectively in social interaction), *concrete intelligence* (the ability to work with things), and *abstract intelligence* (the ability to deal effectively with symbols, abstractions, and ideas). Thorndike and his colleagues theorized that these abilities exist independently, but it soon became apparent that they are correlated in a positive direction. Students who obtain high scores on an intelligence test are likely to be superior in all subjects, although not equally so in all. There is apparently a kind of *general* intelligence in combination with varying degrees of unique aptitudes that affect a person's performance.

The rather simple theory of a pervasive general intelligence was also short-lived, as additional research suggested that there are several factors acting together to make up intelligence. Using techniques of factor analysis in statistically

[21]David P. Ausubel, *Educational Psychology: A Cognitive View* (New York: Holt, 1968), p. 225.

analyzing the results of different tests, Thurston and others identified several intellectual abilities and used these findings in constructing the Primary Mental Abilities test. This test was designed to identify variations in seven areas of intellectual ability: number facility, verbal facility, space relations, memory, reasoning, word fluency, and perceptual speed.

Identification of factors in intelligence has been carried further by Guilford in attempting to describe the total cognitive structure. Through the development of a rather complex model, he and his colleagues have suggested that there are at least some 120 possible abilities and combinations of abilities. These are grouped into three major categories: operations, or the processes a person uses as he reasons; contents, the way in which objects, events, or other materials are handled in the thinking process; and products, the results that emerge from thinking. The operations components are cognition, memory, divergent production, convergent production and evaluation. The contents are either figural, symbolic, semantic, or behavioral; and the products are seen to exist as units, classes, relations, systems, transformations, or implications. Although complex and largely theoretical at this point, Guilford's ideas offer a way to expand our conception of intelligence to include such things as social intelligence, mechanical intelligence, and abilities in special fields such as athletics, music, drama, and speech. With further development and understanding, this approach may offer clues to aid the development of better placed and better organized educational efforts.[22]

It must be admitted that we are just beginning to learn about human intelligence, but from research to this point it is apparent that the term *intelligence* can be used in many ways. A person may have rather high intelligence in a special area, such as social skill or verbal fluency, but special abilities are more or less interrelated and form a general intelligence level, within which may be identified specific strengths and weaknesses.

Measuring Intelligence. The identification and measurement of intellectual abilities has been given a great deal of attention by psychologists and educators from the earliest days of educational psychology. Its value in curriculum planning, individual student placement, and other educational efforts was readily apparent. However, intelligence cannot be measured directly, it must be inferred from observations of how a person performs certain kinds of tasks represented on a test and the relationships between this performance and performance in a training or work situation. All intelligence tests are, therefore, obviously limited in their accuracy and general application.

Tests to determine the approximate level of general intelligence and others designed to measure specific intellectual abilities have been developed, tested, and widely used. Their limited accuracy, inappropriate application of findings to

[22]J. P. Guilford, "Three Faces of Intellect," *American Psychologist* 14 (1959), pp. 469–479; and "Intelligence: 1965 Model," *American Psychologist* 21 (1966), pp. 20–26.

school situations, the changing nature of human intelligence, and other limita-tions in their use have led to much misuse of intelligence test information, but intelligence tests have also been very valuable to educators when used properly to guide educational decisions.

Variation of Intelligence. A wide and continuous range of intelligence, as expressed in typical academic performance or intelligence test scores, is obvious in a normal population. This is consistent with the idea that intelligence, like most other human traits, is determined largely by the cumulative and additive effects of a large number of genes, each exerting a small positive or negative effect on the development of the trait. Thus it has been found, for example, that among 14-year-old students in New York State, mental ages range from 10 to 18, with the midpoint at 14.[23] Expressed in terms of intelligence tests, approximately 64 percent of all IQ scores fall between the range of 85 and 114.[24] Scores above and below this range occur with decreasing frequency, but it can be readily seen that large numbers of students fall into abnormal intelligence categories.

Measured Intelligence and Academic Achievement. The correlation between intelligence, as measured by intelligence or achievement tests, and academic achievement is expected by many teachers and parents to be higher than it actually is. Academic success in various subject-matter fields generally correlates with intelligence or academic aptitude test scores at about the 0.5 level. This means that in only about one-half of the cases do students with high intelligence test scores do equally well in academic achievement. It also means that about one-half of the students with relatively low test scores do better than expected in their academic work. Knowledge of this correlation should impress teachers and parents with the fact that test scores are only indicative of potential and should be used with caution as a guide to achievement prediction or expecta-tion.

The relationship between scholastic aptitude and academic achievement is only moderate for several reasons. In the first place, measures of both are only approximate because of inaccuracies in teacher grading and testing procedures. More importantly, other relevant factors, such as motivation, interests, personal-ity traits, adjustment, and family, peer-group, social class, and cultural influences affect the degree to which academic abilities correlate with academic achieve-ment. Successful students have better study habits, more self-control, "compensa-tory" rather than "protective" ego mechanisms, more realistic levels of aspiration, and personality traits such as dependability, self-reliance, ambition, investigative-ness, and persistence. Knowing this, it would seem that teachers should give more attention to the various factors other than native intelligence which lead to success in school as they seek to help students make the most of

[23]E. L. Cornell, *The Variability of Children of Different Ages and Its Relation to School Classification and Grouping* (Albany: University of the State of New York, 1936).
[24]L. M. Terman and M. A. Merrill, *Measuring Intelligence* (Boston: Houghton, 1937).

their native ability or compensate for intellectual weaknesses.[25]

READINESS TO LEARN. Although it may not have been known as such, the problem of readiness to learn has existed since the dawn of civilization. The controversy about what children can learn at various ages is old, but recent discoveries in psychology have shed considerable light on the problem.

It was not so long ago that children were thought to be miniature adults with adult minds on a small scale. Rousseau was one of the first in modern times to refute this idea and suggest that there are stages in the development of young people at which they best learn various things. No one seriously disputes this idea today, although adults still often tend to overlook the abilities and concepts of the child and impose their image of the world upon him. Especially at a time of national crisis, adults are prone to overcrowd the child's mind with their own intellectual products and concerns to the overall detriment of his total learning experience.

Even though it is still a relatively new field of study, we know much more about readiness to learn now than at the turn of the century. Thorndike, Maslow, Havighurst, Piaget, Bruner, and others have developed theories based on their research which are very helpful to the practicing educator in his efforts to determine proper placement and presentation of learning activities. We now know that readiness is dependent upon both maturation and experience, that it varies with individuals, and that it progresses at a somewhat predictable pace, so that estimates are possible relative to readiness at certain ages or levels of development. Maslow's hierarchy of needs, Havighurst's developmental tasks, Piaget's concepts of concrete and formal operations, and Bruner's proposals about using knowledge of readiness in discovery and inquiry learning all have profound possibilities for use in curriculum planning and in classroom teaching. We cannot go into these theories in detail in this brief discussion, but the serious student of education will make it a point to thoroughly familiarize himself with the work of these and other psychologists, particularly as they apply to specific age levels and academic subjects. Especially important to curriculum builders are the ideas about a "spiral" curriculum and the placement of subject matter and inquiry procedures at various points in the educational system. These ideas will be discussed at greater length further on in this book.

GOALS AND CONSEQUENCES OF BEHAVIOR. One of the more promising approaches to understanding and influencing the behavior of children and adolescents is found in the theories developed by Alfred Adler and adapted for pedagogical use by his followers, notably Rudolph Dreikurs. At the risk of oversimplification we will briefly discuss three of the major concepts involved in this approach: goal-directed behavior, encouragement, and natural consequences.

The foundation of Adler's approach to educational psychology is found in

[25]Ausubel, *op. cit.*, pp. 255–257.

his statement that "every psychic phenomenon, if it is to give us any understanding of a person, can only be grasped and understood if regarded as a preparation for some goal."[26] All behavior is purposive and directed toward the attainment of specific goals. "We cannot think, feel, will, or act without the perception of some goal," and if a person's goals are recognized then the reasons for his actions can be understood.[27]

Dreikurs proposes that there are four basic goals of behavior:
1. Attention (success, recognition)
2. Power
3. Revenge
4. Display of inadequacy

All human beings have a fundamental need for success, for attention, and for recognition. If a person is unsuccessful in achieving this through socially accepted means he will do so through misbehavior or other less acceptable procedures. "Unpleasant by-products like humiliation, punishment, or even physical pain do not matter as long as his main purpose is achieved. Children prefer being beaten to being ignored."

We all also want power. Some have a stronger need for this than others, but the need is universal. This is particularly evident during adolescence when the young person tries to develop a life style of his own which will provide the power to determine his own actions and some control over those around him. Attempts by parents and teachers to "overpower" young people will ultimately be unsuccessful, because the youngster is less restricted in his methods than are adults by a sense of responsibility or moral obligation. When a "victory" is achieved by adults, the young person is even more convinced of the importance of power and becomes more determined to achieve and use it.

Because of frustrated attempts to gain power, or perhaps some other reason, retaliation or revenge may become the basic goal of a person's behavior. Failure to gain success or recognition through approved means may also bring on the desire for revenge, and it will usually be directed at the teacher, perhaps not as a person but as a part of the educational system. Again the teacher is at a disadvantage in combating this goal, because he will not lower himself to the level of behavior or the means used by the student to achieve the desired revenge.

If a person perceives himself to be entirely unsuccessful and unable to achieve other goals, he may attempt to hide behind a display of real or imagined inferiority. This may result in a desire to be left alone, in a totally passive and unresponsive attitude. Inability is used as a protection so that nothing will be required or expected. By avoiding participation or contribution, the student precludes more humiliating and embarrassing experiences.

[26]Alfred Adler, *The Practice and Theory of Individual Psychology*, trans. P. Radin (Totowa, N.J.: Littlefield, 1969), p. 4.
[27]*Ibid.*, p. 3.

In pursuing one or more of these goals, young people may be either active or passive and may use either constructive or destructive methods. In any case, the secret of understanding and correcting the behavior lies in identifying the goal or goals being sought and in helping the student recognize inappropriate means which he may be using or how to change or strengthen potentially successful means for achieving the desired goal.[28]

Encouragement is the second key proposed for helping children to successfully cope with life, both in and outside of school. "Every misbehaving or deficient child is discouraged," according to Dreikurs, and must be helped to regain confidence in his ability, particularly his ability to reach desired goals. So long as constructive and accepted ways maintain confidence in his ability, the child will use them, but discouragement will lead to misbehavior and use of less "acceptable" procedures.

The main reason for discouragement among students lies in the fact that most of our methods of training constitute a sequence of discouraging experiences. They may take the form of overprotection and indulgence, as well as severity, humiliation, and punishment, but the end result is the same—discouragement and a lack of self-confidence. The teacher's most important role then becomes that of adapting and devising ways for students to have experiences of his own strength, of his ability to overcome difficulties and take care of himself. He must learn to depend on himself, rather than on others. Criticism and humiliation (most often expressed in terms of school rules and grades) do not add to a young person's self-confidence and courage, yet they are far more common in the typical school than forms of encouragement and recognition of success.[29]

The best ways to encourage students or to improve their behavior are not found in artificial means or reward or punishment, but rather in the principle of natural consequences. It is easy to confuse encouragement with reward and natural consequences with punishment, but there is an important distinction. Encouragement is not identical with reward, although praise, which can be used as a form of encouragement, may take on the aspects of a reward. Encouragement goes further than reward, however, in that it expresses confidence and faith in the student, even at a time when he is not doing well.

As with encouragement and reward, the same teacher action may be used regarding either natural consequences or punishment. The similarity is superficial, however. Permitting the natural consequences of an act to take place has none of the retaliatory qualities of punishment, nor does it exhibit the personal power and superiority of the teacher characteristic in punishment. Natural consequences express the power of the social order and natural physical laws. In

[28]Rudolph Dreikurs, *Psychology in the Classroom* (New York: Harper, 1957), pp. 12–17.

[29]*Ibid.*, pp. 40–44. For a more complete discussion and examples of how to apply principles of encouragement, see pp. 63–75 and Don Dinkmeyer and Rudolf Dreikurs, *Encouraging Children to Learn: The Encouragement Process* (Englewood Cliffs, N.J.: Prentice-Hall, 1963).

allowing them to take place, the teacher becomes a representative of an order which affects all alike, rather than merely a powerful authority.

The principle of natural consequences offers tremendous potential for teacher application to teaching and learning situations, especially those involving discipline problems. In the classroom, which is itself somewhat artificial, natural consequences are not always possible, but in such cases it is often possible to at least bring *logical* consequences into the situation.[30]

LEARNING HOW TO LEARN. One thing which permeates all of the new curriculum programs is the idea that the most important thing to be learned is "how to learn." Throughout the history of education there has been a small and usually weak minority of educational thinkers who insisted that in addition to acquisition of knowledge students should develop skills for finding out. Knowledge acquisition, transmission of the cultural heritage, and technical skills have been given the dominant concern, however, from kindergarten through graduate school.

Under a variety of labels—discovery learning, independent study, self-directed study, inquiry methods, creativity, and the like—the idea of teaching students how to learn can be traced throughout the history of education if one looks closely. Among the more recent advocates of the idea may be found Maria Montessori, John Dewey, and the Gestalt psychologists. Inquiry as a method of learning was central to Dewey's thinking, in particular. In *How We Think*, he developed the theoretical concept of the nature of inquiry and of reflective thought, identifying learning with thinking, and thinking with active discovery of relationships and organizing principles.[31]

There is substantial agreement among psychologists and educators about the meaning of the term "discovery," with most definitions being similar to that given by Bruner: "a matter of rearranging or transforming evidence in such a way that one is enabled to go beyond the evidence so reassembled to additional new insights."[32] Such a definition incorporates Dewey's earlier statement that the student's experiences with the raw material of what is to be learned generate data, from which he may then proceed to discover ideas.[33]

Discovery learning may thus be seen to differ from the traditional reception learning (rote or meaningful) in several ways. In-reception, the entire content of what is to be learned is presented to the learner in final form. The student is required only to internalize or incorporate the material that is presented to him to that he can reproduce it at some future date. Discovery learning, whether concept formation or rote problem solving, requires that the principal content

[30]*Ibid.*, pp. 50–52, 76–88.
[31]E. Paul Torrance and William F. White (eds.), *Issues and Advances in Educational Psychology* (Itasca, Ill.: Peacock, 1969), pp. 293–296.
[32]J. S. Bruner, "The Act of Discovery," *Harvard Education Review*, 31 (1961), pp. 21–32.
[33]John Dewey, "Thinking in Education," in *Democracy in Education* (New York: Macmillan, 1916), Chapter 12.

of what is to be learned be discovered by the learner *before* he can incorporate it meaningfully into his cognitive structure.

> The distinctive and *prior* learning task, in other words, is to discover something—which of two maze alleys leads to the goal, the precise nature of the relationship between two variables, the common attributes of a number of diverse instances, and so forth. The first phase of discovery learning involves a process quite different from that of reception learning. The learner must rearrange information, integrate it with existing cognitive structure, and reorganize or transform the integrated combination in such a way as to generate a desired endproduct or discover a missing means-end relationship.[34]

Learning by discovery, as it is pursued today, is largely concerned with cognitive aspects—the development and organization of concepts, ideas, and insights. The bewildering and rapidly growing mass of information available in the world points up the need for establishing structures of knowledge so that students can find meaningful relationships among the bits and pieces of knowledge, and even the many comprehensive ideas, with which they are faced in school and in adult life. The traditional struggle with isolated facts has driven the majority of students away from knowledge in the past, and it will do so at a growing rate unless different teaching methods are used today.

In order for students to learn to learn, to think for themselves, to logically attack meaningful problems, and to find reasonably satisfying answers, they must be helped to find out for themselves—to discover. But there must be something to discover that ties all of the facts in the world into comprehensive and understandable wholes. What are they to discover? Behind the new curriculum programs lies the idea that students must be led to discover structure in knowledge. Thus we arrive at the focus and basic approach to curriculum organization of this book.

By emphasizing the discovery approach to learning, teachers will at the same time give opportunity for students to develop creativity and divergent thinking, another idea being stressed among educators today. Also, individual student perception will be given room for growth and expression, providing teachers with the opportunity to better understand individual students and help them gain a better understanding of themselves.

It should be pointed out before closing this brief discussion of discovery learning that although it is extremely important, discovery learning is not the only kind of important learning for students. There are basic skills and facts which students must acquire before they can satisfactorily utilize discovery procedures in a subject area. Also, after generalizations are established through discovery, concrete operations and exercises must often be an important part of further learning in order for the student to adequately understand and be able to apply

[34]Ausubel, *op. cit.*, p. 22.

the knowledge which has been gained. This is especially true in the disciplines of science and mathematics.

Generally Accepted Principles of Learning

The previous discussions of this chapter have shown that there are many explanations for the nature and conditions of learning. No one theory gives us all the answers we need, but each has a contribution to make in our attempts to understand the total field of psychology and educational psychology.

It is of considerable concern to some that psychologists have not reached common agreement and that there are many questions to which we have no definite answers as yet. Those who like things to be in black-and-white order are dissatisfied with the tentativeness and incompleteness of much of our knowledge about how we learn, but human beings—complex and changing as they are—cannot be so easily understood. Our knowledge in the field of educational psychology, and especially in learning theory, will doubtless remain incomplete and subject to change in the forseeable future.

Although somewhat risky and subject to criticism, a summary of the basic agreements among most learning theorists as to educational practices would be useful to the teacher in the classroom. Learning theorists of different schools often agree on desirable classroom practice, although they may disagree as to the reasons behind the practice, and experience often proves the advisability of a pedagogical concept in the absence of scientific explanation. The following statements would seem to be acceptable to most learning theorists, although they might object to wording or suggest qualifications. As a guide to classroom practice, perhaps they may serve satisfactorily.

Individual Differences

1. The abilities of individual students are an important consideration in guiding learning. Students vary in their ability to learn and individual abilities vary according to what is being learned.
2. Students develop in their ability to learn with age and maturation, typically going through similar stages of development, although perhaps at different ages.
3. Each student is unique in his ability to learn and in ways he learns.
4. Human potentialities for learning are much greater than the actual learning usually allowed by the environment.
5. When students are grouped according to one criterion, such as IQ or reading ability, they vary over a range of several grade levels in relation to other criteria.
6. A student's readiness to learn, as determined by previous experience, maturation levels, and the like, enhances or hampers his ability to learn.

7. Learning takes place more easily when the learning tasks are adjusted to individual levels of maturity and other aspects of readiness.
8. Students learn better and more easily that which conforms to their previous attitudes or previous learning.

Perception

9. Recognizing the need for acquiring new ways of behaving is a necessary condition for effective learning.
10. Pupil self-perception strongly influences learning.
11. The quality of the learning experience, as perceived by the student, determines the quality of learning achieved.
12. Meanings derived from a student's experiences in a learning situation depend upon the meaning he brings to the situation.

Motivation

13. Motivation is necessary to learning and may be both general and specific; for example, desire to learn, need for achievement (general), desire for reward or for avoiding threatened punishment (specific).
14. Motivation and effective learning occur more readily when the situation has meaning for the learner.
15. Motivation that is too intense (creating anxiety, pain, fear) may create emotional states which inhibit learning.
16. Intrinsic motivation is moreffective than extrinsic motivation.
17. Reward as a motivational device is usually more effective than punishment or the threat of punishment.
18. Success is a better motivator than failure, and tolerance for failure is best taught by providing a backlog of success.
19. The individual's level of aspiration profoundly influences his success and achievement. Students need help in setting realistic goals.
20. Students work better on a project if they see meaning in it and have helped to choose and plan it.
21. Active participation better facilitates learning than does passive reception.
22. Knowing about a good performance, knowledge of mistakes, and specific information on the nature of successful efforts assist the learner.
23. A good environment for learning, taking into consideration the total classroom situation, is necessary for effective learning.
24. Learners achieve just enough to meet their purposes; often this means that they do only well enough to "get by," unless there is increased motivation.
25. Ridicule, fear of failure, discrimination, and the like are less effective in promoting learning than are guidance, arousal of interests, and encouragement.

Teaching Methods

26. Reinforcement should immediately follow the desired behavior and be clearly related to it.

27. Repetition and drill are necessary for memorizing necessary facts and for learning skills, but they should have meaning for the learner and should include new elements as the practice progresses.

28. There should be continuity of experience from task to task, from subject to subject, and from day to day.

29. Students learn from each other, especially when they have been together for some time. This emphasizes the need for encouragement of good group processes in the classroom.

30. No school subject is particularly better than others in strengthening mental powers.

31. Transfer of learning best occurs if the learner discovers relationships for himself and has opportunity to apply principles of relationships in a variety of tasks.

32. To fix material that needs to be retained for a long time, spaced or distributed recalls are advantageous.

33. If students are led to see that learning has unity, the educational process is greatly facilitated.

34. Concept formation is helped by having the concepts presented in varied and specific situations, followed by experience in trying the concepts in additional different situations.

35. Freedom to make mistakes allows students to explore and to test their thinking. Asking questions that stimulate thinking and imagination also encourages individual thinking and problem-solving.[35]

Selected References

Adams, James F. (ed.), *Understanding Adolescence.* Boston: Allyn and Bacon, Inc., 1968.

Ausubel, David P., *Educational Psychology: A Cognitive View.* New York: Holt, Rinehart and Winston, Inc., 1968.

Bernard, Harold W., *Psychology of Learning and Teaching.* New York: McGraw-Hill Book Company, 1954.

Bruner, Jerome S., *Toward a Theory of Instruction.* New York: W. W. Norton & Company, Inc., 1968.

[35]Adopted from Ernest R. Hilgard, *Theories of Learning,* 2d ed. (New York: Appleton, 1956); Goodwin Watson, "What Psychology Can We Feel Sure About?" *Teachers College Record* 61 (February 1960); and Vernon E. Anderson, *Principles and Procedures of Curriculum Improvement,* 2d ed. (New York: Ronald, 1965).

Bugelski, B. R., *The Psychology of Learning Applied to Teaching.* New York: The Bobbs-Merrill Company, Inc., 1964.

Cole, Luella, and Irma Nelson Hall, *Psychology of Adolescence.* 7th ed. New York: Holt, Rinehart and Winston, Inc., 1970.

Di Vesta, Francis, and George G. Thompson, *Educational Psychology: Instruction and Behavioral Change.* New York: Appleton-Century-Crofts, 1970.

Dreikurs, Rudolph, *Psychology in the Classroom.* New York: Harper & Row, Publishers, 1957.

Havighurst, Robert J., *Developmental Tasks and Education.* New York: Longmans, Green and Company, 1948.

Hilgard, Ernest R., *Theories of Learning.* 2d ed. New York: Appleton-Century-Crofts, Inc., 1956.

Mathis, B. Claude, John W. Cotton, and Lee Sechrest, *Psychological Foundations of Education.* New York: Academic Press, 1970.

McDonald, Frederick J., *Educational Psychology.* 2d ed. Belmont Calif.: Wadsworth Publishing Company, Inc., 1965.

Robison, Lloyd E., *Human Growth and Development.* Columbus, Ohio: Charles E. Merrill Publishing Company, 1968.

Rogers, Dorothy (ed.), *Issues in Adolescent Psychology.* New York: Appleton-Century-Crofts, 1969.

Taba, Hilda, *Curriculum Development.* New York: Harcourt Brace Jovanovich, Inc., 1962, Chapters 6–9.

Torrance, E. Paul, and William F. White (ed.), *Issues and Advances in Educational Psychology.* Itasca, Ill.: F. W. Peacock Publishers, Inc., 1969.

CHAPTER 6

EDUCATIONAL GOALS
AND THE CURRICULUM

American public education today seems to be entering a period which may be either vastly promising or starkley catastrophic. The curriculum, as a large and important part of the educational endeavor, is crucial to the direction taken and the results that occur. Curriculum decisions therefore need to be made competently, on recognized and valid bases, and with the highest degree of consistency possible. We must admit that this has not usually been the case in the past.

The history of curriculum revisions has been one of shifting pieces from one place to another, of adding pieces without removing what should be taken out, of taking out one piece and replacing it with another—all usually without a reappraisal of the whole pattern. The curriculum has become a patchwork, "the amorphous product of generations of tinkering," and this is continuing today. Additions and revisions are made without reconsidering the entire pattern. Acceleration is recommended in one part of the system without corresponding changes in the next. "New" programs are instituted at lower levels in the educational sequence without appropriate changes of the same nature in more advanced programs. Child-centered, society-centered, and subject-centered ideas about curicula vie with each other, when what is needed is a combination including all of these approaches and others as well.

To escape this historical pattern of poorly planned curriculum formation requires rigorous, systematic thinking based on well-established educational goals. Individuals cannot rise above their goals in life, and neither can educational efforts. Jerome Bruner has stated this need and some ideas about meeting it as follows.

> . . . a proper curriculum in any subject (or in the total curriculum of the school) requires some statement of objectives, some statement of what kinds of skill we are trying to create and by what kinds of performances we shall know it. The goal must be plain; one must have a sense of where one is trying to get to in any given instance of activity. For the exercise of skill is governed by an intention and

feedback on the relation between what one has intended and what one has achieved thus far—"knowledge of results." What this means in the formal educational setting is far more emphasis on making clear the purpose of every exercise, every lesson plan, every unit, every term, every education. If this is to be achieved, then plainly there will have to be much more participatory democracy in the formulation of lessons, curricula, courses of study, and the rest. For surely the participation of the learner in setting goals is one of the few ways of making clear where the learner is trying to get to.[1]

Wisely developed, clearly understood goals of education are essential to direction, motivation, and evaluation in curriculum planning and implementation. These are recognized as important determinants of success in our educational efforts, but they often remain obscured by a haze of generalities and good intentions instead of forming the very bone and muscle of school programs.

Critics of public education have enjoyed considerable popularity during the last decade, and many "reformers" are still at work, their vision of the educational task often restricted by out-of-date ideas of what learning is like and how it is encouraged or by a rejection of the democratic nature of public education, or both. Other critics include citizens who are opposed to school taxes, to radicalism or to progressivism, who are concerned about the spread of communism, or who display an obvious fear that cherished customs or ideas about values, morality, or "standards" are being threatened in the schools.

Without a strong sense of direction, educators are at the mercy of the latest and most articulate of these critics. Confusion resulting from tradition, social needs, adolescent needs, power centers in the society, national and international crises, and other forces threatens to eliminate the mediocre sense of purpose now evident among educators unless there is a stronger effort to stand aside and gather perspective, to consider all the elements that should go into curriculum making. Otherwise, curriculum makers will commit themselves uncritically to plans and movements and will take up current modes only to discard them as unthinkingly as they were adopted. Much of the machinery of American education has been developed in the past fifty years in this way, but the current situation and forecasts of the future no longer allow the luxury and waste of similar actions at this time or in the years to come.

In addition to establishing a strong sense of direction, good and accepted goals for education in general and for curriculum development in particular can provide needed motivation, both to educators and to students. Apathy among teachers and students alike is all too common in our schools today, and it is largely due to a lack of perceived and accepted goals—goals which are considered worth reaching.

If goals are needed for direction and motivation, they are no less necessary for evaluation. Students, teachers, local school systems, and the educational

[1]Jerome Bruner, "The Skill of Relevance or the Relevance of Skills," *Saturday Review* (April 18, 1970), p. 68.

system in general have no way of knowing if they are successful unless there are standards by which to measure their progress. These standards must be established in terms of goals—individual, schoolwide, and nationwide—so that evaluation and further progress may occur.

Definition and Description

As in most areas of discussion concerning education, some definition of terms is needed to facilitate understanding and communication. Terms such as function, goal, purpose, objective, and aim are often used somewhat interchangeably in discussions of school operations, but there are some differences in meaning which can lead to confusion if left unexplained.

Functions of the school and of the curriculum are those duties and responsibilities the school assumes—commonly termed the job of the school. This job is fixed by the social group that establishes the school. Within the broad definition of basic responsibilities or tasks to be carried out by the school those responsible for the school's operation identify more specific *goals, aims, objectives,* or *purposes* which they believe will fulfill the basic functions identified by the society. These terms are not identical in their meaning, but for our purposes they may be used somewhat synonymously.

The one basic function of the school is to help young people learn to live in, and improve, their society. "Subfunctions" may be identified which are designed to facilitate the basic function. Downey has suggested that these have four dimensions—intellectual, social, personal, and productive.[2] Within these dimensions, one may identify functions in various ways. Bent and Kronenberg identify the basic functions as being adaptive, integrating, differentiating, or democratizing.[3] Saylor and Alexander are somewhat more specific and detailed, suggesting that the duties and responsibilites of the school consist of

1. Universal schooling.
2. Determination of individual talents, capacities, and abilities.
3. Development of individual potentialities.
4. Transmission of the cultural heritage.
5. Discovery and systemization of knowledge.
6. Inculcation of values, beliefs, and ideals of the social group.
7. Development of character.
8. Preparation for adulthood.[4]

This last listing is approaching what we have defined as goal or purpose identifica-

[2]Lawrence W. Downey, *The Task of Public Education* (Chicago: Midwest Administration Center, 1960), p. 24.

[3]Rudyard K. Bent and Henry H. Kronenberg, *Principles of Secondary Education*, 5th ed. (New York: McGraw-Hill, 1966), pp. 43–45.

[4]J. Galen Saylor and William M. Alexander, *Curriculum Planning for Modern Schools* (New York: Holt, 1966), pp. 126–127.

tion, in that it is more specific and detailed than the typical statement of function. As far as actual classroom work is concerned (and curriculum planning as well), the identification of goals or purposes is more directly applicable. We will deal with this topic in more detail after we have discussed some of the things that go into definition of curriculum goals.

Determining Goals

In earlier chapters we have discussed the origins and development of educational goals throughout history and in various social situations. We have seen how views about educational goals have varied, and even conflicted, depending on the ideas of the times and the social situations encountered. At various times and places more emphasis has been given to the philosophical, the practical, the religious, the esthetic, to education for the masses, for democracy, for mental discipline, or for various other purposes. Questions of individual versus social needs, of the place of subject matter, or the need to actively change society through education have added their part to the controversy. More recently we have seen emphasis given to national defense, to poverty, and to the natural environment in which we live. To reconcile these views seems sometimes almost hopeless, but it must be done if we are to find logical and consistent direction for educational efforts.

Who determines—or who should determine—educational goals? Influence and pressure come from many sources, but they can be generally broken down into those within the local school system and those external to the immediate situation. External sources include federal and state legislatures, state departments of education, accrediting agencies, colleges and universities, organizations of the teaching profession, special-interest organizations, homes, industry, the press, religious organizations, business and technological advances, and the like. Within the local school system, several other sources of goals may be recognized, including school board members, the superintendent, principals, other administrators, curriculum leaders, sometimes bus drivers and custodians, and certainly students and classroom teachers. The relative amount of influence exercised by each of these varies from time to time, but they must all be considered, and others besides, when sources of educational goals are sought.

Before we go further into a definition of educational goals, perhaps it would be well to consider some characteristics of good ones. We need some principles to guide our thinking and help us avoid inappropriate or less desirable objectives. This may also help to shorten the list.

It should be recognized in the beginning that some of the proposed, and even accepted, aims of education are actually incidental, rather than primary. These include: to make more money, to get an easier job, to improve one's social position, to acquire knowledge for its own sake, or to aid in maintaining national prestige. In the course of a good education, one or more of these aims may be attained, but they should be recognized as incidental rather than primary. Some proposed aims, such as the development of mental power through activities involving "mental discipline," are actually false aims and completely unworthy of recognition.

Any list of principles is tentative and incomplete, but we would suggest that good educational aims should exhibit the following characteristics:

1. The society, or at least a significant portion of the society, must approve of them.
2. They must have significance ("relevance," if you please) for students, as well as for teachers and other adults.
3. They must be "teachable," or capable of achievement through instruction. This implies that they must be within the learning capabilities of the students involved.
4. They should be stated in behavioral terms, or at least in terms which may be easily converted to recognizable behaviors.
5. They should be recognized as developmental, representing paths to progress rather than terminal points.

Sources of Curriculum Goals

The foundations of education—history, philosophy, sociology, and psychology—are invaluable sources of information and guidance in the development of goals for education in general and the curriculum in particular. Previous chapters of this book have briefly explored each of these, and at this point we will attempt to draw from each of the foundation areas some goals which may serve as guides to action. Purposes accepted in the past may be also applicable today, while other goals may be developed as a result of recent or current situations.

No attempt will be made to be exhaustive in identifying the curriculum goals which may be developed from the foundations of education, but a representative selection of major objectives from each area will perhaps help the student of secondary school curriculum development in his search for purposes to guide his efforts.

Goals from the History of Education

Some would say that the history of education, in itself, does not establish educational goals, but only indicates how through the ages the philosophical, social, and more recently, psychological forces have acted to influence education. The point is probably valid, but it is through a study of history that one is more impressed with the influence of these forces and becomes better able to see how they have interacted through the years to produce the educational system and the curriculum of today.

They may be mentioned in slightly different form in later sections on the goals of curriculum as derived from the other foundations, but it seems appropriate at this point to indicate some of the aims of education which have been prominent throughout the history of education, even though the particulars of how they have been understood and carried out may have varied with the times. Specific subject matter, organization, and methodology have changed according to the ideas of the time, but most of the basic goals through the years have been the same. The more important ones include the following.

1. To preserve the skills and knowledge required in order to adequately meet needs for food, clothing, shelter, and safety. Within this broader goal might be included those more specifically related to vocational education in more recent times.

2. To preserve the customs, moral standards, and traditions of the society or group. At times, even to the present, this has approached the level of reverence for established ways.

3. To assure that the elders would be respected and cared for by the younger generation.

4. The above three types of purpose required that younger generations be kept under firm control, with little departure from accepted practice allowed.

5. To achieve acceptance and preservation of the status quo.

6. To teach religious customs, rituals, practices, values, and standards.

7. To maintain and carry out some form of initiation rites into adulthood.

8. To fit each person into his established place in society. This usually included keeping women "in their places" and maintaining lines of social class.

9. To maintain a national or cultural identity.

10. To serve the purposes of the state, including producing good citizens, good soldiers, and firm political support.

11. To provide self-understanding and self-realization. Socrates' respected admonition, "know thyself," exemplifies the objective, which has been carried out through the type of curriculum which included the "liberal arts" and the "humanities."

12. For females, until modern times, educational goals usually included only that which was designed to produce good mothers and homemakers.

13. In carrying out objectives related to No. 1 above in more recent times, the curriculum has included the aim of preparing young people for successful lives in business, politics, medicine, law, and the like.

14. To develop the "power to think."

15. To understand the world in which one lives.

16. To prepare young people for college or other higher educational endeavors.

17. To provide opportunity for "upward mobility" in the social and economic system.

18. To help young people "keep up" with modern developments in knowledge, industry, etc.

Goals from Philosophy

Philosophy exists to help man make decisions and take action in an intelligent fashion rather than merely on the basis of tradition, whim, or opinion. The different philosophies treat basically the same topics and questions, but each school of thought has a different approach or suggested answer to a particular issue or question. From the concerns of philosophy, and particularly the philosophy of education, we may identify goals of education and curriculum development as follows.

1. To develop a "way of thinking."
2. To learn to make judgments on the basis of logic, evidence, and experience.
3. To develop the ability to analyze, to clarify ideas, and to identify inconsistencies.
4. To recognize and use accepted sources of knowledge.
5. To evaluate claims to knowledge.
6. To study, evaluate, and contrast values (axiology).
7. To develop a guide to conduct (ethics).
8. To develop an appreciation for beauty (esthetics).
9. To achieve some knowledge of the different philosophies and their application to life.
10. To study the nature of man.
11. To develop concepts about the nature of the "good life."
12. To work toward an understanding of reality.
13. To recognize the importance and implications of problems such as the historical issue concerning the needs of society versus the needs of the individual.

Goals from Social Dynamics

Of the four sources of educational goals, society and social dynamics are probably the most influential and most important. This is true because the school is a social institution, developed by the members of a society to serve the needs of that society. History shows how this has occurred through the years, philosophy helps us to think more rationally about social problems and their implications, and psychology helps us understand how to make the school more effective in fulfilling its social tasks, but the society itself is the basic source of educational goals. To this source of guidance for curriculum development we owe our greatest attention.

No list of educational goals drawn from social dynamics could be complete, and we will make no attempt to be exhaustive in this respect. The following suggestions seem to include the more important objectives derived from the society and may serve to suggest others which deserve special attention.

1. To pass on the culture from one generation to the next. This includes such things as etiquette, language, food habits, religious and moral beliefs, systems of knowledge, attitudes, and values.

2. To pass on the technology of a group of people.

3. To pass on certain ways of life of a subculture existing within an individual community which may be different from the common ways found in the larger society.

4. To teach specific social roles for use by students as they fill their individual places in the community and the larger society. Schools must help students learn about role expectations in particular situations and how to fulfill them.

5. To help students learn to what extent they may be able to change their society and ways in which this may best be done.

6. To help students achieve an accurate and wholesome self-concept, including a feeling of individuality and self-worth. This is particularly important in today's mass society.

7. To help students understand and develop their individual personalities and best use them in their society.

8. To help students recognize and understand the effects of group pressures on individual personality and actions.

9. To help students gain an accurate understanding of the values of their culture relative to success in life so that they may set personal goals more intelligently and in line with personal values.

10. To develop in students an adequate understanding of the social order in which they live, the diversity of cultures found within their society, and how their society is changing.

11. To help students understand and cope with the inconsistencies in their culture.

12. To help students recognize sources of individual direction in the society (tradition, others, and self) and how they may best use each of these sources.

13. To develop an understanding of social class, how it exists in the society, and its importance to the society and to the individual.

14. To help students gain an adequate understanding of American democratic concepts, their importance to the society, and implications for individual daily living.

15. To develop a concept of learning as a "need-fulfilling, goal-seeking, and tension-reducing process."

16. To recognize and effectively utilize the educational importance of other social institutions, groups, and individuals.

17. To develop in students an understanding of the school's role as a socializing agent.
18. To develop in students an understanding of the social problems of the day, their causes, and possible solutions.

Goals from Psychology and Human Development

Educational psychology and information about adolescent growth and development are potential sources of great help for the curriculum planner and for the classroom teacher as he implements the curriculum. These areas of developing knowledge provide concrete and specific suggestions to teachers about how they may best work with individuals and with groups in the classroom to most effectively promote learning. On a broader scale, they also suggest goals for curriculum development in general. Again, the possibilities are endless, so we will confine our efforts to suggesting some of the more obvious and useful curriculum goals which may be drawn from a knowledge of psychology and human development.

1. To help students understand how they learn, how to make the best use of their intellectual abilities, and how to compensate for intellectual weaknesses.
2. To enable students to recognize individual strengths and weaknesses relative to learning, especially as related to preparation for further education or for a vocation.
3. To establish the idea among both educators and students that "education is life, not a preparation for life."
4. To make education purposeful and experiential, stressing application of knowledge more than merely acquisition of knowledge.
5. To adapt the curriculum to individual differences in ability, development, interest, future plans, and the like.
6. To organize the curriculum for best learning in view of what is known about psychology and its application to education.
7. To recognize the idea that "how we learn is part of what we learn," and to make adjustments accordingly in curriculum organization and presentation.
8. To help adolescents understand their own growth and development and implications for personal plans and actions.
9. To apply principles of "readiness" to curriculum development.
10. To develop the curriculum in accordance with what we know about adolescent growth and development—physical, intellectual, emotional, and social.
11. To organize the curriculum in line with theories of adolescent needs and adolescent developmental tasks.
12. To develop the curriculum with attention to basic agreements in learning theory.

13. To recognize and apply implications of the fact that the curriculum is to the individual student what he perceives it to be—neither more nor less.

14. To recognize the need for developing a curriculum which provides for both cognitive and affective learning.

15. To apply within the curriculum the premise that education should capitalize on intrinsic interests of students.

16. To adapt the curriculum to individual student goals.

17. To organize the curriculum so that students will be encouraged in their learning activities, rather than discouraged.

18. To provide within the curriculum the opportunity for every student to experience success and reward.

19. To provide continuity in learning experiences so that students may see that learning has unity and consistency.

20. To facilitate student discovery of structure in the disciplines.

Cognitive-field theories of learning have particularly important implications in organizing the curriculum so as to emphasize structural elements of the disciplines, as we have indicated earlier. Most of the purposes summarized above from psychology and human development are consistent with these ideas and show the importance of understanding field theories and their application to curriculum development. Carrying out these purposes may progress more satisfactorily if considerable attention is given to educational concepts which are supported by cognitive-field theories of learning, such as

1. The concept of educating the "whole child" which has been interpreted as requiring a much broader curriculum and much more comprehensive goals in terms of personality development for teachers in all disciplines.

2. More emphasis by teachers upon helping students to define their educational goals, usually in terms of needs.

3. A movement to integrate the curriculum, interpreted earlier as requiring the elimination of subject disciplines in curriculum organization and the establishment of "core" curricula with subject matter selected for the solution of immediate "felt" problems; more recently interpreted as requiring greater interdisciplinary cooperation, block-time arrangements with disciplinary integrity, and team-teaching.

4. The organization of subject matter for instruction into units which are large blocks of instruction with elements of unity which allows them to be taught and learned as a "whole."

5. Greater concentration upon concepts, generalizations, and complex understandings with the facts being employed as means to the end.

6. The use of overviews and previews in prefacing all courses, units, or teaching objectives, in order to establish a pattern which would facilitate immediate integration of the constituent facts and the derivation of meaning from them.[5]

[5]Wayne Dumas and Weldon Beckner, *Introduction to Secondary Education: A Foundations Approach* (Scranton, Pa.: Intext, 1968), pp. 131–132.

The Disciplines as Sources of Curriculum Goals

A fifth major source of curriculum goals may be found within the disciplines of knowledge. Subject matter has usually been overemphasized in the public schools, but this has largely been an overemphasis on certain uses of subject matter—memorization of facts, excessive attention to details, and so on. Without the disciplines of knowledge, we have little to teach and school becomes only a baby-sitting service.

Chapter 1 of this text dealt with the problem of content in the curriculum, and we do not wish to duplicate what was said there. We will only point out again at this point that from the accumulated knowledge of mankind, whether in the traditional academic subject areas or in other fields of learning, must come the actual content of the curriculum.

We can give proper attention in schools to only a small portion of this knowledge, so care must be exercised in the choices that are made for inclusion in the curriculum. It is our contention that the *structure* of knowledge should receive the most attention in the secondary school curriculum. Instruction in the schools should be aimed at helping students understand the structural elements —to grasp the concepts, generalizations, and methods of inquiry inherent in each discipline and shared among the various disciplines. So that they may grasp these structural elements, students must be led to experience the disciplines, not just learn them. This requires that they have opportunities for personal inquiry, discovery, and experience with a discipline similar to that of scholars.

Statements of Educational Goals

Drawing from the sources discussed above, several statements of educational objectives have been developed by various groups and organizations. Some have gained wide recognition and acceptance, others have been given little attention. The biggest problem in using these statements has been a tendency to state them in very general terms which do not lend themselves easily to classroom application. Those statements which classify desirable outcomes in terms of *behaviors* that people in our society need to master are much more useful.

The earlier statements of educational purpose for American schools were couched in terms prescribing amounts of content in the several subject matter fields. This was better than nothing, but it was soon recognized that something on a broader scale was necessary for the American secondary schools.

A special committee, the Commission on the Reorganization of Secondary Education, was established by the National Education Association in 1912. This committee developed a statement of purposes for American schools which stressed preparation for certain areas of life rather than mastery of certain subject matter. Their report made seven major recommendations, known since that time as the "Cardinal Principles of Education," and it is still considered by many to be among the more valid and useful definitions of secondary school purpose.

1. *Health.* The secondary school should provide health instruction, health habits, organize an effective program of physical activities, regard health needs in planning work and play, and cooperate with home and community in safe-guarding and promoting health interests.

2. *Command of fundamental processes.* Much of the energy of the elementary school is properly devoted to teaching certain fundamental processes, such as reading, writing, arithmetical computations, and the elements of oral and written expression. The facility that a child of 12 or 14 may acquire in the use of these tools is not sufficient for the needs of modern life. This is particularly true of the mother tongue. Proficiency in many of these processes may be increased more effectively by their application to new material than by the formal reviews commonly employed in grades seven and eight.

3. *Worthy home membership.* Worthy home membership as an objective calls for the development of those qualities that make the individual a worthy member of a family, both contributing to and deriving benefit from that membership.

4. *Vocation.* Vocational education should equip the individual to secure a livelihood for himself and those dependent on him, to serve society well through his vocation, to maintain the right relationships toward his fellow workers and society, and, as far as possible, to find in that vocation his own best development.

5. *Civic education* should develop in the individual those qualities whereby he will act well his part as a member of neighborhood, town or city, state, and nation, and give him a basis for understanding international problems.

6. *Worthy use of leisure.* Education should equip the individual to secure from his leisure the re-creation of body, mind, and spirit, and the enrichment and enlargement of his personality.

7. *Ethical character.* In a democratic society ethical character becomes paramount among the objectives of the secondary school. Among the means for developing ethical character may be mentioned the wise selection of content and methods of instruction in all subjects of study, the social contacts of pupils with one another and with their teachers, the opportunities afforded by the organization and administration of the school for the development on the part of pupils of the sense of personal responsibility and initiative, and, above all, the spirit of service and the principles of true democracy which should permeate the entire school—principal, teachers, and pupils.[6]

These principles described the areas of life activity which should be of concern to educators, but they did not elaborate on the behaviors needed to attain these ends. Courses in civics, health, leisure, and home and family were developed in response to the principles of this statement, even though this was not what the Commission had in mind. Some of the courses were worthwhile, but the

[6] *Cardinal Principles of Secondary Education* (Washington, D.C.: Bureau of Education, Bulletin 35, 1918), pp. 11–16.

absence of behavioral terms was a handicap, and resulted in a variety of interpretations and emphases.

The Educational Policies Commission, which was also established by the National Education Association, recognized that a statement of educational purpose needed to combine a recognition of the chief areas of life needs with a description of the behaviors and qualities necessary to attain each, combining ideas about social needs with those about individual needs. Obviously influenced by the 1918 statement, the Educational Policies Commission suggested objectives listed under four main categories describing areas of life needs: the objectives of self-realization, of human relationships, of economic efficiency, and of civic responsibility (1938). Each category includes certain behavioral goals, such as the inquiring mind (an aspect of self-realization), respect for humanity (human relations), and critical judgment (civic responsibility). This was a definite improvement over earlier attempts, but the behavioral objectives were stated in such general terms that little concrete guidance was given to curriculum makers or teachers.[7]

Beginning in the 1930's, several attempts have been made to state and classify objectives in terms of behaviors they represent, differentiating and grouping these behaviors according to the learning processes they require. It was evident that essentially the same types of behavior applied to a wide range of subject-matter content at different levels of education; consequently these behaviors were fitted into a relatively small number of classes, each of which represented distinctions in types of behavior and the ways in which they are learned. This classification differentiates behaviors as acquisition of knowledge, the intellectual skills representing thinking, the behaviors classifiable as attitudes and feelings, and those referred to as academic skills and study habits. This approach yielded statements such as the following grouping of educational outcomes:

1. The development of effective ways of thinking.
2. The acquisition of important information, ideas, and principles.
3. The development of effective work habits and skills.
4. The development of increased sensitivity to social problems and aesthetic experiences.
5. The inculcation of social rather than selfish attitudes.
6. The development of appreciation of literature, art, and music.
7. The development of increasing range of worthwhile and mature interests.
8. Increased personal-social adjustment.
9. Improved physical health.
10. The formulation and clarification of a philosophy of life.[8]

This type of classification presents the scope of curriculum as a range of behavior, not of life needs or of content explicitly. It has been found useful in

[7]Educational Policies Commission, *The Purposes of Education in American Democracy* (Washington, D.C.: National Education Association, 1938), pp. 45–47.

[8]E. R. Smith and R. W. Tyler, *Appraising and Recording Student Progress* (New York: Harper, 1942), p. 18.

determining the areas in which evaluation is needed and in suggesting needed emphasis in curriculum development.

It has probably become apparent to the reader that no single scheme of formulation and classification of objectives covers all the functions that seem important. To specify both the level of expected behavior and the particular content or context in which that behavior is to be applied is probably impossible, except in a particular school and with reference to particular students. The difficulty lies in attempting to describe a behavior and a standard of achievement in general terms at the same time, and in attempting to convey comprehensiveness and specificity simultaneously and in the same order of classification. Some further discussion of this problem seems in order at this point.

Relating Goals to the Classroom

We have seen in the above discussions that the formulation of educational objectives involves a twofold task. The first is that of determining the main aims of education, the broad overall purposes. This task belongs to those qualified to consider the whole field of education and to study carefully the sources from which to derive the aims. Most statements of educational purpose are of this nature. The second task is to define and determine more specific curricular objectives, the context in which they should be achieved, and levels of desired attainment. This task should be assumed by those who develop local curriculum guides and specific units for classroom use, especially individual teachers. To achieve a total result exhibiting consistency, however, requires that specific objectives be directly related to general aims.

Another dimension of the problem of relating goals to the classroom lies in the idea that objectives should be stated as a description of behavior and also as a description of the content to which this behavior applies. When one attempts to clarify the behaviors desired as teaching outcomes, one tends to obscure specific kinds of content required, while emphasis on content usually results in little attention to desired behaviors. Two types of classification developed recently for stating educational goals help overcome this difficulty.

Bloom and others working with him have developed a taxonomy or an overall scheme for classifying and correlating objectives which utilizes three major categories, called *domains*.

The *cognitive domain* involes the acquisition of knowledge and the use of this knowledge in carrying out some intellectual task or solving a problem.

The *affective domain* emphasizes those objectives with an aspect of feeling, emotional behavior, personal disposition, or acceptance or rejection.

The *psychomotor domain* consists of outcomes that constitute muscular or motor skill, manipulation, or neuromuscular coordination.

It is recognized that a student responds and behaves as a total organism and that aspects of all three types of behavioral change may be present in a school activity. However, such a classification scheme, with the subdivisions proposed by the authors, is a useful approach to the formulation of school objectives.[9]

Taba suggests another classification by types of behavior which seems functional as a basis for curriculum development. It includes five classifications of behavior to be included in educational goals.

Knowledge: Facts, Ideas, Concepts. This area of objectives includes the simpler objectives of remembering, or recalling facts, ideas, or phenomena in the form experienced or learned. A broader concept includes the idea of "understanding" or "insight," with the suggestion that knowledge should be mastered to the point that it can be reorganized and used in new situations, that it will involve seeing relationships and making judgments. To be rememebered, used, and adapted to new knowledge, learning of specific facts should be subordinated to knowledge of principles, ideas, and generalizations.

Reflective Thinking. Little disagreement will be found in the idea that people need to learn to think intelligently and independently. Critical thinking involves many different processes, including interpretation of data, application of facts and principles, and logical reasoning.

Values and Attitudes. Few would argue that social and human values should be emphasized in the schools, but confusion and indecision dominate most classrooms in this respect. Functional objectives are difficult to come by in this area, and much additional work is needed to clarify our thinking along these lines. Teaching about values, moralizing, or hoping that values will emerge as a by-product of other things in the school program have generally been the extent to which the teaching of values has advanced. We should not be surprised that school programs have little effect on the development and internalization of important values.

Sensitivities and Feelings. Sensitivity refers to the experiencing of feelings and values instead of descriptive learning about them. It includes a capacity to respond to the social and cultural environment with a personal and unique quality of perception and meaning. It involves the capacity to empathize, to "take the role of the other," in both social and human situations. The ability to respond empathically across barriers of cultural differences results from the development of a cosmopolitan social sensitivity, and is considered basic to social needs in today's world. An important aspect of sensitivity is the extension of feelings— social, moral, and aesthetic. Besides understanding feelings, there is also the problem of generating feelings.

Skills. Identification of necessary skills may range all the way from the basic academic skills, such as the "three R's," to skills necessary for independent and creative intellectual work, those required for problem solving, or the generally

[9]Benjamin S. Bloom (ed.), *Taxonomy of Educational Objectives: The Classification of Educational Goals,* Handbook I: *Cognitive Domain,* and David R. Krathwohl, Benjamin S. Bloom, and Bertram B. Masia, Handbook II: *Affective Domain* (New York: McKay, 1956, 1964).

neglected area of skills pertaining to the management of interpersonal relations and the conduct of groups. With perhaps the exception of basic academic skills, they all deserve more attention than is usually accorded them in the schools.[10]

The Teacher's Task

As the individual classroom teacher attempts to translate general objectives into specific ones for teaching and learning activities, he is faced with questions such as:

1. To which of the general objectives can and should this class contribute?
2. To aid in the realization of the general objectives, what knowledge, thinking skills, values and attitudes, sensitivities and feelings, or skills can be developed in this class?
3. What objectives should be set up for this class that will best fit into the general objectives of education?
4. How can units and other organizational schemes for teaching be best developed in accord with the specific objectives accepted for this class?
5. What activities will best achieve the objectives identified as appropriate to this class?
6. Which teaching methods, illustrative techniques, audio-visual materials, evaluative techniques, and the like are most appropriate to the objectives at hand?

As the teacher attempts to find answers to these and other similar questions he must translate general objectives into specific ones, and specific objectives into classroom efforts in the light of what is both logical and appropriate relative to the subject matter at hand and the growth potential of the given age or maturity level of the students.

Conclusions

The forces in education today have the makings of either a great resurgence in curriculum development or an ignominious retrogression, depending upon the kind of thinking that has the most weight in their shaping and the kinds of goals which are established. Curriculum development is a complex task that requires many kinds of decisions. Decisions must be made first about the general aims which schools are to pursue and about the more specific objectives of instruction. The major areas or subjects of the curriculum must then be selected and specific content to be covered must be identified. Choices must be made about the type of experiences which will be most appropriate for teaching and learning the content selected, for development of understandings and attitudes, and for reaching other desired outcomes. Decisions are needed regarding how to evaluate what

[10]Adapted from Hilda Taba, *Curriculum Development* (New York: Harcourt, 1962), pp. 211–228.

students learn, the effectiveness of the curriculum, and how to make it better. All of these steps require a clear definition and understanding of educational and curricular goals if a reasonable amount of success is expected.

Demanding and lengthy lists of goals such as those suggested on previous pages, especially with the realization that they are incomplete, may very well convince classroom teachers and other curriculum makers that the task before them is beyond achievement. When considered in total, some of the goals appear to be contradictory or incompatable, although this is probably not the major problem. Such lists of goals do impress one with the enormity and complexity of the educator's assignment, and it may be that this is one of the reasons educators so often retreat into the mediocre, but somewhat secure, safety of tradition and the status quo.

As stressed in the beginning paragraphs of this chapter, however, educators must develop and follow some concepts of purpose if they·hope to achieve any kind of worthwhile success. To develop goals for the curriculum they should first learn all they can about the foundations of education and how they should affect educational objectives. The disciplines of knowledge must be included, with emphasis on their inherent structure. Eclecticism, balance, and flexibility may then be utilized as guiding principles for selection, organization, and implementation of a secondary school curriculum that will best serve our society.

Selected References

Alberty, Harold B., and Elsie J. Alberty, *Reorganizing the High-School Curriculum.* 3d ed. New York: The Macmillan Company, 1962, p. 49–79.

Bloom, Benjamin S., and David R. Krathwohl, "Educational Objectives and Curriculum Development," in Edwin Fenton, *Teaching the New Social Studies in Secondary Schools.* New York: Holt, Rinehart and Winston, Inc., 1966, p. 20–32.

Cardinal Principles of Secondary Education. Washington, D.C.: Bureau of Education, Bulletin 35, 1918.

Douglass, Harl R., *The High School Curriculum.* 3d ed. New York: The Ronald Press Company, 1964, Chapter 9.

Downey, Lawrence W., *The Secondary Phase of Education.* Waltham, Mass.: Blaisdell Publishing Company, 1965, Chapter 1.

Dumas, Wayne, and Weldon Beckner, *Introduction to Secondary Education: A Foundations Approach.* Scranton, Pa.: Intext Educational Publishers, 1968, Chapter 6.

Educational Policies Commission, *The Central Purpose of American Education.* Washington, D.C.: National Education Association, 1961.

Educational Policies Commission, *The Purposes of Education in American Democracy.* Washington, D.C.: National Education Association, 1938.

Johnson, Harold T., *Foundations of Curriculum.* Columbus, Ohio: Charles E. Merrill Publishing Company, 1968.

Saylor, J. Galen, and William M. Alexander, *Curriculum Planning for Modern Schools.* New York: Holt, Rinehart and Winston, Inc., 1966, Chapter 4.

Taba, Hilda. *Curriculum Development.* New York: Harcourt Brace Jovanovich, Inc., 1962, Chapters 1 and 13.

Wright, John R., James W. Thornton, Jr., and others. *Secondary School Curriculum.* Columbus, Ohio: Charles E. Merrill Books, Inc., 1963, Chapter 4.

part III

Disciplinary Components of the Secondary School Curriculum

Disciplinary Components of the Secondary School Curriculum

The brief study of educational foundations and their relationships to educational goals included in Part II forms the basis for exploration into more specific aspects of the definition and organization of secondary school curriculum. Although we will not attempt to provide numerous reminders of the importance of history, philosophy, sociology, psychology, and human development to curriculum development, an awareness of these factors will enable the student to grasp a larger understanding of curriculum and how it relates to the world at large. Relationships between curriculum content and the foundations of education may be readily seen if one is alert to the importance of this relationship and sensitive to its existence.

As stated in Chapter 1, for the purposes of this textbook we have identified four major categories or "classes" of disciplines for use in grouping the various fields of learning for the purpose of curriculum determination and organization. Each of these classes—mathematics, natural science, social studies, and the humanities—exhibits distinctive, although not necessarily unique, disciplinary components (content, structure, and methods of inquiry).

Each of the classes of disciplines will be discussed in Part III, with primary emphasis being given to the elements of each discipline and the components which seem to be shared by the various disciplines in each class. Through a recognition of the elements shared by various disciplines, especially those making up a particular class, there is excellent opportunity for correlating subject matter and making it relevant to the student, the society, and the other fields of knowledge.

In studying each of the four classes, and then giving brief attention to the various disciplines within each class, the attempt will be made to identify the elements of content, structure, and inquiry method inherent in the disciplines, although authoritative statements on this subject are often lacking or still in the process of development. To set the stage for these discussions, the definitions of the disciplinary components we have identified should perhaps be repeated. The *content* of a discipline is usually understood to mean the data and factual information which are combined in a logical and natural way to form the *structure*. The structure may be described as a combination of basic concepts and generalizations. The *method of inquiry* refers to a discipline's particular approaches, tools, and methods for discovering and ordering information.

CHAPTER 7

MATHEMATICS

We will begin our discussion of the disciplines with mathematics, primarily because mathematics is more easily seen to logically fit into the mold of a "discipline" that we have described in previous chapters. The elements of mathematics—its content, structure, and methods of inquiry—are more readily apparent than may be the case for the other disciplines, perhaps because it is the most "logical" of the fields of knowledge.

Although the term "mathematics" may have a rather common meaning for most of us, it may be well to start out by attempting to establish a common understanding of the word. Many who have been subjected to the typical high school and college mathematics courses probably see it as ordinary arithmetic with its set rules for computation. Some think of algebra, and may remember it as a collection of special procedures which, by some sort of magic, can be used to get the answer in the book. Others recall geometry, having perhaps been impressed with the idea that it is a mysterious subject full of theorems to memorize and outrageous tricks by means of which we may prove the truth of perfectly obvious relationships in nature. These kinds of concepts may contain some truth, but a more exact and accurate concept is obviously required for an intelligent examination of mathematics as a discipline.

Perhaps we may begin the process of reaching a somewhat common understanding of mathematics by saying that mathematics is a creation of the human mind, concerned primarily with ideas, processes, and reasoning. It is more than the science of numbers and computation (arithmetic); more than the language of symbols and relations (algebra); more than the study of shapes and sizes and space (geometry); and more than trigonometry used to measure distances to stars and to analyze oscillations. It includes statistics (interpretation of data and graphs) and the study of change, infinity, and limits (calculus), but mathematics is also more than what is found in these areas of learning. It is even more than a combination of all these elements.

How, then, may we describe or define mathematics most accurately? Johnson and Rising suggest that mathematics should be thought of as follows:

169

1. *Mathematics is a way of thinking.* It is a way of organizing one's attempts to solve a problem or reach a logical conclusion. It may be used to solve problems in all areas of living and gives insight into the power of the human mind.

2. *Mathematics is a language—a means of communication.* It is a language that uses carefully defined terms and concise symbolic representations to add precision to communication. Mathematics uses a language of ideograms (symbols for ideas) which may be understood by a mathematician of any nationality with clarity and conciseness far beyond any language using phonograms (symbols for sounds). The language of mathematics allows us to perform computations, solve problems, and complete proofs that would be impossible, or at least very difficult, in any natural language.

3. *Mathematics is an organized structure of knowledge.* Each proposition in mathematics is deduced logically from previously proved propositions or assumptions. Fundamental terms, such as *point, line,* and *plane* in geometry, are used to describe essential ideas. Assumptions (called axioms, postulates, properties, or laws) are made about these ideas or operations, and then these assumptions are used to prove theorems.

4. *Mathematics is the study of patterns.* Any kind of regularity in form or idea—radio waves, molecular structures, orbits of celestial bodies, or shapes in nature such as a bee's cell—has a pattern that can be studied mathematically.

5. *Mathematics is an art.* As with any type of art, mathematics is concerned with the maximum expression of ideas and relations with the greatest economy of means. Its beauty can be seen in the organization of a chaos of isolated facts into a logical and understandable order.[1]

History of Mathematics Education in the United States

Mathematics, along with other areas of instruction, has undergone considerable change since its first introduction into American education. The need for mathematics in the early frontier days was rather limited, and consequently, educational efforts in this direction were meager. The common farmer or worker needed little beyond the ability to add, subtract, and multiply. Boys aspiring to a trade needed some knowledge of simple computation, common measure, a few simple fractions, and the use of English and other European moneys. Seafaring men needed to know the basic principles of navigation, clergymen might use astronomy in fixing the dates of religious festivals, and public officials employed surveying skills. From these basic skills came the mathematical instruction in colonial America. Knowing this, it is easy to understand why mathematics received little attention in early elementary schools. Primary emphasis was given

---

[1]Adapted from Donovan A. Johnson and Gerald R. Rising, *Guidelines for Teaching Mathematics* (Belmont, Calif.: Wadsworth, 1967), pp. 4–5.

to reading and writing, with occasional attention to "ciphering," which was little more than the simplest of computations.

It was not until near the beginning of the nineteenth century that mathematics began to receive more attention in American schools, partially due to the rise of commercial interests. The subject matter was logical in its arrangement and unchanging in its presentation to pupils. It consisted primarily of a series of rules to be memorized and applied dogmatically according to rather definite classifications as to type of problem. Few textbooks were available, so the master dictated the problems to be solved and stated the rule or rules to be used. Rote memorization of rules was emphasized, with little concern for understanding of concepts or the significant characteristics of effective reasoning.

Mental discipline assumed a prominent role in early mathematics instruction. The prevailing philosophy of textbook writers and teachers was expressed in typical fashion by Joseph Ray.

> The object of the study of mathematics is twofold—the acquisition of useful knowledge and the cultivation and discipline of the mental powers. A parent often inquires "Why should my son study mathematics? I do not expect him to be a surveyor, an engineer, or an astronomer." Yet the parent is very desirous that his son should be able to reason correctly, and to exercise, in all his relations in life, the energies of a cultivated and disciplined mind. This is, indeed, of more value than the mere attainment of any branch of knowledge.[2]

It is not difficult to see evidence of this philosophy among some teachers of mathematics to this day, even though its validity has been largely discredited.

Discontent and Change

With the growth and development of the public high school during the late 1800's came criticism of the often unplanned and unorganized expansion of course offerings. This criticism extended to mathematics instruction, with colleges and mathematics teachers themselves expressing concern over the lack of student accomplishment in mathematics. Businessmen often doubted the usefulness of typical high school mathematics instruction.

The Committee of Ten on Secondary School Subjects, which was established to study and make recommendations concerning improvement of high school offerings, included in its 1894 report several suggestions relative to mathematics. It was recommended that a course in concrete geometry, with numerous exercises, be introduced at the seventh- or eighth-grade level; that the formal study of algebra begin in the ninth grade and continue in the tenth grade, along with a parallel course in deductive geometry; that this parallel study of algebra and geometry extend through the eleventh grade; that those who did not plan on going to college should study bookkeeping and the technical parts of arith-

[2]Joseph Ray, *New Elementary Algebra* (New York: American Book, 1848), p. iii.

metic after the ninth-grade algebra course; and that a course in trigonometry and advanced algebra be offered to boys who were going into the natural sciences or technical colleges. The suggestion was made that algebra and geometry be taught in parallel fashion so as to encourage coordinated teaching and to improve student understanding of mathematical relationships. With the exception of the parallel teaching of algebra and geometry, these recommendations were largely carried out in the schools as the twentieth century began.[3]

Numerous committees and study groups were activated in the years that followed, but for the most part their efforts had little effect on typical school practice. Perhaps the most influential was the National Committee on Mathematical Requirements, which suggested in 1923 that some of the mathematical studies be moved down to accommodate the junior high school movement, with appropriate adaptations. This group also favored the provision of more elective mathematics courses for students who successfully completed the junior high school requirements.

Mid-Century Developments

As the second half of the twentieth century began, the typical secondary school mathematics program included the following:

Grades 7 and 8: arithmetic and general mathematics
Grade 9: elementary algebra or general mathematics
Grade 10: plane geometry (elective)
Grade 11: intermediate algebra (elective)
Grade 12: solid geometry and plane trigonometry (elective)

Beginning with grade 10, enrollment in mathematics dropped sharply, as only about one-third of the students were enrolled in geometry at this level. This enrollment continued to drop until at grade 12 only about five percent of the students took mathematics.[4]

This state of high school mathematics instruction was not considered satisfactory by many individuals and groups. Criticisms such as the following were common:

> Not enough students were studying enough mathematics. (Twenty states required no mathematics for graduation.)
> The superior student was neglected. (In general, he was taught the same mathematics at the same rate as the average student.)
> Teachers placed excessive emphasis on manipulation and memory and gave inadequate attention to meaning and understanding.
> General mathematics became a dumping ground for those who could not learn algebra.

[3] *Report of the Committee of Ten on Secondary School Subjects* (New York: American Book, 1894), pp. 105–116.

[4] A concise, but adequate, description of the content commonly found in these courses may be found in John J. Kinsella, *Secondary School Mathematics* (New York: Center for Applied Research in Education, 1965), pp. 3–9.

High school algebra was taught as a series of numerous mechanical operations, instead of being organized into a small number of large concepts.

Mathematical proof was confined to geometry. Very few students acquired the notion that the same deductive structure also applied to arithmetic, algebra, and all areas of mathematics.

In most schools there was a lack of coordination among the different mathematics courses.[5]

This kind of criticism, combined with various other forces, brought about a greatly increased demand for change in mathematics education, especially after 1950. Some would date the "new mathematics" movement from the launching of Sputnik I in 1957 and the National Defense Education Act of 1958, but the movement was well under way before those events occurred. It was the result of many forces, some of the most important being:

1. The rapid growth of mathematics during the past one hundred and fifty years.
2. The revolutionary development of science and technology during this century.
3. A growing concern about the neglect of the superior student.
4. The historical tendency for college and university mathematics to move downward to lower grades.
5. A great increase in the collaboration among mathematics teachers at the college and high school levels.
6. An awareness of the great technological and mathematical progress of the USSR.
7. The huge financial support given by the federal government and large foundations to the improvement of mathematics education.
8. The emergence of vigorous and imaginative leadership in mathematics education in various universities and professional organizations.[6]
9. New knowledge about how children learn mathematical ideas.
10. The lack of success of traditional content and method.[7]

The "New" Mathematics Movement

Two characteristics are prominent in changes brought about by the "new" math—a new point of view and a new body of subject matter. A new point of view is evident in the treatment advocated for the portion of traditional subject matter that has been accepted as having valid current educational value. Greater attention is given to basic structure and less attention to mere operational facility. In addition, ways and means have been sought to employ more recently developed concepts and techniques to clarify, simplify, and enrich the presentation of mathematical content.[8]

These two overarching characteristics are evident in the various programs

[5] *Ibid.*, pp. 13–14.
[6] *Ibid.*, p. 15.
[7] Johnson and Rising, *op. cit.*, p. 17.
[8] Charles H. Butler and F. Lynwood Wren, *The Teaching of Secondary Mathematics*, 4th ed. (New York: McGraw-Hill, 1965), p. 55.

developed around the country for the purpose of improving mathematics instruction. Although operating independently and with varying specific purposes, several features are somewhat common among them:

1. A revision of subject matter to eliminate those topics that are relatively unimportant and to introduce new and more useful content, such as probability theory and statistics.
2. Some shifting of subject matter to lower grades, with earlier introduction of abstract concepts.
3. Emphasis on unifying the entire study of mathematics through better integration of topics and emphasis on its fundamental structures.
4. Use of new language and symbols to refine definitions and facilitate concept formation.
5. A change in teaching method that places more emphasis on the deductive process and upon student thought and discovery, with less reliance on teacher instruction and student memorization.
6. Movement away from emphasis on social applications of little importance.

Even though the modern approaches to mathematics education have now been largely adopted across the country, they have not met with universal approval. There is doubtless both good and bad in both the old and the new in mathematics, and the possible contributions of each to the mathematics programs of our schools must be weighed according to their effectiveness for teaching mathematics in a time when technological and scientific patterns are subject to rapid and drastic change. The major criticisms made of the new programs include the following:

1. The applications of mathematics are largely ignored.
2. The limited attention to practice results in inadequate computational skill.
3. The rigor, precision, and symbolism are too great for a large proportion of secondary school students.
4. The content outlined for each grade is too extensive to be adequately presented in the time available.
5. The general objectives of education for citizenship in our democracy are ignored.
6. There are no adequate courses for the low-ability, noncollege-bound, or culturally deprived students.
7. The emphasis on logic and structure has reduced the mastery of basic concepts and operations.
8. The formality of the presentation has resulted in a loss of interest on the part of many students.
9. The new programs are not effective as preparation for college mathematics.[9]

Some, and perhaps all, of these criticisms are no doubt valid to some degree, and further revision of mathematics education programs should take them into

[9]From *Guidelines for Teaching Mathematics* by Donovan Johnson and Gerald Rising. © 1967 by Wadsworth Publishing Company, Inc., Belmont, California, 94002. Reprinted by permission of the publisher.

consideration. However, most serious students of public education today favor the basic approach of the modern mathematics programs, and there is little doubt that it is here to stay. The "revolution" brought about by modern mathematics programs is continuing, however, as mathematicians, educators, and teachers work to improve the new programs. They realize that the ultimate is still to be reached, especially for the average and noncollege-bound student. Current developments suggest that school mathematics is continuing to change in the following directions:

1. New topics will be introduced at all levels.
2. Topics will continue to be introduced at earlier grade levels.
3. Some topics will be eliminated and others reduced to make room for new topics.
4. The language and symbolism will become more precise and more sophisticated.
5. The emphasis on discovery, intuition, and participation of the learner will lead to the development of new instructional aids.
6. The need for evaluating new programs will stimulate research and the development of new measuring instruments.
7. Programs for the slow learner and the culturally deprived will have major emphasis as a result of criticisms and federal support.
8. The new programs will demand a level of teacher competence in mathematics which will result in higher standards in teacher education and certification.
9. The time and attention devoted to drill and manipulative exercises will be drastically reduced.
10. This last point suggests a major item that needs emphasis. *Very little of the classical, traditional mathematics is being discarded.* Number concepts, computation, measurement, algebra, geometry, trigonometry, and analytical geometry will be included in the programs of the immediate future.[10]

Through all the programs developed to date and in the further developments now under way runs a common thread. New insights and new knowledge about mathematics are being used to provide an opportunity for students to learn mathematics more effectively, more pleasantly, and more meaningfully than has usually been the case in the past. Significant progress has been made in a relatively short time, and doubtless we can look forward to even more valuable progress in the future.

Objectives of Mathematics Education

To support arguments for inclusion of mathematics in the school curriculum there must be presented some generally acceptable purposes for its study. For many years, and still to some extent today, the cardinal virtue of mathematical

---

[10]From *Guidelines for Teaching Mathematics* by Donovan Johnson and Gerald Rising. © 1967 by Wadsworth Publishing Company, Inc., Belmont, California 94002. Reprinted by permission of the publisher.

training was alleged to be its role in the development of mental power and facility through "mental discipline." This theory proposes that subject matter is useful in mental training to the extent that it builds the mind through strenuous mental exercise. The gain in mental capacity can then be "transferred" to other situations and problems in other areas. As late as 1956, we see this viewpoint expressed in a UNESCO study which indicated that two-thirds of the sixty-two countries replying to a questionnaire considered mathematics a means of developing the "power of abstraction" and an ability for "logical thinking."[11]

Mental discipline theories have been largely disproved by modern psychology, but the idea does seem to have some value. Logical habits of thought developed in mathematics training can be transferred to a limited extent to other subjects, but only if the possibilities for this transfer are shown to students.

If mental discipline cannot be supported as a prime reason for mathematics study, then what are its purposes? Answers to this question may be suggested from three directions: the liberal arts or cultural aspect; the propaedeutic or preparatory aspect; and the service or practical aspect.

The liberal arts aspect comes from the need for a civilized and educated human being today to know at least as much about mathematics as he does about other cultural subjects and to be able to communicate in mathematics at a comparable level. He needs an appreciation of the power of mathematics and of the role it has played in history through its impact on science, industry, and philosophy.

The propaedeutic aspect stems from the fact that mathematics at one level of understanding is required before a person may develop understanding at a higher level. Mathematics is a countinuing experience, and one phase or "branch" leads to another.

The service aspect is obvious in everyday demonstrations of the need for mathematics of various types in daily life. It is also demonstrated in the use of mathematics to gain a better understanding of the natural sciences, social sciences, engineering, and other areas of learning.[12]

Mathematics for General Education

It is generally recognized that there has been much progress in improving the mathematics curriculum in recent years, but many educators question whether this has been to the general benefit of all students or primarily for the future mathematician, engineer, physicist, or statistician. Mathematics for general education has been almost entirely limited to the junior high school, with

---

[11]Nineteenth International Conference on Public Education, *Teaching of Mathematics in Secondary Schools* (Geneva: UNESCO, 1956), pp. 21–26.

[12]The Conference Board of the Mathematical Sciences, *The Role of Axiomatics and Problem Solving in Mathematics* (Boston: Ginn, 1966), p. 27; and John J. Kinsella, *Secondary School Mathematics* (New York: Center for Applied Research in Education, 1965), pp. 9–12.

the primary function of high school mathematics study being defined in terms of providing opportunities for the beginning of content specialization and the pursuance of one's aptitudes and special interests.

The idea has been generally accepted that a mathematics program which is good for the mathematically capable students is also appropriate for general education purposes if watered down somewhat. The 80 percent of our students who will not pursue vocations which require extensive knowledge of mathematics have been treated to the same basic mathematics education as the 20 percent minority who need advanced training in mathematics. This practice is being widely questioned by those who are continuing to work toward more improvement of the mathematics curriculum.

General Objectives of Mathematics Education

Objectives for mathematics education are usually stated in terms of content to be mastered and understandings to be gained, and these we will not ignore. However, before getting into a discussion of this type goal, we should perhaps suggest the importance of goals related to positive attitudes about mathematics. The attitude a student develops toward mathematics is the key to his success or failure in its study, and should be given prime consideration by the teacher. Desired student attitudes should include the following:

1. *Appreciation* of the power, elegance, and structure of mathematics.
2. *Curiosity* about matematical ideas.
3. *Confidence* in mathematics.
4. *Loyalty* to mathematics, the mathematics teacher, and classmates.
5. *Enjoyment and satisfaction* in learning mathematical ideas.
6. *Respect* for excellence in mathematical achievement by himself and others.
7. *Optimism and cheerfulness* about one's progress in mathematics.[13]

Attitudes such as these can be best developed through a modern approach to mathematics education, one which stresses principles and uses of mathematics rather than looking for (or being shown) a trick to solve a particular type of exercise which is then practiced until thoroughly memorized. In following this approach, mathematics education is consistent with the recent developments in research mathematics which place greater stress on the study of mathematical structure and the role of axioms and definitions. This has been accompanied by more use of logic and more emphasis on the foundations of mathematics and the interrelations between various branches of mathematics. The modern emphasis in mathematics education thus points out that the true essence of mathematics lies in logic, decision making, and systematic search for the underlying structure of any given system or situation. Whereas instruction in mathematics formerly tended toward the search for the solutions of various types of quantitative problems as they arose, the emphasis is now on the search for underlying principles

[13]Johnson and Rising, *op. cit.*, p. 130.

and basic structure as guides to fundamental change.[14]

In attempting to identify mathematics education goals consistent with both the needs of society and the needs of students, various commissions and committees have suggested statements of purpose. One of the more widely accepted statements suggests that the high school program in mathematics should:

1. Provide "the foundations upon which applications to the sciences, engineering, and mathematics itself are built."

2. Allow opportunity for students to become informed in those areas of mathematics which "have become part of what every person should know in order to understand the complex world in which he lives."

3. Give students who do not continue their mathematics program beyond minimum levels some opportunity to develop an understanding and appreciation of the structure and usefulness of mathematics.[15]

A complementary statement, which looks at mathematics education from the perspective of student needs in relation to his society, suggests the following as a basis for identifying mathematical goals:

1. The student needs to know how mathematics contributes to his understanding of natural phenomena.

2. He needs to understand how he can use mathematical methods to investigate, interpret, and make decisions in human affairs.

3. He needs to understand how mathematics, as a science and as an art, contributes to our cultural heritage.

4. He needs to prepare for a vocation in which he utilizes mathematics as a producer and consumer of products, services, and art.

5. He needs to learn to communicate mathematical ideas correctly and clearly to others.[16]

With goals such as these clearly in mind, mathematics teachers and educational leaders can develop programs at the various levels and for more specific purposes that will be much more likely to meet the mathematics needs of students today and adults in the future. The more specific goals and content definitions will be discussed in the following section on the content of the mathematics disciplines appropriate for secondary school programs.

Content

Although mathematics is one of the oldest of man's studies and much of its basic content material long established, recent years have seen its content dramatically revised and expanded. Especially with the "modern" mathematics programs, this revision and expansion have been obvious in the changing pat-

---

[14]Stephen S. Willoughby, *Contemporary Teaching of Secondary School Mathematics* (New York: Wiley, 1967), pp. 32–33.

[15]Adapted from Cambridge Conference on School Mathematics, *Goals For School Mathematics* (Boston: Houghton, 1963).

[16]Johnson and Rising, *op. cit.*, p. 11.

terns of content included in the mathematics curriculum.

Changes in the mathematics content deemed appropriate for instruction in the public schools can be readily observed without going very far back into the past. In 1940, under sponsorship of the major mathematics professional organizations of that time, a commission set up a tentative list of principles and materials as a guide to mathematics instruction in the United States. This statement suggested that mathematics instruction should include the fields of numbers and computation, geometric form and space perception, graphic representation, elementary analysis, logical thinking, relational thinking, and symbolic representation and thinking.[17] Following World War II, several other statements and recommendations were made by various professional groups, resulting in a rather generally accepted content for mathematics education across the country.

At the junior high school level, general mathematics formed the basis for mathematics education, including in the field of arithmetic the ability to:

1. Perform operations involving whole numbers, fractions, decimals, and percentages.
2. Read and interpret numerical tables.
3. Estimate and approximate numerical results.
4. Apply arithmetic to problems of the consumer and citizen.
5. Use ratios.
6. Use and interpret means, medians, and modes.
7. Construct and interpret graphs.

Algebra for general mathematics study at this level was designed to enable students to:

1. Understand and use simple symbols.
2. Write and evaluate formulas.
3. Understand and use positive and negative numbers.
4. Solve simple equations, including proportions.
5. Solve simple verbal problems by means of equations.

General mathematics also was given the responsibility of teaching students geometry and trigonometry to the extent that they could:

1. Identify and sketch basic two- and three-dimensional figures.
2. Perform important constructions with rulers and compasses.
3. Measure with rulers, protractors, squared paper, calipers, and micrometers.
4. Recognize similar polygons and construct scale drawings.
5. Understand and apply the Pythagorean theorem.
6. Obtain the resultant of two vectors.
7. Use the sine, cosine, and tangent in solving problems involving right triangles.

At the ninth-grade level, elementary algebra was the usual course of study, with the following standard topics:

[17]Joint Commission of the Mathematical Association of America, Inc., and the National Council of Teachers of Mathematics, *The Place of Mathematics in Secondary Education*, Fifteenth Yearbook (Washington, D.C.: National Council of Teachers of Mathematics, 1940), p. 61.

1. Simple equations and formulas.
2. The study of dependence through tables, graphs, and formulas.
3. The meaning and use of directed numbers.
4. Operations on monomials and polynomials.
5. Systems of linear equations in two unknowns.
6. Special products of binomials and the factoring of binomials and trinomials.
7. Operations on fractional expressions.
8. Equations involving fractional expressions in one unknown.
9. Ratio, proportion, and variation.
10. Indirect measurement and numerical trigonometry of the right triangle.
11. Powers, roots, and operations on radical expressions.
12. The quadratic equation.
13. The solution of verbal problems.

The mathematics course for grade 10 was almost universally plane geometry, with deductive proof as the major theme. The major topics were:

1. Review of junior high school geometry.
2. Perpendicular and parallel lines.
3. Properties of quadrilaterals.
4. Congruence of triangles.
5. Inequalities in triangles and circles.
6. Properties of line segments and angles in circles.
7. Angles and areas of polygons.
8. Properties of similar polygons.
9. Properties of regular polygons.
10. Measurement of the circle.

At the eleventh- and twelfth-grade levels, mathematics study typically included intermediate algebra, plane trigonometry, solid geometry, and advanced algebra. The topics studied followed. a similar pattern across the country.

Intermediate algebra:

1. Review of elementary algebra.
2. Factoring, graphs, and systems of linear and quadratic equations.
3. The theory of quadratic equations.
4. Fractional and negative exponents.
5. Irrational equations.
6. Logarithms.
7. Exponential equations.
8. The binomial theorem.

Plane trigonometry:

1. Definitions and use of the six functions.
2. Reduction formulas for angles greater than a right angle, and for negative angles.
3. Basic identities: e.g., reciprocal, Pythagorean, and complementary.
4. Formulas for the sum and difference of angles, the double angle, and the half angle.
5. Laws of sines, cosines, and tangents.

6. Trigonemtric identities and trigonometric equations.
7. Applications to surveying and navigation.

Solid geometry:

1. Theorems dealing with lines and planes, and with dihedral and trihedral angles.
2. Mensuration of the prism, pyramid, and frustrum.
3. Mensuration of the cylinder, cone, frustrum, sphere, and spherical triangle.
4. Notions of limit with respect to (3), or Cavalieri's theorem as an alternate.
5. Spherical geometry.
6. Similar solids.

Advanced algebra:

1. Complex numbers and De Moivre's theorem.
2. The linear function, including the concepts of slope and intercept as well as the distance formula.
3. Determinants and systems of linear equations.
4. Theory of equations (including the factor and remainder theorems, relations between roots and coefficients, transformations of equations, character of roots, Descartes' rule of signs, location of roots by graphs and other methods: e.g., Horner's).
5. Permutations, combinations, and probability.
6. Sequences and series, including arithmetic and geometric progressions.
7. Mathematical induction.[18]

Although modern mathematics does not utilize a "new" content so much as it does a new emphasis on structure, there are many new topics, such as probability and statistical inference, algebraic inequalities, linear algebra, vectors, and the use of set language. Much more attention is given to such basic concepts as relation, function, and mathematical systems. More precise terminology and definition, the nature and techniques of induction and deduction, and the construction of mathematical models give additional dimensions to the traditional content, while much less attention is given to the learning of rules, manipulation of formulas and equations, development of computational skills, and the measurement of geometric configurations.

The newer mathematics programs draw upon several areas of mathematics knowledge, including those which are more traditional and some which are not, as noted above, and although each program may be somewhat different in terms of scope, sequence, and means of presentation, there is a common thread of

[18]Adapted from John J. Kinsella, *Secondary School Mathematics* (New York: Center for Applied Research in Education, Inc., 1965), pp. 4–9. From National Council of Teachers of Mathematics, *The Place of Mathematics in Secondary Education*, Fifteenth Yearbook (New York: Bureau of Publications, Teachers College, Columbia University, 1940); Commission on Postwar Plans, "The Second Report of the Commission on Postwar Plans," *The Mathematics Teacher*, 38 (1945); and National Committee on Mathematical Requirements, *The Reorganization of Mathematics in Secondary Education* (Boston: Houghton, 1923).

content material running through all of them. This common content may be briefly identified within each general area of mathematics study as follows.

Arithmetic

Arithmetic may be viewed as more a skill and tool area of study than one of basic content, but much of the more basic study in mathematics is usually identified by this term. It includes:

1. Fundamental arithmetical operations—addition, subtraction, multiplication, and division.
2. Numeration, including whole numbers and fractions (common and decimal).
3. Place value in the decimal system and other systems (particularly the binary).
4. Arithmetic mean.
5. Square root, including methods of approximating square roots of whole numbers.
6. Measurement, including English and metric systems, geometric measurements, use of ruler and protractor, indirect measurements of lengths, areas, volumes, etc.
7. Ratio and percent, making comparisons and scale drawings.
8. Application of correct computation to the solution to genuine problems.
9. Scientific (standard) notation.
10. Estimating.
11. Use of the slide rule.[19]

Algebra

In the modern mathematics programs algebra seems to be assuming the task of common denominator and means of coordination for concepts from the various fields of mathematics. Because it includes such a large field of knowledge, we will not attempt to be exhaustive in outlining the major content material which may be drawn from algebra. Some of the more useful at the secondary school level includes:

1. Set language to describe collections of numbers, and the number line.
2. Algebraic symbols and language.
3. Variables.
4. Equations and inequalities.
5. The properties of commutativity, associativity, distributiveness, inverseness, and identities.
6. Algebraic transformations and manipulations in accordance with the structural properties listed in (5).

[19]Adapted from Charles H. Butler and F. Lynwood Wren, *The Teaching of Secondary Mathematics*, 4th ed. (New York: McGraw-Hill, 1965), pp. 88–89, 251–311.

7. Real numbers.
8. Positive and negative numbers.
9. Polynomial expressions.
10. Rational (fractional) expressions.
11. Factors and exponents.
12. Radicals.
13. Truth sets of open sentences.
14. Functions and relations.
15. Permutations, combinations, and the binomial theorem.
16. Algebraic structures.
17. Fields.
18. Groups.
19. Transformation and composition.
20. Matrix algebra.
21. Vectors.
22. Complex numbers.[20]

Geometry

Geometry has been considered one of the most important subjects in the education of an intelligent man for centuries. Developed by Euclid in 300 B.C., it has changed little since that time. This ability to last through the ages is due to the practical value of this type of study, and more importantly, to its value in teaching a system of reasoning and problem solving. Euclid's geometry was the first systematic treatment of axioms and initiated the procedure of deducing conclusions from premises. Geometry is thus the prototype of a major trend in civilized thought.

Traditional geometry programs have introduced simple geometrical ideas in the elementary school, including formulas for areas and volume. Euclidean plane geometry in the tenth grade and solid geometry in the twelfth grade have been almost universal. Recent proposals and programs for improving the study of geometry in the schools have tended to emphasize the need for attention to geometry outside the Euclidean system. Better articulation of geometry in other mathematics study and the introduction of more advanced geometric concepts have also been characteristic of newer programs.

Content areas for study in geometry include plane, solid, spherical, coordinate, and analytic geometry in both Euclidean and non-Euclidean forms. Modern mathematics programs commonly include the following types of content from geometry:

1. Deductive reasoning.
2. Relationships among geometric elements, such as parallel, perpendicular, intersecting, and oblique lines.

[20]Adapted from Kinsella, *Secondary School Mathematics*, pp. 41–67.

3. Basic postulates and assumptions.
4. Pythagorean and other geometric theorems leading to it.
5. Nonmetric geometry: points, lines, planes, and the relations between them; line segments, rays, angles, triangles.
6. Coordinate geometry: location of points by coordinates; length and slope of a line segment; division of a segment in a given ratio; equation of a line; equation of a circle.
7. Polygons.
8. Polyhedrons: cube, pyramid, prism, etc.
9. Geometric inequalities.
10. Cone, sphere, cylinder.
11. Perpendicular lines and planes.
12. Parallel lines and planes.
13. Loci and constructions.
14. Volumes of solids.
15. Congruence.
16. Cavalieri's theorem.
17. Geometric transformations, such as reflections, rotations, and translations.
18. Graphing.
19. Analytic geometry: loci, straight line, parameters, circle, conic sections, polar coordinates, parametric equations, etc.

Trigonometry

Trigonometry means the science of measuring a triangle, and it was invented for the purpose of measuring inaccessible distances such as heights of mountains and widths of rivers by measuring other distances and angles and then using the formulas of trigonometry. Important applications were also made to astronomy and celestial navigation. The lengthy computations required with arithmetic led to the use of logarithms. Theories developed by mathematicians in studying trigonometry are also used in calculus and other branches of higher mathematics.

Traditional trigonometry courses have emphasized the trigonometric functions, using them to solve right and oblique triangles by means of logarithms. Today there is less emphasis on the solution of triangles and more importance is being attached to the analytic aspects of the subject, such as the variation, graphs, and composition of the trigonometric functions, the inverse functions, proofs of identities, solution of trigonometric equations, polar coordinates and complex numbers in trigonometric form, and a trigonometry of numbers and circular functions. Ideas and procedures of arithmetic, elementary algebra, and geometry form an important part of the content of trigonometry, and by synthesizing these with a few new ideas, concepts, and relations are opened up beyond the scope of earlier courses.[21]

Calculus

Since the turn of the century, various leaders in mathematics education have advocated that elements of the calculus be introduced in senior high school mathematics. There has been no intent to make this experience equivalent to college courses in calculus, but only to provide an introduction to some of the basic ideas and content of this field of mathematics.

Recommendations for the study of calculus are related primarily to a study of rates of change. All things in nature change, and elementary calculus is concerned with questions about how much they change in a given time, how fast they change, whether they increase or decrease, when a changing quantity becomes largest or smallest, and how to compare rates of changing quantities. The calculus of the algebraic polynomial, including ideas of limit, of slope, and of velocity, serve to give an outlook upon the field of mechanics and other exact sciences and provide valuable training in understanding and analyzing quantitative relations.[22]

Appropriate content for a course involving calculus has been suggested as follows:

> The work should include:
> (a) The general notion of a derivative as a limit indispensable for the accurate expression of such fundamental quantities as velocity of a moving body or slope of a curve.
> (b) Applications of derivatives to easy problems in rates and in maxima and minima.
> (c) Simple cases of inverse problems; e.g., finding distance from velocity, etc.
> (d) Approximate methods of summation leading up to integration as a powerful method of summation.
> (e) Applications to simple cases of motion, area, volume, and pressure.
> Work in the calculus should be largely graphic and may be closely related to that in physics; the necessary technique should be reduced to a minimum by basing it wholly or mainly on algebraic polynomials. No formal study of analytic geometry need be presupposed beyond the plotting of simple graphs.[23]

Other Content Areas

To "learn to think" is the most common answer given when students ask why they should study mathematics. Seldom, however, do mathematics teachers actually spend very much time in teaching students the elements of correct

---

[21]Adapted from Carl B. Allendoerfer, *Mathematics for Parents* (New York: Macmillan, 1965), p. 130; Butler and Wren, *op. cit.*, pp. 96, 502, 512.

[22]Report of the National Committee on Mathematical Requirements, *The Reorganization of Mathematics in Secondary Education* (Boston: Houghton, 1923), pp. 57–59.

[23]*Ibid.*, pp. 54–55.

reasoning, or logic. It certainly seems that this should provide a content area appropriate for study in mathematics.

Logic is usually thought of as "the construction of acceptable arguments or proofs." In a more formal sense, proof "is supposed to show that if certain assumptions are accepted, certain conclusions must follow." A proof is thus generally presented in such a way that if we know that one step is true, we are sure that the next step is true, and so on. The *rules of inference* provide the key approaches to this process. Forms of proof include the direct, the indirect, and the contrapositive. These content areas, along with the study of exact wording, variables for statements, and symbols for the various operations provide the basis for the study of logic in secondary school mathematics.[24]

Probability forms another appropriate content area for secondary school mathematics study. It is of interest to people of all ages and is one of the most respected and useful branches of mathematics, particularly in science and insurance. Simply stated, this type of study attempts to make a reasonably intelligent guess and have some idea about the likelihood of its coming true. There is some danger that students may misuse this knowledge through games of chance, but the value to be gained far outweighs this risk.

To help both the potential producer and consumer of statistical reports, mathematics study should include at least the basic concepts from statistics, along with the study of probability. Such study should include both the arithmetical caclulations involved and an understanding of how they can be used to interpret (or misinterpret) data.

Measures of central tendency (mean, median, mode) are basic to understanding of statistics. Also appropriate for study at the secondary school level are topics related to variability and reliability (range, deviation, dispersion, standard deviation, Chebyshev's theorem, standard error, etc.). Pictorial presentations of statistical information provide another useful and important area of content for study.[25]

Structure

Mathematics probably has more obvious structure than any of the other disciplines. In fact, the mathematician's basic purpose is to show how a whole set of seemingly diverse problems have a common form (structure) imposed upon them.

Mathematicians begin with certain undefined terms, such as point, line, and plane in geometry, and use them to describe essential ideas. Assumptions—called axioms, postulates, properties, or laws—are made about these ideas or operations. The terms and assumptions are then used to prove theorems (a type of generalization). In other words, each "branch" of mathematics is based upon:

[24]Willoughby, *op. cit.*, pp. 193–209.
[25]*Ibid.*, pp. 169–170, 358–379.

1. Undefined terms, chosen by the mathematician.
2. Definitions, chosen by the mathematician.
3. Postulates, chosen by the mathematician.
4. Theorems.
5. An underlying system of logic, chosen by the mathematician.

Thus theorems are not chosen by the mathematician and are not under his control. Once the other four items have been agreed upon, a theory is either true or false, regardless of the mathematician.[26]

Concepts, as we are using the term, include in mathematics the undefined terms and also some of the definitions and postulates referred to above. Generalizations may be in the form of definitions, postulates, or theorems, although in most cases we would think of a generalization in mathematics as being somewhat synonymous with a theorem. Some of the more common concepts and generalizations used by mathematicians will be identified as examples of these structural elements of mathematics.

Concepts

A concept has been defined in mathematics as "a mental abstraction of common properties of a set of experiences or phenomena."[27] This definition fits very well with the general idea of a concept which we have been using throughout this book, and may be exemplified in each of the various branches of mathematics. Fundamental concepts which run through all branches of mathematics include set, function, binary operation, field, factor, group, algorithm, and deduction. Particularly in arithmetic and algebra, the following are commonly accepted concepts of importance:

additive inverse	exponent
associative property	factor
cancellation law	fraction
closure	group
commutative property	inclusion
complementation	independence
congruent	inequalities
constant	integer
dependence	integral domain
distributive property	intersection
equation	literal symbols
evaluation	number
numeral	union
rational numbers	uniqueness
real numbers	unity

---

[26]The Conference Board of the Mathematical Sciences, *The Role of Axiomatics and Problem Solving in Mathematics* (Boston: Ginn, 1966), p. 28.

[27]Johnson and Rising, *op. cit.*, p. 47.

relation	universal set
subset	variable
substitution	vector
truth set	zero

Although not necessarily confined to only that branch of mathematics, geometry includes concepts such as:

angle	parallel
Cartesian plane	perpendicular
Cartesian product	point
circle	polygon
collinear points	prism
cone	projections
congruence	pyramid
coordinates	quadrant
coplanar	ray
cylinder	relation
dihedral angle	segment
end points	similarity
intersection	skew lines
line	sphere
locus	triangle
ordered pairs	Venn diagram

Trigonometry naturally is concerned primarily with concepts related to angles and triangles and their measurement. Included are concepts such as angle of elevation, angle of depression, cosine, general angle, polar coordinates, radian, ratio, similar figures, sine, and tangent.

Calculus utilizes several concepts from the other branches of mathematics, and also others which are somewhat unique to calculus, such as:

acceleration	limits
constant	maxima
continuity	minima
derivative	parameter
increment	rate of change
infinitesimal	slope
integral	velocity

It has been pointed out that in the field of mathematics there are basically four types of concepts. These are as follows (with examples):

1. Set concepts (involve objects)—"A number is the common property of equivalent sets."
2. Operational concepts (involve actions)—"Addition is the common property of the union of disjoint sets."
3. Relational concepts (involve comparisons)—"Equality is the common property of the number of elements of equivalent sets."

4. Structural concepts (involve organizations)—"Closure is the common property of a mathematical group."[28]

Generalizations

In mathematics, generalizations may be expressed with words in similar fashion to other disciplines, but they are often given as equations or theorems expressed with algebraic or other notation. The way concepts are taught and then woven into generalizations is indicated in the following example, as the concept of "set" is explained and then used in a generalized statement.

A set of anything is a collection of elements having some characteristic coherence. Some examples of sets are a swarm of bees, a flock of sheep, a covey of quail, a set of dishes, all the positive integers, the rational numbers, the points of a line, or the points of a plane. Equivalence, or one to one correspondence between elements, is thus a basic relation existing between sets.[29]

Generalizations in mathematics are often expressed as "principles" or "laws." A basic principle of addition states that "addition should be used only for combining groups of like things." A principle for the addition of fractions with unlike denominators is: "If the denominators are not alike, make them alike; change the given fractions into new fractions whose values are identical with those of the original fractions but whose forms are changed in such a way that they will all have the same denominator." A principle for the reduction of fractions and raising to higher terms states that "the value of a fraction remains unchanged if its numerator and denominator are multiplied or divided by the same quantity." Similar principles govern the multiplication and division of fractions.[30]

A good example of how generalizations are used in mathematics may be taken from the commutative, associative and distributive laws. These "laws" or generalizations may be expressed either in words or by using algebraic notation in the following manner.

1. Addition or multiplication can be carried on in either order without changing the results:
   (a) Commutative law (addition): For all numbers, a, b, $a + b = b + a$.
   (b) Commutative law (multiplication): For all numbers, a, b, $a \times b = b \times a$.
2. When adding (or multiplying) three numbers, the results will be the same if the third is added to (multiplied by) the sum (or product) of the first two, or if the sum (product) of the last two is added to (multiplied by) the first:
   (a) Associative law (addition): For all numbers, a, b, c, $a + (b + c) = (a + b) + c$.

[28]Adapted from Johnson and Rising, *Guidelines for Teaching Mathematics*, p. 47.
[29]Butler and Wren, *op. cit.*, pp. 61–62.
[30]*Ibid.*, pp. 362–367.

(b) Associative law (multiplication): For all numbers, $a, b, c, a \times (b \times c) = (a \times b) \times c$.
3. The product of a number and the sum of two others is equal to the sum of the products obtained by multiplying the first by each of the others:
Distributive law (multiplication over addition): For all numbers, $a, b, c, a \times (b + c) = (a \times b) + (a \times c)$.

The difficulty of expressing generalizations such as these in words illustrates the advantages of algebraic notation.[31]

From algebra we may take another illustration of how concepts are woven into generalizations to form principles for use in solving mathematical problems. The fundamental operational axioms (generalizations) involved in the solution of linear equations are:

1. If equals are added to equals, the results are equal.
2. If equals are subtracted from equals, the results are equal.
3. If equals are multiplied by equals, the results are equal.
4. If equals are divided by equals other than zero, the results are equal.[32]

Geometry has traditionally been organized around assumptions and theorems, which are simply two types of generalizations, one of which is accepted without question and the other subject to proof. The sequence of basic theorems suggested by the Commission on Mathematics of the College Entrance Examination Board clearly illustrates the use of assumptions and theorems in teaching geometry.

Theorem 1. The base angles of a triangle are equal if and only if the triangle is isosceles.
Theorem 2. An exterior angle of a triangle is greater than either remote interior angle.
Theorem 3. Two lines are parallel if and only if a transversal makes a pair of alternate interior angles equal.
Theorem 4. The sum of the interior angles of a triangle equals two right angles.
Assumption. A line is parallel to the base of a triangle if and only if it divides the other two sides into proportional segments.
Theorem 5. Two triangles are similar if two angles of one are respectively equal to two angles of the other.
Theorem 6. An altitude drawn to the hypotenuse of a right triangle forms two triangles, each similar to the original.
Theorem 7. A triangle is a right triangle if and only if the square on the largest side is equal to the sum of the squares on the other two sides.[33]

To show how they are used in trigonometry, we may use some generalizations concerning the variation of functions.

[31]Willoughby, *op. cit.*, p. 94.
[32]Butler and Wren, *op. cit.*, p. 326.
[33]*Report of the Commission on Mathematics: Program for College Preparatory Mathematics* (New York: College Entrance Examination Board, 1959), p. 38.

1. There is a general similarity in the shape of the graph of any function and its corresponding cofunction.
2. The functions of sin θ and cos θ are always finite and continuous over the entire domain of values of θ, while for certain values of the other functions become infinite and have points of discontinuity.
3. The sine or cosine of an angle can never be greater than 1 nor less than −1, and the secant and cosecant can never have values between these bounds.[34]

Generalizations from calculus, the logic of mathematics, probability, and statistics also serve to form the structure of the discipline and provide the basis for teaching and learning in these areas of mathematics. Illustrations could be given, but in the interests of brevity we will note only that as the study of mathematics becomes more advanced, the generalizations used become more abstract and difficult.

Methods of Inquiry

The mathematician's overall objective is the production and display of a set of theorems which are established by a "proof" of one kind or another. This "proof" usually takes the form of deductive reasoning, by which an organized, systematic, sequential set of statements lead from definitions, postulates and previous theorems to a conclusion in such a way that, if prior definitions and postualtes are accepted, then the conclusion must be accepted. Proof may take any one or more of various forms, including arithmetic, algebra, informal or formal direct and indirect proof, etc.[35]

Although the deductive process provides the technique for drawing valid conclusions and deriving necessary consequences in mathematics, inductive methods of inquiry are also appropriate. Reasoning from the particular to the general, the student may thus speculate upon his observations of a particular situation and reach his own tentative conclusions. Deductive proof is then used to establish the truth or validity (or lack of it) of propositions reached through induction and speculation. Induction and conjecture may thus be regarded as the creative or inventive implement which leads to discovery.[36]

Teaching Mathematics

Changes in the content and presentation of mathematics in the secondary schools have been substantial during the past decade, but the success of the mathematics program still depends upon the quality of the teaching. No program

[34]Butler and Wren, op. cit., pp. 519–520.
[35]Irving Allen Dodes, "Mathematics: Its Structure, Logic and Method," Conference Board of the Mathematical Sciences, The Role of Axiomatics and Problem Solving in Mathematics (Boston: Ginn, 1966), p. 33.
[36]Butler and Wren, op. cit., pp. 70–82.

or organizational innovation can achieve success without this essential ingredient. Students must be brought to the point of learning the various meanings, understandings, and skills, along with the capacity to apply them. Particularly at the point of application, student attitudes and appreciations become crucial, and the development of these is almost entirely dependent upon the quality of teaching which is prevalent. *How* we teach thus again becomes an essential part of *what* we teach. The basic methods of mathematical inquiry are the most important ingredients of mathematics education, and these are taught by example more than as regular content material.

The main purpose of recent changes in mathematics education has been to put emphasis on teaching with understanding in place of rote learning. Good teachers have always done this to some extent, but they were severely handicapped by their lack of training and poor teaching materials. Mathematics study more related to the future lives of nonscientists and nonmathematicians has also been given more emphasis, both through selection of content and through teaching method.

In teaching mathematics, there are four fundamental types of instructional problems. Students must be helped to:

1. Acquire understandings of new concepts and relationships.
2. Strengthen these new understandings so that more than just surface knowledge is developed.
3. Maintain and develop knowledge and understandings they already have.
4. Transfer the use of mathematics understandings and skills to their physical, social, and intellectual environment.[37]

To successfully cope with these problems, the mathematics teacher must select from various instructional strategies those which will best serve the purposes immediately at hand.

In choosing instructional strategies, mathematics teachers need some guidelines. The following suggestions are designed to serve this need.

1. The procedure should be mathematically correct. Only definitions, axioms, and proved theorems previously developed should be used in working with new materials and problems.
2. The procedure should be understandable to the class. Care must be given to assuring that the mathematics being studied and the concepts included are within the grasp of the students and that they understand the things from previous lessons which are needed.
3. A proper learning sequence should be followed. Concrete visual representations should precede and lead to abstract representations, which in turn should lead to generalizations. Each step in the teaching process should rely on a minimum of new concepts, specified conditions, or procedures.

[37]Adapted from Butler and Wren, *The Teaching of Secondary Mathematics*, pp. 133–157.

4. The strategy should provide a satisfying experience for students, rather than a meaningless exercise in manipulation or memorization to complete an assignment.
5. There should be extensive opportunity for future application of the mathematical content and method involved. While some strategies may be more satisfactory mathematically, they may be too sophisticated for the students.[38]

Content Selection

The proliferation of new mathematics programs has made it especially difficult to make decisions concerning the selection of content for the total mathematics program and for specific courses or units. A real danger exists that decisions of this nature will be made on the basis of recency and popularity rather than the needs and interests of specific students. However, such decisions should not be made solely on the basis of value to the student, either. Consideration must also be given to how well the needs of the overall program of secondary education are met, how well the program or content material is adapted to student aptitudes, the potential for stimulation of interest, the level of sophistication of the material, and the relation of the material to student experience.[39]

With these kinds of considerations in mind, a committee of the National Council of Teachers of Mathematics has suggested that the following questions are crucial when decisions about mathematics content selection are to be made.

1. How much emphasis should be placed on the social applications of mathematics?
2. At a particular level, what topics can be most effectively developed and which are most appropriate?
3. What emphasis should be placed on the study of mathematical structures?
4. How rapidly should the student be led from the use of the general unsophisticated language of mathematics to the very precise and sophisticated use of it?
5. What is the relative merit of presenting a sequence of activities from which a student may independently come to recognize the desired knowledge as opposed to presenting the knowledge and helping students rationalize it?
6. What relationship should exist in the mathematics programs between the function of developing concepts and that of developing skill in the manipulation of symbols?
7. At what level should proof be introduced and with what degree of rigor?
8. What provisions can be made for evaluating the changes taking place?[40]

At the level of daily provision of experiences for students, other criteria may serve to guide the classroom mathematics teacher:

[38]Adapted from Johnson and Rising, *Guidelines for Teaching Mathematics*, pp. 26–27.
[39]Butler and Wren, *op. cit.*, p. 83.
[40]Don K. Richards, "Curriculum Development at the Local Level," *Bulletin of the National Association of Secondary School Principals* (April, 1968), pp. 38–47.

1. The topic should be a fundamental concept rather than just a technique.
2. Students should play an active role.
3. There should be opportunity for students to make discoveries.
4. The topic or idea should be appropriate for students' needs at their stage of development.
5. The mathematical concept to be studied should have stood the test of time.
6. The idea should be useful or capable of being applied.
7. The topic should be interesting to the learner.
8. The material should contribute to students' growth and development in understanding a body of knowledge making up a branch of mathematics.[41]

Although there are and should be variations among the programs across the country, it can be said with reasonable accuracy that there is a general pattern of content selection and placement in the public school mathematics programs today.

Grades Seven and Eight. Programs at this level are no longer devoted merely to applications of arithmetic. They now include development of a better understanding of arithmetic with considerable emphasis on properties of the rational number system. New treatments of whole numbers, fractions, decimals, percent, measurement, and graphing are not greatly different from those of the past, but most programs now also include some algebraic symbolism, informal geometry, basic concepts about statistics and probability, indirect measurement and numerical trigonometry, introduction to the solution of equations and inequations, and the basics of deduction and proof.

Grade Nine. Algebra continues to be the major emphasis at this level, with primary attention going to the classical topics—directed numbers, graphs of equations, systems of equations, factoring, quadratics, and radicals. More attention is now given to the use of sets and set operations, work with inequalities and systems of inequalities, and an extension of earlier work with deduction and proof.

Grade Ten. At the tenth-grade level, geometry continues its traditional dominance of the mathematics program, although it is still one of the most criticized parts of secondary school mathematics. It is widely recommended, and carried out to some extent, that algebra should be carried over into grade 10 as an integral part of the geometry course. It is also becoming more common to find that various additional areas of mathematics study are being included in the tenth-grade course.

Because all mathematics courses now emphasize proof and mathematical systems, geometry has lost its significance as a course on the logic and structure of mathematics and must justify its existence on additional grounds. It is therefore being proposed that tenth-grade mathematics programs should continue to develop in students an understanding of the basic facts about geometric figures in the plane, while adding things such as an integrated treatment of plane and

---

[41]Adapted from Richards, *Bulletin of the National Association of Secondary School Principals,* pp. 45–46.

solid geometry, non-Euclidean geometries, coordinate geometry, geometric transformations, more intensive study of proof and mathematical structure, an elementary introduction to analytic geometry, and an introduction to imaginative thinking.

Grade Eleven. In the past, the eleventh-grade mathematics program usually consisted of one semester of solid geometry and one semester of trigonometry (largely limited to defining the trigonometric functions and using them to solve right and oblique triangles by means of logarithms). Modern programs tend to be a fusion of intermediate algebra, including logarithms and complex numbers, with numerical trigonometry. Review of earlier topics is followed with more advanced study of these topics and consideration of additional topics, such as polynomial functions, logarithmic and exponential functions, circular functions, and other functions and relations. Trigonometry is retained but the emphasis is on the periodic nature of its functions. More emphasis is given to the relation of trigonometry to vectors and complex numbers, with much less attention given to triangle-solving, applications to surveying and navigation, and laborious computational experience.

Grade Twelve. The programs for students who follow mathematics study through the twelfth grade continue to be of various kinds. Most schools hesitate to introduce a course in calculus at this level, and so for the most part the twelfth-grade program simply continues the study of topics introduced earlier. Some programs include an introduction to differential and integral calculus and analytic geometry. Probability and statistics, with appropriate related study of permutations, combinations, and the binomial theorem, are sometimes also included at this level.

Teaching Inquiry and Structure

The typical traditional approach to teaching mathematics involved first the statement of a rule. Several examples were then given, followed by problems in which the rule was to be applied. Students were expected to memorize the rule, work the problems and then go on to the next rule with its examples and problems. Rarely were they given an idea about reasons behind the rules or shown how they might have invented the rules themselves. Consecutive rules might have had some relationship, but this was not usually explained. At a prescribed time, students were tested over the accumulation of rules and their applications. As the student proceeded through the year, he usually forgot many of the earlier procedures, requiring frequent review and repitition. All too often, the student thus saw mathematics as a collection of rather stupid, isolated tricks which he was supposed to learn by rote.[42]

The discovery method of teaching (through inquiry) is simply a procedure

[42]Carl B. Allendoerfer, *Mathematics for Parents* (New York: Macmillan, 1965), pp. 10–11.

through which the teacher, by posing appropriate problems, encourages pupils to think for themselves and become more independent. For example, students should have some experience in creating their own theorems and trying to prove them. They should be allowed to conjecture false as well as true theorems, and then test them. They should be allowed to try different axiomatic systems to describe the same situation. This is hardly the same approach as the one in which axioms are given to the class by the textbook or the teacher, whereupon true theorems are presented and pupils are asked only to produce valid proofs for theorems they know to be true, by using axioms they believe to be unquestionable truths.

Students should become aware of a concept before being given a name for it. For instance, at the elementary level pupils may search for properties inherent to all numbers in their number system. One may note that it does not make any difference in which order he adds two numbers, thus "discovering" the commutative law for addition. Later, he might discover that the distributive law for multiplication over addition apparently also applies to all the numbers in the number system (for example, $3 \cdot (5 + 8) = 3 \cdot 5 + 3 \cdot 8$). After working with these and other basic properties, the pupil may begin to use them as axioms or assumptions about his system to prove in an informal way that other properties also belong to the number system. He will thus begin to see arithmetic and algebra as basic underlying structural elements rather than as a series of unrelated tricks he is required to memorize and learn to use adeptly.

As teachers ask questions and guide their learning, students begin to think and learn on their own, becoming independent of the teacher. If the questions the teacher asks are too easily answered, however, students will not be required to think and will remain dependent on the teacher to supply the questions. As the students progress, questions should become increasingly difficult until they must go home and think about the questions, experiment, guess, and try to prove their guesses correct. In this way, pupils will tend to do more and more thinking on their own, and they will also begin to learn to ask their own questions.[43]

Jerome Bruner has observed that "discovery in mathematics is a byproduct of making things simpler. In the main, to understand something is to sense the simpler structure that underlies a range of instances, and this is notably true in mathematics."[44] Following this line of thinking, it may be suggested that we learn mathematical concepts by (1) sorting objects, events or ideas into classes or categories, (2) noticing relationships within the classes or categories, (3) finding a pattern which suggests relationships or structures, (4) formulating a conclusion to describe the pattern of events or ideas, and (5) establishing a generalization by means of a deductive proof.[45]

Leading students through the processes of discovery is not necessarily easy

[43]Willoughby, op. cit., pp. 32–33, 70.
[44]Jerome S. Bruner, On Knowing (New York: Atheneum, 1966), pp. 100, 106.
[45]Adapted from Johnson and Rising, Guidelines for Teaching Mathematics, p. 51.

or without its pitfalls. Several cautions should be kept in mind by the teacher as he proceeds:

1. Be sure that correct generalizations result from student efforts.
2. Do not expect all students to discover every generalization toward which teaching efforts are directed.
3. Discovery takes time—be patient, and don't try to teach all the ideas of a course by discovery.
4. When first discovered, generalizations may not be verbalized by students, and their first attempts at verbalizing them may lack precision and clarity.
5. Discovery activities may need judicious guidance and restraint, although in doing so the teacher must be careful not to stifle curiosity.
6. In guiding discovery activities, avoid overstructuring and keep a balance between freedom and direction.
7. Be careful that students do not jump to conclusions on the basis of inappropriate or too few samples.
8. Maintain in students an awareness of their progress and how their discoveries are important and incorporated in the total structure involved.[46]

Trends in Innovative Programs

Since the first "new math" programs were developed in the early 1950's there have been numerous systems worked out to teach all kinds of mathematics at all levels. Most of these are similar in many respects, although they may vary in particulars of content or presentation procedure. It has not been proven that any one of these programs is better than the others at any level or in any of the areas of mathematics instruction, and it is doubtful that such proof will ever be forthcoming. The needs of individual students and individual schools vary too much for this to occur.

Although there are many variations among programs, several common elements may be identified among them. One of the more important involves the concept of the "spiral" approach to curriculum organization. This concept is discussed more completely in Chapter 14 of this book, so we will at this point indicate only briefly how it may be applied to the mathematics curriculum.

The spiral approach to learning attempts to develop a concept from the intuitive level to the analytic level and from exploration to mastery by spacing instruction so that the teaching of a given topic with its related concepts occurs at several widely separated times, with each new exposure to the topic including both new approaches and a higher level of sophistication. Spiral teaching may be confused with traditional repetition of subject matter at various levels of the school program, but it is not at all the same.

The concept of spiral organization may be illustrated in mathematics by following an organizational pattern for teaching about graphs and graphing. At

---

[46] *Ibid.*, pp. 65–66.

the elementary school level pupils may learn to read graphs of statistical data and to construct bar graphs and distributive graphs. Later on, they plot graphs of points on the number line to represent the truth sets of equations and inequalities. This is followed with instruction related to the more mature concepts of intercepts, slopes, and intersections. These graphs are later related to quadratic equations and to periodic and exponential functions, and at a very mature level graphs may be used to discuss continuity, limits, and probability. Thus concepts and generalizations at one level of understanding are used to support and lead to more advanced consideration of the same or similar topics.[47]

In summary, characteristics of the newer mathematics programs, most of which we have already mentioned, include the following:

1. Many topics found to be obsolete are being deleted.
2. Many new topics are being introduced.
3. An attempt is being made to teach more mathematics in less time.
4. The concern of many efforts is the utmost development of scientific potential of the superior student.
5. Some efforts are aimed at increasing the precision of mathematical language leading to its clarification and simplification.
6. The student is being provided with an opportunity to participate more vitally while learning mathematics—he is becoming more of a doer than a spectator.
7. The student is expected to develop his ingenuity by *discovering* mathematical relations on his own rather than being told what they are by the teacher; carefully designed sequences of questions lead students to make such discoveries.
8. There is more emphasis on the study and recognition of structural characteristics of mathematics; individual concepts and skills are viewed as parts of larger and more significant mathematical structure.
9. Direct involvement of mathematicians, mathematics educators, psychologists, researchers, teachers, supervisors, and administrators has become an accepted procedure in planning curricular reforms.
10. Financial backing of governmental agencies, private foundations, local school systems, and local organizations has become a form of support for curricular reform efforts.[48]

Selected References

Allendoerfer, Carl B., *Mathematics for Parents*. New York: The Macmillan Company, 1965.

Bassler, Otto C., *Learning to Teach Secondary School Mathematics*. Scranton, Pa. Intext Educational Publishers, 1971.

[47]Johnson and Rising, *op. cit.*, pp. 56–58.
[48]Eugene D. Nichols, "The Many Forms of Revolution," *Bulletin of the National Association of Secondary School Principals* (April 1968), pp. 35–36.

Bruner, Jerome S., "On Learning Mathematics," *On Knowing.* New York: Atheneum, 1966, pp. 97–111.

Bulletin of the National Association of Secondary School Principals, April 1968.

Butler, Charles H., and F. Lynwood Wren, *The Teaching of Secondary Mathematics.* 4th ed. New York: McGraw-Hill Book Company, 1965.

Cambridge Conference on School Mathematics. *Goals for School Mathematics.* Boston: Houghton Mifflin Company, 1963.

Conference Board of the Mathematical Sciences. *The Role of Axiomatics and Problem Solving in Mathematics.* Boston: Ginn and Company, 1966.

Dubisch, Roy, *The Teaching of Mathematics.* New York: John Wiley and Sons, Inc., 1963.

Eilber, Charles R., "College Preparatory Mathematics: Preparation for What?" *Bulletin of the National Association of Secondary School Principals,* November 1969, pp. 68ff.

Fehr, Howard F. (ed.), *Mathematics To-Day: A Guide for Teachers.* Organization for Economic Co-operation and Development, 1963.

Johnson, Donovan A., and Gerald R. Rising, *Guidelines for Teaching Mathematics.* Belmont, Calif.: Wadsworth Publishing Company, Inc., 1967.

Kinsella, John J., *Secondary School Mathematics.* New York: Center for Applied Research in Education, Inc., 1965.

Krause, Eugene F., "Homomorphism: A Unifying Concept," *The Mathematics Teacher,* December 1969, pp. 617–622.

Secondary School Curriculum Committee. "The Mathematics Curriculum," *The Mathematics Teacher,* May 1959, pp. 389–417.

Strehler, Allen F., "What's New About the New Math?" *Saturday Review,* March 21, 1964, pp. 68ff.

Willoughby, Stephen S., *Contemporary Teaching of Secondary School Mathematics.* New York: John Wiley & Sons, Inc., 1967.

Wilson, James W., and Jerry P. Becker, "On the Solution of a Problem," *The Mathematics Teacher,* April 1970, pp. 293–295.

CHAPTER 8

NATURAL SCIENCE

Probably no aspect of learning has commanded the attention of the average American in the past decade so dramatically as science. Achievements in space, medicine and health, communications, transportation, agriculture, and countless other areas of scientific endeavor are on every tongue. However, it can be truthfully stated that "as a nation we rely heavily on the products of science, yet, on the whole, we are scientifically illiterate."[1] The significance of science is undeniably evident in all that has happened in the past few decades, yet most students avoid science and look upon the scientific community as somewhat abnormal. Parents continue to display their ignorance of this field almost as a badge of honor, although they acknowledge its importance and often aspire for their children to enter scientific occupations.

What has caused this dichotomy between thought and action among the general populace? Many have claimed that there is an overemphasis on science in our society—and in some respects this is probably true. On the other hand, perhaps our culture suffers from too little emphasis on science for the *average* person, and we thus are unable to relate science to the humanities and everyday life. This is becoming more and more evident as we recognize problems related to environmental mismanagement, pollution, smoking, and similar matters.

Most people can identify pretty well with literature—at least they believe they can read it. This is also true with art, music, history, social problems, and other "humanistic" concerns. Even if not very proficient in these areas, most people can still participate in them in some fashion, either directly or as an observer. Such is not the case with science. Very little scientific knowledge is required for a person to get along quite well in our modern society.

The traditional science curriculum is more suited to an agrarian than a scientific-technological-industrialized society, and to a way of living that no longer exists. We need science curriculum changes that will develop science

[1] Morris H. Shamos, "The Role of Major Conceptual Schemes in Science Education," *The Science Teacher* (January 1966), p. 27.

200

courses more suitable for understanding the nature of the scientific enterprise and its meaning for modern America.

Science Education—An Overview

Ferment in Science Education

It has been said that the greatest threat to education is knowledge, and this is especially true in science. The amount of knowledge in every field is staggering and increasing at an accelerated rate. It is no longer possible to "cover" a science in high school, and it appears equally improbable that even the major principles, laws, and theories of a discipline can be adequately taught in the time normally available for a course. Additions to the science curriculum by accretion have become totally frustrating to both teachers and students. Curriculum innovations are obviously needed to manage the knowledge problem.

The need for change in the science curriculum has focused on the content of subjects, its up-to-dateness and usefulness for modern living, and whether the courses are being taught in an authentic or "scientific" manner. Educators and the general public have recognized the inadequacy of old programs, realizing that they no longer serve the needs of students, the public, or the society. Concern for manpower needs, especially as related to the scientific and economic future and national security, have served to strengthen demands for change.[2]

Defining Science and Science Education

As is true with most definitions, a definition of science is not easily reached. There is no dirth of statements relative to the question, but agreement is often lacking. One of the simpler statements describes science as "the search for order in nature."[3] A prominent authority on science education suggests a threefold definition in proposing that science is "a process of thinking, a means of acquiring new knowledge, and a means of understanding the natural world."[4]

Many authorities draw distinctions among the concepts of science, technology, and technique. Science, or "pure science," is seen as an attempt to understand the laws of nature without regard for application of this knowledge. "Applied science" puts this knowledge to use through technology and technique (the expert use of tools).[5]

To combat a concept often found among the general populace, perhaps a less "scientific" approach to defining science may be appropriate.

---

[2]Paul DeHart Hurd, *New Directions in Teaching Secondary School Science* (Chicago: Rand McNally, 1969), pp. 1–2.

[3]Nelson B. Henry (ed.), *Rethinking Science Education*, Fifty-ninth Yearbook of the National Society for the Study of Education (Chicago: National Society for the Study of Education, 1960), p. 5.

[4]Hurd, *op. cit.*, p. 20.

[5]*Ibid.*, p. 21.

Science is not technology, it is not gadgetry, it is not some mysterious cult, it is not a great mechanical monster. Science is an adventure of the human spirit. It is essentially an artistic enterprise, stimulated largely by disciplined imagination, and based largely on faith in the reasonableness, order, and beauty of the universe of which man is part.[6]

. . . science, like music or fine art, is a wellspring of the divine discontent that stirs man to seek more of life than merely to eat and to sleep. And that discontent is flamed higher by the partner of science, advancing technology, through which we can realistically contemplate the practical achievement of the highest ideals for the condition of man.[7]

Science is asked to take the above concepts, along with related knowledge and attitudes, and make of them appropriate learning experiences for all students. While considering the problems of general education in a free society, the 1945 Harvard Committee formulated a question which still identifies this major concern of science educators, and all other educators. "How can general education be so adapted to different ages and, above all, differing abilities and outlooks, that it can appeal deeply to each, yet remain in goal and essential teaching the same for all?"[8]

The Evolution of Science Education

As is true with all areas of instruction, the history of science education in the United States yields a better understanding of how present goals and practices have developed and how they have been influenced by purposes and programs of the past. Many different purposes for instruction in the sciences have been proposed at different periods, resulting in varying types of curriculum and instruction. These practices and programs have tended to persist to some extent into succeeding periods, resulting in a mixture of old and new in the modern programs. This mixture has not always been a good one, due to the inappropriateness of some older practices to newer concepts of science education.

The history of science teaching in American secondary schools may be traced to the early eighteenth century, although the real beginning is generally credited to Franklin's Philadelphia Academy, founded in 1751. Descriptive, utilitarian, and religious aims formed the basis for this instruction, which generally included natural philosophy, astronomy, chemistry, and geography, with some emphasis upon zoology and geology. Instruction emphasized the memorization of factual material, although Franklin himself had advocated trips to nearby farms and actual practice in gardening as part of the science program.

A second period in the history of science instruction began about 1880 with the adoption of purposes aimed at training the mind. Drill and memorization of

    [6]Warren Weaver, as quoted by Walter Orr Roberts in "Science, A Wellspring of Our Discontent," *The American Scholar*, 36 (Spring 1967), pp. 246–260.

    [7]Walter Orr Roberts, *ibid.*

    [8]*General Education in a Free Society*, Report of the Harvard Committee (Cambridge, Mass.: Harvard U. P., 1945).

factual material continued under the guise of memory training. With faculty psychology and mental discipline as the accepted foundations of learning, science was held to be particularly valuable for training the faculty of observation, promoting the concentration of thought and energy, and providing sense-training through the manipulation of materials. The utilitarian and religious aims formerly accepted were largely displaced with complete concentration on descriptive aspects. Science teaching was carried on with little or no regard for individual interests and needs of students, because the prevailing psychological theories held that all individuals had minds made up of the same faculties which needed to be trained. College preparation was given prime emphasis, partly as a result of the Committee of Ten recommendations.

During this time came the introduction and popularization of the laboratory method as a means of making science teaching vital and effective. Faculty psychology ideas supported these activities in the belief that such work gave opportunity for the cultivation of accuracy in observing changes in phenomena, for developing systematic habits of work, and for training in the power of reasoning. Habits of neatness and precision of expression were supposedly developed through keeping laboratory manuals. To some, laboratory work came to seem as valuable for "discipline" as were Latin and Greek.

The disciplinary aim encouraged the development of formal and systematized subject matter, including meticulous classification of plants and animals, attention to details in laboratory "experiments," and a complete systematization of knowledge. If knowledge in this form was more difficult for the learner, so much the better, as this provided a greater disciplinary value.

A reaction against the disciplinary aim and overemphasis on college preparation ushered in a third period of development, beginning about 1910. There was a tendency to revert to the descriptive and utilitarian aims of earlier times, but attempts were also made to meet the demands of a developing industrial society and mushrooming scientific knowledge. The strong emphases of the faculty psychology period continued to exert much influence, however, even to the present.[9]

As science education moved into the twentieth century, a strong utilitarian motive was evident in such developments as the rise of a civic biology course, sometimes called "toothbrush biology," which was oriented toward improving unsanitary and poor health conditions of that time. The growing industrialization encouraged changes such as that which included in chemistry courses processes such as making steel, mining sulfur, manufacturing sulfuric acid, and smelting ores. Later, the growing use of telephones, internal combustion engines, wireless telegraphy, electrical appliances, and airplanes caused these topics to be included in physics courses. General science was developed to serve as an introduction to

[9]Committee on the Function of Science in General Education, Progressive Education Association, *Science in General Education* (New York: Appleton, 1938), pp. 5–10.

biology, physics, and chemistry and to excite the interest of students in new technological marvels. "Consumer science" was developed as a result of the depression years of the 1930's for the purpose of helping students become more intelligent purchasers of goods and services. "Air-age" biology, physics and chemistry came into being during the war years of the 1940's, but quickly yielded to a concern for technical manpower needs of the 1950's.

The modern period in science education may be said to have begun with the concern for technical manpower needs of the 1950's, which was accelerated tremendously by Russia's orbiting of the first man-made satellite in 1957. The resulting furor of activity related to scientific and technical instruction has usually been well motivated, but sometimes reactionary, frantic, unrelated, and ill-advised actions seem to have been dominant and without total K–12 program planning.

Each major social crisis gaining recognition in American life exercises its influence over science education. For example, current problems of racial integration, poverty, and urban life have created a demand for a science curriculum more suited to the needs of the "disadvantaged" and the "slow learner." New approaches developed to meet the most recent demands of the society are sometimes the result of careful deliberation and thoughtful effort, but such is often not the case. The results of educational research and changes in learning theory seldom get the attention they deserve.[10]

The science education reform of the past decade has brought many new programs and other changes into the typical secondary school, but there is still much disagreement about basic purposes and how to achieve them. These questions will receive our attention in the following pages.

Objectives of Science Education

We come again to the point where an understanding of objectives is required before we can proceed to further consideration of an instructional program for today's young people. The general purposes commonly identified for education in the United States apply, but there is also need for some points of departure more specifically related to the natural sciences.

Most high school graduates arrive at college with a mistaken picture of science, "something like a stamp collection of facts or a game of getting the right answer."[11] This hardly seems appropriate to this scientific age.

To set the stage for a brief discussion of science education goals, we should recognize the fact that science is closely tied to the humanities. The products of science and technology stimulate fundamental changes in human affairs, and the

---

[10]Hurd, op. cit., pp. 12–13.

[11]Nelson B. Henry (ed.), Rethinking Science Education (Chicago: National Society for the Study of Education, 1960), p. 19.

successes of science bring about other types of problems, problems which depend upon the humanities for solution. Numerous examples of this are available: disease control and the resultant problem of population increase, drugs that affect personality, and control of human genetics are typical problems of this type now facing mankind.

William Schram once put the concept we are trying to express very succinctly by saying that "an educated man ought to know science in a humanistic way." Much as he might be expected to know something about history, philosophy, literature, or the fine arts, the educated man should know something about science for his general good and because it is part of his culture. He should feel that he understands his environment reasonably well, and talking with others about science on a nontechnical level should cause no discomfort. It is not necessary that he understand in detail the functioning of the telephone or the automobile, but he should know the difference between science and technology, he should have a command of scientific facts adequate to the purpose of understanding his environment, just as he knows various facts of history, or geography, or literature. Most important, the educated man should know how scientific facts are used in the development of major conceptual schemes, and he should look upon science as a way of understanding, rather than as a distasteful experience that left only educational scars.[12]

Science education for an era of rapid change must be different in character from any of the past. Young people must be educated for living in a modern world, and the purposes for teaching science need to be defined in those terms.

In addition to providing an understanding of current problems, today's science education must also help students recognize and interpret signals for the future. Science educators face the question of how to design a curriculum and develop the intellectual skills and attitudes essential for progress within a system of continuous change. Students must be helped to understand today's world and at the same time be prepared to meet the unknown problems of tomorrow.

Criticisms of Conventional Science Courses

One way to approach a development of objectives for modern natural science education may be to consider some of the criticisms either stated by various people or implied by differences in the new programs. They include the following:

1. Facts are overemphasized—often facts which might be accurately described as trivia.
2. The erroneous assumption seems to be often made that the easiest way to learn science is through technological applications.
3. Bits and pieces of knowledge, without conceptual unity, make up most traditional science courses.

[12]Morris H. Shamos, "The Role of Major Conceptual Schemes in Science Education," *The Science Teacher* (January 1966), pp. 27–30.

4. Laboratory work is poorly related to course objectives and classroom work, consisting most often of exercises designed to develop manipulative skills rather than systematic thinking and to verify rather than to discover.

5. Traditional science courses are usually taught in a dogmatic way, with science being presented as a body of information which is verified and certain.

6. The characteristic features of the scientific enterprise—its modes of inquiry and its human attributes—are both widely neglected.

7. Much of what is taught is only descriptive—the organs or muscles of a frog, the parts of a leaf, the characteristics of halogens, or the particles within an atom.

8. Not only is the investigative nature of science typically relegated to a brief treatment at the beginning or the end of a course, it is also present in an inaccurate way—as a "scientific method," always following certain forms and leading to conclusions.

9. The teaching of science courses is ineffective, often consisting primarily of the instructor "telling" the students, with perhaps a few deviations by means of demonstrations and films. Too many topics are usually treated superficially, with little articulation from topic to topic.[13]

10. Much of what is taught is science of the past.

11. One textbook and one approach to a subject are too often found in science classes.

12. The scientific community has not been adequately involved in producing textbooks and other instructional materials.

General Objectives

Science education has an obligation to present science to students as both producers and consumers of scientific services. All students need a general education in science which will, through a general understanding of the social implications of scientific advancement, assure their effective functioning as citizens. In addition, it should be assured that individuals with the aptitude and desire to enter science as a profession will receive appropriate preparation. The new science programs are designed to do both.

To carry out the two general objectives stated above requires that adequate attention be given to both of the major aspects of science and science teaching —knowledge and enterprise. Observed facts form the secondary phase of science education. Science as inquiry, getting students intellectually involved in exploration and discovery, is of first importance.

[13]Adapted from Hurd, *New Directions in Teaching Secondary School Science*, pp. 44–47.

Attitudes

Lists of objectives for science education have often been put in terms of "attitudes" which should be developed in students. One of the more widely publicized statements came through the Educational Policies Commission of the National Education Association. It stated that the following values (or attitudes) underlie science and should be used in formulating the basic goals of science education:

1. Longing to know and to understand.
2. Questioning of all things.
3. Search for data and their meaning.
4. Demand for verification.
5. Respect for logic.
6. Consideration of premises.
7. Consideration of consequences.[14]

Content

Content selection for the new programs in natural science education is not so much different in kind as in emphasis. The older approaches chose content on the basis of criteria such as "sampling the disciplines" and "meeting the needs of pupils." With the new programs, curricular content is identified more according to the basic nature of the disciplines. Social problems, individual needs, life problems, and the like are not ignored, but they assume a supplementary role.

The present science curriculum reform shows more variation from older programs in its emphasis on the inquiry phase than in some other aspects. A major effort is made to have the active, the knowing, the discovery phase of science as a major element of science study. Previous reforms in science education have been most concerned with updating the content and assuring adequate coverage, but in view of present estimates that the facts of science become obsolete within fifteen years, the notion of coverage or conveying of current knowledge is obviously questionable.[15] Knowing science is more a matter of understanding its modes of inquiry than of inventorying current knowledge. Science may thus be described as "more a verb than a noun."[16]

The Natural Science Disciplines

It appears that there is rather general agreement among most science educators today about the basic content desired. It is described in the 1962 Position Statement of the National Science Teachers Association and the 1964 publica-

---

[14]Educational Policies Commission, *Education and the Spirit of Science* (Washington, D.C.: National Education Association, 1966), p. 15.

[15]Joseph J. Schwab, "Some Reflections on Science Education," *BSCS Newsletter*, No. 9 (September 1961), pp. 8–9.

[16]Hurd, *op. cit.*, pp. 31–39.

tion of the same organization, *Theory Into Action*. Three distinct aspects of the scientific enterprise are indicated: natural history (observation and factual description of nature), science (comprehension and understanding of the observed phenomena), and technology (use and control of phenomena). The importance of inquiry in all three phases is emphasized.

The natural history and technology aspects of these statements have traditionally received considerable attention in typical school programs, but getting students intellectually involved in exploration and discovery so that they may actually understand what science is all about has been largely neglected.[17]

To more specifically identify the content areas appropriate for natural science education, we must resort to somewhat traditional terms. Tykociner has identified the basic sciences as those serving to systematize our knowledge of basic facts and relations: the sciences of matter and energy (physics, chemistry, astronomy, and geology, for example), the biological sciences (primarily botany, zoology, physiology, and genetics), the psychological sciences, and the sociological sciences.[18] Language and mathematics, in some respects, may also be considered sciences, according to the above definition.

The social sciences, language and mathematics comprise disciplinary areas in their own right in our scheme of curriculum organization, although it cannot be denied that certain aspects of these disciplines must be included in study of the natural sciences. Psychology includes areas of study which are appropriate for both social and natural sciences, and should be drawn upon accordingly. This leaves us with a collection of disciplines for the natural science curriculum which is very similar to older designations. One important addition should be pointed out, however, in that what might be called *enquiry into enquiry* is an essential content area of modern science education programs.

Content of the Disciplines

Although they were each developed separately, an examination of the various experimental curriculum projects in science shows some overlap of major science concepts and inquiry processes. This should not be surprising, because each discipline can be subsumed under "science" and should therefore reflect the conceptual network and logical methodologies distinguishing science from other disciplines.

Each of the science disciplines includes subject-matter content and methods of inquiry which, although not necessarily unique to that discipline, provide the basis for organization, investigation, and discovery in that field. Accumulated knowledge is brought into order through models and theories designed to aid problem attack. It is essential that topics be included in the science courses which

---

[17]Shamos, *op. cit.*

[18]Joseph T. Tykociner, *Research As A Science—Zetetics* (Urbana, Ill.: Electrical Engineering Research Laboratory, University of Illinois, 1959), p. 37.

will exemplify scientific methods of inquiry and allow the exercise of them. Some topics should be chosen to illustrate doubts and ignorance in science. These principles of science curriculum selection are well expressed by Hurd.

> The curriculum task is first one of identifying the major overarching ideas that currently characterize the mainstream of thinking within the discipline. The concepts and principles that are to constitute a science course should be those that present a modern picture of the discipline; these may be described as the "key concepts" or "representative ideas." The selection is not random but must represent the logical structure of a discipline. Priority is given to conceptual schemes at the advancing front of science since they are most likely to influence the future of science and be contemporary with the life span of the learner. Since there will always be more knowledge in a discipline worthy of teaching than can be taught in a school year, what is chosen should offer the best promise for allowing the student to learn on his own after he leaves the course.[19]

At this point it seems appropriate to illustrate appropriate content for modern science education programs by briefly describing the more prominent new programs, although no attempt will be made to exhaustively study the many programs now in operation.

EARTH SCIENCES. Rapidly taking the place of the hit-and-miss potpourri of units included in the typical general science course, programs in earth science serve the same general purpose of an introduction and exploration into science for younger students while preserving disciplinary integrity, the inquiry approach, and integration of subject matter. Two programs have thus far reached the stage of development allowing their use in public schools. A brief description of these programs will illustrate the direction being taken in earth science curriculum development.

The *Earth Science Curriculum Project* (ESCP) is an interdisciplinary approach to investigating the earth and incorporates information from several sciences, including astronomy, geology, meterology, oceanography and physical geography. Supported by the National Science Foundation and under the administrative control of the American Geological Institute, planning, writing, and testing of curriculum materials for this program have been under way since 1962. The materials have been prepared for use at about the ninth-grade level.

The ESCP course seeks to represent the unity of the earth sciences, in contrast to the typical general science course composed of special units on astronomy, geology, meterology, oceanography, soil science and physical geography. Material from the several disciplines focuses upon logically related scientific principles, which are organized around two unifying themes: (1) the study of man's environment; and (2) earth science as a process of inquiry.

In an effort to convey to pupils the investigative nature of science as a search

---

[19]Paul DeHart Hurd, *New Directions in Teaching Secondary School Science*, © 1969 by Rand McNally & Company, Chicago, pp. 38–39.

for new and more accurate knowledge about the earth, the curriculum planners
wove three major process schemes throughout the ESCP course:

1. *Science as inquiry:* a search for accurate knowledge and a recognition of the
   incompleteness and uncertainty of present knowledge; unsolved problems;
   logical and systematic development of conclusions from accurate observations and well-chosen hypotheses.
2. *Comprehension of scale:* using scales of measurement or units appropriate to
   the problem; the use of models for the enlargement or reduction of a scale;
   skill in devising and using models; and intuitive feeling for scale in the real
   world and in models.
3. *Prediction:* extrapolation from the known to the unknown in either space or
   time; making logical interpretations of past events from fragmentary records;
   interpreting past events on the basis of given data.[20]

The water cycle and rock cycle are used to organize the subject matter into
conceptual themes, some of which are universality of change, flow of energy in
the universe, adjustment to environmental change, conservation of man and
energy, earth systems in space and time, and uniformity of process. Many concepts from biology, physics, chemistry, and mathematics are introduced into the
course to facilitate an understanding of the forces and processes affecting rocks,
land masses, the oceans, the atmosphere, and the earth in space.

The freedom and encouragement to investigate and speculate on their own
are provided by making the ESCP an activity-centered program. Laboratory
investigations are largely open-ended, allowing for multiple working hypotheses.
Students are encouraged to question, to explain, to extrapolate, and to speculate
as a problem may require.[21]

The *Secondary School Science Project,* also known as the Princeton Project,
has developed a course entitled *Time, Space, and Matter* (TSM). First tested in
grades five through nine during the 1962–63 school year, this program has been
rewirtten and expanded by developers in the department of geology at Princeton
University, in collaboration with chemists and physicists. It was designed for use
at several grade levels in secondary schools, but it is most widely used in the ninth
grade.

The TSM program assumes that science teaching should focus on the inquiry
processes of science, offering students both an account of what has been discovered and (more importantly) a systematic and logical method of thinking. Concepts developed are basic to understanding chemistry, physics, mathematics,
astronomy, and geology.

The course is planned around a series of investigations conceptually and
logically related to each other and building toward a climax of ideas. Students
proceed with investigations, recording their observations, hypotheses, speculations, and conclusions. The notes thus developed comprise the basic content of

20 *Ibid.,* p. 85.
21 *Ibid.,* pp. 143–146.

the course. There is no textbook and none is required, since students essentially write their own. The discovery of relationships, utilizing needed skills of instrumentation and measurement, forms the basic guideline for study.

The TSM course is organized into three major divisions. The first is entitled *On the Nature of Things* and consists of a series of investigations emphasizing observation skills, methods for quantifying data, and inquiry processes such as inferring and theorizing. Content material comes primarily from physics. *Seeking Regularity in Matter*, the second division, draws mainly from chemistry, as students study the occurrence and behavior of matter. The third theme, *Interpreting a World of Change*, incorporates concepts from physics and chemistry to complement principles drawn from geology and develops hypotheses about the composition of the earth and forces producing change. The sequencing of the three phases of investigation is planned to lead students from observations of the concrete in the first series to the abstract in the second and back to the concrete in the third.[22]

BIOLOGY. Recent developments in the field of biology education have been different from those in the other science disciplines in that only one major program to modernize the science curriculum and science teaching in the secondary schools has emerged. Within this one major program are three different sets of materials with different emphases, which developers claim give their program more diversity than many of the others. This program, the Biological Sciences Curriculum Study (BSCS), has been very productive and very influential, and it continues to lead out in the development, testing, and dissemination of materials and procedures for teaching science in general, and biology in particular.

Under the sponsorship of the American Institute of Biological Sciences, the Biological Sciences Curriculum Study began in 1959, guided by a steering committee of about thirty research biologists, high school biology teachers, science educators and school administrators. In the first ten years of its operation over 2,000 biologists and other specialists contributed to the development of the various programs.

The BSCS has been instrumental in the development of numerous programs and various kinds of curriculum materials in some forty adaptations and translations for use around the world. These efforts have been directed to accomplish three primary objectives:

1. Produce modern biology courses (textbooks) for the spectrum of students who take biology in high school.
2. Develop special resource materials for the teaching of these courses, such as films, pamphlets, laboratory blocks, equipment, tests, and new experiments.
3. Formulate programs and materials for both in-service and pre-service

22 *Ibid.*, pp. 140–143.

education of teachers so they may be better prepared to present the new
biological course materials.[23]

Various approaches to the study of biology are preferred by different biologists. Some like to study the "big picture" and focus their attention on the
interrelationships among living things. Others seek explanations about plants and
animals within their molecular structure or take some other approach. This
diversity of interests and resulting variety of ways to study life forms led to the
adoption by the BSCS of a policy leading to the development of three courses
in high school biology. They all have the same goals, conceptual themes, and
objectives; consequently they are more alike than different, with an overlap of
about 70 percent in topics, but the treatment of the topics varies somewhat. The
views of each writing team concerning the structure of biology are represented
in the remaining 30 percent of each course.

A series of themes or conceptual schemes were selected to bind together the
various parts of each course and the three versions. These themes came out of
efforts to seek answers for two pertinent questions:

1. What is the significant knowledge of living things as they are known in modern
   biology: What is the structure of inquiry, processes and concepts that best
   characterizes modern biology?
2. What knowledge of living things, and what attitudes and skills relevant to
   modern biology, will contribute the most to students' personal lives and to the
   execution of their responsibilities as men and citizens?

In answer to these questions, nine themes were selected to represent the major
goals of the BSCS and to identify the direction of teaching.

1. Change of living things through time: evolution.
2. Diversity of type and unity of pattern in living things.
3. The genetic continuity of life.
4. The complementarity of organism and environment.
5. The biological roots of behavior.
6. The complementarity of structure and function.
7. Regulation and homeostasis: preservation of life in the face of change.
8. Science as inquiry.
9. The history of biological conceptions.[24]

From these general goals were developed specific objectives to guide the
writing of the various courses. It was determined that implications for the student
were paramount and that a study of biology should provide him with

1. An understanding of man's own place in the scheme of nature—namely, that
   he is a living organism and has much in common with all living organisms.
2. An understanding of his own body, its structure and function.

[23] *Ibid.*, p. 152.
[24] *Ibid.*, p. 153.

3. An understanding of the diversity of life and of the interrelations of all creatures.
4. An understanding of what man presently knows and believes regarding the basic biological problems of evolution, development, and inheritance.
5. An understanding of the biological basis of many of the problems and procedures in medicine, public health, agriculture and conservation.
6. An appreciation of the beauty, drama, and tragedy of the living world.
7. An understanding of the historical development of biology with examples of concepts to show how these are related to contemporary techniques, technology, and the nature of society.
8. An understanding of the nature of scientific inquiry: science is an open-ended intellectual activity and what is presently "known" or believed is subject to "change without notice"; the scientist in his work strives to be honest, exact —part of a community devoted to the pursuit of truth; his methods are increasingly exact and the procedures themselves are increasingly self-correcting.[25]

The next step taken by the BSCS was the determination that biology could be construed as a number of layers of increasing complexity. Atoms and molecules, the fundamental structural units of matter, are organized into particular systems which make possible the formation of cells. Increasingly higher levels of structure result when various kinds of cells, in different combinations, are assembled to form tissues and organs. Progressing in this fashion from units simpler than the basic components of living systems to the total world of life as we know it, a hierarchical scheme was developed, moving from the less inclusive to the more inclusive:

1. Molecular
2. Cellular
3. Tissue and organ
4. Individual organism
5. Population
6. Community
7. World biome.[26]

A third dimension was added with the idea that all the major kinds of living organisms should be included, identified in simplist terms as protists, plants and animals.

These three dimensions of the BSCS program are illustrated by Fig. 8–1. The intersection of the planes in this diagram circumscribe units of materials for use in constructing courses in biology, which would be arranged in a sequence to provide a logical and teachable whole.[27]

The three versions of the BSCS materials, each developed in accordance with the foregoing principles, take somewhat different approaches to the study

[25] Ibid., p. 155.
[26] Arnold B. Grobman, *The Changing Classroom: The Role of the Biological Sciences Curriculum Study* (Garden City, N.Y.: Doubleday, 1969), p. 77.
[27] Ibid., pp. 76–78.

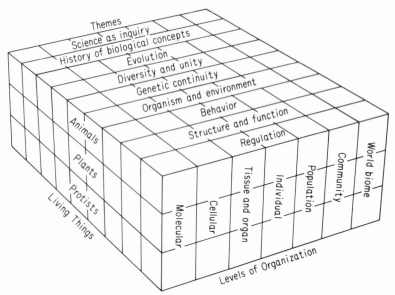

Fig. 8–1. Diagram representing a structure of biology which can serve as a guide to the design of courses in general biology. (From Grobman, *The Changing Classroom, ibid.*, p. 78. Reproduced by permission of The Regents of the University of Colorado.)

of biology. The Blue Version shows a prime concern for physiological-biochemical aspects and consequently has its emphasis at the molecular level. The Green Version stresses ecology and focuses on the community, while the Yellow Version takes the classical development and genetics approach, emphasizing cellular aspects. In all three versions laboratory procedures are dominant.[28]

PHYSICAL SCIENCE. Physics was included in the curriculum of the first American public high school, which opened in 1821. It remained an integral part of the high school curriculum until about 1900, when the growing percentage of young people attending high school lost interest in physics, especially those who did not plan on college. Recent reports indicate that more than 80 percent of today's high school seniors have not taken a physics course. This growing tendency of students to avoid physics has been one of the main incentives behind attempts to improve physical science programs of instruction.

Spurred by students' lack of interest in physics, scholars in this field began the first of the science curriculum reform movements. The *Physical Science Study Committee* (PSSC) began deliberations in 1956 directed toward the production of a new science course which would update and improve physics teach-

[28]Hurd, *op. cit.*, pp. 155–157.

ing. Efforts were aimed at correcting four faults identified in the traditional physics course: (1) it was fifty years out of date; (2) details so overloaded the course that it could not be adequately taught in one year; (3) it was simply a patchwork of individual topics, without unity or conceptual structure; and (4) the true science of physics was obscured by an overemphasis on technology.[29]

Developers of the PSSC physics course were concerned not so much with changing the placement of physics instruction in the high school program as in making it more relevant and better organized. Consequently, the course materials were designed for use at about the eleventh- or twelfth-grade level with a rather select group of students.

A set of goals was identified as appropriate to the accepted purposes of the Committee's efforts. The statement of goals is not radically different from that of earlier textbooks, but the program for their implementation contrasts sharply with traditional methods. The Committee purposed to create a course which would

1. Present physics as a unified yet living and ever-changing subject.
2. Demonstrate the interplay between experiment and theory in the development of physics.
3. Have the students learn the basic principles and laws of physics by interrogating nature itself, thus learning not only the laws but also the evidence for them as well as their limitations.
4. Extend the student's ability to read critically, to reason and to distinguish between the essential and the peripheral, thereby improving his learning skills in general.
5. Provide a sound foundation for those students who plan to study science or engineering at the college level.[30]

Two major themes provide the structure for the course: (1) dynamics of particles under the influence of forces and the conservation laws of momentum and energy, and (2) the superposition principle governing all wave propagation. Some thirty-five major concepts are used to support these themes, with special attention being given to demonstrate the interplay between experiment and theory.

A textbook divided into four parts with thirty-four chapters contains the major material for the PSSC physics course. Part I introduces the student to the world of physics with fundamental concepts such as time, distance, motion, the nature of measurement, the atomic structure of matter, and molecular chemistry. Part II moves into a study of optics and waves, reflection and refraction, particle theory as a possible explanation of light, and the wave model as a possible explanation of optical phenomena. Part III leads into a study of motion through laboratory work related to Newton's laws of motion. This is followed by concepts on gravitation and the laws of conservation of momentum and energy, which lead

[29] Ibid., pp. 186–187.
[30] Uri Haber-Schaim, "The PSSC Course," Physics Today (March 1967), pp. 26–31.

into the development of the kinetic theory of gases. Part IV takes up electricity and magnetism, electrical forces, measurement, the magnetic field around a current, Coulomb's law, energy and motion of changes in an electric field, and a thorough study of the structure of atoms and related phenomena. Throughout the course, opportunity is provided for expansion and reinterpretation of topics as a student's background in physics develops. A knowledge of geometry and algebra is assumed and additional mathematical skills are developed as part of the course.[31]

Project Physics began in 1962 with a series of discussions at Harvard University concerning the need for an approach to teaching high school physics which would be different from either PSSC or traditional physics and attract a larger percentage of students. Further discussions led to a program for developing a course which would be (1) a general education course, (2) built upon "good" physics, and (3) designed for today's educated citizen. "Good" physics is described as that which has a "continuous inherent story line." It is not a collection of details or bits and pieces which are easy to teach, neither is it "soft" or given to overemphasis of everyday technological applications. It stresses human endeavor within the cultural environment and the broader scope of human affairs. It brings out the structure of physics and provides an "encompassing view of the workings of nature." Throughout, it utilizes a historical and philosophical sense as the basis for a coherent view of physics.[32]

Six basic units make up the Project Physics course outline. Beginning with an introduction to the concepts of motion, the student is led into a study of the elements of kinematics and motion in the heavens. With this basis, he learns of the development of the scientific consequences of the triumph of mechanics— the conservation laws of momentum and mechanical energy and the first and second laws of thermodynamics. Electricity and magnetism in the context of fields at rest and in motion form the fourth unit of study, including tracing of the subsequent failure of the mechanistic view. Units five and six deal with the origins of the new physics and the atomic and nuclear models of matter.[33]

Introductory Physical Science (IPS) is a program which was developed after some of the other new science programs had identified several weaknesses in students relative to their knowledge of science principles and procedures. It was designed to remedy the intellectual ills of high school science students, particularly in physics and chemistry. Its proponents claim that it is appropriate either for students who will go on to further study in science or those who will study no more sicence. For the most part, it has been used at grades 8 or 9, although for students who take it as their only high school science course, it has been used at the eleventh-or twelfth-grade level.

[31]Hurd, *op. cit.*, pp. 188–190.
[32]*Ibid.*, pp. 193–194.
[33]Gerald Holton, "Harvard Project Physics," *Physics Today* (March 1967), pp. 31–34.

The IPS program identified several inadequacies found in students who enrolled in more advanced courses. The more prominent problems of this type were

1. Lack of experience in making observations.
2. Inadequate basic laboratory skills.
3. Inability to apply elementary mathematics to experimental results.
4. Inability to correlate an abstract idea with a concrete situation.
5. Lack of familiarity with orders of magnitude.
6. Lack of judgment concerning what is important and what is not.
7. No feeling for approximation
8. No appreciation for the uses of science in real life, especially their own.

Throughout the development of the course, it was kept in mind that the topics included should be useful at several points and that they should be tied together in such a way that students would get the most benefit from their study. Learning materials were selected for their value in helping students learn through their own inquiry. The forming of operational objectives, use of mental models or theories, and development of investigatory skills were considered essential, and the following sequence of major topics was selected as being most conducive to these aims:

Quantity of matter: Mass
Characteristic properties
Solubility and solvents
The separation of substances
Compounds and elements
Radioactivity
The atomic model of matter
Size and masses of atoms and molecules
Molecular motion
Heat[34]

Interaction of Matter and Energy (IME) is another introductory type course for early high school students. It was developed by a group of high school science teachers to emphasize the inquiry system of teaching and learning, and students are given extensive opportunities to observe, investigate, interpret data, and formulate conclusions. Development of hypotheses, use of scientific models, and inductive reasoning are included in a program leading to the acquisition of basic scientific concepts.

Six conceptual themes are used with IME, with appropriate topics selected to make up the course. These themes are:

1. The nature of scientific behavior—experimental design, observation, and interpretation.
2. The nature and use of scientific models.

[34]Hurd, *op. cit.*, pp. 146–148.

3. The particulate and continuous nature of matter.
4. The conversion of energy from one form to another.
5. The continuous interaction of energy and matter.
6. The behavior of matter and energy in living systems.

It may be noted that the course is particularly appropriate for students who go on to enroll in BSCS biology, or it may be used with students who do not take any other science courses.[35]

The *Engineering Concepts Curriculum Project* (ECCP) takes a somewhat different approach to the development of physical science knowledge and abilities in students. It is based on the idea that many students can be taught physical science principles through technology and an understanding of the world man has built. Engineering is concerned with processes, systems, and this type of focus is more likely to attract the typical student than "pure" physics.

The ECCP course is designed to interest those students who would not ordinarily take a physics course, but it cannot be said that it is for all students. It is conceived as a general education course for the typical college-bound student. Two years of mathematics is considered a prerequisite. Its main objectives are to acquaint students with broad theories and techniques which govern technological concepts, including the resources needed to make these successful.

The textbook written for use with the ECCP course is entitled *The Man-Made World*. It is divided into three parts, having to do with the extension of man's mental, sensory, and muscular powers. The divisions and chapter titles as they appear in the text indicate the nature of the course content.

Part A   Logic and Computers
  1. Logical thought and electric circuits
  2. Logic circuits with memory
  3. Plan for a computer
  4. Programing a computer in machine code
  5. Symbolic programing
Part B   Models and Measurement
  1. Models
  2. Models and the analog computer
  3. Data, sensing, and measurement
  4. Dynamic models
  5. Optimization
Part C   Energy and Control
  1. Feedback and control
  2. Amplification
  3. Stability
  4. Energy and the art of the possible[36]

CHEMISTRY. Scholars and teachers in the field of chemistry have also been active during the past ten to fifteen years in developing new approaches to

[35] *Ibid.*, pp. 150–151.
[36] *Ibid.*, pp. 202–208.

teaching science in high schools. Few changes had been made in high school chemistry since 1920, and traditional courses had been criticized in much the same way as other science programs for secondary schools. Course content was often out of date and sometimes incorrect, little use was made of theory, and chemistry was presented in a descriptive way rather than as a dynamic and changing process. Memorization of facts, instead of developing understanding, dominated the teaching activities. Typical experiments simply verified the known, requiring the recording of uninterpreted observations and endless balancing of equations without a real understanding of the relationships and mechanisms underlying the reactions.

Two programs to remedy the ills of traditional chemistry courses have been prominent. They have differed in some respects, but several similarities are evident:

1. They emphasize the principles underlying chemical structure, combination and energy.
2. They establish systematic relations between experiment and theory.
3. They introduce ideas in a tentative fashion and examine them in the light of experimentally derived data.
4. They have an overall internal logical structure for the textbook which makes sampling the book dangerous.
5. They insist upon the value of speculative questions and discussions as a means of promoting and sustaining motivation.
6. They require an inquiry environment in the classroom, and teachers who are heuristically inclined.[37]

The *Chemical Education Material Study* (CHEM Study) is probably the best known and most widely used new program for high school chemistry courses. The emphasis is on structural chemistry and chemical dynamics, following the idea that important concepts and generalizations of chemistry should be developed inductively. It is maintained that data the student can understand should be used and, if possible, gathered directly by him in the laboratory. The experimental nature of chemistry is stressed by utilizing "open-ended" laboratory experiments which allow the student to evaluate and interpret the results of his work. The laboratory is seen as a place where students may seek regularities in what they observe and then raise questions about the observations.

CHEM Study seeks to present chemistry as a science which is representative of human activities. The course focuses on student understanding about the source of facts and their "explanation." In addition, it is intended to produce students who understand the structure system and dynamics of chemistry— electron structure, the geometrical arrangement of atoms, relative sizes and shapes of atoms, the packing of atoms and molecules, the forces between them, and how these conditions influence chemistry. The goals are stated in more formal terms by saying that students are expected

[37] *Ibid.*, p. 186.

1. To accumulate information through experimental observations.
2. To organize information and to observe regularities; to evaluate and to interpret data.
3. To use a model system to account for observed behavior.
4. To communicate experimental findings to others.
5. To appreciate the meaning of uncertainty in science and why certainty is not possible.
6. To recognize a theory or law need not be correct in every context to be useful.
7. To recognize there is no assurance a law established within a certain range of experience applies outside of this experience.
8. To understand the implications of a law (prediction) leading to experiments outside the range of experience upon which the law is based. Interpolation and extrapolation are forms of prediction.
9. To appreciate laws in agreement with presently recognized data may, nevertheless, be changed or abandoned in the future as additional experiments increase our knowledge. Science is not a completed structure but a growing one.
10. To be able to use the simplest cycle of scientific activity—observe; find regularity; find explanations (hidden regularities).
11. To recognize science could not advance if our overwhelming mass of knowledge were not ordered with the aid of theories and laws.
12. To appreciate all scientific knowledge is derived from experimental observations.[38]

Chemical Systems (CBA Chemistry) was developed with the primary purpose of preparing students for further study in chemistry at the college level. It was intended to help close the gap between high school and college chemistry by developing an introductory course presenting modern chemistry at the level of the high school student, bringing students close to the frontiers of chemical knowledge. A strong humanistic orientation is evident in the program, representing a move away from the concept of chemistry as a practical art. The specific goals were defined as

1. To present the basic principles of chemistry as an intellectual discipline and to achieve an appreciation of chemistry as a creative pursuit of human knowledge.
2. To develop facility in analytical, critical thinking—especially thinking which involves logical and quantitative relations.
3. To develop scientifically literate citizens through an understanding of (a) the methods of science and (b) the role of chemistry in society and everyday living.
4. To stimulate an interest in chemistry, to identify promising students, and to provide adequate preparation for further scientific studies.

These goals indicate the intellectual and theoretical aspects of chemistry which are given significant attention throughout the program. Concepts of energy

[38] *Ibid.*, pp. 172–175.

changes and reaction mechanisms, in addition to understanding chemical bonds, provide the core of the course.[39]

OTHER NATURAL SCIENCES. Although the disciplines included thus far supply the major portion of the content material for educational programs in natural science, there are other types of content (considerable debate revolves around their identification as disciplines) which are obviously part of an adequate science education program. Physical education and psychology, in particular, include considerable content material which should be included in the secondary school program, either in the form of separate programs or incorporated into other science courses.

Criteria for Selecting Curriculum Content

As we have already mentioned more than once, one of the major problems in curriculum development is the selection of content material from the vast supply available. With its rapidly expanding store of knowledge, science is a particularly good example of this dilemma. Recognizing the problem, the National Science Teachers Association has suggested the following as criteria for the selection of curriculum materials which are consistent with the purposes of teaching science and consistent with the structure of science.

1. The knowledge must be familiar to the scholar in the discipline and useful in advancing the learner's understanding of science.
2. The content should serve the future as well as the present; therefore the selection of content should focus on the conceptual aspects of knowledge.
3. Every field of science has a basis in experimental and investigative processes. To know science is to know its methods of inquiry.
4. There are connections between the sciences themselves and between the sciences and other subjects. The content for courses needs to be selected to take full advantage of these relationships and to provide wherever possible a logical integration of knowledge. Transdiciplinary skills, intra- and interdisciplinary understanding should rank high as instructional aims.
5. Only a small fraction of the basic knowledge of science can be selected for teaching in a K-12 program; consequently special attention should be given to including those concepts that are most likely to promote the welfare of mankind as well as the advancement of science. This must also include the knowledge that will enable individuals to participate in the intellectual and cultural life of a scientific age.[40]

It may be noted that, although there still is little articulation among the projects, the developers of the various new programs in science education have tended to follow these or similar guidelines. Consequently, natural science educa-

[39] *Ibid.*, pp. 181–183.
[40] National Science Teachers Association, *Theory Into Action* (Washington, D.C.: National Science Teachers Association, 1964), pp. 11–12.

tion is becoming more of a unified endeavor and science curriculum development shows characteristics which are more conducive to the type teaching and learning needed today.

Structure

Again we come to the point of identifying the types of basic concepts and generalizations which are combined to form the structure of disciplines—in this case the natural sciences. As indicated in the preceding section, science educators recognize that general statements about classes of phenomena are the goal of science, rather than statements about particulars. These general statements are called by various names—concepts, constructs, themes, principles, conceptual schemes, generalizations. For purposes of consistency and better understanding of the total curriculum, we will continue to use the terms "concept" and "generalization" to identify the structural elements of the science disciplines, although we will point out how varying terminology is used by some authorities.

As with other disciplines, some very definite although not always agreed upon concepts and generalizations permeate all of science to varying degrees. Presenting factual material in the context of these recurring themes provides a more comprehensive and understandable learning situation. These concepts and generalizations are drawn from mathematics, from space, time, and weight, as well as from more specific areas of the science disciplines. Some are derived from perception (egg, root, etc.), while others are postulated or imagined (gene, atom, electron). Some generalizations are likewise concerned with concepts derived from perception (elements unite chemically in a definite proportion by weight), while others are theoretical (all elements are composed of atoms).[41]

Science concepts may be defined as "abstractions which organize the world of objects and events into a smaller number of categories." They are the vocabulary used by scientists to express themselves (tree, motion, velocity, mass, chemical element). A generalization differs from a concept in that "it states some kind of relationship between two or more abstractions, objects, or events. The statement that 'for every action there is an equal and opposite reaction' is an example of a generalization involving relationship among three concepts, 'action,' 'equal,' and 'opposite.' "[42]

Some authorities use the term "concept" as we have used the term "generalization," or they speak of concepts of varying complexity, using the term "concept" to refer to both concepts and generalizations as we have defined them. Several influential individuals and groups in science education use the idea of a "conceptual scheme" in about the same way that we have defined "generalization." It seems, however, that although some confusion results from this varying

[41]Nelson B. Henry (ed.), *Rethinking Science Education* (Chicago: National Society for the Study of Education, 1960), p. 40.
[42]*Ibid.*, pp. 39–40.

usage of terminology, science educators in the forefront of curriculum and methodology development at the present time utilize two basic levels of structural organization. We will continue to call them "concepts" and "generalizations."

Concepts

Since we have already given some definition of the term "concept" as applied to the natural sciences, including a few examples, at this point we will do no more than suggest some more terms which are illustrative of concepts from the various science disciplines. Some of these concepts are common to all the sciences, while others have more limited use:

approximation	law
atom	length
atomic structure	liquid
bond	magnetic field
classification	magnetism
complementarity	magnitude
compound	mammal
conservation	mass
density	matter
diffusion	measurement
distance	mixture
electricity	model
electron	molecule
element	momentum
energy	motion
entropy	osmosis
environment	pure
equilibrium	reflection
galaxy	refraction
gas	solid
gravitational field	temperature
gravity	time-
heterogeneity	vector
homogeneity	velocity
kinetic energy	weight

Generalizations

By modifying Conant's definition slightly to fit our terminology, we may define science as a series of concepts and generalizations arising out of experiment or observation and leading to new experiments and observations.[43] It must be understood that students do not necessarily learn certain concepts first and then

[43]James B. Conant, *On Understanding Science* (New Haven: Yale U.P., 1947).

combine them into generalizations. Concepts may be learned in the context of generalizations, and thus students gain an understanding of the two structural elements simultaneously. The two should be organized from simple to complex, so that students might progress in accordance with their ability and effort.

Generalizations may be broad in scope and designed for general science education or they may be more specifically related to a particular discipline. The broad type is exemplified in the following six major generalizations which have been proposed for science teaching:

1. Under ordinary conditions, matter can be changed or exchanged but not annihilated or created.
2. Under ordinary conditions, energy can be changed or exchanged but not annihilated or created.
3. There is an interchange of materials and energy between living things and their environment.
4. The organism is a product of its heredity and environment.
5. The universe, and its component bodies, are constantly changing.
6. Living things have changed over the years.[44]

Probably the most inclusive set of generalizations developed recently is that which was suggested in the National Science Teachers Association publication, *Theory Into Action.* These are included in our discussion of curriculum organization in Chapter 14, and we will not repeat them here, but they provide an excellent example of generalizations (or conceptual schemes) for use in science teaching.

Another comprehensive set of generalizations was developed for the K–12 science curriculum in Las Cruces, New Mexico:

1. Everything is made up of natural elements.
2. There are many kinds of living things.
3. Living things are dependent upon their environment.
4. Living things must perform certain functions in order to live.
5. The earth is a small part of a vast universe.
6. The earth's history and current conditions can be studied from its solids, gases, and liquids.
7. There are many forms of energy which can be changed from one to another.
8. Modern society is dependent upon an understanding of natural phenomena.
9. A scientific approach helps to solve problems.[45]

Some less comprehensive generalizations from several different areas of science have been identified as follows:

1. Matter occupies space and has mass.
2. A vertebrate is an animal with a backbone and an internal skeleton.
3. The digestive system is a group of organs with the common functions of preparing food for assimilation.

[44]Joseph Schwab and Paul Brandwein, *The Teaching of Science* (Cambridge, Mass.: Harvard U.P., 1962).
[45]J. Paul Taylor, "K–12 Science Design," *Science Teacher* 31 (March 1964), pp. 29–31.

4. Spermatophyte plants form seeds.
5. Matter may be changed by adding or subtracting energy.
6. The structure of the digestive system of animals varies.
7. Digestion is the process of changing food from an insoluble to a soluble form.
8. The electrical current in a circuit varies with the resistance if the voltage is constant.
9. Matter is made up of particles called atoms.
10. The structure and habits of animals are adaptations that are the result of evolutionary development.
11. In the process of digestion, the molecular structure of the elements contained in the food is changed.
12. Light is an electromagnetic wave.[46]

Examination of these generalizations leads one to see how they could be used in teaching science—as it is defined by Conant and others. By forming, through inquiry, their own concepts and generalizations about the natural world, students can gain an understanding and appreciation of science rather than just a collection of soon-to-be-forgotten facts.

Methods of Inquiry

Natural science has traditionally emphasized inquiry processes, often oversimplified with the term "scientific method." Science education, even though it may have more often advocated problem-solving or inquiry than have some of the other areas of education, still has fallen far short of what might be desired. Understanding science means that a person has a knowledge of its significant concepts and generalizations, a command of its inquiry processes, and appreciates their interaction. We will now turn our attention more specifically to the processes of science and how they relate to science education.

Scientists seek to understand and to explain events found in the natural world. They are interested in seeking knowledge for its own sake. No immediate application of this knowledge may be apparent, but it is sought with the hope that more insight and understanding of human experience will result. Technology purposely emphasizes the practical uses of scientific information, and this problem-solving type of activity has been the prime concern of conventional science courses, rather than "science as inquiry."

The information a scientist acquires becomes intellectually useful only when it is brought into a logical organization. "When a scientist speaks of the 'structure of science' he refers to the conceptual organization of knowledge *and* the inquiry processes giving rise to it; these two phases of science are inseparable."[47] Concepts and processes go hand in hand, making it wise to plan the systematic organization of the curriculum around both.

[46]Milton O. Pella, "Concept Learning in Science," *Science Teacher* 9 (December 1966), pp. 31–34.
[47]Hurd, *op. cit.*, p. 55.

The inquiry methods of science are quite similar from one science to another and therefore provide a means for integration of the science disciplines. A variety of inquiry procedures aid the scientist's search for reliable information, and students should gain some familiarity with several of the more common processes. However, the prime purpose of science education as it is related to inquiry concerns attitude.

Scientific Attitude

The scientific attitude is basically one of refusal to accept too quick or authoritarian explanations. It includes a curiosity as to the why of things, intellectual honesty, suspended judgment, and a belief that phenomena are subject to explanation. Doubt, or at least a degree of skepticism, characterizes the scientist at work, no matter what his special area of interest or investigation.[48]

Several lists of "scientific attitudes" have been proposed. They are all very similar, so perhaps two statements which have received some attention will serve to illustrate the thinking along these lines. Haney has suggested that important attitudes for scientists are

1. Curiosity
2. Rationality
3. Suspended judgment
4. Open-mindedness
5. Critical-mindedness
6. Objectivity
7. Honesty
8. Humility[49]

Another statement contains similar attributes as "values underlying science":

1. Longing to know and to understand
2. Questioning of all things
3. Search for data and their meaning
4. Demand for verification
5. Respect for logic
6. Consideration of premises
7. Consideration of consequences.[50]

Scientific Methods

There developed at one time the idea that there is one scientific method with definite steps to be followed in a sequential order. Conant[51] and others have

[48]Henry, op. cit., p. 43.

[49]R. E. Haney, "The Development of Scientific Attitudes," Science Teacher 31 (December 1964).

[50]Educational Policies Commission, Education and the Spirit of Science (Washington, D.C.: National Education Association, 1966), p. 15.

[51]James B. Conant, On Understanding Science, op. cit.

pointed out that this is not true. Research scientists do not limit themselves to a particular "method." In fact, they deviate considerably. All scientific methods do exhibit the attitudes described above, but their components may vary.

Although the procedures followed by scientists in their research may vary, there do seem to be some common components. The components most frequently mentioned are

1. Recognizing and defining a problem.
2. Clarifying the problem by making appropriate definitions, distinguishing between facts and assumptions, and collecting and organizing relevant information.
3. Formulating possible explanations or solutions (hypotheses).
4. Selecting one or more promising hypotheses for testing and verification.
5. Stating tentative conclusions.[52]

The universality of any procedure, or "method," is unacceptable to most scientists today, because it omits some of the most difficult, creative, and important elements of scientific endeavor. How does one go about "recognizing and defining a problem"? How are decisions made as to what questions should be asked and what data should be sought? How does a person determine what observations are relevant or what hypotheses are tenable? How is it determined that certain conclusions are warranted? A static procedure or "method," may be helpful, especially to less experienced researchers, but its usefulness is definitely limited.

The inquiry processes of science should perhaps be seen as simply the intellectual means by which man inquires into nature. The scientists in each discipline must then decide what should be done by way of discovery and proof, what criteria should be used for measuring the quality of data, how strictly to apply canons of evidence, and in general how to determine the path by which one should move from raw data to conclusions.[53] These scientific thought processes are carried forth on two distinguishable levels—the empirical and rational, with the bulk of the effort going into the rational or constructional realm. Authoritarianism and intuitionism are obviously rejected.[54]

Process Themes

Although it is now generally accepted among scientists and science educators that there are no "rules" to guide the process of scientific inquiry, they do recognize the need for some system of guidelines to help those engaged in inquiry, particularly beginners. The idea of "process objectives" or "process themes" has gained considerable acceptance as a means to this end. Process themes are seen

[52]Henry, *op. cit.*, pp. 43, 47.
[53]Joseph J. Schwab, "Problems, Topics, and Issues," in *Education and the Structure of Knowledge* (Chicago: Rand McNally, 1964).
[54]James T. Robinson, *The Nature of Science and Science Teaching* (Belmont, Calif.: Wadsworth, 1968), p. 114.

as rather general statements which relate to scientific inquiry and the ways that scientists go about their tasks individually and collectively. One of the better-known statements or process themes contains five items.

1. Science proceeds on the assumption, based on centuries of experience, that the universe is not capricious.
2. Scientific knowledge is based on observations of samples of matter that are accessible to public investigation in contrast to purely private inspection.
3. Science proceeds in a piecemeal manner, even though it also aims at achieving a systematic and comprehensive understanding of various sectors or aspects of nature.
4. Science is not, and will probably never be, a finished enterprise, and there remains very much more to be discovered about how things in the universe behave and how they are interrelated.
5. Measurement is an important feature of most branches of modern science because the formulation as well as the establishment of laws are facilitated through the development of quantitative distinctions.[55]

Watson has suggested some additional examples:

1. Man extends his limited sensory capability by the use of various instruments; the invention of novel instruments has opened up large new fields for scientific investigation.
2. Various forms of models and analogues, including working replicas, verbal statements, as well as mathematical formulations, are frequently used to simplify and organize experience.
3. Through journals, meetings, and letters, scientists report and discuss their work with those of similar interests in many countries.
4. Scientific studies are concerned with describing phenomena in parsimonious terms; technology is concerned with practical applications.
5. Since scientists are conscious of the limitations of their generalizations and of the many shortcomings which can occur in generalizing from limited experience, they expend considerable effort upon the testing of generalizations to establish the conditions under which they apply and do not apply, especially the latter.[56]

To summarize this discussion of scientific methods of inquiry, we can say that rather than a series of steps, the scientific method may be described more accurately as a philosophy or idea about investigation. It begins with observation of selected parts of nature, as determined by the scientist's judgment and experience. Questions of "What?," "How?," and "Why?" guide his search for evidence. On the basis of educated guess or observations, one or more hypotheses are formulated to answer one or more of these questions, and subsequent testing by additional observations, experiment, and predication establish the validity or inaccuracy of the hypotheses. All scientists agree that their work is founded upon empirical data and reject authoritarianism, believing that although it may not be

[55]National Science Teachers Association, *Theory Into Action, op. cit.,* p. 21.
[56]Fletcher G. Watson, "Curriculum Design in Science," *Science Teacher,* (March 1963), pp. 13–16.

entirely possible to exclude subjectivity from investigations, objectivity is the ultimate goal of scientific inquiry, utilizing inductive, deductive, and variant types of reasoning as the problem and procedures involved require.[57]

Teaching the Natural Sciences

Although curriculum reform and special training for teachers has now been going on in science for more than a decade, it appears that most of the teachers using textbooks and other materials of the newer varieties are *not* teaching as the authors and developers envisaged. They are still not sure of what should be done to effect inquiry, discovery, and concept learning in the classroom. It thus becomes ever more obvious that changing the organization and materials of a curriculum will not change the curriculum itself unless teachers understand what is required and change their methods of operation.

Teaching Science as Inquiry

The most pressing need among typical science teachers is a change in attitude about the basic purpose of science education. Instead of a storehouse to be filled with information, the student's mind should be viewed as an instrument for thinking. The emphasis must be on the way current learning will influence future performance in the course and in the years to come, rather than on what the student will need to know for the next test. The old assumption was that if students can learn and recall in verbal form all the knowledge prescribed, then all good things in science and life will come. Ample evidence is available to show that this idea is not justified.

Modern science teaching requires that the teacher assume a role which is more than explaining what the book left unclear and testing the student's mastery of what was told. The teacher must help the student learn how to learn. He must impart the art and the skill by means of which the student can teach himself. This includes knowing what questions to ask, when to ask them, and where and how to find the answers. Such skill is attained by relinquishing habits of passivity, docile learning, and dependence on teacher and textbook in favor of an active, doing process in which the textbook and teacher serve as guides, always subject to challenge. Interpretation, rather than application or replication, is the basis of instruction.

The natural sciences are distinguished by a continual flow of new knowledge, by refinements of existing knowledge accompanied by new theories and models. Newer approaches to science teaching reflect these dynamic characteristics by avoiding the presentation of science as dogma and emphasizing the idea that current study is only a phase in the growth of scientific knowledge. Textbooks

[57]Walter A. Thurber and Alfred T. Collette, *Teaching Science in Today's Secondary Schools,* 3d ed. (Boston: Allyn and Bacon, 1968), pp. 2–33.

and other materials use various kinds of phrases to indicate the tentativeness of science, such as "we do not know for sure," "the evidence is not complete," "we are not certain why this happens," or "this is an unsolved problem." Inquiry thus becomes an obvious necessity and science becomes a thinking process rather than a process of memorization.

Teaching science as inquiry also requires opportunity for alternative interpretations of data. Students should see that many questions have no "right" answer but only most probable answers or more and less defensible answers. They should adopt the attitude that the aim of criticism and defense of alternative answers is not to win an argument but to find the best solution to the problem.

Teaching science as inquiry is certainly compatible with current stress on the development of creativity in students. This term is somewhat ambiguous, but it includes fluency of association, expressions, and ideas; spontaneous and adaptive flexibility; penetration; originality; visualization; elaboration; foresight; certain evaluation abilities; and other similar abilities. Few educators would claim that development of these types of attributes is receiving adequate attention in most classrooms.

Attention to some traits which creative persons exhibit may serve to guide our thinking in attempts to improve the curriculum and classroom efforts. The following differences have been noted between persons judged to be more and less creative. It would seem that they should provide implications for the classroom.

1. Creative persons are more self-sufficient, basing their behavior upon their own concept of themselves rather than depending upon close supervision and guidance from others.
2. Creative persons are more independent in making judgments and are willing to stand alone against the group for the sake of accuracy in their reporting.
3. Creative persons are more self-assertive and dominant, more stable, more self-accepting, more aware of and open to their own impulses.
4. Creative persons are more progressive and radical than conservative; more courageous, adventurous, and otherwise more capable of taking greater risks backed by their own efforts in the hope for greater gains.
5. Creative persons are more complex as persons and may stir up group sanctions against themselves as a result of their new ideas, which may be sensed by others as a threat to the status quo.
6. Creative persons are more resourceful.
7. Creative persons are able to tolerate a great deal of ambiguity and can thus live for long periods of time with unsolved problems and with what others often may feel to be confusion.
8. Creative persons are more likely to give unexpected responses, to take new steps forward, to pioneer at the frontiers where trails do not yet exist—indeed, they are attracted to, rather than fearful of, pathfinding and trail-blazing challenges, and like to give them their full attention and effort.[58]

[58]John J. Sullivan and Calvin W. Taylor, *Learning and Creativity, with Special Emphasis on Science* (Washington, D.C.: National Science Teachers Association, 1967), pp. 38–39.

Teaching Concepts and Generalizations

Teaching for the formation of concepts and generalizations rejects ideas of "covering" or even "sampling" a discipline. This is too much like window shopping and lacks significant organization. Disciplines possess a natural pattern of conceptual organization which allows relating new ideas to previous learning and also to what is to come. Following this natural pattern of organization provides for the development of increasingly complex inquiry skills as well as for growth in understanding.

The "unit" system of teaching is another tradition that is inappropriate to the conceptual scheme approach. Textbook writers and teachers find it convenient, but isolated units on heat, weather, sound and light, or living things, for example, usually fail to encourage an understanding of the unity of science. Students quickly forget, even if they once knew, the significance of Boyle's law or of the diffusion of gases or liquids. But they are less likely to forget generalizations related to the overarching scheme of the kinetic-molecular theory of matter.

The unit idea can be woven into the new curriculum, but in most cases it merely serves to strengthen the impression of most students that science is just an endless series of unrelated topics and facts that must be memorized for reproduction on the next test.[59]

Learning concepts and generalizations has characteristics of inquiry and a decision making process. The student takes an array of facts or conditions and must: (1) reduce the differences, (2) find organizational properties for the information, and (3) validate the conceptual organization he gives to the data. This is not a rote process, because the learner must continuously make choices by guessing and testing. He must select a strategy for organizing his information and then decide if it is the only way the data can be related or if there is a way which is more appropriate and more adequate. As he gains a better understanding of concepts and generalizations, the student should be able to distinguish exemplars from nonexemplars, to interpret new situations using this understanding, to make valid inferences, to recode new and relevant information, and in other ways to go beyond the original learning.[60]

Combining the inductive and deductive methods (with variations) brings better results in teaching concepts than either method used separately. At times, it is probably best to use them separately, however. It appears that for relatively easy material the inductive method of deriving the concept out of many specific examples is best, but more difficult material seems to be best learned through a deductive approach in which the presentation of the concept is followed by extensive application.[61]

No amount of methodology will produce the desired results unless the concepts and generalizations selected for teaching are appropriate. These will

[59]Shamos, op. cit.
[60]Hurd, op. cit., pp. 61, 70.
[61]Henry, op. cit., p. 41.

usually overlap in their use into more than one discipline, but they should be authentic in terms of a discipline. Criteria for selecting concepts and generalizations should demand that they

1. Represent the basic ideas and intellectual structure of the discipline as it is known in modern science.
2. Have the greatest capacity for organizing and explaining the widest variety of phenomena and data.
3. Have the most potential for interpreting, generalizing, and inferring, or in other words those concepts with the greatest logical inclusiveness.
4. Can be taught from a variety of exemplars found in a wide range of context.
5. Provide many opportunities for the development of cognitive skills and the logical thought processes which characterize the discipline.
6. Can be used to build other more powerful concepts and principles within science and hopefully provide connections with the conceptual structure of other disciplines.
7. Convey the role of science in man's intellectual achievements.[62]

Concepts and generalizations may be organized according to *conceptual themes.* These are somewhat similar to the older ideas of units or topics, in that they provide an umbrella under which to organize related concepts and generalizations, but correlation among various scientific areas receives much more emphasis. Two examples of conceptual themes may be taken from chemistry and biology.

Biological themes advocated by Bentley Glass include

Interdependence of structure and function.
Regulation and homeostasis.
The genetic continuity of life, its evolution, the diversity of type together with unity of pattern.
The biological roots of behavior.
The relation of organism to environment.[63]

The Chemical Education Materials Study (CHEM Study) program utilizes the following themes:

Energy and its role in chemical reactions.
Conservation of mass-energy in terms of the conservation of atoms and electrical charge.
Kinetics and mechanics of chemical reactions.
Dynamic equilibria.
Competitive factors acting in chemical systems in general.
Electron structure and the geometrical arrangement of atoms.[64]

Several reservations have been expressed concerning the use of conceptual themes or comprehensive generalizations. They may become too general and too

[62]Hurd, *op. cit.,* p. 73.
[63]Bentley Glass, "Renascent Biology: A Report on the AIBS Biological Sciences Curriculum Study," *School Review* 70 (Spring 1962), p. 19.
[64]Hurd, *op. cit.,* pp. 79–80.

hard to relate to scientific disciplines for practical use. Ausubel, for example, proposes that the conceptual scheme approach is sound, but that it should be modified so that a separate set of schemes is made available for each particular discipline. He also suggests that the discovery approach is not good for all learning in the sciences, being too difficult and too slow at times.[65]

This type of caution is often related to a concern that the new science courses are too theory and concept oriented and therefore less practical. This is not true, because in science practical knowledge is derived from basic concepts, laws, principles, and theories. In the use of these basic ingredients, laboratory methods of teaching must be skillfully carried out, however.

These laboratory procedures should be markedly different from the traditional place to illustrate, demonstrate, or verify known concepts and laws. The investigatory approach should follow a spirit of exploring and coping with problem situations more than getting an answer or solving a specific problem. With this approach, laboratory work becomes more than a routine using laboratory manuals filled with blanks requiring "right" answers. It becomes an experience which demonstrates the importance and interrelationship of science with all of life.

Through his laboratory work, the student should gain an ability to relate concepts, theories, experiments, and observations as a means of exploring ideas. Technical skill and precision in carrying out laboratory work are important, but the primary significance is in the meaning this work has for the interpretation of data.

As a place to explore ideas, test theories, and raise questions, the laboratory must provide opportunities for systematic learning about elements of scientific inquiry, such as

1. The variety, characteristics, and limitations of experimental designs.
2. The relationship between experimental options and the nature of the data obtained.
3. The relationships between observed data, experimental results, and the inferences based on the data and results.
4. The tools of measurement and their influence on experimental accuracy.
5. The use of data in generating hypotheses and defining questions and, conversely, the use of hypotheses to guide data collection.
6. The use of theories and models in interpreting data and in making predictions.
7. The analyzing, ordering, and displaying of data in precise and valid ways.[66]

---

[65]David P. Ausubel, "An Evaluation of the Conceptual Schemes Approach to Science Curriculum Development," *Journal of Research in Science Teaching* 3 (1964), pp. 255–264.
[66]National Science Teachers Association, *Theory Into Action, op. cit.*, p. 14.

A practical example of this type of laboratory experience may be seen in what is called open-ended experiments. These experiments do not have a predetermined outcome that the pupil is expected to obtain, as do the typical laboratory exercises, but allow the student to actually carry out a true experiment. True open-ended experiments have the following characteristics:

1. The experiment is used to answer a question.
2. The pupil performing the experiment does not know the outcome of the experiment before performing it.
3. The design of the method for the experiment is frequently determined by the pupil.
4. The pupil makes his own observations and draws his own conclusions.
5. The conclusions drawn by the pupil serve as a basis for formulating new hypotheses which are similarly tested.[67]

EXAMPLES FROM THE DISCIPLINES. Current ideas about science teaching can perhaps be best understood by examining some of the ways in which the newer programs are organized. There is an obvious similarity among them, in that they all follow ideas about conceptual structure or conceptual schemes, but obvious differences are also evident.

The Earth Science Curriculum Project provides one example of subject matter organization for the new science programs. The materials developed by this group are built around the following subject-matter schemes:

1. Universality of change.
2. Flow of energy in the universe.
3. Adaptation to environmental change.
4. Conservation of mass and energy in the universe.
5. Earth systems in space and time.
6. Uniformitarianism: a key to interpreting the past.

Seven conceptual schemes used by the authors of the Biological Sciences Curriculum Study materials show a similar approach to the patterning of content. They are

1. Change of living things through time: evolution.
2. Diversity of type and unity of pattern in living things.
3. The genetic continuity of life.
4. The complementarity of organism and environment.
5. The biological roots of behavior.
6. The complementarity of structure and function.
7. Regulation and homeostasis: preservation of life in the face of change.

Conceptual schemes such as these are approached through classroom activities which seek to maintain an inquiring atmosphere. The CHEM Study program provides a good example of this, in that instead of a course in which the student listens while the teacher talks about chemistry, there is a minimum of lecturing

[67]Thurber and Collette, *op. cit.*, p. 173.

and a substantial amount of class discussion based upon direct observation and reading. Experiments are carried out *before* related readings are assigned in the textbook and before the topic is discussed in class. The prelab discussion before each experiment is done so as not to reveal its outcome, and the laboratory experiments are designed to encourage students to think about their efforts through seeking regularities in their observations and searching for ways to explain them. The experiments have a specified procedure, but they are open-ended in terms of results and interpretations. Conversation among the students during the laboratory sessions maintains the atmosphere of inquiry and this is carried into the following postlab teacher-student discussions.[68]

We have given considerable attention to the idea of interdisciplinary study and the correlation of subject matter from the various science disciplines, particularly through the conceptual-scheme approach. An example from biology illustrates this idea very well.

Instead of a series of isolated courses in zoology, botany, microbiology, genetics, and biochemistry, leading finally up to the concepts and principles of molecular biology, suppose we were to start with the question, What am I, and how do I differ from and resemble, first, other living creatures and, then, other human individuals? This would lead to considerations of the differences and similarities of plants and different animals, of how they are built and how they function, and would include the evolutionary relationships of living organisms. The questions, "How are living creatures built? How do they function?" lead obviously and naturally to molecules and atoms (chemistry) and energy relations (biochemistry-physiology). This in turn leads to ecological relationships (food chains and cycles) and to the relationships between man and his total environment.

The next question, "What determines that I am a man instead of a mouse?" can perhaps be best approached historically through the various steps in the discovery of cells, nuclei, chromosomes, and genes. That genes determine the characteristics of an organism can then be directly attributed to their primary action in cells of all organisms, determining details of their growth and functioning. The final link then comes with the identification of the genetic material as DNA and with recognition of its dual functional role in heredity and in the synthesis of enzymes. This in turn brings in the nature of macromolecules and their interactions.

In following through such a sequence of analysis of "What am I, and how do I work?" practically every area of biology can obviously be touched on and explored to any extent and depth desired and permitted by time. Most importantly, however, by developing the story step-by-step and historically, and by using crucial experiments and concepts, the essential elements of "The Scientific Method"—that is, the analytic approach in gathering data and breaking a problem down to simpler, approachable questions—can be defined and illustrated. At each more complex step and question, this involves building up the previous step and knowledge through formulation of a specific question, logical formula-

---

[68]Hurd, *op. cit.*, pp. 79, 176.

tion of a testable hypothesis, and its experimental verification, refutation, or modification.[69]

INTEGRATION OF THE DISCIPLINES. One of the major criticisms of the new science programs is that the intra-subject connections are weak and the broader meanings of science obscured. The charge is also made that the subject content is no broader than in conventional programs—primarily limited to earth sciences, biology, physics, and chemistry, with little reference to anthropology, oceanography, human ecology, biophysics, and other areas.

For more than ten years scientists and science teachers have been urging that the science curriculum be reformed to provide a more integrated program, but the efforts to develop new curricula in the major disciplines has side-tracked this concern to a large extent. Recently there has been renewed interest in this approach, however, and at least thirty experimental programs are now in operation. They reject the notion of a science education program that perpetuates an artifical separation into discrete disciplines, which is rapidly becoming less valid for scientists themselves, and seek a program that will meet the needs of all students by integrating the whole of science.

Although they vary greatly in detail, all of the unified science projects acknowledge that: (1) the primary function of secondary school science should be a general education in science; and (2) programs should be constructed around concepts, generalizations, and processes that permeate all science. This approach has many advantages, including the following:

1. Better opportunity is provided to pattern instructional materials in a logical and efficient sequence.
2. Repetition can be minimized.
3. Concepts can be developed as they are needed to structure principles at ever-increasing levels of sophistication without restriction to traditional subject-matter fields.
4. More advanced content from any science discipline can be reserved for use at the upper grade levels and with more advanced students while relatively simple content can be used with less advanced students.
5. Material from sciences other than those traditionally included in school programs can be used, thus broadening the students' understanding.
6. Innovative teaching practices are facilitated and encouraged.

Programs utilizing the principles of an integrated science program have been in operation long enough and in sufficient numbers to allow a limited amount of research concerning their effectiveness. This research has shown that in general there has been (1) increased enrollment in high school science, (2) increased scientific literacy among graduates, (3) increased tendency of graduates to enter science oriented courses, (4) no harmful effect on graduates' grades in first-year college level

---

[69]Edward L. Tatum, "Science and Citizens: Horizons for the 70's," *Bulletin of the National Association of Secondary School Principals*, 340 (November 1969), pp. 21–22.

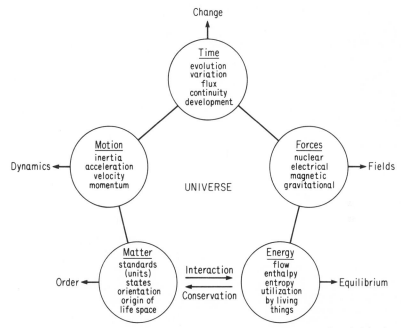

Fig. 8–2. An integrated science program. [From Lincoln-Sudbury Regional High School, Sudbury, Mass., *Unified Science*, (Mineo.), July 1968.]

science, and (5) no disadvantage to graduates in gaining college admission.[70]

No one is advocating the idea that one particular "ideal" integrated course should be developed for all schools. A course suited to all students in all situations is not possible, but diverse patterns of courses, each of which is characterized by a strong commitment to integrating the presently fragmented, specialized science offerings seem to offer great promise.

The diagram of Fig. 8–2 illustrates how the integrated idea for science education might be developed to cut across boundaries of earth science, biology, physics, and chemistry. The inner area of the diagram shows the universe as the central theme, with the five circles indicating how the major concepts of the program relate to the interaction of matter and energy; motion, time and forces. Under each of these concepts are listed the principles developed. Change, fields, equilibrium, order, and dynamics are the broad generalizations developed from these unifying themes.[71]

A program developed at Monona Grove High School, Madison, Wisconsin,

[70]American Association for the Advancement of Science, *Science Education News* (March 1969).

[71]Lincoln-Sudbury Regional High School, Sudbury, Mass., *Unified Science* (mimeo, July 1968).

provides another example of the integrated science approach. This is a four-year, concept-centered program based on the premise that all science is concerned with the nature of matter and energy and with the matter-energy interactions as a function of time. The consequence of these interactions is seen to be change, and this "Process of Change" is the central theme of the program. The diagram in Fig. 8–3 shows how twelve unifying themes dealing with fundamental issues in

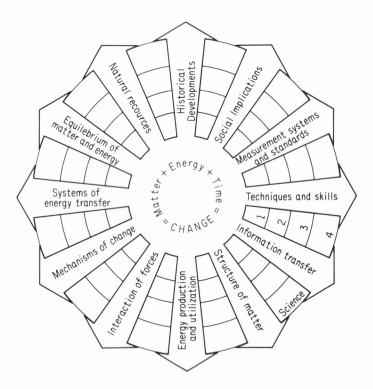

Fig. 8–3. Unifying themes for an integrated science program. [American Association for the Advancement of Science, *Science Education News*, (March 1969), p. 4. Copyright ©1969, by John Wiley & Sons, Inc., Reprinted by permission.]

science have been selected to amplify this central idea and to provide guidelines for the selection and organization of concepts to be incorporated into courses at various levels.

The program developed within this concept encompasses four years, two of which are required of all students. It is structured as follows:[72]

[72] *Science Education News, op. cit.* This and several other programs are described in more detail. For more information and examples, see also Leopold E. Klopfer, "Integrated Science for the Secondary School: Process, Progress, and Prospects," *Science Teacher* (November 1966), pp. 27–31.

Year and course numbers	Major theme
Science IA IB	Matter-Energy and the Process of Change
Science IIA IIB	Matter-Energy Interactions Relating to Life on Earth
Science IIIA	Matter-Energy Interactions in Natural Systems
Science IIIB	The Interaction of Man with His Environment
Science IV	Homeostatic Systems—Mechanisms for Survival

Shifting Emphases in Science Teaching

To summarize and put into perspective the preceding discussion of current science education developments, it seems appropriate to refer once more to the imminent authority on this subject, Paul DeHart Hurd. He suggests that the changing emphases in science reaching over the past decade are the following:[73]

From	To
1. Goals defined in personal-social terms.	1. Goals defined in intellectual competency terms.
2. Problem solving as a specified procedure.	2. Modes of inquiry suitable to exploring a discipline.
3. Student-centered curriculum.	3. Disciplined-centered curriculum.
4. Local responsibility for curriculum development guided by high school teachers.	4. National responsibility for curriculum development guided by scientists working with high school teachers.
5. Major emphasis upon informational aspects of science and minimal attention to the processes of science.	5. An emphasis upon science "as a way of knowing," emphasizing the processes of science as they relate to what is known.
6. A survey of many science topics to acquaint students with the range of knowledge in a subject.	6. A few topics explored in depth and taught to the point of understanding.
7. Descriptive and applied science.	7. Interpretive and theoretical science.
8. "Established" knowledge, with emphasis upon "basic" facts.	8. Knowledge in the mainstream of modern scientific thinking, with emphasis upon models and theories.

[73]Hurd, *op. cit.*, pp. 52–54.

From	To
9. Rote learning and memorization.	9. Concept formation and systematic thinking.
10. Group learning, teacher directed, "telling," and drill.	10. Individual learning, student centered, guided "discovery," and contemplation.
11. The opinion that learning has occurred if information can be repeated.	11. The opinion that learning has occurred if the pupil can use his knowledge in an explanatory or interpretive manner.
12. Subject matter chosen by teachers or textbook authors.	12. Subject matter chosen by research or professional scientists.
13. Personal-social needs of pupils as the criterion base for choosing course content.	13. The conceptual schemes of science as the criterion base for choosing course content.
14. Testing mostly on factual information with a "right" answer.	14. Testing mostly on the use of concepts to interpret observations or provide explanations.
15. Laboratory exercises to demonstrate, visualize, or verify known information.	15. Laboratory experiments to raise problems, test inquiry skills, and provide "discovery" opportunities.
16. Laboratory follows class discussion of topics and is largely divorced from classroom learning.	16. Laboratory work as an integral part of class work with pre- and postlaboratory discussion.
17. Learning capability depends almost entirely on student effort and teacher "telling"; a passive process.	17. Learning capability depends upon organization of curriculum and ability of teacher to match a teaching style with stated goals; an active process.
18. Education focused upon the world as it is today.	18. Education for change and the future.
19. Sequence of learning materials as teacher's arbitrary choice.	19. Sequence of learning materials dependent upon logical structure of discipline.
20. Curriculum improvement through revision and refinement.	20. Curriculum improvement through reform and innovation.
21. Supervision by a curriculum generalist.	21. Supervision by a science specialist.
22. Courses built of instructional units representing a logical organization of information.	22. Courses built around conceptual schemes in a coherent sequence stressing logical unity of discipline.
23. Instruction as information giving.	23. Instruction as information processing.
24. Courses written at a uniform level of conceptualization.	24. Courses written at increasingly higher levels of meaning, building upon previously learned concepts.

Selected References

American Association for the Advancement of Science, *Science Education News*, March 1969.

Andersen, Hans O., *Readings in Science Education for the Secondary School.* New York: The Macmillan Company, 1969.

Brandwein, Paul F., *Building Curricular Structures for Science.* Washington, D.C.: National Science Teachers Association, 1967.

Conant, James B., *On Understanding Science.* New Haven: Yale University Press, 1947.

Educational Policies Commission. *Education and the Spirit of Science.* Washington, D.C.: National Education Association, 1966.

Grobman, Arnold B., *The Changing Classroom: The Role of the Biological Sciences Curriculum Study.* Garden City, N.Y.: Doubleday & Company, 1969.

Hanson, Norwood Russell, "On The Structure of Physical Knowledge," *Education and the Structure of Knowledge.* Chicago: Rand McNally & Company, 1964.

Henry, Nelson B. (ed.), *Rethinking Science Education*, Fifty-ninth Yearbook of the National Society for the Study of Education. Chicago: National Society for the Study of Education, 1960.

Hurd, Paul DeHart, *New Directions in Teaching Secondary School Science.* Chicago: Rand McNally & Company, 1969.

National Science Teachers Association. *Theory Into Action.* Washington, D.C.: National Science Teachers Association, 1964.

Robinson, James T., *The Nature of Science and Science Teaching.* Belmont, Calif.: Wadsworth Publishing Company, Inc., 1968.

Romey, William D., *Inquiry Techniques for Teaching Science.* Englewood Cliffs, N.J.: Prentice-Hall, Inc., 1968.

Schwab, Joseph, and Paul Brandwein, *The Teaching of Science.* Cambridge, Mass.: Harvard University Press, 1962.

Shamos, Morris H., "The Role of Major Conceptual Schemes in Science Education," *The Science Teacher*, January 1966, pp. 27–30.

Sullivan, John J., and Calvin W. Taylor, *Learning and Creativity, with Special Emphasis on Science.* Washington, D.C.: National Science Teachers Association, 1967.

Tatum, Edward L., "Science and Citizens: Horizons for the 70's," *Bulletin of the National Association of Secondary School Principals* 340 (November 1969), pp. 19–34.

Thurber, Walter A., and Alfred T. Collette, *Teaching Science in Today's Secondary Schools.* 3d ed. Boston: Allyn and Bacon, Inc., 1968.

CHAPTER 9

SOCIAL STUDIES

The instructional programs commonly grouped under the term "social studies" or "social sciences" are among the oldest and most respected fields of human study and scholarship, but they are also among the least popular with secondary school students. Because students are tired of memorizing long lists of facts and sometimes questionable generalitions imposed by teachers and textbooks, many have turned their attention to other disciplines—those that present more stimulating materials, more challenging intellectual experiences, and more relevance to current problems and developments.

Intellectual, governmental, and even scientific leaders, in contrast to the attitude of many students, stress the importance of social understanding to the future of democracy and the human race. It has become abundantly clear that more than material affluence, military might, and scientific progress are required to assure rich and peaceful living for the residents of this planet. As a result of this realization, social studies education is receiving increased emphasis, and educational innovators are turning their attention to reform and revision in classroom social studies instruction.

The Path to the Present

Social studies education has been largely determined by the status of the social sciences as they have developed. Soon after the achievement of federal union, the first textbooks in American history and civics (or government) appeared, and throughout the eighteenth and nineteenth centuries, history was the most completely developed and most influential of the social sciences. In addition to American history, attention was turned to Greek, Roman, ancient, English, French, and German history—with the major emphasis on political and military events.

Civics or civil government instruction utilized textbooks which expounded the federal and state constitutions and added variety with equally unappealing details of the terms, salaries, and duties of local officials. Economics acquired enough status to inspire a flow of textbooks after 1820, but never acquired great acceptance as a basic subject for instruction. Geography probably could be rated as a poor second to history in curriculum emphasis during this time and was often pointed in the direction of "sailor geography," which was at least appropriate in communities near the sea. Geography texts were especially prone to the catechetical method, which, when combined with subject matter primarily concerned with lengths of distant rivers, heights of mountains, populations of cities, depths of oceans, and the like, provided little real inspiration to the nineteenth-century student.

Growing concern on the part of college entrance committees culminated in an 1899 report of the American Historical Association's Committee of Seven, entitled, *The Study of History in Schools.* This helped bring some order to the curricular chaos common to most secondary schools. For the four years of high school, the report recommended that social studies education include four "blocks" of history: (1) ancient history, especially Greek and Roman, to A.D. 800 or a few years later, (2) medieval and modern European history to the present, (3) English history, and (4) American history and civil government.[1]

The report of the Committee of Seven in 1899 helped to establish some direction for social studies education, but there was considerable dissatisfaction with its recommendations, especially from the emerging social science professional organizations. Changes in society and in the related needs of young people indicated a need for a social studies program encompassing much more than the historical emphasis advocated in 1899.

With the National Education Association's assumption of leadership in curriculum revision soon after the turn of the century, perspectives on social studies education changed rather rapidly. Various committees and study groups made recommendations which were in many cases quite different in scope and emphasis, but in 1916 these efforts culminated in a report which set a pattern for social studies education that is still dominant.

The National Education Association had established the National Commission on the Reorganization of Secondary Education to provide leadership in curricular reform. A subcommittee of this group, the Committee on Social Studies, released its recommendations in 1916, and the substance of this report clearly mirrored the concerns of the high school teachers, principals, and school superintendents who made up a majority of the committee. Their recommendations emphasized education for citizenship and urged attention to contemporary affairs and problems, with particular reference to local and current circumstances.

Major advances in social studies education were achieved with the 1916 report, in that (1) the general term *social studies* was officially adopted, and (2) the areas to be studied were broadly defined to include not only those relating

---

[1]Erling M. Hunt and others, *High School Social Studies Perspectives* (Boston: Houghton, 1962), pp. 9–10.

to traditional academic concerns, but also those relating more directly to the lives of students. The importance of history as the major area of study was not diminished, but the several disciplines of the social sciences were also included to facilitate perspective and application of historical concepts. The curriculum that emerged in the 1920's as a result of the Committee's recommendations included two cycles of studies, one for grades 7 through 9 and the other for grades 10 through 12:

Grade 7   Geography and American history (the Committee's recommendation of European history gained little following)
Grade 8   American history
Grade 9   Community and Vocational civics
Grade 10   European (often called world) history
Grade 11   American history
Grade 12   Problems of democracy, or of American democracy—social, economic, and political[2]

With minor alteration, this pattern for the social studies curriculum has persisted to the present, as indicated by a recent survey of practices in social studies course offerings of public, private, and parochial schools:

1. Separate course offerings are more usual than broad or block programs.
2. The most prevalent courses are American and world history.
3. There is little variation in grade levels at which the courses are offered.
4. There is an increase in the number of social studies courses being taught.[3]

To summarize the major developments in social studies education, the following trends may be recognized:

1. History as a discipline has persistently formed the core of the social studies curriculum.
2. Subject-matter categories, rather than a broader social science framework, continue to comprise the basic organizational pattern.
3. As a result of this atomistic view of isolated subjects, the curriculum has changed largely by addition and subtraction of subjects and topics.
4. An ethnocentric emphasis is evident in the disproportionate concern with American and European history and politics.
5. Changes in the curriculum have often reflected the power struggles among professional organizations, such as the American Historical Association, the American Political Science Association, and the National Education Association.[4]

[2] *Ibid.*, p. 14.
[3] Willis D. Moreland, "Curriculum Trends in the Social Studies," *Social Education* 26 (February 1962), pp. 73–76; Scarvia B. Anderson, *Social Studies in Secondary Schools: A Survey of Courses and Practices* (Princeton, N.J.: Educational Testing Service, Cooperative Test Division, 1964).
[4] Byron G. Massialas and C. Benjamin Cox, *Inquiry in Social Studies* (New York: McGraw-Hill, 1966), p. 29.

Current Developments

Although slower in getting started and less able to command large national resources of money and manpower, social studies scholars and educators have recently made considerable progress toward substantial curricular reform. Through the efforts of the professional organizations, or the education and academic faculties at universities supported by the U.S. Office of Education through its Project Social Studies, proposed reforms are emerging in abundance. To summarize them is difficult and subject to oversimplification, but perhaps a brief condensation will facilitate understanding of the more important contemporary trends:

1. An increased empirical basis for proposals and practices provides a more substantial foundation for innovative efforts than the past has usually afforded.
2. Emphasis is on teaching basic concepts through use of the "inquiry" approach and other similar functional methods to encourage understanding of the structural elements of social studies disciplines. The amount of material to be covered is reduced and unnecessary repetition is better avoided. In-depth case study materials are often used in these instructional processes.
3. More attention is given to developing a "world view" through study of non-Western cultures as well as the more traditional world studies.
4. More substantive material is being forced down into the primary grades.
5. An ever-increasing number and variety of social studies electives are being offered, especially to seniors.
6. The traditional emphasis on history, geography, and civics is being broken, and interdisciplinary approaches giving more attention to the humanities are rapidly gaining in popularity.

Social Studies Education

The program for teaching the disciplines we have grouped under the "class" of social studies may be termed social studies education. This is a rather general term which is used in a variety of ways, but it seems to best include the disciplines we wish to discuss at this point.

Considerable confusion and controversy are related to the use and meaning of the terms "social sciences" and "social studies." Some would claim that because the disciplines included are not as exact and empirical as the natural sciences the term "science" is misleading and inappropriate. However, because scholars in these fields of study subscribe to similar concepts about problem solving and research, it would not seem necessary to deny them use of the term "science." Some definition of the term does seem advisable, however.

The *social sciences* are those bodies of knowledge accumulated by man from his studies of anthropology, economics, geography, history, political science, social psychology, and sociology. The social sciences are thus a branch of human knowledge, and, to the extent that they are scientific, they are neutral and unconcerned with ethics, practicalities, and the like. The *social studies* are the facts which are selected from the reservoir of truths contained in the social sciences and organized for instructional purposes. They are inevitably concerned with the utilization and application of the knowledge of the social sciences and must consider ethical implications and other realities of the social world in which we live.

Objectives of Social Studies Education

Just as it is difficult to obtain agreement on the definition and scope of social studies, it is equally hard to find universally acceptable statements of objectives for social studies education. No attempt will be made to describe exhaustively the variations in belief concerning social studies objectives. Neither will an attempt be made to presume the wisdom to identify a consensus. We will, however, attempt to arrive at a statement of goals and purposes which seems most compatible with the general philosophy of this text.

The directions set by the 1916 Committee on Social Studies are still basically valid. They are appropriate to the ultimate goal of education in the social studies, which is the development of desirable sociocivic behavior. As stated by Moreland, ". . . social learning consists of the development of those understandings, skills, and attitudes appropriate to successful living in a changing world and to participation in the process of desirable social change."[5]

A general objective as broad as that stated above would seem to require some related "subgoals." These may be conveniently divided into four categories: concepts, generalizations, inquiry skills, and attitudes.

A concept may be defined as ". . . a classification or systematic organization of stimuli, characteristics, or events which have common characteristics."[6] Understanding a concept means that a person can discriminate between appropriate and inappropriate characteristics, and can recognize representations of the concept in other forms. Moreland provides a good example: ". . . the concept 'government' embodies such characteristics as rules for controlling behavior and a focus of authority, and an inappropriate or irrelevant characteristic would be a building. The concept of government may be identified in the family, a church, or a political entity."[7] A grasping of concepts obviously necessitates a prerequisite fund of experience and basic factual knowledge.

A generalization may be defined as a statement of relationship between two

---

[5]Willis D. Moreland (ed.), *Social Studies in the Senior High School* (Washington, D.C.: National Council for the Social Studies, 1965), p. 34.
[6]Frederick J. McDonald, *Educational Psychology* (San Francisco: Wadsworth, 1959), p. 134.
[7]Moreland, *op. cit.*, pp. 34–35.

or more concepts which has broad applicability in space and time.[8] Faulty generalizations often exist in the form of stereotypes (e.g., the Irish have violent tempers, Germans are militaristic, Italians are skilled lovers), which seldom exhibit very much accuracy. More valid generalizations are the result of an accurate understanding of underlying concepts and their relationship to the generalization. A more accurate generalization gleaned from a social studies lesson might be, "The major nations of the world are economically interdependent."

Teaching students to "think" has long been accepted as a prime goal of general education, and social studies education must bear a large share of this responsibility. Students should learn how to weigh evidence, to evaluate alternatives, and to come to their own conclusions. They should understand things, not just know them. Emphasis should be placed on decisionmaking rather than mere remembering. Such a framework entails social analysis, systematic inquiry, multidisciplinary sources of data, and a focus on social issues and judgments.

Inquiry and problem solving in the social studies usually involve attitudes and value judgments. The development of attitudes and values consistent with a democratic society thus becomes another essential ingredient of social studies education. Respect for the dignity and worth of the individual, together with a desire for the kinds of social institutions and processes which best provide for the free and full development of individuals, form the foundation for these democratic values and attitudes.

To conclude this brief discussion of goals for social studies education, a more detailed statement from the National Council for the Social Studies will perhaps be helpful in setting the desired directions for social studies education.

To meet the needs of American society in the late twentieth century, an adequate social studies curriculum must:

1. Identify and emphasize the values and ideals that have guided the American people and nation, with a view to ensuring a reasoned and disciplined patriotism.
2. Be global in scope, encompassing an understanding and appreciation not only of Western civilization and peoples to whom our past is bound, but of the culture and peoples of Asia, Africa, and Latin America with whom our relations are increasingly close. A study of the similarities and diversities of cultures and the different stages of political development and economic growth are required.
3. Provide realism and vitality in the study of American and world society and problems, by deliberately including attention to issues that are unsolved, perhaps divisive, but that require development of informed opinion.
4. Provide continuing opportunity for the development and the continuing application of skills in critical thinking.

To incorporate the findings of scholarship, an adequate social studies curriculum in the late twentieth century must:

---

[8]Theodore Kaltsounis, "Cognitive Learning and the Social Studies," *Educational Leadership* (March 1969), p. 613.

5. Take account of new knowledge and new interpretations in such long-established disciplines as history, geography, political science, and economics and of the findings of the newer behavioral sciences (anthropology, sociology, psychology) and of interdisciplinary (area) studies.
6. In developing courses and units there must be rigorous selection with a focus on the understanding of contemporary society and the skills needed in achieving such understanding.

In applying established knowledge of the teaching and learning process, an adequate social studies curriculum must:

7. Take account of the maturity levels of learners, which advance from year to year but also vary widely within each age group.
8. Both adapt to and capitalize the different learning styles and varied abilities and talents, skills, interests, and backgrounds of learners by drawing upon a wide range of learning experiences, materials, and media, as appropriate.
9. Ensure continuity and consistency through the years of elementary and secondary school, reconciling the necessity for intelligent choice among many possible courses and units with the obligation to realize and to reinforce systematically the gains from the choices actually made.
10. Recognize that learning does not cease with termination of school attendance, and provide the stimulus, skills, and knowledge of sources that are needed if individuals are to continue to learn independently.
11. Provide for flexibility and for carefully planned and evaluated experimentation.[9]

Content of Social Studies Education

The stating of goals for social studies education is all well and good, but no progress can be made toward the fulfillment of such goals without the proper selection of content material to be included in the program, appropriate organization for teaching, and effective teaching methodology. Appropriate aspects of each of these additional essential elements will be discussed briefly at this point.

There is an overabundance of potential subject matter in the field of social studies, and each year the supply increases, because the "knowledge explosion" is by no means limited to the natural sciences. Consequently, the problem of selection becomes ever larger. Choices as to disciplines to be included and then the selection of portions from each discipline's abundance of knowledge provide ample opportunity for disagreement and confusion. The temptation to include a little bit of everything has all too often been dominant, and social studies has become a far-flung, superficial survey lacking in depth, color, humanity, correlation, and relevance. In addition, these surveys have been most often largely limited to ". . . the fact-myth-legend content usually referred to as 'history'."[10]

Recent movements in social studies education have taken the position that

[9]Dorothy McClure Fraser and Samuel P. McCutchen (eds.), *Social Studies in Transition: Guidelines for Change* (Washington, D.C.: National Council for the Social Studies, 1965), pp. 6–8. Reprinted by permission.

[10]Edwin Fenton, *Teaching the New Social Studies in Secondary Schools* (New York: Holt, 1966), p. 113.

the selection of content should emphasize those human affairs fraught with conflict or tension and threatening the integrity of a free society. The most common procedure seems to be identification of major "themes" or problem areas, moving then to the selection of appropriate content from the relevant social and behavioral sciences. Two statements setting down themes for social studies education may be mentioned as typical of the best thus far produced by scholars working to resolve questions of social studies content.

The U.S. Office of Education, through Project Social Studies, established a Curriculum Study Center in 1963 at Harvard University which has developed materials for grades 8 through 10, concentrating on five problem areas of society:

1. The problem of keeping individual and societal conflict within tolerable and reasonable limits.
2. The problem of maintaining a reasonable balance between individual liberty and community cohesion.
3. The problem of maintaining or developing a just priority of privileges among men within society and among nations.
4. The problem of providing a standard of living for all men sufficient to maintain a "civilized" existence.
5. The problem of determining the range of behavior necessary for men to express reasonable dissent in their efforts to effect social change.[11]

This program includes reintroduction and expansion of the five areas at higher levels of complexity by means of a "spiral" curriculum.

Over a period of fifteen years, four successive Committees on Concepts and Values of the National Council for the Social Studies have developed a statement of 15 themes for social studies education, each of which is said to be a societal goal of American democracy. Illustrative concepts and generalizations have been suggested to aid in the development of curricular materials by regional and local educators. The fifteen themes suggested are

1. Recognition of the dignity and worth of the individual.
2. The use of intelligence to improve human living.
3. Recognition and understanding of world interdependence.
4. The understanding of the major world cultures and culture areas.
5. The intelligent uses of the natural environment.
6. The vitalization of our democracy through an intelligent use of our public educational facilities.
7. The intelligent acceptance, by individuals and groups, of responsibility for achieving democratic social action.
8. Increasing the effectiveness of the family as a basic social institution.
9. The effective development of moral and spiritual values.
10. The intelligent and responsible sharing of power in order to attain justice.

[11]Frances A. J. Ianni and Lois S. Josephs, "The Curriculum Research and Development Program of the U.S. Office of Education: Project English, Project Social Studies and Beyond," in Robert W. Heath, (ed.), New Curricula (New York: Harper, 1964), pp. 202–203.

11. The intelligent utilization of scarce resources to attain the widest general well-being.
12. Achievement of adequate horizons of loyalty.
13. Cooperation in the interest of peace and welfare.
14. Achieving a balance between social stability and social change.
15. Widening and deepening the ability to live more richly.[12]

On the basis of problems or themes such as those stated above, there must be a determination of content subject matter appropriate to their study. Each of the social and behavioral sciences may contribute to a functional social studies program, and each should be drawn upon in formulating a program. Although there is room for argument about the wisdom of including such a variety of disciplines within one group called social sciences, the following are usually accepted as the social science disciplines: *anthropology, economics, geography, history, political science, social psychology,* and *sociology*. Certain aspects of some of these may be included in other groupings (such as the natural sciences), but in general this grouping seems reasonably accurate and usable.

Organization of the Social Sciences for Teaching and Learning

Most of the current efforts to reorganize the social studies curriculum utilize the ideas of disciplinary structure which form the focus of this text. Social studies education may be seen to include the four elements mentioned earlier: concepts, generalizations, inquiry skills, and attitudes. These vary to some extent among the various social science disciplines, but there are also many commonalities. The common elements may be utilized to bind the various social science disciplines into a meaningful whole. The need for such an organization for instruction is the basis for the concern which motivates social studies reformers. Samuel P. McCutchen, a recognized social studies scholar, cogently summarizes this concern.

> Our failure to bring coherence to the social studies can quickly be demonstrated by a glance at the past. Taught in a sequence prescribed in 1916, the social studies grew out of history and political science, then history plus geography. As economics and sociology have come to be included the resultant mélange has become more complicated and we have attained a goulash in which the beans, potatoes, and onions are in the same pot but are still not truly synthesized, digested, integrated.
>
> This has been largely due to the fact that social studies teachers have been trying to use the various separate organizations of content, each designed by the logic and for the convenience of the various scholarly disciplines. Failing thus far to achieve and accept a discipline of our own, we have tried to use the discipline

---

[12]Dorothy McClure Fraser and Samuel P. McCutchen (eds.), *Social Studies in Transition: Guidelines for Change* (Washington, D.C.: National Council for the Social Studies, 1965), pp. 10–52.

of history (or occasionally geography) to make the content of economics, political science, and sociology fit into our scheme of teaching, while retaining the multiple frames of content organization.[13]

Social sciences do have basic principles or rules. They cannot meet all the rigorous standards of mathematical principles and cannot be tested in the same scientific manner, but major principles can be identified and used for social studies instruction. The lines of demarcation between disciplines are not as sharp and clean-cut as we are sometimes led to believe.

Concepts and Generalizations

There is not yet, and probably never will be, unanimous agreement on the basic concepts and generalizations of the social studies. There has been enough progress in this direction, however, to provide considerable assistance to the curriculum builder and the classroom teacher. Space will not allow an extensive discussion of common social studies concepts, but a review of the definition of the term and a few examples may suffice to illustrate this element of social studies education.

A social studies concept is usually identified by key words or phrases—sometimes called categories. Social class, leadership, culture, or supply and demand are examples of these categories. A social studies concept, then, is ". . . a word or phrase which has associated with it certain salient, inalienable features."[14] Some more examples of social studies concepts are

1. Revolution	9. Ideology
2. Stratification	10. Family
3. Balance of Power	11. River
4. Diminishing Returns	12. Republic
5. Regional Specialization	13. Government
6. Productivity	14. Institution
7. Cultural lag	15. Customs
8. Nationalism	16. Election[15]

The usefulness of the idea of concept utilization in teaching the social studies is well illustrated by Edwin Fenton.

> Let us suppose, for example, that a student knows four concepts from sociology —social class, status, role, and norms—and wants to analyze the society of Boston in 1750. These four concepts will help to guide his search for data. With them in mind, he will search for evidence about class structure: how many classes existed, and what characteristics distinguished members of one class from those of another. He will try to find out what roles members of each social class played

[13]Samuel P. McCutchen, "A Discipline for the Social Studies," *Social Education*, 27 (February 1963), pp. 61–65. Reprinted with permission of the National Council for the Social Studies and Samuel P. McCutchen.

[14]James G. Womack, *Discovering the Structure of Social Studies* (New York: Benziger, 1966), p. 30.

[15]*Ibid.*

in the society. He will ask himself which roles had high status and which ones ranked at the bottom of the prestige scale. Finally, he will seek evidence about which norms—patterns of behavior—were expected from everyone. The concepts are "imposed conceptions" which guide the search for data toward issues which sociologists have found useful for the analysis of society.[16]

Related concepts may be combined to form generalizations leading to a more complete understanding of the subject. A generalization may be further defined as ". . . a universally applicable statement at the highest level of abstraction relevant to all time or stated times about man past and/or present, engaging in a basic human activity."[17] Characteristics of a generalization have been identified by James G. Womack as follows:

1. Generalizations are derived from social studies content, but they are not content themselves. They not only have content as their source, but their substantiation and proof for being generalizations also come from content.
2. Generalizations have universal application and admit no major exceptions.
3. Generalizations contain no specific references to any particular peoples, places, or times.
4. Generalizations have a thesis; that is, they make a point about the subject for each social science discipline.
5. Generalizations, as principles or rules, comprise the underlying structure for each social science discipline.
6. Generalizations are best discovered by inductive reasoning.
7. Generalizations are abstractions which can be broken down into gradations of complexity and completeness so that they can be understood and mastered, to some extent, even by primary grade students.
8. Definitions and concepts are not themselves generalizations, but may be incorporated into a generalization.[18]

Concepts and generalizations are two different things, but combining the two into one methodology provides excellent educational benefits. One implies the other for maximum learning, as exemplified by the fact that a teacher could introduce concepts while studying or formulating generalizations. Or concept understanding could be approached first, with application of the concepts proceeding through their incorporation into pertinent generalizations.

Understanding of concepts and generalizations is often developed through the use of questions. Those working with the Social Studies Curriculum Project at Harvard University have organized their proposed course of study around man, his nature as a species, and the forces that shaped and continue to shape his

---

[16]Edwin Fenton, *The New Social Studies* (New York: Holt, 1967), p. 14.

[17]Paul R. Hanna and John R. Lee, "Content in the Social Studies," in John U. Michaelis (ed.), *Social Studies in Elementary Schools* (Washington, D.C.: National Council for the Social Studies, 1962), p. 73.

[18]Womack, *op. cit.*, p. 2.

humanity. Three main questions which occur throughout this program provide a means of concept and generalization formulation:

What is human about human beings?
How did they get that way?
How can they be made more so?

These questions lead to generalizations stating that "The five great humanizing forces are . . . tool-making, language, social organization, the management of man's prolonged childhood, and man's urge to explain."[19]

Some additional examples of social studies generalizations may be helpful in understanding the use of this instructional tool. Hanna and Lee have suggested the following as being typical:

Prevention of soil erosion through sound soil management programs will remove soil as a polluting influence on streams. . . .
The development of communication and transportation routes in any area is vitally affected by the physical factors of terrain and climate. . . .
The poorer a family, the greater the proportion of its total expenditure used for food.[20]

Over a period of some fifteen years, Paul R. Hanna, Richard Gross, and several graduate students at Stanford University have identified over 3,000 generalizations deemed important to social studies education. They have been classified into nine "basic activities of man," as follows:

1. Protecting and conserving human and natural resources and property.
2. Producing, exchanging, distributing, and consuming food, clothing, shelter, and other consumer goods and services.
3. Transporting people and goods.
4. Communicating ideas and feelings.
5. Providing education.
6. Providing recreation.
7. Organizing and governing.
8. Creating tools, technics, and social arrangements.
9. Expressing and satisfying aesthetic and spiritual impulses.[21]

The generalizations and the nine "basic activities of man" may be used to define the subject matter to be studied; they also suggest a rudimentary method of inquiry into culture, organized around the nine interrelated parts.

A type of generalization which does not entirely meet the criteria set out above, but which is necessary to social studies education, deserves some attention. It does not meet the general criteria completely in that it has limited rather than universal application. An introductory phrase of the sentence usually indicates the degree of application. For example:

---

[19]Jerome S. Bruner, "Man: A Course of Study," Social Studies Curriculum Project, Educational Services Incorporated, Cambridge, Mass.
[20]Hanna and Lee, *op. cit.*, pp. 75–76, 79.
[21]*Ibid.*, p. 69.

1. In a *capitalist country*, the regulator of supply and demand is the market place.
2. In *fascist countries*, the people are the servants of the state rather than served by the state.
3. In *the Common Market countries*, the principle of regional specialization has led to increased trade with mutual benefit for all.[22]

The teacher must be aware of this type of limited generalization so that he may prevent students' confusing them with those generalizations which have unlimited application.

Methods of Inquiry

We have stated earlier that one of the basic structural ingredients of disciplines is their method of inquiry. How do they go about studying their discipline and gaining new knowledge? How do they prove or disprove ideas concerning the discipline? A math teacher typically concentrates on a principle or theorem, or develops a specific skill. Social studies teachers have traditionally exposed their students to facts, details, and content. Principles or generalizations have rarely been involved.

The newer movements in social studies education are attempting to drastically change this traditional emphasis on facts and content material. Instead of merely following a political or military campaign, faithfully chronicling all the events and dates, attempts are made to raise questions, to hypothesize, and to speculate about people's actions. The techniques and methods of inquiry more common to the behavioral sciences are proving adaptable to the social sciences.

Social studies scholars are consistently moving toward the adoption of inquiry methods identified by the terms "discovery," "problem solving," "reflective thinking," or some similar term. The process itself is not new, but it has seldom been used in the past for social studies education. Educators in other fields, even those who have not done so in the past, seem to be turning more and more to this procedure also.

The inquiry process is sometimes shrouded in difficult language and obscured by hazy procedures, but its elements are essentially rather simple. John Dewey contributed one of the earlier modern definitions when he proposed that the inquiry process is ". . . the active, persistent, and careful consideration of any belief or supposed form of knowledge in the light of the grounds that support it and the further conclusions to which it tends." Using the term "reflective thinking," Dewey went on to point out that this involves "(1) a state of doubt, hesitation, perplexity, mental difficulty, in which thinking originates, and (2) an act of searching, hunting, inquiring, to find material that will resolve the doubt, settle and dispose of the perplexity."[23]

[22]Womack, *op. cit.*, p. 4.
[23]John Dewey, *How We Think* (Lexington, Mass.: Heath, 1933).

Various attempts have been made to classify the cognitive skills involved in the process of problem solving. A condensed version of a scheme developed by Robert Ennis may serve to illustrate this aspect of identifying and organizing social studies materials for teaching. He proposed twelve aspects of critical thinking:

1. Grasping the meaning of a statement.
2. Judging whether there is ambiguity in a line of reasoning.
3. Judging whether certain statements contradict each other.
4. Judging whether a conclusion follows necessarily.
5. Judging whether a statement is specific enough.
6. Judging whether a statement is actually the application of a certain principle.
7. Judging whether an observation statement is reliable.
8. Judging whether an inductive conclusion is warranted.
9. Judging whether the problem has been identified.
10. Judging whether something is an assumption.
11. Judging whether a definition is adequate.
12. Judging whether a statement made by an alleged authority is acceptable.[24]

This list of aspects of critical thinking illustrates the types of cognitive skills which students of the social studies (and other disciplines, as well) should be helped to develop. There is lacking in a list such as this, however, an orderly scheme or strategy for engaging in social inquiry. Without some type of model to help them get organized in their efforts, teachers and students are likely to wander around, become confused in their thinking, and revert to more traditional procedures for studying the social sciences. Several basic models have been proposed in recent years, most of which bear considerable resemblance to the "scientific method" and other similar earlier scholarly procedures. Two of these will be suggested as good examples of procedures to follow in both teaching and using inquiry procedures.

Millard Clements has suggested a basic model which emphasizes the nonroutine character of social inquiry, pointing out that social inquiry depends on both imagination and discipline. "Without discipline there will be no orderly confrontation of evidence." The following tasks are proposed as basic to social inquiry:

1. Invent a mystery. Identify a heuristic question.
2. Find ideas that may be used in the formation and clarification of questions.
3. Using the chosen ideas, translate the heuristic question into general questions which literally direct the inquiry.
4. Translate the general questions into particular questions which focus attention upon evidence.
5. Engage in the cross-examination of the evidence.

[24]Robert H. Ennis, "A Concept of Critical Thinking," *Harvard Educational Review* 32 (Winter 1962), p. 84

6. Write concluding reports or accounts of what has been done, seen, heard, or discovered.[25]

Edwin Fenton, who has been very active in the development of new social studies curricula and teaching materials, suggests a series of steps to be followed by students as they try to learn to organize hypothesis formation and the proof process parts of inquiry. These are termed "Steps in a Mode of Inquiry for the Social Studies."

1. Recognizing a problem from data.
2. Formulating hypotheses.
   (a) Asking analytical questions.
   (b) Stating hypotheses.
   (c) Remaining aware of the tentative nature of hypotheses.
3. Recognizing the logical implications of hypotheses.
4. Gathering data.
   (a) Deciding what data will be needed.
   (b) Selecting or rejecting sources.
5. Analyzing, evaluating and interpreting data.
   (a) Selecting relevant data.
   (b) Evaluating sources.
      (1) Determining the frame of reference of an author.
      (2) Determining the accuracy of statements of fact.
   (c) Interpreting the data.
6. Evaluating the hypothesis in light of the data.
   (a) Modifying the hypothesis, if necessary.
      (1) Rejecting a logical implication unsupported by data.
      (2) Restating the hypothesis.
   (b) Stating a generalization.[26]

Concept and generalization formulation, as discussed earlier, are obviously an integral part of the inquiry process. One cannot proceed apart from the other very well, if at all. For instance, concepts relative to the following terms would be basic to the method of inquiry which social scientists and historians use:

1. Social studies question
2. Hypothesis
3. Fact
4. Data
5. Evidence
6. Frame of reference (also bias and point of view)
7. Generalization
8. Theory
9. Concept[27]

[25]Millard Clements, "The Disciplines and Social Study," in Jean Fair and Fannie R. Shaftel (eds.), *Effective Thinking in the Social Studies*, 37th Yearbook of the National Council for the Social Studies (Washington, D.C.: National Council for the Social Studies, 1967), Chapter 3, pp. 71–72.
[26]Edwin Fenton, *The New Social Studies* (New York: Holt, 1967), pp. 16–17.
[27]Edwin Fenton, *Developing a New Curriculum: A Rationale for the Holt Social Studies Curriculum* (New York: Holt, 1967), p. 14.

An understanding of generalizations concerning the method of inquiry is also required of students before they can adequately and independently pursue knowledge. These *methodological generalizations* comprise the principles or rules which describe the skills or techniques needed to study social studies content. Some examples of methodological generalizations are:

1. Areal geographic relations can be seen most readily by the use of map symbols and scales.
2. Prior to attempting any measurement, as with gross national product or the number of eligible voters, it is important to establish a precise definition of each term to be measured.
3. Inductive thinking in the social sciences has the asset of predictability and the debit of uncertainty, since its focus is on establishing a pattern for a finite number of observable phenomena.
4. Any adequate comparison of political systems demands the establishment of multiple criteria.
5. Few events have single causes or single results.
6. In any system of classification, such as polling, sampling, or establishing categories, one must first establish limits and characteristics for the elements to be included in the classification system.[28]

Attitudes

Education related to attitudes and values, often referred to as the "affective domain," is possibly the most difficult and least successful part of most social studies programs. There has been no lack of exhortation given to this phase of the social studies through the years. Few would deny its importance and place in the social studies curriculum. Still, we must admit that the forming, reinforcing, and changing of values and attitudes has been a largely neglected phase of social studies teaching.

To restate this goal of social studies education, it would seem acceptable to adopt Fenton's proposal that ". . . the affective objectives of social studies education are concerned with the development of attitudes, understandings, and values that will promote a democratic way of life and help each student to develop a personal philosophy."[29] Concepts, generalizations, and inquiry, as discussed in previous sections, are obviously essential ingredients of teaching related to attitudes and values. In practice, they cannot be separated, but for purposes of this discussion we will attempt to deal more specifically with attitudes and values.

It has been suggested that there are three major types of attitudes and values which teachers must consider: behavioral, procedural, and substantive.[30] General agreement could probably be reached concerning the necessity for teaching the first two of these types; many would argue that we have

[28]Womack, *op. cit.*, p. 5.
[29]Edwin Fenton, *Teaching the New Social Studies in Secondary Schools* (New York: Holt, 1966), p. 19.
[30]*Ibid.*, pp. 42–44.

no right to teach the third, although we should probably teach about them.

Behavioral values are those concerned with procedure and conduct in the classroom. Teachers cannot carry out their responsibilities unless students abide by certain behavioral requirements. Procedures concerning class schedules, absentee regulations, and other administrative routines are necessary for the orderly operation of the school and the classroom. The teacher has a right, and a responsibility, to teach attitudes appropriate to these necessities. An appropriate noise level, care of textbooks and equipment, respect for the teacher's authority, refraining from interrupting other students when they are talking, and disciplinary procedures in general must be expected by the teacher and accepted by students before other learning activities can proceed satisfactorily. Every teacher must teach behavioral values, or he will be unable to teach anything else.

Procedural values pertain to the method accepted for discovering and examining evidence in the search for knowledge and validation of ideas. Teachers should be prepared to teach, for instance, that critical thinking is better than uncritical thinking. Prejudices must not be allowed to stand unchallenged by evidence. Experimentation must be accepted as superior to "common sense." The methods by which social scientists and historians arrive at conclusions, through systematic examination of appropriate evidence, must be taught as the superior procedure in social studies inquiry. The need for teaching subject matter is accepted by parents and school officials, but they must also accept the necessity for teaching these types of procedural values if subject matter is to have any real usefulness.

Most of the discussion and argument concerning the teaching of values and attitudes revolves around the third type of values—substantive. Some maintain that teachers do have the right and the responsibility to teach the "accepted" or "common" values and attitudes of the society, or at least those accepted by the dominant group of the society. Others argue just as heatedly that teachers have no right to require or even attempt to gain student acceptance of certain values. Preferences as to type of government, religious beliefs, monetary policy, moral practices, conformity, reading habits, health practices, population control, international government, and innumerable other topics must be considered in the social studies classroom—but there is serious question as to whether teachers should make a conscious effort to persuade students to accept particular beliefs. Such values cannot be avoided in the classroom, but the teacher has a responsibility to be at least as objective as possible in teaching about them. The crucial consideration is the need for teaching *about* these values and attitudes rather than indoctrinating or attempting to persuade students in particular directions. If democratic tenets are valid, the best will prevail if people are allowed to learn about all aspects of a problem and democratically arrive at conclusions and courses of action.

The most comprehensive attempt at identification and classification of desired learning outcomes in the affective domain may be found in a taxonomy which has been very influential in recent years.[31] It is organized on different levels of complexity, and moves on a hierarchial order from the more simple to the more complex. Each level is dependent upon those below it, thus setting up an organizational sequence for teaching. A brief condensation of this taxonomy may facilitate a better understanding of social studies responsibilities related to the teaching of attitudes and values.

1.0 Receiving (Attending)

At this level we are concerned that the learner be sensitized to the existence of certain phenomena and stimuli; that is, that he be willing to receive or to attend to them.

2.0 Responding

At this level we are concerned with responses which go beyond merely attending to the phenomenon. The student is sufficiently motivated that he is not just (willing to attend), but perhaps it is correct to say that he is actively attending. Most commonly we use the term to indicate the desire that a child become sufficiently involved in or committed to a subject, phenomenon, or activity that he will seek it out and gain satisfaction from working with it or engaging in it.

3.0 Valuing

Behavior categorized at this level is sufficiently consistent and stable to have taken on the characteristics of a belief or an attitude. The learner displays this behavior with sufficient consistency in appropriate situations that he comes to be perceived as holding a value.

An important element of behavior characterized by Valuing is that it is motivated, not by the desire to comply or obey, but by the individual's commitment to the underlying value guiding the behavior.

4.0 Organization

As the learner successively internalizes values, he encounters situations for which more than one value is relevant. Thus necessity arises for (a) the organization of the values into a system, (b) the determination of the interrelationships among them, and (c) the establishment of the dominant and pervasive ones. Such a system is built gradually, subject to change as new values are incorporated.

5.0 Characterization by a Value or Value Complex

At this level of internationalization the values have a place in the individual's value hierarchy, are organized into some kind of internally consistent system, have controlled the behavior of the individual for a sufficient time that he has adapted to behaving this way; and an evocation of the behavior no longer arouses emotion or affect except when the individual is threatened or challenged.

The individual acts consistently in accordance with the values he has internalized at this level, and our concern is to indicate two things: (a) the generalization of this control to so much of the individual's behavior that he is described and characterized as a person by these pervasive controlling tendencies, and (b) the integration of these beliefs, ideas, and attitudes into a total philosophy or world view.[32]

[31]D.R. Krathwohl, B. S. Bloom, and B. B. Masia, *Taxonomy of Educational Objectives: Handbook II, the Affective Domain* (New York: McKay, 1964).
[32]*Ibid.*, pp. 176–185.

There are obvious difficulties involved in teaching values, some of which we have already discussed. Research indicates that there is serious doubt that we can really get students to substantially change value judgments. Assuming that we can change them, in what direction should they be changed? A complicating factor is that when we teach certain values we imply that other values or value systems are wrong. On the other hand, if we try to avoid teaching values, or at least teaching about values, we are likely to lead students to believe that no values are worthwhile, that nothing really matters, and that they can do anything their human nature desires. It seems obvious that issues related to values must at least be raised so that students may work out to their own satisfaction the vital matters of life in a social world.

Teaching Strategies

It has been proposed in the preceding pages that social studies education should be concerned with the development of those understandings, skills, and attitudes appropriate to successful living in a changing world and to effective participation in social change. This seems most likely to occur when approached through the teaching of certain concepts, generalizations, problem solving skills, and attitudes. An interdisciplinary approach would seem the most appropriate teaching strategy to follow. *Process* becomes *part of* the *content* with which teachers and students are concerned.

Using an interdisciplinary approach in the teaching of social studies allows students to develop the ability to understand and use the great unavoidable interrelationship of all the social sciences in grasping the "big picture" inherent in a single body of content. It also allows them to use the skills and techniques of social science inquiry. A simple example of this approach to social studies education may better illustrate the point:

> . . . The interdisciplinary approach would say to the teacher preparing to teach a fifth, eighth, or eleventh grade unit from American History—for example, let us say the unit is one on immigration to the U.S.—go ahead as usual and give the time and place dimensions of immigration by using the disciplines of history and geography, respectively. These two disciplines should help the students understand:
> 1. When the various waves of immigration occurred.
> 2. The historical reasons for the waves of immigration.
> 3. The countries from which the immigrants came and the areas of the United States where various nationalities settled.
> 4. Their contributions to the development of our society.
> It is at this point that the teacher usually stops, considering the unit completed. The interdisciplinary approach would now urge the teacher to give students an opportunity to view immigration from one or more of the perspectives of sociology, anthropology, economics, and political science.
> Using one or more of these disciplines, in addition to geography and history, the students might, for the very first time, be exposed to such information,
> 1. From anthropology and sociology as:
>   (a) The Old World cultures of major immigrant nationalities, the introduc-

tion of concepts of tradition-directed societies, patriarchal and matri-
archal societies, and others.
(b) Anthropological differences of nationalities.
(c) Social classes represented by various nationalities, the introduction of
concepts of social class, social stratification, achieved and ascribed
status, and others.
(d) Social problems experienced by immigrants in the United States, and
the social problems caused by immigration.
2. From economics as:
(a) Skills, wealth, and education of various nationalities.
(b) Effects of immigrants on labor unions, United States industrialization,
location of business enterprises, and others.
(c) Effects of immigrants on United States acquisition of territory and
settlement of the frontier.
3. From political science as:
(a) The type of government which existed in the immigrants' native country.
(b) The philosophies of government brought to the United States by
immigrants, the introduction of concepts of anarchism, radicalism,
Fourierism, and Fabianism.
(c) Government problems caused by immigrants, both in domestic and
foreign affairs.[33]

In thinking specifically about how to teach important concepts and generalizations, the average teacher needs some suggestions and guidelines to order his
planning. For teaching concepts, the following guidelines have been suggested:

1. Learning simpler concepts must precede learning of compound concepts of
which they are components.
2. The widely varying prior experiences of students must be taken into account.
3. Real or direct experience, such as a field trip, is more meaningful if preceded
by selective introduction and follow-up analysis.
4. Use of a concept in different contexts enhances learning of it.
5. Examples put life into concepts and make them more real and meaningful.[34]

If a teacher follows the principles of inquiry and discovery, he will give
students the opportunity to arrive at their own meaning of a concept before
giving guidance and direction. Such discovery will increase their understanding,
use, and retention of the concepts.

The same principles that apply to teaching concepts are valid for teaching
generalizations or statements of relationship among concepts. Generalizations
may be acquired by rote or by memorization, but methods utilizing deductive or
inductive reasoning generally achieve higher level retention and better develop
the ability to make application.

Teaching by means of generalizations enables much more efficient articulation of learning experiences throughout students' school years. Generalizations

[33]James G. Womack, *Discovering the Structure of Social Studies* (New York: Benziger, 1966),
pp. 49–51. Reprinted by permission.
[34]Willis D. Moreland (ed.), *Social Studies in the Senior High School* (Washington, D.C.:
National Council for the Social Studies, 1965), p. 40.

can be formulated into varying degrees of abstraction so that their complexity and completeness fit the developmental level of any age student. In this way, generalizations serve as a framework to hold together the total and changing content of the social studies as students move from grade to grade.

Although teaching through generalization development affords many advantages to both teachers and students, there are certain dangers and limitations to be considered:

1. Does the generalization sought really merit discovery?
2. The content included in a unit of study must be such that the particular generalization desired by the teacher can indeed be discovered from studying the content material.
3. A teacher's preconceived list of generalizations must not be allowed to limit students' discoveries, because the teacher's list may not include all, or even the most valuable, generalizations included in the content to be studied.
4. The scope of a unit must be held to a reasonable size, avoiding consideration of too many generalizations, which may tend to confuse and distract students from important understandings.
5. Generalizations proposed must truly meet the requirements of a valid generalization, as suggested earlier in this chapter.
6. The teacher must help students refine their language and understanding of generalizations without yielding to the temptation to dictate the generalizations himself. Even too many hints or too much help to students in their search for generalizations may deprive them of much of the value of discovery learning.[35]

Teaching strategies for helping students develop skill in problem solving, or methods of inquiry, have been much discussed and often little understood. The most commonly accepted ideas are closely related to John Dewey's organization of reflective thinking into five logically distinct steps.[36] Hypothesis making and hypothesis testing by means of information gathering and analysis are central to the ideas of Dewey and also to those of more recent investigations. Information gathering implies skill in library use, the ability to interpret maps, graphs, and charts and to utilize other community sources. Hypothesis formation requires the ability to discern possible courses of action. And hypothesis testing includes the projection of probable consequences of alternative courses of action and evaluation in terms of desired goals.

Probably the most crucial element of problem solving is the long-espoused social studies goal of critical thinking. Students must learn to identify central issues, recognize underlying assumptions, evaluate evidence or authority, and draw warranted conclusions.[37] This can obviously best be done with an actual

---

[35]Adapted from Womack, *Discovering the Structure of Social Studies*, pp. 23–25.
[36]John Dewey, *How We Think* (Lexington, Mass.: Health, 1910), p. 72.
[37]Paul L. Dressel and Lewis B. Mayhew, *Critical Thinking in Social Science* (Dubuque, Iowa: Brown, 1954), p. 1.

problems approach to teaching, and the problems studied must be real, relevant, and important to both the students and the society.

What teaching procedures are most effective in promoting the formation of attitudes and values appropriate to a democratic society? The limited evidence currently available indicates that emotional appeals if not exaggerated, logical arguments with presentation of more than one point of view, and the supplying of factual knowledge can produce attitudinal change to a limited extent. Learning situations in which students actively participate and become personally involved are usually more effective. Role-playing, sociodrama, small-group discussion, and field studies are examples of this type of activity. Reading social novels and viewing films also tend to produce student identification with characters and bring shifts in attitude.

Students change attitudes due to identification with respected adults, such as parents or teachers. Peer pressure often is the source of similar influence, sometimes in a desirable direction, sometimes not.

In the classroom, an atmosphere of mutual respect where each person feels accepted, free to express his own ideas, and important to the learning activities will promote desirable attitude change, especially if each student is offered the opportunity to succeed. Recognition must be given to the importance of the individual's total personality and need to develop toward a mature self-concept.

The Behavioral Sciences

We will begin a more detailed, although necessarily brief, look at the disciplines which compose the class we have designated as the social studies by examining those commonly referred to as the "behavioral sciences"—anthropology, sociology, and social psychology. These studies are all concerned with the "study of mankind," and consequently overlap considerably in subject content. Behavioral science is primarily concerned with contemporary society, particularly the fact that several traits, quantities, or events affect each other and have interacting implications, but this does not rule out considerations from the past —particularly in anthropology. Those who study the phenomenon of man as a social being are thus dedicated to learning the process by which one event or human peculiarity leads to another and the conditions necessary to this process. Human interaction is seen as a totality, in that events are viewed as the consequence of more than one set of causes operating together to produce a given effect or phenomenon.

Most of the concepts crucial to either anthropology, sociology, or social psychology are shared by all three, although at times they are used for different purposes and center on varying generalizations. Culture and related concepts form the core of these studies. Related questions and concepts may be illustrated by the following examples.

In the area of culture:

1. Is culture biologically determined? Does the biology of man dictate the culture's content? Do the different races of man differ in their capacity for culture?
2. Race prejudice, ethnocentrism, and related problems.
3. The variability of culture—differences in language, eating habits, and general cultural facets; the tendency to assume that one's own culture is superior to all others and that customs different from one's own are peculiar or queer.
4. Conformity, especially to the particular mores of a culture, and the ability of these mores to make anything seem either right or wrong to the members of a cultural group.
5. Cultural change and cultural lag.

Pertaining to group interaction:

6. Primary and secondary relations, loyalty, and morale.
7. In-group–out-group relations.
8. Role.
9. Status and social class.

Concerning personality:

10. The idea of self.
11. The significant others.
12. Reference groups and relative deprivation.
13. Learning theory.
14. Psychoanalytic theory.
15. Culture and personality.[38]

Three basic types of study designs comprise the major methods of inquiry found in the behavioral sciences. These may be called the cross-sectional, projected, and ex post facto designs.

When using the cross-sectional approach, controlled comparisons are made for a single date. Judgments may then be made as to differences and similarities, advantages and disadvantages, and the like.

The classical before-and-after approach, usually referred to as the projected experimental design, sets out to study the effects of a program or experiment by surveying a community or group of individuals before the program is implemented and then again after it is has been in operation for a time. The danger of cause-and-effect generalizations is ever present, but significant relationships may be established.

By using the ex post facto design, the researcher is able to generalize from the past to the present by viewing the present situation as an effect of some previously existing set of causes. For instance, the same individuals and families may be compared at present and at some past time. In this way the effects of duration of high school education on economic adjustment or relationships be-

[38]Erling M. Hunt and others, *High School Social Studies Perspectives*, (Boston: Houghton, 1962), pp. 29–51.

tween the type of physical home environment and later social adjustment may be determined. As a variation to this procedure, populations in the same areas at present and at some past date may be compared to determine relationships between such things as changes in socioeconomic factors and their effect on college attendance in a particular geographic area.

Various methods of data collection are used by the behavioral scientist as he studies humanity by means of these research methods. The more common ones include the case study, survey, interview, observation, statistical measurement (psychometric, sociometric), and projective methods such as the sociodrama.[39]

Anthropology

Because it is the oldest of the three disciplines here being considered, we will explore anthropology in greater detail first, before moving on to sociology and social psychology. The "science of culture," as it is often termed, anthropology may be described as "the study of man and his works.[40] A more complex definition describes it as a field "organized around an interest in man seen as something with the characteristics of all life, and around an interest in man seen as something human—a quality not shared, or shared very little, with other forms of life. The quality that induces the second polarity—humanity—is manifest in three basic forms: as it appears in individuals (personality), in persisting social groups or societies (culture), and in all socialized members of our species (human nature)."[41]

The above definitions indicate the breadth of study included in this discipline as it attempts to take a "holistic" view of mankind through his culture. Two main divisions may be recognized—physical anthropology and cultural or social anthropology. Physical anthropology includes human paleontology, which deals with the origins and evolution of our species, and somatology, the branch of study concerned not with our ancestors but with us, in all of our physical aspects, and especially in the study of human varieties (races).

Cultural anthropology may be divided into three main divisions:

1. Linguistics—the study of man's use of symbols, especially language, to communicate.

2. Archaeology—the study of extinct cultures or the past phases of living cultures. The ultimate purpose of archaelogy is like history in that it strives to give us an understanding of the factors involved in the growth, flowering, and collapse of civilizations.

3. Ethnology, which is more concerned with "living" culture, studies the

---

[39]Ernest H. St. Jacques, "The Methods of the Behavioral Scientist as Tools of Learning," *Peabody Journal of Education* (January 1963), pp. 228–235.

[40]Clyde Kluckhohn, *Mirror for Man* (New York: McGraw-Hill, 1949), p. 2.

[41]Robert Redfield, "Relations of Anthropology to the Social Sciences and Humanities," in Sol Tax (ed.), *Anthropology Today* (Chicago: U. of Chicago Press, 1963), p. 456.

ways of life of existing or very recent societies. Sometimes referred to as "social anthropology," its goals are to determine laws for interpreting the regularities of human behavior in certain situations.[42]

Personality psychology, or social psychology, is sometimes grouped under the heading of cultural anthropology also, but we will treat it as a separate discipline.

Key concepts utilized in the study of anthropology include many of those mentioned earlier as common to most of the studies in behavioral science. The following are illustrative:

culture	groups
institutions	group interaction
values	adaptation
role	religion
status	ethnocentrism
norm	citizenship
social class	leadership
culture change	ideology
evolution	

Utilizing these and many other related concepts, generalizations such as the following may be established:

1. It appears that humans everywhere shape their beliefs and behavior in response to the same fundamental human problems and needs.
2. Practically all important differences in human behavior are understandable as variations in learned patterns of social behavior—not differences in biological apparatus, type of blood, or any other genetically inherited mechanism.
3. Every society has regular patterns of behavior that make it possible for individuals to predict each other's behavior and to act accordingly.
4. Man's perceptions of his experiences are strongly influenced by his cultural heritage, and he tends to view his own way of life as the most reasonable and natural.
5. Every human cultural system is logical and coherent in its own terms, given the basic assumptions and knowledge available to the specific community.
6. Man has the capacity to adopt, adapt, and reconstitute present and past ideas, beliefs, and inventions of others who are living or dead.
7. Every cultural system is composed of an interconnected network of behavioral patterns; no system is ever completely static: changes in one area generally lead to alterations in other segments of the system.
8. Personal perceptions, predispositions, and values complicate man's study of man.[43]

The prime method of inquiry for anthropologists is the method of comparison. The use of this method may be illustrated by pointing out that students may better understand the role of the aged in our own society by comparing them and

---

[42]Willis D. Moreland, (ed.), *Social Studies in the Senior High School* (Washington, D.C.: National Council for the Social Studies, 1965), pp. 13–14.

[43]Pertti J. Pelto, *The Study of Anthropology* (Columbus, Ohio: Merrill, 1965), pp. 81–111.

their lives to the elders of primitive tribes. In this and other types of comparison, the purpose is to relate the various elements of our culture by looking at each element as it relates to the whole of life.[44]

The general inquiry method of comparison requires that there be something to compare. The anthropologist gathers the information he needs for such study in one or more of several ways. Field work is usually involved, often in out-of-the-way places. This field work must be followed up, however, with months of painstaking work at home in the library and the laboratory.

Field projects of archaeologists usually involve digging into ancient ruins. More than common digging is involved, however, as a highly developed pattern of techniques must be employed to avoid destruction of objects and clues essential to detailed study.

1. Meticulous care is taken that excavated materials are not damaged in the process of digging.
2. The position and context of every object excavated is recorded by a combination of drawings, notes, and photographs so that the archaeologist can later establish with great accuracy which items found in an excavation belong together in a particular complex of materials for a particular time period, as represented, for example, in the levels of deposited materials—the stratigraphy—of a given site.
3. All significant associated items are collected and recorded: soil samples, remains of animal and vegetable materials, types of rocks and other geological specimens, and all kinds of other materials associated with the monuments, buildings, burial goods, jewels, artwork, stone tools, weapons, or other human handiwork that the archaeologist uncovers.[45]

Physical anthropologists utilize many of the same general methods as archaeologists as they search for evidence about our ancestors. They also carry out research on living communities, measuring and observing human physical types.

In the field of linguistics, research involves collecting samples of the speech patterns employed by a certain group of people. Related languages are discovered by comparison of vocabularies for sound-and-meaning correspondences.

To gather his raw materials, the social anthropologist usually lives for several months in appropriate communities. Variations of two major procedures are usually utilized: interviewing of informants or observation of participants.[46]

Sociology

The behavior of people in groups is the realm of sociology. Institutional functions such as religion, education, family, politics, labor, and various community organizations serve as the focus of this type study. Primary interest is not

[44]Alex Weingrod, "Anthropology and the Social Studies," *Social Education* 20 (January 1956), pp. 5–9.
[45]Pelto, *op, cit.,* p. 34.
[46]*Ibid.,* pp. 37–40.

in the individual, his personality, or his behavior, but in the social forms and structures within which individual behavior takes place. Psychology is concerned with study of the individual, and social psychology focuses on the individual in his social groups, but sociology is primarily interested in the groups themselves and the larger social structures within which both individual and group processes occur.

Sociologists seek general laws or principles about human interaction and association and about the nature, form, content, and structure of human groups and societies. Complete and comprehensive descriptions of particular societies or particular events, as in the case of history, are not sought by sociology, ". . . it is a generalizing and not a particularizing or individualizing science."[47]

As it examines the institutional means by which a society interacts with the forces around and within it, sociology concerns itself with a variety of content areas, of which the following are indicative:

1. Culture, the social processes, social institutions, and social problems.
2. Political sociology.
3. Religion and sociology.
4. Racial and ethnic relations.
5. Communications patterns, the development of leader-follower relations, the process of interaction, and group organizations.
6. Delinquency and crime.
7. The field of communication, including the study of public opinion and mass media.
8. Social change.[48]

Concepts with which sociologists frequently work and with which students should become familiar include most of those mentioned earlier in the general discussion of the behavioral sciences and especially those related to culture, such as primary and secondary groups, deviancy, socialization, anomie, role, status, family, and social class. Theories, such as the life-space or balance theories, are studied to arrive at generalizations such as

1. Man is a social animal who lives always in groups. He may belong to a variety of groups, each of which can be differentiated by its structure.
2. A society exists in the minds of its members and occurs only when there is communication or interaction among those members. The mere grouping or aggregating of people does not produce a society.
3. Man is a flexible, becoming creature. Through the socialization process, he can learn approved ways of behaving in a variety of societies.
4. The interdependence of groups in a complex contemporary society serves as a bond which holds that society together.
5. Every group is a complex of roles. Group members perform given roles and

[47]Robert Bierstedt, "The Science of Sociology," *The Social Order* (New York: McGraw-Hill, 1963), p. 151.
[48]Adapted from Willis D. Moreland (ed.), *Social Studies in the Senior High School* (Washington, D.C.: National Council for the Social Studies, 1965), pp. 29–31.

have some understanding of the expectations associated with those roles. As a member of various groups, a person may learn and assume different roles during a particular period in his life and at various stages in his development and maturation.[49]

In pursuing their study, sociologists generally utilize a method of inquiry involving asking questions or observing. After they have formulated a question in a form to permit its testing, one or more hypotheses are posed in the light of previous study in the field or the best judgment of the investigator. The search for evidence related to the hypotheses may be conducted by gathering data with questionnaires and interviews. Case studies may be appropriate, including comparisons of appropriate cases. Content analysis is often used to determine the emphasis given to attitudes, stereotypes, and ideas in books, movies, newspapers, or advertising. Frequency counts of types of behavior observed in schools, political rallies, or business meetings serve to provide needed data at times. To reach conclusions, sociologists must examine their data and interpret it in relation to the questions being asked. This often involves statistical treatment, both simple and complex, but final judgments are usually reached on the basis of sound reasoning rather than empirical proof.[50]

Social Psychology

The relatively new field of study known as psychology is difficult to classify within the system we are utilizing. It would most logically seem to belong either to the natural sciences or the social sciences, but questions may be raised about placing it wholly in either category. Those aspects which more directly relate to the study of individuals in their social and cultural settings have recently begun to be grouped into a relatively new disciplinary category identified with the descriptive title of social psychology. It seems that the studies falling in this area are those that should logically be included in the social studies curriculum.

Social psychology serves as a bridge between psychology and sociology by maintaining a primary interest in the individual, but its main concern is "... with the way in which the individual behaves in his social groups, how he behaves collectively with other individuals, and how his personality is a function both of his basic physiological and temperamental equipment and of the social and cultural influences to which he is exposed.[51]

In their examination of the effect of the society on the indivudual, social psychologists concern themselves with many of the same content areas, concepts,

---

[49]Caroline B. Rose, *Sociology: The Study of Man in Society* (Columbus, Ohio: Merrill, 1965), pp. 63–93.

[50]Jean Fair and Fannie R. Shaftel (ed.), *Effective Thinking in the Social Studies* (Washington, D.C.: National Council for the Social Studies, 1967), pp. 61–67.

[51]Robert Bierstedt, "The Science of Sociology," *The Social Order* (New York: Mc Graw-Hill, 1963).

and generalizations as do sociologists; they just study them from a slightly different angle. Socialization, personality formation, leadership, perception, conceptualization, attitudes and their development and modification, social interaction, the psychological effects of participation in groups, intergroup conflict, and the relation of sociocultural and social-psychological processes are among the areas of concern typical to this discipline.[52]

In pursuing and validating knowledge in their field of study, social psychologists focus on the development of hypotheses linking personality, culture, and values.[53] These hypotheses are then evaluated by means similar to those common to sociology in general. A significant recent development has been the increased use of experimental methodology in attempts to verify or refute hypotheses.[54]

Political Science

Because they play an active role in public affairs, the people of a democracy must be acquainted with ways of gathering, ordering, and using knowledge about political matters. This need has long been recognized by educators and incorporated in school programs through courses of study generally labeled "civics." Such units or courses have seemingly operated on the assumption that good citizens can be produced through instruction in government, politics, the political process, and the important issues of public policy. The goal is commendable, but there is serious reason to doubt that what has been done in the name of "civics" or "government" has been very successful in its effort to produce good citizens of a democracy. The goal—creation of good citizens—has been too nebulous and too much influenced by many institutions outside the school.

Political scientists seem to largely agree that the best way to promote democracy and democratic citizenship is through study in the whole field of political science, rather than limiting it to civic education. Civics then becomes a part of the total program of political science education for the students, rather than an end in itself. It is not possible to make political scientists out of secondary school students, but perhaps it is possible to teach them something about political science—what it is, what it does, the complexity and difficulty of the problems it deals with. Such an approach will place civic education in approximately the same position to political science that consumer education is to economics. In this way, it is possible to teach students something about what they do not know about politics, government, and public policy, and this in turn may lead to a desire

---

[52]William W. Lambert and Wallace E. Lambert, *Social Psychology* (Englewood Cliffs, N.J.: Prentice-Hall, 1965).

[53]Byron G. Massialas and C. Benjamin Cox, *Inquiry in Social Studies* (New York: McGraw-Hill, 1966), p. 38.

[54]Wilbur C. Miller and Joel E. Greene, "Social Psychology," in Roy A. Price (ed.), *New Viewpoints in the Social Sciences*, Twenty-Eighth Yearbook (Washington, D.C.: National Council for the Social Sciences, 1958), p. 171.

to gain the additional knowledge and adopt the attitudes required of a good citizen.

Political science is an intellectual discipline organized around a body of knowledge about the political behavior of human beings. Legal government, including its history, agencies, processes, structure, functions, composition, rationale, and influence, makes up the main body of subject matter.[55] Fundamental questions of concern to the political scientist include the goals of states, who should rule, the nature of the relationship between the rulers and the ruled, and what kind of social order will best achieve the good life.[56]

Political science studies the authoritative decision making of the political system, including the processes and activities through which a society makes those decisions, chooses men to make them, and influences those who have been chosen. The prime focus is on processes of policy-making in the political system and activities that attempt to influence the system.[57]

Seven major fields of political science have been identified, as follows:

1. Political philosophy—examination of the thought of philosophers relating to the state and the government of men.

2. Comparative government—examination of the political systems of different countries.

3. Constitutional law—concern with how constitutional or basic laws are made and changed, and with their content, intent, and effects.

4. International politics—concern with the political aspects of the relations among nations. This type study includes material that is economic, diplomatic, military, and ideological.

5. American national government—includes all aspects of the American political system, including political parties, pressure groups, public opinion, the legislative, executive, and judicial branches of government, public administration, voting behavior, decision making, civil liberties and civil rights, the federal system, fiscal policy, foreign policy, government and business, and social legislation.

6. State and local government—the structure and functions of local and intermediate governing bodies, including the relations of these agencies to the federal government.

7. Public administration—study of the agencies and procedures by which law is implemented and the behavior of those responsible for its implementation.[58]

[55]Erling M. Hunt et al., *High School Social Studies Perspectives* (Boston: Houghton, 1962), p. 111.
[56]Byron G. Massialas and C. Benjamin Cox, *Inquiry in Social Studies* (New York: McGraw-Hill, 1966), p. 36.
[57]Francis J. Sorauf, *Political Science, an Informal Overview* (Columbus, Ohio: Merrill, 1965), p. 5.
[58]Hunt et al., *op. cit.*, pp. 104–110.

As indicated in the discussions above, political science cannot be neatly confined within hard-and-fast boundaries. The social processes and institutions of the world involve most if not all of the social sciences, and other disciplines as well. Sociologists, along with political scientists, concern themselves with the processes of political socialization by which youngsters acquire attitudes about the political world from their families, teachers, friends, and television programs. With anthropologists, political scientists share an interest in the political systems of primitive and developing societies. Their concern with the political events of the past is shared with historians, and the bases of national power serve as an area of common interest with political geographers.[59]

As with other disciplines, political science is organized around basic concepts and appropriate generalizations. Concepts of concern to political scientists include:

activism	legalism
aristocracy	legislative process
authority	legitimacy
civil rights	policy
communism	political modernization
democracy	political socialization
democratization	political system
elite formation	politics
equality	power
fascism	rights
freedom	secularization
graft	socialism
ideology	sovereignty
justice	state
law	

Utilizing concepts such as these, the political scientist develops generalizations to help him and others better understand the political world of which they are a part. The following generalizations are typical of those which would be of most concern to a teacher of political science.

1. As a minimum condition for its existence a society establishes authoritative institutions that can make decisions which are binding on all the people, provide for the resolution of dissent, and effectively enforce basic rules.
2. The larger a society is, the more an individual must rely upon group membership and representation to achieve his aims. By uniting with others he is able to increase the strength of his voice and improve the chances that his wishes will be made known to those in decision-making positions.
3. The nature of a given society's political system and the nature of its political behavior are closely related to the fundamental system of values to which the society adheres.

[59]Sorauf, op. cit., pp. 7–8.

4. Political ideals, values, attitudes, and institutions develop and change over time.

5. In every society, individuals and groups disagree over some societal goals and directions, over how aims will be achieved, and over the enforcement of standards of behavior.[60]

The appropriateness of the term "science" in "political science" has been argued a great deal, being supported with the contention that the term only calls for the use of the scientific method, which is broadly defined to mean a systematic search for knowledge of the empirical world. Within this context, the political scientist's function is ". . . to study and describe the actions and probable consequences of the actions of modern governments, to study and explain the beliefs and values on which such actions are based, and to evaluate both the beliefs and actions."[61]

In pursuing their study, political scientists utilize methods of study and research appropriate to the type of problem which concerns them at the moment. In selecting appropriate procedures, political scientists borrow a great deal from other social sciences, especially sociology, anthropology, and social psychology. To gather data and information relative to some areas of study, the library and library research skills would be the source of information. In studying voter tendencies or activities, the social scientist would of necessity utilize sampling, questionnaire, and interview techniques. However, although several different types of skills and methods may be found most appropriate to a particular political scientist, they are all committed to the basic tenets of empiricism. It is accepted that knowledge of social behavior and institutions must come from experience, from sense perceptions of events in the real world. Explanatory generalizations are drawn from observations of specific instances and events.[62]

As political scientists study and analyze empirical data, they are largely concerned with finding relationships. This calls for a somewhat nonempirical ability or creative talent which may be termed "insight." In observing a number of events or actions, the political scientist looks for relationships and commonalities from which to deduce general principles or fundamental relationships. Behind this "creativity," however, there must be a background of knowledge and understanding of his subject which comes from rigorous study and experience.

Political scientists use a variety of research strategies, depending upon the type and source of data needed, but four traditional types of research design may be identified:

1. Historical studies—this refers to more than a study of the past or the use of noncontemporary data; it means studies over a time span and organized

---

[60] *Ibid.*, pp. 76–105.

[61] Donald H. Riddle and Robert E. Cleary (eds.), *Political Science in the Social Studies*, Thirty-Sixth Yearbook, National Council for the Social Studies (Washington, D.C.: National Council for the Social Studies, 1966), p. 33.

[62] Sorauf, *op. cit.*, p. 22.

by time sequences (organization of data, description, or analysis by
chronology).

2. Case studies—the examination of some political unit, which may be a
   single political organization, a particular election, a governmental institution, or a court case.
3. Comparative studies—comparison of political institutions, such as political parties or legislatures; processes, such as those of socialization or
   conflict-resolution; or whole political systems.
4. Covariate analysis—a kind of research strategy which focuses on the
   relationship between or among a small number of variables within a single
   political system: for example, determination of the relationship between
   the forms of local governments and the characteristics of the cities.[63]

A more recent approach to inquiry in political science, emphasizing political
behavior, rejects political institutions as the basic unit for research and, instead,
establishes the behavior of individuals in political situations as the basic unit of
analysis. This approach places political science more in line with the "behavioral
sciences," in that the focus is on individuals and groups rather than institutions
and organizations.[64]

The tools of inquiry in political science have been largely borrowed from
psychology and sociology. These include statistical methods, field surveys, and
laboratory or simulated conditions. Probability samples of large populations,
carried out by means of personal interviews conducted by technicians utilizing
standardized interview schedules, have recently assumed a very important role in
political science research, especially that type most familiar to the general public
(voting predictions, voter opinions, etc.).

Economics

Economics is supported as a discipline appropriate for inclusion in the
secondary school program by basically the same general purpose as the other
social studies—the education of students to become responsible citizens of a
democracy. More specifically, its role is ". . . to contribute to an understanding
of society's economic problem and of the economizing processes of the total
society in which all of us live as human beings, and in which we participate as
producers and consumers and as citizens."[65]

Because the term "economics" means any one of several things to those who
use it, perhaps a definition is called for to establish a common ground for the
discussion which follows. All of the more common definitions of the term include
the concept of scarcity—the problem of allocating limited resources among
unlimited human wants. This need to best solve the problem of allocating

[63] *Ibid.*, pp. 34–37.
[64] Hunt et al., *op. cit.*, p. 116.
[65] Ben W. Lewis, "Economics," *The Social Studies and the Social Sciences* (New York: Harcourt, 1962), p. 107.

available resources to maximize the economic welfare of the people seems to be adequately expressed in the following statement.

> Economics is generally described as the study of how society produces and distributes the goods and services it wants. More specifically, it examines the activities that people carry on—producing, saving, spending, paying taxes, and so on—for the purpose of satisfying their basic wants for food and shelter, their added wants for modern conveniences and comforts, and their collective wants for such things as national defense and education.[66]

In pursuing this type of study, students are confronted with three major questions: (1) What shall be produced and in what quantities? (2) How can resources be combined in order to minimize cost and waste? (3) Who should receive the benefits of production? Within these questions lie problems such as deciding which of possible goods and services shall be produced (food, shelter, education, entertainment), how much of each to produce, provision for the organization and distribution of production, what technology and machinery to use, and the proportion of consumer goods to be allotted among the various individuals and groups in the society. These questions of economic policy must be settled by considering three things: (1) how the economic system is operating—its results, (2) how the system should be operating, and (3) proposals relative to what should be done to make what is occurring more nearly match what is desired.[67]

The content of economic education for secondary schools may be debated, but considering purposes such as those above should permit considerable agreement, perhaps disproving George Bernard Shaw's quip that if all the economists in the world were laid end to end they still would not reach a conclusion. A statement prepared in 1961 by the National Task Force on Economic Education seems to best summarize the position of most economists who are concerned with economic education in secondary schools. The economic understanding recommended as essential for citizenship and reasonably attainable in the schools includes:

1. A reasoned approach to economic problems.
2. An overview of the economic system.
3. Problems of maintaining stable economic growth.
4. The distribution of income.
5. Comparison of economic systems.
6. An ability to analyze and think through major economic problems.[68]

Economics cannot tell us what choices to make concerning our economic welfare. It can only tell us what the consequences of our decisions are likely to be. Whether tax dollars should be spent for one thing or another, whether we

---

[66]Marshall A. Robinson, Herbert C. Morton, and James D. Calderwood, *An Introduction to Economic Reasoning*, 4th ed. (Garden City, N.Y.: Doubleday, 1967), p. 2.

[67]Richard S. Martin and Reuben G. Miller, *Economics and Its Significance* (Columbus, Ohio: Merrill, 1965), pp. 11–12, 75.

[68]Adapted from National Task Force on Economic Education, *Economic Education in the Schools* (New York: Committee on Economic Development, 1961).

must tolerate a certain level of unemployment or should have socialized medicine
—answers to questions of this nature must be settled in the political arena in
terms of what is considered best for our society. Economics deals with cause and
effect relationships, and explains the means to reach ends, but it does not deal
with decisions related to the adopting of certain ends.

The National Task Force on Economic Education made a significant contribution to social studies education with its 1961 report, which included, among
several things, a list of important economic concepts which should be taught to
public school students. These form the core of current economics education:

aggregate demand	efficiency
antitrust laws	equation of exchange
balance of payments	exchange
balance of trade	factors of production
balance sheet	farm problem
bank deposits	featherbedding
business cycle	Federal Reserve System
capital formation	fiscal policy
closed shops	government budget
collective bargaining	government expenditures
corporate income tax	gross national product
corporations	income from productive services
demand, supply, price	interdependence
depression, inflation	international specialization
diminishing returns	investment
division of labor	labor unions
economic growth	market, competition, profit
economic security	money
money and real income	profit and loss statement
money costs	property tax
money creation	public debt
monopoly	public utility
national income	real wages, money wages
old-age insurance	sales tax
opportunity cost	saving
other economic systems	scarcity
payroll tax	social security
per capita product	specialization
personal distribution of income	strikes, picketing
personal income tax	tariffs
price level	taxes and resource allocation
private security measures	underdeveloped areas
productivity	unemployment insurance[69]

[69] *Ibid.*

Generalizations concerning economic problems incorporate the above concepts and provide the basic focus for teaching. The following statements exemplify appropriate types of generalizations.

1. Every society has some kind of economic system. This pattern of arrangements involves the production, distribution, and use of goods and services and reflects the values and objectives of the particular society.
2. All economic systems are confronted by the problem of relative scarcity, of unlimited wants and limited resources.
3. Economic conditions and systems change over a period of time.
4. Every economic system possesses regularities which make certain forms of prediction possible.
5. In a modern, complex economic system, individuals are dependent upon others for the satisfaction of many of their needs and wants.[70]
6. It pays the United States, even if we are generally more efficient than other nations, to specialize in the production of those goods in which we are relatively more efficient and trade them to foreigners for the goods that we are relatively less efficient in producing.[71]
7. As a general rule, when more is demanded at some particular price than is being supplied at that price, the price will tend to be bid up by the excess demand until a new price is reached where the amount demanded just equals that being supplied.[72]
8. Businessmen, in striving to make profits, try to produce those goods and services which consumers want; and try to do so at the lowest possible cost, in some cases also seeking to influence consumer demands through advertising and other selling activities.
9. Markets, in which prices rise and fall in response to changing demands and supplies, provide the links which mesh together consumers and businesses, each seeking to make the best of his own position and abilities, into a working system.
10. When individuals and businesses save part of their income and invest those savings in new productive facilities, this increases society's capacity to produce in future periods.[73]

Research in economics involves the analysis of activity which takes place in a constantly changing world. This changing economic world is the laboratory of the economist, and although it will not allow him to use the exacting methods of the experimental science laboratory, he may, by means of thorough observation and recording of economic events and careful analysis of the information gained, suggest hypotheses or tentative explanations. This type of scientific method may not be as exact as some physical scientists would like, but it seems to be the best way so far devised to study the complex and changing economic situation.

Within this framework of the scientific method, inquiry in economics may take one or more of at least three directions. (1) Historical research studies the

[70]Martin and Miller, *op. cit.*, pp. 99–155.
[71]*Ibid.*, p. 79.
[72]National Task Force on Economic Education, *loc. cit.*
[73]Lewis, *op. cit.*, p. 124.

evolution of economic philosophy and of the economic system. Recognition of past trends may give some indication of what to expect in the future. (2) Studies dealing with the functioning of the economic system today investigate the nature and operations of economic components (consumers, businesses, governments, markets) to provide suggestions about current economic problems. (3) Attempts to forecast the future are made on the basis of current knowledge of the economic system and the directions it seems to be taking.[74]

As economic events are studied, three questions may be asked: "What is it? Why is it? What of it? Obtaining answers to these questions involves a three-step procedure:

1. Identify the event by describing it and by comparing it with other events that are similar and familiar.
2. Explore the factors that may have caused the event.
3. Try to discover the implications of the event by considering what the consequences might be under various circumstances.

The problems and questions posed by events of an economic nature also require some type of orderly procedure for solution. Again, following the basic concepts of the scientific method, a series of suggested steps may be followed in making economic decisions:

1. Identify the problem and clarify the issues by studying their background and origin.
2. Identify the objectives and requirements that must be met in treating the problem.
3. Pose the alternative courses of action and analyze their consequences.
4. Appraise the alternatives and decide by determining how well each alternative fulfills the objectives and requirements.[75]

Economists often make use of "models" and graphic devices to illustrate some part of the economic system. By using a model they isolate the main variables in a situation under study and state some of the main relationships among these variables, thus providing a guide to thinking about particular situations or problems. For example, a model might be used to show the relationships involved if the amount of spending for new goods and services by all consumers in the economy depends upon the current level of consumer incomes, the level of consumer prices, the amount of installment debt which consumers owe, and similar factors. Most models are made up of a series of mathematical equations used to express this type of situation, and when considered as a whole, these equations describe the functioning of some part of the economic system.[76]

[74]Richard S. Martin and Reuben G. Miller, *Prologue to Economic Understanding* (Columbus, Ohio: 1966), pp. 63–64.

[75]Robinson, Morton, and Calderwood, *op. cit.*, pp. 13–20.

[76]National Task Force on Economic Education, *op. cit.*, pp. 17–20.

Geography

Geography is one of the oldest fields of study, although it has not always gone by the same name. From earliest recorded history, man has been interested in the features of the land around him, how they are similar, and how they differ from place to place. More recently he has paid more attention to how the various characteristics of places on the earth affect his living. The uniqueness of places and their relationships is thus perceived as it is connected to culture and human behavior. In more formal terms,

> Geography is primarily concerned with the development of meaningful generalizations and concepts about areal arrangements and associations. Beyond the areal concepts is the belief of modern geographers that all physical features of the earth must be interpreted and evaluated in terms of culture.[77]

Although the study of geography has been largely neglected in recent years in our public schools, it, like history, can serve a unique integrative function. What history is to time, geography is to space. Geographers use the map, where historians use the calendar, to furnish a frame of mind to tie the social studies together into a meaningful whole. Through a study of the relationships between man and his environment, students may achieve an understanding and appreciation of how people live and work; how the environment affects their lives, ideas, and customs; and how the characteristics of one region affect those of another. This may be done if students:

1. Become able to look at a globe without finding any large areas about which they are uninformed are unable to predict the kinds of associated features likely to be found.
2. Learn to ask geographic questions, find ways of answering the questions, and test their answers.
3. Become able to both give and receive information by means of the language of maps.[78]

In the past, geography often was limited to the question "What is where?" More recently it has turned to the questions "Why is it where it is?" and "Why isn't it where it isn't?" Further questions now considered important include "Where might it better be?" and "What changes will take place here as a result of such a change here or there?"[79]

In this way the distinctiveness that geography has traditionally possessed as

[77]Byron G. Massialas and C. Benjamin Cox, *Inquiry in Social Studies* (New York: McGraw-Hill, 1966), p. 33.

[78]Adapted from Preston E. James, "A Conceptual Structure for Geography," *Journal of Geography*, Vol. 64, No. 7, pp. 292–298.

[79]Nicholas Helburn, "New Materials and Teaching Strategies: The High School Geography Project," *Bulletin of the National Association of Secondary School Principals* 51 (February 1967), p. 21.

a social science in its concern with the character of "place" has progressed, from simple answers to an oversimplified question of "where," to a perception of "place" as an integrated whole—of a people and its habitat and the interrelations between places. Geography must be seen as more than names of continents, countries, capitals, and crops; more than terms such as meridian, delta, and tropical rain forest; more than elementary map-reading skills and computation of distances by the use of scale. It includes these things, but much more is needed for the study of geography in schools to reach its full potential.

Geography should stimulate a lively curiosity about the earth, its surface, the creatures that inhabit it, how it is changing, and man's relationship to it. Students should be impressed with the mystery, majesty, and beauty of the diverse and ever-changing environment they call home. They should have some conception of the importance of location on the earth, the complexity of the world in which they live, the problems and forces which both divide and unify, and above all, the nature of the relationship between man and his environment.

History has been said to present the drama of human events in time, whereas geography studies the stage on which those events take place. Such an analogy is helpful, but it should also be pointed out that geography is concerned not only with the physical setting of the stage but also with the relations between human events and the stage on which they are enacted.[80] As with history, geography is interested in comprehending wholes, but while the historian thinks mainly in time bonds, the geographer thinks in place bonds. Instead of studying peoples, crops, customs, minerals, towns, or house types for their own sake, he perceives them as parts of an integrated complex that give character to a place. It is the place (region or country) that he wants to understand.[81]

To fulfill their ambitious aims for geographic instruction, geographers utilize several types and divisions of subject matter, including:

1. Biophysical science—a concentration on land forms, climate, and natural vegetation, including attempts to establish cause and effect relationships leading to "laws of nature."

2. Nature-man relationships—attempts to discover how the physical (or natural) environment determines or at least conditions human behavior (sometimes called environmentalism).

3. Human ecology—defines geography as the study of man's adjustment to the habitat. Nature is accepted as a given entity to which man adapts or adjusts according to his wits, through culture and technology.

4. Landscape study—an approach opposed to environmentalism, taking the view that nature is passive and human society is the active agent. According to this view, a society uses its habitat and thereby changes the "natural landscape" into a "cultural landscape."

---

[80]Lorrin Kennamer, "Developing a Sense of Place and Space," in Helen M. Carpenter (ed.), *Skill Development in the Social Studies* (Washington, D.C.: National Council for the Social Studies, 1963), p. 148.

[81]Jan A. M. Broek, *Geography, Its Scope and Spirit* (Columbus, Ohio: Merrill, 1965), p. 4.

5. Population distribution—concern with the distribution of population over the earth's surface and with the different rates of growth of population in various parts of the world. This is related to another area of study —population density, which is to some extent determined by population movements.

6. Urban geography—attempts to establish concepts of location, interaction, circulation, accessibility, distribution, and movement of populations in urban settings.

7. Economic geography—employs the concepts of economics in relating geographic regions, contributing to an understanding of emerging nations, the United States' unique geoeconomic position, the European Common Market, and similar situations.[82]

Concepts inherent in the discipline of geography include many which are rather directly related to the physical characteristics of the earth, but other concepts must also be included to avoid neglect of the cultural and human elements. The following are indicative:

air pressure	location
areal	longitude
arrangement	matriarchal
Asia	migrant
cartography	pastoral
central place	peninsula
climate	population density
continent	population distribution
culture	population growth
distribution	position
economy	projection
elevation	religion
Europe	scale
forest	site
glacier	situation
habitat	sound
hemisphere	strait
internal structure	swamp
island	symbol
isthmus	terrain
latitude	tundra
localization	watershed

Geographical concepts then may be incorporated into generalizations relative to desired geographic understandings. Such generalizations may be stated in simple or more complex terms to fit the learning level of the students. Both types are indicated in the following examples.

[82]Adapted from Broek, *Geography, its Scope and Spirit*, pp. 34–49, 76–79.

1. The shape of the world is round in every direction.
2. There are differences from place to place on the earth's surface.
3. Day and night are caused by rotation of the earth on its polar axis.
4. Cities, streets, towns are shown by symbols.
5. Seasons and varying lengths of day and night are due to revolution of the earth around the sun.
6. The globe is distorted when transferred to a flat map.[83]
7. Mountains have prevented, deflected, or postponed migration, deterred invasions, impeded transportation, hindered agriculture, and retarded population growth.
8. Climate has provided more satisfactory living conditions in some areas than in others, discouraged economic development in some regions, and influenced the choice of new locations for migrants.
9. Rivers have facilitated establishment of travel routes, development of farming, locations and growth of large populations, and (where navigable) have aided in general economic development.[84]
10. Man's use of the land is seldom the result of any single physical factor. Rather, such utilization is determined by the interplay of a number of phenomena, both physical and cultural.
11. The evolution of mankind from isolated, self-sufficient communities to an interdependent whole means ever more trade, migration, diffusion of ideas and practices, and greater importance of relative location or situation.
12. Each culture tends to view its physical habitat differently. A society's value system, goals, organization, and level of technology determine which elements of the land are prized and utilized.
13. Every region is an area homogeneous in terms of specific criteria chosen to delimit it from other regions. This delimitation is always based on an intellectual judgment.
14. The character of a place is the product of the past as well as an interim phase in an ever changing existence.[85]

Geography does not achieve recognition as a discipline from a unique body of subject matter so much as from its point of view and its method of inquiry. Its point of view is defined in terms of the regional concept, and its primary method of inquiry is known as the regional method. A region is defined by geographers as "... an area of any size that is homogeneous in terms of specific criteria and that is distinguished from bordering areas by a particular kind of association of areally related features." These features may be land form, economy, population type, climate, or some other characteristic.[86]

By studying regions thus defined, the geographer seeks to develop meaningful generalizations concerning the areal arrangement and association of things on

[83]Preston E. James (ed.), *New Viewpoints in Geography*, Twenty-ninth yearbook of the National Council for the Social Studies (Washington, D.C.: National Council for the Social Studies, 1959), p. 204.

[84]Jonathan C. McLendon, *Social Studies in Secondary Education* (New York: Macmillan, 1965), p. 138.

[85]Broek, *op. cit.*, pp. 81–113.

[86]Preston E. James (ed.), *New Viewpoints in Geography*, *op. cit.*, p. 16.

the earth. Research procedures include mapping, census taking, graphing, observation, photography, and analysis. By means of quantitative techniques, areal associations between phenomena are possible in rather specific and exact terms. For instance, the two variables of per capita gross national product and per capita consumption of mechanical power may be related. To these two variables may be added a third, such as the percentage of the labor force engaged in agriculture. It is found that there is a strong positive correlation between the first two variables mentioned, but a negative or inverse correlation between the first two variables and the third.By studying such correlations, geographers gain a much better understanding of our world and the way it operates. Various statistical techniques may be used to study correlations of this type. It may be possible to identify cause-and-effect relationships in this way, but caution is required when a correlation is interpreted in terms of cause and effect.[87]

The regional method is appropriate for studying anything that is unevenly distributed over the face of the earth. Earlier studies tended to emphasize the physical features of the earth, but modern geography seeks to blend in human or cultural elements, otherwise it would not be appropriate for inclusion in the social studies. Field investigation plays a large part in geographic study by providing firsthand knowledge of the actual physical or cultural environment.

Cartography—the science of mapping the earth—is a particularly important part of geographic study. A wide range of map-making concepts, techniques, and devices are used as a base for recording data, to facilitate comparison and analysis, and to present ideas and results of research. Landscape patterns are reduced to a size which is more manageable and which permits visualization of the whole more readily.[88]

History

Geography and history have been placed at the end of this discussion of the social sciences because they are generally accepted as the two disciplines which best serve to form a framework around which to relate all social studies inquiry. They are also the oldest and most fully accepted areas of social studies instruction. The twin dimensions of time sequence and areal association form an ideal base for organization of school programs incorporating elements of all the social studies disciplines.

A concise and broadly acceptable definition of history is not easily identified. Voltaire characterized it as "a pack of tricks we play on the dead." Hopefully this is no longer true—if it ever was. The existentialist sees history in terms of man's struggle to realize his freedom. Traditional practices have illustrated a concept of history that is still too much in evidence—that which presents history as past

[87]Brock, *op. cit.*, pp. 58–63.
[88]James (ed.), *New Viewpoints in Geography, op. cit.*, pp. 93–97.

politics or a narration of battles, dynasties, and leaders. Such an approach frames history essentially in chronological and political terms. Modern historians take a much broader approach to their discipline.

In its broadest sense, history encompasses all of the past, whether directly related to man or not and regardless of whether it has been recorded. Historians generally limit their efforts to man's *memory* of the past. This memory of the past is usually in recorded form, but some recorded history has escaped the present memory of man, as it has been lost, discarded, or forgotten. This concept of history may encompass the total record of the past, including literature, law, architecture, social institutions, religion, philosophy, and all else that lives in and through the memory of man.[89]

History may be conceived as an attempt on the part of man to understand the powers of his own mind. This is done as he understands the thoughts and mental powers of men in the past. In this context, history is not a story of successive events or an account of change. Events as such are of no concern at all. They are important only as they indicate an outward expression of thoughts.[90]

The various interpretations of history generally have at least one thing in common—they are attempts to discover patterns and regularities upon which generalizations can be built to explain man and human existence. These generalizations form the structural elements for a system of instruction.

History affords a basis for understanding developments which take place over periods of time. Methods are supplied for studying problems which involve the time dimension and the interrelations of political, economic, social, and intellectual life. Most of the content appropriate to the study of history is shared with sociology, economics, political science, or one of the other social sciences. The uniqueness of history lies primarily in an integrating point of view developed through use of the calendar. History thus becomes significant in the way it is able to take the detached data of the various social sciences and give them related meaningfulness as applied to some particular century or event.

History may be studied through one or more of several different approaches. Traditionally, the following patterns have been utilized:

1. Chronological—a convenient and common approach, this pattern faces the problems of where to start, how divisions should be drawn, and dangers of overgeneralizing about eras. With this approach it may be better to start with the present and work back, instead of vice versa, as is most common.

2. Geographical—also a simple and convenient pattern, this approach studies history by geographical divisions (European, American, Asiatic). The major danger involved is that of leaving out many parts of the world and overemphasizing others.

[89]Henry Steele Commager, *The Nature and the Study of History* (Columbus, Ohio: Merrill, 1965), pp. 1–3.
[90]R. G. Collingwood, "The Idea of History," in T. M. Knox (ed.), *The Idea of History* (New York: Oxford, 1956).

3. Political—particularly prominent since the rise of nationalism in the world, this pattern is also convenient. However, it includes dangers of inculcating a narrow and parochial view, tending to extreme patriotism, exaggerating the role of politics and diplomacy, and neglecting culture, religion, social and economic institutions and other important factors.

4. Cultural—an emphasis on the history of the mind and character of a people, the major ideas which appeared to dominate a society or an age, and the institutions with which we associate the conduct and faith of men. This approach makes great demands on the scholar, as he is called upon to know, understand, and explain the ideas and interests of a whole generation, often in many different societies. To trace manifestations in the whole fabric of history, the cultural historian is required to know the history, art, literature, philosophy, and science of many countries; then he must be able to fuse all of these into a synthesis. Although complex and demanding, this approach probably offers the most potential for real understanding of man and his institutions.

5. Biography—an important and useful approach, because history was much influenced by great men, but the danger of overemphasis must be carefully avoided.[91]

Political, military, and dynastic history, which dominated historical writings up to the middle of the nineteenth century, has given way to these more useful and balanced approaches, although vistages of past weaknesses are still evident in many classrooms. Few today will deny, however, that students receive much greater benefit from studying major problems in history through an understanding of the politics, international relations, science, technology, economics, psychology, and morals which are involved.

Concepts and generalizations may be utilized in teaching history just as usefully as in teaching other social studies, although perhaps somewhat differently. Historians seem to feel more at home with questions to put to data than with lists of concepts, but most analytical questions grow out of concepts. For example, the concept of leadership suggests a number of questions: "Who are the leaders? What are their attributes? How did they gain and maintain support from their followers? What were the 'rules of the game' which they followed?" Questions such as these help historians to bring order to data in thinking about the past. What they study and the conclusions they reach will be largely determined by the questions to which answers are sought.[92]

As with other types of content material, most of the concepts with which historians are concerned are shared with other social sciences. The concepts of culture from sociology, freedom from political science, interdependence from economics, situation from geography, evolution from anthropology, and percep-

[91]Adapted from Commager, *The Nature and the Study of History*, pp. 15–26.
[92]Edwin Fenton, *The New Social Studies* (New York: Holt, 1967), p. 14.

tion from social psychology are examples of the cross-application of ideas among history and all of the social sciences.

Historians, perhaps more than other social scientists, disagree about whether or not one can generalize about their discipline. At one extreme are those who maintain that it is impossible to formulate valid generalizations about history; in which case the historian's task is to simply chronicle the events of the past. At the other extreme are those who believe that it is both possible and necessary to establish generalizations in order to construct timeless laws to guide the future conduct of man.

No doubt, establishing generalizations in history is a risky business, but to gain a better understanding of the past, the historian must generalize. He may be reluctant to attempt to predict the future from the past, but careful analysis will provide valuable insight for understanding the present and determining future action.

> The historian . . . is bound to generalize; and in so doing he provides general guides for future action, which though not specific predictions, are both valid and useful. But he cannot predict specific events, because the specific is unique and because the element of accident enters into it. This distinction, which worries philosophers, is perfectly clear to ordinary men. If two or three children in school develop measles, you will conclude that the epidemic will spread; and this prediction, if you care to call it such, is based on a generalization from past experience and is a valid and useful guide to action. But you cannot make the specific prediction that Charles or Mary will catch measles.[93]

Some historical generalizations characterize the nature of history and transcend particular periods and specific events. Others (sometimes termed "lower level") are less universally applicable or pertain to a rather specific type of situation. Muessig and Rogers have suggested some generalizations of a type that may be used to provide a foundation for curriculum and lesson planning related to history.

1. Continuous and unrelenting change has been a universal condition of human society throughout both remembered and recorded time.
2. History makes men aware of the possible rather than the probable, allowing him to choose among rational alternatives concerning the time in which he lives. History offers no immutable laws, givens, or inevitables, however, upon which to base such decisions.
3. Ideally, the past should be understood on its own terms. Historical events should be examined in light of the standards, values, attitudes, and beliefs that were dominant during a given period and for a given people, rather than evaluated exclusively by twentieth-century standards.
4. Rarely can complex historical events be explained in terms of a simple, one-to-one, cause-and-effect relationship. Rather, a study of the past indicates that multiple causation is the dominant pattern.
5. The record of the past is irremediably fragmentary, selective and biased. The significance of available historical "facts" varies with the individual who

[93]Edward H. Carr, *What Is History?* (New York: Knopf, 1962).

studies them and each generation tends to recreate and rewrite history in terms of its own needs, aspirations, and point of view.[94]

Other, less universal or less encompassing, generalizations also have valuable possibilities for teaching history. They particularly lend themselves to the "discovery" or "inquiry" method of teaching. The following are illustrative:

1. Nations that win wars usually want something besides the satisfaction of victory. So, nations that are the losers pay for their defeat in many ways.
2. To develop civilization, people must settle in a particular place for a long time and live in security.
3. The invention of the printing press began a gradual replacement of superstition with knowledge.[95]
4. A knowledge of past mistakes can guide men in their future actions.
5. Contemporary observers are not the best guides to the meaning and importance of events.
6. In seeking political solutions to economic problems, people often proceed on insufficient evidence.[96]
7. All people express their religious feelings through worship of their own deities.
8. The ability of a people to direct or adapt to basic changes is influenced by their level of education and their application of scientific knowledge.[97]

The historian's methods of finding and validating knowledge are similar in many respects to those of many other disciplines—even the sciences—in that questions are asked and answers are sought and validated.Sciences differ in that they are searching for timeless regularities, while historians search for the beliefs, passions,and actions of men as they lived out certain stages of history involving dramas and episodes of life. Questions asked by historians seek answers about human actions done in the past. The search is for patterns and changes in patterns of men's actions over time and in the past which will enable man to gain more knowledge of himself. This knowledge is then expressed in the form of generalizations with general or limited applicability.

History cannot be called an experimental subject. The term experiential seems more appropriate. The chief occupation of thoughtful historians is a search for the causes of things. Attempts to discover "laws" of history have been largely unsuccessful, but if the student of history accepts the notion of multiple causation and resigns himself to the fact that as yet we do not know enough to explain the causes of many things, the search for causes will itself be an affluent enterprise.

No laws of history command authority, but the study of those manifold forces which ceaselessly play upon history deepens our understanding and brings

[94]Commager, op. cit., pp. 100–139.
[95]Glenn W. Moon and Don C. Cline, Story of Our Land and People (New York: Holt, 1961), pp. 63, 142.
[96]John S. Bowes, "Using Documentary Material in the American History Course," Social Education, February 1964, pp. 88–90, 95.
[97]Donald F. Drummond, Dorothy M. Fraser, and Frank Alweis, Teacher's Guide and Key for Five Centuries in America (New York: American Book, 1964), p. G3.

magnanimity to our judgment. No philosophy encompasses or explains the track-less course of history, but to those who study it with sympathy and understanding and imagination history teaches philosophy.[98]

Historians go about their work by giving attention to three main inquiry concepts: questions, evidence, and interpretation. The teacher's approach to creating a classroom climate which is conducive to critical thinking generally follows an approach including the following phases:

1. *Creation, definition, and clarification of a problem.* Questions relative to a certain historical lesson may be suggested by students or by the teacher. In either case, the attempt should be made to see that they summarize the main points of the lesson. As an example, a teacher initiating inquiry about the Age of Discovery might suggest questions such as these:

> Why does man seek to explore the world around him? Is exploration inher-ent in human nature? Where does he explore and why? Is the term "exploration" to be applied only to the discovery and exploitation of new continents? What factors hinder or strengthen his quest? In what ways and why would exploration and discovery of new lands affect the economic organization and structure of the mother countries and the power relations among them?[99]

2. *Forming alternative hypotheses.* In response to questions, students should offer possible answers. With help from the teacher, each "intelligent guess" should be put into proper hypothetical form, satisfying several basic criteria:

1. It should be testable, i.e., expressed in clear, precise and sometimes quantita-tive language.
2. It should incorporate all the facts of the case under investigation and not just a few of them.
3. It should explain what it sets out to explain;
4. It should have no internal contradictions and it should be simple.[100]

This step in historical inquiry is illustrated by the following hypotheses which were offered by students in response to the questions suggested above:

1. If a country has a monopoly on trade and other countries are not satisfied with the situation, then a great period of exploration will follow.
2. If there is a country whose people make their living from the sea, then these people will be the first to explore and colonize new lands.
3. If the opportunity exists, then it is the nature of man to explore the unknown.
4. If there is exploration, then trade will flourish because of the discovery of new products.
5. If trade increases, then cultural change will be affected.
6. If exploration of previously undiscovered land becomes common, then cer-tain states will fight for the possession of colonies.[101]

[98]Commager, *op. cit.*, p. 94.
[99]Byron G. Massialas, "Teaching History as Inquiry," in Shirley H. Engle (ed.), *New Perspec-tives in World History*, Thirty-fourth Yearbook of the National Council for the Social Studies (Washington, D.C.: National Council for the Social Studies, 1964), p. 637.
[100]Harold A. Larrabee, *Reliable Knowledge* (Boston: Houghton, 1945), pp. 197–204.
[101]Massialas, "Teaching History as Inquiry," *op. cit.*, pp. 637–638.

3. *Testing the hypotheses and their implications.* Through the interpretation of evidence (documents, objects, other sources of information), hypotheses are subjected to tests of logical consistency and empirical verification.

4. *Acceptance of a tenable generalization or conclusion.* As has been pointed out previously, generalizations in history and the social sciences do not have the same preciseness of meaning and anticipated relationship as those in the natural sciences, but this does not preclude their use. The sufficiency of evidence must be constantly considered, and the open-endedness and reconstructive character of historical generalizations should be emphasized.

Before concluding this discussion of inquiry in the teaching of history, perhaps brief mention of the use of historical facts should be made. Much of the criticism and discussion surrounding history as a school subject revolves around the use and misuse of more or less accurate "facts" of history. Few would deny that there is a place for these elements of history, but agreement is usually lacking concerning the proper stress which they should receive. Arnold Toynbee, one of the most prominent and universally accepted historians of recent years, seems to put the problem into proper perspective.

> Facts are an historian's stock in trade, and he has to acquire them in quantities that would be repellent if the facts did not fascinate him. I love the facts of history, but not for their own sake. I love them as clues to something beyond them —as clues to the nature and meaning of the mysterious universe in which every human being awakes to consciousness.[102]

Organization for Social Studies Education

To carry out the type of social studies education suggested in the preceding pages, some type of organizational structure must be devised which will best facilitate the structural approach to teaching. The traditional grade placement of social studies subject matter (primarily history) does not preclude some utilization of this approach, but there seem to be some other systems which may better facilitate such a program.

Various social-studies curriculum projects have made proposals concerning the organization considered best for classroom instruction. Several of them are similar in many respects, although they may differ in detail. A brief description of some representative suggestions may serve to illustrate how the school program could be adapted to better meet the requirements of a modern social studies instructional program.

Building upon an integrated program in the elementary school designed to bring about an understanding of ". . . how men in groups carry on the basic human activities in the expanding communities of men," Paul R. Hanna suggests a five-year program at the secondary school level.

---

[102]Arnold J. Toynbee, "Why and How I Work," *Saturday Review* (April 5, 1969), p. 24.

1. A year's course in world geography is advocated immediately following the elementary program. This would emphasize the concepts, generalizations, and methods of inquiry recognized by geography scholars and adapted by public school teachers for use in the lower secondary school classroom.

2. Following the course in world geography, it is suggested that a year's study in world history should also adhere to the basic tenets of the structural approach.

3. Building upon these world views organized as geography and as history, a semester's study in economics should be required, followed by a required course on political institutions and processes. In each of these courses, major emphasis would be on theory and practice in the United States as it works within a world setting.

4. At the junior level, a required course in United States history would be required.

5. This could be followed by a year's study in "Problems of Society," although it would not be required, as would the other four years of study. Such a course would attempt to study the issues faced by man, selected on an optional basis according to the interests of students.[103]

A less traditional type of organization and sequence, for grades 9 through 12, is exemplified in a new set of materials developed under the leadership of Edwin Fenton.

Grade 9, First Semester: Comparative Political Systems
    A comparison of a primitive political system with the governments of the United States and the Soviet Union, examining the nature of leadership, the institutional setting, decision making, the role of the individual citizen, and ideology.
Grade 9, Second Semester: Comparative Economic Systems
    A comparison of a traditional economy with systems where most decisions are made in the market (United States) and where most decisions are made by command (Soviet Union), focusing upon three basic questions—what is to be produced, how is it to be produced, and for whom is it to be produced.
Grade 10, First Semester: The Shaping of Western Society
    A study of change over periods of time in four areas of Western society— the economic system, politics, the social organization, and patterns of thought.
Grade 10, Second Semester: Tradition and Change in Four Societies
    An examination of four countries—South Africa, China, India, and Brazil— analyzing in each case the traditional society, the impact of Western ideas and institutions, and one major contemporary problem, such as economic growth.
Grade 11: American History
    A study centering on four major themes—the development of the American economic system, the growth of the American political system, the changing American social structure, and the reflection of these developments in the American intellectual tradition.

[103]Paul R. Hanna, "Revising the Social Studies: What Is Needed?" *Social Education* (April 1963), pp. 190–196.

Grade 12, First Semester: Introduction to the Behavioral Sciences
A study of two issues: the methods of inquiry of the behavioral sciences (psychology, sociology, and anthropology), and selected generalizations about the behavior of men as individuals and in groups.

Grade 12, Second Semester: Humanities in Three Cities
A study of the conceptions of the good man, the good life, and the good society revealed in literary and artistic works produced in ancient Athens, Renaissance Florence, and modern New York City.[104]

Dorothy McClure Fraser has suggested a somewhat similar program for the secondary school, founded upon a comprehensive and well-planned elementary school social studies sequence. To give the complete picture, we will include the major topic identifications proposed for the elementary grades, along with a more complete description of the proposed secondary program.

Kindergarten–Grade 1. School Life and Family Life in the Modern World: the school, safety, family life today, in pioneer days and in another culture.

Grade 2. Selected Functions of Living in the Neighborhood, with Appropriate Expansion to the Region, Nation, and World: protection (fire, police), health (doctor, nurse), getting food, communication, transportation, service industries. In connection with study of the neighborhood, children will begin systematic development of geographic concepts.

Grade 3. The Modern Community in Its Broader Setting, with Appropriate Comparisons to Communities that are Removed in Space or Time: geographic features, economic life, transportation, communication.

Grade 4. The Home State in Its Natural and World Setting: typical industries, geography, history.

Grade 5. The Nation in Its World Setting: historical, geographic, and economic elements.

Grades 6–7. Man in His Physical and Cultural Environment (a two-year sequence): world geography, the development of civilization, area study units. Second year to draw heavily on sociology-anthropology (the process of socialization, impact of culture, societal institutions).

Grades 8–9. American Studies—History, Civics, and Economic Life of the United States, including state and local aspects (a two-year sequence): history, economic and technological growth, urbanization, cultural developments, foreign affairs, operation of the political system, civics, economics.

Grades 10–11. Cultures of the World, A Two-Year Sequence Focused on the World Outside the United States, Including Both Western and non-Western Cultures: western civilization, other selected cultures.

Grade 12. Problems of the Modern World (to include both domestic and world problems): interdisciplinary study of such problems as democracy versus authoritarianism, competing economic systems, government and economic life in the United States, population problems, world resources and trade, international organization and world affairs.

Electives. A number of advanced elective courses, most of them one-semester, should be available for senior high school students who have demonstrated their interest and potential ability for social science study: urban geography, international relations, social psychology, The USSR or other regional studies,

[104]Edwin Fenton, *Developing a New Curriculum: A Rationale for the Holt Social Studies Curriculum* (New York: Holt, 1967), p. 3.

or courses dealing with selected periods of history, and advanced placement courses.[105]

From the necessarily brief discussions of change and development in social studies education which have been included in this chapter, it may appear that this part of the curriculum is currently undergoing as much change and revision as any part of the school program. This is probably true, and although many would view this effort as late in coming, certainly considerable progress is being made, and the future promises a much more enticing and constructive experience in social studies learning for the students of our secondary schools than the past has usually offered.

Selected References

Berelson, Bernard, et al., *The Social Studies and the Social Sciences.* New York: Harcourt Brace Jovanovich, Inc., 1962.

Broek, Jan A. M., *Geography, Its Scope and Spirit.* Columbus, Ohio: Charles E. Merrill Books, Inc., 1965.

Commager, Henry Steele, *The Nature and the Study of History.* Columbus, Ohio: Charles E. Merrill Books, Inc., 1965.

Cox, C. Benjamin, and Byron G. Massialas (eds.), *Social Studies in the United States.* New York: Harcourt Brace Jovanovich, Inc., 1967.

Engle, Shirley H. (ed.), *New Perspectives in World History.* Thirty-fourth Yearbook of the National Council for the Social Studies. Washington, D.C.: National Council for the Social Studies, 1964.

Fair, Jean, and Fannie R. Shaftel (eds.), *Effective Thinking in the Social Studies.* Thirty-seventh Yearbook of the National Council for the Social Studies. Washington, D.C.: National Council for the Social Studies, 1967.

Fenton, Edwin, *Teaching the New Social Studies in Secondary Schools.* New York: Holt, Rinehart and Winston, Inc., 1966.

————, *The New Social Studies.* New York: Holt, Rinehart and Winston, Inc., 1967.

Fraser, Dorothy McClure, and Samuel P. McCutchen (eds.), *Social Studies in Transition: Guidelines for Change.* Washington, D.C.: National Council for the Social Studies, 1965.

Gross, Richard E., Walter E. McPhie, and Jack R. Fraenkel (eds.), *Teaching the Social Studies.* Scranton, Pa.: Intext Educational Publishers, 1969.

Hunt, Erling M., et al., *High School Social Studies Perspectives.* Boston: Houghton Mifflin Company, 1962.

[105]Dorothy McClure Fraser and Samuel P. McCutchen (eds.), *Social Studies in Transition: Guidelines for Change* (Washington, D.C.: National Council for the Social Studies, 1965), pp. 56–58. Reprinted by permission.

James, Preston E. (ed.), *New Viewpoints in Geography*, Twenty-ninth Yearbook of the National Council for the Social Studies. Washington, D.C.: National Council for the Social Studies, 1959.

Lambert, William, and Wallace E. Lambert, *Social Psychology*. Englewood Cliffs, N.J.: Prentice-Hall, Inc., 1965.

Martin, Richard S., and Reuben G. Miller, *Economics and Its Significance*. Columbus, Ohio: Charles E. Merrill Books, Inc., 1965.

Massialas, Byron G., and Andreas M. Kazamias, *Crucial Issues in the Teaching of Social Studies*. Englewood Cliffs, N.J.: Prentice-Hall, Inc., 1964.

————, and C. Benjamin Cox, *Inquiry in Social Studies*. New York: McGraw-Hill Book Company, 1966.

Moreland, Willis D. (ed.), *Social Studies in the Senior High School*. Washington, D.C.: National Council for the Social Studies, 1965.

National Task Force on Economic Education, *Economic Education in the Schools*. New York: Committee on Economic Development, 1961.

Pelto, Pertti J., *The Study of Anthropology*. Columbus, Ohio: Charles E. Merrill Books, Inc., 1965.

Price, Roy A. (ed.), *New Viewpoints in the Social Sciences*. Twenty-eighth Yearbook of the National Council for the Social Studies. Washington, D.C.: National Council for the Social Studies, 1958.

Riddle, Donald H., and Robert E. Cleary (eds.), *Political Science in The Social Studies*. Thirty-sixth Yearbook of the National Council for the Social Studies. Washington, D.C.: National Council for the Social Studies, 1966.

Rose, Caroline B., *Sociology: The Study of Man in Society*. Columbus, Ohio: Charles E. Merrill Books, Inc., 1965.

Sorauf, Francis J., *Political Science, An Informal Overview*. Columbus, Ohio: Charles E. Merrill Publishing Co., 1965.

Womack, James G., *Discovering the Structure of Social Studies*. New York: Benziger Brothers, 1966.

CHAPTER 10

THE HUMANITIES

We have left the discussion of those areas of learning classified as the humanities until last, not because they are either inherently inferior or superior to the other disciplines in any way, but because they seem to bind all learning together with a common thread—man.

The Idea of the Humanities

What do we mean when we speak of the humanities? Are they something different from the subjects that high school students normally study, such as English, history, languages, and the like? Why are they considered important? In a practical sense, one may ask, "What can the humanities do for me, for my family, for my business, for my country and the world?" Do the humanities make people better, happier, or more capable? How can the humanities be applied to business, community life, or national concerns? To support proposals for including the humanities as an organized whole in the secondary school curriculum, we must come to grips with these questions. The discussion which follows is designed to at least begin such an effort.

Throughout recorded history there is evidence that man has studied what we might define as the humanities, although the term and concept as used today can be traced with accuracy only a relatively short distance into the past. Romans —notably Cicero and Quintilian—formulated many of the ideas today associated with the term humanities. Aulus Gellius defined "humanity" as "education and training in the good arts," giving us the basic concept which has served since the Renaissance to mark off the humanities from theology, or divine studies, and later from natural science. These studies were considered "good" because they were thought to be particularly adapted to serving the moral nature of man or his practical activities as a citizen or public servant. They were thought to serve ends beyond themselves, bringing about the "humanizing" process in man by developing those virtues and knowledge which separate man from the lower animals.

The Romans, as they adapted ideas from the Greeks, tended to place more value upon those studies which were of most practical use at that time—those

294

involving oratory and statesmanship. The speculative and theoretical tended to be neglected. This fact provides a good example of the major problem associated with the humanities through the years. In general terms, the ends of humane education have been stated in rather consistent form from age to age and from society to society, but the specific means to attain those general ends may be seen to vary considerably, if they are well defined at all.

From the Renaissance to our day, discussions concerning the ends and means of study in the humanities have exhibited similar advocacy of various preferred roads to follow in making man human. Arguments have followed the line that they restore man to humanity and raise him toward God, that they lead to the knowledge of a man's self, with the end of well-doing and not of well-knowing only, that they induce a philosophic habit of mind, or that they lead to a harmonious expansion and interrelation of all the powers which make the beauty and worth of human nature. Some have taken a more utilitarian approach, stating that the value of the humanities is in their aiding the development of a prudent, just, and temperate magistrate; that they fit a man to perform justly, skillfully, and magnanimously all the offices, both private and public, of peace and war; or that they best prepare and discipline men for active life by convincing them that they are men before they are lawyers or physicians or merchants.

The humanities have thus come down to us as instruments to aid the achievement of human ideals. There has been little agreement upon the nature and principles of the disciplines best suited to this purpose or upon the manner in which they should be taught. Therein lies the major difficulty still faced by educators who dare attempt the identification and development of educational means to achieve the lofty goals of humanitarian idealists.[1]

The idea of the humanities still presents a great question. Are they outdated leftovers from past educational ideas, fragments remaining after the physical and social sciences have claimed their subject matter, or do they have a distinct purpose and entity for modern education? Are they a series of distinct disciplines which should be taught by various specialized departments, or do they possess the promise of a means to synthesize accumulated and multiplying knowledge into a consistent system of "humane" values and principles?

Some recent and still developing approaches to answers for these questions take the position that through the humanities we have the best chance to attain an understanding of such enduring values as justice, freedom, virtue, beauty, and truth. We can help man achieve self-awareness and sharpen his sensibilities. We can ". . . stress real persons and cases rather than models, quality rather than quantity, evaluation and evocation rather than observation, beauty and wisdom rather than information."[2] In summary,

> The humanities are a group of subjects devoted to the study of man as a being other than a biological product and different from a social or sociological

---

[1] R. S. Crane, *The Idea of the Humanities*, Vol. 1 (Chicago: U. of Chicago Press, 1967), pp. 155–164.
[2] Jan A. M. Broek, *Geography, Its Scope and Spirit* (Columbus, Ohio: Merrill, 1965), p. 21.

entity. They make certain assumptions about human nature and about history. First, they assume that man lives in a dimension lying beyond science and the social sciences. Second, they assume that his profound sense of individuation is one of the most important things about him. Third, they assume that the better traits of humanity, or, if one likes, the enduring elements of human nature, find typical expression in philosophy, in literature, in language, and in the arts, and that history is both the way by which these expressions are preserved and one of the principal modes of interpreting the meaning of these expressions to and in contemporary life. Fourth, the purpose of the humanities is refining and maturing the individual who studies them sympathetically and intelligently, evidence of refinement and maturation being given by increased sympathy with and understanding of philosophy and the arts in past and present time and increased sympathy with and understanding of man not only as he is but as he has been. Humane studies tend to concentrate upon individual development rather more than upon social judgment, and differ from science in this regard also, since science properly seeks to eliminate the personal equation.[3]

Need for the Humanities

If there ever was a need for study in the humanities, it is magnified today. From every direction we hear the cry that man is being overcome by machines, standardization, and mechanization. As Arnold Toynbee has so aptly phrased it:

> Man has now decisively overcome Nature by his technology, but the victor has been technology, not Man himself. Man has merely exchanged one master for another, and his new master is more overbearing than his former. . . . Nature used to chastise Man with whips, Man's own technology is now chastising Man with scorpions.[4]

Man needs a sense of personal self-realization and also a sense of identity with other men more than ever before. He needs a sense of direction and integrity of purpose derived from his own formulation of values and goals. He needs a fuller understanding of the complexities with which we live, an understanding best gained through the humane studies. Science, intelligence, and physical well-being have their place in the development of a human being, but spirituality, morality, and aesthetic appreciation are even more basic to a full and happy life.

In centering our attention on the humanity of man, the humane studies also possess considerable value as a synthesizing agent. Few students will build their acquired fragments of specialized information into an organic whole without some frame of understanding and appreciation. Such a frame is available through the common denominator of man as he has lived and developed through the ages.

Because of their recognition of the inadequacy of an education dominated

[3]Howard Mumford Jones, *One Great Society* (New York: Harcourt, 1959), p. 17.
[4]Arnold J. Toynbee, "Why and How I Work," *Saturday Review* (April 5, 1969), p. 24.

by science and materialistic concerns, educators have begun to pay much more attention to those traditional, but often neglected, studies we call the humanities. National, regional, and local conferences, task forces, and study groups have been organized to find ways to better fit the proven subject matter of the humanities to the student concerns and the modern educational scene. Financial support from governmental and private sources has not reached anything comparable to that supplied earlier for study in the areas of science and social science education, but progress is evident and future plans are expanding.

Humanities Education

The idea of the humanities is probably acceptable to almost all of those who are interested in education and our educational system. Although their concept of the term may be rather hazy and ill-defined, few would argue against the need for including the humane studies in the public school program. Difficulties arise, however, when the high-sounding phrases of humanistic theorists and philosophers must be put into a form and organizational scheme appropriate for the education of young people. This part of our discussion—humanities education —will be approached in similar fashion to that taken with the other disciplinary areas. Based upon a statement of basic objectives, the structural elements of the humanities—content, concepts and generalizations, and methods of inquiry— will form the outline for the humanities education program considered most appropriate for the times in which we live.

Objectives

The fundamental purpose of humanities education may be stated as the search for an answer to the basic but elusive question: "Who am I?" Through an examination of the records of his past and present experiences, study of the humanities strives to facilitate man's understanding of himself, his relationship to his past, and his place in his own world. Such an understanding has been the goal of man throughout history, but perhaps in no other age has he been so acutely aware of the need for clues to his identity and purpose in the world.

In solving the problems of mankind, science provides us with the "how." The humanities bear the responsibility for choosing what should be solved and for seeking answers to queries of "why?" After they have identified the first-rate questions of society, the humanist treats them as a continuum, with their roots in the past and their branches in the future. When the humanities are successful in their mission, they create that fusion of art and science which produces the whole man, the fulfillment of the Greek aspiration to make of man "a work of art in himself."[5] As H. M. Jones phrases it,

[5]Janice L. Gorn, "Are the Humanities Obsolete?" *Phi Delta Kappan* 49 (January 1968), p. 254.

The purpose of humane learning is to offer those wise enough to want to accept the lesson of human experience an interpretation of the life of man—its tragedies and aspirations, its brutalities and its comic relief. The lesson of human experience in this sense constitutes whatever wisdom man has learned from the processes of history and from those enduring expressions or interpretations of experience we call philosophy, religion in a broad and generous sense, works of literature, and works in the fine arts, including music, architecture, and the dance.[6]

A complete statement of responsibilities appropriate to the basic purpose of humanities education would be long indeed. However, to illustrate the challenge facing educators in this realm, a summary of tasks suggested by Jones may be helpful. He proposes that humanities education is called upon to

1. Teach the rudiments of our own language and foreign languages, both ancient and modern.
2. Acquaint youth with the fundamentals of philosophy, ethics, logic, aesthetics, and, in some cases, religion.
3. Develop in students a competent style in speaking and writing.
4. Inculcate and encourage habits of reading which shall be lifelong, including "serious" as well as recreational selections.
5. Along with the teaching of languages, help students acquire an understanding of the culture, history, social psychology, and needs of the people who use the languages studied.
6. Create and encourage a lifelong taste for the fine arts, music, the theater, literature, good architecture, the dance as an art form, excellent decoration and the like. It is assumed that this will require some familiarity with great names, structures, paintings, and other works of art.
7. Develop in students at least some skill in the theory and practice of criticism (or at least rational judgment upon performances in the arts).
8. Achieve some understanding of the cultural development of the Western world and also that of the Orient, including religions, faiths, cultures, and philosophies.
9. Develop an ethical outlook upon life.
10. Teach "Western democratic traditions," and make "better citizens" out of American youth.
11. Discover and encourage "creativity."
12. Develop a "sane emotional balance" through individual growth in appreciation and understanding.
13. Interpret the general humane, philosophic, or metaphysical significance of modern science and social science, as well as the arts.
14. Create, through humane learning, a balance with technical and scientific learning and emphasis.[7]

[6]H. M. Jones, *op. cit.*, p. 9.
[7]Adapted from Jones, *One Great Society*, pp. 225–227.

In all its aspects, study in the humanities should reinforce the fact that all knowledge is interrelated. Students should be impressed with a sense of the continuity and repetitive quality of the past as they are acquainted with the thoughts, creations, and actions of our predecessors and of our contemporaries. They should be impelled to raise basic questions and to search for answers. And there should be aroused a voracious appetite for more knowledge and understanding—a dissatisfaction with what one knows, curiosity concerning what one does not know, and concern about what is and what might be. In this way will educators help young people learn not only to meet the unexpected and unusual in life but also to live day by day with the expected and usual—perhaps a much more difficult task.

Content

One of the most difficult problems faced by those concerned with humanities education is the identification of appropriate content—usually denoted by the term *subject matter*. Part of the problem is our tendency always to think of content in terms of traditional subject matter divisions, a habit we have already criticized. Being forced to acknowledge, however, that most of us are not going to be able to divorce ourselves from this habitual characteristic, we will continue to utilize this approach to some extent, while pressing for a broader and less subject-boundary-bound approach.

In discussing the objectives of humane learning, it was suggested that the focus of education in this area was man—his acts and works, his thoughts and feelings, and their artifacts. But this opens the boundaries of content material to an almost boundless degree, for all knowledge concerns man in some way. Art, literature, and music would obviously be included in the realm of the humanities, thus defined, but it might also be conceived to include aspects of psychology, cultural anthropology, economics, and archaelogy, which are usually considered sciences rather than humanities.

Can it be rightfully said that any area of study is intrinsically foreign to a humanities program? Could it be that the humanities, rather than being a well-defined group of disciplines, is more correctly a way of looking at things? In this sense, the subject matter of the humanities would not be special, but the aspect of the subject (or subjects) would be special. Subject matter may thus be utilized for its contribution to the study of man as a human being. It would be valued for its contribution to efforts designed to help man become increasingly "humane," rather than animal. This will necessarily involve considerable attention to values, ethics, and morals, not only as they have been and are today but as they should be.

The content for the humanities gains its position in the school curriculum from its value to all men, rather than for its direct vocational or other specific use. Skill and interest in the humanities may enhance vocational opportunities, but placement of the humane studies in the curriculum is justified by their focus upon universal qualities, rather than upon specific and measurable ends.

To further illustrate the approach to subject matter which seems most appropriate to the humanities, it may be pointed out that the really important difference between the humanities and the sciences is not in the subject matter but in the fact that science exhibits a method and a mental attitude of a stabilized subject and an impartial and detached treatment of evidence. The humanities, on the other hand, express the nature of the human involvement with the human world. The sciences are most successful when they seek to move from the diversity and particularity of their observations toward a high degree of unity and uniformity. The humanities reverse this process, as they look for devices of explanation and appreciation to preserve and increase the variety, uniqueness, complexity, and originality that distinguish man from the other animals.[8]

Even though we may agree that the approach outlined above is desirable in attempting to establish a good humanities curriculum, there is still some necessity for thinking in terms of more traditional subject-matter content. Hopefully, the lines of demarcation will be softened and better relationships among the subjects established, but there remains the necessity for some specified data and factual information, and it is probably best to continue to express ourselves in somewhat standard terms in defining these needs.

For the most part, English language and literature, modern and classical foreign languages, music, the graphic and decorative arts, and the performing arts must be included in any type of studies bearing the label humanities. In addition, at least some aspects of history and other social studies must be included as they relate to the interpretation of man and human nature. We must also include those aspects of science and mathematics which widen the understanding of man in relation to his environment and to other men.

Somewhere in the humanities program there must be included a study of religion to some extent if we expect students to gain an adequate understanding of man. It may be that this can best be included within the context of philosophy, the social sciences, or literature, but more than likely there must also be some attention given specifically to religion on a nonsectarian basis.

Although it may not belong to any one field of learning in the truest sense, it would seem that several elements of philosophy should be included in the humanities program for their integrating and synthesizing value. Through its continuous insistence on a type of questioning that is in itself oriented toward synthesis and perspective, philosophy could very likely serve as the best means to relate all humanistic studies into a meaningful whole.

Structure

One of the prime purposes of this text is to develop the idea that concepts and generalizations are essential to the integration and correlation of subject matter, either in a single discipline or a class of disciplines. A cursory examination

[8]Crane, *op. cit.*, p. 12.

of the humanities soon reveals the fact that hundreds of concepts are shared by two or more of the disciplines. Many concepts are common to all of the disciplines we have included in the humanities. The following list is made up of concepts which are shown in the discussions that follow to be a part of the humanities disciplines. Some of them may be utilized in studying any or all of these disciplines. Each of them is shared by at least two of the disciplines.

abstract	logical
accent	love
ambiguity	loyalty
analogy	media
character	metaphor
chronological	model
climax	mood
colloquial	movement
color	opinion
concrete	pattern
consistency	prejudice
consonance	premise
context	proof
contradiction	proportion
contrast	proposition
culture	quality
deducation	reality
design	referent
dignity	religion
dissonance	rhythm
emotive	sacred
evil	secular
evolution	shame
fact	sin
fantasy	sorrow
figurative	style
generalization	subject
harmony	taste
herosim	technique
illusion	texture
implication	theme
induction	tone
inference	transfer
integration	transition
irony	truth
irrelevant	unity
joy	universal
know	validity

literal   value
localism   wisdom

Generalizations which are interdisciplinary in nature may be identified throughout the humanities. Good teachers have always used this approach to give broader meaning to what they were teaching and to help students understand relationships, cause and effect, and relatedness among the activities of man. A more concerted effort to utilize interdisciplinary generalizations will facilitate all teaching and learning in the humanities. The following are examples of the type of generalization which is most useful in study of the humanities.

1. Since no two people have identical experience, communication by means of language, art, music, or other form is unique for each individual.
2. Each person's background of experience adds emotional overtones to his understanding of communications media.
3. Other forms of communication supplement language, with its limitations due to words available, confusion of word meaning, and inexactness of expression.
4. No two people receiving a communication through words, art, music, or other media will understand it in exactly the same way.
5. The use of metaphor vastly extends the power of communication through each media.
6. Form is realized, not taught.
7. Communication through the arts is a blending of the impulse of feeling and the impulse of reason.
8. Response to the arts is both instinctive and cognitive.
9. Cultures and religions have languages of symbols used either to communicate with God or among members of the group.
10. Organization in the arts occurs in response to inner urges.
11. Rhythm and movement are fundamental to all physical expressions.
12. The nature of the materials must be observed by the artist (of any type) as he seeks to express himself.
13. The influence of religion can be traced in all the activities and creative efforts of man.
14. What one believes about God, about man, and about the world has momentous consequences in his life, conduct, and creative efforts.
15. Each of the arts affects the others during any particular historical period.
16. Values and moral standards are expressed by means of all the communicative arts.
17. Through the humanities, man seeks immortality.
18. No work of art can be accurately understood without a knowledge of the times during which it was created.
19. Culture is expressed through the arts, but the arts also affect culture.
20. Man has an innate desire to communicate with his own generation and also with generations to come.

Methods of Inquiry

The humanities, encompassing such a vast array of skills and content as they do, seem to defy the idea that a common approach to inquiry may be identified. If one steps back from the various content areas, however, and takes the broadest possible view, it may be possible to see an all-encompassing approach to inquiry and study of the various disciplines and content areas. No doubt there will be submethods and complementary methods, but perhaps one concept will serve to unify the total study.

In attempting to take this broadest of possible views in the determination of approach to inquiry for the humanities, we have concluded that it is possible to identify an all-encompassing approach. To some, the concept of critical thinking fits the need, and this is indeed a popular emphasis in today's humanities programs. We would prefer the related but larger concept of *philosophical analysis*.

Philosophical analysis is not a new invention or discovery. In fact, it is one of the most ancient and venerable ways of examining knowledge and seeking new understanding. For the most part, it is the method of Socrates, Aristotle, and Thomas Aquinas.

The central concern of the humanities is to get at truth, reality, and the world as we know it and believe it to be. The tools for this task include language (words), music, paints, body movement, religion, reason, and related means of communication. Regardless of the media or the road taken to the determination of truth, the distinctive nature of this approach is derived from a concern for the detailed study of the ways in which man expresses his humanity.

The logical analyst is a critic of all simple and absolute distinctions. He encourages due respect for the subtlety and complexity of ordinary language or other means of expression, while also considering individual perspectives and feelings. Analysis must occur within the total context. For example, it is not consistent with the tenets of philosophical analysis to question the meaning of a word in general. Individual words ordinarily do not have meaning in themselves; sentences do. For this reason the meaning of a word must always be determined by reference to its semantics and the syntax in which it is used, to the kinds of sentences in which its use is appropriate, and to the types of experience to which it is or is not relevant. Neither is a musical phrase or a single feature of a painting analyzed without considering the total work and its largest meaning.[9]

One or more of several different formal precedures may be appropriate to a particular exercise in philosophical analysis. These may be used individually, although more often they complement each other and combine to work toward the overall goal of systematic analysis. Inductive reasoning, for example, is appro-

[9]Charles E. Caton (ed.), *Philosophy and Ordinary Language* (Urbana, Ill.: U. of Illinois Press, 1963).

priate to many types of study in the language arts. Particularly in literature, teachers may direct their students to note particulars and then encourage them to generalize and to hypothesize about the relationships among the particulars and the whole. Instead of telling the student about the literary work in question, the teacher guides him through a study of the composition and leads him to make his own discoveries. The emphasis is on seeing the parts in relationship to the whole.[10]

Deductive reasoning is also appropriate to some types of analysis in the study of the humanities. By starting with a general statement and then illustrating, proving, or applying it, students may practice what they learn as they learn it in any of the disciplines.

Creative thinking assumes the role of an inquiry method, particularly in art, music, and imaginative writing. The created product is then subject to other types of philosophical analysis to determine its merit.

Other types of logical analysis procedures could be mentioned to illustrate the fact that the appropriateness of a specific method of analysis is determined by the problem at hand and the results desired.

Teaching the Humanities

Talking about something is always much easier than doing it, and this is certainly true of teaching the humanities. Planning and organizing a humanities program for a secondary school requires the utmost understanding and coopera-tion among the teaching staff, as they seek to mold and present a program which will sharpen the perception of students toward themselves and the world around them.

A few basic principles are needed to form the foundation for teaching the humanities. In the first place, if the humanities are to aid people in their under-standing of man they must fulfill basic needs and interests arising out of daily living. They must then be presented in such a way that students may achieve more than mere "knowledge about" them. As William James expressed it, there should be developed "knowledge by acquaintance," rather than "knowledge by description." The humanities cannot be learned linear fashion, as science is learned. Students must live with them, soak in them, and thus build richer perceptions of mankind and of life, both personal and universal.

To make the humanities immediately and basically utilitarian, there must be stressed more than mere "aesthetics" and "appreciation." Emphasis must be on concepts and issues, moral and ethical values, and their relation to maintaining and improving society. A constant guard must be maintained to avoid slicing the various humanitarian studies too thin. In dividing a work of art into its elements,

---

[10]William H. Evans and Jerry L. Walker, *New Trends in the Teaching of English in Secondary Schools* (Chicago: Rand McNally, 1966), p. 38.

for example, students are likely to miss that on which the value and contribution of the work exists. As the chemist may destroy water by separating it into its chemical components (which bear no resemblance to water and quench no thirst), so the humanities may be destroyed by singling out subject, formal structure, and other special aspects. The essence of the humanities is lost as soon as we disturb the coincidence of its parts.

Humanities programs are generally organized in one of four ways. The most common is by topic or theme, such as "The Individual and Society," "Freedom and Authority," or "God and Man." A more traditional approach utilizes separate courses in various subjects, with teachers working together to correlate the courses. Aesthetic aspects or categories may form the focus for organization, giving special attention to the subject, style, function, structure, or some other aspect of various works. A fourth type or organization is by chronology, perhaps modified to some extent in relation to specific cultures and cultural periods in history.[11]

A program developed by the Commission on the Humanities of the Commonwealth of Pennsylvania provides an illustration of the topic or theme approach to organization. Six universal issues in human living are suggested:

Man's relationship to society
Man's relationship to the natural world
Man's relation to God
Man's search for truth
Man's search for beauty
Man's search for freedom[12]

With this approach, instruction is based on "the great questions," rather than the "great books," or some other more subject-oriented procedure. Books and other material should be chosen for their value in arriving at answers and for their effect on the emotional and intellectual life of students, rather than their "greatness." The important consideration is the students' approach to the problem raised by a book, the way it is read, not the subject matter alone.[13]

The chronological approach, which is relatively easy to organize, is also used with success in many programs, both at the secondary school and college level. The following chart illustrates how this type of plan might be used to organize teaching and learning in the humanities.[14]

[11]W. J. Hipple, Jr., "Humanities in the Secondary Schools," *Music Educators Journal*, 54 (February 1968), pp. 85–88.

[12]Ross L. Neagley and N. Dean Evans, *Handbook for Effective Curriculum Development* (Englewood Cliffs, N. J.: Prentice-Hall, 1967), p. 172.

[13]Edward J. Gordon, "On Teaching the Humanities," *English Journal* 58 (May 1969), pp. 681–687.

[14]From *The Understanding of Music* by Charles R. Hoffer. © 1967 by Wadsworth Publishing Company, Inc., Belmont, Calif. 94002. Reprinted by permission of the publisher.

Years	Literature	Philosophy
1000 B.C. 1 A.D.	Homer Dionysian festivals; Sophocles, Aristophanes, Euripides Horace, Cicero, Vergil, Plutarch	Socrates, Plato, Aristotle, Epicurus, Zeno
1100 1200 1300 1400	 Dante Petrarch, Boccaccio Chaucer	 Thomas Aquinas R. Bacon
1450	Ariosto	
1500	Rabelais, Spenser Marlowe, Shakespeare	Machiavelli, More, Luther, Erasmus
1600	Cervantes Pepys Milton	F. Bacon, Descartes, Grotius, Hobbs, Spinoza, Locke
1700 1750	Pope, Swift, Defoe, Gray, Goldsmith, Fielding, Burns, Goethe, Schiller,	Voltaire Hume, Rousseau, Kant
1800	Coleridge, Wordsworth, Scott, Byron, Austen, Shelley, Keats, Pushkin, Heine, Cooper, Balzac, Hugo,	 Hegel, Mill, Comte,
1850 1900 1950	Stendhal, Sand, Lytton, Dickens, Poe, Dumas, Thackeray, Longfellow, Hawthorne, Melville, Stowe, Whitman, Tennyson, Eliot, Tolstoy, Dostoevski, Browning, Mark Twain, Ibsen, Stevenson, Wilde, H. James, Maeterlinck, Zola, Kipling, G. B. Shaw, Masefield, Mann, Lawrence, Frost, Maugham, Lewis, T. S. Eliot, Joyce, Dreiser, Fitzgerald, France Malraux, Hemingway, O'Neill, A. Huxley, Benét, Faulkner, Sandburg, Stein, Steinbeck, Thomas, Williams, Miller, Orwell, Cummings, Auden	Kierkegaard, Schopenhauer, Marx, Engels, Thoreau, Spencer, T.H. Huxley, Emerson, Haeckel, Nietzsche, Bergson, Dewey, Pierce, W. James, Spengler, Russell, Santayana Satre, Camus

Musical period	Historical events	Visual arts
1000 B.C. 400 B.C.	Early Hellenic civilization Greek city states	Phidias, Myron, Parthenon

1 A.D.
300
410
600
 	
800
 	
GOTHIC
1200
1300
1400
 	
RENAISSANCE
 	
1500
 	
BAROQUE
 	
1700
 	
CLASSICAL
 	
1800
ROMANTIC
 	
1850
 	
MODERN
 	
1950
	Birth of Jesus; Rome rules
	Constantine declares Christianity
	Rome falls
	Gregory codifies chant; age of
	  monasteries
	Charlemagne made ruler of
	  Holy Roman Empire
	
	Crusades; Magna Charta
	Papal schism
	
	Gutenberg invents movable type
	Columbus and others make voyages
	Protestant reformation
	
	King James Version of Bible;
	Pilgrims land in America
	Newton writes about physical laws
	
	Encyclopedie published
	Watts invents steam engine
	
	Factory system begins
	American Revolution;
	French Revolution
	Napoleon becomes dictator
	Louisiana Purchase
	Monroe Doctrine declared
	McCormick invents reaper;
	Morse telegraph
	Daguerre takes first photographs
	California gold rush
	Darwin writes Origin of Species
	Civil War in United States
	Germany united under Bismarck
	Edison invents electric light and
	phonograph
	Roentgen discovers X-ray
	Spanish-American War
	
	First airplane flight by Wright brothers
	Freud founds psychoanalysis
	World War I
	Einstein writes theory of relativity
	Great depression in U. S.
	World War II
	United Nations founded
	Korean War
	"Sputnik" launched
		Pantheon and Colosseum
		
		Great cathedrals built
		
		Giotto,
		Ghiberti, Fra Filippo Lippi,
		Botticelli, Donatello,
		da Vinci,
		Van Eyck, Dürer,
		St. Peter's built in Rome
		Michelangelo, Raphael, Brueghel
		Titian, Giorgione, Tintoretto,
		Veronese,
		Bernini, Rubens,
		El Greco,
		Rembrandt, Velasquez,
		Van Dyck,
		Poussin,
		Watteau, Hogarth,
		Fragonard,
		Gainsborough
		
		David,
		Ingres,
		Goya,
		Gericault,
		
		Corot,
		Turner, Delacroix,
		Millet,
		Daumier
		
		Manet,
		Degas,
		Renoir,
		Monet, Rodin,
		Seurat, Cezanne, Van Gogh,
		Gauguin, Homer,
		Duchamp, F. L. Wright, Matisse,
		Kandinsky, Braque,
		Picasso, Klee,
		Rivera, Orozco, Rouault,
		Mondrian,
		Miró, Chagall
		
		Lipchitz, Moore

In any type of humanities program, five essentials may be identified:

1. A climate of questioning, creativity, emotional involvement, and individuality —all of which are stifled by examinations and grades.
2. Deemphasis on literary works.
3. Flexibility in methods and materials of instruction.
4. Recognition that affective learning is just as important as cognitive learning.
5. Team teaching to help alleviate the problem of broad teacher preparation and to make the most of several teachers' talents and background.[15]

The variety of activities and projects which may be useful in teaching the humanities is limited only by the imagination and ingenuity of teachers and students. It may include visiting museums, listening to concerts, attending a play, reading anything and everything that seems helpful, and talking. Lots of talking is needed, with teachers and students together, listening to each other, students saying what they are really thinking and feeling, not what they think the teachers want them to say. From this type of activity students will remember ". . . the exquisite moments of insight, the brilliance of beauty recognized and transforming, the heat of exposure of thoughts, at the same time personal and timeless."[16]

Language Arts

Perhaps the characteristic of man which most obviously sets him apart as something special in the world, the most easily recognizable evidence of his "humanity," is his ability to communicate through what we call language—"that intricate, delicately interwoven system of symbols, gestures, and sounds by which the mind of man reaches out to the minds and hearts of other men to communicate feelings, thoughts, desires, and dreams."[17] As it has shaped the past, so language will shape the future of mankind, because through its effects on human thought and behavior language largely determines the success of man's attempts to live with himself and his fellows.

That part of the secondary school curriculum which helps students understand and use the system of symbols, gestures, and sounds which man has developed to communicate by means of the spoken and written word, including gestures and facial expressions, is commonly termed language arts. It consists basically of a description and discussion of how and why we talk and write the way we do, but should also include and differentiate between the two major uses of language—referential (informing or stating facts), and emotive (moving or swaying the emotions).

Although evidence of change is not as pronounced in the language arts

[15]Sheila Schwartz, "Teaching the Humanities," *Clearing House* 43 (April 1969), pp. 508–510.
[16]A. H. Stern, "Humanities: From Aeschylus to Antonioni," *English Journal* 58 (May 1969), p. 677.
[17]Mary Elizabeth Fowler, *Teaching Language, Composition, and Literature* (New York: McGraw-Hill, 1965), p. 47.

programs of secondary schools as may be observed in mathematics, science, or even the social studies, there has been in recent years considerable concern and activity relative to the improvement of language instruction. The heart of the English curriculum is still too often found to be the reading of a few nineteenth-century classics and the study of a grammar inherited from the eighteenth century, but the space age is demanding change. No longer is the once typical program of "literature or book reports on Monday, spelling on Tuesday, vocabulary drill on Wednesday, composition on Thursday, and testing on Friday" acceptable in the language arts classroom. From many directions there come complaints which cannot be ignored:

> College teachers complain that students who enter can neither read efficiently nor comprehendingly, speak effectively, spell or punctuate correctly, write clear, coherent expository prose, or command a fair level of standard English. Many businesses and industries find their employees so lacking in verbal skill that they provide post-public school instruction for them. Surveys of the reading habits of our school and college graduates show appalling figures: not one in ten college graduates reads one book a month; few know how to use their leisure time in reading, viewing movies or television discriminatingly, or how to keep up to date on newspaper and magazine reading. Many homes contain no reading matter of any kind except the daily newspaper. About one-sixth of the child's waking hours from age three until nearly the end of high school are devoted to television, and the fare the networks claim the public demands has been called television's "wasteland." [18]

Objectives

The developing experimental and innovative programs in language arts are based on goals which may be stated rather simply:

1. Clear, thoughtful, and correct speech and writing.
2. Intelligent listening.
3. Critical thinking.
4. Development of a lifelong devotion to literature as a guide to cultural understanding and individual development.

A program based on these goals will raise questions, stimulate students to observe and generalize about their own experiences, and build concepts, instead of being confined to teaching rules and definitions. Grammar will be seen as an important element of language study, but it will be recognized as one part of it —a part which should be taught in direct relationship to effective speaking and writing. It will be understood that language study comes out of students' own speaking and writing, and that language power grows from students' own critical thinking.[19]

---

[18] *Ibid.*, p. 5.
[19] Edward J. Gordon and Edward S. Noyes (eds.), *Essays on the Teaching of English* (New York: Appleton, 1960), pp. 19–29.

Content

Defining the appropriate content for language arts education is certainly not simple. It seems many times that educators use this part of the school program to offer almost anything that doesn't fit well into some other part of the curriculum. This is probably due to the fact that language arts teachers too often have a very hazy idea about just what their efforts should be focused upon and thus fail to develop a unified and coordinated instructional program.

Language arts education, whether in English or in a foreign language, may be considered in the context of two broad and interrelated categories. Ultimate aims of the program are pursued through teaching activities related to what are commonly called "understandings" and "appreciations." The more scholarly among us like to use the terms "cognitive domain" and "affective domain" in referring to these content areas. In more traditional terms, they basically include speaking and listening (speech), reading (literature), and writing (composition).

The second main category of teaching activities may be seen as enabling skills which make possible the achievement of educational objectives in the cognitive and affective domains. They include the skills of talking, reading, grammar and usage, spelling, punctuation, and capitalization. A minimum amount of skill in each of these is required before significant progress can be made toward gaining appropriate understandings and appreciations.

It is fruitless to debate whether minimum mastery of the enabling skills must precede instruction directed toward the cognitive and affective domains. Pupil progress in both categories of language instruction must proceed simultaneously. Skill instruction is boring and irrelevant to students unless it is done in conjunction with activities in speech, literature, and composition. On the other hand, significant learning in the areas of speech, literature, and composition is impossible in the absence of basic language skills.

The concepts and skills of critical thinking should be intertwined throughout all phases of the language arts program. Perhaps this may be viewed as the all-encompassing goal of language arts instruction. Critical thinking cannot be taught apart from the other aspects of the program, but we should probably adopt the view that the other objectives (skills, understandings, and appreciations) have as their ultimate purpose the development of students and adults who can think and act critically and wisely as they go about their daily tasks.

LISTENING AND SPEAKING. The order of the words in this caption may seem to be the reverse of the usual procedure, and indeed listening has been relegated to a subordinate, and often ignored, position in language arts programs. In the sound-filled world in which we now live, however, it is being more widely recognized that we need a filter which will automatically exclude the sounds which are not significant and allow us to listen intelligently. We listen about three times as much as we read, five times as much as we write, and one and one-half times as much as we speak, according to recent studies.[20] Recognition of this fact would seem to justify some reallotment of time and effort in language arts instruction.

Hearing and listening are not the same. Conscious effort is required to listen, and it results in some kind of action. One may hear the sounds of nearby traffic —he listens for the sounds in his own car which may herald mechanical problems. A mother may hear the babble of many children's voices outside her window, but she listens to her own child's cries and takes appropriate action. One hears the endless stream of sound from his car radio as he travels, but he listens when the announcer mentions something of personal interest.

The overall language arts goal of critical thinking comes directly into focus when we think about helping students improve their listening skills, because the need to develop accurate and critical listening should receive prime attention. Students need to learn to evaluate the words and intentions of a speaker, for instance, and ask "Who said it?" "Why is the speaker saying it?" "What does he stand to gain by what he is saying?" "What is his authority for making such a statement?" "What does he really mean?" Discrimination and appreciation, as well as better retention of information, may be expected when critical listening is integrated into the language arts program as a crucial and basic skill leading toward increased understanding and appreciation.

Teachers often neglect listening in their instructional efforts, because they see it as a difficult and complex subject. On the contrary, listening involves fewer skills and is less complicated than speech. Speech instruction necessarily includes many content areas, such as content and organization, vocal quality, pitch, enunciation, pronunciation, and body control. Add to this the required basic skills of grammar and usage and you have a rather complex instructional task. We will not attempt to go into detail concerning these components of a listening and speaking instructional program, although grammar and usage will get some further attention in a later discussion of writing instruction. Suffice it to say at this point that instruction in listening and speech are successful when they develop critical listening and ease, fluency, clarity, and responsibility in speaking.

READING. By far the most important emphasis of elementary school education goes to the teaching of reading. We have seemed to assume that by the time a student reaches the secondary school level his reading skills are sufficiently developed and need no further attention. Reading instruction, if it occurs at all, is usually subordinated to more formal teaching of literature—the novel, the short story, poetry, or drama. Consequently, English teachers have been frustrated in their attempts to carry out established purposes, because most of their students do not read well.

Reading at the secondary school level no doubt should include more than instruction in reading skills, but the teaching of skills must go along with the

[20]J. N. Hook, *The Teaching of High School English*, 3d ed. (New York: Ronald, 1965), p. 402.

attempts to improve understandings and appreciations through the study of literature. In short, the total reading program of the language arts curriculum needs to be broad enough to produce students who exhibit the characteristics of mature readers:

1. A genuine enthusiasm for reading.
2. Tendency to read (a) a wide variety of materials, (b) serious materials on many problems, and (c) intensively in a particular field.
3. Ability to understand words, meanings, and ideas, and to sense mood and feeling intended.
4. Capacity for and making use of all that one knows or can find out in interpreting or construing the meaning of the ideas read.
5. Ability to think critically and analytically about what is read.
6. Tendency to fuse new ideas acquired through previous reading and to translate these into improved behavior.
7. Capacity to adjust one's reading pace to the needs of the occasion and to the demands of adequate interpretation.[21]

Reading skills are among the most complex and important of all learning tasks. The task of improving skill in reading is never completed, no matter how intelligent or educated a person may be. Since most educators acknowledge the importance of reading skill, it is difficult to understand why it has been largely neglected at the secondary school level. Certainly, few would claim that all secondary school students have mastered the skills of reading. In fact, most teachers would support the idea that lack of reading skill is the most common handicap to learning in most fields of instruction.

Skill in reading is much more than the mere recognition or pronouncing of words. Good reading involves apprehension of the meaning, emotion, and purpose of the writer, as related to what one already knows. Reading speed has attracted much attention in recent years, but this is not the sole criterion of excellence in reading; neither is comprehension. The able reader is best characterized as one who is quick to comprehend the purpose, meaning, emotion, and viewpoint of the writer.

There are a multitude of reading skills, and no two people have the same needs relative to their improvement. The use of phonics has inspired much discussion and many claims recently, but reading skill cannot be taught through attention to any one aspect of the problem—no matter how hallowed the practice or idea. Any number of statements are available concerning necessary reading skills. The following program guidelines developed in Pennsylvania seem to include most recommendations for reading skills emphasis:

1. Word Recognition Techniques
   (a) Meaning aids

---

[21]Summarized from William S. Gray and Bernice Rogers (eds.), *Maturity in Reading: Its Nature and Appraisal* (Chicago: U. of Chicago Press, 1956), pp. 54–55, in Mary Elizabeth Fowler, *Teaching Language, Composition, and Literature, op. cit.*, pp. 106–107.

   (b) Visual and structural aids
   (c) Auditory and phonetic aids
2. Comprehension Abilities: reading to
   (a) Retain information
   (b) Organize
   (c) Evaluate
   (d) Interpret
   (e) Appreciate
3. Basic Study Skills
   (a) Locating information
   (b) Use of general references
   (c) Use of visual materials
   (d) Organizing
4. Basic Meaning Development
   (a) Paragraph meaning and organization
   (b) Word meaning[22]

No two people will react in identical fashion to the same set of letters and words presented to them. Consequently, the array of reading difficulties found among our students is somewhat staggering. There are several types of problems which occur quite regularly, however, and they can provide a basis for programs to improve reading skills. A study involving college students and adults and asking them to rank their reading difficulties in order of importance resulted in the following listing, which is typical:

1. Word-by-word reading
2. Vocalizing
3. Backtracking
4. Daydreaming
5. Monotonous plodding (not changing speed)
6. Rereading
7. Word blocking (unfamiliar words)
8. Clue-blindness (ignoring headings, key phrases, etc.)
9. Finger following
10. Word analysis (giving a word more meaning than context necessitates)
11. Head swinging
12. Number attraction (being stopped by a number)[23]

Vocabulary development proceeds in combination with exposure of students to new experiences—in life and in reading. Traditional approaches to teaching vocabulary have tended to occur in a vacuum, because young people often had neither the experiences nor the interests which would facilitate their gaining an understanding of new words. Learning one word a day and using it in a composition, although methodical, is not likely to result in a marked increase in a student's usable vocabulary by the end of the term. It is not so important for a

[22]U. Berkley Ellis, "Developmental Reading in Junior High School," *Journal of Developmental Reading*, 6 (Autumn 1962), pp. 41–49.
[23]John W. Purcell, "Poor Reading Habits: Their Rank Order," *The Reading Teacher*, 16 (March 1963), p. 353.

person to know many words as to thoroughly understand various meanings of a smaller number of words.

Words by themselves are nothing. The word "atom" meant very little to most people before a bomb hit Hiroshima. It was only a word encountered in science class and probably promptly forgotten. Now the word "atom" suggests unbounded energy, destruction, submarines, travel, the hope, or the dread of mankind. In the same way, "subway" for the city dweller, or "silo" for one who lives on a farm are likely to have much more meaning than vice versa. To help students, especially slow students, extend their range of experiences and vocabulary, opportunity should be provided for them to make field trips and in other ways gain new bases for associating words with objects and ideas.

Dictionary skills compose another part of the prerequisite abilities required for successful reading and language study. Many students view the dictionary as a foe rather than a friend, because its use has been taught to them in a fashion similar to that employed for teaching the multiplication tables. It is viewed as an obstacle course—the source of homework assignments—rather than an aid to reading enjoyment.

The ability to find a word quickly is the most important dictionary skill. This necessitates a knowledge of the alphabet and practice in using the guide words. Following the development of minimum skill in locating words, students should learn to analyze dictionary entries and use the wealth of information they contain.

Library skills, in addition to use of the dictionary, form another important prerequisite to reading and literature study. Using tables of contents, indexes, headings, and other typographical cues aid reading. Students also need to learn about other library tools, such as the card catalogue and *Readers' Guide to Periodical Literature*, to facilitate locating information in the library. Other standard sources and research tools should be familiar to students, and they must have experience in making the best use of them.

Expository reading is the most common way in which adults make use of their reading skills. To better prepare them for adulthood, students need to spend more of their time in school learning how to make the best use of nonfiction writing. Learning to distinguish fact from opinion, to find an author's thesis statement and follow his line of argument, to recognize conventions of content and structure of newspapers, magazines, biographies, and other similar sources of information—these types of goals form the basis for teaching and learning in the use of expository reading materials.

Literature, or *imaginative writing*, makes up the major content for most language arts reading programs at the secondary school level. This may take the form of short stories, novels, poetry, or drama, but throughout the study of literature there are interwoven several common threads of purpose. To enjoy reading literature of all kinds and to value it for its humanizing and civilizing influence are among the most important attitudes to be developed in the young reader. He should be led to view literature as a source of information and advice available to those faced with the questions and problems common to man throughout history. The "best that has been thought and said" can thus become something that young people seek and use in their maturing efforts rather than an obstacle course to be completed as quickly and painlessly as possible.

For the average student, the *short story* is probably the literary form best adapted to opening the doors of imaginary writing. The short story compresses a personal crisis and resultant action within a few pages, bringing illumination of great intensity upon the hero's dilemma. Inner conflict and the problems presented by alternative courses of action can be very relevant to the everyday lives of young people. When he knows the problems that agitate the minds of his students, a good teacher can use the short story to dramatize similar dilemmas. Searching questions which are important to developing adolescents provide the foci of attention: "What does this story mean in my life? How does it help me to become a more mature, responsible person? What dangers does it reveal that I also may have to face? What handicap is there in my personality that I can overcome as the hero did? Are there people around me that this story can help me to understand?"[24]

The *novel* also provides an avenue to better understanding of the ideals, emotions, and dilemmas that are common to all men. Sensitivity to beauty and to human feelings, recognition of ethical values, and familiarization with some of the major themes in life and literature can result from the reading and analysis of novels. By analysis we do not mean, however, the typical type of practice which requires that students read two or three chapters a day and retell them in class, emphasizing fact, incidents, and plot. The plot must be seen as only a skeleton around which the living parts of the story are built.

> What does it profit a student to recite all the tags of incentive moment, climax, plot of a novel, not to have seen or felt its inner life? Concentration on the characteristics of the type may result in generalities and pat definitions, in an identification of externals, distracting the student from the experience the novel should bring.[25]

Reading a novel loses most of its attraction and potential for student growth when it is treated as a sum of parts. A novel is an idea presented in action and should relate to a student's problems in his home, school, and community. It may also help him to gain a better understanding of social conditions. Instead, teaching a novel is all to often "something like turning a felled tree into cordwood." First the teacher saws it up into lengths of convenient size for consumption—

[24]Don M. Wolfe, *Creative Ways to Teach English, Grades 7 to 12*, 2d ed. (New York: Odyssey Press, 1966), pp. 283–284.
[25]Edward J. Gordon and Edward S. Noyes (eds.), *Essays on the Teaching of English* (New York: Appleton, 1960), p. 235.

these are doled out as assignments. Each day's supply is then hauled into the classroom and painstakingly scrutinized for knots and other irregularities—hard words, figures of speech, allusions classical and Biblical, freaks of syntax or of rhetoric. Some heat and light may be generated, but by day's end the allotment is reduced to a fine, powdery ash, uniformly dry in texture and gray in color. This type of study results in students' getting the impression that a novel exists to provide a forbidding collection of linguistic oddities which are categorized and labeled, with little or no notion of what function these oddities perform or what place they have in the novel. They may know the difference between a metaphor and a simile, that it is a matter of grave importance, and that lack of such knowledge will end in disgrace on a test. That a metaphor or simile might have some relation to the meaning of the book may never enter their heads.[26]

Students' natural curiosity about themselves and the world around them can also be satisfied through *poetry*, although few students in the typical classroom view it in this fashion. Poetry is simply "language functioning at its highest efficiency." It is an extension of the speech students use, listen to, and read every day. Through intensification of normal language, poetry can more quickly, more exactly, and more profoundly explore the emotional and aesthetic concerns of man.

Poetry is a collection of snapshots of our existence—snapshots which tell us something about ourselves. They remind us of things we may have carelessly passed by or lost through a failure of memory or lack of proper appreciation at the moment. Poetry may tell us of somewhere that we would like to go, or not like to go; or something we would like to see. It is largely subjective and personal, perhaps with rather different meaning and significance for different people, due to their natural individual differences.

To get the most from poetry, students need at least a minimum understanding of the resources by which the poet intensifies language. These may be summarized in two categories—imagery and word music. Within each category are a number of devices which form the basis for more technical study of poetry.

Imagery:	Word Music:
1. Images of color	8. Rhythm
2. Images of sound	9. Rhyme
3. Images of touch	10. Meter
4. Images of smell	11. Alliteration
5. Images of action	12. Assonance
6. Similes	13. Mingling of vowels[27]
7. Metaphors	

Although it is an art form to be seen and heard rather than just read, *drama* should also be included in the imaginative literature program. Modern drama,

[26]Paul Pickrel, "Teaching the Novel: *Great Expectations*," Gordon and Noyes, *ibid.*, pp. 216–217.

[27]Wolfe, *op. cit.*, pp. 262–263.

especially, offers the teacher and student opportunities for studying human nature which are just as promising as other literary forms and generally less taxing. Plays are built on action and excitement. They can be read rapidly and the vocabulary is usually less demanding. Contact with films and television makes it easier for today's student to translate plays into reality than may perhaps be the case for other types of reading.

Drama exists in a wide variety, from realism to fantasy to romance to genre, yet most plays share common qualities: dialogue, entrances and exits, curtains, stage directions, and conflict. In reading and studying drama, there are many possibilities in the way of emphasis. The opening of the play, character studies, study of action, atmosphere and form, and the dramatist's language may be used to provide some organization and form for the study of drama. Regardless of the particular approach, care must be exercised to avoid the ever-lurking literary temptation to disect and digest rather than assimilate and understand. As with the novel, a drama is more than a sum of its parts.

WRITING. The teaching of writing, usually denoted by the more academic term "composition," is almost universally recognized as one of the most important and most difficult assignments given to teachers. Educators, businessmen, administrators, members of various professions, and most others one might wish to question are largely agreed that improvement in written composition should be placed first when thinking about language teaching today. The spoken word receives much attention in our world, but in the conduct of education, business, and other affairs the written word is of crucial importance.

Practice in speaking and listening begins early in life, but development of writing skills is the last to be attempted and is often neglected even then. This tradition of neglect has been challenged, however, by several recent statements, recommendations, and curriculum improvement projects.

Recommendations by James B. Conant have probably had more influence than any other during the last decade. He has suggested that the time devoted to English composition during the four years of high school "should occupy about half the total time devoted to the study of English.[28] The Commission on English of the College Entrance Examination Board has stated that writing should take one-third of the school week in class and outside.[29] Most teachers of English and foreign language generally agree with this emphasis on writing in the language arts curriculum, although they may not be able to carry it out completely.

Many of those who advocate more attention to teaching composition are primarily concerned with the more practical and utilitarian demands of daily private and professional life. The needs for competence in writing of this type must not be neglected, but there are other reasons, perhaps more important, for

[28]James B. Conant, *The American High School Today* (New York: McGraw-Hill, 1959), p. 50.
[29]Floyd Rinker, "Priorities in the English Curriculum," *English Journal*, 51 (May 1962), p. 312.

helping students learn to write well. Current statements of educational goals stress the need for teaching students to think, to understand themselves, and to understand the world around them. Writing offers an excellent means—perhaps the best means—for developing these types of competencies and understandings. "No one knows who he is until he has tried to put himself on paper. And no one knows what his world is until he has tried to describe it."[30] For this reason, we must get our young people to write and keep them writing.

General goals for instruction in writing have been stated in various forms, but it can be safely said that organization, accuracy, clarity, and economy are probably the virtues most in demand. Most teachers would also wish to encourage students to write honestly and responsibly, using language with care, integrity, and sensitivity.[31]

There are at least three basic types of writing, although they are often taught in combination, and probably rightly so. *Utilitarian* writing includes composition related to business and professional letters, letters of complaint, congratulations, request, introduction, and acknowledgment. Skill in writing telegrams, announcements, bulletins, advertisements, minutes, and reports also falls into this category along with other similar business and personal writing activities. *Expository* writing usually gets the most attention in our schools. Here the emphasis is on helping students gain skill in saying exactly what they mean—to inform, interpret, argue, convince, or express an opinion concerning a literary work or an idea. *Imaginative* writing, often called creative writing, is the mode of composition in which the student, aided by his imagination, takes his personal thoughts, feelings, and experiences and expresses them through either prose or poetry. In more formal terms, imaginative writing may be defined as "an act of composition in which the student creates a controlled dramatic voice and an imagined world, without sacrificing the sense of logic and reality. The creation of this world is a process of making concrete the personal experience of the student in the literary form—prose or verse."[32]

Throughout the program for teaching composition, the importance of clear and ordered thinking (logic) should be emphasized. Errors in the mechanics of writing, although not to be ignored, are less important than errors in thinking which permit ambiguity, jargon, or cliché to come between the reader and the idea seeking expression.

The basic skills required for composition, whether in English or in a foreign language, cannot be ignored, although we would like to relegate this phase of the program to the subordinate position it deserves. Skill development should be functional and concerned more with effectiveness of use than "correctness."

[30]Richard B. Sewall, "The Content of Student Writing," in Gordon and Noyes, *op. cit.*, p. 74.

[31]Fowler, *op. cit.*, p. 133.

[32]Gordon and Noyes, *op. cit.*, p. 80.

Appropriate skills should be taught in connection with writing as a direct need for them is evident.

Handwriting, although too often ignored in secondary school instructional programs, is one of the most basic skills required of a writer and deserves more attention than is given to it by most secondary school teachers and students. Simply leading students to see that handwriting reflects the person and that legible handwriting is a matter of courtesy to the reader will encourage students to evaluate their handwriting and perhaps seek to improve it. Poor handwriting seems to have become a source of pride among some individuals, when common sense and practical necessities should produce the opposite attitude.

Spelling presents its own unique problems for language arts teachers. English is notorious for its spelling inconsistencies, and most foreign languages present similar problems. It has been stated that if English were spelled as it is pronounced children could become completely literate in a year or less of schooling.[33] Whether this is completely true or not, it is obvious that any reduction in the vagaries of spelling would accelerate learning. The following poem illustrates the problem well.

English

I take it you already know
Of tough and bough and cough and dough?
Others may stumble, but not you
On hiccough, thorough, slough and through?
Well done! And now you wish, perhaps
To learn of less familiar traps?

Beware of heard, a dreadful word
That looks like beard and sounds like bird.
And dead; it's said like bed, not bead;
For goodness sake, don't call it deed!
Watch out for meat and great and threat,
(They rhyme with suite and straight and debt)
A moth is not a moth in mother.
Nor both in bother, broth in brother.
And here is not a match for there,
And dear and fear for bear and pear,
And then there's dose and rose and lose—
Just look them up—and goose and choose,
And cork and work and card and ward,
And font and front and word and sword.
And do and go, then thwart and cart.
Come, come, I've hardly made a start.

A dreadful language? Why, man alive,
I'd learned to talk it when I was five,

---

[33]N. A. McQuown, "Language-Learning from an Anthropological Point of View," *The Elementary School Journal*, 54 (March 1954), pp. 402–408.

And yet to write it, the more I tried,
I hadn't learned it at fifty-five.[34]

Although few would deny its advantage, it doesn't seem likely that spelling according to the way words sound will become common practice. Even if all should agree to attempt this it could not be fully accomplished, because language is the sum of its many dialects and agreement as to whose dialect should be followed would be difficult, if not impossible, to attain. In addition, languages change with the passage of time, and spelling reform would be obsolete even before it could be universally adopted.

The language teacher must face up to the task of teaching spelling, even though it may seem abnormally frustrating, because poor spelling is recognized quicker and more universally denounced by the average citizen than most other language errors. By any means he can devise, the teacher of language must include instruction designed to:

1. Develop sensitivity to the fact that misspellings look illiterate and create very bad impressions.
2. Encourage students with the idea that spelling facility can be learned through patient study and practice.
3. Develop facility and the habit of using the dictionary to improve spelling.
4. Help students recognize the words which give the most difficulty for the general population and for themselves personally.
5. Learn and use the few spelling rules worth knowing on the basis of their few exceptions.
6. Create the realization that one remembers difficult spellings less by rule than by one's own tricks or devices for associating (e.g., "the principal is your pal," or "a second helping of 's' for dessert").
7. Encourage drill in spelling "demons" and words which give individuals difficulty so that students will master the spelling of words most frequently used in their writing.

Punctuation and capitalization, which are too often overemphasized by language teachers, deserve enough attention to assure that students learn to accept and prefer the conventions of punctuation and capitalization while remaining willing to accommodate conventions to the special demands of what is being said. They should be able to use conventions of punctuating and capitalizing, using handbooks and dictionaries when in doubt about the proper usage.

Grammar and usage are sometimes used rather synonymously in discussing that part of the language program which attempts to teach the conventions of the language. Both terms are subject to loose and varied interpretation, causing much confusion among language teachers. The two concepts can be of much more value if they are better understood as separate but complementing

[34]Author unknown. Reprinted from Harold G. Shane, *Linguistics and the Classroom Teacher* (Washington, D.C.: Association for Supervision and Curriculum Development, 1967), p. 50.

aspects of our attempts to understand and teach language.

Simply stated, grammar is "the study of the way the language works."[35] Any number of other definitions are available, most of them too complex for general use. It may be stated that grammar is "a description of how we talk and write," that it has to do "with word forms and the organization of those words in sentences," or that it "describes how words are used together to convey meaning."[36] All of these definitions share some commonalities, and it must be left to the individual to devise a definition that will best allow him to fulfill the purpose of helping students learn to write effectively. A final suggested definition may be helpful. Laird proposes that grammar "comprises whatever the users of a language do with symbols of meaning (in English, words) in order to express extensive and complicated meanings."[37]

Too much emphasis is placed on grammar by most language teachers, perhaps because it can be rather easily tested. It is often stated that before a student can learn to write he must learn correct grammar. Research to the contrary has been accumulating for more than twenty-five years. A committee studying research on the teaching of composition recently evaluated 485 studies, with this conclusion:

> In view of the widespread agreement of research studies based upon many types of students and teachers, the conclusion can be stated in strong and unqualified terms: the teaching of formal grammar has a negligible, or, because it usually displaces some instruction and practice in actual composition, even a harmful effect on the improvement of writing.[38]

This is not to say that grammar is an insignificant part of language instruction. It simply means that the grammar which can profitably be taught is that which has direct use in speaking and writing. The study of formal grammar should come along in due course as students write, but as auxiliary to the creative process, rather than vice versa. It is an old but invalid assumption that grammar has to do with absolutes of right and wrong, with a monotonous chanting of identifications of parts of speech wholly unrelated to the real problems of oral or written expression, that grammar can be of use to students through dogmatic pronouncements of "correct" and "incorrect" in regard to the use or identification of sentence elements.

A better approach utilizes the concept of *conventions*, rather than *rules*, of grammar. Language does not operate according to fixed, unchanging, and immutable rules, like the rules or laws of mathematics, so the proper approach for today's student of composition will concentrate on the operations of the language, with the realization that language is not a static form controlled by

---

[35]Fowler, *op. cit.*, p. 165.
[36]Gordon and Noyes, *op. cit.*, p. 23.
[37]Charlton Laird, *The Miracle of Language* (New York: Fawcett, 1953), p. 130.
[38]Richard Braddock and others, *Research in Written Composition* (Champaign, Ill.: National Council of Teachers of English, 1963), p. 37.

exercises, but a flexible arrangement of words and structures, usually in constant flow and fluctuation in the utterances of a single person as well as in utterances throughout the history of the language. The conventions of language mechanics exist solely to facilitate communication, and not the other way around.

Usage may perhaps be best studied as a subdivision of grammar, although many authorities prefer to treat it separately. When speaking of usage, the major concern is usually with "the choices speakers make in the forms and meanings of words and the appropriateness of these choices to the situations in which they are used."[39] Whether a speaker chooses to say "I fetched the paper" or "I brought the paper" depends upon his usage preference, as does the choice of the standard word "children" or the colloquial "kids."

When English teachers talk about using "good English" they are usually referring to usage. This "good" English is usually defined rather narrowly. It is suggested, for instance, that good English is "the kind of English that is used by the most respected people, the sort of English that will make readers or listeners regard you as an educated person."[40] Broader concepts are gaining acceptance, and modern usage encourages informality wherever possible, reserving formality for very few occasions.

In the teaching of usage, there is particular cause for rejection of the doctrine of rightness and wrongness, of the correct and the incorrect. As stated by The National Council of Teachers of English, correct usage is "that form of speech which is appropriate to the purposes of the speaker and listener. Bad English is that use of language which is unclear, ineffective, and inappropriate to the language occasion." Simply stated, "Language is the garment or vehicle for thought."[41]

Robert C. Pooley suggests five levels of usage: (1) illiterate—outside the pale of cultured society, not for the classroom; (2) homely—not illiterate and not acceptable; to be modified for the classroom; (3) standard English on the informal level—the usage of cultured, educated people; for the classroom and all ordinary occasions; (4) standard English on the formal level—the goal of expression showing care and restraint; also for the classroom and more formal occasions; (5) literary—usage revealing beauty and grace.[42] In order to judiciously choose the proper usage for a particular occasion and situation, students must learn something about each type and how it can best be utilized.

HISTORY OF LANGUAGES. Although not a normal part of many language arts programs, some knowledge of the history of the English language and of other languages is valuable, not for its own sake, but as illumination, often by contrast,

---

[39]Fowler, *op. cit.*, p. 165.

[40]Bergen Evans and Cornelia L. Evans, *Dictionary of Contemporary American Usage* (New York: Random House, 1957), p. v.

[41]Gordon and Noyes, *op. cit.*, p. 22.

[42]Robert C. Pooley, *Teaching English Usage*, National Council of Teachers of English Publication (New York: Appleton, Inc., 1946).

of present practices. Because of their natural curiosity students are usually interested in knowing where language comes from, and studying this facet of a language will help them better understand who and what we are. Learning about the origins of languages will also facilitate better understanding of other cultures and peoples.

SEMANTICS. Language teachers who stress the importance of critical reading and listening and clear, thoughtful speaking and writing are dealing with semantics, although neither they nor their students may realize it. Because words are symbols that label ideas and objects inexactly, there is a need for helping students understand, through the study of semantics, the transformation and evolution of language and how language can become a more effective tool of communication. It may be that the teacher of semantics has the best opportunity to get away from the normal subject-centered, isolated approach to teaching which this book is designed to alleviate. The teacher of semantics, in fact, may find that he has become the teacher of everything, as he helps students explore the development and meaning of words.

Structure

The combination of concepts and generalizations which comprises the structure of the language arts disciplines has not been as well defined by scholars in the field as is the case with some other disciplines. It may be that the language arts do not lend themselves to this approach as well. It is certainly true that the language arts present a most complex and complicated collection of learning objectives which are in many cases difficult to relate to each other. On the other hand, speaking and listening, reading, writing, language history, and semantics include a multitude of common objectives, concepts, and related generalizations which offer every opportunity for effective teaching and learning.

LISTENING AND SPEAKING. Many of the concepts and generalizations included in the area of listening and speaking are also appropriate to other parts of the language arts curriculum, especially writing, although major emphasis will usually lie in either one or the other. A sampling of concepts appropriate for use in teaching listening and speaking skills might include the following:

ambiguity	content
analogy	contrast
articulation	deductive
body control	dialect
clarity	diction
cliché	discrimination
communication	emotive
comparison	enunciation
fact	organization

figurative language	passive voice
fluency	pattern
formal English	pitch
gesture	point of view
inductive	premise
inference	pronunciation
informal English	self-expression
intonation	shop-talk
jargon	slang
localism	stilted
logic	style
nasality	tone
opinion (judgment)	transition

Concepts such as the above are combined into generalizations. The following are indicative of the type of generalizations which may be utilized in teaching listening and speaking.

1. Language is a means of revealing an individual's values.
2. Tone and approach in language vary with the person to whom one is communicating.
3. Spoken and written language differ in certain ways.
4. Even between two individuals in the same family language varies.
5. Language changes to accommodate a change in society.
6. Professions, trades, and occupations have individual languages.
7. Dialects are prevalent.
8. Cultural referents enrich language.
9. Mass media of language impose certain forms.
10. The sound of language affects the meaning.
11. There are many nonverbal or nonlinguistic "languages."
12. Verbal symbols (words) stand for things and ideas.
13. Language is a system of agreements about meanings.
14. One word may stand for many things or meanings.
15. Meanings develop through experience; individuals may have different meanings for the same words.
16. Generalizations lead to uncritical thinking.
17. Each language has its own peculiar structure.
18. Speech is primary. Writing symbolizes speech/thought.
19. Language has differing social functions.
20. Words convey meaning at various levels of literalness and abstraction.[43]

Some generalizations are especially appropriate for speech activities.

1. One should employ a reflective and analytical technique rather than the argumentative technique in approaching controversial problems.
2. Key words and phrases used in discussion often require definition.
3. General or abstract concepts need reinforcement with appropriate details.

[43]Fowler, *op. cit.*, pp. 64, 66–67, 403.

4. The truth of a solution depends upon the degree to which it corresponds with the basic assumptions.[44]

READING. Reading, or the study of various kinds of writing (literature), has the potential for unlimited benefit to individual students and our society, but this potential seems seldom to be approached in the classroom, probably because most language arts teachers overemphasize the external trivialities of form—type of literary work, plot, climax, meter, and the like. More attention to the structural elements (concepts and generalizations) of literary works will allow teachers and students to gain much more meaningful and useful benefit from reading.

Concepts and generalizations encountered in reading can be almost limitless, because the subject matter of literature is bounded only by the concerns of man. To try to list the concepts and generalizations appropriate to the study of literature is therefore an impossible task. We will attempt only a very brief example of the type of concepts and generalizations that might be included in the classroom where the writings of man form the subject material. Some of the concepts suggested might be useful in studying any literary work—others are probably appropriate only to a particular piece of writing.

Concepts:

authoritarian	loyalty
character	lyric
comedy	mood
connotation	novel
context	patriotism
democracy	plot
denotation	prejudice
dignity	Puritanism
directive	reality
drama	referent
epic	satire
essay	setting
heroism	shame
illusion	sorrow
irony	style
joy	theme
literal	tragedy
literary criticism	truth
literary structure	values
love	wisdom

[44]Adapted from J. N. Hook, *The Teaching of High School English*, 3d ed. (New York: Ronald, 1965), p. 431.

Generalizations:

1. Literature reflects universal elements in human experience.
2. Literature reflects the culture.
3. Literary works may be classified as type-form.
4. A literary work has structure.
5. Literature affects the culture.
6. The relationship of the reader to the literary work is individual and personal.[45]
7. Universal concerns are modified by the American culture pattern from Puritan times to the present.
8. Americans have tended to exhibit a desire to get ahead.
9. All literature can be understood primarily in terms of character, plot, setting, or theme.
10. In a story such as "Old Milon," character is the dominant aspect.[46]

WRITING. The structural elements related to writing are also largely included in speaking, listening, or reading. Writing comes basically from speaking, and consequently many concepts and generalizations related to one are also important to the other. *Concepts* important to teaching composition include:

abstract	literal
active voice	logical comparison
chronological	media
contrast	metaphor
deduction	parallelism
emotive	proof
formal English	rhetoric
grammar	spatial
grammatical construction	stilted
induction	style
inference	subject
jargon	subordination
judgment	transition
language	usage
language structure	usage types
lexical	word order

Generalizations related to composition are usually concerned with the writer's ultimate purpose of self-expression. In writing, one is attempting to communicate thought and feeling which are the result of his experience. Although there is no substitute for practice in writing, several types of generalizations, if understood and practiced, will help improve a person's writing. The following are indicative of the types of generalizations which are helpful to the teacher and student of composition.

---

[45]Fowler, *op. cit.*, p. 403.

[46]Beekman W. Cottrell and Erwin R. Steinberg, *Teacher's Guide Including Inductive Lessons for Insight: The Experience of Literature* (New York: Noble and Noble, 1968), pp. 13–27.

1. Composing requires something to say.
2. Composing involves purpose.
3. Composing involves arranging selected material into a recognizable order.
4. Composing is usually done within recognizable patterns (types).
5. Composing involves the development of an individual style.
6. A combination of grammatical, lexical, and metaphoric meaning results in colorful language.
7. Effective language is composed of skills gained from wide reading, thoughtful listening, and experimental writing.[47]
8. There is a difference between a topic and a subject in composition. A subject necessitates a selection of facts, an interpretation of them, a validated conclusion drawn from them—in short, a subject demands proof.
9. Methods of organizing a composition include chronological, spatial, inductive, deductive, easy to difficult, least to greatest, and reasoning from cause to effect or effect to cause.
10. Development of a composition may be done by:
    (a) Supplying details.
    (b) Using examples.
    (c) Using comparison or contrast.
    (d) Expanding a definition.
    (e) Presenting causes or effects.
    (f) Offering logical proof.[48]
11. Jargon and cliche can be better avoided through use of the active voice.
12. Ambiguity is one of the most common faults of most writers, causing confusion to both the writer and the reader.[49]

LANGUAGE HISTORY. The typical English teacher has tended to decry change in written and spoken aspects of the language. The use of slang, for instance, has been rejected as uneducated and improper, even though it has added color and meaning to the language and is widely used. More progressive language teachers recognize the fact that change in language is inevitable and attempt to make the most of this in their teaching. Showing how language changes and teaching the historical aspects of a language provide motivation, as students see why a given practice is followed, whether in English or a foreign language.

> . . . a study of the history of the language helps to reveal pertinent characteristics of today's English. For example, knowledge of the medieval shift away from numerous inflections tends to clarify why word order is now so important. The growth of complex sentences, replacing many simple and compound structures, has led to the possibility of more precise expression today. The addition of progressive verb forms has lent further enrichment. Most dramatic of all, at least from students' point of view, is the steady growth of vocabulary through the centuries, with borrowings from every continent and almost every nation.[50]

[47]Fowler, *op. cit.*, pp. 64, 403.
[48]Hook. *op. cit.*, pp. 230, 238, 240.
[49]Gordon and Noyes, *op. cit.*, pp. 26, 143.
[50]Hook, *op. cit.*, pp. 10–11.

The English language has been one of the greatest word borrowers in history. About one-half of the words in the English language have been borrowed from Latin and its Romance descendants. During the Renaissance period, alone, words were adopted into English from more than fifty languages.[51] Early settlers in America took over the words they needed from the tongues with which they came in contact. From various Indian tribes came words like *potato, tomato, chocolate, cocoa, canoe, maize, savannah, moose, skunk, terrapin, hickory, pecan, hominy, moccasin, totem, toboggan,* and *mackinaw.* Slaves brought to America from Africa contributed numerous words, including *banjo, goober, yam, chigger, hoodoo, zombie,* and *juke.* Emigrants from various parts of the world, particularly German, French, and Spanish, made their contributions: *sleigh, sauerkraut, kindergarten, Santa Claus, waffle* (German and Dutch); *prairie, chowder, levee, gopher* (French, from American Indian); *mosquito, armada, alligator* (Spanish). Examples such as these can serve to whet the appetite of students and build in them a desire to know more about their language and its use.[52]

Study of the historical development of meaning in language may include the *concepts* of extension (meaning of the word has widened), restriction (narrowing of meaning), pejoration (degeneration), amelioration (elevation, folk etymology, and euphemism by phonetic distortion). Other concepts which may be made a part of language history include: loan words, etymological fallacy, slang, compounding, functional shift, back formation, acronym, onomatopoeia, telescoping, metathesis, generalization, and specialization.

These kinds of concepts may be included in *generalizations* which will help students better understand the language and how it may be used. The following are suggested as being indicative of generalizations which may include various concepts and subgeneralizations:

1. Modern languages are the result of development throughout history.
2. Words get their meanings from various sources.
3. Social, political, and economic events influence language.
4. Languages grow through the addition of loan words and various other vocabulary changes.
5. Words do not necessarily have to continue to mean what they originally meant.
6. Special fields of study develop their own vocabulary.
7. Many new words are coined by adding traditional suffixes and prefixes.
8. Only dead languages cease to change.

SEMANTICS. Semantics, the "science of meaning," lies at the heart of the language arts program. Every good language teacher recognizes the need for teaching not only dictionary meanings but also the emotional implications or

---

[51] Wallace L. Anderson and Norman C. Srageberg (eds.), *Introductory Readings on Language* (New York: Holt, Rinehart and Winston, Inc., 1962), p. 93.
[52] *Ibid.,* Thomas Pyles, "Early American Speech: Adoptions from Foreign Tongues," pp. 93–111.

words and the fact that speakers and writers can influence people not merely by what they say but also by how they say it.

Language is a symbolic process, in that verbal signs are used to represent things in the world of experience. However, these symbols are inexact and may have various meanings or shades of meaning among people of different background or persuasion. When agreement is not reached concerning the meaning of a word, communication becomes difficult if not impossible. For example, the word "democracy," would have widely varying meaning to a Russian, a German, a citizen of ancient Athens, or an American (even various Americans would differ in their interpretation).

As with other aspects of language instruction, the concepts and generalizations which may be included are almost boundless, depending upon the particular objectives at hand. A sampling of each is suggested to illustrate the structural elements of semantics.

Concepts:

Abstraction	euphemism
ambiguity	fact
analogy	generalization
bandwagon	glittering generality
bias word	judgment
circumlocution	loaded words
classification	metaphor
connotation	name calling
context	referent
culture	slanting
denotation	stereotype
directive statement	transfer
either-or dilemma	word magic

Generalizations:

1. There are two broad functions of language: its referential function and its emotive function.
2. Language is a system of symbols and the symbol merely stands for the thing it symbolizes.
3. The meanings for the words he uses are the product of the experiences a person has associated with that word.
4. Words are learned in close association with experiences of love, hate, fear, anger, or security.
5. Since no two people have identical experiences, the language of each individual is unique.
6. Because the meanings for the words we know come from our own experiences, they carry with them many emotional colorings.

7. We have a very limited number of words to stand for an unlimited number of things.
8. Our stock of words is inadequate to represent the complexity of the physical world we perceive through our senses and the myriad feelings, dreams and ideas of which man is capable.
9. A single word often serves to communicate myriad meanings.
10. Although words do not change much, their meanings are constantly changing and extending, as are the things the words stand for.
11. The use of metaphor vastly extends the power and usefulness of language.
12. A primary source of meaning of the words we use in discourse is that of context.
13. Denotative meanings are referential.
14. Connotative meanings are deeply personal and usually emotive.
15. We tend to classify for a single purpose, although a single entity may be classified in several different ways.
16. Most generalizations are false.
17. Invalid generalizations often lead to stereotyped thinking.
18. Wrong inferences result from drawing too hasty or illogical conclusions from incomplete facts.
19. Abstracting is inevitable.
20. Words are often reacted to as magical symbols which might control us or events.[53]

Method of Inquiry

Although they include many skills and content areas, the language arts have as their overall approach to inquiry that process identified as philosophical analysis. Bertrand Russell, along with other philosophers and linguists, has been particularly instrumental in promoting this approach to inquiry in the language arts during modern times.

As language arts scholars seek truth and reality in the world as we know it, they use their own particular tools. The primary tool of the linguist is language (words), but he also employs others as needed.

> The analyst avoids any prescription of method or any comprehensive description of reality. He rather limits himself to the careful investigation of some of the many different ways in which people talk about experience. His attitude is open and tentative. He does not attempt to find any single key to the interpretation of the world, but patiently proceeds to make distinctions and to show relationships among the vast array of possible modes of interpretation.
>
> [The language analyst] warns teachers and students against the temptation to oversimplify language study by a tidy set of labels and a few facile generalizations. In urging the student of language to attend very carefully to the ways speech

[53]Adapted from Royal J. Morsey, *Improving English Instruction* (Boston: Allyn and Bacon, 1965), Wolfe, *op. cit.*, Fowler, *op. cit.*, Hook, *op. cit.*, and other sources.

is actually used, in all its variety and subtlety, he helps him to understand the depth, range and power of human symbolization.[54]

In the study of language (especially grammar and usage), the new forms going under the title of "structural linguistics" are consistent with the concept of philosophical analysis. In this approach to the study of language, four basic assumptions are central:

1. Language is a form or type or aspect of human behavior.
2. Language as a form of human behavior may be studied objectively.
3. From an objective examination of the language it is possible to derive a comprehensive description of that language and moreover a description that will be orderly.
4. Each language has its own unique system or structure, the totality of such structural features being the grammar of the language.[55]

Teaching the Language Arts

Operating on the premise that process is part of the content of teaching and learning, we will briefly explore some of the more current concepts related to the organization and methodology of language arts instruction. Since the purpose of this text is not directly related to teaching methodology, the discussion will only include some examples of trends which seem appropriate to our thesis.

Most language authorities today agree that the language arts program in schools should emphasize the interrelationships of the various language skills, understandings, and appreciations. The frequent separation of the language curriculum into literature, composition, grammar, and speech implies a division of the language process that does not exist in life. The extensive use of handbooks, workbooks, single literature anthologies, vocabulary and spelling lists, standardized tests, and programmed instruction tend to inhibit desirable coordination and stress knowledge *about* language rather than *performance* in reading, writing, speaking, and listening. An integrated program, utilizing the concepts of disciplinary structure, seems more in keeping with current thinking about modern needs relative to language instruction.

> Whether the language we use is heard, spoken, read, written, or studied, the intricate, flexible, and plastic material with which we work is the same: a system of symbols made up of sounds, signal systems, and large and small units of written and spoken words. The modern English program is designed to help the student understand the structure and meaning of the language he speaks, to bring to awareness the unconscious processes he has been using since infancy, and to assist him in using language maturely, responsibly, and effectively.[56]

[54]Philip H. Phenix, "Curriculum and the Analysis of Language," in James B. Macdonald and Robert R. Leeper (eds.), *Language and Meaning* (Washington, D.C.: Association for Supervision and Curriculum Development, 1966), pp. 28, 34.

[55]J. J. Lamberts, "Basic Concepts for Teaching From Structural Linguistics," in Graham Wilson (ed.), *A Linguistic Reader* (New York: Harper, 1967), pp. 3–8.

[56]Fowler, *op. cit.*, p. 48.

Philosophical analysis, the method of inquiry we have suggested as being inherent in language arts study, directly demonstrates how language instruction may be carried out. Analysis is actually an example of education in linguistic usage. Two features of teaching through analysis are especially noteworthy. (1) Through the use of concrete examples, the analyst makes his point by citing cases. By citing characteristic illustrations, he shows what he means and tests the limitations of his generalizations through examples where the generalizations no longer hold true. By using typical cases, the analyst teaches that expressions should be considered in terms of the roles they perform in actual communication rather than in terms of some static rules of grammar or dictionary meaning. (2) The analogy of language with games, as first explained by Ludwig Wittgenstein, (1889–1957), gives additional insight into language and its use. Various kinds of expressions play roles in language similar to the roles associated with the various pieces in a game like chess. Each piece is capable of certain characteristic moves, as defined by the rules of the game. In similar fashion, appropriate uses of various linguistic expressions are governed by the conventions of the language "game."[57]

It has been suggested that language, whether English or foreign, can be more effectively taught if the teacher understands and applies learnings about language as a *process*, a *product*, and an *art*. Teaching language as a process requires an understanding of its use as a symbolic system and the development of the learner in its use. To understand the product requires a knowledge of the spoken and written language, its history, its structural patterns, and the ways that words acquire meanings. To know something about language as an art calls for an understanding of the subtle relationships between words, their meanings, and what verbal symbols tell us about man's thoughts, feelings, and dreams.[58]

One of the most complete programs to be developed thus far as a result of current thinking by language arts educators came through a Project English Curriculum Study Center at Carnegie-Mellon University. The approach developed at this Study Center has helped to define the "New English" movement and stresses the following features:

1. Use of an inductive approach. Instead of telling the student about literature, the teacher guides him through the study of a literary work and leads him to make his own discoveries.
2. A sequential, cumulative approach. Each book is . . . used as part of a sequence, as the program builds unit by unit, grade by grade. Yet the program has been designed with maximum flexibility so that any book may be used without necessary reference to the others.
3. Inclusion of many important long works (as well as many shorter works). Most of the long works are unabridged.
4. Direct confrontation with the literary work. No editorial matter prejudices the work for the student or distracts him from the work itself. Headnotes and footnotes are supplied only when they are essential to understanding.

[57]Phenix, *op. cit.*, p. 34.
[58]Fowler, *op. cit.*, p. 48.

5. All space in the textbooks devoted to literature. In this series all study material is reserved for the Teacher's Guide.

The core of the program is literature, defined as ". . . mankind's record, expressed in verbal art forms, of what it is like to be alive."

The program was developed so that the literature of many nations would be used the first year of a three-year high school program. American literature was designed to come next, and English literature last. However, the materials can be used in any order students or teachers may wish.

The material suggested for the first year concentrates upon some of the universal concerns of man as they appear in world literature—love, heroism, human weakness, social conditions or practices, and the search for wisdom. The eleventh-grade course consists of American literature which reflects how universal concerns are modified by the American culture pattern from Puritan times to the present. The approach is roughly historical but focuses on important aspects of the American character as they are revealed in our literature—aspects such as American Puritanism, the American desire to get ahead in the world, American optimism, and the American social conscience. The twelfth-grade course is primarily made up of English literature. It gives major attention to the most sophisticated perceptions of the nature of literature, those implied in the definition by the phrase "verbal art forms." The treatment is again roughly historical, but this time the focal points are examples of the various literary art forms: story, tragedy, epic, satire, lyric, novel, and drama of social criticism.

The total program is planned to be sequential, cumulative, and spiral. In each of the three years, a different body of literature is presented, but a different approach is emphasized, demanding ever more perceptive responses.

The writing program is based on literature and is also sequential and cumulative. The program considers three concerns of writing: isolation and definition of subject, the effective use of language, and consideration of the particular class of readers for whom the paper is intended.[59]

The newer approaches to teaching literature try to get away from a major fault of most literature teachers—an overconcern with who, what, when, or which, rather than with why. It is recognized that students advance in their reading skill and understanding from a simple grasp of the literal meaning, through a fusing of the meanings of words into ideas, relating and organizing ideas, and understanding related meanings, to a grasp of implied meanings.[60]

The better language teachers recognize that poetry should not be taught as a separate entity, in a unit by itself. This practice tends to indicate a difference between prose and poetry which does not really exist. Poetry is included in a lesson whenever the time seems opportune, when a poem says something related

[59]Beekman W. Cottrell and Erwin R. Steinberg (eds.), *Teacher's Guide Including Inductive Lessons for Insight: The Experience of Literature* (New York: Noble and Noble, 1968), pp. 11–13.
[60]William S. Gray. *The Teaching of Reading and Writing, An International Survey* (Chicago: Scott, Foresman, 1956), pp. 67–70.

to the project under way, in theme or in manner. The poem presented may be the culmination of one of the great themes of human existence traced through an essay, a story, or a novel. In teaching poetry, primary attention is given to the elemental concepts of sound, figurative language and theme.[61]

As to the teaching of writing, or composition, more recognition is being given to the idea that students tend to learn to write by reading widely and by frequent guided practice in writing, accompanied by suggestions for revision and discussion and revision of papers. Teaching composition, which is an art, cannot be done by teaching a set of rules. In the first place, such rules are not wholly valid. If they were completely valid there is little evidence to support the idea that knowledge *about* English usage is accompanied by the ability to speak and write effectively.

Whereas the more traditional formalist stresses the mechanics of writing, newer approaches emphasize the what more than the how. They encourage and help students, by allowing them to grow into an understanding of the structure and possibilities of the sentence and paragraph as they gain experience in writing. The teacher does not lecture on how to write. Rather, by selecting suitable materials and carefully structuring his lessons, he leads the student to discover for himself and then to master the elements of good writing.

Today's student of composition should know what is in the grammar textbooks, but, more important, he should listen to the way the people of his time are establishing meaningful verbal contact with one another. Gifted teachers combine expert teaching of grammar with the power to draw forth the student's deep thoughts. Once a grammatical concept is taught, the student should immediately use his own prepositional phrases in a story, his own predicate adjectives to express his moods, his own participles, infinitives, and adverbial clauses. When thus taught, grammatical constructions become personal possessions. Through composition thus taught, the good English teacher draws from his students stories or themes that reveal to each the unique coloring of his personality and the unique dignity of his experiences.[62]

Perhaps the whole essence of this discussion of the language arts curriculum can be summarized and concluded by saying with the words of Louis Zahner, that the language arts as a whole should be taught so that students may control language to the extent that ". . . experience, reality as it is given us to know it, is not mutilated in its precarious passage through words."[63]

Fine Arts

The fine arts are directly related to the language arts, in that their prime functions are communication and self-understanding, and as man learns to better

---

[61]Gordon and Noyes, *op. cit.*, pp. 274–290.
[62]Wolfe, *op. cit.*, pp. viii, 346.
[63]Gordon and Noyes, *op. cit.*, p. 17.

understand and express himself to his fellow men communication is improved. The arts address themselves to man as an individual creature and also to man as part of the universe. Like language, the arts enable man to know himself and to visualize his position in the world. The artist, like the writer, can be a mirror projecting humanistic values uniquely for all who can understand them.

Artistic activity, whether in the visual arts, music, drama, or some other media, is one of the avenues by which human experience takes on richness and meaning. Throughout the entire history of the human race there is evidence that virtually all peoples have expressed themselves through aesthetic activity. They have varied widely in their particular modes of expression as different people have developed different art forms. Some values of experience in the arts are general, while others are unique, for it is true that while a culture has unique aspects, all peoples derive satisfaction from their arts.

Education through the arts is more than a narrow aesthetic exposure. True art is experience—the actual doing of something. Too much of the aesthetic, or artistic, tends to be seen as something apart from everyday living of the average person. The tendency to relegate art to the museum, the art gallery, or the concert hall is one of the least admirable traits of our society. The consequences of this tendency can be seen in the world we have created around us—the spoiled environment, ugly buildings, and lack of aesthetic appreciation visible in so much of what we make and do. It may be that the major cause of discontent and disharmony in our world today can be traced to our lack of appreciation and fulfillment through the arts. Art has been put on a pedestal, and we are not able to enjoy casual recreations and everyday occupations because of their aesthetic quality.

The tendency to set a glorified fine art upon a far-off pedestal is only one aspect of our culture's seeming determination to separate the ideal or the spiritual from the material and the practical. Because of their remoteness, the objects acknowledged by the cultivated to be works of fine art are seen by the masses as anemic, and they substitute the cheap and the vulgar to satisfy their aesthetic hunger. The same is too often true of religion, expressions of emotion, and other aspects of man which mark him as different from other animals.

Less "civilized" man in the past utilized every aspect of his everyday living as an opportunity to express himself and his finer sensitivities. Domestic utensils, furnishings of tent, house, and cave, various weapons and articles of clothing were wrought with such care and appreciation that today we have placed them in art galleries and museums, according them honor obviously inappropriate to most of today's comparable objects. The arts of the drama, music, painting, and architecture had no peculiar connection with theaters, galleries, or museums. They were a natural part of organized individual and community life.

John Dewey, in his classic treatment of this subject, described the situation as he saw it over thirty-five years ago. His words are still amazingly appropriate.

So extensive and subtly pervasive are the ideas that set Art upon a remote pedestal, that many a person would be repelled rather than pleased if told that he enjoyed his casual recreations, in part at least, because of their aesthetic quality. The arts which today have most vitality for the average person are things he does not take to be arts: for instance, the movie, jazzed music, the comic strip, and, too frequently, newspaper accounts of love nests, murders, and exploits of bandits. For, when what he knows as art is relegated to the museum and gallery, the unconquerable impulse towards experiences enjoyable in themselves finds such outlet as the daily environment provides.[64]

Instead of a concept which sees art as separate and isolated from everyday life, we need one that has its basis in the qualities of ordinary experience. Common human activities can thus become the force needed to transform common human activities into matters of artistic value.[65]

As students of the humanities concern themselves with the various means of human expression, they must learn the languages of the arts so that they may live with them and derive meaning from them. Through such means as exaggeration, distillation, symbolism, and abstraction, the great creators describe the world and man within the world in ways unequaled in any other form.

Our particular trouble, in this "air-conditioned nightmare" which we call civilization, is that we have lost the very notion of cultivating the senses, until butterfingered and tongue-tied, half-blind and deaf to all nervous vibrations, we stumble through life unaware of its most appealing aspects, lost to its intensest joys and communions.[66]

Objectives

As we have indicated above, the role of the fine arts emphasizes expression of the complex of human existence—man's concern with being and what it means to be human. Unlike science, the arts do not quantify existence, they qualify it—trying to express what is involved in consciousness and being. They thus may encompass the total goal of education.

Education may . . . be defined as the cultivation of modes of expression— it is teaching children and adults how to make sounds, images, movements, tools and utensils. A man who can make such things well is a well-educated man. If he can make good sounds, he is a good speaker, a good musician, a good poet; if he can make good images, he is a good painter or sculptor; if good movements, a good dancer or labourer; if good tools or utensils, a good craftsman. All faculties, of thought, logic, memory, sensibility and intellect are involved in such processes, and no aspect of education is excluded from such processes. And they are all processes which involve art, for art is nothing but the good making of sounds, images, etc. The aim of education is therefore the creation of artists— of people efficient in the various modes of expression.[67]

[64]John Dewey, *Art As Experience* (New York: Minton, Balch, 1934), pp. 5–6.
[65]*Ibid.*, pp. 3–19.
[66]Herbert Read, *The Grass Roots of Art* (New York: Wittenborn, 1947), p. 37.
[67]Herbert Read, *Education Throught Art* (London: Faber & Faber, 1943).

It becomes obvious then that the fine arts are to be taught for more than their aesthetic appreciation—their artistic merit. The major aims of education in the arts need to be thought out in terms of the kinds of boys and girls, men and women, we would like to produce with our education system. Through the arts, ". . . we wish to establish certain bonds of sympathy and understanding among them, along with a common interest in absorbing and adding to what is great and good in our civilization."[68]

In summary, the major aims of education through the fine arts may be stated as follows:

1. Broadening the student's aesthetic horizons through relating the major achievements of our cultural heritage to his experiences.
2. Pointing up the interrelationship among the arts.
3. Developing critical evaluation of the arts in their worldly setting through directed training of the eye and the ear.
4. Assisting the student in developing aesthetic values which may serve as guides in his adult life.
5. Developing sensitivity to artistic creations in contrast to or as affected by the mechanical and utilitarian aspects of societies.
6. Guiding the individual person toward a greatly enriched life based on deep pleasure and life-enhancing aesthetic values.[69]

The fine arts have as their major purpose the development of a student's sensitivity to the world around him. This awareness—of himself and his environment—is best achieved through the maximum use of a student's whole set of senses. The fine arts provide mediums through which the individual can express his ideas—his reactions to the impressions he receives—and, by expressing them, learn to evaluate them. In this way ". . . vague impressions are brought into sharp focus, puzzling impressions are understood, fragmentary ones are completed and alarming ones are faced so that fear is overcome." The fine arts thus allow us to examine what we are thinking and feeling, our imaginative powers of observation are stimulated, and understanding of ourselves and the world around us is extended and deepened.[70]

OBJECTIVES IN ART. Art education in the United States began with an emphasis on the precise execution of "object drawings." A particular sequence of problems was pursued to develop a set of skills growing out of absolute principles. Later this changed to an aesthetic orientation based on nineteenth-century absolutes of beauty. Finally the shift was made to the modern concept

[68]Thomas Munro, "The Interrelation of the Arts in Secondary Education," *The Creative Arts in American Education* (Cambridge: Harvard U. P., 1960), p. 32.
[69]Detroit Public Schools, "Fine Arts Adventure," in William Raymond Sur and Charles Francis Schuller, *Music Education for Teen-Agers*, 2d ed. (New York: Harper, 1966), p. 82.
[70]R. N. Pemberton-Billing and J. D. Clegg, *Teaching Drama* (London: U. of London Press, Ltd., 1965), p. 17.

which seeks to develop sensitivity to visual relationships. Students are led to "... an awareness of their visual experiences and to development of their capacity to communicate personal understandings through aesthetic form." Art in general education is now designed to be less a body of subject matter composed of certain skills and more a way of working and a way of seeing. Ample opportunity is given students to make personal judgments, discover their own meanings, and create harmonious relationships in their own way.[71]

A core of common goals for art education at all levels may be identified which will help refine the sensibilities of students and extend their capacities to perceive aesthetic qualities. Barkan has stated that such a core of common goals should include the following:

Sensitivity to visual relationships
The visual organization of shapes, positions, colors, tonal values, and textures.
The use of materials to achieve particular qualities of visual organization.
Sensitivity to communications embodied in works of art
Emotional impact.
Symbolic meanings.
Meanings in particular qualities of visual organization.
Attitudes of adventure and discovery in processes of working and observing.
Visual cues from the environment as sources for stimulation.
The character of materials and tools as guidelines for action.
Unforeseen possibilities that become apparent in any work in process.
Elements of speculative play, uncertainty, struggle, and resolution as aspects of working process.
Insight into aesthetic qualities in works of art
Similarities and differences in works of art from a variety of traditions in our artistic heritage.
Similarities and differences among the forms and characteristics of works of art in our own time.
Similarities and differences in works of art produced by children and youth.
Insight into aesthetic qualities of visual experiences.
The work of artists, craftsmen, designers, film makers, architects, and city planners, with the implications of their efforts for day-to-day experiences of people.
Skills for control and fluency.
The nature of tools and materials, and ways to control the intended meanings for making works of art;
Processes that encourage discovery, reconstruction, and refinement in work, observation, and analysis.[72]

---

[71]Manuel Barkan, *A Foundation for Art Education* (New York: Ronald, 1955), pp. v–vi, 4, 13.

[72]Manuel Barkan, "Curriculum and the Teaching of Art," in Jerome J. Hausman (ed.), *Report of the Commission on Art Education* (Washington, D. C.: National Art Education Association, 1965), pp. 77–78.

OBJECTIVES IN MUSIC. In music study through the humanities program, the student is led to *listen* more acutely and with a greater comprehension of the kinds of meaning with which music is concerned. This goal is analogous to that in art, whereby the student is helped to *see* more meaningfully.

Music is a common part of everyday living today, and it would seem that music education would be faced with no great obstacles. On the contrary, because its presence in the background of our activities is so pervasive, the tendency to hear without listening becomes a formidable barrier to true music understanding and appreciation. Comparatively few people are accustomed to actively and consciously listening to music against a background of silence and with the purpose in mind of exploring its deeper meanings and implications.

An additional difficulty results from the fact that most students' experience in music has emphasized performance rather than the aesthetic values of the music itself. Music as a part of the humanities program is not intended to threaten performance; it will, in fact, facilitate its development. The performing aspects of music education are reinforced as students gain a broader understanding of music and the other arts, because they become increasingly aware of the need for higher standards of performance, individually and as group members.

Music in a humanities program should reach the music student and deepen his understanding of what good music is and what it takes to produce it, but it should also draw into music the students presently not touched by the music offerings in the school. Music can thus become more closely related to other areas of instruction, creating a learning experience that broadens the education of all who participate in it.

The purposes of teaching music, as they seek to meet the musical needs of students, may be thought of in four basic terms: listening, performing, creating, and evaluating. More specifically, desired outcomes of music education may be said to include:

1. Positive attitudes toward music.
2. Development of standards of discrimination.
3. Respect for others' musical tastes.
4. An awareness of America's musical heritage.
5. An awareness of the musical contribution of other nationalities.
6. Active use of musical instruments.
7. Understanding of the adolescent and adult voice.
8. Good listening habits.
9. Muscular coordination through rhythmic activities.
10. Realization of the therapeutic value of music.
11. An appreciation of the importance of music reading.
12. A desire for serious study and group participation.[73]

[73] J. J. Weigand, "Experiences in General Music," in Archie N. Jones (ed.), *Music Education in Action* (Boston: Allyn and Bacon, 1960), p. 96.

OBJECTIVES IN DRAMA AND LITERATURE In the areas of drama and literature, it is obvious that the fine arts and language arts overlap. This is true to some extent in all of the subject areas involved in the humanities, which supports the approach to curriculum organization we are following in this book. We will not duplicate at this point what was said in the discussion of the language arts concerning the purposes and program of literature in the curriculum; however, it does seem appropriate to further explore the field of drama, as it is usually classified as part of the fine arts curriculum.

Drama can make significant contributions to the development of a well-rounded, productive, and happy adult. The knowledge, skills, habits, understanding, attitudes, and character traits essential for rich personal living, for sound choice of an effective participation in a vocation, for satisfying human relationships, and for responsible, contributing citizenship can be encouraged and developed through drama and related activities in ways perhaps impossible otherwise. Classroom work in dramatics emphasizes expression and appreciation of the arts, and is intended to develop those skills which are important in everyday communication. In addition, the teamwork necessary for the achievement of a dramatic performance develops traits related to cooperation, directed effort, and loyalty.

Drama is basically a narrative art—it presents a story. The stories presented give pleasure and entertain, but they also have a wide range of other functions. "They may, for example, conserve [the society's] legends, order its laws, explore its problems, demonstrate its codes, ridicule its weaknesses, or extend its knowledge."[74]

A total list of desirable objectives for drama in the humanities program would be too long for inclusion here, but perhaps a brief selection will serve to indicate the possibilities of this too often neglected discipline. A good drama program should lead students:

1. To respect drama as an art form to be seen and heard rather than just read.

2. To learn something of theater as it exists and develops, not only in our own country but throughout the world.

3. To become aware of, or in a position to assess, the nature of the theater, its associate arts, its actual function in the world, its place in varying cultures and societies, and its essential elements, origins and development.

4. To recognize that their own culture and achievements relative to the theater are not the best measures of theater in other countries, ages, or cultures.

5. To understand that illusion of reality (credibility) is more important in drama than reality itself.

6. To understand the various forms of drama—tragedy, comedy, farce, melodrama—and their typical forms and uses.

[74]Lynn Altenbernd and Leslie L. Lewis, *A Handbook for the Study of Drama* (New York: Macmillan, 1966), p. 1.

7. To understand the theories of katharsis and empathy—that by identifying with certain characters and their human condition, by feeling pity, terror, horror, or joy, a person purges himself of inhumanities and develops more admirable traits.

8. To be able to follow a play performance and to grasp elements of character, motive, and the relationship of one character to another.

9. To explore the inner nature of man.

10. To recognize in drama archetypes and archetypal experiences.[75]

OBJECTIVES IN FILM AND TELEVISION. Most of the objectives appropriate to education in drama and the theater are also appropriate for study in the fields of film and television. Although largely ignored in most school programs, so far as the official program is concerned at least, it would seem justified to give more attention to this form of communication. It has been established that the average child watches television about twenty hours per week, and few would deny that current films require some intelligent assessment and evaluation.

In addition to objectives such as those suggested for the study of drama and the theater, goals such as the following seem fitting as guidelines in the development of film and television aspects of the humanities program.

1. To increase understanding and enjoyment of television and the cinema.

2. To increase awareness of our common humanity and individual uniqueness.

3. To provide a measure of self-defence against commercial and other exploitation.

4. Where possible, to encourage self-expression not only in traditional forms (speaking, writing, drawing) but in the language of the screen (making films).

5. To encourage viewers to become more selective in their choice of program.

6. To help viewers to become more aware and discriminating in their responses and to develop their power of judgment so that they may benefit from those programs, both imaginative and factual, which have the capacity to enrich their lives[76]

Content

The fine arts may be said to include all areas of study and achievement regarded as aesthetic. To narrow the range of content material for the fine arts, perhaps it would be well to adopt the position that the question of appropriate subject matter for inclusion in the arts is basically one of determining what mediums are acceptable for expression of man's experiences. "Art" popularly tends to denote painting, and "artist" one who paints. To the contrary, every work of art has a particular medium by which expression is made and man attempts to communicate with his fellow man and with himself. The question

[75]Adapted from E. J. Burton, *The Student's Guide to World Theatre* (London: Herbert Jenkins, 1962), p. 5; and Arnold Lazarus and Rozanne Knudson, *Selected Objectives for the English Language Arts* (Boston: Houghton, 1967), pp. 45–50.

[76]A. W. Hodgkinson, *Screen Education* (Paris: United Nations Educational, Scientific and Cultural Organization, 1964), pp. 26, 78.

of content for education in the arts then becomes a question of media. Every art has a medium of its own: ". . . painting cannot exist without color, music without sound, architecture without stone and wood, statuary without marble and bronze, literature without words, dancing without the living body."[77]

The fine arts share the common purpose of communicating experience—through the most appropriate available medium. As they seek to fulfill this purpose, five content principles may be identified in each of the arts. These elements serve to provide a common bond and point of correlation. They are:

1. The subject—what it is about.
2. The function—what it is for.
3. The medium—what it is made of.
4. The organization—how it is put together or arranged to form a pattern to express some meaning.
5. The style—the personality, individuality, mood, or temper of the work.[78]

To achieve the ultimate understanding of the arts also requires a knowledge of current concepts from psychology, sociology, anthropology, cultural history, and philosophy if this aspect of the study of man is to be complete. We thus see again the necessity of a holistic approach to the humanities and their interpretation of human beings.

The concept of process as content is critical to instruction in the arts, perhaps as in no other field of instruction. The art teacher, for example, does not teach "oil painting" or "water color" per se. He introduces students to these media as possible means for personal expression. Content, in terms of activities such as painting, graphics, ceramics, weaving, singing, satire, or characterization, is misleading. These are only means of expression and communication. The content is the ". . . interrelation of many factors in experience—visual, aural, tactile, emotive—and within the individual—sensitivity, imagination, questioning."[79]

The basic content areas of *art* are color, form, texture, and space. These are the artist's means of communicating.[80] The skills and techniques which comprise his tools of expression include drawing, painting, sculpture, architecture, graphic arts, applied design, embossing, etching, lithography, photography, ceramics, and other media of expression.

Experiences which should be provided in the secondary school *music* program include singing, playing, rhythms, listening, music reading and other musical learnings and insights. These experiences are composed of theory, acoustics, harmony, form or design, folk music, choirs and choruses, conductors, the human voice, popular music, performance, instruments, musical travelogs, composers, musical Americana, and the like.

---

[77]John Dewey, *Art as Experience* (New York: Minton, Balch 1934), p. 196.

[78]Louise Dudley and Austin Faricy, *The Humanities*, 3d ed. (New York: McGraw-Hill, 1960), pp. 1–3. Succeeding chapters discuss these elements as related to the various arts.

[79]Jerome J. Hausman (ed.), *Report of the Commission on Art Education* (Washington, D.C.: National Art Education Association, 1965), p. 98.

[80]*Ibid.*

Drama, according to Aristotle, includes six major elements in combination: action, character, thought, language, music, and spectacle. These elements seem to still comprise the major content areas for drama instruction.[81] Supplementary content areas include the origins and development of drama and the theater, drama and the theater today, philosophy of drama, types of drama, the stage, actors, plays, dramatic techniques, stage techniques, and dramatic theory.

Content areas for studying the role of *film* in the fine arts include many things in common with drama and the theater, art, and music. These may be studied as they are adopted and adapted in television and motion picture. In addition, there are several aspects of the art which are unique to film, such as the following suggested areas for study of film as an art form:

> Editing
> Camera angles
> Special effects
> Film in the theater—35 mm
> Film in the community—16 mm
> Film in the home—television
> Philosophy of film
> Psychology of film
> Techniques of film
> The experimental film
> The documentary film
> The changing form and function of film
> Film as an agent of social change.[82]

Structure

Although the subject matter of the fine arts is quite different from that of the social studies, or even language arts, the same approach can be used to organize and understand its content as that which we have advocated for other disciplines. The concept and generalizations which form the structure of the arts and relate them to each other give the coherence and understandability required for the average person to benefit very much from their study. In addition, the unifying principles of basic concepts and generalizations facilitate the establishment of value criteria by which the lasting can be sifted from the mediocre.

Many of the concepts and generalizations appropriate for fine arts study in secondary school are common to all of the fine arts—and the language arts as well. Others are somewhat unique to a particular discipline, such as music or drama. Both types will be briefly discussed to illustrate this approach to organization of the fine arts curriculum.

---

[81]Altenbernd and Lewis, *op. cit.*, pp. 2–3.
[82] David C. Stewart (ed.), *Film Study in Higher Education* (Washington, D.C.: American Council on Education, 1966), pp. 19–33, 69.

CONCEPTS. Concepts important to the fine arts are generally related to ways and means of communicating ideas and feelings, because this is the basic purpose of the arts. Concepts which may be seen to be common among the fine arts, and which thus provide a means for coorelation and coordination, include:

abstraction	intensity
absurd	light
accent	line
appreciation	media
association	model
balance	movement
climax	organization
color	pattern
comprehensiveness	profoundness
consistency	proportion
consonance	quality
counterpoint	recreativity
creativity	rhythm
criticism	space
design	structure
dissonance	style
distillation	surrealism
emphasis	symbolism
exaggeration	taste
expression	technique
fantasy	texture
form	theme
gracefulness	timbre
harmony	tone
imagery	unity
integration	universality

Each art form includes some concepts which are by and large unique to that form. In art, most of the basic concepts seem to be shared with the other arts, but music, for instance, includes concepts such as sound, pulse, metre, melody, interval, scale, antiphonal, and chromatic which are somewhat unique to music. Music and the theater arts share concepts like phrase, pitch, tempo, empathy, dynamics, dialogue, diphthong, denouement, exposition, and acoustics. Theater, drama, and film may claim as their own such concepts as characterization, plot, protagonist, antagonist, confidant, foil, soliloquy, banter, stichomythy, comic relief, peripety, stock character, pantomime, and foreshadowing.

GENERALIZATIONS. As with concepts, many generalizations hold true for most or all of the fine arts. Others are somewhat unique to a particular art form. Generalizations held in common include the following:

1. The fine arts form a universal language.

2. Art is an activity.
3. Form is realized, not taught.
4. Form has unity and variety.
5. Organization occurs in response to inner urges.
6. A work of art portrays the times in which it was produced; yet its portrayal is not literal or complete in the usual sense.
7. A work of art interprets rather than describes.
8. Art's subtle insight often conveys the essence of a period more forcefully than do detailed historical descriptions.
9. Although a work of art is usually the creation of one man, it reflects the feelings of many men.
10. The most important qualities in works of art are those which are profound, lasting, and unique.
11. Cultures and religions have had their languages of accepted symbols.
12. Every art work speaks with symbolic overtones.
13. Discriminative choices are necessary to the development of the artistic choice of expression.
14. Art is a blending of the impulse of feeling and the impulse of reason.
15. Response to art is both instinctive and cognitive.[83]

Some generalizations are primarily related to only one or two of the arts:
1. Even the most "realistic" art is but a symbol of reality.
2. When, through art, we give form to our experiences, we put them in an aesthetic mold of color, shape, texture, light and space.
3. Art observes the nature of materials.
4. Rhythm and movement are music's most fundamental physical expressions.
5. Illusion of reality (credibility) is more important in drama than reality itself.
6. Many masterworks of drama operate on several levels of meaning simultaneously—usually on the literal level and allegorical or symbolic levels.
7. The final meaning of a play is the product of its total impression.
8. A particular play often leads the audience toward a philosophic statement, either expressly or by implication.
9. Many times one character of a drama is the author's "mouthpiece."
10. Screen media, although usually controlled by "the few," are directed towards "the many," and because they are couched in terms which are understandable by, and acceptable to, the majority, they are bound to make their appeal to the lowest common denominator.[84]

[83]Adapted from Howard Conant, *Art Education* (Washington, D.C.: Center for Applied Research in Education, Inc., 1964), pp. 20–23; Hausman, *op. cit.*, pp. 86–88; and other sources.
[84]Adapted from Hausman, *Report of the Commission on Art Education*, pp. 85–103; Conant, *loc. cit.*; Burton, *op. cit.*, p. 6; Lazarus and Knudson, *op. cit.*, pp. 45–49; Hodgkinson, *op. cit.*, p. 26.

Method of Inquiry

The comprehensive method of inquiry for the fine arts is the same as that for all of the humanities—philosophical analysis. It may encompass more of the creative aspects than some of the other disciplines in this class, but the basic approach is the same—getting at truth, reality, and the world as we know it and believe it to be. Whereas the main tool for this task is language in the language arts, the fine arts utilize graphics, sound, movement, and related media. The methods and tools of logic (induction, deduction, criticism) applied to analysis of the art forms are utilized in basically the same way as in other areas of humane studies. Any work of art may thus be exposed to questions such as "Why did the artist create it? What did he want to show? What experience was he trying to make clear? What had intrigued him so much that he wanted to share it with others? Did he satisfactorily communicate? Are his ideas, as communicated through the work, valid, universal, and true of man throughout time and geographic location?"[85]

Teaching the Fine Arts

In the fine arts, as in perhaps no other area of learning, it is obvious that *how* we teach is part of *what* we teach—process is a part of content. Whether taught as craftmanship, beauty, communication of ideas, entertainment, or an expression of feelings and ideas, the fine arts exemplify the necessity for students to create and perform. The reciprocal actions of seeing, hearing, feeling, and organizing form the core of this process, as students learn how their feelings about these processes affect their actions as they strive to organize materials and media into aesthetic form.

> The art experience, whether it be creating art or understanding the art created by others, is a process of interaction involving the individual, the idea, the tools and materials, and the evolving art form. There is constant interaction among these factors; yet they function in no absolute sequence.[86]

More and more, good teachers of music, art, drama, and the other fine arts are realizing that good teaching ought to be a translation of what professionals in these fields demonstrate and what scholars explain about the nature of these arts. With this study process, involving both process and product from the professional's viewpoint, the student must discover the content of his studies through his own work and out of the depths of his own experience. He will become aware of the need to give attention to the interplay of three factors: (1) the theme or idea that serves as his stimulus, (2) the medium or material he chooses to use and manipulate, and (3) the component elements of form he is able to bring into being. Nuances of ideas and feelings find expression as the

---

[85]Dudley and Faricy, *op. cit.*, pp. 9–10.
[86]Mary Adeline McKibbin, "Art in the Secondary Schools," in Hausman (ed.), *op. cit.*, p. 93.

student learns to utilize to the fullest advantage the art form he prefers at the moment.[87]

The development of two attributes—creativity and critical ability—comprises the main focus of teaching in the arts. To fulfill these two purposes there are three main types of study and instruction in any art. Although they of necessity must be mentioned one at a time, the three should proceed simultaneously and in correlation with each other. (1) Practice, including performance, as in painting or playing the piano, is one of these types of study. It may include creative production, as in composing music or painting an original picture. Especially at the lower levels of the secondary school, this part of the program should get the most emphasis. (2) The second approach is historical—teaching the chronological development of a single art or a group of them, such as the visual arts, through a period of time in some part of the world. (3) The third part, which may be termed the theoretical, includes the principles of criticism and may develop into philosophical and scientific aesthetics for advanced students.

In teaching the fine arts as related to the humanities, teachers should be careful to be sure that the principles of the arts are constantly related to their operation in the everyday world.

> If the principle under investigation should be "line" the student might expect to learn about line as it operates in fashion design, in popular music, in the literature of both poets and advertising men, in cars and houses, and of course in the best examples of all of the arts as well. If "balance" is being studied, the focus will be on the role played by this principle in both the visual and the auditory arts, again with many everyday examples.[88]

To help students develop a feeling for the arts and their relationship to the everyday world, the teaching process may be constructed around such broad questions as the following:

1. What is art?
2. To what extent do literature, art, and music reflect the spirit of an age?
3. What are the various approaches to or treatments of tragedy and comedy in the arts?
4. What are the enduring qualities that are inherent in classics and that account for their universal appeal?
5. When has prose been the predominant mode of literary expression?
6. When has poetry been the predominant mode of literary expression?
7. How do trends in prose and poetry relate to the art and music of the day, and in what way?
8. What conclusions can be related to the world in the twentieth century?[89]

Utilizing approaches to curriculum organization and teaching methodology based on the structural elements of the disciplines, the creative teacher may devise many ways to make use of the endless variety of possibilities inherent in

---

[87]Manuel Barkan, "Curriculum and the Teaching of Art," in Hausman (ed.), *ibid.*, p. 71.
[88]Sur and Schuller, *op. cit.*, p. 79.
[89]*Ibid.*, p. 81.

348 Disciplinary Components

the fine arts to help students sharpen their perception of the people and world around them. Guidance and direction can be given to students in the use of all their senses to better understand themselves, their fellow men, and the world in which they live, resulting in happier and more productive lives.

Religion

Because of the range of religious pluralism in the United States, religion's place in the public schools is one of the continuing problems in American education. During the early years of our nation, religious education and secular education were practically one and the same, because almost all formal education was sponsored by the churches. Religious ideas and symbols were common throughout the school curriculum. So long as most of the people accepted similar religious beliefs this presented no serious problem, but diversity of religion, rather than homogeneity, has become characteristic of our society today, and separation of the functions of church and state in education has proved to be a most perplexing problem.

The First Amendment to the Constitution of the United States was intended as a guide toward the treatment of religion, but it has been interpreted in various ways. In attempting to (1) prohibit any established religion in the United States, and (2) guarantee complete religious freedom, this Amendment was adopted as follows:

> Congress shall make no law respecting an establishment of religion, or prohibiting the free exercise thereof; or abridging the freedom of speech, or of the press; or the right of the people peaceably to assemble, and to petition the Government for a redress of grievances.

When applied to public school practices, the two main purposes stated in this Amendment sometimes are found to be in conflict. The result has been much confusion among educators.

The problem seems to be to find a way in public education to give proper recognition to the place of religion in our culture while at the same time holding to the principle of separation of church and state. This principle was never meant to exclude all study of religion from the school program, as this would be as much a violation of religious liberty as teaching which advocates or supports a particular religious belief. To be silent about religion may actually make the public school an antireligious factor in the community.

It would seem that perhaps the best way to solve this problem would be to teach religion as a field of study and scholarship within the humanities program. The intellectual life of man has never been far removed from the manifold concerns of religion, because they both include speculation on man's nature, his possibilities for good and evil, his conduct, his eventual destiny, and the nature of a supreme or ultimate being. Education *about* religion has been specifically encouraged by the courts as a way to maintain our cultural heritage without advocating or teaching any religious creed. A statement by the National Education Association is to the point:

> Knowledge about religion is essential for a full understanding of our culture, literature, art, history, and current affairs. That religious beliefs are controversial is not an adequate reason for excluding teaching about religion from the public schools. . . .[90]

A more recent statement by the American Association of School Administrators is more specific as to how acceptable goals of religious instruction may be achieved.

> The desirable policy in the schools . . . is to deal directly and objectively with religion whenever and wherever it is intrinsic to learning experience in the various fields of study, and to seek out appropriate ways to teach what has been aptly called "the reciprocal relation" between religion and the other elements in human culture. The implementation of that policy calls for much more than an added course, either for teachers or for the high school curriculum itself. It requires topic-by-topic analysis of the separate courses, and cooperative efforts by the teachers to give appropriate attention to these relationships.[91]

Objectives

The objectives of religious education in the public schools are indicated, and to some extent stated, above. They may be summarized under four headings:

1. *Perennial Questions*—acquainting students with the perennial questions which man has raised and attempted to answer concerning meaning and destiny, including the reflection of these questions in systems of thought, cultic acts, and characteristic attitudes and beliefs.

2. *Evaluation and Criticism*—developing in students an ability to distinguish and assess the various forms of religious, philosophical, and theological statements, as evidenced in arguments, presuppositions, convictional utterances, myth, symbol, and the like.

3. *Religion and Culture*—achieving recognition and understanding of the role of religion and the religious in literature, history, the arts and other cultural manifestations; relating religion to cultural forces.

4. *Respect for Others*—encouraging tolerance for the religious convictions and practices of others and then going beyond mere tolerance so that students can understand and value people for their differences, honoring their religious convictions and practices.[92]

[90]Educational Policies Commission, *Moral and Spiritual Values in the Public Schools* (Washington, D.C.: National Education Association, 1951), p. 5.
[91]American Association of School Administrators, *Religion in the Public Schools* (Washington, D.C.: American Association of School Administrators, 1964), p. 60.
[92]Adapted from Clyde A. Holbrook, *Religion, A Humanistic Field* (Englewood Cliffs, N.J.: Prentice-Hall, 1963), pp. 70–85. American Association of School Administrators, *Religion in the Public Schools, op. cit.*, pp. 27–30.

Content

The nature of religion is so pervasive an element in human culture that drawing boundaries becomes at once imperative and almost impossible. As with other major areas of human culture such as fine arts, literature, or history, religion touches many facets of human life and profoundly interacts with them. Its interplay with philosophy, music, art, and literature, as well as with government, economics, and other disciplines requires of the student a breadth of view seldom encountered in public education.

> Stated in comprehensive terms, religion embraces the study of those forms of conviction, belief, and behavior and those systems of thought in which men express their concerned responses to whatever they hold to be worthy of lasting and universal commitment. Religion takes for its province of study not only the normative beliefs, practices, and literatures of the world religions as commonly classified, but also manifestations of religious attitudes which impinge upon cultural contexts—political, economic, or artistic—often considered foreign to religious aims.[93]

Those who have attempted to reduce the boundaries of religion instruction to manageable proportions have utilized various approaches, one of the more common being to focus on several types of questions which are common to all religions. They include:

1. A scheme of salvation—identifying the source, nature, and appropriate methods for removal of some evil believed to afflict human life. Equal concern is given to how to achieve or receive the gift of some "blessedness," release, or fulfillment which transcends the evil in either this world or the next, and possibly both.

2. The theological question—dealing with the nature of supreme beings or being, or whatever functions as the ultimate reality.

3. The anthropological question—concerning the nature and possibilities of man.

4. The epistemological question—knowledge of the divine will, including how to communicate with diety and how diety makes known its will to man, as through prayer, vision, sacred literature, intuition, or reason.

5. The ethical question—raising the issue of appropriate forms of conduct toward deity and fellowmen. Beliefs are often stated in terms of codes, norms, or laws.

6. The eschatological question—deals with the end or limits of history, culture, and time and with death and the possibility of immortality.

7. The cultic question—refers primarily to the nature and the meaning of those acts by which a religious faith assumes public embodiment. The cultic question in its broadest sense may include modes of worship, social organization of the religious community, roles and functions of special religious personnel, and ways in which proper group and individual con-

[93] *Ibid.*, p. 36.

duct are assured. It may also include consideration of the place of symbols, characteristic gestures, forms of speech, and effects of religious belief upon architectural and art forms.

8. The cosmological question—relates to man's theories and visions of the creation, nature, and form of the world and his place in it.[94]

Structure

Religion can be best studied in the same way as the other disciplines—by giving attention to the structural elements: concepts and generalizations. Concepts involved in the study of religion would include

baptism	faith
Christian	God
church	idol
creation	indoctrination
creed	liturgy
cultic	monotheism
doctrine	ordinance
ecclesiastic	orthodox
ecumenical	Protestant
evil	puritan
religion	sect
ritual	secular
sacred	sin
sacrament	theology
salvation	worship

Generalizations which might be employed in the teaching of religion are exemplified in the following, which have been suggested by several different authorities. They are not listed in any particular order, except by reference.

1. Man, at any point in his development, has a need for religion.[95]
2. Every religious system or outlook is in some sense a scheme of salvation, whether or not the term appears in its literature.
3. Often, since the cultus offers the assurance of salvation to its members, the acts of worship themselves are regarded as sacred or at least as necessary steps to the goal of salvation.[96]
4. The history of Europe in the Middle Ages is in great part the history of the Christian church.
5. Religion implies an ultimate reality to which supreme allegiance must be given.
6. What one believes about God, about man and about the world has momentous consequences in life and conduct.

---

[94]Adapted from Holbrook, *Religion, A Humanistic Field*, pp. 72–75.

[95]American Council on Education, *The Function of the Public Schools In Dealing with Religion* (Washington, D.C.: American Council on Education, 1953).

[96]Holbrook, *op. cit.*, pp. 72, 74.

7. Religion expresses itself in institutions which organize themselves about the function of group worship.[97]
8. According to traditional doctrine man is created from the dust of the earth. His life is enmeshed with nature, dependent upon natural processes, subject to natural caprice.
9. Biblical thought [says] that man's creation is in the image of God. Man is not merely a part of nature. He transcends the natural processes in which he is involved.
10. In biblical thought man, though created to love, is sinful. His historical existence is precarious, and in trying to make it secure he resorts to various stratagems in which he exalts himself and his institutions in defiance of God and his fellow men.[98]

For a World History course, where the great religions are considered in their historical settings, generalizations such as the following may be employed for teaching religion as an experience of mankind.

1. Religion has been a universal experience of mankind.
2. Religion has been a great cultural force in man's history.
3. Religion has made great contributions to our ethical heritage.
4. Those aspects of the various religious groups which are common to all should be emphasized, rather than the differences which are divisive.
5. We should recognize the right of all men to choose the forms of their religious expressions.
6. We should understand and respect the religions and religious practices which differ from our own.[99]

Method of Inquiry

The methods of inquiry utilized by those who study religion are not unique to religion. There are no techniques for investigation or evaluation which are peculiar to it or which set it apart from other humanistic studies. A diversity of methods are employed as they are appropriate. For example, the methods used to analyze a passage from the Bible or the Rig Veda are basically the same as those employed by a classics scholar in studying a text or other similar type of writing. Methods particularly appropriate to the study of history may be used either to investigate the relation between seventeenth-century English sectarianism and the rise of religious toleration or to study the military campaigns of General Grant. Comparing Buddhist and Christian goals of human existence demands no more or less unique devices than does comparing Sir John Mandeville's and Jean Jacques Rousseau's outlooks upon life. Archaelogical or anthropological procedures employed in opening and presenting the Dead Sea Scrolls are no different than those used to unearth and prepare other types of ancient manuscripts for study.[100]

---

[97]American Council on Education, *The Relation of Religion to Public Education: The Basic Principles* (Washington, D.C.: American Council on Education, 1947), pp. 2, 11.
[98]Amos N. Wilder (ed.), *Liberal Learning and Religion* (New York: Harper, 1951), pp. 70–72.
[99]American Council on Education, *The Function of the Public Schools in Dealing with Religion*, *op. cit.*, p. 30.
[100]Holbrook, *op. cit.*, pp. 37–38.

One of the strongest justifications for placing the study of religion in the humanities program comes from the fact that the methods for studying religion are common to other disciplines of the humanities. All of these methods are fundamentally incorporated in the concept of philosophical analysis, which is the basic method of inquiry for the disciplines of the humanities.

Teaching about Religion

It is difficult to say that a certain tendency relative to instruction in religion is common, because there is great diversity of practice and these practices are changing, due to court decisions and other influences. Policies in particular school districts may range all the way from avoidance of any religious instruction or religious emphasis (including Christmas programs and baccalaureate services) to planned programs of instruction emphasizing a particular group of religious beliefs. Most schools which attempt religious instruction try to emphasize the factual study of religion, a common core of religious beliefs, and moral values.

Those who attempt to teach religion inevitably face the highly charged issue of indoctrination. Teachers of economics, government, sociology, philosphy, or history may be just as likely to seek to bypass critical judgment in order to elicit a desired response to certain ideas, beliefs, or attitudes, yet when religion is inserted in the curriculum there is immediate concern about indoctrination. Many parents and community members even maintain that instruction in religion automatically involves indoctrination in specific religious beliefs and attitudes and consequently regard religion as totally incompatible with the purposes of a liberal education.

Religion instruction in the classroom activities of the curriculum may include only incidental references to religion as a part of regular coursework. It may be restricted to teaching moral and spiritual values in some fashion. On the other hand, religion instruction may be carried out in more direct fashion through courses designed specifically to teach religion, Bible reading practices (even though this has evidently been declared unconstitutional by the Supreme Court), homeroom devotional exercises, or units on religion in regular coursework.

Activities outside the regular classroom which are designed to teach religion include baccalaureate services, regular chapel or morning devotional exercises, assemblies devoted to religious exercises or featuring speakers on religious topics, observance of religious holidays (with various preholiday activities in the school), excusing students for religious holidays of their faiths, lunchtime blessing, or display of religious documents and materials. More and more question is being raised by citizens and by the courts concerning the legality or wisdom of these types of practices, but few schools seem to have changed them significantly in recent years.

Taking the position that religion instruction should be a part of the humanities curriculum tends to avoid charges of sectarianism and questions of legality, but there is little precedent to guide those who wish to organize such a program.

Content areas should probably include some concepts and generalizations from many areas of study, including:

Religious ideas
Religions of the world
The heritage of the Bible
The Bible as literature
History of Christianity
Motifs of Hebraic-Christian thought
Christian ethics
The relation of religion and culture (in America and elsewhere)
Religion and science, art, music, literature, architecture, etc.
Problems of religion
Philosophy of religion

Utilizing concepts and generalizations as the structural elements, religion instruction may take any of several different forms of organization and procedure. An illustration of the way one high school attempts to deal with religion in a coordinated program of instruction in art, history, literature, music and in an experimental seminar on religions for seniors may be helpful.

A World Culture program of studies includes all tenth-, eleventh-, and twelfth-graders, with the tenth-grade social studies course covering man from his earliest beginnings down to about 1800. Also at the tenth-grade level, the literature course surveys the religious literature, including the Bible as an anthology of Hebrew and Early Christian literature, Greek literature, the Koran, some of the sacred writings of the Orient, and the religious classics of early Europe, the Middle Ages, the Renaissance, and Puritan literature.

Throughout the program, the teachers of English, history, art, and music correlate their teaching. The various types of music developed by religious groups are touched upon by the music teacher. Other forms of art evolved by religious groups are examined by the art teacher. The English teacher leads students in reading and interpreting the underlying philosophies of the various religions, while the history teacher establishes the historical setting and tries to correlate the learning activities through discussion sessions. Five basic understandings form the core of the whole program:

1. Why man, at any point in his development, has a need for religion.
2. How man has used religion.
3. The geographic and historic environment in which different religions have developed.
4. The similarity and differences between major religions of the world. (This is aimed at bringing about more tolerant attitudes through better understandings.)
5. The influence of religion upon history.[101]

[101]American Council on Education, *The Function of the Public Schools in Dealing with Religion, op. cit.*, pp. 30–32.

Another example may serve to illustrate a less extensive program which may be carried out as part of a course in social studies or some other area. In this case, a unit on "Philosophy and Religious Values" includes the following section headings:

1. What is religion?
2. Where do I get a system of values to guide my life?
3. Why should I be understanding toward the beliefs of others?
4. In what do I believe?
5. What is the relationship between religion, morals, and character?
6. What does religion contribute to society?
7. What is prayer?
8. What are some of the great stories of religion?
9. Why should I have a religion?
10. What is the place of religious values in my plan of action?[102]

Adjusted to the level of understanding and maturity of the students, educators need to see that religion instruction assumes its rightful place as a very crucial part of the humanities program. The concepts and generalizations found in religion may serve to coordinate many other areas of study as students use them in a program of inquiry into the humanities.

Philosophy

Although not always recognized as such, philosophy is a basic ingredient of all good humanities programs. To philosophize is to try to understand, to explain, and to relate—all of which must be included in various aspects of study in the humanities. In fact, it may very well be that in philosophy we have the best means for integrating and relating the various disciplines.

Philosophy means literally "love of wisdom." It is not equivalent to wisdom, but it implies a desire to pursue and study wisdom. Wisdom, in turn, is most often defined as truth. One who studies philosophy, then, is in pursuit of truth—regardless of the academic field of inquiry.[103]

Eduard C. Lindeman, of the New York School of Social Work, supported the idea of teaching philosophy in secondary schools almost thirty years ago in words which still have an authentic ring:

> In an age of high-powered propaganda and pressure group methods it becomes imperative that citizens should reclaim the democratic function of doing their own thinking. . . . Philosophy is the discipline required. Philosophic instruction should be introduced at an early age, certainly in secondary education. I doubt whether individuals ever think as clearly or as logically as they do in early adolescence. Nor do I believe that individuals ever again raise more important

---

[102]Richard B. Dierenfield, *Religion in American Public Schools* (Washington, D.C.: Public Affairs Press, 1962), p. 57.

[103]Van Cleve Morris, "The Philosophy of Education," in Van Cleve Morris and others, *Becoming an Educator* (Boston: Houghton, 1963), p. 52.

questions about life and its meaning than they do at this age. I do not mean to imply that formal instruction in philosophy should be introduced at this period. On the contrary, I merely ask that teachers be so prepared as to be able to discuss, with students, the philosophic phases of all issues which rise to importance in the minds of youth. Certainly, the basic principles of logic, ethics and esthetics will have direct application to the entire secondary school curriculum.[104]

Mark Van Doren has made the statement that in the construction of a "liberal" curriculum, ". . . philosophy is the first need everywhere."[105] Whitehead earlier supported this view with his definition of education as ". . . the acquisition of the art of the utilization of knowledge."[106] "Utilizing" the mass of knowledge now being poured down upon the heads of young people requires some system of ordering and assimilating not usually supplied by the typical secondary school curriculum. Students have difficulty in trying to see the whole picture of life. They can't "see the woods for the trees." Philosophy can provide ideas as trees by which to see the woods, thus fulfilling another of Whitehead's admonitions that the purpose of education ". . . is to make the pupil see the wood by means of the trees."[107]

In summary, the teaching of philosophy is desirable for the following five reasons:

1. It may make a great contribution to the coherence of general education, by establishing a connection between the various subjects and by giving the mind a basis for assessing the place of separate items of knowledge in the system of knowledge as a whole.
2. It promotes reflection which calls for and develops independence of judgment, refusing to be satisfied with hasty and superficial answers to serious problems—it teaches the student to "think for himself" and to form judgments neither detached to the point of indifference nor yet too dogmatic.
3. It clarifies and refines the appreciation of humanistic values and establishes their universality.
4. It inspires respect for others' freedom of thought and promotes efforts to achieve tolerance and deeper understanding among men.
5. It helps the individual to form ideas on all the problems of thought and action, which enable him to take his proper place in contemporary society, and the community of mankind.[108]

Purposes

The fundamental purpose of instruction in philosophy at the secondary school level is to teach students to think, a purpose widely accepted as the basic goal of the total educational program. The special province of philosophy in

---

[104]Brand Blanshard et al., *Philosophy in American Education* (New York: Harper, 1945), p. 284.

[105]Mark Van Doren, *Liberal Education* (New York: Holt, 1943), p. 114.

[106]Alfred North Whitehead, *The Aims of Education* (New York: Macmillan, 1929).

[107]*Ibid.*

[108]Georges Canguilhem (ed.), *The Teaching of Philosophy, An International Enquiry of UNESCO* (Paris: United Nations Educational, Scientific and Cultural Organization, 1953), p. 187.

teaching students to think for themselves lies in the area of how man ought to live. Through philosophy, students may first learn to be critical about the sources and the methods of obtaining knowledge. They may then learn to investigate the fundamental methodology inherent in arriving at values of any kind.

Study in philosophy should encourage and assist students with speculation on their own ideas or on those of others concerning questions such as : What is the meaning of human life and the significance of the world in which man finds himself? What is the general nature of the universe in which human life has its setting, in so far as that character has a bearing on human destiny? What is that destiny? How far can man affect it by his own actions; and, within the limits of his choosing, what activities and pursuits should he follow? What kind of life is more worthwhile leading, individually and collectively?[109]

As an acquaintance with, and an appreciation of, philosophical problems and terminology are developed, the learning activities should be built around the student's personal problems and his philosophy of life, with emphasis on the functional rather than the academic. At the same time, the student will gain valuable experience in reading and analyzing somewhat difficult writing.

Content

Philosophy as a field of study has not been widely adapted for use at the secondary school level, and to do so requires considerable ability and ingenuity on the part of teachers. Many of the terms and concepts commonly used by philosophers are very abstract and for adolescents to benefit from their study they must be approached from their level of understanding and interest. The following statement indicates the content appropriate for such a program.

1. The relation of philosophy to the liberal arts, and the definition and value of philosophy.
2. The nature and function of ethical theory, ethics as a systematic search for principles or standards of moral evaluation, free will, theories as to the nature of right action, the nature of moral obligations and moral responsibility, egoism and altruism, and application of ethical principles to social problems.
3. Current criticisms of education practices and theories, definition of education, the ends toward which education should be directed, and definition of a liberal education.
4. Definition of art, aesthetic contemplation, categories of aesthetic value, the value of art, and criticism of the arts.
5. The nature of knowledge, the acquisition of beliefs, the nature of evidence, scientific method, the structure of a developed science, the general presuppositions of science, the nature and criteria of truth, and some theories as to the nature of knowing and evidence.
6. Problems of the philosophy of religion, typical features of religion, typical

[109]John Herman Randall, Jr. and Justus Buchler, *Philosophy, An Introduction* (New York: Barnes & Noble, 1942), pp. 5–6.

religious ideas, the legitimacy of faith, and the positive and negative values of religion.

7.Metaphysics.[110]

The material for study and discussions related to the above areas of study are drawn from one or more of the traditional branches of philosophy:

Ontology—the study of the nature of the real world. This includes *metaphysics*, which deals with the technical question of existence.

Epistemology—the study of knowledge and of how knowledge is gained. Closely related to epistemology is the science of *logic*, which deals with the exact relating of ideas.

Axiology—the study of values and of how values are determined. The field of axiology embraces two regions of value: the ethical and the aesthetic. *Ethics* is concerned with the nature of good and evil, the evaluation of human behavior, and the principles which control this behavior. *Aesthetics* is involved with principles governing the creation and appreciation of beautiful things.[111]

In treating the many questions and concerns of philosophy, attention should be given to various views and systems of philosophy as they relate to the particular topic at hand. Naturalism, idealism, realism, and pragmatism, with their religious, educational, artistic, and humanistic implications, provide the basic content areas for this approach to the inclusion of philosophy in the humanities curriculum.

Structure

Few concepts are unique to philosophy, because, as we have stated previously, philosophy is related to all areas of learning. The following list of concepts is illustrative of this structural element in philosophy. A complete list would form a book in itself.

aesthetics	irrelevance
altruism	know
ambiguity	logical
analogy	metaphysics
conclusion	naturalism
consistency	non sequitar
contradiction	pragmatism
converse	premise
cosmology	probability
deduction	proposition
egoism	realism
ethics	religion
evolution	supernatural

---

[110]John Henry Melzer, *Philosophy in the Classroom: A Report* (Lincoln, Neb.: University of Nebraska Press, 1954), pp. 44–45.

[111]Van Cleve Morris (ed.), *op. cit.*, pp. 54–57.

fallacy	syllogism
idealism	truth
implication	universals
induction	validity
inference	value

Philosophical concepts go into generalizations related to the question and concerns appropriate to this study. The following are typical.

1. There are two general views one can take about human nature: (1) that it is fixed and definable, or (2) that it is changing, evolving, and always in question.[112]
2. The general character of our philosophy influences our attitude in the interpretation of values, and the converse is equally true.
3. On the Hebraic-Christian view, moral standards are revealed to us by divine authority.
4. If pleasurable emotion were the criterion of goodness in conduct the consequences of our acting according to it would more than likely interfere with rather than promote our interests in the *long run,* our *total* interests.[113]
5. The validity of an informal argument may be assessed by considering the content of each of the statements made in it and asking whether a conclusion or inference *does* follow from its premises.
6. The widest range of informal fallacies [occur because] the premises are irrelevant to the conclusions; that is, the conclusions do not follow logically from them.
7. An appeal to authority is in itself irrelevant, because an argument is strong or weak, valid or fallacious, regardless of its author.
8. An argument falsely attributing cause where none exists commits a fallacy of irrelevance in the sense that its premise or premises do not justify a conclusion asserting a causal connection.
9. The fallacy of begging the question is the fallacy of assuming in a premise the very point one is attempting to establish.
10. Deductive inferences follow "necessarily" from their premises and are true if their premises are true; inductive inferences from particulars are no more than probable.[114]

Method of Inquiry

Philosophy (through philosophical analysis) is particularly valuable as an integrator in the humanities because of its insistence on a type of questioning that is oriented toward synthesis and perspective. It tries to consider all sides and aspects of a question and thus may involve many traditional subject areas in studying a particular question or problem.

Philosophy is primarily concerned with two types of inquiry or research. One

[112]*Ibid.,* p. 64.
[113]Randall and Buchler, *op. cit.,* pp. 244, 251, 256.
[114]L. M. Brown, *General Philosophy in Education* (New York: McGraw-Hill, 1966), pp. 24–28, 65.

360 Disciplinary Components

may be called *analytical philosophy* and the other *speculative philosophy*. Analytical philosophy examines the nature, methods, procedures, and foundations of all human reflection, whether in art, science, religion, or some other field, and subjects it to criticism, clarification, and definition. Speculative philosophy has as its concern the unification of all phases of human experience into a comprehensive and meaningful whole through synthesis and interpretation. Both types of inquiry are, of course, intimately interrelated.

Observation is the basis for inquiry by philosphers. This is, however, a much broader type of observation than that employed by the sciences. Philosophy appeals to the broadest and most fundamental features of experience for verification.[115]

Teaching Philosophy

Philosophy is not so much a subject alongside other subjects, to be taught in similar fashion, but a kind of reflective activity that may integrate and illuminate all subjects. Philosophy is relevant to all activities in secondary education, because the desire to understand is relevant to all teaching and learning. It has often been said that teaching English is every teacher's business. So it is every teacher's business ". . . to encourage the questioning mind, to argue things out with all who wish it, to justify his tastes on demand or even without demand, to regard fact at every point as an invitation to theory."[116]

Philosophy is a basic ingredient of all human activity and should be an active and integral part of all study. We can appropriately place the phrase "philosophy of—" before practically any general noun of broad application, such as music, history, politics, law, physics, civil rights, journalism, or business, thus showing the place of philosophy in education.

Selected References

Altenbernd, Lynn, and Leslie L. Lewis, *A Handbook for the Study of Drama*. New York: The Macmillan Company, 1966.

American Association of School Administrators, *Religion in the Public* Schools. Washington, D.C.: American Association of School Administrators, 1964.

Anderson, Wallace L., and Norman C. Srageberg (eds.), *Introductory Readings on Language*. New York: Holt, Rinehart and Winston, Inc., 1962.

Beggs, David W., III, and R. Bruce McQuigg, *America's Schools and Churches, Partners in Conflict*. Bloomington: Indiana University Press, 1965.

[115]Randall and Buchler, *op. cit.*, pp. 40–41.
[116]Blanshard et al., *op. cit.*, p. 93.

Blanshard, Brand, et al., *Philosophy in American Education.* New York: Harper & Row, Publishers, 1945.

Boles, Donald E., *The Bible, Religion, and the Public Schools.* New York: Collier Books, 1963.

Brown, L.M., *General Philosophy in Education.* New York: McGraw-Hill Book Company, 1966.

Butler, J. Donald, *Four Philosophies and Their Practice in Education and Religion.* 3rd ed. New York: Harper & Row, Publishers, 1968.

Childers, J. Wesley, *Foreign Language Teaching.* New York: The Center for Applied Research in Education, Inc., 1964.

Conant, Howard, *Art Education.* New York: Center for Applied Research in Education, Inc., 1964.

Crane, R. S., *The Idea of the Humanities,* Vol. 1. Chicago: University of Chicago Press, 1967.

Dewey, John, *Art As Experience.* New York: Minton, Balch & Company, 1934.

Dierenfield, Richard B., *Religion in American Public Schools.* Washington, D.C.: Public Affairs Press, 1962.

Dudley, Louise, and Austin Faricy, *The Humanities.* 3rd ed. New York: McGraw-Hill Book Company, 1960.

Educational Policies Commission, *Moral and Spritual Values in the Public Schools.* Washington, D.C.: National Education Association, 1951.

Evans, William H., and Jerry L. Walker, *New Trends in the Teaching of English in Secondary Schools.* Chicago: Rand McNally & Company, 1966.

Fowler, Mary Elizabeth, *Teaching Language, Composition, and Literature.* New York: McGraw-Hill Book Company, 1965.

Glenn, Neal E., and Edgar M. Turrentine, *Introduction to Advanced Study in Music Education.* Dubuque, Iowa: Wm. C. Brown Company Publishers, 1968.

Gordon, Edward J., and Edward S. Noyes (eds.), *Essays on the Teaching of English.* New York: Appleton-Century-Crofts, Inc., 1960.

Graeffe, Arnold Didier, *Creative Education in the Humanities.* New York: Harper & Row, Publishers, 1951.

Hausman, Jerome J. (ed.), *Report of the Commission on Art Education.* Washington: National Art Education Association, 1965.

Hodgkinson, A. W., *Screen Education.* Paris: United Nations Educational, Scientific and Cultural Organization, 1964.

Holbrook, Clyde A., *Religion, A Humanistic Field.* Englewood Cliffs, N.J.: Prentice-Hall, Inc., 1963.

Hook, J. N., *The Teaching of High School English.* 3rd ed. New York: The Ronald Press Company, 1965.

Jewett, Arno (ed.), *Improving English Composition.* Washington, D.C.: National Education Association, 1965.

Johnson, Francis R. (ed.), *The Humanities Chart Their Course.* Stanford, Calif.: Stanford University Press, 1945.

Jones, Archie N. (ed.), *Music Education in Action.* Boston: Allyn and Bacon, Inc., 1960.

Jones, Howard Mumford, *One Great Society.* New York: Harcourt Brace Jovanovich, Inc., 1959.

Lanier, Vincent, *Teaching Secondary Art.* Scranton, Pa.: Intext Educational Publishers, 1964.

Lazarus, Arnold, and Rozanne Knudson, *Selected Objectives for the English Language Arts, Grades 7–12.* Boston: Houghton Mifflin Company, 1967.

Macdonald, James B., and Robert R. Leeper (eds.), *Language and Meaning.* Washington: Association for Supervision and Curriculum Development, 1966.

Marckwardt, Albert H., *Linguistics and the Teaching of English.* Bloomington: Indiana University Press, 1966.

Melzer, John Henry, *Philosophy in the Classroom: A Report.* Lincoln, Neb.: University of Nebraska Press, 1954.

Morris, Van Cleve (ed.), *Becoming an Educator.* Boston: Houghton Mifflin Company, 1963. Chapter 3.

Morsey, Royal J., *Improving English Instruction.* Boston: Allyn and Bacon, Inc., 1965.

Munro, Thomas, and Herbert Read, *The Creative Arts in American Education.* Cambridge, Massachusetts: Harvard University Press, 1960.

Pemberton-Billing, R. N., and J. D. Clegg, *Teaching Drama.* London: University of London Press, Ltd., 1965.

Randall, John Herman, Jr., and Justus Buchler, *Philosophy, An Introduction.* New York: Barnes & Noble, Inc., 1942.

Stewart, David C. (ed.), *Film Study in Higher Education.* Washington, D.C.: American Council on Education, 1966.

Stroup, Thomas B. (ed.), *The Humanities and the Understanding of Reality.* Lexington, Ky.: University of Kentucky Press, 1966.

Sur, William Raymond, and Charles Francis Schuller, *Music Education for Teen-agers.* 2nd ed. New York: Harper & Row, Publishers, 1966.

"Symposium: Religious Education as a Discipline," *Religious Education* 62 (September–October, 1967), pp. 387–430.

Taylor, Marvin J., *Religious and Moral Education.* New York: Center for Applied Research in Education, Inc., 1965.

Whitehead, Alfred North, *The Aims of Education.* New York: The Macmillan Company, 1929.

Wilder, Amos N. (ed.), *Liberal Learning and Religion*. New York: Harper & Row, Publishers, 1951.

Wilson, Graham (ed.), *A Linguistics Reader*. New York: Harper & Row, Publishers, 1967.

Wolfe, Don M., *Creative Ways to Teach English, Grades 7 to 12*. 2d ed. New York: The Odyssey Press, Inc., 1966.

part IV

Other Components of the Secondary School Curriculum

Other Components of the
Secondary School Curriculum

In addition to the traditional academic components of the secondary school curriculum, the majority of schools offer students the opportunity to avail themselves of additional experiences and services under the sponsorship of the school. Among the more common are: the acquisition of vocational and technical skills, participation in school activities, and receiving guidance and counseling from trained personnel.

The purpose of including a discussion of vocational and technical education, student activities, and guidance and counseling is that these elements are an integral part of the secondary curriculum. Although they may differ in nature and function from the more traditional aspects of the curriculum, these components make a positive contribution to the development of the student.

Chapter 11 deals with the subject of vocational and technical skills. The emphasis of this chapter is on the relationship between vocational and technical education and the total school curriculum, the content of current programs, and the role of government involvement in shaping the nature of such programs in the schools.

Chapter 12 is concerned with the student activity program and, again, the emphasis is placed upon the nature and function of the activity program in relation to the total curriculum. Major topics included in this chapter are the place of student activities, typical student activity programs, administration of student activity programs, and improving student activity programs.

The last chapter in Part IV discusses the topic of guidance and counseling. Although not generally discussed in connection with the secondary school curriculum, the authors feel that it is a part of the curriculum, since its nature and functions make a direct input to the total curriculum. The major topics included in Chapter 13 are the relationship of guidance and counseling to the curriculum, the definition and scope of guidance programs, their development, functions, and organization; and the teacher in relation to the guidance program.

CHAPTER 11

VOCATIONAL AND TECHNICAL SKILLS

Vocational education is an established part of the secondary curriculum. Although varying in degrees of emphasis from school to school and from region to region, vocational and technical programs can be found in almost every secondary school in the country.

A Definition

The meaning of vocational education, as well as its place in the secondary curriculum, is not agreed upon by all who concern themselves with the secondary program. Basically, there are three positions relative to the definition of vocational education.

First, there are those who place vocational education in the same category as any other subject in the curriculum. This position holds that any educational endeavor is vocational in nature in that the basic concepts and skills taught in secondary schools are necessary for present-day employment. For example, the ability to read, write, and do simple calculations is a basic requisite to the work world; therefore reading, writing, and arithmetic are vocational in nature.

A second position takes the point of view that vocational education is confined to training students to work with their hands. Those who hold this view visualize the vocational programs in secondary schools as courses where students learn how to do specific physical manipulative operations, such as repairing a small motor.

A third position, and the most popular one today, is that vocational education is that phase of education that endeavors to prepare an individual in all aspects related to a specific occupation. From the standpoint of uniqueness from general education, no clear division is attempted. Rather, the distinction is more one of objectives and focus than one of pure distinction.

Vocational education encompasses many of the same concepts as general

369

education but relates more to the chosen occupation of the learner. For example, one might study angles in mathematics for the purpose of general education or from the standpoint of the needs of a carpenter in framing a house. The distinction, then, is one of focus, rather than content.

Ingram lists five characteristics which distinguish vocational education from general education.

1. Education is vocational when it is designed specifically to improve the efficiency of an individual in a specific occupation—either as preparation for employment or supplementary to the duties of employed workers.
2. Education is vocational when it is taught and learned in its relationship and application to the actual job requirement of a specific occupation.
3. Education is vocational when it is of more value to persons who will pursue, or are pursuing, a specific occupation than to other persons.
4. Education is vocational when it is timed so that the learner can apply it at the time it is learned to useful and productive work in a specific occupation.
5. Education is vocational when the necessary skills and knowledge of a particular occupation are being taught and learned in their practical and proper application to the work.[1]

In summarizing the essential characteristics of vocational education, Ingram states:

Briefly, education is vocational when it provides instruction in the "why" and "how" to persons engaged in or preparing to enter a specific occupation rather than instruction "about" things to those who might be interested. If these are the purposes and intent of vocational education, there can be no other explanation of its characteristics.[2]

It is evident, then, that a variety of definitions of vocational education exist but the latter one offered by Ingram appears to be the dominant one today. The broader definition of vocational education recognizes that programs must include a variety of experiences which will aid students in becoming more efficient in any type of vocational work while focusing their attention on a specific occupation.

Place of Vocational-Technical Education in the Total School Program

The place of vocational-technical education in the total school program remains a point of controversy even though programs of this nature have existed in the secondary school for many years.

At one end of the spectrum there are those who hold the position that the sole purpose of the secondary school is to provide a strong academic program and

[1] J. Fred Ingram, *What Makes Education Vocational* (Washington, American Vocational Association, Inc., 1965), p. 3.
[2] *Ibid.*

the place for vocational training is in postsecondary institutions such as trade schools. Reflective of this position is a statement produced by the Council for Basic Education. Although recognizing that vocational education is presently a part of the secondary program in almost every school, the Council states:

> That vocational training is offered in due subordination to the school's fundamental purpose of intellectual discipline, and that standards of achievement are maintained as rigorously in vocational as in academic fields.[3]

The statement by the Council for Basic Education is based, perhaps, on the long-standing issue of vocational versus liberal education. The liberal education position supported by such men as Robert Hutchins and Arthur Bestor asserts that the school exists to perform an intellectual function, therefore, the content of the school curriculum should be intellectually oriented. For one to become "liberated" one must confine his studies to such subjects as history, mathematics, biology, language, literature, philosophy, and religion. Those who hold this position believe that through this type of curriculum a person acquires the ability to understand the world about him and function more effectively within that world. The argument extends to the idea that specific training for a vocation can best be accomplished after a strong academic background.

In refuting this position, Horn states:

> I know of no incontrovertible evidence that demonstrates that engineers and journalists, for example, can't think as well as individuals who have majored in literature and history, that they aren't as good citizens, or that they fail to have as broad interests. On the contrary, the psychologists have long since disproved the theory that certain subjects such as mathematics and languages teach the individual to think more effectively; but most liberal arts people have never heard of the evidence or have conveniently put it from their minds. . . .[4]

Another view which fails to support the position of the "liberalist" is offered by Geiger.

> That concern with the present is illiberal is of a piece with the idea that "vocational education" presents the grand antithesis: Here is the illiberal bogey always available for drubbing. Now, it is very easy to sneer at the alleged vocationalizing of much modern education. Lofty contempt for practical subjects is the watermark of too many self-defined scholars. The examples chosen are calculated to get a laugh—pie-making, camp leadership, window-cleaning, prepharmacy, salesmanship. Certainly there will be no apology here for the evident abuses of overvocationalism in many sections of present-day education. But to assume that training for making a living has no place in liberal education is to assume that education has no context.[5]

[3]Council for Basic Education, "Statement of Purpose," in Robert O. Hahn and David B. Binda, *Secondary Education: Origins and Directions* (New York: Macmillan, 1965), p. 6.
[4]Francis H. Horn, "Higher Learning and the World of Work," in Henry Ehlers and Gordon C. Lee, *Crucial Issues in Education* (New York: Holt, 1965), pp. 231–232.
[5]George R. Geiger, "An Experimentalist Approach to Education," in *Modern Philosophies and Education* (Chicago: National Society for the Study of Education, 1955), p. 153.

Regardless of the arguments against it, vocational education has established a place in the secondary curriculum. With the continued interest on the part of government to provide funds for vocational and technical programs, vocational education will not only become more entrenched but will continue to expand. The issue of whether or not vocational education has a place will continue but chances are slight that the impact of the controversy will be noticed. What remains now, it seems, is working out some of the problems in order to provide a quality program for persons selecting to pursue vocational education. Some of the more pressing problems are discussed in the following sections.

Keeping Pace with Current Needs

Changes in the world of work have continued to multiply, particularly since 1950. These changes have required curriculum workers in the area of vocational education to restructure and update programs in line with these changes. For example, Table 11-1 reveals the projected shift in occupational needs from 1960 to 1975.

Table 11-1

CHANGING OCCUPATIONAL NEEDS*

Occupation groups	Percent of total economy, 1960	Percent of total economy, 1975
Service workers	12.5	14.4
Managers, officers, proprietors	10.6	10.2
Professional technical	11.2	14.6
Farm workers	8.1	3.8
Clerical	14.7	16.7
Sales	6.6	6.7
Craftsmen and foremen	12.8	12.8
Operatives	18.0	16.7
Nonfarm laborers	5.5	4.3

*National Industrial Conference Board, 1969.

With respect to the importance of this type of information to vocational education, the table reveals:

1. A drop in the need for farm workers.
2. A drop in the need for most kinds of blue-collar workers.
3. A growth in the need for white collar workers, particularly professionals, technicians, and clerical workers.
4. A growth in the need for service workers.

The changes that constantly occur in the world of work present special problems to those who plan vocational-technical programs. There is a tendency for society to look to the schools for solutions to economic and social problems. In terms of economics, for example, when unemployment is high the schools are often called upon to find a solution to the problem. Although the secondary school can contribute to the solution of such problems, it is limited because it is only one of the many agencies needed to work on the problem. The problem is one of determining how best to keep pace with the changes taking place in the world of work. To compound the problem, it is estimated that many of the vocations now in existence will not exist in the future, being replaced with vocations not now in existence. How, then, can a student be prepared for a vocation that, at the present, does not exist?

Recognizing the possibility of training students for a vocation that may not exist in the future, vocational educators has been moving in the direction of what is known as the "cluster approach." In essence, the plan involves exposing students to a preparation program centered around several vocations that have elements in common. In other words, a student trains for a cluster of occupations rather than one specific vocation.

Providing Balance Between Vocational and General Education

Another problem that concerns curriculum planners in the area of vocational-technical education is the distribution of time and emphasis that should be given to vocational education. At one point there were those who advocated that in order to produce persons fully qualified to enter a specific vocation on the completion of high school, the program would have to occupy a substantial part of the student's school time. The emphasis given by this approach was that a student should spend the majority of his time training for the vocation with the remaining time spent meeting the minimum requirements for graduation. Although advocated for many years, this approach has never fully been accepted as a workable plan.

A more acceptable plan is one of considering vocational education as an integral part of the total school program. In this respect, vocational education exists to serve the special needs of certain students while providing exploratory experiences for others. Occupations that require postsecondary training are increasing every year, making it less feasible to train highly skilled workers in the secondary schools. Another factor in lending support to this approach is the generally accepted idea that vocational education and general education should be brought closer together in the preparation of persons for the world of work.

Current Vocational-Technical Programs

Vocational-technical programs in the secondary schools have grown rapidly in recent years. While vocational education per se for any given student consists of those courses chosen to further his vocational choices, the primary areas of interest today are:

1. Business education
2. Vocational home economics
3. Vocational agriculture
4. Vocational technical education

Business Education

Business education is the generic term which describes the entire program of education for business. It includes those courses which provide for personal skill development, citizenship, and consumer economic understanding.

Americans today are living in a business-oriented society that is assuming an ever-increasing importance in our lives as the complexity of civilization grows. Very few Americans can escape contact with the business community, indeed, the production, distribution, and consumption of goods and services bring most of us into daily contact with the business world.

It is generally agreed that business education programs offered at the secondary level exert tremendous influence on the lives of many young people. Because of the important contributions it affords in the educational development of all young people, business education commands a prominent place in modern secondary school programs—a position it has maintained for many decades, both in terms of meaningful and vital course offerings and in terms of sizable enrollments.

Effective programs of business education consist of courses and activities in the area of business which are specifically designed to meet the exploratory needs of the junior high school student, the vocational needs of the senior high school student, and the common needs of all students.

Basic business courses are generally available to any student who has aptitude, interest and needs for vocational business education. These courses are designed to develop knowledge, skills, habits, attitudes, and ideals necessary for successful entrance into and advancement in business occupations.

Successful programs of business education must effectively provide training for general education as well as for business education. While primarily designed to further the vocational training of a student, business education should also serve to help a student to (1) live more effectively. (2) acquire a sense of responsibility to his employer, his nation, and himself, and (3) develop a capacity for thinking and reasoning which will enable him to meet the challenges of today as well as those of tomorrow.

Authorities in the field of business education advocate two guiding principles of curriculum construction. First, a curriculum should serve the needs of young people who take business courses. Second, a curriculum should serve the needs of the employing community. Concomitant with these two premises is the concept that the business education curriculum should serve the following three basis purposes:

1. General education—all students should have an understanding of today's business-oriented economy. This concept is best developed through general business or social business courses.
2. Personal use education—all students benefit from certain courses used in personal life experiences. An example of such is notehand, more commonly referred to as typing for personal use.
3. Vocational education—most students need preparation for a job upon leaving high school since less than 50 percent go on to posthigh school training. Four basic vocational preparation programs in business education are suggested to meet this need—bookkeeping, clerical, stenographic, and distributive.[6]

A sound secondary program of vocational business education contributes significantly to general education. For example, vocational business training contributes to general education through the development of

1. Self-assurance through increased proficiency in the skills of written and oral English and in problem solving abilities.
2. Direct appreciation of the responsibility of earning a living in our society.
3. A philosophy of human relationships based on respect for the accomplishments and rights of others, as well as increased ability to work and live with other individuals.
4. Emotional and physical well-being as a result of emphasis upon correct posture, personal grooming, personal appearance, and other qualities prerequisite to successful employment.
5. Mental health and ethical character resulting from a realization of the values of a sound psychological climate for coping with unpleasant situations tending to occur in any occupation.
6. An increased understanding and appreciation of the economic problems of business and everyday life.[7]

GENERAL OBJECTIVES OF BUSINESS EDUCATION. The objectives of general business education include preparation of students to

1. Become well acquainted with opportunities and requirements in business occupations.
2. Acquire understanding of the nature and function of the American business system and its essential role in the maintenance of the socioeconomic well-being of our people.
3. Become intelligent consumers aware of business goods and services.
4. Utilize in business situations, both as workers and as consumers, such basic skills as arithmetic and English and to maintain and improve these skills.

[6]Fred S. Cook and Martha L. Mead, "Expectation for Development of the High School Business Education Curriculum," *National Business Quarterly*, Vol. 35 (Summer 1967), p. 11.
[7]C. J. Zuehlke, "The Contribution of Secondary School Vocational Business Education to General Education," *National Business Education Quarterly*, Vol. 33 (Summer 1965), p. 69.

5. Engage in business practices and activities related to other aspects of our society.
6. Enter training in business beyond the secondary level[8]

These objectives may be met through proper selection of courses to be offered, and by guiding students in planning an orderly sequence of courses.

CONTENT FOR BUSINESS EDUCATION PROGRAMS. The program in business education should be based upon individual student needs. Therefore, some schools may find it possible to enrich the business curriculum by alternating some course offerings from year to year.[9]

Four suggested program arrangements are as follows:
1. General Electives
2. Vocational Clerical Program
3. Vocational Stenographic Program
4. Vocational Distributive Education Program

A common pattern designed to meet general educational objectives, includes one or more of the following courses: typewriting (eighth or ninth grade) general business, business arithmetic, typewriting I (first year high school), bookkeeping I (first-year high school), business law, and economics.

To meet the vocational objectives for business education, a program should provide a variety of sequences or patterns of courses. A comprehensive business education curriculum might be organized on the basis of grade placement and sequence as follows:

Grade 10	Grade 11	Grade 12
Introduction to Business I and II	Bookkeeping I and II	Office Practice
Typewriting I and II	Shorthand I and II	Shorthand III and IV
	Typewriting III and IV	Office Internship
	Marketing and Merchandising I and II	Marketing and Merchandising III and IV
		Marketing Internship
		Marketing Laboratory

Numerous business education courses have value for all students, regardless of vocational goals and plans. Every high school student deserves the opportunity to enroll in those business education courses which will be of most value to him. Objectives of general electives in the area of business education are

1. To provide experiences that will help the student to realize his potential as a contributing member of society.
2. To provide experiences that will contribute to student knowledge and understanding of business and economics as an essential part of general education.

[8]Lloyd V. Douglas et al., *Teaching Business Subjects* (Englewood Cliffs, N.J.: Prentice-Hall, 1965), p. 31.
[9]*Ibid.*

3. To provide experiences that may serve as a foundation for advanced study.
4. To provide an opportunity for each student to develop an appreciation of high standards of moral and ethical behavior in business.

The Vocational Clerical Program. The vocational clerical program is designed to prepare students for employment as clerk typists, file clerks, general and office clerks, office machine operators, receptionists, and other related occupations. Instruction includes machine operation, record-keeping, filing, clerical routines, and business techniques. Emphasis is placed also on the development of habits and desirable personality and character traits. Occupational competencies should result from acquired skills, human relations insight, and knowledge of sound business principles. General objectives for this type of program are to

1. Provide opportunities and experiences necessary for the development of marketable clerical skills needed for initial employment and advancement.
2. Provide meaningful experiences for students of varying abilities and needs, stimulating each to progress toward his maximum potential.
3. Provide an opportunity for each student to develop an appreciation for high standards of moral and ethical behavior in business.

The vocational clerical program enables students to explore career opportunities in office occupation through a sequence of courses extended throughout the senior high school.

Three examples of programs showing possible arrangements and sequences of clerical education courses which a school might develop to provide quality preparation for clerical occupations are

Grade 10	Grade 11	Grade 12
Introduction to Business	Bookkeeping I and II	Office Practice
Typewriting I and II	Business Elective	Office Internship
		Typewriting III and IV
Introduction to Business	Bookkeeping I and II	
Typewriting I and II	Business Elective	Office Practice
		Typewriting III and
		Office Machines or
Introduction to Business	Bookkeeping I and II	Typewriting III and IV
Typewriting I and II	Typewriting III and IV	
		Office Practice

Electives: Business Law, Business Organization and Management, Consumer Economics, Economics

The Vocational Stenographic Program. The vocational stenographic program is intended to prepare students for employment in office occupations which require stenographic skills. In addition to developing knowledge of basic dictation and transcription, students receive opportunities for developing skills in machine operation, bookkeeping, filing, and business techniques.

Objectives of vocational stenographic education are to

1. Provide opportunities and experiences necessary for the development of marketable stenographic skills needed for initial employment and advancement.

2. Provide the essential technological foundations and occupational skills for students pursuing a continuing educational objective required for professional business careers.

3. Provide an opportunity for each student to develop an appreciation for high standards of moral and ethical behavior in business.

Examples of stenographic programs showing possible arrangements and sequences of courses that might be utilized to provide quality preparation for stenographic occupations are

Grade 10	Grade 11	Grade 12
Introduction to Business Typewriting I and II	Bookkeeping I and II Shorthand I and II	Stenographic Office Practices Office Internship
Introduction to Business Typewriting I and II	Bookkeeping I and II Shorthand I and II	Shorthand III and IV Office Internship
Introduction to Business Typewriting I and II	Bookkeeping I and II Shorthand I and II	Office Practice Shorthand III and IV
Introduction to Business Typewriting I and II	Bookkeeping I and II Shorthand I and II	Stenographic Office Practice Shorthand III and IV Typewriting III and Office Machines

Electives: It is recommended that one of these additional business electives be included in grade 11 and 12: Business Law; Business Organization and Management; Consumer Economics; Economics

The Vocational Distributive Education Program. Vocational Distributive Education entails a program of education concerned with subject matter unique to the function and field of marketing, merchandising, and management. Specific study of problems in retailing, wholesaling, and service occupations is of fundamental importance.[10]

The basic instructional goals of such a program primarily involve the acquisition of basic understandings, attitudes and skills; student adjustment to the adult world of employment and responsibility, and occupational advancement of meaningful employment, growth, and satisfaction.

Assessment of student success in distributive education must be based on those factors that relate to development of pertinent aspects of employability. Social, basic skills, technical, and marketing competencies, coupled with an understanding of the profit structure of American business, should provide each

[10]Ralph E. Mason, *Methods in Distributive Education* (Danville, Ill.: Interstate Printers and Publishers, 1962), p. 15.

individual student with the necessary skills for employment in entry level or career level occupations.

Marketing is that area of business administration dealing with activities which direct the flow of goods and services from producer to consumer. Included among these activities are buying, selling, advertising, display, public relations, and management.[11]

Marketing programs provide an opportunity for students to explore possibilities in marketing through sequential courses extending throughout the three or four-year senior high curriculum.

The option of employment and training through internship programs is an added feature of distributive education. Close supervision by the school's teacher-coordinator and by a training sponsor designated by the employer enables the trainee to develop marketable skills and a mature outlook toward the world of work.

Following are examples of programs showing possible arrangements and sequences of courses which schools might adopt to provide quality preparation for distributive education and marketing.

Grade 10	Grade 11	Grade 12
Introduction to Business Typewriting I and II	Marketing and Merchandising I and II	Marketing and Merchandising III and IV Marketing Internship or Marketing Laboratory
Introduction to Business Typewriting I and II	Marketing and Merchandising I and II	Marketing and Merchandising III and IV Marketing Internship or Marketing Laboratory

Electives: Typewriting I and II, Bookkeeping I and II, Business Law, Economics, Speech

Vocational business education is an integral part of the total secondary school curriculum. The general education learnings and opportunities presented by business education programs labeled vocational should be made available to those secondary school students who are to continue their education, as well as those students who enter terminal programs. The essential activities of life are of such a nature that many of the skills, attitudes, and understandings learned in vocational business education have specific value in the nature of general education.

Many states are carrying out laudable programs aimed at helping students prepare for entering and advancing in business careers. No two states use the same procedures and techniques or follow the same organizational path.

[11]Karl A. Elling, *Introduction to Modern Marketing—An Applied Approach* (New York: Macmillan, 1969), p. 5.

Individually meeting the needs of citizens while striving to work out the problems of a new orientation, the different states have made substantial progress. As states exchange ideas and work cooperatively together with federal and regional office educators, they are afforded excellent opportunities for serving the nation.

Business education has an important responsibility in modern public education. Business educators must be continually aware of this particular responsibility of public education and assist in fulfilling its goals.

Vocational Homemaking Education

Home economics has from its beginning been conceived as a professional field concerned with service to society. Its aim has been one of action, relating theoretical knowledge to particular problems and situations. The basic end or aim of home economics is the creation and enhancement of viable family life. The guiding purpose of vocational education in home economics is to prepare youth for the responsibilities and activities involved in homemaking and in achieving family well-being. The general objective of vocational education in home economics is to provide instruction that will enable families to improve the quality of their family life through more efficient development and utilization of human and material resources.

The challenge of change is perhaps greater for home economics than for any other body of knowledge. This challenge is necessitated not only by the rapid technological, social, and economic developments in modern American living but also by the rapid increase in educational institutions which offer instruction in home economics, and by the expansion of their research programs and extension services.

CURRICULUM CONTENT FOR VOCATIONAL HOME ECONOMICS EDUCATION. As an applied professional field dedicated to professional service, home economics as a disciplinary area does not possess a single distinct body of knowledge. Rather it has an overall structure consisting of metaknowledge, theory drawn largely from the basic sciences, and practical knowledge borrowed from other fields.

Metaknowledge consists of knowledge about a given field of study. Such knowledge identifies (1) the field, (2) how it is related to other fields, and (3) how it is differentiated from them. In essence, metaknowledge consists of knowledge of the basic aim or purpose of a field, the basic concepts of a field, their interrelationships, and the modes of inquiry used to validate such.

Theoretical knowledge is dependent upon metaknowledge and consists of abstract knowledge about the objects of study in a field. Thus, theoretical knowledge is relevant to the purpose of a field and to the structure around the basic concepts with which a field is concerned. It includes terminology and definitions of terms, classifications, sets of data, generalizations drawn from data, and theories which organize generalizations into sets.

As an applied science, home economics is concerned with the practical use of the knowledge it produces and teaches. This implies concern not merely for student understanding, but for understanding, predicting, and controlling or assisting in practical decision making. Such practical knowledge is often called technical knowledge or technology. The skillful use of such knowledge in diagnosis and treatment involves craftsmanship.

In order to prepare youth for the continuous task of adapting to the realities of rapidly changing society, vocational home-economics education can be effectively organized into the following subject areas or courses of study:

1. Human development and the family
2. Housing
3. Foods and nutrition
4. Textiles and clothing
5. Home management and family economics

CURRICULUM STRUCTURE FOR VOCATIONAL HOME ECONOMICS EDUCATION. Curriculum structure refers to identifiable shapes or categories which are interrelated to form a pattern. Structure applied to conceptual thinking and knowing refers to the form or logical pattern of the concepts involved.

Discussion of the structure of a curriculum is a discussion at the level of metaknowledge. In seeking and discovering knowledge, the basic aim or purpose of a field and the basic concepts of a field determine what questions to ask and seek answers to in research, what data to seek, what investigations to perform, what criteria to use in judging data, how to interpret the data, and what kind of conclusions to draw from analysis of the data. Metaknowledge is again called into use in planning and implementing a curriculum for teaching because it indicates what subject matter to offer on the basis of available intellectual resources and moral obligation.

In summary, metaknowledge gives direction to (1) creating and organizing abstract substantive knowledge relevant to the field, and (2) identifying and dealing with the specific, practical problems with which those in a service-oriented profession are concerned. Theory helps in identifying and classifying practical problems. It remains for practical knowledge to bridge the gap between the findings of basic research by invention and development of strategies, techniques, and materials or facilities.

The basic concepts upon which the substantive content of home economics is based are those involved in analysis of family structure and functioning. In 1961 the Home Economics Education branch of the U.S. Office of Education brought together a representative group for the purpose of identifying basic universal concepts and related generalizations in the field of home economics. The group proposed the following conceptual framework for use in designing the structure of a home economics curriculum:

Subject area	Concepts
Home Development and the Family	Universality of individuals and families Uniqueness of individuals and families Development and socialization of the individual

Subject area	Concepts
	Challenge and creative possibilities of change
Housing	Influence of housing on people—physical and psychological, social
	Factors influencing the form and use of housing—human, environmental
	Processes in providing housing—designing, selecting, building, financing, furnishings, and equipment, managing, maintaining
Foods and Nutrition	Significance of good as related to cultural and sociocultural influences, nutrition, physiological and psychological satisfactions
	Nature of food—chemical and physical properties, factors effecting change in properties of food
	Provision of food—production, consumer practices, protective measures, management of resources
Textiles and Clothing	Significance of textiles and clothing to the individual in society—interrelationships of clothing and culture, social and psychological aspects of clothing, clothing as a medium for artistic perception and expression, textiles and clothing in the economy, psychological aspects of textiles and clothing
	Nature of textiles and clothing—textiles, garments
	Acquisition of textiles and clothing—selection, use and care, consumer responsibilities
Home Management and Family Economics	Environmental influences on individual and family management—societal, economic
	Managerial processes—decision making, organization of activities
	Effective elements in management—resources and their utilization
	Values, goal, and standards

The generalizations related to each proposed concept are far too numerous to include in this section. It will suffice to say that all of the proposed generalizations express an underlying truth, have an element of universality, and usually indicate relationships. A few examples of generalizations pertaining to vocational home economics education are as follows:

As more services are built into foods, the control of industry over the kinds and quality of food increases while that of the home decreases.

The size, design, and construction of housing are affected by zoning ordinances, building restrictions, and by other housing in the community.

The resources available for meeting clothing needs include available goods and services, purchasing power, personal information, ability, time, and energy.

The attitude and information of the meal planner about food and nutrition influence the nutritional adequacy of the food served.

Housing is a resource used in attaining individual and family goals.

Counter space between work areas helps reduce steps by providing a stacking, loading, and holding zone.

Vocational Agriculture

Agriculture programs represent one of the oldest vocational offerings in the secondary school. Originally designed for future farmers, vocational agriculture programs have grown to include a variety of farm related experiences.

The Smith-Hughes Act of 1917 provided the basis for vocational agriculture and exerted tremendous influence on the shape of programs offered in the secondary schools for nearly five decades. With the changing status of farm occupations, changes had to take place in vocational training programs. For example, during the period 1947 to 1962 agricultural jobs decreased approximately three million, making it necessary to change emphasis. With farm jobs continuing to decrease by approximately 250,000 per year, the chance for productive employment on farms is becoming increasingly difficult.

The Vocational Act of 1963 made a substantial contribution to correcting the problem by providing support for training in farm-related occupations, such as food processing, irrigation methods, marketing, and equipment sales and repair. These programs, many of which are currently offered, provide at least a partial answer to providing realistic employment opportunities for youth desiring to enter the agriculture field in some capacity other than as farmers.

CONTENT FOR VOCATIONAL AGRICULTURE. Three broad categories of programs provide a base for describing the content of current vocational agriculture programs.

First, the original intent of vocational agriculture, preparation for farming, has been retained. The aim of vocational agriculture is still to train present and future farmers in the art and science of farming. Programs of this nature are designed to prepare youth to

1. Learn how to enter the field of farming and make a success of it.
2. Learn how to produce farm products in the most efficient and profitable manner.
3. Learn how to market farm products in the most profitable manner.
4. Learn how to make the best use of the soil and to conserve it for future use.

5. Learn how to participate in farm related leadership activities.[12]

A second category of vocational agriculture is often referred to as off-farm vocations. These programs include training in the various aspects of business management and commercial operations such as service and supply, processing marketing. Specifically, programs of this nature are designed to

1. Develop a body of scientific information related to farm occupations.
2. Provide an opportunity to acquire experience in applying the scientific knowledge gained in work experiences related to the farm.[13]

A third category is the technical and professional vocations related to vocational agriculture. This area generally provides exploratory experience for those desiring to continue their education beyond the high school. In an effort to achieve this purpose, programs in this category include

1. Opportunities to develop knowledge of the scientific principles of agriculture.
2. Opportunity to develop interest in the variety of professional and technical opportunities available.[14]

An example of content of current vocational agriculture programs is presented in the following outline.

I. Agriculture Orientation
II. Agriculture General Shop
   A. General Shop
   B. Woodworking
   C. Selecting Woodworking Projects
   D. Simple Sketching and Drawing
   E. Electricity and Electronics
   F. Sheet Metal
   G. Elementary Arc Welding
   H. Glazing and Painting
   I. Safety in Shop
III. Principles of Crop Production
   A. Plant Science and Soils
   B. Plant Food and Fertilizers
IV. Rural and Urban Living
   A. Home and Family Living
V. Youth Organization
   A. Leadership development through instruction and individual activities.
     1. Organization

[12]Adapted from Roy W. Roberts, *Vocational and Practical Arts Education* (New York: Harper, 1965), p. 178.
[13]*Ibid.*
[14]*Ibid.*, p. 179.

2. Leadership
3. Contest and Awards

VI. Principles of Livestock Production

VII. Supervised Practice Program

VIII. Conservation of Natural and Human Resources

The purposes of vocational agriculture in the public schools are twofold—to contribute to the broad educational objectives of the public school system, and to provide education needed for employment in agriculture. The following objectives are generally agreed upon as valid guidelines for all vocational agriculture programs.

1. To complement the broad educational objectives of the public school system by making practical and intellectually appealing application of the academic subjects, particularly science, mathematics and economics, as they are related to the problem of the agriculture student.

2. To develop responsibility, leadership, citizenship and cooperation through the teaching of the life sciences and the social sciences.

3. To provide basic education for high school youth who will later go into agricultural business occupations requiring an agriculture background.

4. To provide basic education in agriculture for the high school youth who plan to engage in some type production agriculture, or who now live on farms.

5. To assist with the occupation and vocational guidance of high school youth.

6. To provide an opportunity for high school youth to develop the knowledge, skills, and abilities required in gaining proficiency in general shop and agriculture mechanics.

7. To provide instruction that will better prepare students for posthigh school training, in area schools, trade schools and colleges.

Although considerable progress has been made in vocational agriculture programs, many problems still exist. Tenney offers a list of suggestions for improving programs in this area.

1. Vocational agriculture programs should be modernized in view of the constant technological changes taking place in this country. There needs to be greater emphasis on the principles of farm science and farm management practices, including expanded supervised work experience and leadership training.

2. Programs offered at the high school level should be expanded to include a larger clientele, since the range of farm-related occupations for which some farm training is useful has been greatly expanded.

3. Programs are needed for both young farmers striving to get started and established farmers who need training to increase their proficiency. Programs are also needed for farm-related workers already employed.

4. Special programs in agriculture technology are needed to better prepare

persons to enter employment in agriculture-related industries and businesses.

5. Programs are needed to upgrade leadership. This can be accomplished through youth organizations for those who plan to enter an agriculture occupation.[15]

Although the suggestions listed above represent only a few of those currently being advocated, the feeling is that a general expansion of vocational agriculture programs at the secondary level is needed. However, care should be taken to provide the kinds of programs that are current with the needs of the times.

Technical Education

The need for persons trained in a technical speciality has become more and more evident in recent years. In response to this need, educational programs have been developed aimed at training workers in occupations that require technical knowledge and skills of a different nature than those needed by professional workers such as scientists or engineers.

Most modern occupations require the employment of some manipulative skills and the application of a variety of technical information such as those concerned with the design manufacture, sale, and servicing of products.

In general, technical education is designed to train persons for occupations for which posthigh school training, particularly graduation from college, is not required for entry into the occupation. Most technical programs offered at the secondary level are considered terminal and geared to meet the needs of various vocations that require specific skills.

The need for technicians is evident in a variety of fields. Examples given in the following list represent only a few of the opportunities but illustrate the types of occupations that might be termed technical.

1. Industry—engineering aides, science aides, inspectors, production and maintenance supervisors, technical salesmen, and factory technicians.
2. Business—special machine operators, advertising and display technicians, secretarial aides with special knowledge, and operators of motels.
3. Agriculture—farm managers, for specialized operations, livestock breeder, broiler-plant operator, supervisor of processing plant, machinery operator, inspectors, estimators, surveyors.
4. Health—medical technicians, dental technicians, physical therapy aides, X-ray technicians, practical nurses, nurses' aides.
5. Home economics—child-care aides, specialist in food preparation and preservation, interior decoration.

Technical education programs are on the increase but remain in much the same position as that of vocational education of several decades ago. The major

---

[15]Adapted from A. W. Tenney, "Agricultural Education," in *Sixty-Fourth Yearbook of the National Society for the Study of Education* (Chicago: U. of Chicago Press, 1965), pp. 117–118.

opposition to the growth of technical education was the reluctance to recognize the existence of a level of work between the skilled trades and the professions. The professional field of engineering was one of the first to recognize the need for technicans, but other fields such as medicine have come to realize the necessity of encouraging training for technicians.

Technical education can now be found in some high school programs but has not made the progress that the proponents of this type of training had hoped for. However, with an increase in programs evident, it appears that technical education is beginning to make a place for itself in the secondary program.

It is clear that most secondary schools cannot produce trained technicians for numerous occupations. It can, however, select those that hold the most promise for employment and exert effort to develop programs.

Government Involvement in Vocational Education

The federal government has a long history of concern for vocational and technical education. This concern is reflected in the numerous legislative acts passed by the Congress making available huge sums of money over the years to insure operation and maintenance of such programs in the schools. The following legislative acts constitute the basis for support of current vocational-technical programs.

Smith-Hughes Act

The Smith-Hughes Act represents the first major attempt by the federal government to provide direct support for vocational programs. Passed in 1917 and signed by President Wilson, the Act appropriated approximately $7 million for assistance in vocational agriculture, trades and industry programs, and home-economics education. Although the Act today represents only a small portion of the available assistance currently allocated to vocational-technical education, its impact, both past and present, is notable.

The situation in America at the time the Act was passed was one where a large portion of the work force was engaged in farming and related occupations. Therefore the funds were directed toward programs for students preparing to work on the farm and for those preparing to work in a farm-related trade. A portion of the money was also set aside for home economics instruction for students preparing to enter work in the home.

The rigid manner in which the Act was written has produced a relatively uniform program which has tended to remain fairly constant over the years. With the exception of three short-term supplements to the Smith-Hughes Act and the 1963 amendment, the program outlined in 1917 continues much the same today.

George-Barden Act

In 1946 Congress passed the George-Barden Act which was designed to supplement the provisions set forth in the Smith-Hughes Act. It made available $29 million to be used in the same manner as the $7 million already available for vocational programs. In respect to spending priorities, the George-Barden Act followed the same pattern set with the earlier act in that vocational agriculture received the most support with home economics, trades, and industry, and distributive occupations following in that order. In 1956 the Act was amended to include fishery occupations and practical nursing.

Although the GI Bill for World War II veterans provided money for vocational programs in an indirect way, little effort was made to provide additional support for vocational education until the late 1950's. It is interesting to note that as late as 1957 the federal government's financial commitment to vocational programs totaled approximately $37 million. The programs, at least in terms of financial support, remained substantially static during forty years of operation. In fact, attempts were made to reduce the existing financial commitments during the economy drives of the 1930's and as late as the early 1950's.

In assessing the characteristics of vocational programs during the early years of its operation, Venn states:

1. The program was "of less than college grade." The original intent of the drafters of these laws clearly was to make this a secondary school-level program. All vocational courses had to be "terminal" in nature, and, no matter where taught, credit for them could not be applied toward the baccalaureate degree.
2. The program was heavily weighted toward rural areas. Over 60 percent of the funds were channeled into vocational agriculture (apportioned on the basis of the states' farm population) and home economics (apportioned on the basis of rural population).
3. Funds were made available only to that part of the program that was of "immediate" value to the vocational training of the students. Money could not be used for the capital expenses involved in setting up such a program, nor for the expenses of conducting a well-rounded program of related knowledge and general education.
4. All courses had to be "useful" and "practical." Vocational agriculture students had to participate in at least six months of directed or supervised farming practice, while at least one-half of the instruction time of trades and industry students had to be given to shop work on a useful or productive basis.[16]

The National Defense Education Act

The situation in regard to federal funding for vocational-technical education remained at a relatively low level for many years. However, an event that served as a catalyst for numerous changes in education in general also had a significant impact on vocational education. That event was the launching of Sputnik I by

16Grant Venn, *Man, Education, and Work* (Washington, D.C.: American Council on Education, 1964), p. 114.

the USSR in 1957. The event caused worldwide attention, but especially it triggered a series of events that changed the rather dormant interest in vocational-technical education.

When the implications of the launching of Sputnik were fully realized and the clamor of excitement quieted down, the spotlight was turned on the schools in an attempt to identify the problem. It was determined, it seems, that the schools were not training enough people to enter the highly skilled jobs necessary to the nation's defense effort. This lack of manpower became a serious concern in regard to the threat it posed to the United States space and defense programs. It was also determined that although the population and economy had shifted from the rural-agricultural to the urban-industrial, the types of programs sponsored by the government had not kept pace with this change. The result of the reevaluation of vocational education was the passage of the National Defense Education Act in 1958.

The impact of this Act came about in the form of area vocational programs under Title VIII of the NDEA. It authorized $15 million to be used for the training of highly skilled technicians particularly in fields where acute shortages were present and where the shortage was critical to national defense.

In the process of implementing Title VIII of NDEA, the authority for administration was placed under the same statutes and limitations as Title III of the George-Barden Act.

Venn again offers several significant comments relative to the importance of this move:

1. The Act still provided for programs of less than college grade. As in the case of the previous programs, the vocational courses offered had to be terminal and not apply toward the baccalaureate degree.

2. The new Act provided funds for area vocational educational programs which allowed any public institution willing to offer defense-related programs, programs of less than college grade, and accept students from areas not served by vocational programs to participate. The result was that articulation between secondary education and postsecondary education became confused due to the overlap in programs.

3. By linking Title VIII funds to the provisions set forth in the George-Barden Act, no distinction was made regarding vocational education and technical education. Many persons, particularly in technical education, felt this was a mistake because of the distinct requirements in course content, faculty, and standards. The argument followed that the administration and control of these programs should be in the hands of technical educators, and in the case of vocational education, in the hands of vocational educators. The feeling is that this restriction has tended to distract the attention from the work that needs to be done, particularly in technical education.[17]

17 *Ibid.*, pp. 115–117.

It is generally agreed, however, that the funds provided for vocational-technical education by the NDEA acted as a positive influence on most states to improve their programs in these areas.

A supplement to the NDEA was passed in 1961. Known as the Area Redevelopment Act, the program made available funds for vocational training of the underemployed and unemployed. This supplement represented, perhaps, the first indication of a shift in emphasis from rural-oriented programs to more urban-related programs. A stipulation of the Act included the restriction that the funds were to be used for training and retraining of persons in redevelopment areas.

Manpower Development and Training Act

The major limitation of the Area Redevelopment Act was the restriction on the population eligible for assistance. While the ARA supported programs for persons in depressed areas, the realization emerged that a need for technical training was not confined to specific areas but rather was a national problem. The result was the authorization of additional funds to support training programs for unemployed and underemployed persons who lacked the skills to be employed or to advance into more responsible and better paying jobs. The major difference allowed for the MDTA to operate without restrictions in regard to the location of potential participants.

In 1963 Congress passed several amendments to the MDTA in an effort to correct some of the flaws that were identified as hindering the program from realizing its full potential. Several limitations were identified, but basically they revolved around the lack of basic general education. The programs were geared to training in a specific skill; however, to benefit from the training offered a minimum of competency in basic education skills was required. Among others, the basic skills included the ability to read, communicate, and do simple arithmetic. As a result of these requirements, a large number of unemployed and underemployed persons were not participating in the programs. The thrust of the new amendments was aimed at correcting this situation by providing provisions for the programs to devote time to basic education skills.

Reappraisal of Vocational-Technical Programs

Probably the first major reappraisal of federal activity in vocational and technical education came about as a result of a task force appointed by President John F. Kennedy in 1961. The task force completed its work and a report was published in 1963. Among the more significant recommendations were

1. The level of federal spending for vocational and technical education be increased approximately seven times. The recommended amount for supporting quality programs to meet future needs was set at $400 million.

2. The existing programs should be expanded to include preemployment training in such areas as distributive and agricultural occupations.
3. Programs should be directed toward high school age youth with various handicaps, especially those with socio-economic and academic handicaps.
4. Programs should be expanded to include posthigh school vocational and technical education for both youth and adults. The recommendation included the suggestion that funds be made available to support the establishment of special training centers to be located in areas plagued with a high degree of unemployment or underemployment.
5. Programs should include short-term training courses for youth and adults that are unemployed or underemployed and for persons needing occupational updating.
6. Programs should be initiated designed to improve teaching efficiency, instructional materials, and other related features relative to vocational-technical education.[18]

Vocational Education Act of 1963

Many of the recommendations offered in regard to the improvement of vocational and technical education programs became a reality with the passage of the Vocational Education Act of 1963.

In an effort to overcome some of the limitations of past vocational programs, the Act provided for the extension of present programs but provided support for the development of new and innovative ones and encouraged research efforts to expand the knowledge base in this area. The Act also authorized the development of work-study programs designed to encourage youth to pursue vocational education.

The amount of money appropriated for these programs is striking in comparison to past amounts made available to vocational education. The Act of 1963 covered the expenditure of $60 million for the year 1964 with the stipulation that the support be increased to $225 million for the year 1967. This in itself marked a turning point for the expansion of vocational and technical programs and assured this area of education substantial support for years to come.

Impact of Federal Involvement

In respect to the significance of federal legislation and vocational education, Mobley and Barlow state:

> It is clear that the vocational education program has advanced more rapidly with federal funds than would have been the case without them. States that had

---

[18]Adapted from U.S. Office of Education, *Education for a Changing World of Work* (Washington, D.C.: Government Printing Office, 1963).

lagged in developing vocational education programs were induced to take action.[19]

In respect to the specific contributions of federal involvement in vocational-technical education, the authors of the previous quotation elaborate.

1. *Promotion of the national welfare.* The fruits of federal involvement in vocational-technical education have been realized during the times of war and crises. In times of war, for instance, the manpower needs to produce the necessary materials were trained and placed on the job. Whenever the national welfare has been threatened due to shortages in trained manpower, federal funds have provided a means for meeting these needs.

2. *Development of standards.* As a result of federal involvement, uniform standards have been developed for vocational programs which at least assure a minimum of quality for all programs.

3. *Improvement of administration and supervision.* In response to federal legislation, a framework for administering and supervising the programs was developed. The accountability for support created the necessity for effective administration and supervision in order to maintain the desired level of quality.

4. *Development of standards.* A positive result of federal activity has been the creation of national standards to provide programs with operating guidelines. The establishment of the Federal Board for Vocational Education contributed significantly to promoting standards for federally supported programs.

5. *Development of teacher education.* The employment of federal funds in vocational programs made it necessary to up-grade teacher education programs, both preservice and inservice. The result has been a substantial growth in the quality of such programs. For example, national and regional conferences called by the U.S. Office of Education, Division of Vocational and Technical Education, have provided an excellent means for exchanging ideas and methods relative to effective teacher preparation.

6. *Evaluation.* As in the case of most areas of education, evaluation seldom reaches a desired level until a need arises to do so. Evaluation in vocational-technical education was no exception. However, with increasing use of federal funds, the need for more adequate information regarding the effectiveness of programs arose. Although not a specific requirement of the federal acts until 1963, sufficient encouragement existed to inspire those concerned to strive for more accurate evaluation of programs. In

[19]Mayor D. Mobley and Melvin L. Barlow, "Impact of Federal Legislation and Policies Upon Vocational Education," *Sixty-Fourth Yearbook of the National Society for the Study of Education* (Chicago: U. of Chicago Press, 1965), p. 191.

this day, which some refer to as the age of accountability in federal funding, the need for better evaluation of programs is more acute.[20]

Although opposition has always existed regarding the use of federal funds for educational purposes, it appears that the general impact of federal involvement in vocational and technical education has yielded positive results. It also appears that the trend toward greater federal involvement in such programs is likely to increase during the years to come.

Vocational Guidance

With vocational programs expanding in the secondary school a need has arisen for expanded guidance services for students. The aim of such programs is to provide guidance for the student in the problems and techniques in choosing an occupation and in becoming adjusted to it. More specifically, vocational guidance performs the function of providing students with information that will help them to make wise decisions concerning the selection of vocational courses and the relationship of this selection to future goals. Bent and Unruh list several factors that influence the selection of vocational programs or individual courses for which students may need professional help.

1. *Future intentions of students.* A prime factor in selecting a vocational program or a course in vocational education is the probable future intentions of the student. The problem, of course, is that the student is not always sure of future goals. Different vocations require different types of training. Some are mastered on the job, some through specialized programs, while others require considerable formal schooling. The task of vocational guidance is to help students become aware of the requirements for various vocations so they may plan their preparation accordingly.

2. If students plan to attend a trade school after graduation they might be guided into one of the prerequisite courses. If they plan to enter a vocation immediately after graduation or before, the proper selection of courses will help them in securing a job. In some cases, students who plan to go to college may elect to take a vocational course for personal satisfaction or some simply as a matter of interest.

3. *Projected time in school.* Often it is possible to identify, rather early, those persons who may not remain in school to graduation. Students who do not remain in school until graduation often find it difficult to find productive employment due to the lack of a salable skill. Vocational programs can help in this respect but the student often requires help in identifying the need for such training. Students who plan some formal training after graduation from high school may require different types of

[20] *Ibid.*, pp. 193–195.

vocational training than those who plan to enter the world of work before graduation.

4. _Success in nonvocational subjects._ In general, students who are not successful in general education often find it difficult to achieve in college. Whether they graduate or not, students who pursue a general education program at the secondary level with a low degree of achievement often find it difficult to find productive employment in the world of work. In this respect, vocational guidance plays a significant role in helping students to select experiences that will aid them in securing and maintaining employment.

5. There is a considerable difference between directing students into vocational courses and just placing them in such courses because they were not achieving well in academic subjects. In the past, this practice was responsible for fostering the attitude that vocational education was a dumping ground for all students who could not succeed in the academic area. A strong vocational guidance program can do much to remove attitudes of this nature.[21]

Vocational Guidance Services

There is, of course, some overlap between general guidance programs and those specifically designated as vocational guidance services. Often the functions of vocational guidance and general guidance are performed by the same person. With specific reference to vocational education, the services performed by vocational guidance are

1. Making available to students information pertaining to their abilities, interests, and other information that might be useful in making a decision concerning a vocation.

2. Providing comprehensive information to students regarding educational and occupational opportunities open to them.

3. Providing counseling services to individuals regarding educational and occupational problems.

4. Providing programs for aiding in the placement and adjustment of students entering the world of work.

It is generally agreed that a valuable addition to any school staff is a person whose primary responsibility is in the area of vocational guidance. Too often vocational education is used for purposes such as assigning students with academic or disciplinary problems to vocational education. When this occurs both the student and the vocational program suffer.

A final point regarding vocational education is that the movement toward a closer relationship between this phase of education and the total school cur-

[21]Rudyard K. Bent and Adolph Unruh, _Secondary School Curriculum_ (Lexington, Mass.: Heath, 1969), pp. 161–162.

riculum moves us closer to a truly comprehensive secondary school, a goal we have talked about for a long time but have attained in only a few instances. Flexibility, individualization of instruction, and a variety of experiences to fit the needs of all students are the means by which a comprehensive curriculum is achieved.

Selected References

Barlow, Melvin L. (ed.), *Vocational Education: The Sixty-Fourth Yearbook of the National Society for the Study of Education.* Chicago: The University of Chicago Press, 1965.

Bent, R. K., and Adolph Unruh, *Secondary School Curriculum.* Lexington, Mass.: D. C. Heath & Company, 1970, Chapter 7.

Ehlers, Henry, and C. Lee Gordon (eds.), *Crucial Issues in Education.* 3d ed. New York: Holt, Rinehart and Winston, Inc., 1966, Chapter 4.

Miller, Robert (ed.), *Education in a Changing Society.* Washington, D.C.: National Education Association, 1964.

National Committee on Secondary Education, *Educating For Work.* Washington, D.C.: National Association of Secondary School Principals, 1967.

Roberts, Roy W., *Vocational and Practical Arts Education.* New York: Harper & Row, Publishers, 1965.

Rosenberg, Jerry M., *Automation, Manpower, and Education.* New York: Random House, Inc., 1966, Chapter 4.

Venn, Grant, *Man, Education and Work.* Washington, D.C.: American Council on Education, 1964.

CHAPTER 12

STUDENT ACTIVITIES

The basic purpose of the early schools in this country, and the sole basis for their existence, was the development of scholarship. This pattern of schooling existed until the turn of the century, when a type of dualism emerged in American secondary schools in relation to the objectives and the manner in which these objectives were implemented. In addition to emphasis on scholarship, a whole series of activities developed in an effort to provide students with worthwhile experiences outside the classroom setting.

The exact origin of student activities in the secondary school remains obscure, but the basic expansion of such programs in American secondary school began during the early part of this century. The rapid development of such programs in secondary schools can be attributed, in part, to two factors.

1. The desire of parents to see their children perform either in an athletic contest or in some related school activity.
2. The belief, on the part of educators, that many of the basic needs of students could best be met outside the formal classroom.

With the backing of parents and educators, the student-activity program in secondary schools has flourished. It is rare today to find a school without some type of activity program even in schools where only the bare essentials of an academic program can be offered.

A variety of terms are used to describe this facet of secondary education, but one of the most common used today is "student activities." Others commonly used are: extracurricular, cocurricular, and extraclass. Terms used to describe a particular program are not always accurate in describing the intended meaning. In this case the different terms can be used to gage the changing emphasis on such programs. The term *extracurricular*, for example, denotes curricular status but implies the activities that come under this term are outside the regular curriculum. The more recent term *cocurricular* implies a closer relationship with the regular curriculum.

Another term for modern activity programs is *extraclass*. The term suggests that everything a student does under the auspices of the school is a direct extension of classroom experiences. The term does not imply that the same

396

experiences occur in extraclass activities that occur in regular classrooms but rather that these additional experiences are included in the curriculum to help achieve the overall objectives of the school. Using this definition, the educational outcomes for a math club and a mathematics course are not the same. The math club, however, might be a direct outgrowth of the mathematics class and operate to satisfy a need that cannot be achieved in the regular classroom. Although the term "extraclass" is more definitive of the nature of modern programs than the earlier terms, it still denotes an "extra" activity.

Unfortunately, there appears to be little uniformity in terminology when referring to these programs, which may account for the variety of terms used to denote such activity. A rather general term, yet one that is gaining in popularity, is simply "student activities." In employing this term, Robbins and Williams define student activities as "an aspect of the curriculum which is voluntarily engaged in by students, which is sponsored by the faculty, and which does not carry academic credit toward promotion or graduation."[1]

Place of Student Activities

Before proceeding to a more specific discussion of the place of student activities in the secondary school curriculum, it may well serve a purpose to review some of the basic assumptions on which the student activities program is based.

1. Student activities provide an opportunity for students to engage in worthwhile activities under the professional supervision of adult leadership.
2. Student activities serve as a safety valve for student energies that might otherwise be channeled into underdesirable avenues.
3. Student activities furnish the student with additional opportunities to satisfy psychological needs such as the need for recognition, the need for acceptance, the need for approval, and the need for success.
4. Student activities provide an opportunity to extend the academic curriculum by providing experiences not available in regular classrooms.
5. Student activities serve as a motivating force for keeping students in school who might otherwise drop out.
6. Student activities offer a variety of opportunities to develop creative talents.
7. Student activities offer students the opportunity to fulfill the need to socialize that often cannot be met in the regular classroom.
8. Student activities provide an opportunity for teachers to become better acquainted with students and offer many chances for informal guidance.
9. Student activities provide an excellent training ground for the development of citizenship.[2]

[1]Jerry H. Robbins and Stirling B. Williams, *Student Activities in the Innovative School* (Minneapolis: Burgess, 1969), p. 42.
[2]Peter F. Oliva, *The Secondary School Today*, 2d ed. (Scranton, Pa.: Intext Educational Publishers, 1972), pp. 174–175

Developing or maintaining a student-activity program in the secondary school is usually justified on the basis of the foregoing assumptions. Although some empirical evidence exists to support these claims, all do not enjoy such support. However, the logic employed to justify such programs apparently has been strong enough to convince most of the worth of such experiences.

The precise relationship between the student-activity program and regular classroom activities has never been clearly defined except for the generally accepted idea that a relationship should exist between them. In an attempt to place the student-activity program in the total school program, several points of view are held by those who plan and execute school programs.

One position extends the idea that the basic curriculum is the heart of a school and the very reason for its existence; therefore any activity sponsored by the school should be directly related to the basic classroom program. In other words, the student-activity program should exist as enrichment for the subject areas that constitute the core of the curriculum. For example, math clubs should exist in order to enrich the basic instruction in mathematics by allowing students the opportunity to explore ideas outside the classroom setting.

Another position, quite opposite to the enrichment idea, is that a relationship does not have to exist between the student activity program and the regular classroom. According to this position, a certain body of subject matter constitutes the core of the school's program and should stand as the central focus of the school. Activities outside this central focus may be thought of as avocational activities without any direct relationship to the subject matter curriculum. The position does not negate the value of the student-activity program but rather places it as secondary to the regular program of studies. For example, activities such as sports, hobby clubs, and the like are justified on the basis of leisure-time training or simply enjoyment but exist separate and apart from the subject curriculum and contribute to a different set of objectives.

While the enrichment idea is rather rigid in the types of activities permitted, the avocational position is quite flexible. The avocational position follows the idea that a clear-cut distinction exists between the subject matter curriculum and the student activity program.

A third position concerning the place of student activities might be called that of immediate interest.[3] The advocates of this position hold that the learning experiences of youth are conditioned by their readiness to learn and their interest in pursuing certain types of activities. Following this position, the student-activity program should be governed by student interests and activities provided that will help satisfy these interests.

Although some merit exists in each position, taken alone they leave something to be desired. The modern view appears to draw from all three positions

[3]Frederick C. Gruber and Thomas Beatty, *Secondary School Activities* (New York: McGraw-Hill, 1954), p. 10.

when talking about the place of student activities. The current view, at least that shared by many leading educators, is that the student-activity program should be an educative experience. Activities should be planned and executed on the basis of principles and practices calculated to bring about the greatest contribution to educational objectives. The key to this view is educational objectives. Educational experiences, in or out of the classroom, should be determined on the basis of objectives rather than some preconceived notion about student activities per se.

We may then conclude that student activities may grow out of the subject curriculum, may consist of activities designed to supplement the subjects, or may be independent of them.

Typical Student-Activity Programs

There are few regulations regarding the types of student activities that might be included in any secondary school program. However, state agencies, regional accrediting associations, college entrance requirements, and tradition contribute heavily toward a rather uniform regular curriculum in the secondary school. Although these outside influences are not mandatory in determining a student-activity program, a high degree of uniformity exists in student-activity programs in the country. This uniformity is due, at least in part, to the proven success of certain types of programs which has led to a common acceptance of such programs as valuable components of student-activity programs.

Although considerable flexibility exists, there are several broad classifications of activities that are included in the majority of secondary school programs. These are: student-council activities, school assembly activities, athletic activities, publishing activities, clubs, and individual activities. The extensiveness of specific activities included under these broad classifications varies considerably from school to school, from state to state, and from region to region depending upon the interests of the students involved, the interests of the community involved, and the resources available to a given school to promote such programs.

Student-Council Activities

One of the chief purposes of public education in America is to develop well-informed individuals that can function effectively in a democracy. One means of accomplishing this goal is through active participation by students in school affairs. This idea is based on the premise that democratic citizenship can be learned much in the same manner as history, mathematics, or any other subject.

The terminology used for this aspect of student activities is again reflective of changing emphases. An earlier term used to denote student participation in school affairs was "student government." The term implied that students were being given the responsibility for self government in many aspects of the school's operation including major decision making, discipline, and the like. This idea lead to the discussion of how far students should be allowed to go in the area of self-government. In some cases discipline was turned over to students and the result was largely unsatisfactory.

With the changing emphasis on student participation in school affairs, a more descriptive term has arisen to describe this aspect of the student-activities program. The term used most often today is "student council," which denotes a type of organization similar to that of a neighborhood council.

Using this term, the basic function of the student council is not to run the school but to determine the wishes and desires of the student body and make them known to the administration and faculty.[4]

PURPOSES OF THE STUDENT COUNCIL. The student council should be comprised of a group of elected students with responsibility for determining student affairs that are outside the classroom but within the jurisdiction of the school. In this respect, the student council can provide an excellent training ground for democratic living as well as provide a meaningful means for participation in affairs of the school.

Among the more specific purposes of the student council are:

1. To provide specific citizenship training in preparation for life in a democracy.
2. To provide a means for students to actively participate in the management of their own affairs.
3. To encourage closer relationships between students, faculty, administration, and the community in general.
4. To provide a means for students to satisfy certain needs that cannot be met in a regular classroom situation.
5. To provide a means for students to become more self-directive by allowing for meaningful responsibility and initiative.
6. To provide a means for learning social cooperation and sharing.
7. To provide a means for building school morale by giving students a say in their own affairs.
8. To provide a means for students to develop qualities of leadership and followership.[5]

Bear summarizes these purposes well in the following statement:

> The main function of the student council is to provide learning experiences for students. Its principal contribution to learning is the development of good citizenship which is one of the cardinal objectives of the schools, both public and

---

[4]Arthur Kent, "And Finally—A Definition of Student Council," *School Activities* (May 1969), p. 11.

[5]Adapted from Robbins and Williams, *Student Activities in the Innovative School,* p. 81.

nonpublic. For this reason the student council is no longer considered to be extracurricular or an adjunct to the curriculum, but an integral part of it.[6]

During the later part of the 1960's a change in attitude toward student participation in school affairs began to emerge. Tied to youthful unrest in general, charges were brought against student councils stating that this was largely a meaningless activity. Proposals were made ranging from complete control over school affairs to at least providing students the opportunity to participate in the major decision-making process of the school. Educators have responded in a variety of ways, but the most common has been to hold to the more traditional view of the role of students in the operation and maintenance of the school.

Probably, many of the complaints brought against the student council are based on fact. No doubt, many student councils are "window-dressing" and contribute little to student involvement in school decision making. However, there are many student councils that do make a significant contribution to the decision-making process by working within the boundaries set for them.

For educators to abdicate their responsibility for running the school would be an error. However, much is to be gained by recognizing the contribution of the student council, assuming its representiveness of the student body, and incooperating their ideas and suggestions into the total school program.

School Assemblies

One of the traditional types of student activities that have contributed greatly to the total school program over the years is the assembly program. Administrative assemblies are considered of a different nature in that the primary purpose of this type of activity is to accomplish an administrative purpose rather than to meet the needs of students.

School assemblies are an excellent vehicle for students to express themselves in a variety of ways and provide one of the most forceful means of developing and maintaining school unity. They can be a means for accomplishing many purposes that could not be achieved in any other manner. For example, the assembly can provide a means for diffusing the ideas, thoughts, and talents of students to the total student body while meeting a social purpose necessary in the lives of young people.

Specifically, the purposes of the assembly program in secondary schools are these:

1. To cultivate school spirit and unity.
2. To provide a means for students to develop leadership training.
3. To provide a means for emphasizing proper audience habits.
4. To recognize worthy achievement.

[6]Williard Bear, "Functions, Objectives, and Basic Principles of the Student Council," *The Student Council in the Secondary School* (Washington, D.C.: National Association of Student Councils, 1962), p. 7.

5. To acquaint students with school and community affairs.

6. To provide entertainment for students.

There are other purposes for the assembly program but the six mentioned above serve the purpose. The main point, however, is not so much what takes place at assemblies but who plans and executes the programs. One of the consistent complaints of students regarding assembly programs is that they are constantly placed in the role of spectators rather than participants. If it is recognized that the school has the final authority over the assembly prógram, much can be gained by giving students the responsibility for planning and executing programs of special interest to them. The role of the school should be one of providing assistance where needed while assuring that programs presented meet with the standards set for the school.

Athletics

The vast majority of secondary schools have some form of athletic program. Types of programs range from highly competitive programs in all sports to one-sport schools that compete on a rather low level. Most schools, both large and small, incorporate some type of intramural program into their school.

There is little doubt that the athletic component of the student-activity program commands the most attention and support in schools today. More specifically, interscholastic football and basketball have emerged through the years as the main aspects of the activity program. This has resulted in a problem of maintaining a proper balance between these two activities and the remainder of the programs. There are numerous reasons for this situation, two of which are described in the following statements:

1. Americans are sports-loving people. This love is reflected both in the way people participate in sports and the large number of avid sports spectators. America is a competitive society and this is also reflected in the leisure-time activities of people. It does not come as a surprise, then, when ten thousand people will attend a football game, probably the most competitive game of all, and a ping-pong match may go begging for spectators. In essence, Americans thrive on competitive activities, either as participants or spectators, and lend their support to the maintenance of these activities in the schools.

2. Money is also a factor. Schools with thriving programs of football and basketball enjoy considerable income that would not be forthcoming if the major emphasis was placed on individual sports or less competitive activities such as gymnastics. Although all programs of this nature are not self-supporting, they do manage to support a large proportion of the costs of such programs, and in some instances, have enough left over to help support other activity programs of the school. This becomes a strong argument for those who advocate major emphasis on certain activities.

Operating under the assumption that interscholastic competition is here to stay, the primary concern of schools should be the attempt to provide as many additional activities as possible for students who do not participate in the major sports.

Desirable physical activities that schools should consider in addition to major sports include

1. *A strong physical education program.* The physical education program of a school is distinguished from the major sports program in that activities should be provided for all students. The major objective of this program should be that of physical training. In addition, the program should provide opportunities for students to gain skill and appreciation for activities that have a carryover value to later life. Examples of this are golf, tennis, and badminton. For this type of activity to be effective, a well-organized program must exist and must not be an adjunct to the major sports program.

2. *An organized intramural program.* This highly desirable extension of the basic physical education program provides opportunities for students to compete in a variety of activities among themselves. Programs of this nature can include both individual and team sports but should avoid approaching the level of competition found in the major sports. The emphasis should be on active participation for all and not for the few that can perform the best.

3. *An active supportive program.* In an effort to involve as many students as possible in this type of student activity, it is desirable to develop a set of supportive activities built around the athletic program. This is especially necessary in relation to major sports where only a few of the student body actually participate. These activities might include booster clubs, cheerleaders, marching organizations, and other types of organizations and activities that can be built around the athletic program.

Publishing Activities

The degree of publishing activities engaged in by schools varies considerably depending primarily on the size of the school. The three most common school publications are school newspapers, annuals, and handbooks.

The basic justification for including such activities in the school program is to give students the opportunity to participate in a worthwhile learning experience. Students participating in this type of activity learn to gather news, compose articles, write editorials, and acquire the experience in all aspects of production of printed material. The activity also makes a significant contribution to those not actually participating in that the product is of immediate interest to them.

In recent years students have become critical of the controls placed upon them in regard to student publications. A by-product of this criticism has been the rather recent phenomenon of the "underground" publication. The issue of control is not new but seems to be more in the forefront today. Controls placed upon student publications vary in intensity but most are justified on the basis of insuring "proper taste" for student publications. The issue is becoming a real problem for schools and will continue to be for some time to come. There is no quick solution, but it seems proper to assert that schools do have authority over student publications and should act accordingly.

Clubs and Individual Activities

There are many needs and interests of students that cannot be met in the regular classroom. However, many of these needs and interests can be met in organized clubs and individual activities outside the classroom. Activities of this nature may be classified as hobby, social, service, subject matter, or preprofessional. In some cases the activity might be individual. For example, where no organized club exists, a student may pursue his interest on his own. A well-planned set of club and individual activities contributes significantly to enrichment of the total school program. This type of activity should be encouraged in that the educational and other benefits achieved by students far outweigh the problems associated with such programs. The basic criteria for creating clubs should be student interest and school and community acceptance. The most effective activities of this nature are those created and maintained by students themselves with faculty and administration participating in a helping role.

Administration of Student-Activity Programs

One of the major administrative decisions that must be made concerning the student-activity program is the selection of activities to be included in the program. Several factors are involved in this type of decision, but the ultimate responsibility rests with the administration. Bent and Unruh offer a set of criteria, expressed in question form, that appear helpful in making this type of decision.

1. To what extent does the activity contribute to the major aims and purposes of secondary education?
2. Is it desired by the students rather than imposed on them?
3. Is an interested and qualified teacher available for sponsoring the activity?
4. Are time, facilities, and space available?
5. If it is a group activity or many students are needed for successful participation, as in athletics, are a sufficient number of students interested who are capable of participating?
6. Is it approved by society?
7. Is it in keeping with state and local laws?
8. Is there danger involved?
9. Is it costly to pupils?
10. Is it democratic? Open to all?[7]

[7]Reprinted by permission of the publisher, from Rudyard K. Bent and Adolph Unruh, *Secondary School Curriculum* (Lexington, Mass.: Heath, 1969), p. 143.

Careful selection of student activities are necessary to insure a well balanced and successful program. Seeking honest answers to the preceding questions can be extremely helpful to those who have to make the decisions.

From an administrative standpoint, several other factors must be considered in planning and maintaining a successful student-activity program. Among the more important ones are personnel, resources, and control. Other factors must also be considered, but for the purposes of this brief description, the three mentioned will suffice.

Personnel

To insure a successful activity program, a number of people must involve themselves in the program. The number and the degree of involvement will depend largely on the size of the school and the emphasis placed upon student activities. It is necessary, then, that each school provide the most efficient type of organization within its capabilities and needs. Regardless of size, the following personnel should be involved in a student-activity program.

1. *The Principal.* By virtue of his position, the principal is responsible for everything that goes on in the school. In terms of the student-activity program, the principal maintains the same authority as with any other program of the school. In some cases he may delegate this authority to an assistant principal or, in the case of larger schools, to a director of student activities.

2. *Faculty Sponsor.* Probably the most important ingredient in a successful student-activity program is the faculty sponsor. The primary duty of the sponsor is to provide guidance for the conduct of an activity. Basically, there are three methods for selecting faculty sponsors. First, faculty members may be allowed to select activities they wish to sponsor. Second, students may be allowed to select the faculty sponsor. Third, the school administration selects faculty sponsors. Without question, the most common method of selecting faculty sponsors is administrative selection. The justification used for following this practice is that the administration is in the best position to monitor teaching load and to utilize teacher qualifications most effectively. To be effective, however, this method of selection should also take into account teacher willingness and student acceptance. An unhappy faculty sponsor or a faculty sponsor not compatable with students involved in the activity are not ingredients that make an effective program.

Resources

The allocation of resources is an administrative decision necessary for the operation of an effective activity program. While the financial aspects of the program usually command the most attention, other factors are equally important. In addition to finances, factors of space and time must be dealt with if an effective program is to emerge.

In many instances, student-activity programs have grown faster than the resources available for support. This is particularly true in the case of finances. The usual sources of revenue for activity programs include:

1. Proceeds of athletic events.
2. Funds specifically budgeted for the activity program.
3. Sale of such items as candy, school supplies, and the like.
4. Student fees, assessments, and fines.

In recent years, funds for many programs have been lacking, partly as a result of a sagging economy. However, students have an ingenious way of providing resources for programs they deem worthwhile.

Funds secured from the sale of tickets for athletic contests, various productions, and similar programs should be sufficient to meet the expenses of an activity program. However, this is not always the case. Probably the best method of financing the activity program is through the regular budgetary channels of the schools. The danger of relying on fees, assessments, activity cards, and the like is that many students may be excluded from participation due to the cost involved. If an activity is deemed worthwhile, the school should provide the major portion of the cost.

Space is another factor that often presents serious problems for schools. While schools manage to provide space for the major competitive sports, this is not the case for most of the other activities. In the design of a new building, consideration should be given to providing space for the activity program. A club room, office space for the student council, and an activities workroom are examples of the kind of space needed. In existing buildings it is sometimes possible to find usuable space by converting a storage area or by partitioning part of a classroom.

Determining the time to be alloted to activities presents another problem for schools. Robbins and Williams comment on this factor when they say:

> If student activities are valuable enough to be sponsored by the school, if they are legitimate means of accomplishing the objectives of the school, student activities can, and should, be scheduled for students and teachers just as the more formal curricular experiences.[8]

Control

The problem of administrative control of student activities is becoming more intense in today's schools. The direct control of the student-activity program operating within a school is the responsibility of the principal. Some of this responsibility is delegated by the principal to faculty and students. To offset many of the problems associated with administering an activity program, school ad-

[8]Jerry H. Robbins and Stirling B. Williams, *op. cit.*, p. 219.

ministrators have formed associations to aid in regulating this component of the school program. The earliest associations grew out of the need to regulate competition in major sports and has spread to include the entire activities program. The value of associations of this nature is that some consistency can be provided in regulating the various activities both on and off campus. When rules and regulations are fostered in conjunction with others, the problems associated with administering the program are lessened.

Another element involved in the control of student activities is law. Although the United States Constitution is silent on the matter of education, the states do reserve the right to regulate education. Specific legislation regarding the activity program in schools is rare, but inferences to related legislation is often used when making decisions regarding some aspect of the program. For example, a decision to permit a certain kind of activity to exist in a school might be based on "liability" statutes even though the specific activity is not mentioned in the law.

One way of easing the tension regarding the control of student activities is to include students in the decision-making process. Student representation on the regulatory bodies seems to be a step in the right direction.

Improving Student-Activity Programs

Student activities are an established part of the secondary school curriculum. To aid in planning and maintaining a worthwhile program, schools need to address themselves to the following factors.

Involvement

The factor of involvement can be addressed from two directions, teacher involvement and student involvement. It is generally agreed that involvement in student activities, for both staff and students, is desirable. However, a problem can and often does arise concerning overinvolvement or underinvolvement.

In many schools today a wide variety of activities exist. For some people involvement is a way of life and this type of attitude carries over into the activities program. Although teachers as well as students fall into this category, students have a greater tendency to become overinvolved, since teachers are normally well occupied during the day with regular classroom activities. The danger of overinvolvement, at least in many instances, is that when students become too involved with activities regular classroom work suffers. When this occurs, and it does, the basic reason for the existence of an activity program is violated. Another danger of overinvolvement is that when a few students participate in many activities, chances for others to participate, who may need the experiences more, become less.

Schools use a variety of methods for controlling involvement of students in activity programs. One method which has met with varying degrees of success is the point system. Basically, the point system is designed to distribute participation in the activities. The system involves awarding a certain number of points for membership in an organization. Additional points are given for work in a leadership capacity or for holding office. Schools vary in terms of the number of points they will allow a student to accumulate but most attempt to set a total in line with the student's other responsibilities.

Many educators feel that underinvolvement is a more serious problem than overinvolvement. Some have charged that in our quest for controlling student involvement we have neglected to encourage those who could greatly profit from the activity experience. The majority of dropout studies, for example, show that students dropping out of school have not participated, to any extent, in the school's activity program. Several factors have contributed to this lack of participation. Among the prime causes of underinvolvement are entrance requirements and scheduling. Many schools have traditionally set requirements for students to meet before becoming involved in an activity. Central among these requirements has been grade point average, which automatically eliminated some students from participation. The difficulty, of course, is that many students who cannot perform well in regular classwork are not allowed to pursue an activity in which they are interested and wherein they may have an opportunity for success. Denying an opportunity for a chance to succeed in the case of students who fail to succeed in the regular classroom often results in negative consequences.

The time alloted to student activities, particularly in situations where activities are scheduled after school or on Saturdays, tends to eliminate some students from participation. Students who must work or lack the transportation to attend activities find it difficult, or impossible, to become a part of some activity. In any case it seriously limits the type of participation possible to the student.

Balance

The most common criticism brought against the activity program can be traced, at least in part, to the overemphasis of one or more activities. Due to the high interest of student activities to students, parents, and others, the temptation is ever present to place undue emphasis on some programs, particularly those with great spectator appeal. Activities that seem to cause the most problems are the competitive sports. However, in some schools, activities such as band tend to become overemphasized.

The importance of establishing specific and well-defined objectives for the total school program again becomes evident when the problem of overemphasis arises. A community that is enthusiastic about competitive sports or band competition, for example, may directly or indirectly influence undue emphasis on such programs. Some schools have let themselves become so involved with one activity, usually football or basketball, that their entire program of student activities, and often aspects of the academic program, are planned to favor this activity. Excessive expenditures for stadiums—their use being almost exclusively for athletic contests—and salaries for coaches exceeding, by a significant degree in some cases, those for other teachers of equal competence and experience are only the outward signs of such imbalances. The answer, again, can be found in the overall objectives of the school and in attempting to provide experiences that will aid in achieving these objectives. If this is taken seriously, a proper balance can be maintained.

Evaluation

Evaluation of the student-activity program should command the same attention as evaluation in any other aspect of the curriculum. Unfortunately, evaluation of the secondary school curriculum, in general, leaves much to be desired, and evaluation of the student-activity program has suffered the same fate.

For evaluation to be effective it should be both objective and continuous. The program should be examined at the end of each year, or at least every two years, at which time recommendations concerning changes or improvements should be made. The evaluation should be objective, but not necessarily geared to a rigid design, and should involve students as well as the faculty and administration.

To aid in developing evaluative procedures for student-activity programs, the following general criteria should prove helpful.

1. The student-activity program should grow out of and augment the regular classroom program of the school.
2. The student-activity program should provide students with the opportunity to develop those characteristics recognized as objectives of the total school program.
3. The student-activity program should provide a balanced program for all students.[9]

The following are some of the more specific items that should be examined when evaluating student-activity programs.

1. Are student needs and interests given special attention in planning and maintaining the program?
2. Does the program reflect the presence of democratic ideals and processes?
3. Is the program designed to serve all students?
4. Do such factors as cost inhibit participation of some students?
5. Are teachers assigned to activities on a fair and equitable basis?
6. Are fund-raising procedures held within acceptable limits?

In the final analysis, the major criteria that should be employed is whether or not the activity program is contributing to achieving the objectives of the school.

[9]Adapted from Lindley J. Stiles et al., *Secondary Education in the United States* (New York: Harcourt, 1962), p. 286.

In terms of evaluation procedures, a number of acceptable methods are available. Some are more formal than others, but selection should be made on the basis of local needs and the utilization of acceptable practices. The following list illustrates some of the possible methods available for evaluating the activity program. Among the more common are:

1. Questionnaires, check lists, rating scales, and the like.
2. Evaluation by outside groups such as visiting committees or individual experts.
3. On-site visits to other schools for the purpose of gathering comparative data.
4. Conferences with faculty groups and individual faculty members.
5. General observations and impressions of student reactions relative to the effectiveness of the program.
6. Formal evaluation of the program, i.e., employing acceptable design and analysis procedures.[10]

For evaluation to be effective, the results must be used to improve the program. Dumas and Beckner state:

> Based on the best judgment of those making the evaluation, conclusions must be drawn about the effectiveness of the activities. If the evaluation is a periodic, more formal effort, a committee composed of both students and faculty will usually make this judgment and suggest ways to make improvements. Continuous evaluation in the light of these considerations would be part of each student's and sponsor's everyday attempts to improve the program. In the final analysis, the value of the activities program will be evidenced in the attitudes and growth of students, the approval of the faculty, and the enthusiasm of the community for the program.[11]

Summary

The sole justification for the student-activity program of any school is the contribution it makes to the overall objectives of the school. In planning a student-activity program the first step should be to identify the objectives of the school to which student activities can contribute. Too often activities are selected and then, as an afterthought, matched with some objective. The outcome is not always desirable and often leads to an unbalanced program.

The next step in planning and maintaining an effective program is to select those activities that best reflect the stated objectives. Ideally, this step should be accomplished with the participation of students, faculty, and the administration.

Finally, the student-activity program should be continually evaluated in order to assess the effectiveness of the activities in achieving the objectives of the

---

[10]Adapted from Wayne Dumas and Weldon Beckner, *Introduction to Secondary Education* (Scranton, Pa.: Intext, 1968), p. 232.

[11]*Ibid.*, p. 233.

school. The evaluation should result in changes and modifications as the information dictates.

It should be noted that the overall attitude of young people toward school and school activities is changing. At one extreme is the student revolt that has been a part of the school scene during the late 1960's and the early 1970's. The results have ranged from open confrontation with school authorities to violent action on the part of the students and others. At the other extreme is the sincere expression of concern for needed changes in the school program. Regardless of the means used to express their concern, students seem to be saying the same thing—we want more participation in school affairs. As a result of the changing attitudes of young people, it seems accurate to say that the organization and operation of student activities, particularly activities such as the student council and student publications, will undergo some drastic changes in the near future.

Selected References

Frederick, Robert, *Student Activities in American Education.* New York: Center for Applied Research in Education, 1965.

_____, *The Third Curriculum.* New York: Appleton-Century-Crofts, Inc., 1959.

Graham, Grace, "Student Activities: An Overview and A Rationale," *Bulletin of the National Association of Secondary School Principals* 48 (October 1964).

Robbins, Jerry H., and Stirling B. Williams, *Student Activities in the Innovative School.* Minneapolis: Burgess Publishing Company, 1969.

CHAPTER 13

GUIDANCE AND COUNSELING

The need for guidance grows as the secondary school continues to expand and change. The need for guidance and counseling in the areas of course selection, vocational choices, and solving personal problems and value conflicts continues to increase for students.

Relationship of Guidance to the Curriculum

Assuming the definition of curriculum as all the experiences encountered by students under the supervision of the school, the guidance program of a school becomes an intergral part of the total curriculum. In recent years this relationship between guidance and the curriculum has been recognized and has resulted in increased emphasis on guidance programs in schools. There is little doubt that many of the adverse effects of school experienced by a growing number of students is tied, at least in part, to the curriculum. For example, recent studies have indicated a significant relationship exists between the curriculum and such factors as failure, retardation, truancy, dropouts, and others. Even without substantial cause-and-effect data, the information is strong enough to warrant action. The action needed, and being taken in some schools, is the activation, or reactivation, of an effective guidance and counseling program to aid students in achieving a greater degree of harmony with the curriculum. Mathewson supports this position with the following statement:

> The whole rationale of the developmental phases rests upon the provision of a wide variety of curricular and extra-curricular experiences for students and the evaluation of these by each individual in relation to his own needs and goals. Subject-matter instruction, individual study, cocurricular activities, student government, athletics, and other aspects of the school curriculum may affect student development favorably or adversely.[1]

[1]Robert H. Mathewson, *Guidance Policy and Practice,* 3d ed. (New York: Harper, 1962), p. 289.

This increased awareness of the necessity for guidance in achieving the objectives of education has led to a closer working relationship between the principal component of the curriculum, the teacher, and the guidance program of the school. In too many instances in the past, the role of the teacher and the role of guidance personnel were considered separate. Teachers have been traditionally looked upon as imparters of knowledge with the secondary purpose of looking after the needs of the student. The proportion of time spent by teachers imparting knowledge has far outweighed the time spent in guidance activities with students. The reason, of course, is that a teacher with a daily pupil load of 150–200, working with thirty or forty students in five, six, or even seven classes per day can scarcely know little more about the pupils than their names.

If the guidance program of a school is to be effective, a closer working relationship between teachers and counselors must emerge. This relationship should arise because of the common professional goal shared by all school personnel—the total well-being of the student. The need exists for both teachers and guidance personnel to realize that they share common goals. Such an awareness should result in a more effective working relationship and enhance the benefits received by students when the curriculum and student guidance are planned to complement each other.

Definition and Scope of the Guidance Program

Any attempt to define guidance must take into consideration that guidance is both a group of services and a point of view. A guidance point of view might be summarized in the following statements:

1. Awareness of and respect for the fact that all individuals are different.
2. Respect for the worth and dignity of each individual.
3. Recognition of the right of every individual for self-growth and self-development.
4. Recognition that nothing should limit an individual's development and mobility other than ability, effort, and the security of the rights of others.
5. Recognition of the interrelatedness of the individual and group welfare.
6. Recognition of the right of every individual for the opportunity of social and economic mobility within the prevailing occupational and class structure.[2]

These statements reflect the view that guidance is a service dedicated to working with individuals in an effort to assist them in achieving their full potential. This view is consistent with an educational philosophy common in this country. Some of the basic tenets of this philosophy state that:

1. Each pupil is a person and has value as such.

[2]Adapted from Edwin E. Vineyard, "Toward a Philosophy of School Counseling," *The School Counselor*, Vol. 2 (March 1964), pp. 179–180.

2. Each pupil learns as an individual what he experiences.
3. Each pupil has the right to an opportunity for the highest level of education from which he is capable of profiting.
4. The total development of the individual, rather than academic progress alone, is the concern of the school.
5. The school is a socializing agency concerned not only with individual development but also with integration of the individual into the larger society.
6. To meet the differing needs for self-realization of varied pupils, the school must offer a varied and comprehensive program of experiences.
7. To meet the differing needs for self-realization of varied pupils, the school must offer, in addition to the teaching or instructional service, various other specialized and augmenting services.[3]

Guidance is also a program of services. Usually, the guidance program of a school consists of the following:

1. The counseling service.
2. The individual inventory
3. The information service
4. The placement service
5. The follow-up service.

Probably the most important part of the guidance program in any school is the counseling service. This part of the program is designed to assist students in self-understanding and self-management, both of which are necessary for proper adjustment to school and to life outside the school. The individual inventory is a procedure for securing information about the student which is used in guiding the student both academically and personally. This phase of the program normally includes both the testing program and the activities associated with it. The information service is designed to provide information for students in planning their educational and vocational futures. The placement service operates to aid students in moving to the next step, whether it be outside or inside the school program. The final service of guidance programs is the follow-up, and consists primarily of keeping track of students in order to provide feedback for the school. These functions, and others, are discussed more fully later in this chapter.

Development of the Guidance Program

Before the turn of the century relatively few students attended secondary school. Since most of the students who did attend had intentions of going to college, the curriculum emphasized a program of studies that would help students to achieve this goal. Few provisions were made for students who had other goals

[3]Sidney Hook, *Education for Modern Man* (New York: Dial, 1946), p. 2.

or for those who lacked the ability to pursue the traditional secondary curriculum.

Shortly after the turn of the century a rapid increase in secondary enrollment occurred. Along with the rapid increase in enrollment came diverse types of students. While students attending secondary school before 1900 were mostly interested in preparation for college, many students attending secondary school during the early part of the 1900's had little interest in or aptitude for college attendance. A large number of students had no clear purpose in view following completion of secondary school, while others had intentions in the direction of a vocation which required a type of preparation quite different from that which constituted the curriculum of that day.

In an effort to deal with these changing conditions, secondary schools were faced with the task of expanding the curriculum to meet the changing needs of the students. As the curriculum expanded, students were faced with the problem of selecting the course of study, or simply several courses in some cases, that would best fit their needs.

The increased expansion of the curriculum created a number of problems not associated with the single-purpose schools of the past. One of the most pressing problems was maladjustment. Often students found themselves in courses for which they had no interest and which they were not prepared to handle. The result of this mis-selection was serious loss of time for many students, but more significantly, emotional disturbances and frustrations often occurred. The situation also resulted in an accelerated dropout rate that has continued to modern times. The situation was further aggravated by the fact that teachers were trained as subject specialist and came from educational backgrounds that were oriented toward college preparation. The subject-matter orientation of most teachers of that day provided little preparation for helping students in matters outside their field of specialty, leaving students with the task of solving their problems themselves.

One of the first major efforts to deal with educational and vocational problems in an organized manner was made during the latter part of the first decade of this century. In 1908 Frank Parsons of Boston established a vocational placement service for out-of-school youth. Parsons' first efforts were concerned with helping young people find employment in keeping with their abilities, skills, and interests. Through the efforts of Parsons, the Boston Vocational Bureau was created to carry out the task of matching the skills of young people with jobs.

Another person instrumental in the development of guidance was Jesse B. Davis. Noted primarily because of his work with student counseling in Michigan, Davis helped establish a program designed to teach educational and vocational guidance to students. His program was explained in a book entitled *Vocational and Moral Guidance* published in 1914.

From the early attempts to organize guidance services, geared almost exclusively to vocational guidance, a program has emerged that provides a variety of services for students.

Functions of the Guidance Program

The functions of an effective and comprehensive guidance program include the following:
1. Studying the individual.
2. Providing information.
3. Counseling students.
4. Following student progress.
5. Enhancing home, school, and community relationships.
6. Testing of students.
7. Providing services to teachers and other school personnel.
8. Conducting research.

Although services provided for students will vary from school to school, the functions listed above are believed to be necessary functions of an effective guidance program. A discussion of each function is presented in the following sections.

Studying the Individual

In order to effectively guide students, it is necessary to understand them. This can best be accomplished by accumulating as much information both qualitative and quantitative as possible and using this information to help students. The primary goal of this function is to systematically gather information about students and help teachers to make use of it, since it is impossible for guidance personnel alone to make the best use of all the information.

Information about students can be derived from a variety of sources. The most common types of information gathered by guidance personnel are psychological and scholastic test scores, records of past achievement, information relative to family background, and information concerning the student's interests, attitudes, aptitudes, behavior, and other partinent characteristics. Gathering information of this type is the responsibility of the guidance specialist, but teachers contribute significantly to the process by collecting information about students through classroom tests, evaluations of past achievements, anecdotal records kept by teachers, and the general impressions of students gained through day-to-day contact with the student.

Although the function of studying the individual is a difficult and time-consuming task, the process is of little use unless the information is employed by school personnel to help students understand themselves and to make appropriate choices. Too often test scores and other valuable information about students are not used in the most efficient manner, thereby negating the effort expended in collecting the information.

Providing Information

Another function of a guidance program is supplying students with educational and occupational information. Because of the ever-expanding curriculum, expanding postsecondary school opportunities, and increasing need for planning by students who plan to attend college, students in the secondary school today are frequently faced with difficult and important choices to make concerning these matters. Students need to know what they must do to fulfill their goals, or in many cases, help them to establish some goals. In addition, students need help in selecting the proper courses to meet their interests, future goals, and specific requirements set forth by the school. The larger the school the more important this function becomes.

Students who plan to enter college upon graduation from high school must plan their program in order to meet entrance requirements and students who plan to enter the world of work after graduation need information regarding the specific kinds of preparation needed. Guidance personnel and teachers can provide this kind of information to students and help students to profit more from their high school experiences.

To aid in accomplishing their function, secondary schools should complete libraries of educational and occupational information, and these libraries should be easily accessible to all students. The libraries should include current catalogs of colleges and universities in the area and a selected group of catalogs of institutions in other parts of the country. Occupational information should be available for students who plan to enter the labor market upon graduation. Several excellent systems of files based on the *Dictionary of Occupational Titles* are available and offer information pertaining to almost every occupation in existence.

Another excellent means of dispensing educational and occupational information is by inviting persons affiliated with colleges, professions, or occupations to come to the school for sessions with interested students. This can be done on a continuous basis or by sponsoring career days or other such special occasions where individuals or groups are invited to visit the school for the purpose of telling students about career possibilities. Probably the most effective way is to use a combination of both.

Counseling Students

Most educators consider the counseling function as the core of the entire guidance program. One of the primary tasks of the counseling function is to work with students who have adjustment problems. Every school has students whose attitudes and actions are markedly out of line with normal behavior and who are desperately in need of constructive help. Often the solution to problem behavior, for example, lies more in finding out why the problem occurred than in bringing action against the offender. This is particularly true with students who are unusually shy, belligerent, dishonest, rude, overagressive, or emotionally unstable. In most cases students exhibiting consistent behavior of this nature are experiencing adjustment problems which, if allowed to continue, bring harm to both the individual and the school. To work effectively with students with more severe problems, persons with special training are needed. Unfortunately, many counselors spend less time performing this function than on other phases of the guidance program.

Although working with adjustment problems is a major part of the counseling function, other types of activity also are performed. Generally, secondary school guidance personnel are expected to work with students in the areas of educational counseling, vocational counseling, as well as personal and social counseling. Educational counseling involves helping students to make wise educational plans and constitutes one additional step beyond dispensing information. Educational counseling also means working with students to help them discover their own interests, desires, and future goals. The counselor then guides the student to plan his educational program in line with these insights.

Vocational guidance involves helping students discover vocational possibilities. This often entails guiding the student to establish realistic vocational goals in line with the many factors that effect a decision of this nature. Counseling also involves helping students work out personal and social problems. Although not experiencing severe adjustment problems, many students of secondary school age experience numerous personal and social problems that can affect their school achievement. Among the more common are boy-girl relations, the student's role in an adult society, peer relationships, grooming, and home and school problems.

The degree of counseling that actually takes place varies considerably from school to school. Some schools have recognized that a real need exists to work with students on a more personal basis and have established unique programs to help accomplish this goal. With the problems of youth intensifying, schools should work toward the development of imaginative programs that will benefit both the individual and the school.

Following Student Progress

When guidance personnel occupy their time with such functions as collecting information on students, providing educational and vocational information to students, counseling them, and helping them to find their places after graduation from school, it seems logical that a necessary function would be to find out what effect these efforts have had on the student as reflected in his postsecondary school life.

The process of following students after they leave the secondary school is not merely to collect information but rather to find out if the current programs provided for students are meeting their needs. The information gathered should be used to evaluate the school program and bring about change when the information dictates.

The most common type of follow-up used in secondary schools today involves former students attending college. The reason for concentrating more on the college population than students following other pursuits is the relative ease in getting information. Most colleges provide the secondary school with a record of achievement of their former students and often include additional information regarding their success, or lack of it, in the college environment. College achievement, when used alone, leaves much to be desired as a means for evaluating a school program, but this type of information does provide some insight into the college-preparatory aspect of the curriculum.

Follow-up studies of students who do not continue their education beyond the secondary school is a more difficult task. The reason for this difficulty is that students scatter into a variety of occupations and into many parts of the nation. The difficulty in locating these students, the cost involved in contacting them, and the difficulty in getting responses from students make this type of follow-up less effective than studies of the college population. Another aspect which has to be considered is that studies have shown that former students who are not achieving well will not respond to inquiries from their former school. This results in information gathered only on those former students who are doing well. However, it is important for schools to contact students entering all kinds of endeavors in order to provide the kinds of data necessary for effective decision making.

In terms of using follow-up studies for evaluation purposes, it has been suggested that the most effective time for gathering such data is several years after the students have left school. The reason given for this suggestion is that former students who have been away from the secondary school for a number of years are more likely to respond in a more objective manner. Another suggestion for making follow-up studies more effective is to study the former student more than one time. The goal of this procedure is to gain insight into the changes that take place over a relatively long period of time.

Guidance personnel and schools in general need to follow their former students into the world outside the school if the school is to discover the extent to which it is achieving its stated purposes. The follow-up study appears to be the most effective means for accomplishing this purpose at the present.

Enhancing Home, School, and Community Relationships

Another important function usually assigned to guidance personnel is building good relationships between the school and the community. Since guidance personnel have frequent opportunities to meet with community members and since guidance personnel, as a result of the functions they perform, pose little threat to students or parents, they are in a unique position to carry out this function. It is for these reasons that guidance personnel are frequently assigned the task of coordinating the home, school, and community relations program.

Normally when a community is kept informed about its schools it is more likely to support them. Several procedures for accomplishing this task have been used to good advantage by schools. For example, PTA groups, business groups, and professional groups are usually interested in what is going on in the schools. This yields an excellent opportunity for school representatives to talk to such groups and explain new programs, long-range plans of the school, and other topics of interest to the community. Another procedure that has met with some success is the information bulletin published periodically by the school. This device, if used properly, is an excellent means of communicating to the public.

Testing Students

A function that is usually a part of the guidance program of a school is the administration, scoring, and deployment of standardized tests. In some schools, testing has become such an enormous task that it occupies more time than any other aspect of the guidance program. Although testing is important, that it commands such emphasis in some schools is unfortunate. Part of the problem lies in the necessity of persons trained in testing to carry out the task, and since guidance personnel usually are the best trained for the job, the major portion of the testing program becomes the job of guidance personnel. The most common tests given in schools today include

Intelligence tests
Tests of general ability
Special ability tests
Interest tests
Personality tests
Achievement tests
Attitude tests
Prognostic tests

The number of tests used and emphasis placed on tests varies from school to school, but because of the rather large number of students involved, guidance personnel must rely on teachers for some of the work of administering the tests. For this to be effective, teachers must be trained in order to insure that the tests are administered correctly. For example, if one teacher allows students more than the allotted time on a test, the outcome will be biased. Therefore, guidance personnel must assume an added function—that of training teachers to correctly administer the tests. This adds to the burden but helps make the testing program more effective.

A final task associated with the testing program for which guidance personnel must take the initiative is the interpretation and use of the information gained. Too often a massive efforts is put forth to gather test information and then this information is not used. Guidance personnel must take the initiative in informing teachers of test results and in helping them to use this information to the best advantage of the student.

Providing Services to Teachers

Because of the type of specific training most guidance workers possess, they are in a position to provide a variety of services to teachers and other school personnel. For example, guidance personnel are uniquely situated to offer help to teachers in the area of classroom relations, or as the case may be, to help in working with an unusually difficult student. There are numerous other areas where the experience and training of guidance personnel can be of unique service to teachers.

For this type of interchange to occur, the atmosphere in the school should be such as to encourage teachers and guidance personnel to interact freely. When the guidance program of a school is looked upon in the same manner as other aspects of the curriculum, the contribution of this phase of the school program is enhanced.

Research

A final function of the guidance program to be discussed in this section is that of research. Although schools are not noted for their research involvement, when such activity does occur it most often originates with or at least involves guidance personnel. Again, one reason for this is the training that persons in this type of position receive, as well as the nature of their work. Having access to data on a wide variety of school situations is conducive to stimulating research activity, since careful scrutiny of information received by guidance personnel cannot help but raise questions.

Organization of the Guidance Program

Considerable variation exists in regard to the organization of guidance programs at the secondary level. This variation is due to two major factors. First, the size of the school dictates the type of organization that is needed. For example, some large high schools have elaborate organizations consisting of numerous functions and personnel. In other situations, especially small schools, the guidance program might consist only of a part-time person assigned to carry out a few functions. The second factor is the amount of money available for support of a guidance program. Some schools that could well support an extensive program do not, while others do more than they can actually afford. The criteria in most instances is emphasis. How those in the position to allocate money perceive the guidance program of a school makes all the difference in the amount of money they are willing to set aside for such programs. Nevertheless, if guidance is to be included in the total curriculum of a school, regardless of the size and support, an appropriate organization must be present if the program is to be effective.

Some general principles that should influence the organization of a guidance program in a school are offered by Zeran and Riccio.

1. The administration must believe in, understand, and want a program of guidance services.
2. The staff must feel the need for an organized program of guidance services and be willing to participate in the activities.
3. The guidance services are designated for a specific school.
4. The guidance services are for all boys and girls . . .
5. The program of guidance services must be predicated upon the competencies possessed by the existent staff and the time available for the performance of these services.
6. The existent guidance services should be evaluated and a program designed to meet local needs as well as to utilize the staff skills.
7. One individual, by virtue of preparation, personal or other characteristics, and acceptance by the staff, should be responsible for the program of guidance services.
8. A program of guidance services will not meet all pupil difficulties.[4]

Although some specific types of organizational patterns exist for guidance, the preceding principles imply a need for individual attention in terms of organization. Each school should have an organization that is tailored to meet the needs of the students served. Most guidance programs are sufficiently similar to permit classification, and most programs reflect the use of one of three types of organization—centralized, decentralized, or a combination of both. The following sections briefly describe these types of patterns.

Centralized Organization

When guidance services are separated in terms of organization from other aspects of the school and when the program is under the direction of designated guidance personnel, the centralized pattern is in operation. This type of organization is designed primarily for efficiency but often requires more money to operate than the other types. A centralized program in a school may be organized so that one person or a group of persons is assigned the specific tasks of operating the program. The persons functioning in these roles may be given various tasks such as testing, counseling, imparting formation, or public relations. The lines of authority run from the principal to the guidance director and to the other personnel working in the guidance program.

---

[4]Franklin R. Zeran and Anthony C. Riccio, *Organization and Administration of Guidance Services* (Chicago: Rand McNally, 1962), pp. 205–208.

Decentralized Organization

In contrast to the centralized pattern of organization, the decentralized plan places the responsibility for all guidance functions on the school staff. Hollis and Hollis describe this type of organization in the following manner.

> The program is decentralized to the extent that each teacher becomes in theory a guidance specialist. . . . Since these who work with the pupils are the ones who should know them best, teachers are in a particularly advantageous position to offer guidance when it is most appropriate. A guidance staff is not usually employed, and the coordination duties within a building are performed by the principal or the assistant principal.[5]

Although part of the logic behind this type of organization is sound, particularly that of teachers being in a position to know their students, the decentralized pattern of organization is rarely seen in the secondary schools today. Part of the reason for its absence is the accrediting agencies and the departments of education in the states. Probably the only schools that might adopt the decentralized plan would be small schools where the centralized or the combination patterns would not be feasible.

Combination Organization

The combination approach to guidance organization is a hybrid of the centralized and decentralized plans. This type of organization is becoming more popular and may become the most widely used approach in the years to come.

The major emphasis of the combination approach is to provide specialists in guidance and counseling and utilize these persons for consultation with other members of the school staff. Even though the guidance specialists work directly with students, a considerable amount of their time is spent in working with teachers. The objective is to involve teachers in guidance and counseling but also to provide them with sufficient training and information to do an effective job with some functions of guidance without the direct assistance of the guidance specialist.

When the combination approach is used, the responsibilities for the guidance program are distributed among the various members of the staff with the goal of working together to accomplish the defined guidance functions. The guidance specialists may work directly with the teacher in the classroom on such items as test administration, test interpretation, and other matters that might require joint effort. The essence of the combination pattern is the attempt at division of labor regarding the guidance functions and striving to promote team work among all members of the staff.

[5]Joseph W. Hollis and Lucille U. Hollis, *Organizing for Effective Guidance* (Chicago: Science Research Associates, 1965), p. 92.

The Teacher and the Guidance Program

The role of the teacher in guidance and counseling has changed considerably. Until recent years, teachers were responsible for this type of activity in addition to their teaching because no one else was available to do the job. The emergence of guidance and counseling as a separate field of study and the availability of persons trained to work with students in this manner led to a shift in responsibility from the teacher to the guidance specialist. In some instances the roles of the teacher and guidance specialist became completely separated and very little communication existed between them.

The role of the teacher in the guidance program is still an issue in many quarters, but in recent years attempts have been made to bring about a closer working relationship between the two. The growing use of the combination type of organization reflects the success of these efforts. To many, the teacher plays a vital role in the guidance program of a school regardless of the extensiveness of the program. In the day-to-day contacts with students, the teacher is in a position to make significant contributions to the program.

Some specific contributions that the teacher can make to the guidance program include homeroom guidance, subject counseling, observation and referral, and, in some instances, test administration.

Summary

The theme of this brief chapter on guidance and counseling is that the guidance program of a school is related to the curriculum and should be considered as an intergral part of the total school program. The details of organization, functions, and approaches used in the various programs may differ from school to school, but the essence of an effective guidance program depends more on tailoring these aspects to local needs than on adherence to one specific type of organization or approach.

The guidance and counseling program of a school can be a significant factor in achieving the objectives of the school. For this to occur, however, the guidance program must be thought of and utilized in relation to the total curriculum of the school.

Selected References

Boy, Angelo V., and Gerald J. Pine, *The Counselor in the Schools.* Boston: Houghton Mifflin Company, 1968.

Byrne, Richard H., *The School Counselor.* Boston: Houghton Mifflin Company, 1963.

Hollis, Joseph W., and Lucille U. Hollis, *Organizing For Effective Guidance.* Chicago: Science Research Associates, Inc., 1965.

Kowitz, Gerald T., *Operating Guidance Services for the Modern School.* New York: Holt, Rinehart & Winston, Inc., 1968.

Mathewson, Robert H., *Guidance Policy and Practice.* 3d ed. New York: Harper & Row, Publishers, 1962.

Zeran, Franklin R., and Anthony R. Riccio, *Organization and Administration of Guidance Services.* Chicago: Rand McNally & Company, 1962.

part V

Implemen-
tation of the
Curriculum

Implementation of the Curriculum

Two topics of major concern to students of curriculum are discussed in Chapters 14 and 15. The topics are curriculum organization and administration, and curriculum evaluation and improvement.

Chapter 14, on curriculum organization and administration, takes a look at a variety of organizational patterns for implementing the curriculum and attempts to present these patterns in such a manner that the reader can gain an overall view of the possibilities that exist for curriculum implementation. The major topics covered in the chapter are traditional patterns of curriculum organization, varient patterns of curriculum organization, and content structure and curriculum organization.

The intent of Chapter 14 is to provide curriculum planners and students of curriculum with a view of the available means for implementing the curriculum and to stress the point of the necessity of attending to the objectives and structure of the curriculum before the mechanics of organization are determined. In line with the general theme of the book, content structure, one pattern of organization, the spiral, appears to be particularly adaptable for a curriculum using this approach.

Chapter 15—the final chapter of the book—is concerned with the topic of curriculum evaluation and improvement. The general theme of the chapter is that for meaningful improvement to occur a sound system of evaluation must be present. While the terms "evaluation" and "improvement" are treated separately for the purpose of clarity, the intent is to stress the relationship between the two.

The major topics covered in the section on evaluation are the process of evaluation, problems and prospects of curriculum evaluation, and illustrative evaluation projects. The major topics covered in the section on curriculum improvement are the nature of curriculum improvement, factors influencing change, factors hindering change, and a model for facilitating change.

CHAPTER 14

CURRICULUM
ORGANIZATION

How may we best organize the curriculum in order to achieve optimum results? This question, along with several others posed in the preceding chapters, is of considerable importance to curriculum study and constitutes the basic extension of the discussions relating to content structure and determination.

Many aspects of the general field of education remain obscure, but the idea that a plan must exist for implementing the curriculum is an aspect commanding almost total agreement among those concerned with the education of American youth. Agreement, however, ends at this point. A variety of ideas and plans exist, but it appears that a single answer to the question regarding the best way to organize the curriculum is still beyond us and, indeed, may remain so, because a single answer may not be what we are looking for.

An acquaintance with some of the basic terminology used in conjunction with the study of curriculum organization appears necessary to acquire some measure of common understanding before pursuing the subject at greater length. The terms, *scope, sequence,* and *articulation* are particularly pertinent and will be defined in the following paragraphs.

Scope refers to what the curriculum or- some segment of the curriculum includes. For example, a college preparatory secondary school would have a much narrower scope than a comprehensive secondary school.

Sequence refers to the order in which content is arranged for instruction. The possibilities for sequential arrangement of subject matter consists of organizing content according to levels of complexity, according to chronology, or according to some other system of logical order. These possibilities also relate to any other facet of the curriculum.[1]

Articulation refers to the manner in which the various components of the

[1]Wayne Dumas and Weldon Beckner, *Introduction to Secondary Education* (Scranton, Pa.: Intext, 1968), p. 189.

curriculum relate to one another. A curriculum possessing good articulation is one where the transition from one segment of the curriculum to another is smooth and where unnecessary duplication or difficulties are absent. At this point the consideration of articulation must involve two types of basic school organization, vertical organization and horizontal organization. *Vertical organization* involves the classification of students for their movement through the school program from the time of admission to the time of completion. *Horizontal organization* refers to the way in which "segments of these vertical units are arranged side by side providing both a pupil-to-teacher ratio and a basis for assigning students and teachers to available space."[2]

Older Patterns of Curriculum Organization

Writers in the field of curriculum have given a variety of names to the patterns of organization used by schools to implement the curriculum. The nomenclature offered by Spears, however, appears to be adequately descriptive of the various organizational patterns. In a book published some years ago, Spears categorized curriculum organization into six types. The categories included the subject curriculum, the correlated curriculum, the fuzed curriculum, the broad-fields curriculum, the core curriculum, and the experience curriculum. He further suggested that the order in which the organizational patterns are listed represents a type of sequence ranging from the more traditional, or reactionary, to the more revolutionary.[3]

Aside from being adequately descriptive of the traditional patterns of curriculum organization, the categories listed by Spears constitute an interesting base from which to study current practices and proposals.

The Subject Curriculum

The subject curriculum is the oldest and most commonly used types of curriculum organization. The roots of this type of organization are long, ranging from ancient Greece and Rome, through the monastery and cathedral schools of the middle ages, to the schools of America in the 1970's. The subject-centered type of curriculum organization remains the most commonly used approach for implementing the curriculum.

Basically, the subject curriculum is a means of organizing the content of education into subjects of instruction. In its basic form, the subject curriculum consists of a set of subjects compartmentalized into bodies of knowledge and

[2] John I. Goodlad, "Individual Differences and Vertical Organization of the School," *Individualizing Instruction* Sixty-first Yearbook of the National Society for the Study of Education, Part I (Chicago: U. of Chicago Press, 1962), p. 209.
[3] Harold Spears, *The Emerging High School Curriculum* (New York: American Book, 1940), p. 52.

taught in isolation from one another. For example, history is taught as a separate subject without regard to other subjects that might have some relationship to it, such as geography, economics, or sociology. This is also true of all other subjects because each subject is believed to have a logic and organization all its own.

CHARACTERISTICS OF THE SUBJECT CURRICULUM. Smith, Stanley, and Shores list two distinctive features of the subject curriculum that tend to set it apart from the other organizational patterns. These are

1. That the subject matter is classified and organized in accordance with the divisions of labor in research.
2. That this curriculum emphasizes expository discourse and techniques of explanation.[4]

The idea that subject matter is classified and organized on the basis of research implies a direct relationship between the accumulation and classification of knowledge. This implication is given further substance by Smith and others when they state:

> As men found out more and more about their world, the point was reached at which it became desirable to classify their learning in order to make reference to it more easily, to use it more effectively in further study of their environment, and to explain to others the knowledge they have gained.[5]

It should be understood that the purpose behind this type of organization is to increase the student's understanding of the world about him. No attempt is made to relate the information involved to any practical situation. Subject content is selected and organized for instruction on the basis of the inherent worth of the material to be studied. It is assumed that the student will be able to make application on his own whenever the need arises.

The assumption that the subject curriculum can be distinguished from other types of curriculum organization on the basis of the feature of emphasizing expository discourse and techniques of explanation is illustrated by Smith and others by defining four types of exposition.

> The first is that which proceeds from the simple to the complex. The simple is defined as that which contains few elements or subordinate parts, as a one-celled animal is simpler than a many-celled animal. . . .
> The second is an expository order based upon prerequisite learnings. This principle is followed particularly in subjects consisting largely of laws and principles, such as physics, grammar, and geometry.
> The third form of exposition is that which proceeds from the whole to the part. Geography frequently begins with the globe, with the idea that the earth is a sphere, because this conception serves to interpret many geographic observations, such as differences in time and seasons.

[4]B. Othanel Smith et al., *Fundamentals of Curriculum Development*, (New York: Harcourt, 1957), pp. 230–231.
[5]*Ibid.*, p. 230.

The fourth kind of exposition is chronological. Facts and ideas are arranged in a time sequence so that presentation of later events is preceded by discussion of earlier ones.[6]

Observation of subject-matter curriculum organization presently in operation in a large number of secondary schools today tends to support the preceding discussion of the distinctive features of this type of organization.

CRITICISMS OF THE SUBJECT CURRICULUM. Although the subject curriculum has been in existence for many years, it has not been void of serious criticism. Some of the more common objections to this type of curriculum organization are

1. Much of the material considered essential to researchers and scholars is often meaningless to students who have little experience or interest in the subject. When the subject becomes the prime objective, the students' special abilities and interests are neglected.
2. The compartmentalization of subject matter results in fragmentary learning. The student tends to learn pieces rather than wholes, which results in his inability to properly see the relationship of what he has learned in each subject. To gain an understanding of the causes of the Civil War, for example, requires understandings from several subjects other than history.
3. The subject curriculum neglects the study of significant social and environmental problems of concern to the student. In the process of studying what is considered the essential elements of a subject, little time is left to consider current events.
4. The subject being taught often becomes more important than the student. In this type of situation, it becomes more difficult to understand the students with whom the teacher works.
5. The subject curriculum often does not emphasize thinking. The study of a particular subject often requires memory, drill, and understanding of information placed in logical order by others, thereby emphasizing the thoughts of others and causing them to command a more prominent position than individual or independent thinking.

The responses to the criticisms of the subject curriculum are many and varied. The subject curriculum remains, however, the dominant pattern for organizing the secondary curriculum. Some of the more common factors contributing to the persistence of this type of organization are presented in the following statements.

1. The subject curriculum has strong support from all parties concerned with education primarily because it is the kind of organization with which they are most familiar.
2. The teacher training institutions tend to perpetuate this type of organiza-

[6]*Ibid.*, p. 233.

tion with the general pattern of certification required of prospective teachers. One prepares to be a history teacher, for example, by specializing in that subject, and when certified, becomes a teacher of history.

3. The textbooks and other types of education materials are developed for use in accordance with a specific subject area.
4. The professional associations of teachers tend to lend support for this type of organization by bonding together persons teaching specific subjects.

Alberty and Alberty offer additional information regarding the major arguments that have contributed to the longevity of the subject curriculum. These are

1. Systematic organization is essential to the effective interpretation of experience.
2. The organization of the subject-centered curriculum is simple and easily understood.
3. The subject-centered curriculum is easily changed.
4. The subject-centered curriculum is easily evaluated.
5. The colleges have generally approved and perpetuated the subject-centered curriculum through admission requirements.
6. The subject-centered curriculum is generally approved by teachers, parents, and students.[7]

The Correlated Curriculum

An extension of the basic subject-centered type of curriculum organization is the attempt to show relationships between two or more subjects without destroying the subject boundaries. This type of organization is most often referred to as the *correlated curriculum.*

The idea of subject correlation is based on the assumption that an inherent relationship exists between facts, concepts, and other aspects of a given subject and similar types of information found in other subjects. For example, a common effort to correlate subject matter has occurred in such fields as history, literature, mathematics, science, and others. The attempt centered around showing relationships between, say, a certain event in American history and the literature of the period. No attempt is made to destroy the uniqueness of either subject, but rather to show how one complements the other. One might study Margaret Mitchell's *Gone With the Wind* for its literary value and at the same time emphasize the historical value.

In regard to the value of this type of curriculum organization, Bent and Unruh present several reasons why the correlated curriculum has value for students.

1. The transfer of training is facilitated. Pupils cannot transfer classroom-acquired knowledge to their everyday lives without help, and if this transfer does not

[7]Harold B. Alberty and Elsie J. Alberty, *Reorganizing the High School Curriculum*, 3d ed. (New York: Macmillan, 1962), pp. 173–180.

take place, there is little possibility that the materials learned in school will function in their lives outside school.

2. Pupils are more likely to be motivated if they can see the relationships between subjects. Students are not equally interested in all subjects; therefore, teachers should employ interests expressed in one subject to motivate interests in others.

3. Students obtain greater depth of knowledge and their studies are immensely enriched through correlation of subject matter.

4. Most units, topics, and activities cannot be fully understood if they are studied from one point of view only.[8]

Although the basic purpose of the correlated curriculum was to reduce compartmentalization and framentation of subject matter in order to achieve the above listed values, there is little evidence to indicate that this has been achieved to any significant degree. It is generally recognized that some degree of incidental correlation is found in any curriculum, but planned and systematic programs designed to achieve this purpose have been noticeably absent.

The Fused Curriculum

The fused curriculum represents, in the Spears continuum of curriculum organization, the second step away from the subject-matter organization. It consists, basically, of an attempt to create a subject, or course, based on the content previously taught in separate units. In other words, the combining of two or more subjects into one but still retaining the basic content of each subject. The plan is similar to correlation but differs in that it attempts complete integration rather than incidental or planned correlation. "Teaching several subjects as one" is a phrase often used to describe the fused approach.

The major criticism that has been voiced against the fuzed curriculum is that it too often consists of a combination of courses rather than the intergration for which it was designed. However, fusion, at least the basic assumptions of it, appears to hold definite opportunities for the integration of learning.

Probably the most notable attempts to move in this direction have occurred in the fields of science and social science at the secondary level. Combining zoology and botony into biology was one of the earliest attempts with government, sociology, and various other combinations drawn from the social sciences into courses in American Democracy or American problems as examples of more recent attempts to bring content from several related areas together for the study of a common problem. The same idea can be found at more advanced levels with course titles preceded by "a survey of."

Again, the key element of the fused curriculum is that the combined subjects are taught "as one." As in the case of the correlated curriculum, little evidence

---

[8]Reprinted by permission of the publisher from Rudyard K. Bent, and Adolph Unruh, *Secondary School Curriculum* (Lexington, Mass.: Heath, 1969), pp. 63–64.

exists indicating to what extent this has actually occurred to a significant degree.

The Broad-Fields Curriculum

This approach to curriculum organization is based on the assumption that there are essential studies that all students should pursue. A natural extension of the correlated and fused curriculum, the broad-fields approach emerged as an attempt to bring together content from several subject areas and to then arrange this content into a broad general course. The major difference between this approach and the correlated and fused approaches, is that the broad-fields concept goes beyond combining two courses and attempts to bring about broader understandings by stressing relationships among a number of subjects and how the content of these subjects relates to the understanding of a broad concept.

Some of the broad concepts for which the broad-fields approach has been used are: Problems of American Democracy, Social Relationships, Effective Communication, and Man and Society. Often, more general terminology is used to represent this concept. Some of the more common are language arts, social studies, and general science. By whatever name, the general purpose of organizing the curriculum in this manner is to retain the values of logical, systemized knowledge while at the same time allowing greater freedom of action within the context of a broad field. This same idea can also be seen at the college level in numerous courses entitled "a survey of," or "an introduction to."

ADVANTAGES OF BROAD-FIELDS ORGANIZATION. Although never extremely popular, the broad-fields approach to curriculum organization did find its way into a number of high schools. For those who tended to support this type of organization, the justification for doing so centered around the following points.

1. The broad-fields approach provides a planned way for insuring that students will relate content of the various subjects to each other and to concepts including several areas of content. For example, in the language-arts field, spelling is reinforced due to its being related to reading and writing; mathematics is reinforced when related to science, and so on.

2. The broad-fields approach gives the student an opportunity to select the most significant information contained in each of the subject areas considered, thereby eliminating the study of insignificant material.

3. The broad-fields approach emphasizes the understanding of generalizations and principles rather than memorizing facts in isolation.

CRITICISMS OF BROAD-FIELDS ORGANIZATION. Those who found fault with this type of approach usually pointed to one or more of the following shortcomings.

1. The creation of a broad-fields curriculum does not automatically result in

subject-matter integration. The ingredients necessary to make this type of organization work have been missing in many past efforts.

2. Teachers are too often poorly prepared to help students see the relationships among several subjects as they might relate to a broader concept.

Persons representing the various subject fields have also voiced objection to having their subject integrated with other subjects. Typical of this position is the criticism of the broad fields organization offered by Bestor.[9] Writing about the field of history, his main objection was based on the idea that when a subject like history is submerged into something called "social studies" the result is often a loss of identity and a garbled perspective of historical chronology.

The resistance to the broad-fields approach has perhaps contributed to the lack of widespread use of this plan in the secondary schools, but organizations of this type continue to flourish at the college level.

The Core Curriculum

The fifth type of curriculum organization presented in the Spears classification scheme is the core curriculum. Of all the attempts to break from the traditional subject curriculum mentioned previously, the core approach has probably been the most successful, particularly at the junior high school level. Other labels used to describe this particular type of organizational arrrangement are: common learnings, block-of-time, general education, and unified studies.

There is and has been considerable confusion among the students of curriculum regarding the distinctive features of this type of organization. Many advocates of the core curriculum have contended that the distinctive feature lies in the emphasis upon the present-day needs of society. The general acceptance of this idea by curriculum theorist or practioners certainly has not been universal.

Another interpretation of what the core curriculum is, or what it should be, revolves around the idea of common learnings. This interpretation is based on the assumption that there are certain specific types of learning experiences that should be considered basic for all students. A definition of the core curriculum reflecting this interpretation is offered by Neagley and Evans.

> In this curriculum design one subject or group of subjects becomes the core around which all other school subject areas are organized. . . . It is more precisely defined in terms of a program of general education or common learnings under fewer teachers than the separate subject curriculum would require.[10]

Reflecting the more socially oriented interpretation of what the core is, Douglass offers several distinguishing characteristics of this type of organizational pattern.

1. The core curriculum utilizes the experience-centered approach to curriculum development.

---

[9]Arthur Bestor, *The Restoration of Learning* (New York: Knopf, 1955), pp. 126–129.
[10]Ross L. Neagley and N. Dean Evans, *Handbook for Effective Curriculum Development* (Englewood Cliffs, N.J.: Prentice-Hall, 1967), p. 3.

2. The change of behavior with which the core is concerned centers on growth necessary to function as an effective citizen in a democracy.
3. The basic class procedure is problem solving.
4. The content is drawn from social and personal problem areas considered as significant phases of general education.
5. The subject matter of the core cuts across subject boundaries.
6. The emphasis on teaching skills is based on need.
7. The procedure of teacher-pupil planning is used.
8. The provision for cooperative planning by teachers is made possible.
9. The core class is scheduled for a longer block of time than the single period.
10. The guidance function is an integral part of the core.
11. The core class includes pupils of various abilities.[11]

Another difference in the two interpretations of the core presented in this section is that, in one instance, subject-matter integrity or distinction is maintained, whereas in the other instance subject matter is utilized only where it is appropriate and needed to fulfill the goals of the program.

Growth and Current Status of Core Curriculum. We have mentioned that the core approach to curriculum organization has probably had more acceptance as a means of breaking subject-matter lines than any of the previously mentioned approaches. However, although it was far from successful in breaking the traditional subject-matter orientation, unlike fusion, for example, the core approach managed to find its way into practice in a number of school programs.

The core curriculum began to be employed by a few schools during the 1930's and continued to grow through the 1940's and the early part of the 1950's. During this period of growth the approach found acceptance and use primarily in the junior high schools.

The popularity of the core curriculum began to wane during the late 1950's, to be replaced, at least in conversation, with other types of curriculum organizations. The loss in popularity has been attributed to the schism that developed between the designers of the broad-fields approach which advocated the reorganization of traditional subject matter and the promoters of the "experience core," which advocated the needs of adolescents as the prime base for curriculum determination.[12]

In attempting to explain the decline in popularity of the core, Overton offers the following observation:

> . . . The unsettling effects of a rapidly realigning world order [during the 1950's] gave rise to a morbid anxiety and cynicism that led citizens to seek a Communist under the covers of every social studies textbook, and public education became

[11]Harl R. Douglass (ed.), *The High School Curriculum*, 3d. ed. (New York: Ronald, 1964), pp. 248–252.

[12]Harvey Overton, "The Rise and Fall of the Core Curriculum," *The Clearing House* 40 (May 1966), p. 533.

fair game for a rising host of critics, from cranks seeking self-aggrandizement to college professors seeking to restore learning as undefiled deliberation in the pristine subject matter of the traditional school. After Sputnik I in 1957, the era of reassessment of American public education began in earnest, and the core curriculum, along with most of the formal trappings of progressivism, slid into its niche in educational history as an event to be recorded and explained.[13]

Despite the decline in popularity, there are signs that the core is not dead. In a recent article, Vars comments on the state of affairs by saying that "although somewhat shaky from its recent bout with the 'academie-itis' that swept American education in the early sixties, core today shows a renewed vigor of body and spirit."[14] In an effort to give substance to this statement, the author offers several points to illustrate the presence of the core.

1. The core idea is an integral part of current organizational schemes such as team teaching, humanities programs, middle school, and special programs for the disadvantaged.

2. The core ideas of problem-centered learning, student involvement in learning, student involvement in instruction, and education as a humanizing experience are a part of curriculum programs today.

3. Surveys by the U.S. Office of Education have shown an increase in the use of core programs from 1940 to 1960, but recent studies suggest that the block-time arrangement has declined. This, however, does not suggest a wholesale abandonment of the idea.[15]

Probably the most common instance of the use of the core curriculum today is the block-time arrangements found in many junior high schools. In most cases the organization consists of a combination of social studies and language arts taught by one teacher utilizing two or more periods daily. The practice is found most often at the seventh-grade level, occasionally at the eighth-grade level, and rarely at the senior high levels. One reason for this limitation may be due to the idea that the seventh grade normally is considered the transitional period whereby students move from the self-contained elementary classroom into a more departmentalized situation. The block-time arrangement is assumed to facilitate articulation from one phase of the school program to the next. Little evidence exists regarding the types of programs actually employed in the block-time arrangements, but a conjecture would be that the "true" core is in the minority.

CRITICISMS OF THE CORE CURRICULUM. The objections voiced toward the core curriculum, or at least against the theoretical premise of the core, revolve around the following points:

1. Teachers have not been trained to work effectively in a core program. Most teachers are trained in subject-centered programs at the college and

---

[13]*Ibid.*

[14]Gordon F. Vars, "The Core Curriculum: Lively Corpse," *The Clearing House* 42 (May 1968), p. 515.

[15]*Ibid.*

university level and find it difficult to break the pattern when they begin teaching.
2. Subject content is "watered down" in the process of integration.
3. There is little or no provision made for sequential learning, which results in a haphazard accumulation of knowledge.
4. Most schools do not have adequate materials and facilities to conduct core classes.
5. The degree to which student interest and needs should be used in planning the instructional program for the core has not adequately been determined. The result has ranged from too much to not enough recognition, depending upon the position of the critic.

The problems and conflicts surrounding the core curriculum have been many and varied and have not yet been resolved. It appears, however, that the basic idea of the core was sound but suffered from overexposure to discourse and lack of exposure to sufficient testing and evaluation.

The Experience Curriculum

The most extreme break from the subject curriculum was the experience curriculum, also referred to as the activity curriculum or the child-centered curriculum.

In 1940, Spears viewed the experience curriculum in the following manner:

> The experience curriculum is the one type which definitely turns its back upon a subject-matter approach. It begins with a philosophy of the learning process, against which all the school's practices must be measured. In short, it sees education as a continuous life process, as the growth of the whole individual in accordance with his environment, and it aims toward a more intelligent participation of that person in his culture.
> Since this culture or environment is constantly changing, the experience curriculum cannot be a fixed curriculum. Instead, it is a series of experience situations, each offering possible growth factors and understandings which the learner may carry forward to help him meet future experience situations. . . . The curriculum begins with pupil interests and felt needs, sees growth as coming from purposeful activity, and emphasizes the importance of an integrated individual so that he may constantly adjust himself to a changing culture.[16]

The general idea of the experience curriculum assumes that the attitudes and skills necessary for a student to solve a problem or satisfy a need are those that can be learned best and most effectively when the curriculum relates to the specific experiences of youth. In this respect the curriculum cannot be planned in advance, since each group of students possess different needs and interests. The curriculum is planned for and by each class as needs and interests arise or are discovered.

The experience curriculum has found little acceptance at the secondary level.

[16]Spears, op. cit., p. 26.

Many of the same arguments pointed against the other attempts to break from the subject curriculum were also voiced against this approach. Two major criticisms of this approach that are somewhat unique are as follows:

1. It is beyond a teacher's capacity to determine, for each class she teaches, the needs and interests to a degree that could serve as a basis for curriculum planning.
2. It is impossible to provide a well-rounded education when the curriculum is based on students' needs and interests.

Further discussion of the experience curriculum as it pertains to the secondary curriculum seems irrelevant because of its almost universal absence from the secondary program. It should be added, however, that the idea of capitalizing on students needs and interests has been a part of all attempts to organize the curriculum but has not been, nor is it today, the focal point for curriculum determination.

Close examination of the types of curriculum organizations presented will reveal considerable overlap, making it difficult to single out any one of the attempts to integrate the curriculum as being unique. The one element they do have in common, however, has been the attempt to break the traditional subject-matter approach to curriculum organization.

It seems safe to say that the subject curriculum has managed to survive throughout the attempts to change it. It is interesting to note that current writings on curriculum organization center around the subject-centered approach with modifications. It is possible that the old saying, "If you can't beat 'em, join 'em," may have considerable meaning for curriculum planners during the decades to come. The evidence of the reemphasis on the subject-centered organization is found in all of the more recent curriculum projects now in operation or in planning. The "new" math projects, the various science projects, the social studies projects, and others all are based on the subject approach with certain modifications. It is also interesting to note the acceptance and use of the "new" ideas in school programs, an occurrence not afforded such ideas as fusion or correlation. It should be noted, however, that many of the newer approaches to curriculum organization are utilizing some of the ideas of these approaches while attempting to retain the basic integrity of the subjects.

Emerging Patterns of Curriculum Organization

It appears that the majority of the newer plans for organizing the curriculum are not attempts to break subject-matter lines but rather to strengthen the manner in which the subjects are presented to students. Close observation of most of the more recent organizational schemes reveals little that is completely new. In most cases the newer approaches are extensions or modifications of the older patterns of curriculum organization. For example, a nongraded plan of curriculum organization may be primarily subject centered with no attempt at integration. However, a nongraded approach might also be centered around a broad-fields plan or a core plan.

The newer types of organizational patterns being talked about today, and in some cases actually being practiced, fall in both the horizontal category of organization and the vertical pattern of organization.

The Nongraded Curriculum

The nongraded curriculum is one of the most talked-about vertical patterns of curriculum organization to emerge in recent years. The concept of nongraded or ungraded curriculum refers to the type of organization whereby the student is allowed to proceed through the school program at his own rate. The student's continuous progress in achievement is regulated by goals or objectives set for him by the school and based upon the individual needs and abilities of the student.

The idea of nongradedness is based on the assumption that achievement will be greater if the student is allowed to proceed at his own rate in his quest for subject-matter coverage and mastery. It is further assumed that a student's higher rate of achievement can be traced to his feelings of adequacy and satisfaction derived from the absence of artificial barriers placed before him, resulting in enhanced motivation.

The nongraded plan of organization is generally a reaction to the traditional graded plan characteristic of the American school system since the mid 1800's. With the establishment of evidence relative to individual differences in ability and other human characteristics, dissatisfaction with the graded pattern of organization began to appear. The nongraded type of organization is an outgrowth of this dissatisfaction.

The idea began appearing in print during the late 1950's and began to be employed on a limited basis in schools during the early 1960's. As with most of the innovations appearing in education today, a number of variations exist. In spite of these variations, the following characteristics appear to be a part of most of the nongraded programs.

1. Grade designations are removed from classes.
2. Pupils move at their own optimum rate for a period of two or more consecutive years under a continuous progress scheme.
3. Progress is based largely on the pupil's success in reading, language, and arithmetic.
4. Individual differences in pupils are recognized and provision is made for them.
5. Pupils may remain with the same teacher for two or three years.
6. Although external standards exist, they are treated as broad guides.
7. External standards are related specifically to the individual rather than to the group.[17]

[17]Ross L. Neagley and N. Dean Evans, *Handbook for Effective Curriculum Development* (Englewood Cliffs, N.J.: Prentice-Hall, 1967), pp. 111–112.

A number of programs designed around the nongraded concept exist today ranging from comprehensive programs found in such schools as Nova High School, Fort Lauderdale, Florida; Melbourne High School, Melbourne, Florida; John Glenn Junior High School, San Angelo, Texas, and numerous others, to programs of a rather limited nature.

It should be noted that merely eliminating grade levels does not necessarily constitute a significant change in curriculum organization. Unless changes in the curriculum itself accompany the change in organization, little difference can be noted other than that more hurdles are added for students. A major argument against this type of arrangement is that some of the so-called nongraded secondary schools are not that at all but rather schools where many additional levels have been substituted for the usual grades. In other words, nongradeness may or may not constitute a changed pattern of curriculum organization depending upon what is done with the content involved.

The Dual-Progress Plan

A pattern of curriculum organization that grew out of a concern for preparing teachers to cope with the increasing sophistication of knowledge has resulted in a type of horizontal organization known as the dual-progress plan. Originally developed for the elementary school, the plan has found its way into the junior high school in a few instances in recent years.

The dual-progress plan is a semidepartmental arrangement whereby students are exposed to teachers of special subjects while remaining part of the day in a self-contained situation. For one-half of the day, pupils are grouped by ability with one teacher who is responsible for instruction in the social studies and language arts and for performing certain homeroom duties such as record keeping and counseling. The remaining portion of the school day is devoted to specialized instruction in subjects such as science and mathematics. In the specialized areas of study, students are grouped by ability, achievement, and progress in a nongraded manner.

The dual-progress plan developed by George Shoddard at New York University,[18] constitutes two broad areas of study. The first area is called *cultural imperatives* and consists of instruction in language arts and social studies. The idea for this grouping of subjects is to provide students with mastery of communication skills in order to give them the necessary skills to participate fully as a member of society. This grouping is conducted on a graded basis in order to insure a sufficient attainment of these basic skills. The second area is referred to as *cultural electives* and includes specialized study in science, mathematics, arts and crafts, music, and other more specialized subjects. The assumption for offering these subjects in a nongraded pattern is that it is believed that a student's

[18]George D. Stoddard, *The Dual Progress Plan* (New York: Harper, 1961).

level of achievement in such subjects is largely dependent upon individual ability, interest, and motivation. When cultural electives are organized in a nongraded pattern, the variations in student's abilities and interests can best be accounted for in the instructional program. In essence, the plan offers two alternatives for progressing through the curriculum, graded in the imperatives, and nongraded in the electives.

The primary advantages of the dual-progress plan as seen by those that advocate its use is the possibility of utilizing both the traditional departmental pattern of organization and the more recent nongraded pattern at the same time. In doing so the plan allows for teacher specialists, consistency in the amount of instruction offered in the basic areas, and a variety of opportunities to pursue areas of special interest in the elective plan.

Although developed for the elementary school, the dual-progress plan appears to hold promise as a pattern of curriculum organization at the secondary level. Schools who find it difficult to go all the way to a nongraded pattern may find this type of arrangement worth considering.

The Track Curriculum

Tracking, as a pattern of curriculum organization, consists of a procedure for organizing the curriculum into levels and placing students in the specified levels according to ability, past achievement, and interest.

Organizing the curriculum in "tracks" is not a recent innovation but rather a borrowed concept from European schools. However, its limited use in the schools of this country began in the relatively recent past.

An illustrative example of the track pattern of curriculum organization is the four-track curriculum initiated in the Washington, D.C., senior high schools in 1956. The program operates under the assumption that students of all ability levels need instruction in the basic skills and that these can best be taught when the range of differences is reduced within classes. The four curriculum sequences used in this program were as follows:

1. *Honors*—for the more able student. This track consists of a total requirement of 18 hours of honors courses including four years of English, four years of foreign languages, four years of mathematics, three years of science, and two and one-half years of history and government.

2. *College Preparatory*—for the college-bound student not qualified or not desiring the honors program. In this program, the student would complete a total of 16 units including four years of English, two years of mathematics, foreign languages, and sciences, and one and a half years of social studies.

3. *General*—for the student not qualified or not desiring the college preparatory curriculum. Students placed in this track would be required to com-

plete a total of 16 units including four years of English, one year of science, and one and a half years of social studies.

4. Basic—for the academically retarded high school student. This program also requires 16 units but the standard subjects are geared to remedial work. The program also includes one year of basic business practices, and one year of basic shop for boys and basic home economics for girls.[19]

In a statement of objectives of the four-track curriculum, Carl F. Hansen, superintendent of schools in Washington, D.C., expressed the desired outcomes of this pattern of curriculum organization.

1. The track system provides a planned curriculum for individual differences. It replaces the improvisations now resorted to at the high school level.

2. It provides a total rather than a partial curriculum program for students of different ability levels. For example, instead of only a remedial English class for retarded readers, there are also classes in history, arithmetic, and business for the same retarded readers. Similarly, it provides an across-the-board program of studies for the academically gifted.

3. It increases the teachability of classes by reducing the range of differences in academic abilities within them.

4. It stresses education in the fundamental subjects systematically organized and taught. It is counterrevolutionary in respect to life-adjustment education. It steps up content and performance as an antidote to a prevailing "let the kids be happy" doctrine.

5. It requires instruction in the basic academic content for the bright, average, and slow. Thus the common learnings are stressed at varying levels of difficulty for all pupils. The bright are not encouraged to loaf through school or the slow to waste their time in improvised nonacademic subjects.

6. It requires the bright student to take sequences of the rigorous "hard" subjects rather than to select subjects at random from an educational smorgasbord. It reduces the temptation to elect easy subjects by cutting down on the number of elective choices.

7. It gives the bright student the right to excel in classes with students of his own capacity rather than grow lazy and indifferent to scholarship which is currently debased in the comprehensive high school.

8. It gives the slow learner a curriculum program which leads to completion of high school at the same time that it offers opportunity for upgrading achievement. Because it removes the anonymity of school retardation, it stimulates pupils to step up their effort.

9. It preserves the democracy of the comprehensive high school at the same time that it challenges educational achievement at various levels within it. The comprehensive high school is doomed unless specific plans are made to step up the quality of learning for the bright, the average, and the slow.

10. It encourages specialization in the preparation for teaching the gifted and the slow. Without systematic curricula for the gifted and the slow, special teacher education in these fields will not be developed. Our present ineptitude in teaching the gifted and the slow will then be indefinitely perpetuated.

11. It is as modern as automation because it encourages general competence

[19]Carl F. Hansen, *The Four-Track Curriculum in Today's High Schools* (Englewood Cliffs, N.J.: Prentice-Hall, 1964), p. vi.

among all pupils as the best preparation for vocational adaptations expected in the future. More education in the communications and arithmetic arts is demanded of all citizens for successful vocational retraining. The ability level system of instruction makes profitable education in these fields available to all pupils through high school.[20]

Much criticism of the tracking pattern of curriculum organization has been voiced in recent years. The primary objection to the plan seems to be centered around the placement of students in the various tracks. A long-standing value associated with public education in America has been that every student should be given an equal opportunity for acquiring as much education as desired. Those opposed to tracking have voiced the opinion that when students are placed in a track, even though they can change to a track other than the one designated, it violates the concept of equal opportunity for all. In the face of continued criticism it seems doubtful that much use will be made of this plan.

The preceding discussion of emerging organizational patterns is not intended to be all-inclusive. It simply illustrates the types of efforts that are being made. Recently numerous ideas have been advanced and a number of projects initiated in an effort to find more effective patterns for organizing the curriculum. Notable among these efforts is the "Trump Plan," which combines ideas about continuous progress, team teaching, and modular scheduling into a scheme which is gaining considerable acceptance in various adaptations. Most of the other recent innovations in curriculum organization have been limited to particular subject areas, such as biology (BSCS), physics (PSSC), chemistry (CHEM Study), mathematics (SMSG), or social studies (Fenton series). These and other approaches were previously discussed in Part III. They are helpful, but there is a danger that the total perspective of the desired curriculum may be lost in these specialized efforts.

Because these newer developments are as yet largely unproven and our space in this text is limited, we will not attempt to explore these plans in detail. Current literature in the field, especially publications of the Association for Supervision and Curriculum Development (ASCD), will provide the inquiring student with current information on recent developments. The following discussion of content structure and the spiral curriculum describes what the authors of this text believe to be a most promising approach to curriculum organization revision.

Content Structure and Curriculum Organization

A relatively new approach to curriculum organization, presently more talked about than practiced, is the spiral pattern. References in the literature concerning this type of organization are few, but the idea seems to hold promise as an organizational pattern for implementing a curriculum based on the concept of disciplinary structure.

[20] *Ibid.*, pp. vii–viii.

The idea of disciplinary structure, to which this book is directed, is based on the assumption that every subject contains certain basic concepts that constitute the basis for a complete understanding of the subject. The assumption further implies that a thorough understanding of the structure of a subject will enhance the process of drawing implications and relationships from the study of the subject. A curriculum based on this idea, then, would consist of the basic concepts inherent in each subject and presented to students in such a manner as to insure repeated exposure to the extent deemed necessary. The spiral approach to curriculum is a procedure for implementing this idea of disciplinary structure.

The idea of the spiral approach to curriculum organization can be traced, in part, to the work of Jerome Bruner. In explaining the rationale of the spiral curriculum, Bruner states:

> If one respects the ways of thought of the growing child, if one is courteous enough to translate material into his logical forms and challenging enough to tempt him to advance, then it is possible to introduce him at an early age to the ideas and styles that in later life make an educated man. We might ask, as a criterion for any subject taught in primary school, whether, when fully developed, it is worth an adult's knowing, and whether having known it as a child makes a person a better adult. If the answer to both questions is negative or ambiguous, then the material is cluttering the curriculum.[21]

Bruner follows this statement regarding the rationale for content structure with an hypothesis that sets the stage for utilizing the spiral pattern of curriculum organization. The hypothesis states that

> . . . any subject can be taught effectively in some intellectually honest form to any child at any stage of development.[22]

Assuming this hypothesis can be supported, the curriculum should be organized around the great issues, principles, and values that a society deems important. [23]

Implementing the Spiral Curriculum

One of the first decisions that has to be made before a spiral organization can be implemented is determining what major concepts constitute the heart of each subject. Some subject areas, notably science, have moved more rapidly in identifying major concepts for study than have other areas. Probably the best sources for information of this nature are the various curriculum committees associated with the subject areas.

A primary factor in making a decision regarding the major concepts of any subject area is the determining of the source of authority. As in any phase of education, some disagreement exists regarding what major concepts should be

---

[21]Jerome Bruner, *The Process of Education* (Cambridge, Mass.: Harvard U.P., 1960), p. 52.
[22]*Ibid.*, p. 33.
[23]*Ibid.*, p. 34.

emphasized; however the same disagreement exists regarding the content to be emphasized under any type of organization. In any event the decisions regarding content must be made by persons knowledgeable in the area under consideration. In this respect, a collective decision by experts is usually superior to one made by an individual.

Once the decision regarding content is determined, the next step in implementing the spiral organization is to organize the content in terms of levels of complexity, ranging from the basic ideas associated with the concept to the degree that the students involved can profit. For example, if the plan is to include grades 7 through 12, the levels of difficulty would begin with what is considered basic to understanding the subject with levels of intensity increasing each year until the highest degree of concentration desired is achieved. This would then provide the desired amount of repeated exposure to the same concept at various levels of difficulty.

As was mentioned earlier, the area of science has probably moved more rapidly toward identifying the basic concepts of the field and organizing these concepts according to levels than any other area of study. A 1964 publication of the National Science Teachers Association Curriculum Committee attempted the task of identifying basic science concepts and defining the emphasis to be given the concepts at various levels. The following is an example of their efforts to structure the concept of matter on seven levels.

I. All matter is composed of units called fundamental particles; under certain conditions these particles can be transformed into energy and vice versa.
II. Matter exists in the form of units which can be classified into hierarchies of organizational levels.
III. The behavior of matter in the universe can be described on a statistical basis.
IV. Units of matter interact. The bases of all ordinary interactions are electromagnetic, gravitational, and nuclear forces.
V. All interacting units of matter tend toward equilibrium states in which the energy content (enthalpy) is a minimum and the energy distribution (entropy) is most random. In the process of attaining equilibrium, energy transformations or matter-energy transformations occur. Nevertheless, the sum of energy and matter in the universe remains constant.
VI. One of the forms of energy is the motion of units of matter. Such motion is responsible for heat and temperature and for the states of matter: solid, liquid, and gaseous.
VII. All matter exists in time and space, and, since interactions occur among its units, matter is subject in some degree to changes with time. Such changes may occur at various rates and in various patterns.[24]

Following this structure, a spiral organization could be implemented by organizing the identified content into major units of study to be presented at various points in the curriculum. For example, the levels might correspond to

[24]NSTA Conference of Scientists, "Conceptual Schemes," *Theory into Action in Science Curriculum Development*, (Washington, D.C.: National Science Teachers Association, 1964), p. 20.

grade levels or, in the case of a nongraded organization, stages of individual performance required of each student. Figure 14-1 provides a visual illustration of the spiral approach.

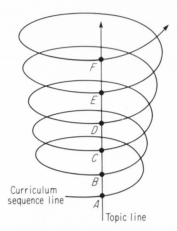

Fig. 14–1. Visual illustration of the spiral approach. (Adopted from Donovan A. Johnson and Gerald R. Rising, *Guidelines for Teaching Mathematics*, Wadsworth Publishing Co., Belmont, Calif., 1967, p. 67.)

Advantages and Disadvantages of the Spiral Pattern

Because of the lack of experimentation with the spiral pattern of curriculum organization, talking in terms of advantages and disadvantages may be premature. However, a description of certain assumed strong points and speculated weaknesses will be attempted.

A major assumption that might be used to support this type of organization is that repeated exposure to the same topic or experience increases the chances of exposure at a time when students are in the best position to profit from the activity. This assumption is supported to a degree by current research and thought on the relationship between growth patterns and learning.

A second advantage of the spiral pattern is that it provides repetition, which is generally considered a necessary component to meaningful learning. The question of the value of repetition in the learning process has been mooted for many years with considerable variation in answers. It seems, however, that the key to the value of repetition is what is being repeated. If one repeats meaningful information the experience should be profitable but if the material repeated has no lasting value, then it should not be repeated. In relation to the idea of structure, the spiral organization emphasizes repetition of the same basic concepts deemed important to understanding the subject but at different levels of complexity. The degree of repetition is planned to correspond with the changing interests of youth and their increasing ability to understand abstraction. Therefore, the sequence of the curriculum under a spiral pattern would consist of presenting material relative to the identified concepts from the simple and concrete to the more complex and abstract.

A major disadvantage of the spiral pattern of curriculum organization is the possibility of the students becoming bored with repeated exposure to the same topics. However, this is also a problem in the traditional subject-oriented curriculum where students do encounter the same topics in several places in the curriculum. The key to overcoming this problem is a well-defined and planned structure which avoids exact duplication of material while treating the same basic concepts.

Summary

There are numerous ways of organizing the curriculum for instructional purposes. Among the possibilities discussed in this chapter are the subject curriculum, the correlated curriculum, the fused curriculum, the broad-fields curriculum, the core curriculum, the experience curriculum, the nongraded curriculum, the dual-progress curriculum, the track curriculum, and the spiral curriculum.

It is clearly evident that the most popular pattern of curriculum organization used by secondary schools in America is still the subject-centered curriculum. Although numerous attempts have been made to break from this pattern, it appears that the subject curriculum has successfully survived these attempts and remains the dominant pattern of curriculum organization. The most promising attempts to get away from the subject curriculum seem to utilize approaches identified by the term *spiral curriculum.*

Selected References

Alberty, Harold B., and Alberty, Elsie J., *Reorganizing the High School Curriculum.* New York: The Macmillan Company, 1962.

Bent, Rudyard K., and Adolph Unruh, *Secondary School Curriculum.* Boston: D. C. Heath & Company, 1969.

Bestor, Arthur, *The Restoration of Learning.* New York: Alfred A. Knopf, 1955.

Bruner, Jerome S., *The Process of Education.* New York: Vintage Books, 1960.

Douglas, Harl R. (ed.), *The High School Curriculum.* New York: The Ronald Press Company, 1964.

Hansen, Carl F., *The Four-Track Curriculum in Today's Schools.* Englewood Cliffs, N.J.: Prentice-Hall, Inc., 1964.

Inlow, Gail, *The Emergent in Curriculum.* New York: John Wiley & Sons, Inc., 1966.

Neagley, Ross L., and N. Dean Evans, *Handbook for Effective Curriculum Development.* Englewood Cliffs, N.J.: Prentice-Hall, Inc., 1967.

Overton, Harvey "The Rise and Fall of the Core Curriculum," *The Clearing House* 40 May 1966.

Saylor, J. Galen, and William M. Alexander, *Curriculum Planning for Modern Schools.* New York: Holt, Rinehart and Winston, Inc., 1966.

Smith, B. Othanel, et al., *Fundamentals of Curriculum Development* (New York: Harcourt Brace Jovanovich, 1957).

Spears, Harold, *The Emerging High School Curriculum.* New York: American Book Company, 1940.

Stoddard, George D., *The Dual Progress Plan.* New York: Harper & Row, Publishers, 1961.

Trump, J. Lloyd, and Dorsey Baynham, *Guide to Better Schools: Focus On Change.* Chicago: Rand McNally & Company, 1961.

—— and Delmas F. Miller, *Secondary School Curriculum Improvement: Proposals and Procedures.* Boston: Allyn and Bacon, Inc., 1968.

Vars, Gordon F., "The Core Curriculum: Lively Corpse," *The Clearing House* 42 *(May 1968).*

CHAPTER 15

CURRICULUM EVALUATION
AND IMPROVEMENT

Knowing whether a school is a good school, whether a teacher is a good teacher, whether students are learning what they should be learning, and whether a curriculum change is better than what it replaced are such fundamental factors in good curriculum development that no one may brush them aside lightly. Yet, finding imaginative and comprehensive answers to those questions has plagued curriculum planners for generations.[1]

The preceding statement, made by one of the leading educators in America, clearly illustrates the role and scope of curriculum evaluation and its relationship to curriculum improvement. The factors mentioned in the statement also point to the fact that the process of curriculum evaluation and improvement is a complex endeavor marked by perennial pitfalls. The logic, however, is clear. Evaluate the school to find out if it is a good school. If it is not, seek ways to improve it. Evaluate a teacher to find out if the teacher is a good teacher. If the teacher falls short of what is defined as a good teacher, then some form of change directed toward improvement must be initiated. Evaluate a new program to find out if it is more effective than the present program. If the new program proves to be more effective, replace the old program with the new. Following the same procedure, if students are not learning what they should be learning, initiate changes to improve the situation.

Unfortunately, this simple and rather straightforward analysis of the relationship between curriculum evaluation and improvement is beset with problems of considerable magnitude which inhibit its total transferral to actual practice. The remainder of this chapter is devoted to the discussion of these problems, dealing first with curriculum evaluation, followed by a discussion of the process of curriculum improvement, and concluding with a suggested model for improving the curriculum.

[1]J. Lloyd Trump and Delmas F. Miller, *Secondary School Curriculum Improvement* (Boston: Allyn and Bacon, 1968), p. 339.

Curriculum Evaluation

Perhaps the most comprehensive definition of curriculum evaluation to appear in some time is offered by Stake.

> The purpose of educational evaluation is expository; to acquaint the audience with the workings of certain educators and their learners. It differs from educational research in its orientation to a specific program rather than to variables common to many programs. A *full* evaluation results in a story, supported perhaps by statistics and profiles. It tells what happened. It reveals perceptions and judgments that different groups and individuals hold—obtained, I hope, by objective means. It tells of merit and shortcomings. As a bonas, it may offer generalizations ("The moral of the story is . . .") for guidance of subsequent educational programs.
>
> Curriculum evaluation requires collection, processing, and interpretation of data pertaining to an educational program. For a complete evaluation, two main kinds of data are collected: (1) objective *descriptions* of goals, environments, personnel, methods and content, and outcomes; and (2) personal judgments as to the quality and appropriateness of those goals, environments, etc. The curriculum evaluator has such diverse tasks as weighing the outcomes of a training institute against previously stated objectives, comparing the costs of two courses of study, collecting judgments of the social worth of a certain goal, and determining the skill or sophistication needed for students commencing a certain scholastic experience. These evaluative efforts should lead to better decision making; to better development, better selection, and better use of curricula.[2]

Curriculum evaluation may be seen then as a continous process revolving around the attempt to objectively assess the worth of school experiences. The logical extension of this process is the development of projects designed to improve the educational experiences of youth, which in turn is followed by reevaluation. Thus the process continues with the ultimate objective of providing data regarding the following three factors:

1. The overall quality of the educational program. The program involved may be one school, one school system, or possibly the educational program of the entire nation, such as the National Assessment Program currently underway.

2. The quality of one or more aspects of the curriculum. This might involve the social studies program of a particular school or school system, the methods, or method, used to present the content of the curriculum, or the materials, or specific set of materials, used for instruction. Again the program may be defined as local, regional, or national in scope.

3. The effectiveness of programs designed to replace or supplement certain portions of the existing curriculum. This might consist of an experiment

[2]Robert E. Stake, "Toward a Technology for the Evaluation of Educational Programs," in Ralph Tyler, Robert Gagne, and Michael Scriven, Perspectives of Curriculum Evaluation, (AERA Monograph 1), © 1967 by Rand McNally & Company, Chicago, p. 5.

designed to test the effectiveness of a new course of study for civic education.

The Process of Curriculum Evaluation

To gain a better understanding of the process of curriculum evaluation, it may be helpful to consider the major components of the evaluative process. First, a specific definition of the product must be made. This component is usually referred to as *objectives* or *goals*, and its purpose is to define specifically what the product should look like. This effort is generally accomplished by determining the specific qualities desired for students after they complete the educational experience in question and expressing these desired qualities in the form of descriptive statements. If an entire school program is being evaluated, objectives regarding the qualities desired, or in one sense a profile, are used as the basis for evaluation. Second, the means used to achieve the stated objectives must be considered. This component is concerned with the methodology of evaluation, the specific methods that will be employed to assess the stated objectives. Third, the standards or norms used to judge the adequacy of the product must be established. Standards are usually expressed in terms of specific behaviors or certain learning outcomes. Table 15–1 illustrates the relationship between the components of the evaluative process and the basic components of the school curriculum.

Table 15–1

RELATIONSHIP BETWEEN THE COMPONENTS
QF THE SCHOOL CURRICULUM AND THE COMPONENTS
OF THE EVALUATIVE PROCESS

School curriculum	Evaluative process
Objectives	Objectives
Content and processes	Methodology of evaluation
Outcomes	Criteria of judging the outcomes

Consider an analogy to the evaluative process drawn from the world of industry. Before any product reaches the point where it is ready to sell to the consumer, a specific set of plans are drawn regarding (1) what the product will be, (2) what the product will look like, (3) what the product is designed to do, and (4) how the product is to be used. In other words, the designers know in advance the specific details of the finished product. The next phase in production is to gather materials, design machines, and outline specific procedures for the manufacture of the product. When the product is complete, its adequacy is judged by certain predetermined criteria. If the product is an automobile, for example, the criteria for judging adequacy of the finished product might include general performance, sales, repair needs, and so on.

Although curriculum evaluation deals in the realm of human behavior rather than automobiles, the process is basically the same, or should be. The roles each of the three components play in the evaluative process are discussed separately below.

THE ROLE OF OBJECTIVES. One of the more popular concerns of educators today revolves around the subject of objectives. The primary focus of these concerns lies in the direction of insisting that goals and objectives of the total school program, as well as specific programs, be restructured in terms of the specific behaviors the programs are designed to cope with. As it applies to curriculum evaluation, the position follows the line of reasoning that unless objectives are spelled out in terms of specific behaviors, evaluation becomes a difficult if not meaningless task. With this view in mind, curriculum evaluation becomes the task of assessing educational outcomes which are based on predetermined objectives.

Objectives generally fall into two categories: (1) objectives designed to lend direction to the "whole" educational program, and (2) objectives designed to lend direction to specific programs contained within the framework of the school curriculum.

Whole-program objectives constitute statements regarding the expected outcomes of an entire school program. In other words, they describe the characteristics a person completing the school program should possess. The objectives also characterize the qualities of the student presently participating in the program —in essence, a model of the educated man.

Attempts to define the educated man have occupied the thoughts and actions of educators and other interested parties for many years. Although numerous organizations and individuals have attempted to define the qualities that products and participants of the secondary school program should possess, probably the organization that has had the greatest impact on the development of educational objectives was the Commission on the Reorganization of Secondary Education. In 1918 the Commission issued a statement of goals which are still recognized as valid purposes of secondary education and for which most of the subsequent statements are based. The Commission defined the educated man as one that

> Recognizes the importance of good health and demonstrates this knowledge by practicing good health habits.
> Possesses a command of the fundamental processes and demonstrates this by his ability to apply the fundamentals of reading, writing, and arithmetic to the study of new material.
> Recognizes the importance of worthy home membership and demonstrates this by his ability to effectively function as a family member.
> Is prepared to enter the world of work as demonstrated by his ability to select his vocation wisely.

Possesses the qualities to act well his part as a member of neighborhood, city, state, and nation.

Is equiped to secure from his leisure the re-creation of body, mind, and spirit, and the enrichment and enlargement of his personality.

Possesses high ethical standards as demonstrated by a sense of personal responsibility, initiative, and spirit of service to the principles of democracy.[3]

The significance of these statements is that they have been used, and are still used, as a basis for secondary school development. The content and processes of the secondary school curriculum today greatly reflect the qualities contained in these statements. To judge the effectiveness of the curriculum, then, assumes the ability to determine how well the curriculum is achieving these purposes.

The second type of educational objectives may be classified as specific program objectives. Objectives of this nature are those that lend direction to the various aspects of the curriculum, and ideally grow out of the whole-program objectives. For example, the objectives of the social studies program or a single course in social studies, say civics, may relate to one or more of the whole-program objectives. Some recognized objectives of a social studies program are:

1. To understand movements, events, and personalities that have influenced the history of the United States.
2. To understand the economic system.
3. To understand the interdependence of individuals and nations.
4. To develop skills for recognizing harmful propaganda.
5. To develop skills for using maps, globes, and charts.
6. To develop favorable attitudes toward basic American beliefs.
8. To develop favorable attitudes toward our American heritage.[4]

Each facet of the curriculum has, in some form, objectives similar to the ones cited for the social studies. Objectives of this type command similar significance to whole program objectives in that they become the basis for evaluation. To decide if a specific curricular program is effective is to determine how well the objectives are being achieved. In this respect, the desired outcomes of whole program evaluation and specific program evaluation are the same.

METHODOLOGY OF EVALUATION Before proceeding to the discussion of various methods used in curriculum evaluation, it may well serve a purpose to point out a distinction that is often made between the terms "curriculum evaluation" and "curriculum research." Although considerable ambiguity exists in the use of the terms, the general distinction is often one concerned with the precision involved.[5] For example, one might "evaluate" the effectiveness of a particular course of study in a variety of ways, ranging from pure subjectivity to controlled

---

[3]Commission on Reorganization of Secondary Education, *Cardinal Principles of Secondary Education*, Bulletin No. 35 (Washington, D.C.: Government Printing Office, 1918).

[4]Adapted from William B. Ragan, *Modern Elementary Curriculum* (New York: Holt, 1966), p. 293.

[5]David A. Abramson, "Curriculum Research and Evaluation," *Review of Education Research* 36 (June 1966), p. 392.

experimentation. Somewhere along this continuum a line might be drawn to separate evaluation and research. It is extremely difficult, however, to make this distinction when reviewing the literature dealing with curriculum research and evaluation. Perhaps there should be no distinction at all.

Our discussion of the methods used in curriculum evaluation will proceed from the more subjective methods to the more highly structured research procedures.

Probably the most subjective means for evaluating the curriculum might be called *explanatory methods*. The use of the term "explanatory" in this context refers to those methods in which subjective judgment is the sole basis for evaluation. Perhaps the best example of this procedure is the current practices employed by accrediting associations. The procedure involves examining the school program and judging its adequacy by how well it meets certain standards predetermined by the association.

For instance, the criteria used by most associations to evaluate secondary school programs are based on the evaluative criteria set forth by the National Study of Secondary School Evaluation. These criteria are centered around the major aspects of a school program:

1. The philosophy and objectives of the school.
2. The relationship of the school to the community.
3. The specific educational program and related activities.
4. The physical plant.
5. The school staff and administration.[6]

The quality of a school program, then, is judged on the basis of the degree, determined subjectively, to which the program is meeting these criteria. The decision regarding adequacy is normally determined by a reviewing committee, and based on this judgment, the program is evaluated.

To further illustrate this procedure, consider the following specific criteria, selected from the total set under the heading "Program of Studies" that are employed in the evaluation of a school program. A program of studies is judged adequate if:

1. Proper recreational opportunities are available.
2. Professional consultants are used in curriculum development procedures.
3. Opportunities are available for developing favorable attitudes toward home and family living.
4. Instructional activities provide for extensive use of the library.
5. Opportunities are available for acquiring a knowledge for and appreciation of the cultural heritage.[7]

---

[6]Adapted from National Study of Secondary School Evaluation, *Evaluative Criteria for the Evaluation of Secondary Schools* (Washington, D.C.: National Study of Secondary School Evaluation, 1969).

[7]*Ibid.*, p. 55.

The specific criteria, of which the preceding are representative, concludes with four statements that the evaluator must judge in determining the overall effectiveness of the program of studies.

(a) To what extent does the curriculum serve the needs of all students?
(b) To what extent is the curriculum organized in a sequential manner?
(c) To what extent is the curriculum responsive to change?
(d) To what extent is the curriculum adapted to the different ability levels of students?[8]

An abridgement of an actual committee report pertaining to the program of studies is presented below and may be viewed as somewhat typical of the explanatory method of curriculum evaluation.

PROGRAM OF STUDIES

The reviewing committee has carefully examined the section on the Program of Studies of the Evaluative Criteria prepared by the administration and faculty of Catholic High School.

The instructional program at Catholic High School is of a college preparatory nature. The school offers 32½ units of credit courses.

It is evident that many varied techniques and approaches which are being used in the presentations of instructional materials have proved very effective and conducive to learning.

Result of the observation made in the classroom and the study of the annual report, the committee feels that the students of Catholic High School are being instructed and directed by a very highly certified and qualified staff.

The committee feels that the instructional program seems to be flexible enough to allow for the improvements that are necessary from time to time, and that the teaching is so planned as to develop knowledge, understanding, attitudes, ideals, habits and skills which are vitally important in helping the individual secure a firm grip and place in our American Society.

The committee noted overloaded classes in various areas but realizes the faculty is aware of this deficiency and that corrections and adjustments are forthcoming. After making overall observations, discussing the instructional program with faculty members and students, and reviewing the self-study evaluation as submitted by the faculty, the committee offers the following observations, commendations and recommendations in the various subject matter areas of the Program of Studies:[9]

Another frequently used method of this nature is *simple observation.* Although similar to the preceding method, it differs by its lack of structure. Simple observation consists primarily of observing the curriculum in action and making a judgment according to some preconceived notions. For example, some key questions mentioned by Doll relating to curriculum evaluation are often answered

[8] *Ibid.,* p. 39.
[9] Report of Reviewing Committee for Southern Association of Colleges and Schools, Catholic High School Report (Baton Rouge, La., 1966), p. 6.

using observation as the principal method. How much movement in the curriculum is present? Is the curriculum moving toward its goals? How fast is the movement occurring? What precisely can be said about direction of the movement?[10]

Obviously, the major weakness of this procedure is the lack of structure and control. For example, to judge the effectiveness of such critical aspects of the curriculum as the classroom climate, materials for instruction, evaluation procedures, methods of teaching, teaching effectiveness, and the like, requires considerably more precision than is possible from simple observation.

A second group of methods available for use in curriculum evaluation may be classified as *descriptive methods*. The techniques that fall in the descriptive classification are those designed for: (1) assessing the current status of the curriculum, (2) comparing the curriculum with internal and external criteria, and (3) relating the various components of the curriculum to each other and to short and long-range goals. The degree of precision achieved from the use of these methods is considerably higher than simple explanatory procedures. There remains, however, considerable variability in the degree of precision the descriptive method can produce.

One of the more common descriptive procedures for determining the current status of the curriculum is the survey. The degree of precision of this method is limited but it does contain a certain amount of structure, thereby allowing the evaluation to be more systematic. Surveys have been employed to answer questions relating to "what exists" and "how much of what is being evaluated exists." The what exists question normally revolves around attempting to answer such questions as the following:

1. How many courses and of what type are currently offered in the curriculum?
2. What types of materials are available for the instructional program?
3. What is the general status of the teaching staff?
4. What methods are most commonly employed in the teaching-learning situation?

Answers to these questions and others like them provide a general view of the quantity involved in the program but provides little information regarding the quality of the program.

Surveys are also used to solicit opinions from persons involved in the school program. For example, surveys can be quite helpful in assessing the general feelings of teachers, students, and parents regarding the school program.

A descriptive method with somewhat more precision is the *comparative approach* to curriculum evaluation. If employed in the descriptive sense, the

---

[10]Ronald C. Doll, *Curriculum Improvement: Decision-Making Process* (Boston: Allyn and Bacon, 1964), p. 321.

comparative approach allows the evaluator a yardstick to aid in judging the adequacy of the curriculum. This is accomplished by using another program or programs to determine what differences if any exist. The common procedure for applying this technique is to select two or more groups representing various points on the continuum in order to identify the significant factors that distinguish one group from another. Comparisions can be made, for instance, between graded schools and nongraded schools with the purpose of attempting to isolate significant factors associated with each.

This approach was used in a recent study by Nelson when he attempted to compare school achievement among adolescent children with working and non-working mothers. Specifically, the author sought answers to the following questions:

1. Is there a difference in school achievement among children from homes where the mother works full-time, part-time, or not at all?
2. Do boys and girls differ in school achievement among the maternal employment groups?[11]

In general, the casual-comparative approach is used when evaluation questions are of the nature that require the program being evaluated to be compared with some internal or external criteria.

A third descriptive technique for providing information regarding the school curriculum is the *correlational* or *predictive* approach. It differs primarily from the comparative approach in that instead of looking for differences between and among groups, it concerns itself with the discovery of relationships. For example, to discover the degree of relationship that exists between the amount of time spent doing homework and school achievement provides a base for making decisions regarding the role of homework in the school program. The relationship between certain aspects of the school curriculum and student success in college is another example of how this procedure might be applied.

The most precise procedure for evaluating the curriculum is the *experimental approach*. To illustrate the nature of the experimental method in curriculum evaluation, a brief summary of a recent study is presented.

A study which appeared in an educational research journal was designed to compare achievement scores of eleventh-grade students when instructed by a teaching team with the achievement scores of similar students taught in traditionally arranged classes on a standardized examination in American History. It was hypothesized that those students taught by a teaching team of three teachers possessing a variety of competencies would achieve significantly higher scores on questions requiring factual recall or recognition, as well as on questions requiring reflection, than would students taught by individual teachers, each working

[11]Dean D. Nelson, "A Study of School Achievement Among Adolescent Children with Working and Non-Working Mothers," *The Journal of Educational Research* 62 (July-August 1969).

independently in traditional classroom groupings. The subjects used in this study were 164 eleventh-grade students with no prior experience with teaching teams. The researcher first divided his subjects into two groups, an experimental group and a control group, that were approximately equal on certain measures important to the outcome of the study. The students in the experimental group were assigned to large classes, small classes, or into individual study according to the combined professional judgment of the members of the team. Flexible scheduling, flexible grouping, and teacher teams were applied.

The second group, the control section, was treated quite differently. These students were divided into classes ranging from 25 to 30 students and met daily in the traditional manner. They were taught by the same teacher operating independently with individual classrooms and teaching materials were utilized at the descretion of the individual teacher. At the conclusion of the experiment, the students were given a standardized one-semester examination in American History especially prepared for this study.

After the test scores were in, the researcher proceeded with the tasks of analyzing the data through appropriate statistical techniques, organizing and presenting his data, and drawing conclusions based on the data.

Is the team approach superior to, equal to, or inferior to the conventional approach in achieving higher scores on questions requiring factual recall or recognition, as well as on questions requiring reflection of eleventh-grade students in American History? The researcher concluded that no significant differences were found between the two groups on questions requiring factual recall or recognition. Questions requiring reflection, however, yielded significant differences. The researcher further concluded that teaching teams may indeed be more effective than conventional classroom arrangements in producing certain types of learning.[12]

The foregoing example is illustrative of the application of the experimental approach to curriculum evaluation. The approach differs from the descriptive approach primarily on the basis of time and control. In other words, the experimental approach allows the investigator to assume command of the situation and exert control over those factors that might influence the outcome of the evaluation other than the specific aspect of the curriculum being evaluated. For example, if the effect of team teaching on achievement is to be tested, those factors that might influence achievement other than team teaching must be isolated and controlled. When this is accomplished, a more accurate decision can be made regarding the impact of this type of teaching method.

The meaning of controlled experimentation is expressed well by Stanley:

> The word "experimentation" has come to have many meanings for educationists. The most common one of these might be termed "experiENtation, trying

---

[12]Jack R. Fraenkel, "A Comparison of Achievement Between Students Taught by a Teaching Team and Students Taught in Traditional Classes on a Standardized Examination in American History," *The Journal of Educational Research* 61 (September 1967).

new approaches and subjectively evaluating their effectiveness. My concern here is with a more structured type of inquiry, akin to that carried out in many of the sciences. It involves control by the experimentor of at least one variable, such as teaching arithmetic, that he can *manipulate.* Thus, experimentation of this kind differs from observation of naturally occurring events in that the stage has been set by the experimenter so that the possibly differential effects of at least two "treatments" can be observed in a situation where assignment of *experimental units* (often pupils or classes) to the several treatments has been made without bias.[13]

CRITERIA OF EVALUATION The third component of the evaluation process is the criteria or standards by which the total curriculum, or some part of it, is judged. For example, if the objective of a particular social studies program is to produce better citizens, some means of judging the degree of citizenship possessed by the individuals in the program must be found.

One of the more common criteria used for evaluating the curriculum is the statement of criteria developed by the Cooperative Study of Secondary School Standards. Although mentioned in the preceding sections of this chapter, the fact that they are used both for determining objectives and for establishing standards justifies a brief treatment here. The guide for secondary school evaluation, first published in 1940 and revised in 1950 and 1960, expresses its function in the following statement:

> The study has developed a proved way of recognizing that schools which are quite different may be equally good. This involves the basic principle that a school should be evaluated in terms of what it is striving to accomplish (its philosophy and objectives) and in terms of the extent to which it is meeting the needs of the students who are enrolled or for whom it is responsible. . . . The evaluations resulting from the use of materials and procedures suggested by the National Study of Secondary School Evaluation may be considered as ratios of accomplishment where the quality and nature of work done in a school are related to what should be done in order to satisfy the philosophy and objectives of the school and the needs of the youth who are served by the school.[14]

With this objective, the *Evaluative Criteria* contains a set of statements by which the school program is to be judged. In one sense, the criteria set forth serve as a bais for all phases of the evaluative process.

Another common criteria used in curriculum evaluation involves quantitative norms or standards. This approach employs pupil performance as a means of evaluating the curriculum and uses as a basis for judgment a comparison with local or national norms. By *norms* we mean the procedure for establishing performance levels for a particular group.

Norms are established by administering tests, say achievement tests, to a large group of students over a period of time. From the results of these tests, a

[13]Julian C. Stanley, "Elementary Experimental Design: An Expository Treatment," *Psychology in the Schools* 4 (July 1967), p. 195.

[14]National Study of Secondary School Evaluation, *op. cit.,* p. 4.

normal distribution of scores is obtained. The distribution represents the performance of students on a particular test. The significance of this kind of distribution whether conducted on a local level or on a national level, is that it provides a yardstick by which to measure individual or group performance. An individual test score, then, becomes more meaningful when it can be compared with some norm or standard.

Figure 15–1 illustrates the use of the normal distribution in establishing norms. It can be noted that the entire area under the curve represents the total number of scores in the distribution. Vertical lines appear on the curve and represent the major subdivisions to the right and left of the average score. The numbers printed in these subareas are percents—percentages of the total number of people. Thus 34.13 percent of all cases in the normal distribution have scores falling between 0 and one standard deviation. The fact that 68.26 percent of the cases fall between + or − one standard deviation gives rise to the common statement that in a normal distribution roughly two-thirds of all cases involved in the educational enterprise might be expected to perform at the average level.

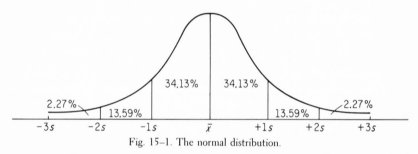

Fig. 15–1. The normal distribution.

When using this approach for curriculum evaluation, one measures pupil performance directly, which in turn is used to reflect on the adequacy of the curriculum. If pupils perform well (at least average or above) it is assumed that the curriculum is performing accordingly. For example, if senior pupils take the College Entrance Examination Board (CEEB), their performance is judged by a comparison with the national norms (distribution) set for that particular examination. This can be observed in Fig. 15–1. For instance, if a student's score is 500, a comparison with the national norm would reveal that his performance was the average—that is, he performed above 50 percent of those taking the test before him and below 50 percent of those taking the test before him. If a group of students taking the test performed in a manner closely approximating the normal distribution, it might be said that the students performed in the expected fashion. If the student's distribution differed from the normal, the interpretation would be made in accordance. In any event, the outcome of the comparison is considered indicative of the adequacy of the school curriculum.

It should also be mentioned that many school systems construct similar distributions on the local level which are used in a like fashion as described above.

A third criteria that may be used in evaluating the curriculum is postschool performance. This is considered, by many, to be the most significant criteria for judging the school curriculum. Postschool performance is probably the most difficult (consequently less used), because of the difficulty in measuring the performance of the product. For example, if the curriculum is being evaluated in terms of its objectives, certainly many of these objectives cannot be measured while the student is still in school. Schools with more specialized purposes can often use criteria of this type more effectively. A college preparatory school, for example, might set various aspects of college performance as criteria. The curriculum of the school could then be evaluated in this respect. Schools with more comprehensive objectives, many of which may be nonacademic, have a more difficult time in using postschool criteria.

Problems and Prospects of Curriculum Evaluation

One of the major problems associated with curriculum evaluation is the differences that exist regarding its *role* and *function* within the total framework of the school curriculum. In introducing a review of research on curriculum evaluation, Baker expressed a common view regarding this matter.

> The past three years have netted little in the way of definitive empirical research dealing with curriculum. To be sure, many papers have been written on the evaluation of specific programs, and reports have been made of the differential efficacy of a variety of instructional procedures. However, curriculum research and evaluation as a subject matter has not yet been defined and bounded.[15]

A promising procedure for defining the function of curriculum evaluation is offered by Scriven. In offering a distinction between *goals* and *roles* of evaluation, the procedure emphasizes that these functions be referred to as "formative" evaluation and "summative" evaluation. The lack of such a distinction, the author believes, is partially responsible for the lack of productivity in past efforts to systematically evaluate the curriculum.[16]

Formative evaluation is defined as evaluation procedures which are employed for the purpose of revising the curriculum while it is still in development. For example, formative evaluation would concern itself with answering questions about educational instruments in the following manner:

1. How well does the instrument perform?
2. How does the instrument compare to some other instrument?

[15]Robert L. Baker, "Curriculum Evaluation," *Review of Educational Research* 39 (June 1969), p. 339.

[16]Michael Scriven, "The Methodology of Evaluation," in Ralph W. Tyler et al., *Perspectives of Curriculum Evaluation* (Chicago: Rand McNally, 1967), p. 43.

3. What specific effects does the instrument have on other educational variables?

4. Is the instrument worth what it is costing?[17]

In order for this type of evaluation to be effective, a planned and continuous program of evaluation must be built in with the overall plan for curriculum development. This type of activity "permits adjustments to be made in the curriculum on the basis of deficiencies identified enroute. It also suggests a trial-revision cycle based on predetermined standards of enroute student performance or a defined nonstudent outcome."[18]

Summative evaluation refers to the evaluation activity that attempts to arrive at an overall estimate of the curriculum. This might involve an evaluation of a course of study, or even the entire curriculum. In essence, it is an attempt to evaluate the product of the curriculum.

Another persistent problem in curriculum evaluation centers around *objectives*. More precisely, what objectives should be used, who should formulate them, and how should they be stated? It should be noted that this is not a problem unique to curriculum evaluation but rather a problem common to all aspects of the educational enterprise. However, since it is generally agreed that the process of curriculum evaluation is one of determining the outcomes of objectives, the subject of objectives becomes of prominent importance.

In respect to evaluation activity, the major problem revolves around how the objectives are to be stated. To understand the nature of this problem, one must remember that for any type of meaningful evaluation to occur some measurable entity must be present. To develop an objective which merely states a vague generality in respect to a proposed outcome can only expect a generality when its effectiveness is judged. For example, educational objectives at all levels have traditionally been on the basis of understanding, appreciating, becoming aware of, and so on. However noble these outcomes may be, they are not measurable and therefore cannot be adequately evaluated.

In recent years a considerable effort has been made to enhance the use of educational objectives in the evaluation process. Basically, the efforts have included attempts to (1) classify educational objectives according to order of complexity, and (2) rephrase objectives in terms of specific behavioral outcomes. Probably the most notable attempt at classifying objectives is to be found in the *Taxonomy of Educational Objectives, Handbook I: Cognitive Domain* developed by Bloom[19] and *Handbook II: Affective Domain* developed by Krathwohl.[20]

Although not enjoying complete acceptance, and certainly not complete

[17] *Ibid.*, p. 40.

[18] Robert Baker, *op. cit.*, p. 353.

[19] Benjamin S. Bloom (ed.), *Taxonomy of Educational Objectives Handbook I: Cognitive Domain* (New York: Longmans, 1956).

[20] David R. Krathwohl et al., *Taxonomy of Educational Objectives Handbook II: Affective Domain* (New York: McKay, 1964).

agreement, the movement toward stating objectives in behavioral terms has gained widespread notice in recent years. The primary advantage of stating objectives in this manner is to allow greater specificity of measurement. This can be seen in the following example illustrating an objective stated in general terms and the same objective stated in terms of specifics.

General Objective   To understand the period prior to the start of the Civil War

Behavioral Objective   When students complete the study of the period prior to the start of the Civil War, they will be able to: (1) relate the major causes of the Civil War, (2) . . .

It can be seen that the objective stated in terms of specific outcomes lends itself to measurement to a greater extent than the objective stated in more general terms.

In the area of evaluation methodology, a consistent concern has been the *lack of control* in curriculum evaluation activities. Lack of control in evaluation activities means that factors other than what is being evaluated operate to influence the outcome, thereby distorting the desired results. When loose control is present during evaluation, it becomes difficult to determine if the outside factors influenced the outcome more than the factor being evaluated. For instance, if posttest scores are being used to evaluate the effectiveness of a set of instructional materials, a large number of factors, other than the set of instructional materials, operate to influence performance on the posttest. These are the factors that must be isolated and controlled before an accurate judgment regarding the instructional materials can be made.

The concern for lack of control in evaluation activities stems primarily from the common practice of employing descriptive techniques and quasi-experiments in curriculum evaluation. When descriptive techniques are used, such as a causal-comparative study conducted after a program is underway or completed, it is extremely difficult if not impossible to properly equalize the subjects being compared on the relevant factors that might influence the outcome of the comparison other than the primary target of the comparison.

A final note concerning problems and prospects in the area of evaluation criteria. Traditionally, the chief criteria for evaluating the worth of educational programs has been test performance. Measurement specialists have expressed for years that if it exists in quantity, it can be measured. This follows the line of reasoning that if an educational program has an impact, that impact can be measured. From this exercise, standards can be set that reflect the general achievement distribution of students. Therefore, criteria based on test performance are an adequate means for assessing the curriculum.

The problem, of course, is the notion that our measurements are not perfectly complete and the instruments used in measurement are primarily developed to provide discrimination among individuals. However important discriminating among individuals may be for instruction and guidance, it is a rarity when standardized tests are available that discriminate among curricula.[21]

Illustrative Evaluation Projects

The purpose of this section is to present several evaluation projects, both past and present, to illustrate some of the procedures employed in curriculum evaluation. Selecting representative projects from the many that have been conducted, and are presently underway, is, in itself, a hazardous task. No attempt was made to be all-inclusive, but rather, to select a few of the projects that have made, or have the potential of making a significant contribution to educational practice. A second criteria used in selecting the projects was the basic approach used. An attempt was made to select projects that employed somewhat different techniques. The five projects selected were: The Eight-Year Study, Project Talent, The Conant Report, Project Physics, and the National Assessment Project.

THE EIGHT-YEAR STUDY. The purpose of this project, undertaken by the Progressive Education Association, was to obtain evidence regarding the relationship between the type of high school program students were exposed to and success in college. At the time this study was undertaken, colleges and universities governed the curriculum of the high school, as they do to a great extent today. It was believed by some that if this restriction could be removed the secondary schools could improve their program. The opposite viewpoint contended that to be successful in college a student must pursue a curriculum designed specifically for college preparation. The Eight-Year Study was designed to seek a solution to this controversy.

In 1932 a number of colleges and universities agreed to participate in the project by agreeing to accept students from a group of thirty selected secondary schools without entrance examinations and without regard to the normal requirements for admission—i.e., so many courses in math, English, foreign language, and so on. The only requirements for admission were recommendation of the principal, record of past achievement and class activities, and scores on aptitude and achievement tests. The plan was to allow students to follow a variety of curricular patterns during their four years in high school and then assess their progress during their four years of college.

The schools selected to participate in the study were thirty secondary schools, both public and private, and were representative of size and geographic location. Each school was given a free hand in developing programs for its students.

The procedure for the study consisted of comparing graduates from the experimental schools with graduates of the conventional high schools. The students were equated on the basis of sex, age, socioeconomic status, intelligence, and other relevant variables. The object of this exercise was to equate all of the factors

[21]Stake, *Ibid.*, p. 6.

that might influence the outcome of the study other than the type of college preparation experienced by each of the participants. This effort resulted in 1,475 matched pairs of subjects. During the college experience, the students were compared on the following factors:

1. Intellectual competence as measured by grade point average, honors, and other intellectual pursuits beyond the classroom.
2. The manner in which the students used their leisure time.
3. Competence in judgment, adaptability, and other practical aspects of college life.
4. Philosophy of life, ideals, standards, goals.
5. Emotional stability.
6. Social skills.
7. Awareness and sensitivity to social problems.
8. Physical fitness.

The study was completed in 1940 with the following general conclusions:

1. The graduates of the experimental schools were not handicapped in their college work.
2. Departures from the prescribed pattern of subjects did not lessen the student's ability to cope with the responsibilities of college.
3. Students from the experimental schools that made the most curriculum revisions achieved distinctly higher than students of equal ability with whom they were compared.
4. The basic assumption of the study—that success in college does not depend upon the study of certain subjects for a certain period in high school—was substantiated by the findings of the study.[22]

THE CONANT REPORT. A noted educator, James Bryant Conant, launched a curriculum evaluation study that has had profound effect on the curriculum of the American high school. His first attempt at curriculum evaluation resulted in the widely read book *The American High School Today*, published in 1958.[23] This work was followed by *Education in the Junior High School Years* in 1960, *Slums and Suburbs* in 1961, and *The Education of American Teachers* in 1963. However one feels about the methodology of these investigations, primarily that of structured observation, the studies have influenced the secondary curriculum to a considerable extent.

The forecasts of William Alexander, made shortly after the publication of the first report, have been extremely accurate. He predicted:

1. That this report will be widely read and even more widely cited.
2. That it will be used effectively to resist movements toward establishing selective academic high schools.
3. That it may aid proponents of school consolidation efforts. . . .

[22]Adapted from Wilford M. Aikin, *The Story of the Eight-Year Study* (New York: Harper, 1942).
[23]James B. Conant, *The American High School Today* (New York: McGraw-Hill, 1958).

4. That the twenty-one specific recommendations will be used to support and refute many local proposals.

5. That, most important, this report may mark the completion of an already significant turn in the public press and in public discussions away from attacks on secondary education and toward realistic appraisal of the financial and personnel problems involved in improving secondary education in the United States.[24]

The original study consisted of a survey of previously identified comprehensive high schools located in twenty-six of the most populas states. The basic question the study was designed to answer was:

> Can a school at one and the same time provide a good general education for *all* the pupils as future citizens of a democracy, provide elective programs for the majority to develop useful skills, and educate adequately those with a talent for handling advanced academic subjects—particularly foreign languages and advanced mathematics?[25]

To answer this question, the investigators conducted a structured interview, accompanied with visits to classrooms of the participating schools and school systems. On the basis of the data collected, the guiding question for this study was answered in the affirmative. However, it was found that the majority of the schools surveyed were not achieving the comprehensiveness desired, yet possessed the potential of doing so if certain modifications were made. These modifications, expressed in terms of recommendations, centered around the following headings: the counseling system, individualized programs, required courses for all, ability grouping, a supplement to the regular high school diploma, English composition, diversified programs for the development of marketable skills, special consideration for the very slow reader, programs for the academically talented, highly gifted pupils, the academic inventory, organization of the school day, prerequisites for advanced academic courses, rank in class, academic honors list, developmental reading programs, summer school, foreign languages, science courses, homerooms, and twelfth-grade social studies. The study suggested that if positive changes were made in these areas a truly comprehensive high school could be a reality.

In view of the many innovations and changes that have emerged since this report was published, it is evident that the impact of the study has been substantial. Many of the improvement projects currently underway have been greatly influenced by the study and the subsequent recommendations.

PROJECT TALENT. Another project of considerable importance to the secondary curriculum is Project Talent. Directed by John C. Flanagan of the American Institute for Research and the University of Pittsburg, the study represents an

---

[24]William M. Alexander, "The Conant Report: A Preliminary Appraisal," *Phi Delta Kappan* 40 (March 1959), p. 249.

[25]Conant, *op. cit.*, p. 15.

effort to examine youth on a national scale relating to their human talents and characteristics. The project sought information regarding students' interests, their career plans, and the relation of their high school courses to their life goals. The specific objectives of the study were:

1. To survey available talent.
2. To identify interests, aptitudes, and background factors.
3. To determine effects of lack of interest and motivation.
4. To identify factors affecting vocational choice.
5. To identify predictors of creativity and productivity.
6. To determine the effectiveness of various types of educational experiences.
7. To study procedures for realizing individual potential.[26]

The project was also concerned with determining why so much potential is lost and to probe some possibilities for reducing the loss.

The project sample consisted of 5 percent of the public and private high schools throughout the nation. Data were gathered by administering a large battery of tests consisting of approximately 2,000 questions asked of 440,000 high school students. A questionnaire was also administered to 1,353 secondary schools relating to a variety of school characteristics.

A large amount of data has already been collected by the investigators but the real impact of this study will come as a result of the follow-up studies planned for one, five, ten, and twenty years after the high school students have graduated.

The long-range outcomes, as they relate to the curriculum, are thought to be:

1. To provide and compile a comprehensive inventory of the characteristics related to the talents of the youth of America.
2. To develop a set of standards aimed at improving the educational and psychological measurement of human characteristics.
3. To develop a comprehensive guide to be used in the counseling of high school students.
4. To gain an understanding of the factors that influence a young person's choice of their life work.
5. To gain an understanding of the educational experiences which prepare students for their chosen life work.[27]

NATIONAL ASSESSMENT PROGRAM. Probably the most ambitious effort to evaluate the curriculum is in the beginning stages at the time of this writing. Known as the National Assessment of Education, the project has as its primary purpose the assessment of what people can do. More specifically, the major objective is to determine the percentage of people who have certain levels of

---

[26]John C. Flanagan, and others, *The Identification, Development, and Utilization of Human Talents: The American High School Student* (Cooperative Research Project No. 635, University of Pittsburg, 1964), pp. 1–3.
[27]*Ibid.*

knowledge, understanding, and attitudes. It is believed that this effort will prove an accurate estimate of how well we are doing in education and, after further assessments, how we are progressing toward improving the products of education.

Ralph Tyler, a prominent figure in the assessment program, comments about assessing the progress of education:

> Because of its primary importance, our people are seeking information to guide their thinking and action in support of education. The need for information of this sort by teachers, administrators, school heads, and the general public is a legitimate one. There is some misunderstanding of the nature of an assessment of educational progress because it is confused with the typical achievement testing programs used in many schools. Current testing programs seek to measure the relative achievement of individual pupils, while the assessment of educational progress seeks to describe what has been learned by various groups representing different geographic areas and different sections of the population.[28]

The procedure for the assessment program consists of providing comprehensive information, with the use of specifically designed achievement tests, about what is being learned. The areas to be assessed are literature, science, social studies, writing, citizenship, music, mathematics, reading art, and vocational education. The objectives which will guide the assessment in each of the areas were developed under contract by the American Institutes for Research, Educational Testing Service, The Psychological Corporation, and Science Research Associates.

An example of the type of objectives developed for the study is as follows:

> Respects the views and feelings of other people and can tell why this respect is desirable.[29]

An example of the exercises developed for the study is as follows:

> You are going to hear a piece of music.
> You will be asked what instrument is playing.[30]

In regard to communicating the results of the assessment of educational progress, the following hypothetical example is offered:

> For a sample of thirteen-year-old boys of higher socio-economic status from large cities of the northeast region, it was found that:
> 91 percent knew two-thirds of the following important ingredients in a persons' diet.
> 52 percent could plan an appropriate experiment for testing hypothesis like the following. . . .[31]

---

[28]Ralph Tyler, "Assessing the Progress of Education," *Phi Delta Kappan* 47 (September 1965), p. 14.

[29]The Committee on Assessing the Progress of Education, *How Much Are Students Learning* (Ann Arbor, Mich.: The Committee, November 1968), p. 9.

[30]*Ibid.*, p. 11.

[31]*Ibid.*, p. 15.

The project, when completed, will constitute one of the largest (testing of 120,000 to 140,000 individuals) efforts of this nature ever undertaken.

Curriculum Improvement

Improving the curriculum of the school has always been a major concern to persons interested in the education of young people. To say, however, that improvement of the curriculum has progressed on an upward plane throughout the history of American education is an overstatement. There have been periods of notable change but there have also been long periods where attempts to improve the curriculum proceeded at an extremely slow pace. Secondary education probably falls into the latter category more than any other level of education, at least in terms of content offerings. A look at the basic course offerings of Chicago High School (Central) in 1884 lends some support to this idea.

First year	Algebra, Latin or German Physical Geography
Second year	Geometry, History, Latin or German, Natural History, Botany
Third year	Natural Philosophy, Rhetoric, Latin, German, or French, Chemistry, English Literature
Fourth year	Astronomy, Civil Government, Latin, German, or French, Study of Authors, Geology, Mental Science, Reviews, Political Economy

Source: John A. Clement, *Principles and Practices of Secondary Education* (New York: Appleton, 1924), p. 189.
Note: The course of study was divided into three terms allowing for variation in time for each course offered.

The end of World War II marked the beginning of a movement that has progressed more rapidly and included more significant attempts to improve the curriculum than any other period in the history of American education. The decade 1960–70 was particularly productive in regard to the generation of ideas and projects aimed at curriculum improvement. If the present trend continues, as it is almost certain to do, the decade 1970–80 should be exciting indeed.

Any attempt to cover all of the changes that have taken place is an impossible task as far as this text is concerned. Therefore, an attempt will be made to deal with the nature of curriculum improvement, factors influencing change, and factors hindering the ongoing process of curriculum improvement.

It should be mentioned at this point that the terms "improvement" and "change" are not always synonymous. A number of changes that have taken place have not brought about significant improvement, and conversly, a number of attempts to improve the curriculum have not resulted in meaningful change.

Nature of Curriculum Improvement

Several areas appear to be the basis for much of the curriculum change taking place today. Even with the wide diversity in subjects and settings, the most common elements appear to be:

1. Reorientation of content emphasis.
2. Organization for teaching and learning.
3. Role of the student in the process of education.

CONTENT EMPHASIS. Although a number of content changes, in the form of deletions or additions, have occurred in modern times, the basic courses presently offered in junior and senior high schools in the United States are not markedly different from the course offerings of schools several decades ago. The major change that appears to underlie many of the projects currently underway is the attempt to restructure the content in an effort to make it more "relevant." Current literature in the area of curriculum makes considerable use of this term. Basically, the phrase "making content more relevant" implies that a need exists to take the basic content, such as science and mathematics, and restructure it in order to concentrate more on understanding of basic concepts and their general applicability to other fields and present and future life situations. In other words, the changes in this direction that are taking place appear to be following the idea that subject matter, in itself, has less to offer when viewed in discrete units, unrelated to the total realm of knowledge. This idea represents a marked difference from the traditional liberal arts approach to subject matter so prevalent in teaching subject matter in the past.

For example, some of the "new mathematics" programs stress the desirability of dissolving the traditional compartmentalization of subjects like algebra or geometry and replacing them with problem-solving approaches that require the use of interrelated facets of the entire field of mathematics. This "interrelatedness" is viewed as a means of making the subject matter in this field more relevant. This same idea is becoming more noticeable in a number of fields of study.

The idea of structure and relevance is expressed well by Goodlad. He states:

> If previous areas of curriculum development can be described as child-centered or society-centered, this one can be designated as subject- or discipline-centered. The ends and means of schooling are derived from organized bodies of knowledge. Further, the curriculum is planned by physicists, mathematicians, and historians, and students are encouraged to think like these scholars. The word "structure" has replaced "the whole child" in curriculum jargon. [See G. W. Ford and Lawrence Pugno, (eds.), *The Structure of Knowledge and The Curriculum* Rand McNally, Chicago, 1964.]

> Many curriculum builders seek to organize their fields around the primary

structural elements of each discipline: the concepts, key ideas, principles, and modes of inquiry. It is assumed that understanding these elements (rather than merely possessing the facts) gives the student the intellectual power to attack unfamiliar problems and enables him to grasp intuitively the relationship of new phenomena already experienced.[32]

In general, the current movement in the area of subject matter is to improve the curriculum by updating content, reorganizing the subject matter, and initiating some rather unique approaches to methodology. This type of activity can be seen in some of the relatively new programs, such as Project English, Physical Science Study (PSSC), Biological Sciences Curriculum Study (BSCS), Earth Science Curriculum Project (ESCP), and others.

ORGANIZATION FOR LEARNING. Traditionally, secondary schools have operated on the basis of one teacher being responsible for the instruction of 25–30 students in a particular subject. This is still the most popular means of curriculum organization in junior and senior high school in America. However, the idea that the most efficient way to organize the learning environment is to group students by grade level and subject has been seriously challenged in recent years. This renewed interest in curriculum organization has resulted in numerous attempts to improve on the existing patterns.

One of the most widely publicized attempts to change the traditional organization for learning is the move to replace the graded organization with nongraded organization. Basically this approach involves allowing the student to progress at his own rate of speed without regard to grade-level barriers. A number of variations to this approach exist but a common element with all of them is that the traditional concept of the grade level is seen as a barrier to efficient learning.

The school philosophy of Nova High School, Fort Lauderdale, Florida, one of the pioneers in nongraded programs, is illustrative of the philosophy behind the movement.

Nova places major emphasis on the areas of communication, mathematics, pure and applied science, humanities, and social studies. However, it is recognized that, while mastery in these areas is important in itself, the educative process demands more from the teacher than mere formal presentation of the material. What a student is learning at any given time is determined by his past experiences, by his present interests, needs, and capabilities, and by the kind and quality of the interaction which takes place between the student and his environment during the learning process. Therefore, to effectively attain the school's general objectives, the learning situation must be structured to establish a continuity between what is to be learned and what has been learned; to provide opportunities for the fruitful interaction—intellectual and sensorial—between the student and the subject he is studying, his peers, and his teachers; and to foster a set of desirable attitudes toward the subjects.[33]

---

[32]John I. Goodlad, *The Changing School Curriculum* (New York: Fund for the Advancement of Education, 1966), pp. 14–15.

[33]*Nova Teacher's Handbook*, 1966.

There have been several other changes designed to alter the traditional organization for learning, such as the middle school, but in most cases the changes are more administrative than basic in nature.

An area that has received considerable attention and where some very fundamental changes have taken place is in the methodology of instruction. The interrelateness of methodology and curriculum organization make the subject of teaching methods germane to this discussion. In many situations the type of curriculum organization present dictates the type of methodology used in instruction. In graded organizations, for instance, methods of teaching are centered around one teacher and a fixed number of students pursuing knowledge in one subject. The element that appears to be at the heart of the attempts to deviate from this normal pattern of instruction is the recognized need to improve upon the utilization of teachers' time and talents. It is also recognized that as content changes occur, so must the other phases of the curriculum.

One of the changes relative to methodology that has gained widespread publicity has been the introduction of team teaching as a means of facilitating the break from the traditional mode of curriculum organization.

This procedure, and the several variations similar to it, is based at least in part on the assumption that the role and function of the school professional must be changed in order to bring about significant improvement. For example, the professionalization of teaching is based on what teachers do. The manner in which teacher competencies have traditionally been utilized, and the necessity to perform certain tasks considered detrimental to full professional competency have tended to weaken the professional status of teachers. Trump alludes to this point when he says:

> The professional concept requires that teachers have enough time and the proper facilities for such activities as preparing for their professional tasks. Keeping up to date, conferring frequently with colleagues, conducting research and innovation, and improving the evaluation of what they do and what their pupils accomplish. Team teaching aims to develop these requisites for the professionalization of teachers—as well as improved learning for individual students. Its goals are to reconize better the individual differences among teachers and to utilize better the competencies of each person.[34]

The plan involves an arrangement in which two or more teachers and various supportive personnel, such as teacher aids, join together to plan, instruct, and evaluate in one or more content areas, drawing on each team member's special talents and utilizing a variety of technical aids, large-group instruction, small-group discussion, and independent study.[35]

ROLE OF THE STUDENT. A changing concept of the role of the students has resulted in a number of changes in the secondary school. Basically, the changes

[34] J. Lloyd Trump and Delmas F. Miller, *op. cit.*, pp. 317–318.
[35] *Ibid.*, p. 318.

have followed the direction of allowing students more responsibility for their own learning. The idea of independent study and structured inquiry is not new, of course, but it has gained considerable favor as an instructional technique and reflects changing attitudes regarding the role of the student.

Traditionally, students have assumed the passive role in the educational process, both from an instructional standpoint and from an administrative standpoint. Recent developments, however, appear to be recognizing the potential of allowing the student a more active role in the planning and implementation of the curriculum.

The assumptions that seem to be behind many of the current programs designed to activate student participation in the activities of the curriculum are based on various learning theories that have been known for quite some time. However, there appears to be a renewed interest in planning ways for these ideas to be implemented. The more basic of these assumptions are as follows:

1. That all students do not have the ability, or the capacity to profit from the same instruction.
2. That all students do not have the same needs for and interest in a particular subject.
3. That all students are heterogeneous with respect to past achievement and in rate of learning.

The more sophisticated forms of independent study and structured inquiry involve the use of some type of programmed materials, either in the form of a machine or prepared guides. Regardless of what kind of materials are used, the purpose is to allow each individual student to pursue his subject at his own rate and to allow him the freedom to explore topics of special intetest to him. The nongraded concept makes extensive use of this idea.

Although interrelated with many of the other changes taking place, the impact of technology on the curriculum merits special mention. The harnessing of the computer for instructional use, tape machines, television and videotapes, various types of teaching machines, and other such devices have influenced changes in many schools. Even though research consistently fails to support the superiority of these techniques over the more conventional means of curriculum implementation, it appears that a possible explanation for this is that we have not reached an advanced point in the scientific design for the use of such equipment and that the use of technology in the curriculum has largely been rather unimaginative and uncreative.[36]

Any attempt to judge the direction of curriculum change in American secondary schools is indeed hazardous. Also, any attempt to make a positive statement regarding the impact of curriculum changes on the improvement of the curriculum is equally hazardous. Only time and a concentrated research

---

[36]"Radio and Television in the Secondary School," *The Bulletin of the National Association of Secondary School Principals* 50 (October 1966).

effort can reveal the effectiveness of the curriculum changes now taking place and determine their future use.

That changes are occurring in the secondary schools of America is obvious, even to the casual observer of the secondary scene. It is also obvious that the tempo of change is increasing and is likely to accelerate in the years to come.

Factors Influencing Change

Before proceeding to the discussion of some of the more specific factors influencing curriculum change, mention should be made of a few general values deemed important to persons in this country. A consideration of these values is important because they provide the base for any type of change in the curriculum to take place. Four of these values that appear to be most pertinent to the curriculum are as follows:

1. The unchanging belief of the majority of the American people in the democratic way of life. Democracy is built upon the premise that society is composed of individuals free to explore the truth. The concept of an open society as opposed to a closed one is conducive to experimentation into ways of improving the curriculum.

2. The concept of equality of opportunity is a fundamental value of American society. This value has given impetus to the constant concern for providing educational opportunities for everyone who can benefit from them.

3. The belief in material progress has influenced the schools to constantly strive to improve themselves and to hold out the idea that the best is yet to come.

4. The value regarding the importance of education in a democracy has provided symphatic support, although not always to the extent desired, to the cause of education. Without the support of the people, the schools would wither and die.[37]

A number of specific factors are operating today that act to influence changes in the curriculum.

CHANGES IN SOCIETY. Although fundamental changes in the fabric of American society have long served as an agent for curriculum change, changes in recent years appear to have been more intensive than during many periods in the past.

Schools in America have always been considered a function of society—that is, they exist to fulfill a basic need of society, education. Therefore the schools are subject to change when the needs and desires of society change.

To illustrate the influences changes in society have on the curriculum one can look at the changes that have taken place in two social institutions, home

[37]Adapted from Richard I. Miller, "An Overview of Educational Change," in Richard I. Miller (ed.), *Perspectives on Educational Change* (New York: Appleton, 1967), pp. 2–5.

and church, and see the impact these changes have had on a third social institution, the school. There was a time in our society when some of the functions now performed by the school were considered a function of the home. Two examples of this are home economics and driver education, both of which are now established parts of the secondary curriculum. The question might be asked as to why the shift in responsibility from home to school. Any number of answers might be given, but a rather simple one that cannot be overlooked is that society wanted it that way. In the case of driver education, a problem existed in society that needed to be solved and the holder of the responsibility at that time was apparently not doing the job, so the social institution most in control by society, the school, was awarded the responsibility. Many functions now performed by the school were acquired in a like manner. In essence, the mood of society, including its major concerns at any given time, is a potent force in setting the direction for curriculum change.

INCREASED KNOWLEDGE. The "knowledge explosion" has become a common expression among educators whenever curriculum change is discussed, and is credited, as much as any one single factor, with the present ferment in education.[38] The phenomenal advances in the sciences, coupled with the passage of time, have resulted in problems of considerable magnitude regarding the organization and presentation of curricular content. In the area of history, for instance, the inescapable fact that time "marches on" imposed an almost impossible condition for teachers attempting to cover, say American history, in the traditional manner. As new knowledge is added, alterations have to be made in dealing with the old. One way of doing this, of course, is to add new courses. But under traditional school organization, when something is added something usually has to be subtracted. The decision about what to add and what to subtract is awesome indeed.

In the case of the sciences, new discoveries must constantly be evaluated in light of present knowledge to determine if the new knowledge negates the old. This, too, is a task that most teachers and administrators, even expert curriculum planners, find difficult to accomplish on a continuous basis.

There are several other factors influencing curriculum change, such as the population increase and increased mobility of the population. However, the two factors mentioned above appear to be the prime forces behind present-day attempts to change and improve the curriculum.

Factors Hindering Change

The attempt to change and improve the educational experiences of youth is often met with resistance, both from within the profession and from sources outside of education. Some of the more prominent factors that inhibit curriculum

[38] *Ibid.*, p. 6.

improvement efforts are educational philosophy, tradition, economics, and administrative resistance.

PHILOSOPHY. Philosophy is generally defined as a set of beliefs or ideas that influence individual or group behavior. As applied to education, the general set of beliefs one holds concerning what young people should learn and how they should be taught has a marked influence on the school curriculum. Although a detailed discussion of the various educational philosophies is beyond the purpose of this chapter, two philosophies that exert considerable influence on educational change will be briefly mentioned.

The compelling forces of idealism and pragamatism have long operated as stabilizers of the curriculum on the one hand and as catalysts for change on the other. Idealism operates under the premise that certain absolute truths exist. A school curriculum influenced largely by a philosophy of idealism, which has been mostly the case in the past, is one primarily occupied with passing on the heritage of these truths from one generation to another. On the other hand, a school curriculum influenced by pragmatism is usually more inclined to favor a curriculum suitable for present and future needs without much regard for retaining or preserving any particular set of beliefs. The curriculum, under the influence of pragmatism, is more apt to be receptive to experimentation of new ideas and procedures.

The dominant force in American secondary education today remains that of idealism. Therefore, many of the current efforts to change the curriculum that are in opposition to the basic beliefs of idealism meet with considerable resistance.[39]

TRADITION. Somewhat related to philosophy yet different in some respects is the factor of traditionalism as a hindrance to educational change. The reluctance to depart from the familiar is certainly not a phenomenon unique to the school curriculum, but it does figure prominently in any effort to bring about significant changes in the curriculum.

Tradition and experience are often synonymous and the influence of past experience has frustrated many a curriculum planner.

> The comfortable rut of experience . . . can serve a strong deterrent to effective change, as depicted by the teacher who said: "My students have become good citizens hitherto under current practices and there is no reason to think a few new ideas are going to change our world of reasoning."[40]

ECONOMICS. Economics as an impediment to educational change must be considered as a prime factor in any discussion of this sort. Although conflicting evidence exists regarding the relationship between cost and improvement, the fact remains that many of the newer educational innovations require additional

---

[39]For an excellent discussion on this matter, see J. Donald Butler, *Four Philosophies*, (New York: Harper, 1968).

[40]Miller, *op. cit.*, p. 11.

money to operate, at least initially. This is particularly true when the improvement project requires the acquisition of new equipment and materials.

ADMINISTRATIVE RESISTANCE. Administrative convenience in the form of rules and regulations that school administrators deem necessary for smooth operation of a school often comprise another roadblock to curriculum improvement efforts. For example, any new program that may require a departure from the master schedule may be met with considerable resistance. It is a fact that the key person in any attempt to improve the curriculum is the school administrator. For this reason any successful curriculum change must have the blessing and cooperation of the administration. This situation is due in part to the idea that the school administrator, a building principal for example, is ultimately responsible for what goes on in the school. If the outcome of the project is favorable, he may be praised, but if the outcome of the project leaves much to be desired the administrator must bear the responsibility.

If the general atmosphere of the school and community is not conducive to change, the school administrator will most likely be governed by administrative convenience and be somewhat reluctant to change a pattern of operation that has proven safe.

A final consideration in regard to the hindrances to change is the factor of inadequate planning by administrators and supervisors. A vivid illustration of the effect this factor can have on the success of a new project occurred several years ago in a school that had recently adopted a "new math" program. A supervisor visited a mathematics class in the school and related the experience of observing a class in math where all of the students were using the new materials while the teacher was using the old textbook. When confronted by the supervisor, the teacher related that upon returning to school for the start of the new term, she had been told that the materials had arrived for the new program. This was her first knowledge of the ensuing change. The reason for the situation became clear. This illustration may represent an extreme case, but enough evidence exists to indicate that it may be more typical than we might like to think.

Educational change must involve a reeducation of teachers, administrators, and all concerned with the school program if any curriculum improvement project is to be successful and result in meaningful change. This involves not only reeducation in terms of content but also reeducation directed toward changes in attitudes. Unless the persons involved in the change understand it and believe that it has merit, the chance for success is minimized.

A Model for Facilitating Change

It is generally recognized that no one procedure for bringing about meaningful curriculum change is available, but it is also true that significant curriculum improvement rarely occurs without systematic planning. The following model consists of a series of statements, gleaned from a number of writers in the area

of educational change, with added modifications designed to guide in the process
of curriculum improvement efforts.

1. *Examine the school philosophy and objectives.* It is exceedingly important that those who attempt to improve the curriculum have a clear
   understanding of what the school stands for and what it is attempting to
   accomplish. It is also important to determine if the objectives of the
   school are compatable with the general philosophy and that they are
   stated in measurable terms.

2. *Conduct an evaluation of the curriculum.* This step should involve a
   concentration of summative evaluation activities with other phases of the
   evaluative process utilized as deemed necessary. Included in this step
   should be the determination of the criteria to be employed in the evaluation.

3. *Determine curriculum needs.* Based on the results of the evaluation,
   curriculum needs are identified and the determination of priorities are set.

4. *Select improvement projects.* After the needs have been identified and
   the priorities established, a search should be launched to identify the
   appropriate innovations that appear to hold promise for inclusion in the
   program.

5. *Plan for the implementation of project.* This may be one of the more
   crucial steps in the improvement process. Basically, it involves the education or reeducation of all persons concerned with the project.

6. *Implement the project.* A major point of concern at this point is that the
   project has been thoroughly planned and sufficient time has been allotted
   for its execution.

7. *Evaluate the project.* The major concentration at this point should be on
   controlled evaluation. A second point of note is that the evaluation of the
   project should be intergrated throughout the entire process. To evaluate
   the project experimentally, plans must begin when the project begins so
   that the necessary controls to be executed.

8. *Decide if a more permanent change is warranted.* On the basis of the
   evaluation, a decision must be made regarding the next step. If the
   evaluation was favorable or unfavorable, a decision must be made to
   include the innovation in the curriculum, modify it or try something
   different, or continue without the innovation.

Some valuable suggestions for implementing curriculum change, offered by
the late Kimball Wiles, are as follows.

1. The tasks of basic research, program design, and field testing should be
   accomplished by outside forces, because of the need for a variety of
   expertise and money which may be more than a single school or school
   system can underwrite.

2. Major instructional innovations should be introduced by the administration, because they possess the authority to make the necessary decisions
   for the conduct of the project.

3. The prepackaged instructional system can be introduced despite opposition of some instructional staff, because those who oppose it will eventually accept it.

4. The informal communication system of a school must be dealt with during the process of planning and implementing new programs. The prestige of those who accept have a marked influence on those who originally oppose.

5. The innovator's real or assumed identity is a major factor in the acceptance of a new program.

6. The key to successfully implementing new programs is providing assistance to teachers as they begin to operate in the new program.

7. The most persuasive experience that can be provided to convince school personnel of the value of a new program is to allow them to observe a successful new program in action.

8. A continuous in-service program must be available to allow for new teachers brought into the school system.[41]

Conclusion

As this book is being prepared, a new decade is upon us that promises to be even more challenging, than that of the Sixties. The increasing complexity of the world we live in will continue to become more complex, requiring education to continually strive for ways of improving the educational opportunities available to youth. Sound curriculum evaluation and improvement must play a significant role if meaningful progress is to be made.

Selected References

Baker, Robert L., "Curriculum Evaluation," *Review of Educational Research*, Vol. 39 (June 1969), Chapter 4.

Beatty, Walcott H., *Improving Educational Assessment*, Washington, D.C.: Association for Supervision and Curriculum Development, 1969, Section I.

Foshay, Arthur W., "Shaping Curriculum: The Decade Ahead," *Influences in Curriculum Change*, (Washington, D.C.: Association for Supervision and Curriculum Development, 1968).

Goodlad, John I., *et al.*, *The Changing School Curriculum*. New York: Fund for the Advancement of Education, 1966.

Miller, Richard I. (ed.), *Perspectives on Educational Change*. New York: Appleton-Century-Crofts, Inc., 1967.

[41]Adapted from Kimball Wiles, "Contrasts in Strategies of Change," in Robert R. Leeper (ed.), *Strategy for Curriculum Change* (Washington, D.C.: ASCD, 1965), pp. 7–8.

Leeper, Robert R. (ed.), *Strategy for Curriculum Change*. Washington, D.C.: ASCD, 1965.

Tyler, Ralph W., *et al.*, *Perspectives of Curriculum Evaluation*. Chicago: Rand McNally & Company, 1967.

Verduin, John R., *Cooperative Curriculum Improvement*. Englewood Cliffs, N.J.: Prentice-Hall, Inc., 1967.

INDEX